D0088033

Words Their Way™ with Struggling Readers

Word Study for Reading, Vocabulary, and Spelling Instruction, Grades 4–12

Kevin Flanigan
West Chester University of Pennsylvania

Latisha Hayes
University of Virginia

Shane Templeton
University of Nevada, Reno

Donald R. Bear
University of Nevada, Reno

Marcia Invernizzi
University of Virginia

Francine Johnston
University of North Carolina at Greensboro

Boston Columbus Indianapolis New York San Francisco Upper Saddle River
Amsterdam Cape Town Dubai London Madrid Milan Munich Paris Montreal Toronto
Delhi Mexico City Sao Paulo Sydney Hong Kong Seoul Singapore Taipei Tokyo

This book is dedicated to the memory of our teacher, Edmund H. Henderson.

Vice President, Editor-in-Chief: *Aurora Martínez Ramos*
Senior Development Editor: *Hope Madden*
Editorial Assistant: *Meagan French*
Marketing Manager: *Amanda Stedke*
Production Editor: *Annette Joseph*
Editorial Production Service: *Omegatype Typography, Inc.*
Manufacturing Buyer: *Megan Cochran*
Electronic Composition: *Omegatype Typography, Inc.*
Cover Design: *Diane Lorenzo*

Credits and acknowledgments borrowed from other sources and reproduced, with permission, in this textbook appear on appropriate page within text.

Copyright © 2011 Pearson Education, Inc., publishing as Allyn & Bacon, 501 Boylston Street, Boston, MA, 02116. All rights reserved. Manufactured in the United States of America. This publication is protected by Copyright, and permission should be obtained from the publisher prior to any prohibited reproduction, storage in a retrieval system, or transmission in any form or by any means, electronic, mechanical, photocopying, recording, or likewise. To obtain permission(s) to use material from this work, please submit a written request to Pearson Education, Inc., Permissions Department, 501 Boylston Street, Boston, MA 02116, or email permissionsus@pearson.com.

Printed in the United States of America

10 9 8 7 V056 14 13

www.pearsonhighered.com

ISBN-10: 0-13-513521-4
ISBN-13: 978-0-13-513521-1

About the Authors

Kevin Flanigan is an associate professor in the literacy department at West Chester University of Pennsylvania. He works in the WCU Reading Center, where he and master's students assess and teach children who struggle to read and write. A former middle grades classroom teacher and reading specialist/coach, he researches and writes about developmental word knowledge and struggling readers.

Latisha Hayes has taught students with reading disabilities in the primary through middle grades as a special educator and reading specialist. Now an assistant professor at the University of Virginia, she teaches courses on the diagnosis and remediation of reading difficulties. She works with preservice and inservice teachers at the McGuffey Reading Center, where students across the grades receive diagnostic and tutoring services. Her interests have focused on the support of struggling readers through university-based programs and partnerships.

Shane Templeton is Foundation Professor of Curriculum and Instruction at the University of Nevada, Reno, where he is program coordinator for literacy studies. A former elementary and secondary teacher, his research focuses on the development of orthographic knowledge. He has written several books on the teaching and learning of reading and language arts and is a member of the usage panel of the *American Heritage Dictionary.* He is author of the "Spelling Logics" column in *Voices from the Middle,* the middle school journal of the National Council of Teachers of English.

Donald R. Bear is director of the E. L. Cord Foundation Center for Learning and Literacy, where he and preservice teachers, master's students, and doctoral students teach and assess children who struggle to learn to read and write. Donald is a professor in the department of educational specialties in the College of Education at the University of Nevada, Reno. Donald has been a classroom teacher and he researches literacy development and instruction. He is an author of numerous articles, book chapters, and books.

Marcia Invernizzi is a professor of reading education at the Curry School of Education at the University of Virginia. Marcia is also the director of the McGuffey Reading Center, where she teaches the clinical practica in reading diagnosis and remedial reading. Formerly an English and reading teacher, she works with Book Buddies, Virginia's Early Intervention Reading Initiative (EIRI), and Phonological Awareness Literacy Screening (PALS).

Francine Johnston is a former first grade teacher and reading specialist who learned about word study during her graduate work at the University of Virginia. She is now an associate professor in the School of Education at the University of North Carolina at Greensboro, where she teaches courses in reading, language arts, and children's literature. Francine frequently works with regional school systems as a consultant and researcher. Her research interests include current spelling practices and materials as well as the relationship between spelling and reading achievement.

Contents

Preface

In the United States alone, there are eight million students in grades 4 through 12 who struggle to read on grade level (NCES, 2003).

Although *word knowledge* is only one component of literacy, it is an absolutely essential factor that underlies and affects many other areas of literacy. It is critical to success in the upper grades curriculum and across the content areas because these word-level skills are foundational to other literacy skills, such as reading fluency and comprehension. If you consider the challenges that content area textbooks present to students in grades 4 through 12, it is not surprising that even skilled readers will need support and effective instruction in order to shoulder the conceptual load.

Words Their Way™ with Struggling Readers: Word Study for Reading, Vocabulary, and Spelling Instruction, Grades 4–12 takes the framework and research behind the phenomenally successful word study approach of the parent text, *Words Their Way™: Word Study for Phonics, Vocabulary, and Spelling Instruction,* by Bear, Invernizzi, Templeton, and Johnston, but focuses the attention squarely on the needs of struggling adolescent readers.

Intended for the classroom teacher, this handy book provides specific guidance, strategies, and tools for helping struggling students, grades 4 and up, catch up with their peers in literacy. The thrust is intervention—specifically, utilizing word study with its hands-on, assessable approach to aid students struggling with the reading and writing demands of middle and secondary classrooms. This text will help you determine student needs; provide you with the strategies to guide each student toward success in reading, spelling, and content area vocabulary; and even outline ideas for fitting these strategies into your crowded schedule. You'll have the following tools to help your students acquire the literacy skills they need to meet the ever-increasing demands of school life:

- Focus on the specific needs of struggling readers in upper elementary, middle, and high schools
- Teacher-directed but student-centered instruction based on a developmental model of word knowledge
- A two-pronged approach to word knowledge instruction: (1) reading and spelling knowledge (including phonics and decoding) and (2) vocabulary knowledge
- Vocabulary activities to address needs across the content areas: math, science, social studies, and English
- Teacher-friendly, ready-to-use activities in each of the instructional chapters

This book will help you target instruction where it is most needed and equip you with the specific methods you'll need to help your students get up to speed in their reading ability. Using a powerful and highly engaging approach to word knowledge instruction—word study—you will be able to directly target the reading, vocabulary, and spelling needs of your older struggling readers.

- Word study is a highly active and powerful approach to reading, vocabulary, and spelling instruction.
- The approach helps older struggling readers become more excited about words and more motivated to learn about how words work.

- Word study actively engages students in applying critical thinking skills by comparing and contrasting words and word patterns.
- Through the targeted assessment opportunities provided in these pages, word study becomes developmental.
- Word study combines the best of systematic, explicit instruction with hands-on opportunities for student practice and exploration of words.
- Word study can exponentially boost students' vocabularies by teaching students how to unlock the meaning system that permeates the English language.

Organization of This Text

When working with older struggling readers, it is helpful to organize word knowledge difficulties into three primary, interrelated areas of need: (a) difficulties in *spelling and reading knowledge,* (b) difficulties in *vocabulary knowledge,* and (c) *lack of motivation and engagement* to learn about words and the concepts they represent.

Part I: Introduction to Word Study with Struggling Readers, Grades 4–12

Chapter 1: Word Study with Older Struggling Readers

This chapter discusses three main areas that affect reading performance: *orthographic knowledge, vocabulary and comprehension knowledge,* and *motivation/engagement.* It highlights the critical needs of our older struggling readers and writers and briefly introduces you to the power of word study to improve their spelling and reading knowledge, vocabulary knowledge, and motivation and engagement. The chapter ends with a brief overview of the stages of development.

Chapter 2: Core Word Study Principles and Practices for Spelling, Reading, and Vocabulary Instruction

Our second chapter is divided into three parts. The first part introduces you to the five core principles of word study instruction for older struggling readers. You will also learn about practices to enhance your spelling and reading instruction in the second part of the chapter. The third part will guide you through core practices for vocabulary instruction. Highlights from this chapter include developing engagement and motivation, encouraging higher-level thinking about words, and adjusting your instruction along a continuum of support.

Part II: Word Study Assessment and Instruction for Spelling and Reading

Chapter 3: Assessment: Spelling and Reading

This chapter outlines word knowledge assessment for spelling and reading. You will learn how to administer and interpret qualitative spelling inventories as well as analyze reading errors. You will also learn about using assessment data to group your students for instruction and how to put together a manageable schedule to meet group needs.

Chapter 4: The Within Word Pattern Stage

This chapter highlights effective instructional practices that promote phonics, spelling, and decoding knowledge for students in the within word pattern stage of development.

Chapter 5: The Syllables and Affixes Stage

Building on Chapter 4's coverage, Chapter 5 highlights effective instructional practices that promote phonics, spelling, and decoding knowledge for readers and writers in the syllables and affixes stage of development.

Part III: Word Study Assessment and Instruction for Vocabulary

Chapter 6: Generative Vocabulary Instruction: Teaching Struggling Readers to Crack the Meaning Code in English

Our first of three chapters dedicated to vocabulary development highlights effective instructional practices that promote vocabulary knowledge. Our focus is teaching students how to tap into the power of Latin- and Greek-derived prefixes, suffixes, and roots to exponentially increase vocabulary knowledge.

Chapter 7: Word-Specific Vocabulary Instruction

The second vocabulary chapter highlights effective instructional practices that promote the more sophisticated vocabulary found in grades 4 through 12 content areas. Our dual focus includes general core academic vocabulary and vocabulary specific to math, science, social studies, and English.

Chapter 8: Vocabulary Assessment and Organization

This chapter outlines various informal vocabulary assessments that can target both generative vocabulary knowledge and content-specific vocabulary knowledge.

Companion Volumes

We believe that the hands-on word sorting approach to word study is an invaluable literacy tool for you and your students. Broaden your word study understanding and instruction with the variety of additional materials available.

For Older Readers

- *Words Their Way™: Word Study for Phonics, Vocabulary, and Spelling Instruction* (4th ed.), by Donald R. Bear, Marcia Invernizzi, Shane Templeton, and Francine Johnston
- *Vocabulary Their Way™: Word Study with Middle and Secondary Students,* by Shane Templeton, Donald R. Bear, Marcia Invernizzi, and Francine Johnston
- *Words Their Way™: Word Sorts for Syllables and Affixes Spellers* (2nd ed.), by Francine Johnston, Marcia Invernizzi, Donald R. Bear, and Shane Templeton
- *Words Their Way™: Word Sorts for Derivational Relations Spellers* (2nd ed.), by Shane Templeton, Francine Johnston, Donald R. Bear, and Marcia Invernizzi
- *Words Their Way™: Word Sorts for Within Word Pattern Spellers* (2nd ed.), by Marcia Invernizzi, Francine Johnston, Donald R. Bear, and Shane Templeton

For English Learners

- *Words Their Way™ with English Learners: Word Study for Phonics, Vocabulary, and Spelling Instruction,* by Donald R. Bear, Lori Helman, Shane Templeton, Marcia Invernizzi, and Francine Johnston
- *Words Their Way™: Emergent Sorts for Spanish-Speaking English Learners,* by Lori Helman, Donald R. Bear, Marcia Invernizzi, Shane Templeton, and Francine Johnston

- *Words Their Way™: Letter Name–Alphabetic Sorts for Spanish-Speaking English Learners,* by Lori Helman, Donald R. Bear, Marcia Invernizzi, Shane Templeton, and Francine Johnston

Additional Titles

- *Words Their Way™: Letter and Picture Sorts for Emergent Spellers* (2nd ed.), by Donald R. Bear, Marcia Invernizzi, Francine Johnston, and Shane Templeton
- *Words Their Way™: Word Sorts for Letter Name–Alphabetic Spellers* (2nd ed.), by Francine Johnston, Donald R. Bear, Marcia Invernizzi, and Shane Templeton

Acknowledgments

We begin by thanking Linda Bishop for her vision and leadership in getting this book off the ground and Hope Madden for her continued guidance and support throughout. We would also like to thank the educators whose review and feedback helped to shape this text: Debbie Cottle, Columbus Academy, Ohio; Jacqueline Glasgow, Ohio University; James Johnston, Central Connecticut State University; Margot Kinberg, National University; Timothy Shanahan, University of Illinois at Chicago; David Smith, University of Nevada, Reno; and Roderick Winters, Winona State University. We would also like to thank all of our teachers, students, and colleagues who have taught us so much and our families, who have given us so much support.

chapter 1

Word Study with Older Struggling Readers

In the United States, there are *eight million* students in grades 4 through 12 who struggle to read at grade level (NCES, 2003). This shocking number, along with a host of related factors, has prompted experts to conclude that we are in the midst of an adolescent literacy crisis (Biancarosa & Snow, 2006; Deshler, Palincsar, Biancarosa, & Nair, 2007). When dealing with a massive number such as eight million, it is easy to overlook the individual students, the fact that each of these eight million is a young person with a name and story. To put a name and a face to this group, one of the authors—Kevin Flanigan—will share his experience working with James, a fifth grade struggling reader.

> It was the beginning of my third year as a middle grade classroom teacher, but the first time I had ever had a student like James. James was an outgoing and intelligent fifth-grader who played point guard on his basketball team and had an easy and contagious laugh that immediately put others at ease. However, James's normally upbeat personality drastically changed whenever he was confronted with any activity that required him to read or write. Initially, he became tense and quiet and, after ten minutes or so, began to sigh, drop his head to one side, and stare away from the book or paper.
>
> I first noticed James's difficulties in his writing. Writing took a great deal of effort for James, whether constructing a graphic organizer, answering questions from the social studies textbook, or composing a story during writing workshop. He would tightly grip the pencil, hunch over the paper, and begin to sigh as the activity dragged on. His written work, which often took two to three times as long as his classmates', was unorganized and usually lacking in detail and sophisticated vocabulary—he nearly always chose basic words like *walked* instead of more mature, specific vocabulary like *strolled, swaggered,* or *shuffled.* His papers were so full of misspellings that I sometimes experienced difficulty reading back what he wrote. Although he often did well on the Friday spelling tests, he rarely spelled these words correctly the following week or transferred this knowledge to his writing.
>
> Along with his writing and spelling difficulties, James struggled to read—even in my lowest-achieving group reading at the third grade level. Not only did James find most school reading difficult, he simply didn't like to read. During independent reading time, despite my best efforts to find books he would find interesting and could read independently, I would often catch James staring out the window or glancing furtively at the clock, waiting for the next activity to begin. James was not motivated to read and was doing little reading for meaning in my classroom.
>
> Worse than small-group and independent reading—where at least the books were a little easier and he was afforded some choice—was the dreaded social studies textbook, a rather dry and difficult text for even my strongest readers. I'll never forget the day I sat down with James and first heard him read the textbook aloud to me. He painstakingly read one paragraph, word by word, with me supplying many multisyllabic words he was unable to decode himself. Just as striking as his inability to decode many of the words was his lack of familiarity with the essential meanings of the vocabulary words in the social studies passage. As we discussed the passage together afterward, it

quickly became apparent that he didn't know the meanings of keywords and concepts like *pioneer, produce,* and *however*—words absolutely essential to an understanding of the paragraph.

At the end of our discussion about the social studies passage, James quickly turned his head away from me, embarrassedly wiping away the tears welling up in his eyes, and asked, "Mr. Flanigan, why is this so hard for me?" It was this moment—actually hearing James attempt to read aloud and discuss something that was clearly so inappropriate and frustrating for him—that brought home to me the complete mismatch between what James needed and what I was doing. It was no wonder that James found reading such a negative and humiliating experience.

However, James possessed an important strength that became readily apparent—he loved being read to aloud, particularly from adventure and sports-themed books and most nonfiction books about animals. In addition, with support, he could understand most of what was read aloud to him. He also thrived on hands-on activities and cooperative group learning—comprehending higher-level science concepts we had explored during experiments and remembering important historic events we had role-played in cooperative groups.

I was at a loss for how to help James. Despite his many strengths, his inability to spell and decode words accurately and fluently, combined with his significant lack of vocabulary knowledge, was having a devastating impact on his learning across the curriculum. Even more importantly, it was destroying his motivation and belief in his ability to learn. What I was doing was not working for James; however, I felt that I was caught in a catch-22 between what the curriculum required me to teach James and what James needed.

- I was required to teach James social studies, but he couldn't read the social studies textbook.
- I was required to teach James science, but he couldn't read the science manuals.
- I was required to teach James to write an organized, coherent five-paragraph essay, but he couldn't spell simple one-syllable words.

Put simply, James was required to *read to learn* the content information in order to succeed in school, but in my mind, he hadn't *learned to read* yet. (As I learned more about literacy development and instruction, I found that James—although well behind his peers—did indeed possess some important literacy skills that I could build on; however, this was my initial feeling at the time.)

The Statistics on Older Struggling Readers

Unfortunately, James's difficulties are not uncommon for many middle grade and high school students. As mentioned above, there are millions of older struggling readers in our nation's schools. According to National Assessment of Educational Progress (NAEP) data from the 2007 reading test, only 33 percent of fourth-graders and 31 percent of eighth-graders performed at or above the proficient level (NCES, 2007). The remaining students, who scored below the proficient level, are identified as achieving only "partial mastery" of grade-level reading skills and knowledge. If we define "partial mastery" as reading below grade level, then adolescent literacy experts are accurate in estimating that *nearly 70 percent* of fourth and eighth grade students are reading below grade level (Biancarosa & Snow, 2006, p. 7).

This staggering statistic has far-reaching consequences for individual students and our society as a whole:

- Nearly 7,000 high school students drop out every day (Alliance for Excellent Education, 2006). Experts cite the lack of adequate literacy skills necessary for success in high school as a primary reason for this high dropout rate (Kamil, 2003).

Figure 1.1 Why Grades 4 through 12?

Many different terms are used to identify struggling readers beyond the primary grades (K–3), including *adolescent*, *older*, and *secondary*. In this book, we use the terms *older struggling readers* and *middle grades and high school struggling readers* to refer to struggling readers in grades 4 through 12. We focus on this group because the literacy challenges we discuss in this book—including the increased vocabulary and conceptual load, more sophisticated multisyllabic words, and the specific demands of content area learning—usually begin in fourth grade and continue into the middle grades and high school (Carnegie Council on Advancing Adolescent Literacy, 2010).

- "A large percentage of young dropouts are unemployed. Many end up in prison" (Deshler et al., 2007, p. 4).
- The picture does not improve for many students after high school; 42 percent of postsecondary students take some type of remedial coursework (Adelman, 2004), and approximately 40 percent of high school graduates do not possess the literacy skills that employers want (Achieve, Inc., 2005).
- In recent years, the demand for unskilled labor has decreased; at the same time, the fastest-growing professions require more extensive skills (ACT, 2005; Levy & Murnane, 2004).
- According to the U.S. Department of Labor, low literacy skills have resulted in nearly $225 billion a year in lost productivity (Grimsley, 1995).

In light of these alarming statistics, it is not an exaggeration to say that we are experiencing an adolescent literacy crisis of epidemic proportion in the United States.

The Importance of Word Knowledge for Struggling Readers

Older struggling readers and writers are not a monolithic group—there is no one "typical" profile of these students. In fact, they may struggle with different literacy skills for a number of reasons. For instance, some students may have great difficulty decoding unfamiliar multisyllabic words. Others may be able to decode these more difficult words but are not able to read grade-level text with adequate fluency—the ability to read with appropriate accuracy, rate, and phrasing to support comprehension. Still others may not possess the vocabulary and background knowledge to enable comprehension of a science textbook or to craft a well-written persuasive essay. A large proportion of older struggling readers experience difficulty with important comprehension processes, such as identifying the main idea in a text, making inferences, or summarizing key content information. Of course, if you have worked with older struggling readers, you know that it is not uncommon for these students to have needs in more than one area.

Many struggling readers, like James from the preceding vignette, struggle with words, whether it is fluently spelling words, accurately and automatically decoding words, or accessing the meanings of words (Biemiller, 2003; Chall & Jacobs, 2003; Leach, Scarborough, & Rescorla, 2003). This book is intended to help those older struggling readers who experience primary difficulties in the area of word knowledge. We use the term *word knowledge* here to refer to three related areas of knowledge about how words work: spelling knowledge, reading or decoding knowledge, and vocabulary knowledge (see Figure 1.2). As the figure indicates, word knowledge develops in the context of contextual reading, writing, speaking, and listening. There is a reciprocal relationship between the development of word knowledge and meaningful experiences reading and

Figure 1.2 Three Areas of Word Knowledge: Spelling, Reading, and Vocabulary

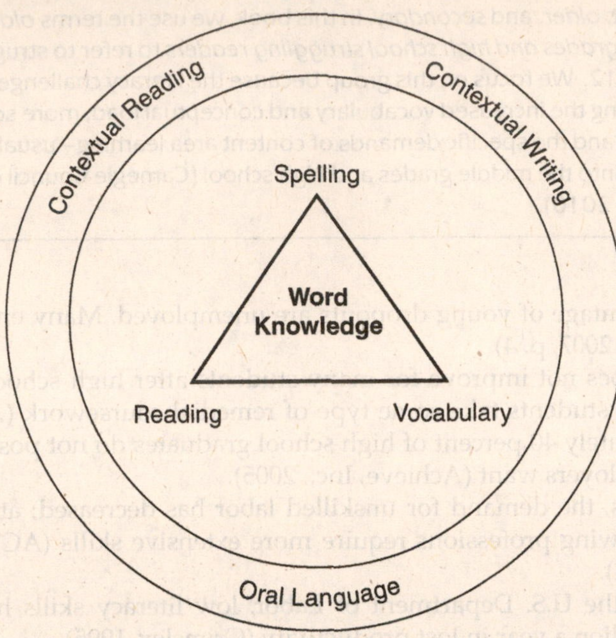

writing in context; gains in one area promote growth in the other area. Although word knowledge is only one component of literacy, it is an absolutely essential foundation that affects many other areas of literacy and is critical to success in the upper grades curriculum and across the content areas.

- Students who cannot accurately and fluently spell words will be less likely to write as much as their peers, will have more difficulty focusing on and communicating their intended message in their written work, and will be less motivated to write.
- Students who cannot accurately and automatically read words will struggle to read fluently, will likely experience difficulty comprehending what they are reading, and will be less motivated to read more.
- Students who do not possess strong vocabularies will be less likely to comprehend what they are reading; less likely to write with powerful, precise word choice; and more likely to experience difficulty grasping abstract content area concepts and information in English, science, math, and social studies.

The Word Knowledge "Domino Effect"

Students who have difficulties reading and spelling words accurately and quickly are likely to struggle in all areas of literacy (Deshler et al., 2007). This is because these word-level skills are foundational to other literacy skills, such as reading fluency and comprehension. Because these skills build on each other, they are akin to a set of dominos; if the first domino topples, subsequent dominos are likely to come tumbling down. Figure 1.3 shows how inadequate decoding knowledge can affect other literacy skills.

How exactly does this domino effect happen? How might lack of word knowledge skills negatively impact other critical literacy skills? Take the case of Sasha, a skilled eleventh grade reader, attempting to read this in her American history textbook:

> Despite the many compromises reached by northern and southern politicians over the previous 40 years, and despite the best efforts of some politicians, the intractable differences between the northern and southern states became too great for the country to handle.

Figure 1.3 Word Knowledge "Domino Effect"

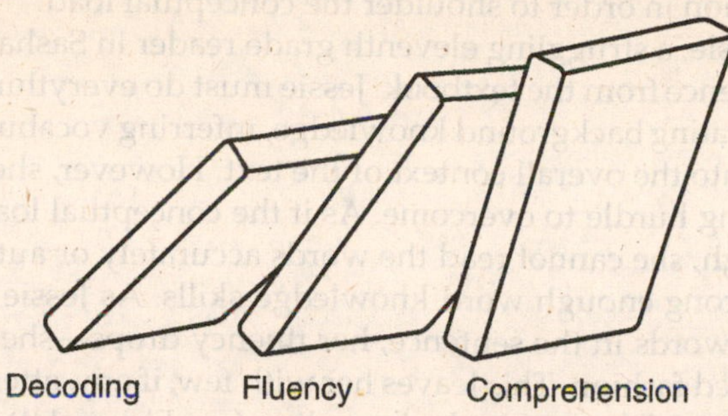

As Sasha reads this sentence, she, like all readers, has only a limited amount of attentional resources to devote to the act of reading. Decoding and comprehending compete for these limited attentional resources (LaBerge & Samuels, 1974; Perfetti, 1985). Fortunately, Sasha possesses such strong word knowledge that she can recognize nearly all of the words in this sentence accurately and automatically; decoding the words requires little conscious effort on her part. This enables her to read the sentence fluently and thus, "spend" the majority of her attention comprehending the sentence. Figure 1.4 shows how Sasha's decoding knowledge takes few of her attentional resources, allowing her to focus the majority of her attention on comprehension.

Focusing on comprehension is crucial, because Sasha is going to need all of her comprehension skills in order to make sense of such a complex sentence. At the very least, she will have to

- Activate her background knowledge about the historical context alluded to in the sentence (what compromises over the last 40 years?)
- Access or infer the meanings of vocabulary words (what does *intractable* mean?)
- Exercise her knowledge of syntax (how do the two introductory dependent clauses relate to the independent clause?) and text structure (how does this sentence fit in to the overall structure of the section and chapter?)

Figure 1.4 Comprehension and Decoding Resources of a Skilled and Struggling Reader

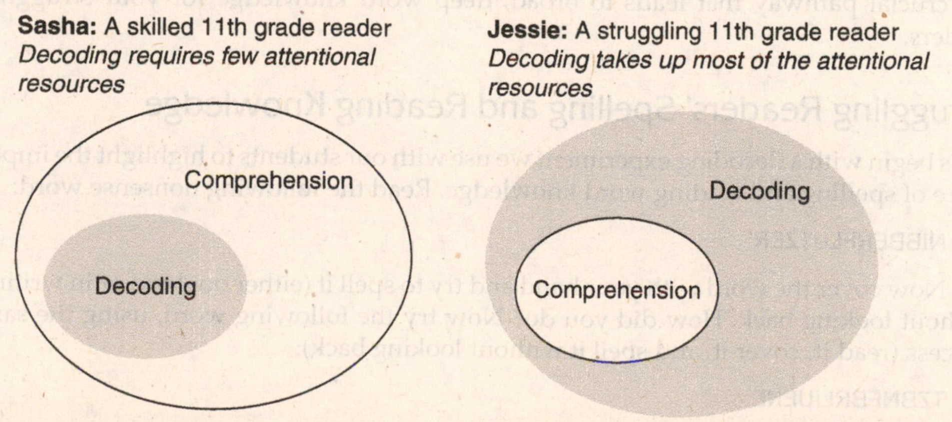

Source: Adapted with permission from Morris, 2008.

When we look closely at the challenges that content area textbooks present to students in grades 4 through 12, it is not surprising that even skilled readers will need support and effective instruction in order to shoulder the conceptual load.

Now imagine Jessie, a struggling eleventh grade reader in Sasha's class, attempting to read the same sentence from the textbook. Jessie must do everything that Sasha needs to do in terms of activating background knowledge, inferring vocabulary meanings, and fitting the sentence into the overall context of the text. However, she has an additional, potentially devastating hurdle to overcome. As if the conceptual load presented in this sentence is not enough, she cannot read the words accurately or automatically because she does not have strong enough word knowledge skills. As Jessie struggles to recognize and decode the words in the sentence, her fluency drops—she begins to read in a word-by-word, labored fashion. This leaves her with few, if any, attentional resources to devote to making sense of the words she is reading (see Figure 1.4). It is not surprising that Jessie's comprehension, and motivation to learn, will suffer. Put another way, by the time Jessie reaches the end of the sentence, she will have difficulty remembering what the beginning of the sentence said.

The Difficulties Facing Older Struggling Readers

When working with older struggling readers, it is helpful to organize their word knowledge difficulties into three primary, interrelated areas of need: (1) difficulties in spelling and reading knowledge, (2) difficulties in vocabulary knowledge, and (3) lack of motivation and engagement to learn about words and the concepts they represent. Reflecting this organizational structure, this book will describe how the word study approach to instruction can effectively target these three components: spelling and reading knowledge, vocabulary knowledge, and engagement with words (see Figure 1.5).

Part I (Chapters 1 and 2) of this book will introduce core instructional principles and general practices for word study. Part II (Chapters 3, 4, and 5) will describe word study assessment and instruction that targets students with spelling and reading needs. Part III (Chapters 6, 7, and 8) will describe word study assessment and instruction that targets students with vocabulary needs. In Figure 1.5, an arrow connects spelling and reading knowledge with vocabulary knowledge—highlighting how these different components of word knowledge work together so that gains in one area promote growth in the others. A common theme that runs throughout this book is the critical importance of creating an engaging environment that motivates your students to learn more about specific words and about how words work. In Figure 1.5, notice that *engagement* links word study instruction to spelling, reading, and vocabulary knowledge; we did this to emphasize our strong belief that engagement provides the crucial pathway that leads to broad, deep word knowledge for your struggling readers.

Struggling Readers' Spelling and Reading Knowledge

Let's begin with a decoding experiment we use with our students to highlight the importance of spelling and reading word knowledge. Read the following nonsense word:

NIBBERFLUTZER

Now cover the word with your hand and try to spell it (either out loud or in writing) without looking back. How did you do? Now try the following word, using the same process (read it, cover it, and spell it without looking back):

TZBNFBRLIUERE

How did you do? Which word was easier to spell? Which was more difficult?

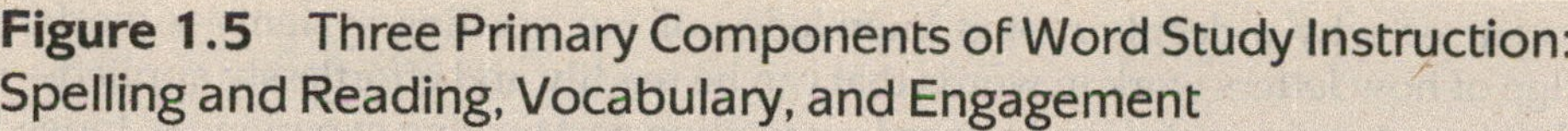

Figure 1.5 Three Primary Components of Word Study Instruction: Spelling and Reading, Vocabulary, and Engagement

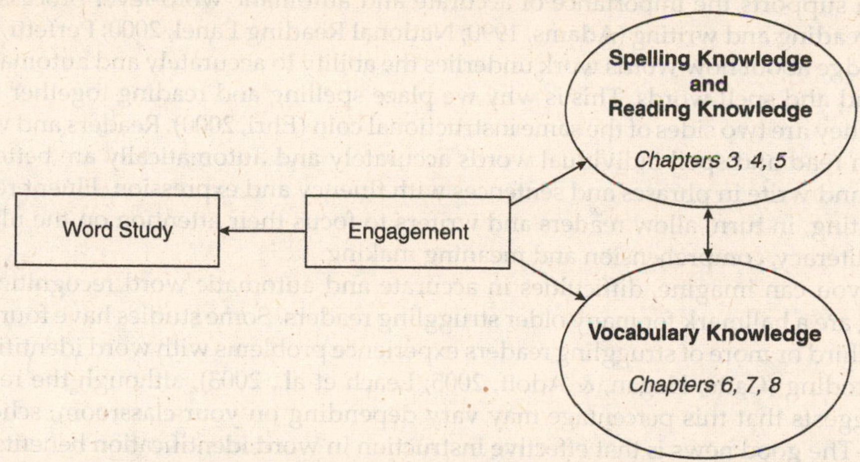

Chances are, you were better able to read and spell the first word, NIBBERFLUTZER, than the second word, despite the fact that (a) you have never seen either word before and (b) both words contain exactly the same 13 letters (go ahead and check). Why is this so? The answer illustrates an important insight into how our reading mind makes sense of the English spelling system: Our minds are not cameras; our minds are pattern seekers. If our brains worked like a camera, we could simply look at a word once, take a "picture" of it, and remember it exactly as it is. This would be analogous to what is sometimes referred to as having a "photographic memory." If our minds worked this way, then both words would be equally easy to recognize and spell because they both contain exactly the same letters.

However, as we discussed, our brains do not take "pictures" like cameras; we remember words by looking for known spelling patterns in words. For example, even though you had never seen the nonsense word NIBBERFLUTZER before, you were able to spell it (or come close) after seeing it only once because you recognized familiar spelling patterns, or chunks of letters in the word. Your underlying orthographic knowledge—knowledge of the spelling system—enabled you to easily read, store in memory, and spell this word. In this case, the NIB part of the word is similar to other words you already know like *rib* and *bib*. The FLUTZ part of the word shares a similar spelling pattern with *klutz*. And, of course, the ER pattern in the second and final syllables is familiar in many words like *butter* and *miser*. So instead of having to remember 13 separate letters for NIBBERFLUTZER, you only had to remember three or four familiar letter sequences, or spelling patterns—a much easier job for your memory. On the other hand, the second nonsense word, TZBNFBRLIUERE, is much more difficult to decode, remember, and spell because you probably did not recognize any familiar spelling patterns. (Does the TZBNF letter sequence remind you of any other English word? We can't think of any.)

Reading and Spelling Difficulties for Older Struggling Readers

Now imagine that you are a struggling reader like James from the opening vignette and are asked to read, day in and day out, textbooks that contain multisyllabic words that are extremely difficult for you to decode and spell, like TZBNFBRLIUERE. What would this do to your ability to read fluently? To finish your homework assignments on time? To comprehend what you are reading? To your motivation to read?

You can see why a deeply rooted knowledge of our spelling system—a working knowledge of how letters work in words that can be readily and effortlessly applied—is essential to fluent, meaningful, and rewarding reading and writing experiences. Indeed, research supports the importance of accurate and automatic word-level processing in skilled reading and writing (Adams, 1990; National Reading Panel, 2000; Perfetti, 1985). Knowledge about how words work underlies the ability to accurately and automatically both read and spell words. This is why we place spelling and reading together in this book—they are two sides of the same instructional coin (Ehri, 2000). Readers and writers who can read and spell individual words accurately and automatically are better able to read and write in phrases and sentences with fluency and expression. Fluent reading and writing, in turn, allow readers and writers to focus their attention on the ultimate goal of literacy, comprehension and meaning making.

As you can imagine, difficulties in accurate and automatic word recognition and spelling are a hallmark for many older struggling readers. Some studies have found that up to a third or more of struggling readers experience problems with word identification and decoding (Catts, Hogan, & Adolf, 2005; Leach et al., 2003), although the research also suggests that this percentage may vary depending on your classroom, school, or district. The good news is that effective instruction in word identification benefits older students who struggle in this area (Wexler, Edmonds, & Vaughn, 2008).

In Part II, we describe how the word study approach (Bear, Invernizzi, Templeton, & Johnston, 2008) can improve your struggling readers' ability to accurately and automatically read and spell words. In these chapters, we lead you through the process of diagnostically assessing your students' needs, identifying their word knowledge stage of development, and targeting instruction to directly meet those needs.

Struggling Readers' Vocabulary Knowledge

In addition to being able to spell and read words accurately and automatically, middle grade and high school students need to know the meanings of literally tens of thousands of words, particularly the more sophisticated vocabulary that permeates the upper grade content areas. To get a flavor for the daunting vocabulary challenges posed by the middle grade and high school curriculum, read the following end-of-section exercise from a high school geometry textbook:

> The **segments** that join the **midpoints** of **consecutive** sides of a **rectangle** form a **rhombus.** The **segments** that join the **midpoints** of **consecutive** sides of a **rhombus** form a **rectangle.** What type of **quadrilateral** is formed by **segments** that join the **midpoints** of **consecutive** sides of a square? Use the **diagram** on page 339 to **justify** your answer. (Aichele, Hopfensperger, Leiva, Mason, Murphy, Schell, & Vheru, 1998, p. 343, emphasis added)

In just the first sentence from this exercise, we counted five vocabulary terms that might pose a problem for a high school student, particularly a struggling reader: *segment, midpoint, consecutive, rectangle,* and *rhombus.* In the following three sentences, we counted three additional vocabulary terms that might be unknown: *quadrilateral, diagram,* and *justify.* Each word represents a potential stumbling block to comprehension for the reader who does not know its meaning—eight potential stumbling blocks to overcome within the space of a few sentences.

Now read the following end-of-chapter problem from a high school chemistry textbook. The reader is asked to take a chemical reaction that is described in words and convert it into a chemical equation using scientific symbols.

> 54. Write a **balanced chemical equation** for each of these **reactions.** Use the necessary symbols from table 7.1 to describe the reaction completely.
>
> a. Bubbling **chlorine gas** through a **solution** of **potassium iodide** gives **elemental iodine** and a **solution** of **potassium chloride.** (Wilbraham, Staley, & Matta, 1995, p. 203, emphasis added)

In just the directions and part a of a four-part question (we did not include parts b, c, or d), we counted at least seven potentially difficult vocabulary words and concepts: *balanced chemical equation, reactions, chlorine gas, solution, potassium iodide, elemental iodine,* and *potassium chloride.* Inadequate knowledge of even one of these concepts, like *balanced chemical equation* or *potassium iodide,* would leave the student with very little chance of answering the question and successfully converting the words into a balanced chemical equation.

These math and science textbook examples illustrate a finding that reading researchers—and middle grade and high school content area teachers—have known for years: vocabulary knowledge strongly influences reading comprehension (Anderson & Freebody, 1981; Davis, 1944). This makes perfect sense. A reader who understands the meanings of these words and concepts is much more likely to grasp the gist of the exercise or passage; along the same lines, a reader with a superficial knowledge of those vocabulary terms and concepts will likely experience significant difficulties comprehending the text. It is not surprising then that students with an impoverished vocabulary will struggle greatly in reading comprehension, writing, and content area learning.

Not only are vocabulary knowledge and reading comprehension highly correlated, but vocabulary knowledge becomes increasingly important to academic success as students move through middle and high school and beyond, as indicated by the following:

- Some high school chemistry texts introduce more new vocabulary than the typical foreign language class (Holliday, 1991).
- To adequately comprehend a text, 90 to 95 percent of the total word meanings of that text must be known (Carver, 1994; Nagy & Scott, 2000).
- Among many struggling older readers, limited background knowledge and vocabulary contribute to poor reading performance (Biemiller, 2003; Chall & Jacobs, 2003).

Clearly, the increased vocabulary load of the middle and high school curriculum poses a major obstacle for older struggling readers. Students with strong vocabularies are at a distinct advantage; students with weak vocabularies are at a great disadvantage. One way to view the magnitude of this vocabulary disadvantage is through the vocabulary gap.

The Vocabulary Gap for Struggling Readers

How big is the vocabulary gap for our struggling readers? Specifically, how many words do struggling readers need to learn to catch up to their on-grade-level peers? Research in vocabulary acquisition can give us a sense of the massive numbers involved. Researchers have estimated that school-age children learn approximately 2,000 to 3,000 new word meanings per year, resulting in a 40,000 word reading vocabulary for the "average" high school graduate (Nagy & Herman, 1987; Stahl & Nagy, 2006). This is equivalent to the "average" student learning approximately seven new word meanings per day, an astonishing rate of growth. However, it is important to remember that these estimates are averages. Higher-achieving readers are likely (and incredibly) learning more than this, and lower-achieving readers are likely learning much less, resulting in a vocabulary gap between the two.

Table 1.1 compares the vocabulary growth, in the number of word meanings known, between two hypothetical students: Jose, a normally achieving reader, and Cody, a struggling reader. For this example, we assume that Jose and Cody entered third grade with equivalent vocabularies of 13,000 words. However, around fourth grade a major change takes place in vocabulary acquisition: From this point on, the majority of a student's vocabulary growth will come not from oral language, but from the new vocabulary the student picks up while reading written language. This includes the more sophisticated words and concepts students encounter in content area texts, newspapers,

Table 1.1 Vocabulary Growth of Two Students

Grade Level	Jose (a Normally Achieving Reader)	Cody (a Struggling Reader)	Vocabulary Gap
3	13,000	13,000	0
4	16,000	14,500	1,500
5	19,000	16,000	3,000
6	22,000	17,500	4,500
7	25,000	19,000	6,000
8	28,000	20,500	7,500
9	31,000	22,000	9,000
10	34,000	23,500	10,500
11	37,000	25,000	12,000
12	40,000	26,500	13,500

and magazines, such as *portrait, slither, pharaoh,* and *evolution.* These are words not typically used in day-to-day conversation but rather most likely encountered in books or in conversations about books.

The fact that reading will be the primary source of new vocabulary growth from about fourth grade on puts Cody at a great disadvantage for two reasons: (1) Cody, as a struggling reader, is not reading as much as Jose, and thus won't be exposed to as many new vocabulary words as Jose, and (2) Cody is not able to read and understand more advanced texts like Jose, and thus won't be exposed to the richer and more sophisticated vocabulary found in those books. Given this lack of vocabulary exposure, it is not unreasonable to assume that Cody will be learning half as many new word meanings each year as Jose (1,500 words per year for Cody as compared to the average 3,000 words per year for Jose).

As you can see in Table 1.1, the vocabulary gap between the two students widens very quickly. By sixth grade—in only three years—Cody is already 4,500 vocabulary words behind Jose. By ninth grade, Cody knows as many word meanings as Jose did back in sixth grade. By twelfth grade, there is a *13,500-word vocabulary gap* between the two students.

As this example illustrates, the vocabulary gap between lower- and higher-achieving students is a reality that educators must face. In one classic study, it was found that high-achieving high school seniors knew approximately *four times* as many words as their lower-achieving peers (Smith, 1941). Stahl and Nagy estimate that higher-achieving fifth-graders "may know thousands, perhaps even 10,000, more words" than their lower-achieving classmates (2006, p. 27). Whichever estimate you point to, the critical point is sobering: the vocabulary gap for lower-performing students is real and significant.

However, as with reading and spelling, the good news is that quality vocabulary instruction, coupled with large amounts of appropriate and engaging reading and writing, can make a real difference in student success. Effective vocabulary instruction not only significantly improves student learning of the individual words and concepts taught, but also promotes reading comprehension of the larger passages containing those words (Beck, Perfetti, & McKeown, 1982; National Reading Panel, 2000). In Part III, we will describe effective vocabulary assessment and instruction that will motivate your struggling readers and ties directly to their content area learning, with the power to exponentially boost their vocabulary knowledge.

Struggling Readers' Engagement

Picture the struggling readers and writers in your classroom. Do they enjoy reading the textbook, or any other school text for that matter? Do they choose to read or write in their free time? Are they excited about learning and using new words and concepts? Do they collaborate with, question, or actively discuss ideas with other students in your classroom? Perhaps most important, do they believe that their hard work will result in academic success? For too many of our nation's struggling readers, the answer to these questions is a resounding "No."

Lack of engagement in school and motivation to read is perhaps *the* defining characteristic of older struggling readers. As one high school teacher we worked with put it, "Motivation is *everything* with older kids." Because engagement is so critical to academic success, we will discuss it here in some depth. According to Guthrie and Wigfield (2000) and Guthrie (2004), reading engagement includes the following three dimensions (see Figure 1.6):

1. *Cognitive.* Engaged readers can apply their knowledge and strategies to make sense of their reading and gain conceptual understanding.
2. *Socially interactive.* Engaged readers actively participate in a literacy community and can discuss what they are reading with peers and teachers to jointly construct meaning.
3. *Internally motivated.* Engaged readers are intrinsically motivated to read for many personal goals, including gaining informational knowledge and reading for pleasure.

You can pick out the engaged readers in your classes. These are your students who are intrinsically motivated to read more about a topic of interest; they can apply their background knowledge strategically to learn new information; they enjoy the challenges of deeply thinking about and discussing new knowledge and thought-provoking ideas with others; they get "lost" in their books, absorbed in the story or the text. Perhaps most important, they believe that *they are in control* of their own learning and success in school. The contrast between our most and least engaged readers could not be more striking. Not surprisingly, the research in this area highlights the stark differences between the most and least engaged students and the strong links between reading engagement and achievement (Guthrie, 2004):

- Engaged readers spend 500 percent more time reading than disengaged readers.
- Incorporating motivational practices into comprehension strategy instruction significantly increases students' reading comprehension.
- Studies have found that the correlation between reading comprehension achievement and engaged reading "was higher than any demographic characteristic, such as gender, income, or ethnicity" (Guthrie, 2004, p. 5).

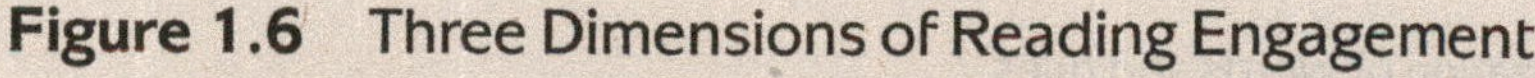

Figure 1.6 Three Dimensions of Reading Engagement

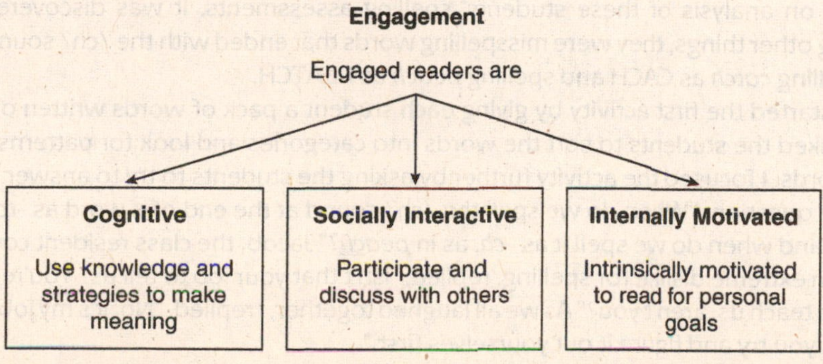
Engagement
Engaged readers are
Cognitive
Use knowledge and strategies to make meaning
Socially Interactive
Participate and discuss with others
Internally Motivated
Intrinsically motivated to read for personal goals

This last point is perhaps the most incredible finding from the research on engagement—that *engagement can trump powerful risk factors* such as low socioeconomic status and low education level of parents. Simply put, engagement powers the engine of reading comprehension and content area learning. Engagement is also critical in learning about words. Vocabulary researchers refer to a related concept, *word consciousness*, to describe a person's positive disposition toward words and word learning (Stahl & Nagy, 2006). These two important concepts, engagement and word consciousness, are at the core of this book and should be at the core of any serious effort to work with older, at-risk students. Creating a lively and engaging classroom atmosphere for word learning is critical to the success of our struggling readers. This type of teaching and learning will lead to deep, long-term word knowledge; it will also make teaching and learning more enjoyable and rewarding for you and your students.

engagement LINK

Throughout the chapters, we will include engagement links in the margins like this one to highlight motivational practices.

We know that engaging our least engaged students can be a very difficult task; however, there are specific, research-based practices that we have used and found effective in both classroom and clinical settings. In Chapter 2, we introduce these core motivational practices—such as providing student choice, self-directed learning and goal setting, and collaborative activities—that you can incorporate into your classroom to ignite a word learning spark in your students. Throughout the remainder of the book, we will further highlight and elaborate on these motivational practices with "engagement links" in the margins to provide you with more specific ideas.

Word Study Instruction with Older Struggling Readers

In the first half of this chapter, we described three areas of word knowledge difficulty for older struggling readers: (1) difficulties in spelling and reading knowledge, (2) difficulties in vocabulary knowledge, and (3) lack of motivation and engagement to learn about words and the concepts they represent. In the second half of this chapter, we introduce you to a powerful and highly engaging approach to word knowledge instruction that directly targets the spelling, reading, and vocabulary needs of your older struggling readers—word study.

> Perhaps the best way to give you a sense of the potential power of this approach with struggling readers is to share an early personal classroom experience with word study. One of the authors [Flanigan] was working with a small group of sixth grade struggling readers who had significant difficulties spelling and decoding words and had been turned off by traditional approaches to spelling instruction—approaches that were based on
>
> - Whole-class instruction
> - Identical spelling lists for every student, regardless of any individual's level of word knowledge
> - Rote memorization of words and rules
>
> Based on analysis of these students' spelling assessments, it was discovered that, among other things, they were misspelling words that ended with the /ch/ sound, such as spelling *catch* as CACH and spelling *peach* as PEATCH.
>
> I started the first activity by giving each student a pack of words written on cards and asked the students to sort the words into categories and look for patterns across the words. I focused the activity further by asking the students to try to answer the following question: "When do we spell the /ch/ sound at the end of a word as *-tch*, as in *catch*, and when do we spell it as *-ch*, as in *peach*?" Jacob, the class resident comedian with an extreme dislike for spelling, replied, "Isn't that your job to tell us? You're getting paid to teach us, aren't you?" As we all laughed together, I replied, "No, it's my job to help you as you try and figure it out yourselves first."

The energy level in the room immediately picked up and the discussion became lively as the sixth graders began moving the word cards into different categories, pointing out patterns that they noticed, asking questions, and discussing their thinking. After a few minutes the students had sorted the words into two categories like this:

catch	peach
hatch	coach
pitch	roach
blotch	teach
twitch	beach
stretch	screech
clutch	reach
latch	speech

Most students immediately saw that the words on the left all ended in *-tch* and those on the right all ended in *-ch*, but couldn't tell much more. I provided more support by asking, "Are there any other differences you see between these words? Any differences in how they look or sound that might give you a clue as to when to spell the /ch/ sound at the end of a word with a *-tch* or a *-ch*?" The students began to closely examine the words and read down the list again. I reminded them to look at other parts of the word, including the beginning and the middle.

After a short time, Jacob jumped up and replied, "The words on the left all have only one vowel in the middle, and the words on the right all have two vowels in the middle!" I congratulated Jacob (who now sported a smug grin on his face) on his insight into how the spellings of the two words looked different, but again asked the class, "How about the sound differences?" With additional prodding and examination of the words, Jessie excitedly added that she had found the "rule" for words ending in the /ch/ sound: "If the word has a long vowel sound in the middle, like *beach*, you should spell it *-ch*. If the word has a short vowel sound in the middle, like *witch*, you should spell it *-tch*." At this point, Jacob bolted up out of his seat and, with a look of extreme exasperation on his face, asked, "How come no one ever told us this stuff before? It actually makes some sense!"

Because the students were clearly motivated to continue, I told them that there are at least four words in the English language that do not follow the rule and challenged them to find all four. I was surprised as the students dove right in and diligently began brainstorming words, finding some that did follow the pattern (like *patch*) and eventually finding all four words that didn't follow the pattern: *rich, such, much,* and *which*. As another student pointed out, if these oddball words had followed the pattern, they would be spelled RITCH, SUTCH, MUTCH, and WHITCH. I was astounded, having never seen these normally apathetic students so excited about spelling before! We wrote these oddball words on cards, so the sort now looked like this:

		?
catch	peach	rich
hatch	coach	such
pitch	roach	much
blotch	teach	which
twitch	beach	
stretch	screech	
clutch	reach	
latch	speech	

As the students were about to leave class, Jacob asked, "How do you know that there are only four words in English that don't follow the pattern? What if I find another one tonight? What will we get?" Not wanting to miss this teachable moment, I promised the class an extra break the following day if anyone was able to find another oddball word for homework. The next day, Jacob strutted into the classroom with a look of supreme confidence on his face and announced that he had found a fifth oddball word. The entire class, including the higher-achieving students, was riveted as Jacob strode to the front of the classroom and wrote the following word on the board—*sandwich*—and explained that the second part of the word did not follow the pattern. If it had, it would be spelled SANDWITCH. I argued that *sandwich* did not count because we were only discussing one-syllable words. Jacob argued that I had not said anything about the number of syllables yesterday and appealed to a jury of his peers—the rest of the class. The jury agreed with Jacob and the class received their extra break.

How Word Study Differs from Traditional Approaches to Spelling, Reading, and Vocabulary Instruction

It is clear from the preceding experience that word study is a highly active and powerful approach to spelling, reading, and vocabulary instruction. Initially, the most striking realization from this first experience with word study was that older struggling readers could actually become excited about words and motivated to learn more about how words worked. Even before we knew the terms *engagement* and *word consciousness*, it was apparent from this experience that making words come alive like this—getting normally disengaged students like Jacob to passionately argue about words—was essential to have any chance of getting through to this or other groups of struggling readers. Developed by Edmund Henderson (1981) and his colleagues at the University of Virginia, word study goes beyond traditional modes of instruction, which tend to emphasize rote memorization of spelling rules and vocabulary definitions, in a number of other critically important ways:

- Word study actively engages students in applying critical thinking skills by comparing and contrasting words and word patterns.
- Word study is developmental, meaning that an informed analysis of students' word knowledge can help teachers determine what spelling features to teach and when to teach them.
- Word study combines the best of systematic, explicit instruction with hands-on opportunities for student practice and exploration of words.
- Word study can exponentially boost students' vocabularies by teaching students how to unlock the meaning system that permeates the English language.

Word Study Actively Engages Students in Higher-Level Thinking

As you noticed from the vignette, the students were the ones doing much of the work in the lesson; they were the ones categorizing the words, questioning the teacher and each other, making tentative hypotheses about spelling patterns, and manipulating the word cards. By comparing and contrasting the two spelling patterns (*-tch*/*-ch*), they came up with generalizations about these spelling patterns that they could apply to future words they will encounter. Categorizing, questioning, hypothesizing, manipulating, comparing, contrasting, generalizing—these are exactly the types of higher-level thinking skills we want our middle grade and high school students to develop and use in class. And this is exactly the type of higher-level thinking and engagement that will lead to real, long-term, deep knowledge about words. Sadly, this type of instruction is too often missing for our lowest performing students—the very ones who need it the most.

Word Study Is Developmental

In the example, you may have noticed that the teaching of this group of struggling sixth-graders did not blindly start from lesson 1 of a prescribed, off-the-shelf phonics program.

This type of one-size-fits-all teaching doesn't work. It would be akin to a ski instructor taking a group of skiers of different ability levels and starting them all off on the same intermediate-level slope. For the most skilled skiers, the intermediate slope would quickly become boring because it presents no challenge, no room to grow. For the least skilled skiers, the intermediate slope would quickly prove frustrating, possibly even dangerous, and would probably not result in a return trip to the slopes any time soon. Thankfully, effective ski instructors don't do this; what they do is find out *your* ability level and start you off on the appropriate slope with instruction tailored to fit *your* specific skill level.

In the same way, it was necessary to first find out what these particular students knew about the spelling system prior to any decision on where to start instruction. So a diagnostic spelling assessment was used to help identify the spelling features our students were ready to examine. (Chapter 3 describes how to assess your students in this way.) This type of precise, timely teaching that allows teachers to differentiate and individualize instruction is another important way in which word study differs from many other programs. Diagnostic teaching is also beneficial because it enables us to build on what students already know rather than focus solely on what they do not know.

Word study is based on developmental spelling theory and research, which shows that students learn spelling patterns in a developmental progression that can be organized into stages (Bear et al., 2008). The word study approach to phonics and spelling instruction is a systematic approach based on this predictable scope and sequence of phonetic and spelling features that parallels students' growing knowledge of English orthography. Students' spellings help guide teachers in their instructional decision making and allow them to differentiate effective, efficient instruction based on their students' present knowledge. As in the example, students should begin instruction where their assessments indicate, and teachers should address each student at his or her instructional level. This student-based instruction is especially important for struggling readers/writers/spellers (Morris, Blanton, Blanton, Nowacek, & Perney, 1995).

Word Study Combines the Best of Systematic, Explicit Instruction with Hands-On Opportunities for Student Practice and Exploration of Words

The experience with the sixth-graders also debunks the unspoken myth among many that explicit instruction in spelling and phonics skills must necessarily include boring drills, rote memorization, and lower-level thinking. In fact, one great benefit of word study is that teachers can balance explicit instruction with hands-on exploration of words in an engaging and thought-provoking manner.

Systematic and Explicit Instruction

Explicit instruction is commonly accepted as an effective mode of instruction in phonics and spelling (Moats, 2000; National Reading Panel, 2000) and should involve a direct connection to reading and writing. This mode of instruction includes opportunities for repeated practice that are both teacher-guided and student-led. Explicit instruction is commonly defined as a manageable presentation with "how to" information and modeling, guided practice and feedback, independent practice, and repeated practice as necessary (Duffy, 2003; Rosenshine, 1986). The lesson previously described included multiple opportunities for the sixth-graders to repeatedly practice reading, manipulating, and thinking about the words. Teacher support was provided through questions (Do you notice any sound differences in the word?) that focused the students' attention on particular parts of the word. If the students needed it, the lesson could have been made even more explicit by modeling how to sort the first two to three words in each column and explaining our thinking as we did so.

Time, of course, is of the essence because struggling readers are already behind their peers in reading and writing achievement. Explicit instruction can provide an efficient method for skill development, if carefully planned and executed to address areas (i.e., phonics and spelling) that are most highly associated with later literacy outcomes as well as more global literacy areas such as comprehension. Instruction that is more explicit and complete produces greater effects, especially with students experiencing difficulties (Duffy et al., 1987).

Hands-On Practice and Application

In addition to explicit instruction within a systematic scope and sequence, students who struggle to acquire literacy skills also need a lot of hands-on practice and application. The categorization aspect of word study makes it particularly beneficial for these students as it affords them the opportunity to manipulate specific word features and apply critical thinking skills. The word study approach teaches students how to look at words so that they can construct an in-depth understanding of how written words work as they make generalizations.

Through word study, teachers guide their students to compare and contrast words based on similarities and differences, just as the sixth-graders did in the vignette when comparing words like *patch* and *stitch* with words like *peach* and *reach*. In this way, word learning is a conceptual process that requires children to recognize and use the similarities and differences among words through comparisons. This type of categorization is a fundamental cognitive activity that leads to forming the concepts making up our knowledge base (Gillet & Kita, 1980). Categorization allows us to organize new information in relation to known information and then make generalizations about the characteristics of all members of a certain category (Bruner, Goodnow, & Austin, 1966). For example, children who know the word *round* can apply their understanding of the *-ound* phonogram when reading or spelling new words like *sound, ground,* and *hound.*

Considerations for English Learners

Determining Language Experiences

In our nation's schools, there has been dramatic growth in the percentage of students from diverse language backgrounds. Just as struggling readers are not a monolithic group, neither are these English learners—they can enter your classroom with a wide range of language and literacy experiences and with different levels of competency in both English and their home language. Bear, Helman, Templeton, Invernizzi, and Johnston (2007, pp. 5–6) discuss four different examples of literacy proficiency among English learners:

- Some English learners enter school already proficient in their native oral and written language.
- Bilingual English learners demonstrate oral language competencies in both English and a second language.
- Some learners may be proficient speakers in their first language, without being literate in that first language. These students must acquire basic reading skills while learning to speak English at the same time.
- Some English learners may not have a solid base of language development in their first language.

As you can see from these examples, there can be significant educational differences and varying needs among your English learners. Because of this, it is important to find out what language and literacy experiences your students have already had. This will help you to better meet their needs while simultaneously building on their strengths. In terms of instruction, the research on diverse learners has identified a common set of teaching principles and practices that promotes successful learning for all students, including language-minority students (Center for Research on Education, Diversity and Excellence, 2004). In Chapter 2, we will discuss how general principles and practices for English learners overlap with instructional principles and practices for struggling readers.

Word Study Can Exponentially Boost Students' Vocabulary Growth

The sixth grade example showed how word study can effectively target students' ability to read and spell words, but how can word study help to close the vocabulary gap for struggling readers? In contrast to vocabulary programs that emphasize teaching words one at a time, word study can exponentially boost students' vocabularies by also teaching them the meaning system that underlies these words.

By way of example, we were working with a small group of middle grade students, examining words that all shared the root *spect* (e.g., *spectator, spectacles, inspector*). These students were trying to discover the root's underlying meaning by comparing the meanings of the individual words. After a lively discussion, one of the students blurted out, "I've got it. You use *spectacles* to look at something, an *inspector* looks into things, and *spectators* look at or watch a game. So they all mean to look at something! *Spect* must mean to look." A few minutes later, another student, who had attended basketball games at the *Spectrum* (the professional basketball arena where the Philadelphia 76ers used to play) many times, screamed aloud when she realized why the basketball arena was called the *Spectrum*. She kept repeating, "I was a *spectator* at the *Spectrum*. I was a *spectator* at the *Spectrum*." To which another student queried, "Were you wearing your *spectacles*?"

We have found this engagement and excitement in learning about words a natural byproduct of the active nature of word study. In addition to the development of this word consciousness, these students are learning the meanings of the specific words examined in the lesson and, just as importantly, are learning about how to generalize their knowledge to new words in reading and writing. For example, learning only one high-frequency root, like *spect*, can help students unlock the meanings of many more words, like *spectacular, speculate, respect, disrespect, specter, circumspect, prospect,* and *introspect*. Figure 1.7 is an example of how students can generate 15 words from only one root, *spect*, using a root web activity—notice how all of these words share a common meaning (*spectacular*—something that is worth looking at; *spectator*—one who looks). In addition, as Figure 1.7 shows, students can take root webs to a second level of generation (generating *respectful, respectable,* and *respective* from the base word *respect*). This activity gives you a flavor for the potential power and excitement of generative vocabulary instruction—in which we teach students how they can generate literally thousands of words from a relatively small number of roots. Chapter 6 describes activities and teaching strategies that will support this type of learning in your classroom.

Figure 1.7 Root Web of *Spect*

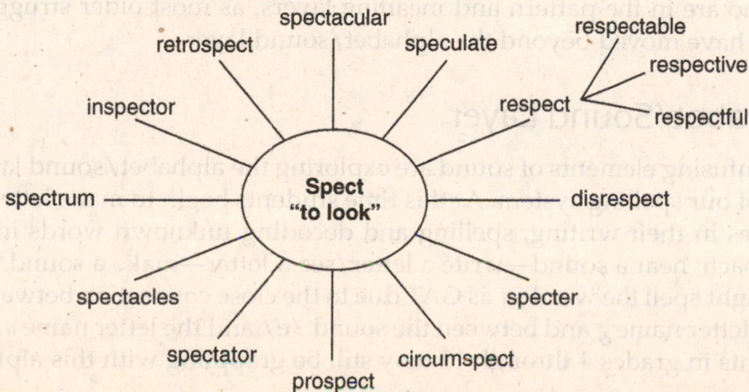

The Basis of Word Study

Historically, traditional spelling instruction was based on memorization, because written English was commonly accepted as being extremely unpredictable. This belief is not uncommon among teachers today. Many still believe that once letter sounds and a limited number of "rules" about letter patterns (e.g., "when two vowels go walking, the first one does the talking") are learned, students must resort to rote memorization.

Starting in the 1960s, a number of researchers began to find that the English spelling system was much more regular than originally thought (Chomsky & Halle, 1968; Hanna, Hanna, Hodges, & Rudorf, 1966; Venezky, 1970). For example, Venezky (1967) provided support for the assertion that written English is predictable when considering patterns of letters, rather than individual letters, with his idea of *functional spelling units* (e.g., considering *gain* as *g-ai-n* rather than *g-a-i-n*). In building on this corpus of work, Henderson and his colleagues at the University of Virginia introduced the learner's developing knowledge of these regularities as an additional consideration (Henderson & Beers, 1980; Templeton & Bear, 1992).

At the same time that Henderson and his colleagues were examining students' spellings, the linguist Charles Read began investigating students' writing in the late 1960s, which ultimately changed the face of early literacy instruction. Specifically, Read (1971) investigated preschool students' invented spellings. He found that their spellings were not random, as was initially thought, but were based on the students' tacit knowledge of English phonology. This research was pivotal in the burgeoning work of Henderson and his colleagues; Henderson's growing corpus of students' invented spellings showed similarities to the observations of Read—a logical system to students' spellings that evolve over time. This predictable progression of spelling development has been observed in various groups of students from preschool students (Templeton & Spivey, 1980) to adults (Bear, Truex, & Barone, 1989), as well as in students across dialects (Cantrell, 2001; Stever, 1980) and other alphabetic languages (Gill, 1980; Temple, 1978). Students who experience difficulty learning to read also appear to go through this same progression of development (Worthy & Invernizzi, 1989).

Three Layers of English Orthography

A critical observation made by Henderson and his colleagues was that students and adults tend to move from confusion over elements of *alphabet/sound* (JAT for jet), to confusion over elements of *pattern* (MAIK for *make*), to confusion over elements of *meaning* (RECUTATION for *recitation*). This progression occurs for all learners of written English—including English learners, struggling readers and writers, and students with learning disabilities—varying only in the rate of acquisition. This progression, as noted in Figure 1.8, mirrors the historical evolution of written English and follows three layers of knowledge—alphabet/sound, pattern, and meaning. In this book, we focus on students who are in the pattern and meaning layers, as most older struggling readers (but not all) have moved beyond the alphabet/sound layer.

The Alphabet/Sound Layer

Students confusing elements of sound are exploring the alphabet/sound layer, the most basic level of our spelling system. At this time students begin to make letter–sound correspondences in their writing, spelling and decoding unknown words in a primarily linear approach: hear a sound—write a letter/see a letter—make a sound. A student at this level might spell the word *jet* as GAT due to the close connection between the sound /j/ and the letter name *g* and between the sound /e/ and the letter name *a*. Some struggling students in grades 4 through 12 may still be grappling with this alphabet/sound

Figure 1.8 Three Layers of English Orthography: Sound, Pattern, and Meaning

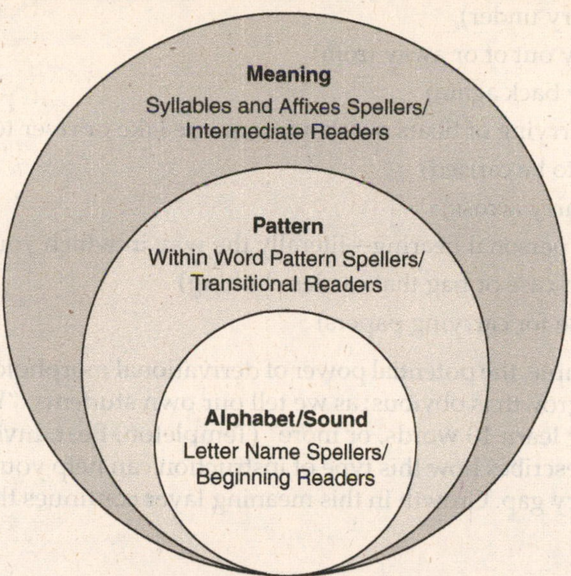

layer. However, most students should be mastering concepts commonly confused in this layer by the end of first grade. Because most older struggling readers will have moved beyond this stage, the alphabet/sound layer will not be a focus in this book.

The Pattern Layer

The second level of our spelling system is the pattern layer. Students who are clear on letter–sound connections and starting to explore elements of the pattern layer are beginning to understand that letters in single-syllable words are combined in various patterns. For example, three long *a* vowel patterns students examine at this stage are the *e*-marker in *cake,* the *ai* in *rain,* and the *ay* in *tray.* Later in the pattern layer, students begin to investigate the patterns of syllable combinations, such as the open syllable pattern in *pi-lot* and the closed syllable pattern in *bon-net*. These pattern issues should be cleared up around the end of fifth grade. However, in our experience, the bulk of students experiencing difficulty in grades 4 through 12 are clustered at this level. Part II of this book describes word study assessment and instruction for struggling readers in the pattern layer.

The Meaning Layer

The meaning layer of our spelling system takes the *morphology* (the study of *morphemes,* or meaning units) of our language into account. Morphological knowledge takes center stage with middle grade and high school students as they examine how meaningful chunks of language combine. The student confusing elements of morphology is first investigating *inflectional* morphology, which indicates verb tense (adding *-ed* to a verb such as *jump* to indicated past action—*jumped*) and number (adding an *-s* to *dog* to make the plural form—*dogs*). Students then begin to consider *derivational* morphology, in which the addition of affixes allows us to derive many additional words from a single base word or root. For example, from only one root like *port* (meaning "to carry"), the following 12 words can be derived by adding prefixes, suffixes, or attaching to other roots. Notice how all of these words share a common meaning: "to carry."

porter (one who carries)
export (to carry out)
import (to carry in)
support (to carry under)
deport (to carry out of or away from)
report (to carry back again)
portage (the carrying of boats overland from one lake or river to another)
portable (able to be carried)
transport (to carry across)
comportment (personal bearing—literally the way in which you carry yourself)
portmanteau (a case or bag that carries clothing)
portfolio (a case for carrying papers)

From this example, the potential power of derivational morphology to exponentially boost vocabulary growth is obvious; as we tell our own students, "When you learn one word, you actually learn 10 words, or more" (Templeton, Bear, Invernizzi, & Johnston, 2010). Chapter 6 describes how this type of instruction can help your struggling readers close the vocabulary gap. Growth in this meaning layer continues throughout students' academic careers.

Word Study Is Developmental—Even for Struggling Readers

The word study approach is inherently systematic, based on a scope and sequence of these layers, and parallels students' growing knowledge of orthography. Word study differs from the approaches of many systematic commercial programs, because word study (1) is based on a developmental continuum of word learning and (2) differentiates instruction for students based on their achievement relative to this developmental continuum. Students are first assessed to determine their instructional level within the word study continuum (i.e., where they fit in the developmental sequence of orthographic development). Bear and colleagues (2008) maintain that students must be taught at their stage of development or instructional level, the level at which they know enough to profit from instruction no matter what their age or grade level. There are five developmental stages or instructional levels of word knowledge that further differentiate the three layers of English orthography (*emergent, letter name–alphabetic, within word pattern, syllables and affixes,* and *derivational relations*). Each stage corresponds to certain grade levels, as shown in Figure 1.9. Within each stage, there is a progression of phonic and spelling features as illustrated in Figure 1.10 (Bear et al., 2008).

As students progress through the developing stages of spelling knowledge, they also move through a predictable continuum of reading development. Reading, writing, and spelling have a reciprocal relationship; they are dependent on and reinforce one another. Emergent spellers are not yet reading, and their spelling attempts do not represent any letter–sound correspondences. The letter name speller relies on the names of letters to spell words and functions in a beginning stage of reading development. Within word pattern spellers are more conventional in their spelling attempts as they begin to rely on letter patterns for various sounds. Additionally, these students are working on developing their reading fluency as transitional readers. Students who have reached the syllables and affixes stage are learning about patterns within and across syllables in multisyllabic words. Students at this stage would be considered intermediate readers. The last stage, derivational relations, involves the understanding of spelling–meaning

Figure 1.9 Spelling and Reading Stages and Grade Levels

Alphabet *--------->* ***Pattern*** *--------->* ***Meaning***

Emergent Stage
Emergent Reading
Pre-K to middle of 1

Letter Name–Alphabetic Stage
Beginning Reading
K to middle of 2

Within Word Pattern Stage
Transitional Reading
Grade 1 to middle of 4

Syllables and Affixes Stage
Intermediate Reading
Grades 3 to 8

Derivational Relations
Advanced Reading
Grades 5 to 12

Figure 1.10 Spelling and Reading Stages

Alphabet ——> **Pattern** ——> **Meaning**

Emergent Spelling
Emergent Reader

Prereading *(Chall, 1983)*
Logographic *(Frith, 1985)*
Prealphabetic *(Ehri, 1997)*

Letter Name–Alphabetic Spelling
Beginning Reader

Stage 1: Initial Reading & Decoding *(Chall, 1983)*
Alphabetic *(Frith, 1985)*
Partial-to-Full Alphabetic *(Ehri, 1997)*
Phonetic Cue *(Spear-Swerling & Sternberg, 1996)*

Within Word Pattern Spelling
Transitional Reader

Stage 2: Confirmation & Fluency *(Chall, 1983)*
Orthographic *(Frith, 1985)*
Consolidated Alphabetic *(Ehri, 1997)*
Automatic Word Recognition *(Spear-Swerling & Sternberg, 1996)*

Syllables and Affixes Spelling
Intermediate Reader

Stage 3: Reading to Learn *(Chall, 1983)*
Strategic Reading *(Spear-Swerling & Sternberg, 1996)*

Derivational Relations Spelling
Advanced Reader

Stage 4: Multiple Viewpoints *(Chall, 1983)*
Stage 5: Construction & Reconstruction *(Chall, 1983)*
Proficient Adult Reading *(Spear-Swerling & Sternberg, 1996)*

connections in derivationally related words. Consistent with this stage of spelling is the advanced stage of reading.

The Synchrony of Literacy Development

Students progress through increasing levels of reading competencies in relation to these stages of word knowledge development. Many studies have found that spelling knowledge contributes to reading growth (e.g., Cataldo & Ellis, 1988; Ehri & Wilce, 1987; Morris & Perney, 1984). This makes sense; a student who has a grasp of the *oa* spelling pattern as in *soap* will be more likely to successfully decode words like *groan* and *floating* while reading. Many researchers have factored word knowledge into their reading stages (Chall, 1983; Ehri, 1997; Frith, 1985; Spear-Swerling & Sternberg, 2000), as you can see in Figure 1.10. The stages put forth by these researchers describe a similar progression of reading that follows a child's development from prereader to skilled reader.

The synchrony of development clearly demonstrates the connection between reading and spelling. You may, however, be wondering about words your students may be able to read but find difficult to spell. Consider the example of a student who spells the word *mouth* as MAOTH but reads it correctly in the following sentence: "The cheese fell out of the crow's *mouth*." How could a student be able to read *mouth* accurately but not spell it correctly? This phenomenon can be explained simply. Based on this student's spelling, the vowel pattern poses the most difficulty. The student uses known elements of the word—the consonants—along with the context of the sentence to accurately identify the word *mouth*. Reading is a recognition task and is, therefore, easier to perform relative to the productive task of spelling. When asked to spell the word, however, every letter counts. The following section outlines the stages of spelling and their reading stage connections that will be used throughout this book.

The Emergent Speller and Emergent Reader

As outlined in Figure 1.11, students in the alphabet/sound layer are first in the emergent stage of spelling development and the emergent stage of reading. These students do not use letter–sound correspondence when attempting to spell. They will scribble, use letter-like forms, or write random letters when asked to spell a word. For example, a child at this level might spell the word *cat* as RT4KS3, exhibiting no letter–sound correspondence or awareness of individual sounds or phonemes. This "pretend" way of dealing with the task of spelling is why Chall (1983) used the term *prereading* for this stage.

Similarly, the emergent child's reading does not reflect any letter–sound knowledge. When asked to read text, these students will be unable to match their speech to the print and may not even have a sense of directionality of print (left-to-right progression of text). Often children at this stage of development recognize words or phrases as a "logo." For example, a child looking at a stop sign might say, "Look mommy—it says *stop!*" This is not a result of reading; it is due to recognition of the logo/picture. As a result, Ehri (1997) coined this phase of development the *prealphabetic stage* and Frith (1985) used *logographic stage*. Typically, children at this stage of reading and spelling are in prekindergarten through kindergarten; however, learners exhibiting these characteristics are in this stage of development regardless of grade level. Because the majority of struggling students in grades 4 through 12 will have passed beyond this stage, we do not address the specific needs of emergent readers/writers in this book.

The Letter Name Speller and Beginning Reader

Later in the alphabet/sound layer, students move to the letter name stage of spelling and the beginning stage of reading. Children at this stage tackle a word in the following manner: hear a sound—write a letter/see a letter—make a sound. The problem

Figure 1.11 Synchrony of Literacy Development in English

ALPHABET/SOUND

PATTERN

MEANING

Reading and Writing Stages/Phases:

	Emergent	Beginning	Transitional	Intermediate	Advanced
	Early Middle Late	*Early Middle Late*	*Early Middle Late*	*Early Middle Late*	*Early Middle Late*
Reading	Pretend read	Read aloud, word-by-word, fingerpoint reading	Approaching fluency, phrasal, some expression in oral reading	Read fluently, with expression. Develop a variety of reading styles. Vocabulary grows with experience reading.	
Writing	Pretend write	Word-by-word writing, writing moves from a few words to paragraph in length	Approaching fluency, more organization, several paragraphs	Fluent writing, build expression and voice, experience different writing styles and genre. Writing shows personal problem solving and personal reflection.	

Spelling Stages/Phases:

Emergent → **Letter Name–Alphabetic** → **Within Word Pattern** → **Syllables and Affixes** → **Derivational Relations** →

Examples of misspellings:

Word	Emergent	Letter Name–Alphabetic	Within Word Pattern	Syllables and Affixes	Derivational Relations
bed	*MST E*	*bd bad*	*bed*		
ship	*TFP S*	*sp sep shep*	*ship*		
float	*SMT F*	*ft fot flot flott*	*flowt floaut flote float*		
train	*FSMP G*	*jn jan tan chran tran*	*teran traen trane train*		
bottle	*B*	*bt botl bodol*	*botel botal*	*bottel bottle*	
cellar	*S*	*slr salr celr*	*seler celer seler*	*celler seller cellar*	
pleasure	*P*	*pjr plasr plager*	*plejer pleser plesher*	*pleser plesher plesour*	*plesure pleasure*
confident				*confadent confiednet*	*confedent confendent confident*
opposition				*opasishan oppasishion*	*opositian oposision opposition*

arises in their limited knowledge of individual sounds in words and of letter sounds. Letter name spellers have a developing awareness of individual phonemes, meaning that they may sometimes exclude a sound due to their inability to parse out that particular sound in the word. Initially, these children will represent word boundaries when asked to spell single-syllable words. For example, if asked to spell the word *date,* the early letter name speller would write DT. These students have progressed from pretend reading to real reading. However, they read with partial cues as evidenced in their spelling. For example, a child functioning early in this stage may read the word *cake* in "The boy ate the cake" as *cookie* or *candy* due to this limited knowledge of letter sounds and partial phoneme awareness. Therefore, books for children at this stage must be extremely supportive with predictable and easily memorized text. Due to these defining characteristics, Ehri (1997) called this portion of the stage the *partial alphabetic phase.*

As children move through the stage, their awareness of individual sounds (phonemes) in words becomes more fully developed. At this point, children will include the medial vowel of single-syllable words in their spelling even if it is not accurate. For example, when spelling the word *champ,* the letter name speller might omit the *m* in the *-mp* blend, spelling the word as *chap.* These spellers also rely on the names of letters to spell words. For example, when spelling the word *job,* the letter name speller might represent the word as GIB. The sound of the *j* in *job* sounds like the the letter *g,* the short *o* sound is close to the name of the letter *i,* and the sound of *b* leads the letter name speller to the letter name *b.*

As letter name spellers progress through this stage, they are developing a bank of words that they know automatically. These children are able to firmly establish a word in their memory because of their more developed knowledge of letter sounds and their growing phonemic awareness. However, without a sizeable bank of known words, these readers are characteristically disfluent readers, meaning they read aloud in a word-by-word, unexpressive fashion as they finger-point text. This portion of the stage corresponds to Ehri's (1997) *full alphabetic phase.* Even though children with these characteristics can be found in any grade, this stage of development generally coincides with first grade expectations. As in the emergent stage, the majority of your struggling readers and writers in grades 4 through 12 will probably be beyond this letter name speller/beginning reader stage. Therefore, this stage will not be a focus in this book.

The Within Word Pattern Speller and Transitional Reader

Our colleague Regina Smith calls the within word pattern stage "the black hole of reading" because so many older struggling readers get stuck here in their literacy development. Roughly equivalent to the second through fourth grade literacy levels for "average" achieving students, this stage focuses on mastering knowledge of single-syllable word patterns. Bear, Invernizzi, Templeton, and Johnston (2004) estimate that 25 *percent of the adult population* in the United States is at this stage. In Chapter 4, we discuss specific principles and practices for working with students in this stage.

At the within word pattern stage, students begin to investigate vowel and consonant patterns in single-syllable words. No longer are they tied to the very linear approach of the beginning reader/letter name speller; students at the pattern layer know that they may need more than one letter per sound heard in a word. For example, a letter name speller might spell the word *train* as TRAN, using one letter for each sound. However, a within word pattern speller might spell *train* as TRANE, realizing that the long *a* pattern must be accompanied with a silent letter. Although both students' spellings of *train* are incorrect, you can see how much more sophisticated the within word pattern student's word knowledge is. Students at this stage are studying the sound and pattern simultaneously as they learn that the long *a* sound can be represented with a variety of letter patterns (e.g., *cake, rain, tray, weight*).

Within word pattern spellers simultaneously move into the transitional stage of reading development. As with spelling, these readers have consolidated single letter–sound units into larger chunks/patterns as they process progressively higher-order units of word structures to read and spell (Chall, 1983; Ehri, 1997; Frith, 1985). For example, the transitional reader would chunk the word *clamp* as *cl-amp* rather than *c-l-a-m-p,* becoming able to store words more efficiently in memory and read and spell words more accurately and fluently.

Transitional readers also have a sizeable store of words they know automatically, which frees up more of their attention resources while reading to devote to building fluency and comprehending more difficult text. They begin to read silently, and their reading develops a more prosodic quality. They are beginning to read in phrasal units, but still sometimes must revert back to word-by-word reading when confronted with more difficult text. Children at this stage of development are generally in second grade and are transitioning out of this stage sometime in third grade. It is important to remember, though, that children with these characteristics can occur at any grade and that many struggling adolescent readers find themselves stuck at this stage searching for the tools they need to progress.

The Syllables and Affixes Speller and Intermediate Reader

A large number of struggling readers and writers at the middle grade and high school level will have a solid understanding of the single-syllable pattern words examined in the within word pattern stage, but will still experience difficulty decoding and spelling multisyllabic words such as *maintain, cascade,* and *respectable.* These more advanced spellers and decoders are ready for instruction in more sophisticated skills that focus on developing an awareness and knowledge of multisyllabic words. In Chapter 5, we discuss specific principles and practices for working with students in this stage of literacy development.

Students at this stage have transitioned from a single-syllable word focus to patterns in two-syllable words. For example, they might spell the word *bonnet* like BONET if they have not yet reached the understanding that a stressed syllable with a short vowel must be closed by a consonant, the vowel-consonant-consonant-vowel spelling pattern. With multisyllabic words comes the issue of syllable stress. The syllables and affixes speller must make decisions about whether a syllable is stressed and what happens to vowel patterns in either situation. For example, say the following two words aloud: *contain* and *fountain.* As you can hear, the *ai* in *contain* sounds quite different from the *ai* in *fountain* due to the stressed syllable.

These types of spellers are known as intermediate stage readers, among whom silent reading dominates. Readers in this stage can adjust their reading pace and attention based on the changing demands of text. With a high level of cognitive energy available, students can focus more readily on content area learning and strategic reading (Chall, 1983; Spear-Swerling & Sternberg, 2000). They will process words at the syllable level when faced with an unknown word, dividing words into syllables and determining how those constituent parts fit together. For example, when faced with the unknown word *trample,* the reader at this stage will divide the word into *tram-ple.* Readers and spellers at this stage are typically found in grades 3 through 5, although many struggling adolescents will also find themselves in this stage. These struggling readers often have a difficulty mastering this stage. For example, they may be able to read books at the fourth grade level but not with the same speed as average developing intermediate readers.

The Derivational Speller and Advanced Reader

Late syllables and affixes spellers are also considering word components relative to the meaning layer as they compare various morphemic units. For example, students at this stage learn about plurals (*cakes, foxes, ponies*), inflected endings (*coaching, hopping, skating*), and common affixes (*rewrite, taller*). Later in the meaning layer, students become derivational relations spellers and advanced readers. As spellers, they are investigating meaning chunks in derivationally related words. For example, children at the beginning of this stage might spell the word *composition* as COMPASITION. As they progress through this stage, they learn a powerful principle—that words that are related in meaning are often related in spelling. In the case of the word *composition*, they make the connection to the word *compose*—a word that is related in both meaning and spelling. Readers at this stage are very accomplished in their reading skills and learn many new concepts and vocabulary words while interacting with text. They are critical readers who not only consolidate new information, incorporating it into already known concepts, but also make decisions about what information they feel is important to consider (Chall, 1983; Spear-Swerling & Sternberg, 2000).

These types of readers/spellers are most often found in the middle grades and high school (grades 6 through 12). Struggling readers, by definition, will not be advanced readers and thus the majority will not be found at this stage. However, all upper grades students—including struggling readers—can capitalize on the built-in meaning system in English to boost their vocabulary knowledge. This type of generative vocabulary instruction is described in Chapter 6.

chapter 2

Core Word Study Principles and Practices for Spelling, Reading, and Vocabulary Instruction

It is fifth period at Bennett Middle School, team planning time for one of the eighth grade middle school teams. The assistant principal, Janette Maxwell, has called the teachers together to discuss how to best support the at-risk eighth-graders on the team who failed to score "proficient" on the state reading tests in past years. She begins the meeting by asking the teachers, "What are the main literacy problems you are seeing with these students? What, specifically, are they having difficulty with in your classroom?"

"Reading comprehension," immediately replies Tim Jackson, the eighth grade science teacher. "Nearly all of my struggling readers can't understand the science textbook, or understand it enough to get a basic gist of the key information. They are much better at grasping the main science concepts if I guide them through a science experiment beforehand. So, I've begun using a lot of experiments and other hands-on activities. The experiments really seem to work and motivate them; however, I'm worried, because if I rely *only* on experiments to get the information across, my students won't learn how to read science texts, or any science information, for that matter. I'm not really teaching them how to read or write in science—skills that will be even more critical next year in high school."

"Tim, can your at-risk students even read your science textbook fluently?" asks Macy Caldwell, the eighth grade civics teacher. "I've found that a lot of my struggling readers can generally understand our civics text when I read sections *aloud* to them in class, but they simply don't have the decoding skills to read many of the words on the page—if you can't decode the words, you won't be able to comprehend the text. Those struggling readers that *can* decode the words can't do it quickly enough—it takes them so long to decode the words, by the time they get to the end of a paragraph, they've often forgotten what the beginning of the paragraph said! And a lot of these same students don't write a lot—writing is a chore for them. They have trouble spelling words that most eighth-graders should know by now. But I just don't have the time to go back and teach them these basic reading and writing skills *and* still be able to cover the content I need to teach."

"Now that you mention it, a number of them do read in a choppy, word-by-word manner," agrees Tim. "Even more of a problem, at least in my mind, is that they don't *want* to read—and I really can't blame them. I mean, these are good kids—and many try really hard. But I wouldn't want to read a textbook, day in and day out, that was that frustrating either. After a while, I'd probably start to give up, too."

Ms. Mayor, the eighth grade English teacher, who had been quiet until now, chimes in, "You know, for many of my at-risk students, lack of decoding skills is only part of their difficulty. I'm continually surprised at the vocabulary words they don't know and the background knowledge that I assume they already have. And I'm not talking just about my content area vocabulary—I don't expect most of my students to be familiar with many new English concepts like *quatrain* and *red herring*—that's what I'm here to teach them. I'm talking about vocabulary you would find in regular middle school books, regardless of the content area—words like *however, although, produce, disgusted,* and *approve.* Being able to decode these words doesn't help much if you don't know what they mean!"

The issues brought up by the teachers in the vignette are not uncommon for teachers who work with older struggling readers. As we discussed in Chapter 1, while there is no one single profile of an older struggling reader, many older struggling readers have difficulties with *words*—whether it is fluently *spelling* words, accurately and quickly *reading* words, or accessing the *meanings* of words. Because word knowledge is so foundational, word knowledge difficulties can pose a devastating barrier to acquiring and developing many other critical literacy skills, including reading comprehension and skilled writing—two components of literacy that are essential for learning across the content areas in middle and high school. We cannot ignore this word knowledge domino effect and simply hope it goes away. If we are serious about changing the academic careers of our struggling readers, we need to do something different. We need to provide our at-risk students with effective and motivating instruction that directly and precisely targets their areas of need.

So what exactly can you do? What specific teaching strategies and activities can you use in the classroom to help your older struggling readers? In this chapter we present core word study principles and practices for spelling, reading, and vocabulary instruction. These core principles and practices will serve as the foundation for the rest of this book. (For more in-depth discussion of spelling and reading word study instruction, see Part II. For more in-depth discussion of vocabulary word study instruction, see Part III.) This chapter will be divided into the following three parts:

1. Five core principles of word study instruction
2. Core word study practices that build struggling readers' spelling and reading knowledge
3. Core word study practices that build struggling readers' vocabulary knowledge

Five Core Principles of Word Study for Spelling, Reading, and Vocabulary Instruction

We focus on five core principles of word study instruction for struggling readers. As Figure 2.1 indicates, these five principles apply to spelling, reading, and vocabulary instruction and thus will serve as the instructional backbone of this book. Use these principles to guide you—as your "teaching compass"—as you apply and even extend or modify the activities in this book with your struggling readers.

Use Assessment to Guide "Just Right" Instruction

As we discussed in Chapter 1, word study is not an off-the-shelf phonics program in which every student starts in the same place and moves forward in lockstep fashion. Rather, the power of word study comes from a diagnostic approach to teaching in which students begin instruction where the assessments indicate—just as an effective ski instructor begins instruction based on the level of the student's skiing skill. The following sections give you a sense of how assessment can guide instruction in spelling and reading and in vocabulary.

Assessment-Based Instruction in Spelling and Reading

How do we know where to start word study instruction that is "just right" for our students, instruction that provides the optimal level of challenge necessary for growth without causing frustration or leading to failure? As mentioned in Chapter 1, a student's

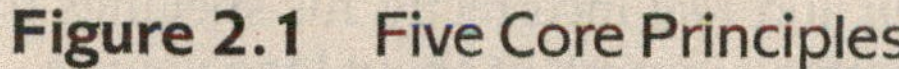

Figure 2.1 Five Core Principles

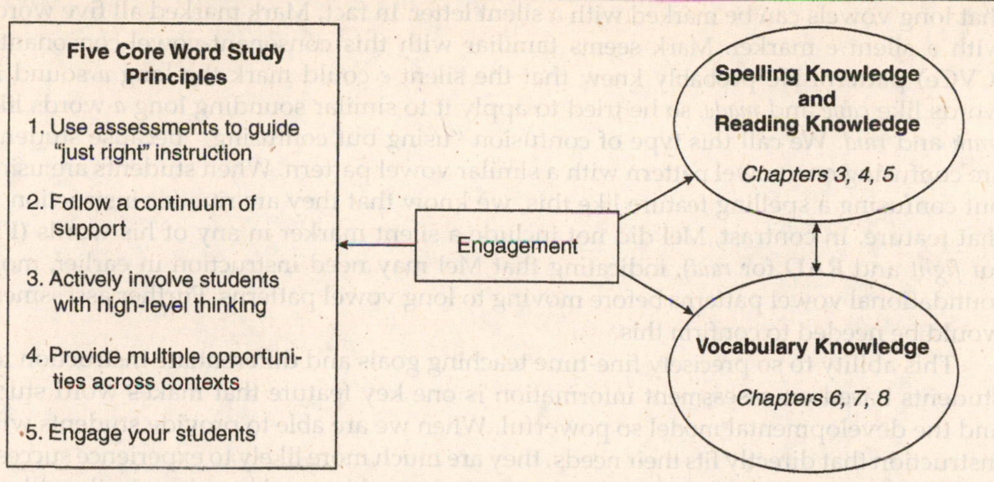

spelling inventory (see Chapter 3 for a step-by-step guide to administering and analyzing spelling inventories) provides excellent diagnostic information about the student's current level of word knowledge. From this assessment, we can determine what spelling features the student already knows solidly and what spelling features he or she is ready to examine next. In this way, you can establish a "just right" goal with your struggling readers—a goal that is not so easy that it will become boring nor so difficult that it will cause frustration. To give you a very small taste of how a student's spellings can help you determine his or her optimal level of word study instruction, look at how three students spelled the following five long vowel pattern words in Figure 2.2: *fight, raid, made, float, train,* and *suit*.

Lynne, in the left-hand column, correctly spelled all five words, indicating that she most likely has a solid knowledge of long vowel patterns. If these spellings are consistent with her ability to read and spell these patterns in context, then Lynne probably does not need much work with this particular spelling feature. Now, let's compare Mark's and Mel's spellings, in the middle and right-hand columns. If you were just marking these two columns for correct/incorrect spellings, both Mark and Mel would receive the same score: zero correct. However, a closer look at their spellings reveals that Mark's spellings are more sophisticated and "nearer the mark" than Mel's.

Figure 2.2 Three Students' Spellings

Lynne	Mark	Mel
fight	fite	fit
raid	rade	rad
float	flote	flot
train	trane	tran
suit	sute	sut

For example, even though Mark spelled *train* and *raid* incorrectly, his spellings of TRANE and RADE reveal that he does know something important about long vowels—that long vowels can be marked with a silent letter. In fact, Mark marked all five words with a silent *e* marker. Mark seems familiar with this consonant-vowel-consonant-*e* (CVCe) pattern. He probably knew that the silent *e* could mark the long *a* sound in words like *cane* and *made*, so he tried to apply it to similar sounding long *a* words like *train* and *raid*. We call this type of confusion "using but confusing," because students are confusing one vowel pattern with a similar vowel pattern. When students are using but confusing a spelling feature like this, we know that they are ripe for instruction in that feature. In contrast, Mel did not include a silent marker in any of his words (FIT for *fight* and RAD for *raid*), indicating that Mel may need instruction in earlier, more foundational vowel patterns before moving to long vowel patterns. Further assessment would be needed to confirm this.

This ability to so precisely fine-tune teaching goals and differentiate instruction for students based on assessment information is one key feature that makes word study and the developmental model so powerful. When we are able to provide students with instruction that directly fits their needs, they are much more likely to experience success. Initial success will lead to motivation to continue working and learning. As the old adage goes, "success breeds further success." Chapter 3 clearly explains step-by-step procedures for administering assessments and analyzing your students' spelling/reading word knowledge needs so you can plan effective word study instruction.

Assessment-Based Instruction in Vocabulary

How do we know if students are ready for instruction in a vocabulary word or a particular concept? Chapter 8 discusses vocabulary assessment in depth, but Beck, McKeown, and Kucan (2002) give the following sage piece of advice—if you can explain the vocabulary word or concept to the student in other words and concepts that the student already knows, the word is probably appropriate. If not, you may need to back up and provide foundational knowledge that is necessary to grasp that particular concept. For example, a *rhombus* could be defined as "an oblique-angled equilateral parallelogram." If your students don't already know the concepts of *oblique*, *equilateral*, and *parallelogram*, this definition will not be of much help. You may need to back up and provide this foundational information first.

Follow a Continuum of Support, Balancing Teacher-Directed Explicit Instruction and Student Exploration

Assessment-based instruction designed to meet your students' needs (as in the spelling example in Figure 2.2) should follow a *gradual release model* (Fisher & Frey, 2008a). To implement this model, you first assume all of the responsibility for the lesson but then gradually release control as your students assume more and more of the responsibility. This gradual release can occur over the course of a month, a week, or even a day. Notice in Figure 2.3 how you move from modeling in the "I do" phase of the model to guiding with "we do," followed by implementing student-led group work with "you do it together," and eventually providing independent practice with "you do it alone." As you work with students, you may find that you move back and forth within the model as dictated by student response, from independent practice back to guided work with teacher support if students are having difficulty with a concept.

Sometimes instruction, especially in the middle grades and high school, includes teacher-led instruction immediately followed by student practice. For example, a math teacher might demonstrate how to find the area of a circle and then expect the students to independently apply the skill in practice items from their math text. However, notice that the math teacher skipped guided instruction and student-led groups, two phases

Figure 2.3 Gradual Release Model

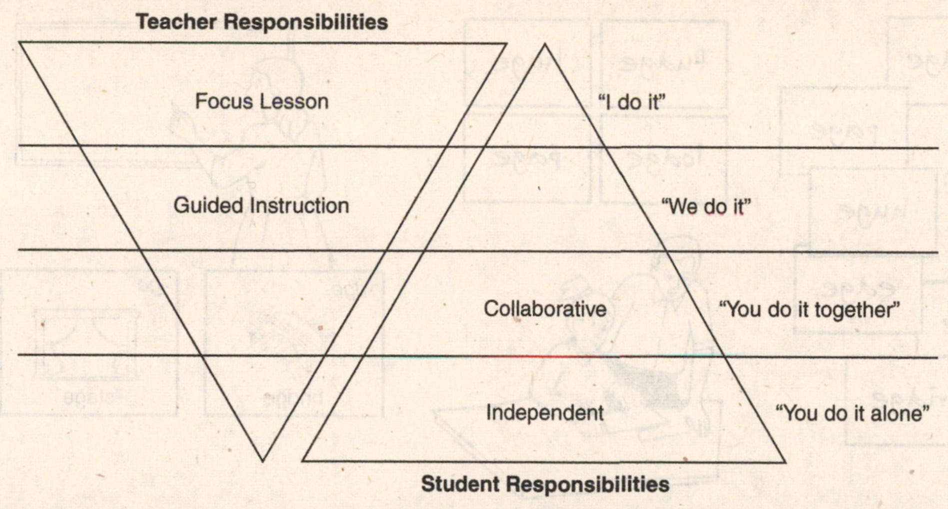

Source: Fisher & Frey, 2008a.

of the model that are crucial to effective implementation. Guided instruction allows you to set high—and appropriate—expectations while providing the necessary support for those expectations to be met. Student-led groups provide a stage for your students to collaborate with peers as they apply features to new contexts.

The first phase of the model—explaining and modeling—is the time you would introduce the concept, skill, or strategy that you have targeted for instruction. For word study lessons, this will generally comprise orthographic features for spelling and reading or vocabulary for meaning. Fisher and Frey (2008a) assert that this phase of the model is "designed to make the learning transparent to the learners" (p. 17). You can think of your instructional stance as moving along a continuum of support (see Figure 2.4). As with all students, there will be times when your instruction needs to be more or less explicit, depending on their knowledge and the information to be learned. To explain this concept, consider three types of instructional approaches: (1) open sort, (2) Guess My Category, and (3) closed sort. Starting at the left, you first encounter the open sort, which is a student-constructed—and student-centered—sort in which students create their own categories with the set of words. Approaching the middle of the continuum, you will see "guess my category," an approach that not only provides the words but also presents the words already placed in their respective categories, without, however, explaining why the words are in their categories. Looking to the right of the continuum, you will find the closed sort, which is the most explicit, providing explicit explanations of the "why" regarding each of the categories being considered. Note that although we will be discussing sorts in terms of sorting words, they can also include pictures or objects.

Open Sort

The open sort is the least explicit approach. It still offers support, because you are stacking the deck by supplying the words to be sorted. However, this sort is student centered rather than teacher directed. In an open sort, your students test their own hypotheses about the sorting categories, leading to discussions that are very rich; students' explanations of why they sorted the way they did reveal much insight into their developing knowledge about orthography. In order to maximize the time spent open sorting, make

Figure 2.4 Continuum of Support

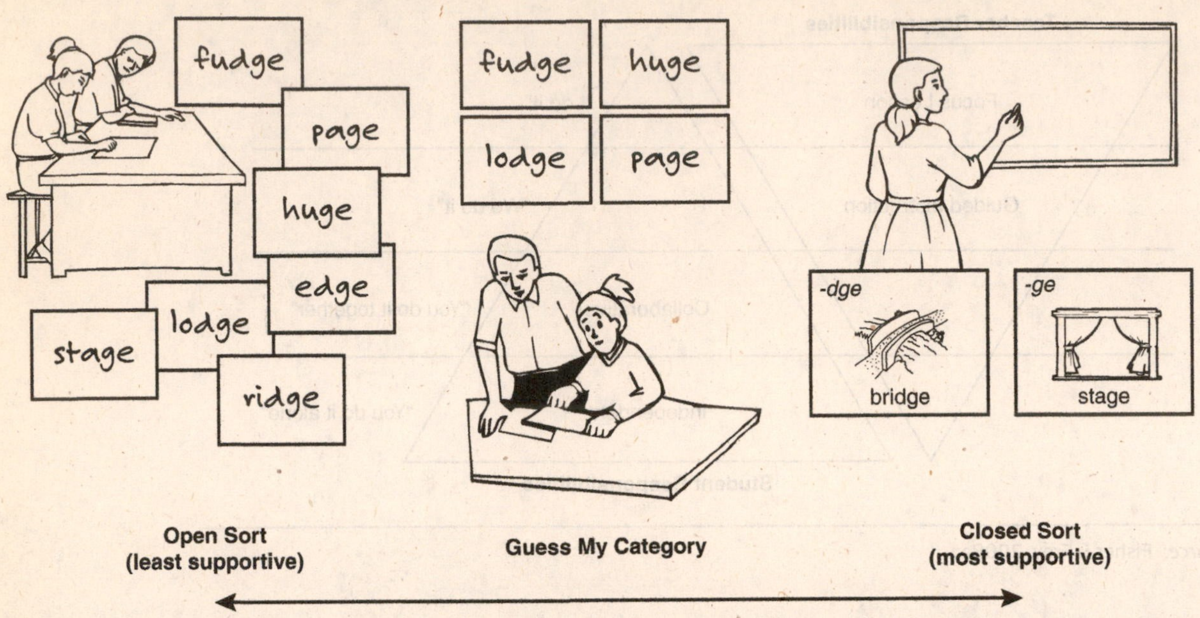

sure your students are familiar with sorting and are adept at finding commonalities among words (or pictures or objects). As a word of caution, your students must have some level of knowledge about the features to be considered in order for them to benefit from the exercise. Stack the sorting deck with words that exemplify the features you are targeting. For example, to encourage consideration of the endings *-dge* and *-ge*, simply give students the following list of words: *fudge, page, huge, lodge, stage, edge, ridge.* Then ask the students to sort the words and try to find categories.

Guess My Category

The Guess My Category approach requires more support from the teacher. Like open sorts, you provide the words to be sorted. An additional provision of the approach is that the words are already placed in categories. You can choose to sort only a few of the words, leaving unsorted words for your students to continue the sort or you can choose to provide the completed sort in its entirety. In either case, the goal is for students to explain why the words have been placed in each category. Guess My Category is particularly useful while working with content-specific vocabulary, but the approach is also effective when considering orthographic features. For example, let's reconsider the *-dge* and *-ge* example from the open sort. You would supply the first few words in the two categories:

fudge	page
lodge	huge

Then give them another word (like *ridge*) and ask where they would put it and why. When the students can explain your categories, they have "guessed the category."

Closed Sort

When working with older struggling readers, time is of the essence, and explicit instruction provides an efficient method for skill development. The most explicit of the three approaches is the closed sort, which is generally used when considering new features. A closed sort stands in direct contrast to the open sort. You not only supply the words to be manipulated in a closed sort but also supply direct instruction on the categories. Teachers model the comparisons and contrasts through the categorization task of sorting. Roehler and Duffy (1984) use the term "direct explanation" rather than "direct instruction." "Explanation" does not involve explicitly *telling* students the rules. As William James admonished, "teaching is not telling" (1899/1958). Word study can be seen as explanatory by teacher modeling and by providing opportunities to investigate and manipulate words according to commonalities and differences in order to make decisions through teacher guidance. In other words, explain the patterns but not the rules. As Fullan, Hill, and Crevola (2006) so plainly put it, we do not need more *prescriptive* teaching but rather more *precision* in our teaching.

After the target features are explained, you then model the sorting process. To do a closed sort with our *-dge* and *-ge* words, you would begin by introducing those features and modeling a few placements, explaining why certain words go in certain categories. Throughout this process, you are engaging your students and encouraging their involvement, which will allow you to gauge your students' understanding of the categories. When your students demonstrate a level of control, you release the sorting task to them. As they work, you discuss the categories and their commonalities, as well as their differences. Corrective feedback is offered when necessary.

Contrary to popular belief, closed sorting can be extremely engaging for your students. Struggling adolescent students tend to be highly engaged when working within their *developmental levels* and on the receiving end of direct, clear explanations of information that has long been an enigma to them. We are reminded of a high school student who responded to a clearly delivered closed sort by asking, "Why didn't anyone tell me this before?"

Choose Activities That Actively Involve Students in Higher-Level Thinking and Deep Processing of Words

According to noted cognitive scientist Daniel Willingham (2009), "Memory is the residue of thought" (p. 41). In other words, we *remember* what we *think about*, and we remember *best* what we think about *most deeply*. In terms of word learning, the more we can get students to think deeply about word meanings and spelling patterns, the better they will be able to truly "own" them and use them in their reading and writing. This is why memorizing definitions for a vocabulary test does not work and we forget half the words by the following week—memorizing definitions does not require us to really *think* about the words.

So if memorizing definitions or spellings does not work, what does?

- Connect new to known
- Categorize words and concepts

Connect New to Known

Give yourself about ten seconds to review the list of items below. Once your ten seconds is up, cover the list and write down all you can remember.

dog	hammer	apple	grape
nail	hamster	rabbit	cat
orange	wrench	pencil	crayon
paper	banana	glue	screw

Now review the next set of items. Again, give yourself ten seconds for review. Then cover and write down all of the items you remember from this list.

rose	fork	cow	river
daisy	spoon	chicken	ocean
tulip	knife	pig	pond
lily	ladle	sheep	lake

Which list resulted in more items remembered? Most likely your answer is the second because it was actually organized by categories whereas the first list showed the items in a random order. The organizational structure allowed you to remember more items. Helping your students see the connections among the items being studied as well as how those items fit into their overall knowledge of the concept will likewise help them remember.

People possess *categorical rules* that they use to interpret the world. New information comes in and is immediately processed by how it fits into these rules, or one's *schema*. Schema theory was first introduced by Piaget in 1926 and expanded later by Anderson (1977). Many others have built on the theory since then (e.g., Rumelhart, Smolensky, McClelland, & Hinton, 1985). The basis of this idea is that people develop schemata (or categorical rules) that are organized in a meaningful way. Information is added, subtracted, ignored, or transformed depending on how it relates to the schema. Therefore, in order to build knowledge, one must have existing, well-constructed schemata (or prior knowledge) with which to make connections. If prior knowledge is absent, then often the new information is ignored or not understood. If the prior knowledge is poorly constructed or organized, again, the information is most likely lost on the learner. The end result is an elaborate network of mental maps, if you will, of our conceptual understandings. Consider an unorganized file drawer. Folders that are misfiled are difficult to find and ultimately utilize. Your students need to have a nicely organized "file drawer" so that they can easily pull out the schema needed, make connections among the folders and items within, and add new items as needed.

You can take this theory and apply it directly in your classroom. First, you need to assess your students' prior knowledge of a subject prior to beginning instruction. For example, you would need to administer one of the qualitative spelling inventories found in Chapter 3 in order to determine their level of orthographic knowledge. Once you have an idea about their current knowledge, you can then decide how to build new knowledge. But, remember, part of building is helping to organize this information, or *make connections* between previously learned and new information. Graphic organizers can be especially helpful to struggling students by helping them visualize these connections and see the big picture. Figure 2.5 provides an example of the schema involved in the various long *o* vowel patterns. This big picture provides you with a powerful visual to illustrate your explanation while you are moving through the gradual release model.

Categorize Words and Concepts

Sorting is a natural application of schema theory to instruction and provides a framework for the explanation and demonstration found in the first phase of the gradual re-

Figure 2.5 Big Picture

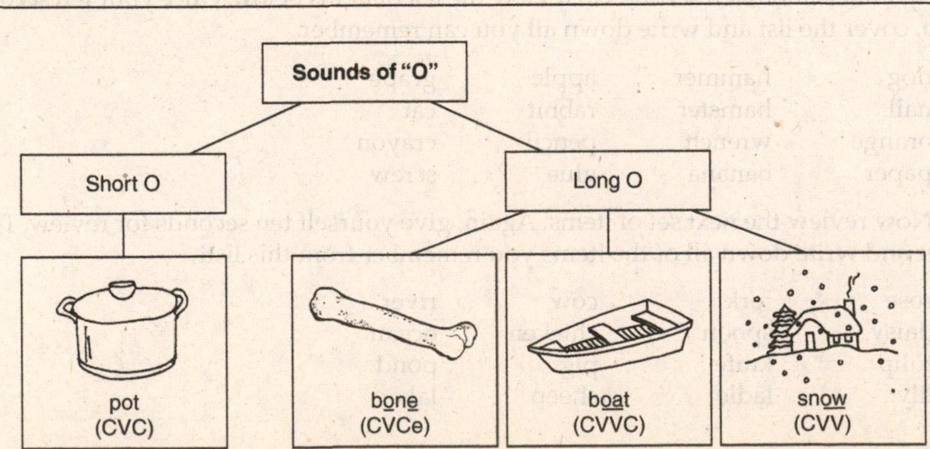

lease model. Sorting also provides your students with a hands-on activity to work either with peers or alone to test their understanding as you move into the guided practice and student-led practice portions of the gradual release model. As you read this book, you will see many examples of sorting activities because of the power of connecting and categorizing. Word learning is a conceptual process that requires your students to recognize and use the similarities and differences among words through comparisons. Sorting is at the heart of word study as teachers guide students to compare and contrast words based on similarities and differences.

Categorization allows us to create order by considering new information in relation to what is already familiar; this process ultimately leads to making generalizations about the characteristics of all members of a certain category (Bruner, Goodnow, & Austin, 1966). For example, students who know the word *chain* can apply their understanding of the *-ain* ending chunk when reading or spelling new words like *brain, stain,* and *strain.* A problem-solving atmosphere during phonics instruction is effective and motivating for students. Word sorting creates this type of atmosphere by providing hands-on opportunities to make cognitive connections about the similarities and differences among the targeted features.

Sorting can be used across the stages. Within word pattern spellers/transitional readers will benefit from sorting words based on vowel patterns. Sorting words by syllable patterns or affixes with similar meanings is an activity suitable for syllables and affixes spellers/intermediate readers. Students who are performing at the derivational relations spelling and advanced reading stage would profit from sorting words based on Greek and Latin stems and roots that share common meanings. As your students move through the stages of spelling, they will learn how to consider words in different ways while making decisions about their sounds, patterns, and meanings. Consider the ancient proverb, "I hear and I forget, I see and I remember, I do and I understand." Word sorting involves *doing* something with words.

Provide Multiple Opportunities for Students to Manipulate Words across a Variety of Activities and Contexts

Repeated practice is built into the model of gradual release that is incorporated into the word study approach. Not only will your students be involved in repeated practice sorting words, as discussed, but they will also participate in extensions of the sorting through generating and analyzing words in a variety of contexts that allow for collaborative and independent work. For example, generating from the keyword *pound,* your students would brainstorm related *-ound* words like *found, round,* and *hound.* When analyzing, you might teach students how to break down a whole word like *ground* into the onset (*gr*) and high-frequency ending chunk *-ound.* Repeated exposures do not mean repetition with worksheets and drills. The activities must be intentional and purposeful. The ultimate goal is for your students to not only learn the information but be able to apply it in various contexts and retain it across time. Repeated practice void of intent and purpose may result in mastery as measured by weekly tasks, but it will not likely translate into retention over time.

At its best, repeated practice must also include teacher and/or peer feedback. This constructive feedback must be timely and should provide specific observations and recommendations. For example, a group of your students may be working with the unaccented ending /er/ in two-syllable words (e.g., *doctor, stellar, longer*). You might notice one of your students writing *stellar* as *steller* while completing a writing sort independently. At this point, you might say, "I see that you have written *stellar* as *s-t-e-l-l-e-r.* Nice job using one of the patterns we discussed that can spell that sound. We talked about *er, or,* and *ar.* Remember, we talked about how confusing it is when we have many options for spelling one sound and that there are meaning connections to help us here. What part of speech is *stellar?* Yes, it is an adjective. Now I want you to go back to your notebook where you recorded the feature explanations for the three spelling options. Which one applies to adjectives?" Notice that this feedback was clear and specific. Not only did the feedback include some level of positive reinforcement (thinking about the spelling options even though the right pattern was not used), but it also included a recommendation for how to remedy the problem.

The process of working with words (sorting, generating, and analyzing) provides struggling readers with repeated opportunities to manipulate words as they participate in guided practice and student-led work. Multiple opportunities to investigate the target features are crucial to struggling readers. Sorting alone doubles or even triples the number of opportunities in a shorter amount of time compared to traditional activities. When students have repeated practice with letter sequences that occur in many different words, these sequences are eventually perceived as whole units (Ehri, 1994). For example, repeated occurrence of the letters *t-i-o-n* results eventually in *-tion* being perceived as a unit. Students can then use this unit to decode analogous unknown words. Providing multiple exposures to words is also critical in vocabulary instruction. Research by McKeown, Beck, Omanson, and Pople (1985) suggests that students need at least 12 meaningful exposures to a word to reliably improve comprehension of a passage containing that word.

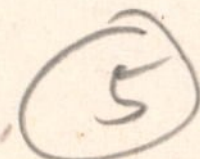

Engage Your Students

As we discussed in Chapter 1, engagement provides the critical pathway to reading comprehension and academic success, particularly the success of our older struggling readers who have so often been turned off by school. In fact, "motivation is everything" with our older students. So what, exactly, can you do in your classroom to create active, engaged learners? Guthrie (2004) and his colleagues, who have done the seminal research in engagement, have identified a number of instructional practices that can promote student engagement in your classroom. Based on the work of Guthrie (2004), Deshler and colleagues (2007), and our own experiences, we present five instructional practices to promote student engagement in word learning (see Figure 2.6).

Engagement Practice 1: Use Assessment to Plan Successful Learning Experiences

We have already discussed how assessment can guide instruction, but what does assessment possibly have to do with engaging your students? The short answer is that we are

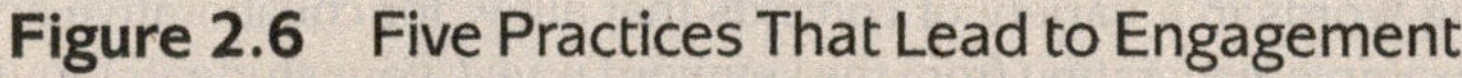

Figure 2.6 Five Practices That Lead to Engagement

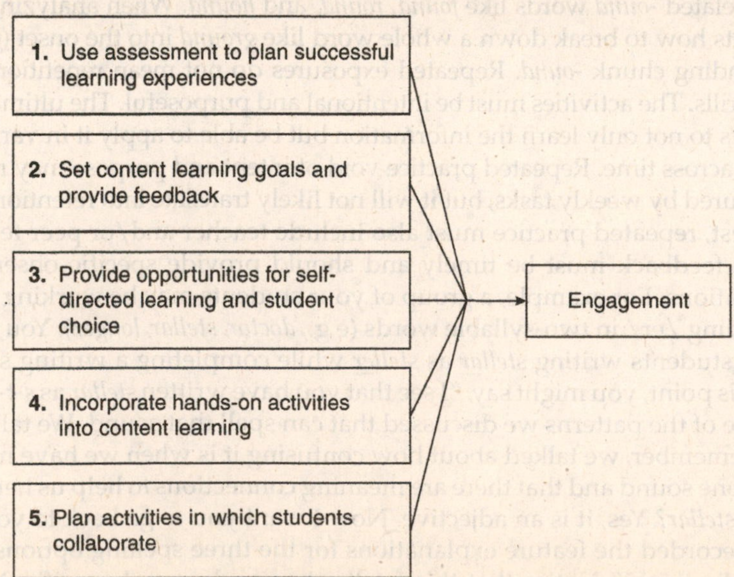

Figure 2.7 16 Spelling Words

bwlch	Eglwys-fach
dyffryn	Ffridd Fawr
eglwys	Eglwys Wen
llwyn	Ffridd
llys	mynydd, fynydd
Eglwys y Drindod	Ffridd y Foel
Ffriddisaf	llyn
ystrad	Llanfairpwllgwyngyllgogerychwyrndrobwllllantysiliogogogoch

engaged and motivated when we successfully complete a task that presents the appropriate level of challenge—difficult enough to learn from, but not so difficult as to cause frustration and failure, and not so easy as to result in boredom. This concept of "just right" instruction, or *instructional level,* is a powerful guide to providing appropriate and precise teaching. How do we find a student's optimal level of instruction? *Assessment.*

Read the list of 16 words in Figure 2.7. What if we told you that you would be tested on the spellings of these 16 words next Friday? And then we told you that you would receive 20 more words of similar difficulty the following week? And from that week on, until the end of the year, you would get 20 to 25 spelling words every week, increasing in difficulty as the year went on? How would that make you feel? Would you be motivated to learn more about spelling? Would you be able to spell these words in your contextual writing, or recognize them while reading a month later? A week later? The next day?

If you were like most of us, you would probably quickly become frustrated with studying the list in Figure 2.7 for at least two reasons: (1) These words hold no meaning for you, and (2) you don't recognize many (if any) familiar spelling patterns in the words. So studying for the Friday test becomes a task of brute memorization. If you were one of the few students motivated enough to study for the Friday test, you would likely forget most the spellings by the following week.

In fact, the words in Figure 2.7 are real words from Welsh, a language notorious for its long spellings and "jawbreaker" words. Unless you know something about the Welsh language, you were probably daunted by these words, because you are not familiar with common Welsh spelling patterns (remember the NIBBERFLUTZER/TZBNFBRLIUERE decoding experiment from Chapter 1). Hard as it may be to believe at first glance, there *are* patterns in these words. Look closely and you will see some (for example, *eglwys* means "church" in Welsh, so it makes sense that *Eglwys-fach* translates as "little church" and *Eglwys y Drindod* means "Trinity church"). By the way, one of our favorite words is *Llanfairpwllgwyngyllgogerychwyrndrobwllllantysiliogogogoch,* the name of a Welsh town that translates as "the church of St. Mary in the hollow of white hazel trees near the rapid whirlpool by St. Tysilio's of the red cave." How's that for a spelling demon!

This example gives you a sense of what spelling and decoding instruction is too often like for our struggling readers. They are asked to study spelling patterns that are too difficult for them, because they do not have knowledge of foundational spelling patterns in place, just as you probably lack foundational knowledge of Welsh spelling patterns in the Figure 2.7 example. It is like trying to teach calculus to someone who does not have a firm grasp of basic algebra—it will not lead to long-term learning and will quickly lead to frustration for both student and teacher.

Engagement Practice 2: Set Content Learning Goals with Your Students and Provide Feedback on Progress toward Those Goals

Wiggins and McTighe (2005) tell the story of a high school student who ran on the school track team. Although she wasn't one of the fastest athletes on the team and didn't win many races during high school, she stuck with track for all four years of high school.

When her coach asked at the end of her senior season why she kept at it for four years, without much competitive success, she replied, "But I *was* successful, coach. My times got better each year."

As this example illustrates, even lower-achieving individuals can be motivated by appropriate, attainable, clear goals and specific, timely feedback on progress toward those goals. If the track runner's goal was to beat other runners who were naturally much faster than her, she might have given up after her freshman year. However, the track runner was motivated to beat *her* time; in essence, she was competing against herself. Her running times every practice and meet were clear measures of her progress toward her goal. Importantly, she believed that her *hard work* would result in improvement and success. This is the same reason weight loss programs have participants weigh themselves at the outset of the program and then weigh themselves periodically throughout the program. If you can see that you are making progress toward your goal, you will be motivated to keep working toward that goal. If you see that your hard work results in no progress, you will likely stop.

In the same way, we can motivate our struggling readers with clear, appropriate, attainable spelling, reading, and vocabulary goals and specific, timely feedback on their progress toward those goals. When students have a clearly established content goal for learning—whether in spelling, reading, or vocabulary—they have a real purpose to read, write, think, and collaborate with others.

Engagement Practice 3: Provide Opportunities for Self-Directed Learning and Student Choice

As much as possible, make your students partners in their own learning by providing them with choice—one of the easiest and most powerful ways to motivate your students. Choices, even small ones, are powerful motivators because they give students some control over their learning. Choices can be made about content (what you will learn), activities (how you will learn them), and time (when you will learn them). According to Guthrie (2004), "With minor forms of ownership over their literacy, students dig deeper for meaning, monitor their understanding, and express their newfound knowledge more elaborately than do students without these choices and decisions about their learning" (p. 12). Following are some examples of how you might use choice in your word study instruction.

- *Activity Choice.* We often provide students with some choice of activities in spelling and reading word study instruction. For example, we might give our students a choice from a number of possible word study activities that day: speed sort, writing sort, or blind writing sort (these activities are described in the spelling and reading section of this chapter).
- *Content Choice.* Sometimes, it makes sense to split up vocabulary work, allowing small groups to choose two or three vocabulary words they want to study from a class list of ten words assigned that week. Using the jigsaw method, each group studies their words, becomes an "expert" on them, and shares their vocabulary knowledge with the other groups (Aronson, 1978). The teacher monitors, facilitates discussion, and clarifies or adds information on the concepts as needed.
- *Time Choice.* Sometimes, you may not care in what order a set of activities gets done, as long as they are completed by a certain deadline. In these cases, you may consider giving students the choice of when they want to do them.

Engagement Practice 4: Plan Hands-On Activities as Anchors and Springboards for Word Learning

Science experiments, social studies debates, math activities that involve manipulatives, field trips to museums—these are all examples of motivating hands-on activities that can be used as a springboard to content learning. Hands-on activities like these are important for a number of reasons, including the following: (1) They can provide critical background knowledge for struggling students who may not have had the same educational opportunities as other students in your class; (2) they provide a concrete experience to ground abstract concepts; and (3) they are often fun and motivating in their own right, giving the spark necessary to jumpstart a lesson or unit of study. The following examples are hands-on activities that could be used to prime the pump for student learning of key vocabulary concepts (vocabulary words/concepts that are targeted for instruction are in italics).

- Math. Fifth grade students use a geoboard—a math manipulative—to illustrate the following key concepts: finding the *area* and *perimeter* of a *rectangle* and *triangle* and deriving the *formulas*.
- Social Studies. Twelfth grade government students break into groups to debate controversial issues, such as the tension between the authority of the police to conduct *search and seizure* of students and their lockers versus the students' *right to privacy*.
- Science. Ninth grade students in an earth science class create a cloud inside a bottle to investigate the following related key science concepts: *water vapor, humidity, saturation, condensation, cloud formation.*
- English. Eighth grade English students, studying roots as part of their vocabulary instruction, sort words into categories based on their study of two roots: *aer* (meaning "air") and *hydra* (meaning "water"). Word sorting is a hands-on way to make abstract word concepts, like Latin and Greek roots, concrete and visually explicit for students.

Aer ("air")	Hydra ("water")
aerosol	hydrant
aerate	hydrate
aerial	hydra
aerobics	hydrogen
aerodynamic	hydroelectric
aeronautics	hydraulic
aerospace	hydroplane

Engagement Practice 5: Plan Collaborative Activities

Research shows that well-designed collaborative learning significantly improves student motivation and comprehension (National Reading Panel, 2000). Students learn from each other and are more engaged when they bounce ideas off their peers, receiving affirmation, feedback, and clarification of their thinking. With this in mind, nearly all of the word study activities described in this book can be done in groups, including pairs. The activities we describe provide structure and focus to this work so that group time will be time well spent. In addition, the gradual release model explained previously includes many opportunities for students to work together and with teachers, including guided practice (teacher provides feedback as students try out a new process or activity) and small-group work (students work together).

Core Word Study Practices That Build Spelling and Reading Knowledge

It is the beginning of third period, and Mrs. Ruiz is working with a small group of struggling readers at the back of her English classroom. The rest of her eighth-graders are at their seats, independently reading books and responding in their literature journals. As she does every other Monday, she takes about 15 minutes to introduce a new word sort to the small group in order to work on their spelling and decoding knowledge—two

Considerations for English Learners

Guiding Principles for English Learners

Students learning to read and write in a new language face many challenges. English learners benefit from small, differentiated group instruction designed to meet their specific developmental literacy needs and whole, heterogeneous group instruction targeting language. Regardless of the group setting or the instructional purpose, your diverse learners will benefit from teaching based on the following guiding principles (Bear, Helman, Templeton, Invernizzi, & Johnston, 2007). As you read through these principles, you will notice a great deal of overlap with the five core principles for struggling readers.

- *Utilize explicit and systematic instructional techniques.* Students learning English benefit from instruction that targets their instructional level and follows a gradual release method (explicit instruction, modeling, and guided practice). Specific to diverse learners, you must contextualize lessons (clarify instruction with real-life objects, expressive body language, role playing, and so on) and modify language to make the message more accessible to learners who are overwhelmed by a fast-coming stream of speech.

- *Engage your students in a learning community.* Diverse learners must feel comfortable working in instructional settings with others (you and their peers) and valued as members of the learning community. Opportunities to ensure student interaction require all students to communicate. Using your assessment data helps you determine appropriate goals for them to establish within the community.

- *Highlight connections.* When English learners know how new knowledge connects to their prior understandings, your instructional efforts will be most beneficial. Connecting new knowledge to previously learned knowledge is known as building schemata, an activity where you can simultaneously show the big picture of how things fit together. You can use graphic organizers to make these connections more concrete.

- *Provide opportunities for active construction of knowledge.* Hands-on activities not only actively engage your students but also provide nonverbal support for your diverse learners. These opportunities do not always have to mean manipulatives; hands-on activities can also refer to settings that allow for student interaction, both oral and written. Students engage with a topic and share their understandings with others. During these interactions, you may need to make use of modified questioning strategies. Questions are adapted to meet the needs of the student so that the response might require a yes or no answer, a one- or two-word response, a sentence response, or an open-ended response.

major areas of need for these particular students. This Monday, Mrs. Ruiz has given each student a pack of word cards to sort, as shown in Figure 2.8.

After going through each card to make sure everyone can read the words and knows their meanings, Mrs. Ruiz says, "Remember that we're starting out today with an open sort. So I'm going to give you a few minutes to try and look for the patterns in the words and categorize them on your own. You can work with a partner if you'd like." The partners spread the cards out on the table and begin discussing the words, organizing them into columns and looking for patterns. Mikah remarks that all of the words have two syllables. Jessie explains to the group that she organized the words by the vowel found in the first syllable (*a*, *e*, *i*, *o*, *u*), as she shows them her categories:

a	e	i	o	u
bacon	message	pilot	common	human
cabbage	recent	blizzard	copper	butter
mammal	legal	spiral	robin	humid

Mrs. Ruiz responds, "I really like your thinking on this sort, Jessie. I like the way that you are looking at words, taking into account both the syllable and the vowel

Figure 2.8 Sort for Mrs. Ruiz's Class

at the same time. That is exactly the type of thinking that will help you decode longer words and spell more difficult words. Did anyone find another pattern in these words?"

After a few more students describe their thinking about the words, Mrs. Ruiz decides that she needs to start providing more support in order to hone in on the target feature of the sort. She says, "OK, you've noticed many interesting things about these words, but I'm thinking of another pattern in these words. This is the pattern that we are going to focus on for the next few weeks. So, let's play Guess My Category. I'm going to start placing the words in two categories, but I'm not going to tell you why I'm putting a word in a certain category—you've got to figure that out."

Mrs. Ruiz places the following four words in two categories, reading each word aloud as she slides it into place:

pilot	cabbage
bacon	button

She says, "OK, let's read down these two columns together. Remember the three core questions we need to ask ourselves when looking for a pattern in words:

- What about the words *looks* the same?
- What about the words *sounds* the same?
- *Where* is the pattern in the words (beginning, middle, end)?"

As the students read down the words, two hands shoot up. Picking one, Mrs. Ruiz says, "Jamal, you think you can guess my categories? Don't tell me the pattern yet. Tell me which column you would put this word in." She hands Jamal the card showing *humid,* and he places it in the same column as *pilot* and *bacon.* Next, Mrs. Ruiz places the word *copper* on the table in front of the group. "How about this word? Jessie, do you want to try?" Jessie places *copper* under *cabbage* and *button.* After two more student turns, the sort appears as follows:

pilot	cabbage
bacon	button
humid	copper
spiral	blossom

At this point, it appears that most of the group is "getting it," so Mrs. Ruiz asks, "OK, so how are the words in the first column alike? Exactly! The words under *pilot* all have only one consonant in the middle. How about the words in the second column?

Right again, the words under *cabbage* in the second column all have two consonants in the middle. In fact, because the two consonants are the same, or doubled, we call them *doublets*. OK, so you've answered two of the three core questions we ask ourselves when looking for word patterns: (1) What about the words *looks* the same? and (2) *Where* is the pattern in the word? But, you still haven't answered the third question: (3) What about the words *sounds* the same? Let's read down the columns and see if we can find a sound pattern."

The students read down the columns aloud, but no one volunteers an answer. So Mrs. Ruiz says, "Let's read down the words again, and let's focus on just the vowel sound in the first syllable in the words, kind of like Jessie did when she showed us her category at the beginning of the lesson." As they read down the words the second time, Jamal blurts out, "I've got it—the words in the first column all have *long* vowel sounds in the first syllable, like the *i* in *pilot* and the *a* in *bacon*, and the words in the second column all have *short* vowels in the first syllable, like the *a* in *cabbage* and the *u* in *button!*"

The group continues to sort the words as Mrs. Ruiz passes them out. Tammy says, "I've got an oddball" as she places *cabin* by itself, off to the right of the other two columns.

pilot	cabbage	cabin
bacon	button	
humid	copper	
spiral	blossom	
legal	message	
recent	mammal	
human	blizzard	
local	dessert	
rumor	sudden	
solar	butter	
	common	

"Good eye, Tammy. What makes you think *cabin* is an oddball?"

"Well, *cabin looks* like it should go in the first column with *pilot* and *bacon* because it has only one consonant in the middle of the word, but it doesn't *sound* like *pilot* and *bacon*—the *a* in cabin is short, while the *i* and *a* in *pilot* and *bacon* are long. On the other hand, *cabin sounds* like it should go in the second column with *cabbage* and *button* because it has a short vowel sound in the first syllable, just like they do. However, *cabin* doesn't *look* like *cabbage* and *button* because it doesn't have two consonants in the middle. If it followed the pattern for this column, *cabin* would be spelled with two *b*'s in the middle: *c-a-b-b-i-n*. So it doesn't fit anywhere!"

"Great job, Tammy, and let's remember *cabin* for our next sort in a couple of weeks. Sometimes words that we initially think are oddballs turn out to be entirely new patterns as we find more examples. Now, let's see if we can come up with a way to describe the patterns we discovered in our own words . . ."

Before the small group returns to their desks, they copy the words by column into their word study notebooks. They also write down, in their own words, the spelling pattern they discovered together (e.g., "In a two-syllable word, when the vowel in the first syllable is short, you will usually have two consonants following the vowel"). The students will work with this same set of words in various ways over the course of the next two weeks, re-sorting the words, writing the words by category, timing themselves sorting with "speed sorts," and playing various review games to reinforce their word learning. At the end of the two weeks, Mrs. Ruiz will assess their learning with a writing sort.

The Power of Word Sorting with Struggling Readers

The simple but powerful process of sorting words into categories is at the heart of word study. In *Words Their Way*, Bear and colleagues (2008) state, "Categorizing is the fundamental way in which humans make sense of the world" (p. 51). As the students in Mrs. Ruiz's class sorted words, they were actively engaged in comparing, contrasting, and analyzing words—all *higher-level thinking processes* that lead to a greater breadth and depth of word knowledge. Word sorting activities like the one just described help students make generalizations about how words work, generalizations that they can then apply while spelling words as well as to new words they encounter in their reading. Because sorting is a foundational process used throughout this book, we will describe it in depth here.

The following practices offer additional help when embarking on a word sorting approach with struggling students:

- Discuss strategies for spelling and reading.
- Use consistent keywords for features.
- Generate, analyze, and sort words.

Discuss Strategies for Spelling and Reading

As discussed earlier, the first step in the gradual release model is explanation and modeling. A key component of modeling is thinking aloud. When you think aloud, you are verbally talking through your own thinking, a process known as metacognition. Modeling your own strategy use, rather than simply telling your students what to do, will result in deeper understanding. Your students will have a better idea about when to apply certain strategies, how to apply them, and how to evaluate whether or not they are right. See Figure 2.9 for an example of an explicit explanation of strategic spelling. This modeling demonstrates how a strategic speller/reader approaches unfamiliar words when sorting, writing, or reading.

Use Consistent Keywords for Features

Good readers often use an analogy process when faced with an unknown word. In fact, Ehri (1991) suggests that analogy is not only a common way readers decode unknown words but is also one of the most effective ways. For example, a student may not know the word *voucher* right away while reading, "Jake lost his *voucher* to get into the movie." Using an analogy approach, the student might refer back to the keyword *cl<u>ou</u>d* from previous sorting when considering the *ou* in *v<u>ou</u>cher*. Similarly, this same student might refer to *cloud* again when spelling *council*. Using consistent keywords will help your students store these words in memory so that they are more likely to use them during sorting while spelling and reading. Chapters 4 and 5 offer suggestions for keywords to use for each feature discussed.

Generate, Analyze, and Sort Words

The gradual release model incorporates many opportunities for repeated practice (teacher guided, peer assisted, and individual). For struggling readers, the repeated practice must include generating and analyzing words in addition to the sorting. Students need to have opportunities to analyze words into their orthographic components (e.g., the *ou* in *ground*) and eventually meaning components (e.g., the *un*, *ground*, and *ed* in *ungrounded*). Further, they need experience using their knowledge to generate new words using target features (e.g., thinking about the common syllable pattern consonant-*le* and how it works across the words *circle*, *bubble*, and *able*). Sorting provides this repeated practice.

There are two basic types of sorts commonly used during word study: sound sorts and pattern sorts. These sorts and their variations allow students to use their growing knowledge while reading and also apply this knowledge to writing, with practice to

Figure 2.9 Strategic Spelling: Lessons to Encourage Students to Spell

To help struggling students feel more comfortable attempting to spell words they do not know, conduct a few lessons using the theme "Strategic Spelling." If you want students to produce quality writing, you need them to be willing to take risks in their spelling. You do not want them to rush through without thinking and you do not want them to labor over spelling. You also do not want them to avoid using words they cannot spell. Any of these scenarios can, and often do, result in students missing out on the reward of expressing themselves. Your lessons should follow these three steps:

1. Encourage invented spelling.
2. Spell words together.
3. Model spelling strategies.

Encourage Invented Spelling

You can begin by talking openly about spelling words you do not know, such as at the beginning of a writing lesson. For example, you have been studying traditional fairy tales and have deconstructed many tales that you have read. You are now working on writing fairy tales using your class's blueprint for fairy tales. As a class, you start planning a class-constructed tale. While you are writing on the board, you might say, "You know, when I write, I sometimes want to use a word that I don't know how to spell. What are some things you do to help you spell a word you don't know?" Students might say things like "Ask someone" or "Skip it." Older students often know how to talk the talk, so they might say, "Sound it out." The problem is that they know that phrase ("sound it out") but do not know how to sound out a word. They do not know, for example, how to use analogy to a known word or how to break a word into syllables. Ask your students the procedure they use for sounding out words. If they are unable to articulate an answer, talk to them about how you will help them learn about and implement some key strategies for spelling unknown words. Be specific that we need to be "strategic."

Spell Words Together

Continue with your class-constructed fairy tale. "See right here. I'm thinking of the evil character. I want to use the word *fiendish.* But, I don't know how to spell that word. Let's see. My first step would be to see if there are any parts I can take off to help me get to the base word. Are there any parts to take away?" If your students do not come up with *-ish,* tell them that the *-ish* is an ending often used to make a noun into an adjective. "That *-ish* ending on *fiendish* is used to make a noun an adjective. Like the word *sluggish.* A *slug* is a small creature that looks like a snail but doesn't have a shell. The word is therefore a noun. Putting *-ish* on the end of that word changes it to an adjective to describe something or someone who is slow moving. I can take off the *-ish* in *fiendish* and get *fiend.* Okay, so let's think about *fiend.* Let's be strategic here. I'm going to first think about a word I know that is like it. Usually you can think of words that rhyme with it if one doesn't come to mind right away. However, I can't think of any that will help me. So now I will think of all of the sounds I hear because this is a single-syllable word: /f/ /ē/ /n/ /d/. So I know I have *f, long e, n, d.* To spell long *e,* I have some options: *ee, ea, ie.* I'm going to write all three versions and see if I recognize the right one: *feend, feand, fiend.* I know that *ee* is more common but *ie* is the one that looks right to me. So now I have *fiend.* To get *fiendish,* I just need to add *-ish.*"

As your students become more comfortable with this process, invite them to think aloud while spelling with the group. Occasionally, a student might be critical of another's attempts. In such cases, it will be vital for you to address this criticism. You might say, "The important thing is that you have written the word and that you can reread it. We are all learning here, and there will be times when you don't know how to spell a word you want to write. That's part of the process. It is important for us to think through our strategies for figuring out how to write these words. We need to talk them through together. The more we think through our spellings and the more we write, the better we will be."

Model Spelling Strategies

One lesson discussing spelling will not achieve the results you want. Lessons discussing strategic spelling will permeate your academic day and should be a formalized part of your English or language arts work. Some key strategies include the following:

1. If it is a single-syllable word:
   a. *Think about another word you know that rhymes with the word.* If you know one, use it to help you. For example, a student might be trying to spell *frown.* Thinking of other words that rhyme will help: *town, down, clown,* and so on. Using analogy to known words will enable the student to identify *-own* as the ending chunk.
   b. *If you can't think of another rhyming word, then break it up into its constituent sounds.* The student trying to spell *couch* may break it up into /c/ /ou/ /ch/ and come up with a few versions based on knowledge of ambiguous vowel patterns: *couch* and *cowch.* At this point, direct the student to see which one "looks right." Success in identifying the accurate spelling is, of course, dependent on reading practice.
2. If it is a multisyllable word:
   a. *Think about common syllable patterns to help you break the word into its syllabic parts/chunks.* A student knowing about the common open vowel-consonant-vowel syllable pattern (e.g., *pi-lot, ro-bot, ra-dio*) will be able to use this knowledge to spell the word *vacant.* See Chapter 5 for a more in-depth explanation of syllable types.
   b. *Use what you know about single-syllable words to help.* Once the word *delight* is broken into its syllabic parts (*de-light*), the student can apply information about common long *i* patterns from their single-syllable within word pattern study. So knowing that *-ight* is a common ending (e.g., *light, right, sight, bright, might*) will lead the student to apply the *-ight* ending to *delight.*

Figure 2.10 Sound Sort

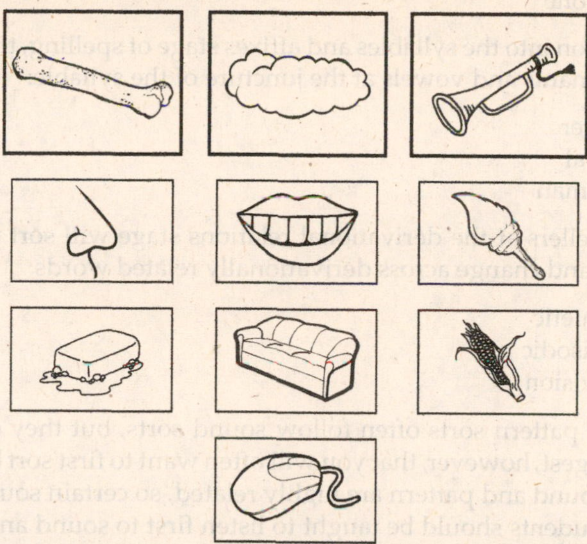

develop automaticity. Use the continuum of support (open sorts, Guess My Category sorts, and closed sorts) to vary the level of scaffolding with the sorts or variations described in this section.

Sound Sorts

Sorting by sound enables your students to make sense of the alphabetic nature of the English language. Sound sorts are particularly helpful when introducing a new or difficult sound contrast. The printed word can sometimes be a giveaway for the category. For example, when sorting open and closed syllables, your students could simply look at the juncture of the two syllables to see if there is one consonant (open syllable in *pilot*) or two consonants (closed syllable in *hammer*). To avoid this, you can sort using pictures. For example, when investigating long vowels, your sorts should include short and long contrasts. This comparison of sounds can be accomplished through picture sorts or word sorts. See Figure 2.10 for an example of a sound sort created to teach the ambiguous *o* after having studied short *o* and long *o*. As you can see, this picture sort is *stacked* to highlight the sound contrasts among these three features. You can use sound sorts during the introduction of your weekly features and follow the sound sort with an introduction of the spelling patterns (see the following pattern sort discussion).

Sound sorts sometimes have a key picture as a label; we recommend key pictures for the same reason we recommend keywords: They provide a consistent reference point for struggling readers. This key picture should be consistent each time a particular feature is sorted. For example, you may be targeting the sound difference among various sounds of the vowel *o:* /ō/as in *bone,* /aů/ as in *cloud,* and /ȯr/ as in *horn.* These key pictures would head up their corresponding categories each time these sounds are studied. Having consistent key pictures will provide your students with an anchor to support their learning of sounds.

Pattern Sorts

When students have the printed form of the word available, they can sort by the orthographic features. The sophistication of the features studied will depend on the developmental stage of spelling. Within word pattern spellers will sort words by vowel patterns:

coach	stroke
roast	choke
roam	throne

As students transition into the syllables and affixes stage of spelling, the pattern of study moves to the consonants and vowels at the juncture of the syllable:

button	fever
tunnel	local
hammer	human

More advanced spellers at the derivational relations stage will sort words by the patterns of constancy and change across derivationally related words:

athlete	athletic
episode	episodic
revise	revision

As mentioned, pattern sorts often follow sound sorts, but they can also be standalone sorts. We suggest, however, that you will often want to first sort by sound and then move to pattern. Sound and pattern are highly related, so certain sounds correspond to certain patterns. Students should be taught to listen first to sound and then to consider alternative ways to spell that particular sound. While sorting, you will want your students to ask themselves if the words look right *and* sound right; these questions require them to be reflective and encourage them to look for connections between the sound and pattern. Consider the student trying to spell *slouch.* By first thinking about the sound /aů/, this student can then think about the spelling options for that sound: *ow* and *ou.* The student then writes out the word: *s-l-o-u-c-h.* Looks right, sounds right.

Keywords containing the target orthographic patterns should be used to label each category. These keywords should carry over the key pictures from the sound sort. For example, your keyword cards for a sort contrasting the /ȯr/, /ō/, and /aů/ sounds would include the key pictures used during the sound sort: *horn, bone,* and *cloud.* The difference now is that the keyword cards will include the printed word and highlighted pattern (see Figure 2.11). The students would then complete the sort by matching the pattern in each word to the pattern in the keyword at the top of the category. Recurring patterns should be represented as an abbreviated code that stands for the consonant and/or vowel patterns being studied. Consider the keyword card for /aů/ as in *cloud.* Notice that the card also has the CVVC pattern (consonant-vowel-vowel-consonant) included on it. Talking about these universal patterns (along with the *ou* ambiguous vowel pattern) can help your students. Keyword cards can therefore include three components: keyword, picture, and pattern.

Figure 2.11 Sound Sort to Pattern Sort

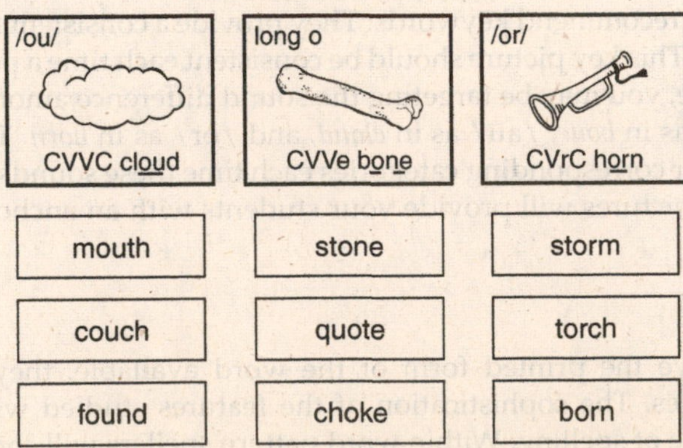

Not all words will fit the targeted features in a sort. If you included *worm* as one of your sorting words in the sort comparing /ȯr/, /ō/, and /aů/, you have a word that does not fit your /ȯr/ category. It looks right but does not sound right (the /ər/ in *worm* does not match the /ȯr/ in *horn*). These words are called *oddballs.* Often this is the case with an oddball; they look right (or follow the pattern) but do not sound right. Including oddballs is a very effective way to consider function words. These are words that serve grammatical functions but have little identifiable meaning. They include prepositions *(about, to, under),* pronouns *(they, we, she),* conjunctions *(and, but, or),* articles *(a, the, an),* auxiliary verbs *(were, be, have),* and particles *(thus, as, if, then).* Studying function words like *ought, though,* and *through* as oddballs while considering /aů/ as in *cloud* will support your students' learning. Chapter 3 has more discussion of function words.

Variations of Sorts

There is a variety of sound and pattern sorts that you can encourage students to apply to reading and writing and use to develop automaticity.

- Writing sorts
- Blind writing sorts
- Speed sorts
- Word hunts
- Brainstorming

Writing Sorts The motoric act of writing a word reinforces the association of the letters and orthographic patterns with the sounds and meanings. In fact, young students often take part in the practice of tracing and writing the letters of words while verbalizing the letter names or letter sounds. The technique of writing words to support learning has been well established in the field. You will want to provide your struggling students multiple opportunities to write the words they are studying. However, having students write words five or more times can turn into a simple practice of copying and become a mindless activity. If *thinking* is not involved, then *learning* will not likely follow. A simple modification can make a big difference. Having your students write words into the target categories accomplishes two goals. First, your students will be involved in the physical act of writing. Second, they will have to continue to think about the sounds and patterns as well as the characteristics specific to each category. This attention to the characteristics of each category reinforces the analogy to the keyword as a clue for the spelling of words with the same sound and pattern.

A writing sort begins with writing the keywords for the target features at the top of each category. The words are then written down in their corresponding categories (see Figure 2.12). Your students do this by turning over one word at a time from their sort and then writing it down. Or you may wish to have your students complete a blind writing sort.

Blind Writing Sorts The blind writing sort is a commonly used variation of the writing sort. A blind writing sort begins in the same way with keywords written as labels for each category. However, instead of students reading the card *before* writing the word down (as in a writing sort), the words are called out by a peer or teacher. The student's job is to spell the word correctly and place it in the appropriate column. Looking at the word card afterward can serve as a check. Blind sorts can, and should, be done throughout the week. Do not expect correct spellings at first but do expect accuracy to increase as your students have more practice with the sort. Blind writing sorts can also take the place of the traditional spelling test; keywords would be written before students write and sort the words as they are called.

Figure 2.12 Writing Sort

r-Controlled
CVC
car (ar)
chart
harm
carve

Long a
CVCe | CVVC
cake (a_e) | rain (ai) | vein (ei)
brake | stain | weight
blame | trail | beige
shape | chain | veil

Oddball
break
great
said

engagement LINK

Not only do speed sorts help support automaticity, but they are also very motivating.

Speed Sorts Speed sorts can help your students develop fluency and automaticity. You will first want to ensure a level of accuracy before your students embark on sorting with speed. The procedure for speed sorts is the same as with any sorting except that your students will time themselves using a stopwatch. You may find that your students make occasional mistakes while speed sorting. It is helpful to have a completed sort typed out on paper for them to check their sorts when done. Encourage students to try to beat their personal times. Figure 2.13 shows a student's efforts across a week of speed sorting as he charted each of his times. As you can see, he sorted in well under a minute by his third try, demonstrating automaticity.

Word Hunt It cannot be assumed that your students will make the connection between spelling words and reading words. Words hunts can help make this connection. They can also show how useful word study can be for reading and spelling development. A word hunt requires your students to hunt through previously read texts or their own written drafts for words that follow the target features. Using previously read texts is critical so

Figure 2.13 Speed Sort Chart

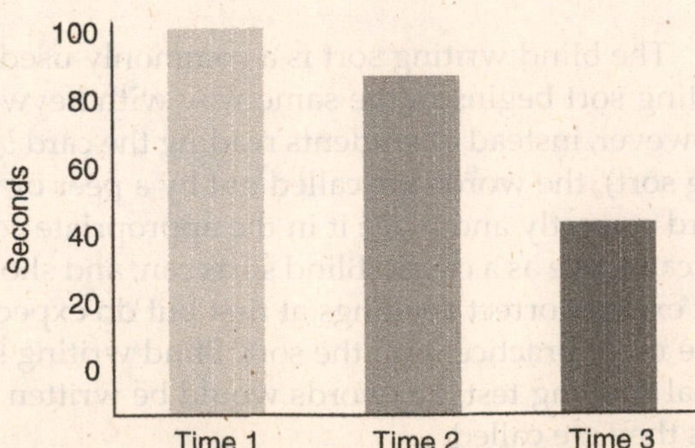

Figure 2.14 Word Hunt

that your students do not confuse skimming for words with reading for meaning. Each found example should be recorded in a sort. Figure 2.14 shows a partially completed word hunt for words that end in *-le* and *-el (buckle, sparkle, bushel)*, thus demonstrating how word study efforts can ultimately benefit reading. Some patterns are common and found easily in virtually any text; however, others are less common and harder to find. Therefore, some features lend themselves to word hunts better than others.

The purpose of the hunt (to demonstrate the connection between spelling and reading) can be met within a few minutes. Time is of the essence in the classroom, so you want to focus your word hunt. One way to do this is to provide the pages from specific books in which you want students to hunt. We have found previewing texts and offering pages with multiple examples to be helpful in keeping the focus during the hunt and maximizing time. A few minutes can be sufficient for making your point.

Hunting for words in their own written pieces is an excellent activity to help students connect spelling to writing. You could choose to have them hunt through a working draft with an editor's eye during the editing phase of the writing process, looking for correct spellings and even incorrect spellings of the target features. Your students can also hunt through finished pieces for examples to include in their hunts. Struggling readers are not overwhelmed because they are only hunting for words following certain targeted features. They may choose to hunt through each other's writing; however, we recommend allowing that to be their decision, as your students may be sensitive about their writing.

engagement LINK

Students will be engaged while hunting through their *own* writing. To further motivate your students, award them points for finding words that are spelled correctly. They should also get points for finding misspelled words and correcting them.

Regardless of whether your students are hunting in texts or their own writing, it is important to set up the hunt and afterward debrief the hunt. You will want to model word hunting before expecting your students to do so. Once your students are hunting on their own, you will need to build in debrief time. These debriefs can be with you or with a peer. Likewise, the hunts can be guided by you, done in small groups, or completed individually. We have found that group hunts are particularly motivating and beneficial. When a word comes into question, the discussion that follows can be very powerful. Have reference materials, such as dictionaries, available to resolve any questions.

Brainstorming Occasionally, you may want to have your students brainstorm lists of words that follow the features they are studying. Brainstorming can illustrate the value in your word study lessons and help make connections to words that they may already know that follow the same features. Brainstorming is an alternative to word hunts when the features of study are not frequently found in text. For example, if you are studying the simple prefix *non-*, you may not be able to find multiple examples in the available texts. Instead, have students brainstorm a list of words: *nonstop, nonsense, nonfiction.*

Brainstorming can also be used to resolve questions that may arise while conducting word study lessons. For instance, while studying long vowels, your students may notice that some words end in *-ce* (*rice*) and others in *-se* (*wise*). A student asks how you would know to use *-ce* or *-se*. You could then ask your students to brainstorm a list of words with those endings. As the students call out words, record them in categories, as in the sort below.

rice	wise
face	chose
place	phase
brace	those
price	these
slice	close
advice	chase
	erase
	excuse

Now you are incorporating a Guess My Category approach. The combination of brainstorming and Guess My Category will allow your students to make a discovery about the endings. Words ending in *-ce* have the /s/ sound while words ending in *-se* often have the /z/ sound, with a few exceptions (e.g., *chase* and *erase*).

Dealing with Mistakes With any of these sorts, your students will occasionally make mistakes. We suggest the following rule of thumb when you notice sorting mistakes.

- If the mistake occurs early in the sort, then correct it. Sometimes mistakes that occur early result in subsequent mistakes due to students cueing off of the initial error.
- If the mistake happens later in the sort, then let it stand as is. See whether students catch their own mistakes while reviewing the sort. Then ask why the sorting placement was a mistake and how it can be corrected.
- You may find mistakes after the fact while reviewing your students' writing sorts or word hunts. In these cases, you may find it helpful to have your students complete a reflection chart (see Figure 2.15).

This reflection chart provides the opportunity for students to make their own clarifications and even generate new questions. In Figure 2.15, the student questions why

Figure 2.15 Reflection Chart

What word was misplaced?	Why? Where should it go?
water	I found water and put it in the VCV open syllable pattern but it is open without the right sound. The a is not long. It should be an oddball. But why isn't it long?
many	I put many in the VCV syllable pattern. This is wrong because it is closed. The a isn't long. But it isn't short either. Right?
busy	I put this one in the VCV open syllable too. I got it wrong because it has VCV but not open. It is closed. But this one is weird too. It isn't short.

the vowels in the first syllable of each of the words (*water, many, busy*) are neither long nor short. To answer the question about *water,* you could do a quick brainstorm with the student. Showing the words *water, war, warm, wand, want,* and *wash* can illustrate how a *w* preceding an *a* can change the sound of the *a* to make it closer to short *o*. This, of course, is not universally true, as in *wag* and *wait*. However, knowing this sound change can happen is helpful when spelling and decoding.

Core Word Study Practices That Build Vocabulary Knowledge

"Look up the definition and write it in a sentence." At one time or another in your school career, you have probably heard these words and been assigned this task as a standard part of your vocabulary work. Yet how effective is this activity? Does it lead to long-term deep word knowledge? To get a sense for how well this activity works in building students' vocabulary, read the actual samples of student sentences in Figure 2.16. Each example includes the dictionary definition provided to the student, followed by the student's attempt to write the word in a sentence.

These humorous and telling examples come from a well-known study by Miller and Gildea (1987) in which they looked at thousands of sentences written by fifth- and sixth-graders (as cited in Adams, 1990). The students were provided dictionary definitions of vocabulary words and then asked to write sentences that included the words. The researchers found that 63 percent of the student sentences were "odd." Why did so many students find it difficult to write an acceptable sentence when provided with a dictionary definition? Part of the answer is because there is much more to knowing a word than simply memorizing a definition. Moreover, as Stahl and Nagy (2006) caution, if our vocabulary instruction consists solely of asking students to memorize definitions, our students will fall prey to the "phone number" syndrome, remembering a definition (phone number) only long enough to take the test (dial). After the test is taken or the phone number dialed, all is forgotten.

What does effective vocabulary instruction—instruction that moves beyond dictionary definitions—look like? The last section of this chapter will introduce you to effective and engaging word study instruction that helps our struggling readers build a broad, rich, and deep base of vocabulary knowledge that they can use across the content areas.

Figure 2.16 Student Sentences Incorporating Vocabulary Words

Dictionary Definition	Student's Sentence
correlate. 1. Be related one to the other: *The diameter and the circumference of a circle correlate.*	"Me and my parents correlate, because without them I wouldn't be here."
meticulous. Very careful or too particular about small details.	"I was meticulous about falling off the cliff."
erode. 1. To eat out.	"My family erodes often."

Source: Miller & Gildea, 1987, as cited in Adams, 1990, and Stahl & Nagy, 2006.

The Nature of Words: Three Types of Vocabulary

One of the first steps in making instructional decisions regarding vocabulary is identifying the nature of the words you will teach. Knowing the nature or type of word being taught will guide you in deciding how to best teach that word (see Chapter 7). Figure 2.17 presents the three major categories, along with related information, that vocabulary researchers currently use to classify types of vocabulary words. In keeping with the work of Templeton and colleagues in *Vocabulary Their Way* (2010), we use the following terms for these three major types of vocabulary:

- Conversational vocabulary
- Core academic vocabulary
- Content-specific vocabulary

Conversational vocabulary includes the most common and frequently occurring words in our spoken language, such as *is*, *dog*, and *run*. Vocabulary researchers Beck, McKeown, and Kucan (2002) label these words "tier 1" vocabulary because they typically require no instruction and are so easily acquired indirectly as part of typical oral language development. The remaining two types of vocabulary, core academic and content-specific, are the two categories that all students, including struggling readers, need to be directly taught in school.

Core academic vocabulary encompasses words that may not occur often in everyday spoken language, but are at the heart of written language and learning in the middle and high school grades (and beyond) because they occur frequently across the content areas in textbooks, novels, lectures, and class discussions. Examples of core academic words include *solitary*, *drenched*, *solemn*, *stampede*, *glare*, *thrust*, *dissolve*, *dispel*, and *haphazard*. As you can see, these more mature, sophisticated vocabulary words could be found in texts on almost any subject. For example, *dissolve* could be used during a science experiment (salt *dissolving* into water), found in a social studies textbook (the Civil War *dissolved* the bond that tied the North and South together), or encountered in a story from the class English anthology (the young man *dissolved* in tears upon hearing the tragic news). Students often have the basic concept that underlies these words but may lack the label (e.g., students may understand the basic concept of "breaking down or disintegrating" without necessarily possessing the label *dissolve* or understanding its particular connotations in different contexts). Beck and colleagues (2002) wisely advocate targeting these "tier 2" vocabulary words for instruction because of their high utility across content areas, their frequency in more mature reading material including newspapers and magazines, and their usefulness in allowing students to more precisely express themselves in written language and general academic discourse. Core academic vocabulary instruction is usually viewed as the purview of English or language arts teachers.

Content-specific academic vocabulary refers to words and concepts that are specific to disciplines and content areas such as the *Magna Carta* in history, the *dual parallels theorem* in math, *half-life* in science, and *quatrain* in English. Labeled "tier 3" vocabulary by Beck and colleagues (2002), these words often represent new concepts—as opposed to the more familiar concepts of core academic vocabulary—and thus will often take more time and effort to teach and learn. Subject area teachers are usually responsible for teaching this type of vocabulary. These content-specific words have very precise meanings in their respective content areas and represent the essential concepts and "big ideas" of their subjects.

Of course, these three vocabulary categories are not intended to be rigid and ironclad but are simply meant to give you a way to think about the nature of words as you teach vocabulary. For example, you will find words that overlap between different categories. The word *parallel* might be introduced in geometry as applying to "two straight lines lying in the same plane but never meeting." In this sense, *parallel* is a content-specific word. However, students also need to know the more general sense of parallel, illustrated in the following sentence: "Jessie and Mike had *parallel* careers—going to the same schools, working for similar businesses, and holding the same management positions." In this case, *parallel* is a core academic word that means "similar, having the same direction or course."

Overview of Core Vocabulary Instruction

Once you have a sense of the nature of the words you will teach, you need to decide *how* to best teach them. The following guidelines will help you as you implement the activities described in the following section (Blachowicz & Fisher, 2010; Stahl & Nagy, 2006):

- Move beyond basic definitions
- Help students make connections
- Work with words in context

Move beyond Basic Definitions

As illustrated in Figure 2.16, a dictionary definition only provides the "tip of the iceberg" in terms of information about a word. To really "own" a word, students need to dig deeper for meaning and move beyond a basic dictionary definition. Generating synonyms and antonyms, comparing and contrasting shades of meaning among related words, and thinking of examples and non-examples of a word are all ways to get students actively engaged in deeply processing word meanings.

Figure 2.17 Three Types of Vocabulary

***Vocabulary Their Way* (Templeton et al., 2010)**	**Beck, McKeown, and Kucan (2002)**	**Other Names for Vocabulary Categories**	**Examples**	**Student Knowledge**	**Where Can I Find These Words?**	**Who Is Responsible for Teaching?**
Conversational Vocabulary	Tier 1 (basic words)	General vocabulary	*dog* *run* *is*	Usually known	Higher-frequency words found on General Services List (West, 1953)	
Core Academic Vocabulary	Tier 2 (high-frequency words for mature language users)	High-utility vocabulary (Stahl & Nagy, 2006)	*tangible* *cultivate* *random* *sanctuary*	Students often have a basic underlying concept, but lack a label	Found across content areas; Academic Word List (Coxhead, 2000)	English/ language arts teachers
Content-Specific Vocabulary	Tier 3 (low-frequency words, usually related to specific content area or domain)	Technical vocabulary	*cirrus* *half-life* *rising action* *parallelogram* *Civil Rights movement*	Often represent concepts and labels that are new to students	Specific to a content area (textbooks)	Content area teachers

Help Students Make Connections

When students make connections between related words and the concepts that they represent, they are creating stronger schemata—more elaborate and tightly woven conceptual networks that can be readily activated when reading, writing, thinking, and discussing. Helping students make these connections can go a long way toward improving word learning. For example, your students may not be very familiar with the word *anguish,* but they have undoubtedly experienced "acute distress or pain" at some point in their lives. Asking them to tell of a time in which they have been in anguish helps personalize this word and put it into context by connecting the word to a personal experience.

Work with Words in Context

It has been said that "words live in context." This is true. The ability to use words *in context* is perhaps the ultimate test of word learning. Superficial knowledge may allow a student to choose the right definition for a word on a multiple-choice test, but deep understanding is needed to use the "just right word" in one's writing to communicate the intended message to an audience. We learn words best when we see them used and applied in context, whether the context is a sentence in an English text, a discussion in math class, or a science experiment write-up. Activities that encourage students to (1) notice rich, powerful vocabulary words in their contextual reading, (2) use words that "pack a punch" in their writing, and (3) incorporate sophisticated words in their class discussions help them to gain a fuller, richer understanding of a word's meaning.

Core Vocabulary Activities

What do these guidelines look like in action? The following core word study activities help build the vocabulary knowledge of your struggling readers. These activities will also serve as the foundation for additional activities that are presented later in this book.

- Concept/meaning sorts
- Vocabulary self-collection strategy
- Have you ever?

Concept/Meaning Sorts

The concept sort is one of the most effective, engaging, and readily adaptable vocabulary building strategies we have used with our students. Struggling readers find concept sorts extremely helpful because they make connections between abstract concepts concrete and visually explicit—a student's thinking is literally "laid out on the table" for all to see. Concept sorting, in which students categorize vocabulary terms by meaning, promotes vocabulary learning and deepens conceptual understanding in the content areas. These types of sorts are easily applicable across the different disciplines, requiring students to categorize math words, social studies terms, or science concepts and to explain the rationale behind their decisions—higher-level thinking that requires deeper processing of word meanings. For example, during a social studies unit on the Civil War, students might be asked to categorize important historical figures from this era such as Frederick Douglass, Abraham Lincoln, and Robert E. Lee under the "header words" *Union Leaders, Confederate Leaders,* and *African American Leaders.* As they sort these words, the students can discuss how each figure fits within each category.

Concept sorts can also be used at the beginning of a unit to assess and build students' background knowledge and to serve as an advance organizer for learning. For example, a science unit on ecosystems might begin with students categorizing the following words into related groups: *owls, trees, deer, stream, rocks, bushes, moss, sunlight, air, worms, bacteria, fungi, climate.* As they group the words, the students should label each category. The lack of teacher-provided header words makes this an open sort because the possibilities for categories and labels are open-ended (e.g., *Living* vs. *Nonliving* or *Plants, Animals,* and *Other*). The ensuing discussion, in which students explain the rationale behind their thinking, can provide the teacher with valuable information regarding her students' background knowledge as well as set the stage for future learning. Later in the unit, the teacher can "close down" the sort to highlight the core concepts of the unit. By doing this, the students would classify these same words, or a subset of these words, using teacher-provided labels that she wants the students to focus on (e.g., *Producers, Composers,* and *Decomposers*). The final sort in this ecosystem unit might look like this:

Producers	Consumers	Decomposers
trees	deer	fungi (mushroom and molds)
flowers	owls	bacteria
algae	squirrels	

The possibilities for concept sorts are limitless. In English class, words can be sorted by parts of speech. In civics, characteristics of different types of government (e.g., "representatives are elected by the people to make decisions") can be sorted under categories such as *Direct Democracy, Representative Democracy,* and *Dictatorship.* In health class, foods can be categorized as *Protein, Fat,* or *Carbohydrate.* Concept sorts can be used before a lesson or unit to both assess background knowledge and serve as the students' "prediction" about how the vocabulary terms are related, during a unit as students refine their knowledge, and at the end of a unit as a review. They can even be used as a prewriting strategy to help students organize ideas before writing. See Chapter 7 on word-specific instruction for more in-depth information about concept sorting, including step-by-step procedures, additional examples, and extensions of concept sorting that can be applied across content areas and grade levels.

The power of this method can be attributed to providing these older students some ownership and choice in the words chosen and the richness of the teacher–student and peer-to-peer interactions and discussions.

Vocabulary Self-Collection Strategy (VSS)

The vocabulary self-collection strategy (Haggard, 1986; Ruddell & Shearer, 2002) is a powerful method for increasing struggling readers' motivation to learn words as well as the depth and breadth of their vocabulary knowledge. In this activity, students are asked to find and nominate words to the class that they find interesting and would like to learn more about. In their study, Ruddell and Shearer found that struggling middle school students placed in an intensive reading intervention program chose and gained deep long-term knowledge of academic words such as *nebula, lustrous, paunch, melancholy, serene,* and *tranquil.* The procedures for VSS are as follows:

- Once per week, ask students to find and nominate words that would be "good for the class to learn" for the weekly class list. These words can come from any source, such as textbooks, independent reading, newspapers and magazines, comic books, music, or TV. This is an excellent way to encourage students to notice words in context.
- When nominating words, students tell the class (1) where they found the word, (2) what they think the word means, and (3) their argument for including the word on the class list.
- As a class, choose a final set of words, come to consensus on a common definition for each (use the dictionary as necessary), and record the words and definitions in student learning logs or vocabulary notebooks.
- Over the course of the week, examine the words repeatedly, using a variety of methods, including semantic feature analysis, semantic mapping, or whatever strategy

best fits the words, your students' needs, and the learning goals. These and related activities can be found in Chapter 7.

Have You Ever?

"Have you ever?" is one of our favorite methods for connecting newly learned words with students' previous experiences. It is perfectly suited for core academic vocabulary terms that are new to students but for which students already have a basic underlying concept. Developed by Beck and colleagues (2002) this often humorous activity can be done in a relatively short amount of time with powerful results. We often use this activity after reading a story, returning to the text and examining the selected word in the context of the story with the students and then providing a brief definition and example from our own lives.

engagement LINK

The humor and built-in connection to students' own experiences make this a highly engaging activity.

- After reading a story or section of text, go back to the text and point out to your class a few carefully selected core academic words (e.g., *agog* and *saturnine*).
- Ask the students, based on the context, to infer the words' meanings.
- Briefly and clearly define the vocabulary in words your students can understand.
  - *agog* means "highly excited by eagerness and anticipation"
  - *saturnine* means "gloomy, dark, moody"
- Provide an example from your life. "I was *agog* when I learned that we were going to have our third child, but briefly became *saturnine* after I calculated the number of diapers that would need changing over three years."
- Ask the students for times when they "experienced" or "saw" the word.
  - "When I found out that our lacrosse team was going to state, I was *agog*!"
  - "I was totally *saturnine* when my parents told me I couldn't go to the party this weekend."

"Have you ever?" can be done as an in-class activity or a homework activity. The power comes from students' linking the new words to personal experiences, sharing their sentences with each other, and discussing the word meanings. When students create their own sentences, they are putting the words back into context. After hearing the words used again and again in meaningful contexts by their peers, students are much more likely to really grasp the words, comprehend them while reading, and use them later in discussion and writing.

Additional Core Activities That Move beyond Basic Dictionary Definitions

In addition to the vocabulary strategies just described, there are a number of common practices vocabulary researchers have identified that lead students to think deeply about words (Stahl & Nagy, 2006). Often, teachers will introduce a new vocabulary word by providing a basic, student-friendly definition of the word. Then the class, usually in small groups, will do some combination of the following:

- *Generate synonyms and antonyms of the word.* Teaching, discussing, and generating synonyms and antonyms of a word can be helpful in fleshing out a word's meaning. For example, when examining the word *dilapidate,* students might come up with synonyms and related words like *disintegrate, fall into ruin, decay,* and *destroy.* Antonyms might include *grow, flourish,* and *mend.* By connecting this new word to related words that are known, students make connections and begin to get a better idea of the word's meaning. This is an excellent opportunity for students to use a dictionary and thesaurus. Of course, not all words will have antonyms.

- *Compare and contrast shades of meaning among related words.* No two words have exactly the same meaning, including synonyms. For students to really "own" a word, they need to know how it compares and contrasts with related words. This will help them to think more precisely about each word's meaning and pinpoint the critical characteristics of a word that differentiate it from related words. From the *dilapidate* example, we could discuss with students that *destroy* implies complete annihilation, usually as a result of a more active process, like a fire, earthquake, or war (the city was *destroyed* by the army), whereas *dilapidate* implies a state of ruin resulting from neglect and is usually thought of as occurring more gradually (the abandoned house was *dilapidated*).

- *Generate examples and non-examples of a word.* When we ask students to come up with examples and non-examples of a word, they must move beyond the definition and think about how the word applies in the world. This type of situational thinking lends itself perfectly to connecting to student's personal experiences. For example, students may not know the word *dilapidate,* but they have no doubt seen a dilapidated house, building, car, or bus sometime in their lives. Student-generated examples and non-examples often spring from personal experiences and act as anchors for new word learning.
- *Act out the word.* In charades, students provide clues about a word by acting out the word. Teammates must try to guess the word from the clues. In the classic version of charades no words are allowed, so physical gestures and miming must be used to convey meaning to fellow team members. A variation allows students to use word clues but not the vocabulary word itself. The act of creating clues requires students to apply words to situations and context and personalize word learning. It is also one of the most high-energy, motivating activities we have used with students.
- *Draw a picture of the word.* It has been said that "a picture is worth a thousand words." Even simple pictures can give students a visual link that can trigger a word's meaning. More complex concepts can often be visually summarized with pictures and graphics. (Think of a rendition of the solar system or a visual of an atom.)

Figure 2.18 is the front and back of a vocabulary graphic organizer that shows how many of the practices just described can be combined in a format that allows students to dig deeply into a word's meaning. This graphic is a modification of a four-square activity that will be discussed in more detail in Chapter 7 (Eeds & Cockrum, 1985). Often, the teacher starts the discussion off by providing a basic definition of a word and may also provide some examples and non-examples from personal experience. Then small

Figure 2.18 Vocabulary Graphic Organizer

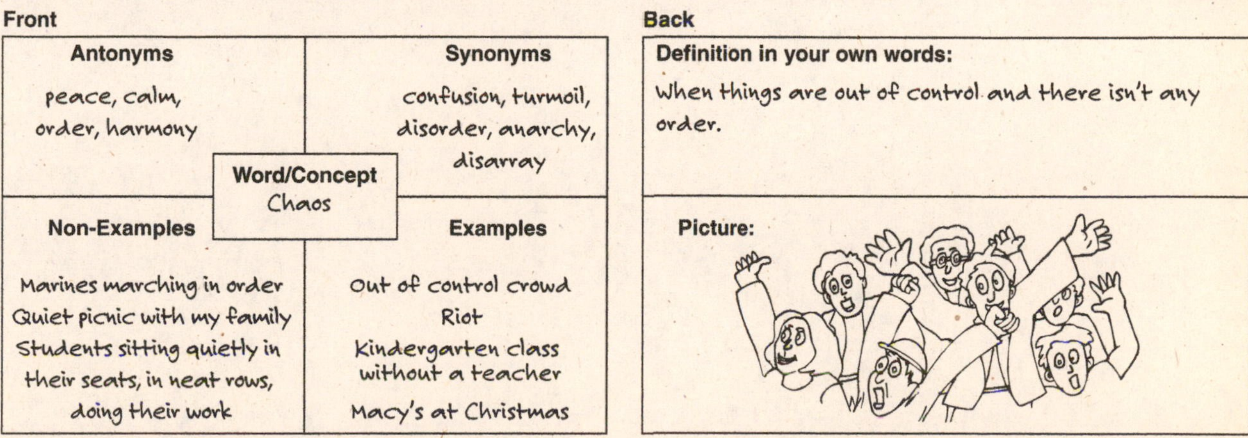

Front
Antonyms
peace, calm, order, harmony
Synonyms
confusion, turmoil, disorder, anarchy, disarray
Word/Concept
Chaos
Non-Examples
Marines marching in order
Quiet picnic with my family
Students sitting quietly in their seats, in neat rows, doing their work
Examples
Out of control crowd
Riot
Kindergarten class without a teacher
Macy's at Christmas
Back
Definition in your own words:
When things are out of control and there isn't any order.
Picture:

Source: Adapted from Eeds & Cockrum, 1985.

groups of students work together to complete the graphic organizer, generating synonyms, antonyms, examples, non-examples, student definitions, and drawings or visual representations of the word. Dictionaries and thesauruses, whether hard copies or online versions, should be used. Discussions are often lively and humorous (see examples in Figure 2.18) during this small-group work, as the teacher monitors and facilitates. At this level, the activity is more about the higher-level thinking and discussion generated by the graphic organizer than about the graphic organizer itself. At the end, small groups can share their work with the whole class, with the teacher confirming, praising, and clarifying student responses.

chapter 3

Assessment: Spelling and Reading

"Why Are They Spelling *Pounce* as *Panse*?"

Ms. Dishner wanted to get more information about her eighth grade English/language arts students' word knowledge, so she gave them the Upper-Level Spelling Inventory from *Words Their Way* (see Appendix A) at the beginning of the year. Scoring the inventories, she noticed that many of her below-grade-level readers spelled *pounce* as PANSE or PANCE. She thought that the *a* for *ou* error must not be random because many of these students made the exact same error. Further investigation of their errors revealed that these particular students were within word pattern spellers, a stage that normally achieving students usually pass through in second and third grades. This finding made sense due to their reading behaviors; all of these students were reading significantly below grade level with a choppy reading style, moving between word-by-word and phrasal reading. Referring to Chapter 4, the chapter concerning the within word pattern, she read how students at this stage often revert to their previous letter name–alphabetic tendencies when faced with a sound whose pattern is completely unfamiliar.

Why Developmental Assessment?

To provide the most effective instruction for your students, assessment should become a part of your professional routine. As teachers, we are often faced with two contradictory goals. First, we are expected to teach students certain skills or concepts for a particular grade level or type of content. Second, we are expected to individualize instruction to meet the needs of our particular students. These competing goals can sometimes cause tension. You may be a ninth grade English teacher expected to teach your students how to develop different methods of composition, such as narrative, expository, and informational writings with multiple purposes. Through this work, your students are supposed to not only produce coherent, organized pieces, but they are also expected to use a style sheet method (i.e., Modern Language Association or American Psychological Association) for citing sources (English Standards of Learning for Virginia Public Schools, 2002). However, your students come to school with wide variations in language skills, amounts of background knowledge, levels of motivation, and so forth. Many of your students come to class ready to tackle grade-level writing tasks with ease, and others come experiencing difficulty constructing a coherent paragraph. Utilizing your assessment data can help you target instruction and balance the need for developmentally targeted skills instruction with the curriculum.

As opposed to traditional testing that indicates students' percentage of mastery or how students perform based on a local or national standard, developmental assessment provides information teachers can use for decisions about the type of instruction that students need. Knowing which students require which type of instruction will allow you to better meet the needs of your students, especially those struggling to achieve growth

engagement LINK

Struggling students are sometimes disengaged due to years of feeling frustrated by their difficulties. Assessment allows you to tailor instruction to meet student needs. Because this instruction is within their developmental grasp, your students will experience success and see progress. The end result is more engaged students.

Table 3.1 Which Assessment Should You Use?

	What Is the Purpose?	How Much Time Is Involved?	Who Should Administer It?	Is It Group or Individually Administered?
Qualitative Spelling Checklist (Appendix A)	• Check for application of word study instruction in writing • Get information about orthographic knowledge	• Minimal	• English teachers • Special education teachers • Literacy specialists	• Individually
Qualitative Spelling Inventories (Appendix A)	• Assess orthographic knowledge growth	• Minimal	• English teachers • Special education teachers • Literacy specialists	• Whole group • Small groups • Individually
Reading Error Analysis (Appendix C)	• Check for application of word study instruction in reading • Get information about orthographic knowledge	• Minimal	• English teachers • Special education teachers • Literacy specialists	• Individually

in literacy. The assessment measures outlined in this chapter address two goals: (1) guiding instructional planning and (2) monitoring progress. Your students are more likely to respond to your instruction, become motivated, and get involved in class and with assignments if your instruction meets their developmental needs. Some testing should be done at the semester's start and end. Other testing should be implemented on a more frequent basis to monitor your students' progress and response to your instruction.

The time you have to teach each of your students is precious; however, the time you have for your struggling students is arguably more valuable. These students need to make up ground at the same time that they are trying to meet grade-level expectations. Therefore, your instructional decisions need to be strategic, which begins with assessing your students to ensure that you are providing the most timely and appropriate instruction. In this chapter, we offer ways to assess your students' orthographic knowledge while spelling and reading. See Table 3.1 for guidelines on choosing the right assessment for the right purpose, as well as other considerations (e.g., time involved). These assessments will help you determine which reading and word study activities will be most productive for your students.

Strategically Observe Spelling

A fundamental step in the assessment of reading, spelling, and vocabulary is observation of student performance. Observing your students' oral and written language will give you insight into their word knowledge, both orthographic knowledge (reading and spelling) and semantic knowledge (vocabulary). Indeed, observation is the most frequently employed type of assessment found in classrooms; you observe your students every day in their interactions with their peers and you, in their written work, and while reading texts, among others. They may be involved in independent reading during content area classes or more teacher-directed reading during language arts or literature. Likewise, your students are involved in a variety of writing activities, such as journaling, responding to reading, or writing content area summaries. In this section, we offer tools to make your observations more systematic. Once this information is collected, you will be able to analyze specific errors and identify error patterns to guide instruction.

When seeking to discover what students know about English orthography, teachers generally use spelling assessments. Although these assessments provide insights into their orthographic knowledge and experience with words, you can also gain insight as you informally observe your students' writing. Generally, we look at writing in terms of grammar and composition, but you should also consider your students' spelling attempts while writing.

You have opportunities each day to observe your students as they write for a variety of purposes, providing a record in which they reveal many of their understandings. As your students are writing, observe their errors and the strategies they use while spelling unknown words. Unfortunately, many of our struggling students write shorter pieces, partly because the task of writing can be quite laborious for them. They expend a great deal of energy thinking about the spellings of words and therefore often choose words that they are more comfortable spelling. However, these writing samples are still valuable as you look for transfer of your word study instruction. For example, you would expect a student who has been working with syllable patterns in word study to accurately spell words like *pilot* and *hammer*.

In Figure 3.1, we see a writing sample from a ninth-grader, Dominique. In this sample, he is telling the story of how he got a scar on his forehead when he was younger. When we look for what Dominique knows about words based on his spellings, we see that he has mastered simple consonant blends and digraphs but not complex consonant clusters like the *-tch* in *stitches*. He also demonstrates knowledge of short and long vowels in single-syllable and many multisyllable words. Other vowel patterns in multisyllabic words are a challenge (MYSCHEVEOUS for *mischievous*). In addition, we can see that he did not double the final consonant when adding the inflected endings *-ed* and *-ing* (SLAMED for *slammed;* RUNING for *running*). Occasionally using a checklist like the Qualitative Spelling Checklist (see Figure 3.2, p. 63) will provide a systematic way to record your students' spelling attempts while writing. The checklist can help you confirm the application of features studied during word study instruction. The features covered in the checklist for within word and syllables and affixes spellers are explained in detail in Chapters 4 and 5.

The Qualitative Spelling Checklist is a series of questions organized in a progression through the orthographic features of spelling. Using this checklist, you can see clearly what features your students are using in their writing. You can also locate the spelling stages of your students from the late letter name–alphabetic to the derivational relations stages.

The checklist is organized with guiding questions on the left and columns for you to check on the right. The questions all relate to specific orthographic features and are divided into corresponding stages of spelling. The columns allow you to check whether or not the feature is used correctly all of the time, often, or not at all. Start with the first question and continue until *No* responses start to be checked (or until the features are not

Figure 3.1 Dominique's Writing Sample

When I was 4-6 years old I was at my grandparents house and I had a little toy tractor thing that blew bubbels and I was quite myscheveous so I decided that I wanted to try to go as fast as I could through the kitchen. Little did I know there was a chair in my "run way" so stupid as I was I came rocketing down the floor and I slamed into this chair. My grandparents came runing. They said that I was bleeding over my right eye. I had to go get stiches over my eye and I still have a scar today.

present in the particular sample). The checklist follows a developmental progression, so it should be apparent when the features are outside of a student's realm of knowledge. A student should at first get many "Yes" responses and then begin to accumulate some "Often" marks until eventually receiving a few "No" responses in a row. This is not to say there will not occasionally be a "Yes" followed by a "No" and then back to "Yes" with the very next feature. This will occur with older struggling readers who have memorized the spelling of sight words but have not mastered the underlying spelling or orthographic principles. To be conservative, and to find students' true instructional levels, observe when there are several "No" and "Often" responses.

Let's consider Dominique's checklist (see Figure 3.2). Notice that he begins the checklist with a series of checks in the *Yes* column. He demonstrates in this sample that he can correctly spell features in the late letter name–alphabetic stage (e.g., short vowels) and almost all features in the within word pattern stage (e.g., long vowels). He begins to have checks in the "Often" and "No" columns in the syllables and affixes stage, where he shows confusion with adding inflected endings when he fails to double the final *m* in *slammed* yet correctly adds inflected endings to words requiring him to drop the *e*-marker (e.g., *decided*). Continuing through the questions, Dominique confuses unaccented final syllables when he confuses the *le* in *bubbles* (e.g., BUBBELS for *bubbles*). At this point, no more checks are assigned in the columns on the right. Dominique does not spell any words using the features probed in the remaining questions; therefore, no responses are given. Based on this checklist, Dominique is spelling in the syllables and affixes stage. This finding would be confirmed using the appropriate qualitative spelling inventory. The checklist, in this way, can provide you with a benchmark on the qualitative spelling inventory that would be appropriate for students when you have little or no other information about their orthographic knowledge.

Qualitative Spelling Inventories

Using inventories, you will be able to identify a student's stage of developmental spelling and what spelling feature instruction within that stage would best meet the student's needs. Fresch and Wheaton (2002) explain more systematic assessments as those that compare apples to apples because they allow you to use students' spelling to check progress over time using consistent and comparable evidence. Observations, on the other hand, are more likely to compare apples to oranges because mediating factors may influence performance (e.g., dictionaries and friends). Qualitative spelling inventories are important systematic checks that present you with a clear and complete picture of your students' orthographic knowledge. Taken together, informal reading/writing observations along with qualitative spelling inventories provide you with a rich collection of information that will guide you in developing a comprehensive instructional plan for your students.

Qualitative spelling inventories are made up of lists of words chosen to represent a variety of orthographic features at increasing levels of difficulty, spanning multiple stages of spelling. The words are chosen specifically to assess a student's knowledge of features that relate to the different stages of spelling. However, the lists do not assess all spelling features and are therefore not exhaustive. The features probed are the ones most helpful in identifying a stage of spelling. Qualitative spelling inventories are administered like a traditional spelling test, and the results are analyzed for each student.

Edmund Henderson and his students at the University of Virginia developed the first qualitative spelling inventories in the 1980s and 1990s. Perhaps the best known of these early inventories is the McGuffey Qualitative Inventory of Word Knowledge (Schlagal, 1992). Schlagal's inventory consists of graded lists (first through eighth grades) and can be useful for circumstances where reporting spelling achievement in terms of grade level is necessary or desired. A feature guide has not been developed to help analyze this inventory, so you must analyze errors yourself to determine which features are being used correctly and which are used but confused.

Figure 3.2 Dominique's Checklist

Use this checklist to analyze students' uncorrected writing and to locate their appropriate stages of spelling development. Examples are in parentheses. The spaces for dates at the top of the checklist are used to follow students' progress. Check when certain features are observed in students' spelling. When a feature is always present, check "Yes." The last place where you check "Often" corresponds to the student's stage of spelling development.

Student Dominique Observer Hayes

Dates 2/2009

	Yes	Often	No
Letter Name–Alphabetic			
Late			
• Are short vowels spelled correctly? *(bed, ship, when, lump)*	✓		
• Is the *m* or *n* included in front of other consonants? *(lump, stand)*	✓		
Within Word Pattern			
Early			
• Are long vowels in single-syllable words used but confused? (FLOTE for *float*, TRANE for *train*)	✓		
Middle			
• Are most long vowel words spelled correctly, while some long vowel spelling and other vowel patterns are used but confused? (DRIEV for *drive*)	✓		
• Are the most common consonant digraphs and blends spelled correctly? *(sled, dream, fright)*	✓		
Late			
• Are the harder consonant digraphs and blends spelled correctly? *(speck, switch, smudge)*			✓
• Are most other vowel patterns spelled correctly? *(spoil, chewed, serving)*	✓		
Syllables and Affixes			
Early			
• Are inflectional endings added correctly to base vowel patterns with short vowel patterns? *(shopping, listed)*			✓
• Are junctures between syllables spelled correctly? *(cattle, cellar, carries, bottle)*	✓		
Middle			
• Are inflectional endings added correctly to base words? *(chewed, marched, shower)*		✓	
Late			
• Are unaccented final syllables spelled correctly? *(bottle, fortunate, civilize)*			✓
• Are less frequent prefixes and suffixes spelled correctly? *(confident, favor, ripen, cellar, pleasure)*			
Derivational Relations			
Early			
• Are most polysyllabic words spelled correctly? *(fortunate, confident)*			
Middle			
• Are unaccented vowels in derived words spelled correctly? *(confident, civilize, category)*			
Late			
• Are words from derived forms spelled correctly? *(pleasure, opposition, criticize)*			

If your intent is to analyze spellings by orthographic features, then other spelling inventories may better meet your purpose (Bear, 1982; Ganske, 1999; Invernizzi, 1992; Invernizzi, Meier, & Juel, 2003; Morris, 1999; Viise, 1994). Many of these have a transparent system for analyzing errors by orthographic feature, and, like the McGuffey Qualitative Spelling Inventory, they have continuous lists of words sampling orthographic features across spelling stages. These inventories have been used to document the developmental progression of spelling for students with learning disabilities (Invernizzi & Worthy, 1989), students diagnosed with dyslexia (Sawyer, Wade, & Kim, 1999), and functionally illiterate adults (Worthy & Viise, 1996).

Qualitative spelling inventories not only provide you with information regarding your students' stages of spelling development, but they also offer you information about their reading levels. As discussed in Chapter 1, spelling and reading are closely intertwined. Many studies have shown that scores on qualitative spelling inventories are consistently related to, and predict with great accuracy, the reading achievement of school-age children and even adults (Bear, Templeton, & Warner, 1991; Bear, Truex, & Barone, 1989; Edwards, 2003; Ehri, 2000; Ellis & Cataldo, 1992; Morris, Nelson, & Perney, 1986).

Using Qualitative Spelling Inventories

Sometimes teachers feel overwhelmed when first learning about spelling inventories with transparent orthographic features to analyze. Many teachers we work with are amazed at how many features there are as they begin analyzing spelling inventories and worry about their unfamiliarity with some of the features. The analyses in this chapter will provide some of the information, and you can look to Chapters 4 and 5 for detailed explanations of the within word pattern and syllables and affixes stages and the features within.

In this chapter, we offer three spelling inventories to assist you in your assessment routine: The Primary Spelling Inventory (PSI), the Elementary Spelling Inventory (ESI), and the Upper-Level Spelling Inventory (USI). The Primary Spelling Inventory (PSI) consists of 26 words beginning with simple consonant-vowel-consonant words *(gum)*, moving to vowel patterns (e.g., *coach*), and ending with inflected endings (e.g., *camped, riding*). This inventory is often used with students who have instructional reading levels ranging from first to third grade. The Elementary Spelling Inventory (ESI) is designed to probe features through the derivational relations stage of spelling, beginning with simple consonant-vowel-consonant words *(bed)* and ending with words having Latin and Greek roots *(opposition)*. The ESI is used with students reading instructionally at approximately the third through fifth grade levels. The Upper-Level Spelling Inventory (USI) is used with students performing in the upper stages of spelling—syllables and affixes and derivational relations. It begins with words containing vowel and consonant patterns (*switch*) and progresses to words with Latin and Greek roots (*irresponsible*). Generally, students reading instructionally above a fifth grade level will need the USI. Table 3.2 outlines these inventories and the stages they address.

Table 3.2 Selecting a Spelling Inventory

Spelling Inventory	Reading Achievement Level by Grade	Word Knowledge Range
Primary Spelling Inventory	1–3	Letter Name–Alphabetic Within Word Pattern
Elementary Spelling Inventory	3–5	Within Word Pattern Syllables and Affixes
Upper-Level Spelling Inventory	5 and up	Syllables and Affixes and up

Considerations for English Learners

Assessing English Learners

To determine their level of word knowledge, English learners should participate in assessments such as the spelling inventories described in this chapter. These inventories provide you with the information you need to determine word study goals and design targeted lessons. Bear, Helman, Templeton, Invernizzi, and Johnston (2007) offer the following guidelines for administering spelling inventories to English learners.

- Ease your students' worries about spelling words that they do not know how to spell. Many English learners have been in educational settings where misspellings were discouraged. Therefore, some of your students may be uneasy about attempting to spell unknown words. To help alleviate such concerns, you can model strategies for spelling unknown words for your students (see Chapter 2).

- Make sure to read the provided sentences and offer additional support. You want to ensure that your English learners know the meanings of the words you are asking them to spell. If a word's meaning is unknown, provide additional sentences, show pictures, provide a synonym, or use movement to clarify meaning. For example, for the word *drive*, you could show a picture of someone driving a car or act out steering with your hands on a wheel. Bear and colleagues (2007) provide a Picture Spelling Inventory—a qualitative spelling inventory that uses pictures and visual cues to demonstrate the word you want them to spell.

- Have your students verbalize words as they spell them. This practice may help them make connections between English and their primary language.

- Invite your students to put a question mark by words when they are unsure of their meanings. This process will provide you with insight into their vocabulary knowledge.

Bear and colleagues (2007) also provide error types that are commonly found among English learners. You can refer to these error types to better understand misspellings.

- Some misspellings reflect minimal contrasts between English and a student's primary language. For example, /s/ and /z/ are minimal pairs in English, meaning the two sounds are the same except in one way. They are articulated in the same way, but /z/ is voiced and /s/ is not (/z/ produces a vibration of the vocal cords while /s/ does not). If a sound in English does not exist in the student's primary language, the student will substitute a close match from their primary language. Consider /z/ and /s/. Chinese does not have the sound /z/; therefore, many Chinese speakers will spell /z/ with an *s*, its minimal pair.

- English learners frequently substitute whole words. For example, a student may write WHAT for *when*. This error type is often more common with students who have learned a more transparent orthography like Spanish—an orthography that has fewer sounds and highly consistent spellings. It has not been necessary for them to develop fine-tuned sound discriminations, and, as a result, they may not recognize the sounds at the ends of words or syllables.

- English learners often sound out words, especially if their primary language has a transparent orthography. These students expect each sound to have a letter match, or that each letter will be sounded. At the same time, they look for consistency between their primary language and English. This often results in deleted or added sounds. For example, many English words follow the CVC closed syllable pattern (*cat* in a one-syllable word and *basket* in a two-syllable word). Spanish, on the other hand, has few instances of the CVC pattern. Therefore, Spanish speakers often leave off ending consonants. Some languages do not have consonant blends similar to the ones found in English, so students may add vowel sounds between consonants while they are trying to represent those sounds. For example, Chinese speakers may insert a vowel sound between *s*-blends (SINAK for *snake*).

- The spelling of English learners may appear inconsistent. For example, students may spell more complex words correctly (like *happy*) and other, less advanced words incorrectly (like BEAD for *bed*). This may happen because older English learners sometimes memorize the spellings of words that are beyond their level of word knowledge.

- Students learning English may not take advantage of contextual information. For example, a student who hears the sentence "The dog chewed my favorite sweater yesterday" may not represent the *-ed* ending in *chewed* if they are unfamiliar with the inflected endings commonly found in English. A student proficient with the structure and vocabulary of English will be alerted by the word *yesterday* and know to pay attention to any marker of the past tense.

Not only are these inventories packed with a wealth of information about your students' orthographic knowledge, but they are also easy to use and quick. Many teachers find these inventories to be the most helpful and easiest-to-use assessments they administer. Designed for group administration, the time involved in giving the inventories is minimal. Likewise, the analysis of the inventories is not time intensive. The inventories are well constructed; studies have found them to be reliable and valid measures of your students' orthographic development. Table 3.1 provides information about the purpose of using a spelling inventory relative to other assessments of orthographic knowledge.

When your students are comfortable spelling unknown words, you can feel confident that their performance on the spelling inventories will provide reliable information. To use any of the spelling inventories, follow these six steps (see Figure 3.3).

1. Create a comfortable environment.
2. Select a spelling inventory.
3. Administer the inventory.
4. Score and analyze the samples.
5. Organize groups.
6. Determine instructional goals.

Step One: Create a Comfortable Environment

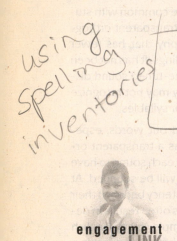

When students feel like they are in control of their own learning, they are more likely to be engaged and motivated to participate in school. A first step to helping your students take control is creating a safe environment for taking risks.

Students' educational experiences through the grades have a profound effect on them. Students who struggle academically all too often become disengaged in school and expect failure. As first-graders, they probably labored over reading and spelling willingly. They believed that their efforts could result in academic success. However, as the years passed, these struggling students may have become increasingly frustrated by their difficulties and their lack of progress relative to their peers. Often, students who struggle to read eventually come to the conclusion that they are not good readers and that reading is too difficult (Chapman, Tunmer, & Prochnow, 2000). Years of failure result in students' feeling as if their achievement is not controllable. In other words, they think they do not have the ability to do well, developing feelings of learned helplessness—the belief that nothing you do can lead to success (Dweck, 1987). In fact, they begin to interpret their failures as indicators of low ability, choosing to avoid activities that could provide further evidence of their deficiencies and disengage from tasks associated with failure (Henderson & Dweck, 1990).

The good news is that there are exceptions to these findings. Children who struggle but still believe that they can do better as a result of their own efforts do achieve at higher levels compared to those who feel that their efforts are for naught (Kistner, Osborne, &

Figure 3.3 Steps to Using the Spelling Inventories

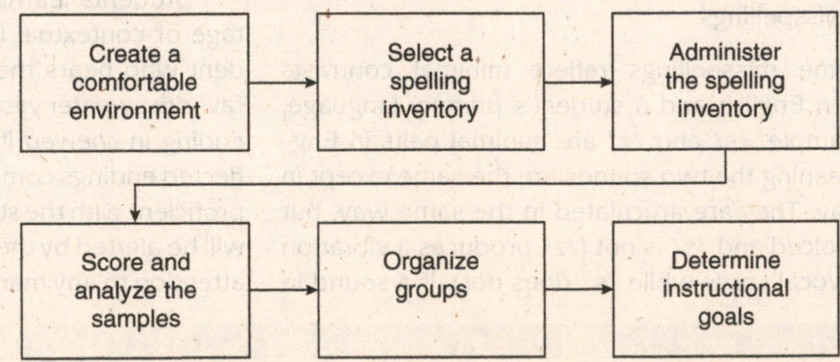

LeVerrier, 1988). Teachers can help students by making them aware of how their academic successes are related to their own efforts—effort matters. Students need to know that school is about becoming better rather than being the best. They need to know that people learn by trying hard and failure is just a natural part of learning. In addition, they need to feel as if they can safely participate. With failure comes vulnerability. Your students should feel that your classroom is a safe place to take risks and to fall sometimes, knowing that you (and their peers) are there to help pick them back up.

Assessments are often associated with failure, but you can help alleviate the fear that often comes with assessments by creating a comfortable environment that encourages effort and sees students as their own agents of change. Another simple step that can ease these fears is to let them know you will not be assigning grades to their papers. Let them know that instead you will be using the information to understand how to help them learn more about spelling and reading words (see Step Three: Administer the Inventory for more on this). Encourage them to be strategic in their efforts to spell unknown words (see Chapter 2).

Step Two: Select a Spelling Inventory

Select a spelling inventory by considering the grade level and reading achievement of your students. With struggling readers and spellers, you should put more weight on their achievement level. See Table 3.2 for guidance on using reading levels as a guide. For example, if you were Ms. Dishner in the opening vignette, you would consider the reading level of the students first and then their grade level. Recall that the group she was considering was at a third grade reading level. Using Table 3.2, Ms. Dishner was directed to choose either the Primary Spelling Inventory or the Elementary Spelling Inventory. She decided on the Elementary Spelling Inventory due to the actual grade level of these students—eighth grade.

Another option to assist you in selecting an inventory is the Qualitative Spelling Checklist, which can give you a spelling stage estimate. You can use that information along with Table 3.2 to make an informed decision. For example, we can use Dominique's checklist in Figure 3.2, which was based on a writing sample. Because the checklist shows Dominique to be a syllables and affixes speller, Table 3.2 directs you to either the Elementary Spelling Inventory or the Upper-Level Spelling Inventory. Knowing Dominique's reading level can help you decide between the two inventories.

You may not have achievement information readily available to you at the start of the year. In this case, you may find starting each student at the same level and adjusting as needed your best option. After you administer a list, shift to small-group administration of other lists if necessary. Keep in mind two points. First, your students must generate a number of errors in order for you to determine a spelling stage. Second, you do not want to consider inventories on which students make too many errors. When a list is too difficult, students may make errors on features they have previously mastered due to the interference of sophisticated features beyond their developmental reach. A good rule of thumb is to administer an easier inventory if your students' percentage correct is less than 50 percent. Viewing Ms. Dishner's classroom composite form in Figure 3.4, you can see that Henry, Suzanne, Kayla, Jose, and Damien all scored less than 50 percent on the Elementary Spelling Inventory. She should consider giving them the Primary Spelling Inventory.

Step Three: Administer the Inventory

Begin administration by preparing your students for testing. These inventories are not designed for grading purposes; students should not study the words before or after the inventory is administered. Have them number a paper as they would for a traditional spelling test. Then provide them with an explanation similar to the following to give a reason for taking the inventory and to assuage any nervous feelings.

Figure 3.4 Ms. Dishner's Classroom Composite

Elementary Spelling Inventory Classroom Composite

Teacher Dishner School Roswell Middle Grade 8th Date Sept.

SPELLING STAGES →	EMERGENT LATE / EARLY	LETTER NAME–ALPHABETIC MIDDLE	LATE		WITHIN WORD PATTERN EARLY	MIDDLE	LATE	SYLLABLES AND AFFIXES EARLY	MIDDLE	LATE	DERIVATIONAL RELATIONS EARLY	MIDDLE	
Students' ↓ Names	Consonants	Short Vowels	Digraphs	Blends	Long Vowels	Other Vowels	Inflected Endings	Syllable Junctures	Unaccented Final Syllables	Harder Suffixes	Bases or Roots	Correct Spelling	Total Rank Order
Possible Points	7	5	6	7	5	7	5	5	5	5	5	25	87
1. John	7	5	6	7	5	7	5	5	5	4	4	24	84
2. Grace	7	5	6	7	5	7	5	5	5	4	4	23	83
3. Lucy	7	5	6	7	5	7	5	5	5	4	4	23	83
4. Eli	7	5	6	7	5	7	5	4	5	3	4	21	79
5. Maria	7	5	6	7	5	7	5	4	4	4	4	21	79
6. Bai	7	5	6	7	5	7	5	3	4	4	4	20	77
7. Adriana	7	5	6	7	5	7	5	4	4	3	3	19	75
8. Preston	7	5	6	7	5	7	5	4	4	3	2	18	73
9. Kazuma	7	5	6	7	5	7	5	3	4	3	3	18	73
10. Claire	7	5	6	7	5	7	4	3	3	2	2	18	69
11. Lijuan	7	5	6	7	5	7	4	3	3	2	1	18	68
12. Antonia	7	5	6	7	5	7	4	3	3	2	1	17	67
13. Talia	7	5	6	7	5	7	4	3	3	2	2	16	67
14. Yanmei	7	5	6	7	5	7	4	3	2	3	1	16	66
15. Alicia	7	5	6	7	5	7	4	3	3	2	0	13	62
16. Sophia	7	5	6	7	5	7	4	3	2	2	0	13	61
17. Karl	7	5	6	7	5	7	3	3	2	3	0	13	61
18. Janie	7	5	6	7	5	7	4	3	2	2	0	12	60
19. Jack	7	5	6	7	5	7	4	3	2	2	0	12	60
20. Isabella	7	5	6	7	5	7	4	3	2	2	0	12	60
21. Henry	7	5	6	7	5	5	3	2	2	1	0	10	53
22. Suzanne	7	5	6	7	4	5	3	2	2	2	0	10	53
23. Kayla	7	5	6	7	4	5	3	1	1	1	0	10	50
24. Jose	7	5	6	7	4	4	3	1	1	0	0	9	47
25. Damien	7	4	5	7	2	1	1	0	0	0	0	6	33
Highlight for Instruction					1	5	6	17	15	18	8		

Note: *Highlight students who miss more than 1 on a particular feature; they will benefit from more instruction in that area.

> I am going to ask you to spell some words. You may have not studied these particular words. Some of the words may be easy and others may be difficult. Do the best you can while you use your strategies. I will not give you grades on these papers. Your work will help me understand how you are learning to read and write. This will let me know how I can help you.

You want to get the best effort from your students to make sure that you are getting an accurate view of their word knowledge. Many older struggling students rush through spelling words they do not know without giving them much thought. This type of behavior may be due to a learned helplessness that develops after years of failure, as discussed earlier. It may also be due to a lack of knowledge when it comes to strategically approaching a word they do not know. Regardless, you want to avoid this type of behavior. Before administering the spelling inventories, you may want to incorporate lessons like the ones described in Chapter 2 (see Strategic Spelling) during your writing time to provide a natural setting for negotiating spelling words they may not know. These lessons will encourage students to use strategies to assist them when spelling unknown words; tacking a statement like "If you don't know the word, then spell it the best you can" onto the instructions for the inventory will not achieve the effect you are seeking.

Now you are ready to begin calling out the words on the inventory. Pronounce each word naturally without drawing out the sounds or breaking words into syllables. Say each word twice and use it in a sentence. It is critical to use the word in a sentence if you are calling out a homophone; using *cellar* in a sentence is important so the student will not confuse it with *seller.* It is absolutely appropriate to alert them to these words; you could say, "Listen to this sentence so you know which *cellar/seller* I am talking about." As you will notice, sentences are provided with the inventories in Appendix A. Saying the sentence with every word is not always necessary and, in fact, can be distracting. If you do not feel it is necessary, do not read the sentence.

It will be necessary to monitor your students while administering the inventory. Move around the room as you call the words aloud to not only monitor their work but to also observe their behaviors. Note students who are writing quickly. These students may not require "think time" because they know the correct spelling, or they may be students who are not exercising any of their strategies and are simply not giving it their best effort, deciding to "bag it." Look for words that you cannot read due to poor handwriting. Ask students to rewrite any words you cannot read or to tell you any questionable letter. Or ask a student to print rather than write in cursive if their cursive is particularly difficult to read.

Help your students keep up with the words. Say the number of a word prior to calling it out. Students sometimes skip a word and saying the numbers aloud may bring this to their attention so that you can redirect them. While moving around the room, you can look out for any skipped words.

Once you have finished the inventory, you may want to give your students a second opportunity with the words. You can do this simply by calling out the words one more time, leaving a bit of time between words to allow students to revisit any words about which they are unsure. Students are allowed to reflect on their work through this re-examination, and their additional attempts give you even more information about their growing orthographic knowledge.

Most of your students will be able to complete one inventory in about 20 minutes. You want to give your students sufficient time to respond, but at the same time, you want to keep the pace. In most cases, you will administer the entire selected inventory, for two reasons: (1) It is better to have too many words than too few, and (2) your students will want to "save face" rather than be singled out to stop. Students who score less than 50 percent on a given inventory should take an easier inventory. Take a look at Kayla's spelling inventory (Figure 3.5). She scored 40 percent on the Elementary Spelling Inventory. Given this score, it might be useful to have her take the Primary Spelling Inventory. Students who score above 90 percent on the inventory should take a more

Figure 3.5 Kayla's Elementary Spelling Inventory

bed	
ship	
when	
lump	
float	
train	
place	
drive	
brite	(bright)
shoping	(shopping)
spoyle	(spoil)
serving	
chooed	(chewed)
caryes	(carries)
marched	(marched)
shower	
botel	(bottle)
faver	(favor)
rippun	(ripen)
seler	(cellar)
plescher	(pleasure)
forchunate	(fortunate)
confdant	(confident)
sivilise	(civilize)
opozishun	(opposition)

difficult one. So the Upper-Level Spelling Inventory should be administered if 90 percent or more was achieved on the Elementary Spelling Inventory. Those students scoring between 51 and 89 percent do not need additional inventories; you should have enough information to make a stage determination and formulate instructional goals.

Step Four: Score and Analyze the Inventories

Once you have administered the inventories and collected your students' papers, the next step is to score them. You will obtain two scores: a power score and a feature score. Scoring is not simply quantitative, not simply determining whether your students spelled a word right or wrong. The process of scoring is also qualitative and will give you information about specific orthographic features within the individual words. For example, Kayla spelled the word *chewed* as CHOOED. This error shows that she is unfamiliar with the *ew* spelling pattern, but it also shows that she knows the initial digraph (the *ch*) and the inflected *-ed* ending. She will get points for the initial digraph and the

-ed ending. This type of scoring and analysis provides you with qualitative information about the specific spelling features your students know and what they are ready to study next. Many of the features probed on the inventories are explained in detail in Chapters 4 and 5.

Find a Power Score You will first establish a power score by marking each spelling as right or wrong. You should also write the correct word by any misspelled word, which will draw your attention to the features that are right and wrong. Having the correct spellings will also help when sharing a student's inventory with another teacher or a parent. Then add up the number of words spelled correctly. This is your power score. Kayla (see Figure 3.5), for example, had a power score of 10.

Power scores will give you a rough estimate of your students' spelling stages. As discussed earlier, the spelling inventories were developed as a stage-by-stage assessment; each inventory consists of groups of words containing features that will be learned in successive spelling stages. Consider the Elementary Spelling Inventory, for example: The first group of words consists mostly of short vowel, single-syllable words consistent with features mastered in the letter name–alphabetic stage of spelling. The next group includes single-syllable words that contain vowel patterns acquired in the within word pattern stage. As the list progresses, words are provided to probe the syllables and affixes and derivational relations stages.

Consider Kayla's spellings of the first four words on the Elementary Spelling Inventory. She demonstrated her ease with features at this stage. She correctly spelled blends and digraphs (e.g., *ship, float*), short vowels (e.g., *bed*), and preconsonantal nasals (e.g., *lump*). These features are all acquired in the letter name–alphabetic stage of spelling. Therefore, Kayla would be considered independent at the letter name–alphabetic stage, as shown by her correct spellings:

bed
ship
when
lump

With the fifth word in the inventory, the stage shifts from the letter name–alphabetic to the within word pattern stage. The next group of words explores vowel patterns (e.g., *float, train, place, drive, bright*), which is the main feature in the within word pattern stage. Kayla correctly spells all of these words except one—BRITE for *bright*. Because she only makes one error, we can say that she will need a brief review of long vowel patterns.

float
train
place
drive
brite (bright)

The next group of words contains features consistent with the late within word pattern and early syllables and affixes stages. These words have ambiguous vowel patterns, including diphthongs (e.g., *spoil*), schwa-plus-*r* (e.g., *serving*), and lower-frequency vowel patterns (e.g., *chewed*). In this group, we can see Kayla got very few words right and most wrong, spelling only *serving* and *shower* correctly. However, she demonstrated some knowledge of early syllables and affixes features. Kayla correctly represented inflected endings despite not applying doubling principles (*shopping* as SHOPING). She correctly represented the single *v* in *favor* (FAVER) but did not double the *l* in *cellar* (SELER) or the *t* in *bottle* (BOTEL). She also incorrectly doubled the *p* in *ripen* (RIPPUN). Finally, she did not accurately spell the final unaccented syllables in *cellar* (SELER), *bottle* (BOTEL), *favor* (FAVER), or *ripen* (RIPPUN).

shoping (shopping)
spoyle (spoil)
serving
chooed (chewed)
caryes (carries)
martched (marched)
shower
botel (bottle)
faver (favor)
rippun (ripen)
seler (cellar)

The last group of words sample features from the derivational relations stage of spelling. These words have advanced features that are typically studied in the middle grades and beyond. For example, a feature probed here is a vowel or consonant sound change with the addition of a suffix (e.g., changing *please* to *pleasure*). As can be seen in Kayla's sample, she misspelled every word in this section, indicating that instruction at this level would be a clear area of frustration for her.

plescher (pleasure)
forchunate (fortunate)
confdant (confident)
sivilise (civilize)
opozishun (opposition)

Table 3.3 shows the relationships of the power scores on the three qualitative spelling inventories. The table will help you use the power score to determine an estimated stage and even refine development as being early, middle, or late within the stage. As you can see, Kayla's power score of 10 on the ESI places her in the late within word pattern stage. This finding is consistent with the preceding discussion. Given this analysis, you may feel comfortable with the information you have on Kayla using the ESI and, therefore, decide not to administer the PSI.

Determine Feature Scores A feature guide is provided for each of the three spelling inventories to help you consider your students' samples (see Appendix A). The feature

Table 3.3 Power Scores and Estimated Stages

Spelling Inventory	Emergent	Letter Name			Within Word Pattern			Syllables and Affixes			Derivational Relations		
		E	*M*	*L*	*E*	*M*	*L*	*E*	*M*	*L*	*E*	*M*	*L*
Primary (PSI)	0	0	2	6	8	13	17	22					
Elementary (ESI)		0	2	3	5	7	9	12	15	18	20	22	
Upper-Level (USI)					2	6	7	9	11	18	21	23	27

guides help you analyze errors and confirm the stage designations suggested by the power score. Kayla's feature guide in Figure 3.6 shows you how to complete (and score) the feature guide.

As you can see, the top portion of the feature guide shows the stages and divides them into early, middle, and late. The header row lists the spelling features as they correspond to the stages, following the developmental sequence. The words from the inventory are listed in the far left column. For each word, check off each feature of the word that is represented correctly. For example, because Kayla spelled *ship* correctly, there is a check for the ending consonant, the short vowel, and the digraph, for a total of three feature points. Kayla also gets a point for spelling the word correctly; this is recorded in the far right column. Because Kayla spelled *bright* as BRITE, she gets a check for the blend but not the long vowel spelling pattern *igh*. So for *bright*, Kayla would get one point for the correct blend but no other points. Even though Kayla used the wrong spelling pattern, she did mark the vowel as long in *bright*, using *i-e*. This shows that Kayla is using but confusing this feature since she used a reasonable representation of the feature rather than not marking the long vowel at all.

You will notice that not every feature is scored in every word (e.g., *bright* is scored for "Blends" and "Long Vowels" but not "Final Consonants"). The features sampled, however, are sufficient for identifying the stages of spelling. After scoring each word, add the checks in each column and record the total score for that column at the bottom. This score is a ratio of correct features to the total possible features. You can adjust this ratio of correct features to total possible features if you do not call out the entire list of words for that particular inventory. Then add the total feature scores across the bottom and the total words spelled correctly. This will give you an overall total score. The total score can be used to rank order students and to compare individual growth over time.

Identify Stage of Spelling After completing the feature guide for all of your students, you will use that information to determine a developmental stage. The continuum of features across the top of the guide shows gradations for each developmental level. These gradations allow you to be more precise in your assessment of students' orthographic knowledge and will help you determine more appropriate instructional goals for word study. Simply put, if a student spells most of the features relevant to a stage correctly, then that student is probably late in the stage. If a student is beginning to use the key features of a stage but still has some misspellings from the previous stage, then the student is probably at the early part of the new stage. This is illustrated in Kayla's feature guide. She is beginning to use some features in the late within word pattern stage but still has some misspellings consistent with the middle of that stage. Therefore, she is most likely transitioning from the middle within word pattern stage to the late within word pattern stage. As you can see on Kayla's feature guide, the developmental stages are circled in the row across the top of the guide. Her use of short and most long vowels is noted as correct. She is confusing some other vowel patterns. This has been circled in the top row. In cases like Kayla's, taking a step backward is often a good first step. Therefore, you should choose to consider her to be a middle within word pattern speller and design instructional goals accordingly. You would then refer to Chapter 4 for further guidance.

Let's look at Javier's spelling inventory as an example of a student spelling at the syllables and affixes stage (Figure 3.7 on p. 75). Based on his power score of 18 on the ESI and using Table 3.3, Javier's stage of spelling would be late syllables and affixes. Qualitatively, we can see that he correctly spelled many of the words probing features at the within word pattern stage (e.g., "Long Vowels" and "Other Vowels") and some features at the syllables and affixes stage (e.g., "Inflected Endings"). He began using but confusing features that would fall in the latter portion of the syllables and affixes stage, such as "Syllable Junctures" (e.g., RIPPEN for *ripen*) and "Unaccented Final Syllables" (e.g., FAVER for *favor*). Please see Figure 3.8 (on p. 76) to see Javier's Feature Guide.

Figure 3.6 Kayla's Feature Guide

Primary Spelling Inventory Feature Guide

Student's Name Kayla Teacher Dishner Grade 8th Date Sept.

Words Spelled Correctly: 10 /25 *Feature Points:* 40 /62 *Total:* 50 /87 *Spelling Stage:* WWP

SPELLING STAGES →	EMERGENT LATE	EARLY	LETTER NAME–ALPHABETIC MIDDLE	LATE	EARLY	WITHIN WORD PATTERN MIDDLE	LATE	SYLLABLES AND AFFIXES EARLY	MIDDLE	LATE	DERIVATIONAL RELATIONS EARLY	MIDDLE		
Features →	**Consonants Initial**	**Consonants Final**	**Short Vowels**	**Digraphs**	**Blends**	**Long Vowels**	**Other Vowels**	**Inflected Endings**	**Syllable Junctures**	**Unaccented Final Syllables**	**Harder Suffixes**	**Bases or Roots**	**Feature Points**	**Words Spelled Correctly**
1. bed	b ✓	d ✓	e ✓										3	1
2. ship		p ✓	i ✓	sh ✓									3	1
3. when			e ✓	wh ✓									2	1
4. lump	l ✓		u ✓		mp ✓								3	1
5. float		t ✓			fl ✓	oa ✓							3	1
6. train		n ✓			tr ✓	ai ✓							3	1
7. place					pl ✓	a-e ✓							2	1
8. drive		v ✓			dr ✓	i-e ✓							3	1
9. bright					br ✓	igh							1	
10. shopping			o ✓	sh ✓				pping					2	
11. spoil					sp ✓		oi						1	
12. serving							er ✓	ving ✓					2	1
13. chewed				ch ✓			ew	ed ✓					2	
14. carries							ar ✓	ies	rr				1	
15. marched				ch ✓			ar ✓	ed ✓					3	
16. shower				sh ✓			ow ✓			er ✓			3	1
17. bottle									tt	le			0	
18. favor									v ✓	or			1	
19. ripen									p	en			0	
20. cellar									ll	ar			0	
21. pleasure											ure	pleas	0	
22. fortunate							or ✓				ate ✓	fortun	2	
23. confident											ent	confid	0	
24. civilize											ize	civil	0	
25. opposition											tion	pos	0	
Totals		7 /7	5 /5	6 /6	7 /7	4 /5	5 /7	3 /5	1 /5	1 /5	1 /5	0 /5	40 /62	10 /25

Figure 3.7 Javier's Elementary Spelling Inventory

bed	
ship	
when	
lump	
float	
train	
place	
drive	
bright	
shopping	
spoil	
surving	(serving)
chewed	
carries	
marched	
shower	
bottle	
faver	(favor)
rippen	(ripen)
seller	(cellar)
plessure	(pleasure)
fortunate	
confedent	(confident)
civilize	
oposision	(opposition)

Step Five: Organize Groups

Grouping is a critical component of word study instruction. Determining instructional levels would be a moot point if the instruction that followed continued to teach district- or state-created standards to the whole class. Small-group instruction is an alternative, allowing you to provide timely, appropriate instruction. Elementary teachers are often very familiar with grouping, and their school days are often set up in a way to more easily allow for grouping. On the other hand, grouping for instruction can be a challenge to implement, especially in the secondary grades. Grouping can sometimes have negative connotations. Students may feel stigmatized when placed in lower groups, and research has shown that lower groups sometimes receive ineffective instruction (Allington, 1983; Stanovich, 1986). However, developmentally appropriate instruction is beneficial for all students, especially struggling students.

engagement LINK

Small, differentiated grouping not only allows you to implement assessment-based instruction, but it also provides your students with a group of peers similar in development. This type of group may be a first for them as they have most likely spent a great deal of time in whole-group settings, where their difficulties are enhanced. Small groups based on students' developmental needs allow them to see that they are not alone.

Figure 3.8 Javier's Feature Guide

Elementary Spelling Inventory Feature Guide

Words Spelled Correctly: 18 /25 *Feature Points:* 55 /62 *Total:* 73 /87 *Spelling Stage:* Syllables & Affixes

SPELLING STAGES →	EMERGENT LATE	LETTER NAME–ALPHABETIC EARLY	MIDDLE	LATE	WITHIN WORD PATTERN EARLY	MIDDLE	LATE	SYLLABLES AND AFFIXES EARLY	MIDDLE	LATE	DERIVATIONAL RELATIONS EARLY	MIDDLE		
Features →	Consonants: Initial	Consonants: Final	Short Vowels	Digraphs	Blends	Long Vowels	Other Vowels	Inflected Endings	Syllable Junctures	Unaccented Final Syllables	Harder Suffixes	Bases or Roots	Feature Points	Words Spelled Correctly
1. bed	b ✓	d ✓	e ✓										3	1
2. ship		p ✓	i ✓	sh ✓									3	1
3. when			e ✓	wh ✓									2	1
4. lump	l ✓		u ✓		mp ✓								3	1
5. float		t ✓			fl ✓	oa ✓							3	1
6. train		n ✓			tr ✓	ai ✓							3	1
7. place					pl ✓	a-e ✓							2	1
8. drive		v ✓			dr ✓	i-e ✓							3	1
9. bright					br ✓	igh ✓							2	1
10. shopping			o ✓	sh ✓				pping ✓					3	1
11. spoil					sp ✓		oi ✓						2	1
12. serving							er	ving ✓					1	
13. chewed				ch ✓			ew ✓	ed ✓					3	1
14. carries							ar ✓	ies ✓	rr ✓				3	1
15. marched				ch ✓			ar ✓	ed ✓					3	1
16. shower				sh ✓			ow ✓			er ✓			3	1
17. bottle									tt ✓	le ✓			2	1
18. favor									v ✓	or			1	
19. ripen									p	en ✓			1	
20. cellar									ll ✓	ar			1	
21. pleasure											ure ✓	pleas	1	
22. fortunate							or ✓				ate ✓	fortun ✓	3	1
23. confident											ent ✓	confid	1	
24. civilize											ize ✓	civil ✓	2	1
25. opposition											tion	pos ✓	1	
Totals		7 /7	5 /5	6 /6	7 /7	5 /5	6 /7	5 /5	4 /5	3 /5	4 /5	3 /5	55 /62	18 /25

Students taught at their instructional level regardless of whether the instruction is "below grade level" make more progress than when they are instructed at levels that are too difficult (Morris et al., 1995). For example, it would be difficult for students to study vowel patterns in unaccented syllables (e.g., *baggage*) if they are still grappling with vowel patterns in one-syllable words (e.g., *stage*). We advocate flexible developmental grouping for parts of the day to accomplish specific purposes like word study. Other areas of literacy instruction, such as vocabulary development, are best addressed with heterogeneous whole-class grouping. We offer two ways to help you create your developmental groups: classroom profiles and spelling-by-stage classroom organization charts.

As you complete the feature guides for your students, you will most likely notice that students often span two or more stages, revealing quite a range of word knowledge. After analyzing students individually, you can create a classroom profile, which allows you to record the individual assessments on a single chart so that you can easily see how your groups might be formed. These groups should be fluid; students should not remain tracked in their original groups for the rest of the school year. If some students are not challenged or are frustrated, then the groups should be reorganized. While you are meeting with groups, the other students can be involved in many different activities such as journaling, independent reading, projects related to content areas, and so forth. Examples of grouping with inclusive classrooms, block scheduling, and period scheduling are addressed at the end of the chapter.

You can use the following general guidelines when considering grouping formats in your classroom. First, teachers generally should have three or four groups. Five or more groups are often unmanageable, resulting in less instructional time. Second, the size of group is a consideration. Groups of six to eight make it easier for you to observe day-to-day work and for your students to be involved in discussions. However, you will find that some groups will have to be larger, depending on your class size. If you have a group working far below grade-level expectations, you may want to consider a smaller group size so that you can provide more intensive instruction. Third, you may find a large range of instructional levels in your class, which may result in some students not being placed exactly at their developmental stage. For example, consider Damien from Ms. Dishner's class (see Figure 3.4). He is at the lower end of the developmental continuum and an outlier in the class. No other students are functioning at the early within word pattern stage. However, it would be impractical to place him by himself. Therefore, Ms. Dishner has placed him in the closest available group for instruction. Damien may work with a partner who can help him read and sort words. Also, hopefully, Damien is also receiving additional work outside of class with a specialist. His work can be supported in that setting as well.

The following five-step procedure is a good method for determining your groups.

1. Begin by stapling each student's spelling tests to his or her feature guide. This will help keep you organized so that you can quickly and easily pull a particular student out for review if needed.
2. Put the student papers in order from highest to lowest by power score (number of words spelled correctly) or by the total feature score (sum of all of the feature scores). Record the students' names from top to bottom on the classroom composite form (see Appendix A) in this order.
3. Record each student's scores from the bottom row of his or her feature guide in the row beside his or her name on the classroom composite chart.
4. Highlight the cells on the chart in which the students make more than one error on a particular feature. Let's look at Kayla (Figure 3.4). Notice that her "Long Vowels" cell is not highlighted (she scored 4 out of 5, missing only one) but "Other Vowels" is highlighted (she scored 5 out of 7, missing two). The understanding here is that a student spelling all but one long vowels correctly may have an adequate

understanding of that feature. In contrast, students misspelling two or three of the long vowels will need more work on that feature. Do not highlight cells where the students score a zero because they are not using the feature at all, indicating that the feature is at their frustration level. Focus your instructional time, instead, on features with two or three errors.

5. Finally, determine your instructional groups. You will frequently find that your groups will correspond to particular stages or to features within a stage. If you rank order your students and record them on the composite chart accordingly, you can find clusters of highlighted cells that can be used to determine groups. Using the classroom composite, Ms. Dishner created three word study groups: (1) a group of early to middle derivational relations spellers—John, Grace, Lucy, Eli, Maria, Bai, Adriana, Preston, and Kazuma; (2) a group of early, middle, and late syllables and affixes spellers—Claire, Lijuan, Antonia, Talia, Yanmei, Alicia, Sophia, Karl, Janie, Jack, and Isabella; and (3) a group of middle to late within word pattern spellers—Henry, Suzanne, Kayla, Jose, and Damien. After you make decisions about your students' instructional levels, you can also fill in the spelling-by-stage classroom organization chart (see Appendix A). See Figure 3.9 for Ms. Dishner's spelling-by-stage classroom organization chart.

Many teachers find this chart easier to use than the class composite chart when determining groups. To fill this chart out, simply refer to the stage circled on your students' feature guides. You would then record each student's name underneath the corresponding spelling stage on the chart, differentiating among early, middle, or late. Once you have recorded the names, you can begin to determine your groups. Notice Ms. Dishner has circled three groups for word study. You can see that Ms. Dishner has used arrows to indicate that those students may go to a higher or lower group. Using reading and spelling observations can help make these determinations as well. A general rule of thumb is to put students early in a stage with the strongest of the previous stage rather than with their same stage group; the instructional goals for a student early in a stage are quite different from spellers late in the stage. You may even want to consider factors other than word knowledge, such as self-esteem and dynamics of the group, to help solidify your decisions.

Step Six: Determine Instructional Goals

In order to set goals, it is important to consider expectations for developmental spelling stages and corresponding grade levels. Table 3.4 can guide you on the typical developmental stages expected within each grade level and expectations for the end of the year. These guidelines are provided as a reference point as you consider the developmental

Table 3.4 Spelling Stage Expectations by Grade Levels

Grade Level	Typical Spelling Stage Ranges within Grade	End-of-Year Spelling Stage Goal
K	Emergent—Letter Name—Alphabetic	Middle Letter Name—Alphabetic
1	Late Emergent—Within Word Pattern	Early Within Word Pattern
2	Late Letter Name—Early Syllables & Affixes	Late Within Word Pattern
3	Within Word Pattern—Syllables & Affixes	Early Syllables and Affixes
4	Within Word Pattern—Syllables & Affixes	Middle Syllables and Affixes
5	Syllables and Affixes—Derivational Relations	Late Syllables and Affixes
6+	Syllables and Affixes—Derivational Relations	Derivational Relations

Figure 3.9 Ms. Dishner's Spelling-by-Stage Chart

Spelling-by-Stage Classroom Organization Chart

SPELLING STAGES →	EMERGENT			LETTER NAME–ALPHABETIC			WITHIN WORD PATTERN			SYLLABLES AND AFFIXES			DERIVATIONAL RELATIONS		
	EARLY	MIDDLE	LATE	EARLY	MIDDLE	LATE	EARLY	MIDDLE	LATE	EARLY	MIDDLE	LATE	EARLY	MIDDLE	LATE
								Damien	Henry	Alicia	Claire	Adriana	Eli	John	
									Suzanne	Sophia	Lijuan	Preston	Maria	Grace	
									Kayla	Karl	Antonia	Kazuma	Bai	Lucy	
									Jose	Janie	Talia				
										Jack	Yanmei				
										Isabella					

all sorts: – teacher structures groups, identifies target feature and provides words w/ target feature
– explicitly state purpose
– students engaged – collaborative
– check + reflect
– extend

) Open sort – teacher provides words. Asks students to sort them and asks students to test their hypotheses about each category

spelling stages of your students. They are not, however, provided as the end-of-the-year expectations for your struggling students, which may not be reasonable one-year goals for these students.

Teacher-Determined Goals You can think of goals in two ways: long-term goals for the year and short-term goals that will ultimately lead you to your long-term goal. Generally speaking, long-term goals reflect your stage expectations and short-term goals reflect the features necessary for study to reach the designated long-term goal. When thinking about goals, you need to consider a few points: set specific, measurable goals; include time expectations; and remain realistic. Make it clear what you are working to accomplish. For example, you may set a long-term goal for one of your seventh grade English/language arts groups to move from the late within word pattern stage to the middle syllables and affixes stage by the end of the year. A short-term goal for students in the early syllables and affixes stage may be to accurately add inflected endings to single-syllable words following the CVCe (*bike* to *biking*), CVVC (*rain* to *raining*), CVC (*slip* to *slipping*), and CVCC (*lift* to *lifting*) patterns.

In order to ensure that goals are met, you must set time expectations. Teachers often find it easy to have short-term goals that are evaluated quarterly. Weekly evaluation of goals is not practical because many features take multiple weeks to fully investigate. Your goals along with their time expectations must be realistic. For example, it is unrealistic to expect your ninth grade students still achieving at the within word pattern stage to progress to the derivational relations stage in the course of one year. However, it is highly probable that they could reach the middle syllables and affixes stage. Additionally, your short-term goals should have an eye to the feature breakdown of the developmental continuum. For example, you would not establish a beginning short-term goal for your early syllables and affixes group to correctly spell open and closed two-syllable words. Using the suggested sequences found in Chapters 4 and 5 (Tables 4.1 and 5.1) will be very helpful.

Feature guides should be used to help determine instructional goals for each group. Use the stage determinations (with early, middle, and late designations) to develop your long-term goals. Then turn to your short-term goals. Look across the feature columns from left to right; instruction should begin at the point where most of the students in the group begin to make two or more errors on a feature. You may find it necessary to start with the feature on which the first child in the group starts to falter. As you look at the totals across the bottoms of the feature guides for the group, consider what the students know and what they are using but confusing. You can also use the class composite chart showing the feature totals for each student.

Let's return to Ms. Dishner's class composite (Figure 3.4). Take a look at Kayla's group. This group, as a whole, has all feature points for short vowels. On the long vowels feature, most in this group have one misspelling (and in Damien's case three errors). The group begins to collectively make more than one error on the other vowels feature. Given Damien's needs and the students missing one of the long vowel words, a review of long vowel patterns may be an appropriate place to start, and would therefore become one of your instructional goals for the group. One of your first short-term goals for the group could be that students will correctly represent long vowel patterns including CVVC (*soap; rain*) and other common long vowel patterns (*snow; tray*). See Chapters 4 and 5 for suggestions on starting places within a stage based on power and feature scores.

Involving Your Students Your students can also be involved in goal setting. Doing this makes them more accountable for their own achievement; you can celebrate their success with them as you track growth over time. Involving them in this process allows them to be self-directed in their own learning, resulting in more engagement and increased motivation. They will feel more in control, rather than recipients of expectations placed on them from sources outside themselves. Having a visual to guide conversations about goals may be helpful. Your students will be able to see their progress and think about future goals. See Appendix B for stage-by-stage goal-setting charts that can be used during conversations with your students (and even parents). Your assessment using the qualitative spelling inventories and the guidance of the feature pacing guides found in Chapters 4 and 5 will help you set realistic *and* reachable goals.

We suggest officially checking in with your students on a regular basis; again, quarterly will most likely be often enough (please see the Progress Monitoring section later in this chapter). During these conversations, not only will you assess short-term goals and create future goals, but you also should talk about how your students need to be persistent and determined. The stage-by-stage goal-setting charts can help you show where the long-term goal will lead them; seeing their ultimate goal is very motivating. We have found it additionally motivating to check or cross off features on the list as you and your students find evidence of sustained mastery. Nothing is quite as satisfying as crossing something off of your list; students feel that same sort of satisfaction and ultimately pride. Talking about persistence and determination naturally brings up obstacles and setbacks. However, you can be reassured that setbacks will not regularly occur because of your consideration of developmental needs. Involving your students in determining and assessing goals helps them see how their efforts result in success and progress.

engagement LINK

Involvement in goal setting is an important step in helping your students feel that their efforts affect their learning, in contrast to feeling as if their ability to learn is predetermined (and out of their control). You will see your students take more initiative and responsibility for their learning.

Strategically Observe Reading

Although assessment of spelling appears to be the most direct view into your students' orthographic knowledge, reading can also provide a window into their understanding. Figure 3.10 shows how spelling and reading knowledge spring from the same underlying word knowledge. Your students' developing word knowledge factors into their ability to read words just as it affects their ability to spell words (Ehri, 1998; Perfetti, 1992). Remember the NIBBERFLUTZER example from Chapter 2? You were able to read and spell this word—a word you had never seen before—because of your underlying orthographic knowledge of the common spelling patterns found in this word.

You will notice, however, that your students' ability to read words is slightly ahead of their spelling accuracy. The contextual support of books accounts for this discrepancy between reading and spelling. Spelling samples provide us with a very conservative measure of what a student knows about words whereas reading could be considered a more liberal measure. If a student can spell a word, we can be certain that he can read that word. The reverse is not necessarily true. For example, your within word pattern students can accurately read many two-syllable words (e.g., *tripping, circle, mountain*). If asked to spell those words, however, you might see *tripping* misspelled as TRIPING, *circle* as CERCOL, and *mountain* as MOWTUN. Take Timothy, a sixth grade student performing in the within word pattern stage of spelling. He might spell the word *wrinkles*

Figure 3.10 Student's Word Knowledge: Spelling and Reading

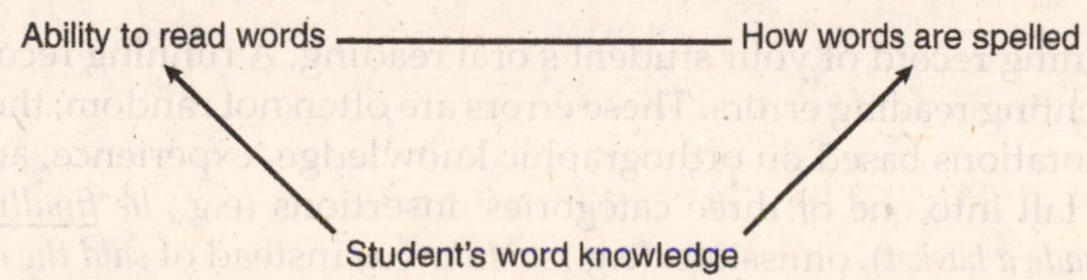

Source: Adapted with permission from Morris, 2005.

as RINKELS. However, when faced with the following sentence from *Stone Fox* by John Reynolds Gardiner—"Her skin was tan, and her face was covered with wrinkles"—he can read *wrinkles* accurately and possibly without hesitation.

During times when your students are reading silently, have selected students read aloud to you for a couple of minutes. You can expect to hear certain reading errors at different developmental levels. Understanding developmental word knowledge will help you better perceive, and therefore respond to, your students' errors. For example, let's again consider Timothy, the within word pattern speller/transitional reader just discussed. He might substitute *growled* for *groaned* in the sentence, "Jason groaned when he missed the ball." Timothy is obviously attending to many features of the word *groaned.* He is considering the *gr* at the beginning, the *o* vowel pattern in the middle, and the *-ed* ending. When combined, these considerations result in a word that would make sense in the sentence: *growled.* His incomplete knowledge of vowel patterns accounts for his *oa*/*ow* confusion.

Your response to this error depends on two main factors. First, Timothy should be reading in texts at his instructional level; this is the level at which he will be able to read most words in the text accurately. Generally, a text is considered at a student's instructional level if he or she is able to read at least 90 to 95 percent or more of the words correctly (Betts, 1954; Mesmer, 2008; Stauffer, Abrams, & Pikulski, 1978). This assurance also means that the student should be able to use orthographic knowledge along with context to figure out most unknown words. Second, because you know that Timothy is a within word pattern speller/transitional reader, you can feel confident in guiding him through the long *o* vowel pattern. You might prompt him to look at the word again, paying attention to the *oa* pattern. For students who have not progressed into the within word pattern stage of development and are in the letter name–alphabetic stage, you would not prompt them to reconsider the *oa* spelling pattern, because they would not be familiar with vowel patterns and the sounds they make.

Analyzing Reading Errors

A qualitative analysis of reading errors may be helpful in thinking about the pattern of orthographic errors your students exhibit while reading. Specifically, an error analysis allows you to see whether your students are transferring word study instruction to their reading. We acknowledge that there are a variety of ways to analyze errors students make, including meaning errors, while reading (see the *Qualitative Reading Inventory-4* by Leslie and Caldwell, 2005, for an example of a more comprehensive error analysis). In this chapter, we are only considering the errors made while reading that can provide information about your students' orthographic knowledge.

You may want to have your struggling students periodically read aloud to you from instructional-level text. It is unrealistic to complete an error analysis of each student's reading. We suggest analyzing the errors of those students who are the most in need of appropriately targeted instruction or those who seem to have difficulty transferring word study instruction to a different context—their reading. In addition, the passages do not need to come from formal reading inventories but can instead be pulled from the books already being read in class. These need not be long passages; lengths of 125 to 150 words have been found to be sufficient (Klesius & Homan, 1985).

Take a running record of your student's oral reading. A running record is a written record documenting reading errors. These errors are often not random; they are, instead, logical representations based on orthographic knowledge, experience, and context. Errors generally fall into one of three categories: insertions (e.g., *he finally made a basket* instead of *he made a basket*), omissions (e.g., *said the boy* instead of *said the angry boy*), and substitutions (e.g., *she begun to run faster* instead of *she began to run faster*). Substitutions are the errors we will focus on.

Coding these substitution errors can help you make determinations about the pattern of errors your students are making. To complete the error analysis (see Appendix C for a blank form), first record all substitution errors and the corresponding text. Next, go through the guiding questions from each column in the error analysis. These questions are designed to guide you through an analysis of substitution errors, the errors that give you insight into orthographic knowledge. If you answer yes to a guiding question, then place a check in that column. If the answer is no, then leave the column blank. Substitutions can be coded in a variety of ways:

- Consonant patterns
- Vowel patterns
- Syllable patterns
- Morphemic units
- Function words

You first want to consider if the student is confusing consonant patterns in the words. For example, reading *wed* for *wedge* shows a confusion with the consonant pattern *-dge*. In this case, you would place a check for this word in the column titled "Does the error involve a consonant pattern confusion?" The error *begun* for *began* mentioned above would not be checked because the error lies in the vowel, not the consonants.

The next question in the error guide, "Does the error involve a vowel pattern confusion?" should be checked for any error that involves a mispronunciation of a vowel pattern in either a one-syllable word or in the accented syllable of a multisyllable word. For example, if the student misread *roast* for *roost* you would check it here. Likewise, if the student read *selling* for *ceiling,* you would mark it here. You would not, however, mark the student reading /'me-nās/ for *menace* here. Such an error occurs because of the lack of stress on the second syllable of *menace,* resulting in the *a* becoming a schwa or "uh." When a syllable is not stressed, vowel patterns are unreliable. The *menace* error would be coded as a syllable pattern confusion. See Chapter 5 for more explanation about the unaccented syllable.

Syllable pattern confusion is a common category of reading errors, a type that involves any error in multisyllable words that can be explained by common syllable patterns, such as the open C-VC pattern in *diner,* or by accent. For example, reading *diner* as *dinner* shows a syllable pattern confusion because the long vowel sound in open V-CV words was not used. Errors involving accent can be seen in words like *baggage* (the second syllable pronounces the *a* as a schwa rather than the long *a* as would be indicated by the *e*-marker). Errors such as these would be checked in the syllable pattern column. You may also see syllables, or parts of syllables, omitted when a student is attempting to read a multisyllabic word, such as reading *sumersion* for *submersion.* This would also be coded as a syllable error because confusion occurs at the syllable level; it is not a consonant issue because the student would be able to read *sub* correctly without any hesitation.

Another common error type involves morphemic units, which are units that hold meaning or affect the meaning of a word. For example, plurals and past tense markers are morphemic units. Therefore, errors such as *table* for *tables* and *walk* for *walked* would be considered errors of morphemic units. Notice that these errors involve the omission of the units, which is what you will most likely observe in errors involving morphemic units. Other errors may involve contractions (reading *are* for *aren't*) or prefixes and suffixes (reading *taller* for *tallest*).

The last column in the reading error chart is for function word errors. Students with reading difficulties often misread these words (Shaywitz, 2003). Function words occur frequently in text. They are referred to as "functional" because they hold little meaning and generally have the purpose of supporting another word. They are most often articles (*a, an, the*), determiners (*both, neither*), quantifiers (*much, little*), pronouns (*he, they*), prepositions (*in, between*), conjunctions (*and, although*), auxiliary verbs (*be, are*), and

Figure 3.11 Function Word List

a	at	each	if	near	per	those	where
about	be	either	in	neither	plus	though	whereas
above	because	enough	including	nevertheless	several	through	wherever
according	been	every	inside	no	shall	throughout	whether
across	before	everybody	instead	nobody	she	thru	which
after	behind	everyone	into	none	should	thus	whichever
against	being	everything	is	no one	since	till	while
ahead	below	except	it	nor	so	to	who
albeit	beneath	few	its	nothing	some	toward	whoever
all	beside	for	itself	of	somebody	under	whom
along	between	from	less	off	someone	underneath	whomever
although	beyond	had	like	on	something	unless	whose
am	both	has	little	once	such	unlike	will
among	but	have	many	one, etc.	than	until	with
an	by	he	may	onto	that	unto	within
and	can	hence	me	or	the	up	without
another	certain	her	might	other	their	upon	would
any	consequently	hers	mine	ought	them	us	yet
anybody	could	herself	more	our	themselves	wanting	you
anyone	did	him	most	ourselves	then	we	your
anything	do	himself	much	out	therefore	what	yourself
are	does	his	must	outside	these	whatever	
around	down	however	my	over	they	when	
as	during	I	myself	part	this	whenever	

degree adverbs (*very, too*). In total, there are fewer than 300 function words (see Figure 3.11 for a list).

After coding all of the errors, tally up your checks. Count the checks placed in each column and write your column total in the bottom row labeled "Column Total." If you notice a preponderance of errors of a certain type, you will need to incorporate activities into your instruction to meet that particular need. The last row, "Where Can I Find Out How to Teach This?" provides you with the chapters in this book that will help you address those instructional needs.

In Figure 3.12, you can see ninth-grader Catherine's errors made while reading a passage at her instructional level from the *Qualitative Reading Inventory-4* (Leslie & Caldwell, 2005). We can see that she had errors from all of the orthographic error types. She misread consonant patterns (reading *running* for *writing*), vowel patterns (reading *quite* for *quit*), syllable patterns (reading *constation* for *conversation*), morphemic units (reading *did* for *didn't*), and function words (reading *with* for *my*). When these errors are tallied up and considered by frequency, we can see that a preponderance of her errors involved function words. She had 10 function word errors out of a total of 22 errors compared to two to four errors in the other categories.

Understanding developmental word knowledge will allow you to interpret your students' reading errors and to make appropriate instructional decisions. Catherine demonstrated a pattern of function word errors. Her specific weakness in this area would prompt you to include more function words within your day-to-day word study work. For example, she misread *thought* and *through* for *though*. While studying abstract vowels (those that are neither long nor short), such as the *ou* in cl<u>ou</u>d and the *ow* in c<u>ow</u>,

Figure 3.12 Error Analysis Coding Guide

Text	Error	Does the error involve a consonant pattern confusion?	Does the error involve a vowel pattern confusion?	Does the error involve a syllable pattern confusion?	Does the error involve a morphemic unit confusion?	Is this a function word error?
convey	con-vee		X			
Elijah	ah-lee-jah		X			
articulate	ar-tik-ah-late			X		
writing	running	X	X			
begun	began					X
conversation	constation			X		
didn't	did				X	
had	was					X
though	thought/through					X
had	has					X
sentences	sentence				X	
quit	quite		X			
also	only					X
the	—					
painstaking	paintaking			X		
myself	me					X
what	that					X
the	that					X
suppose	supposed				X	
has	was					X
wedge	wed	X				
my	with					X
Column Total		2	4	3	3	10
Where Can I Find Out How to Teach This?		Chapter 4	Chapter 4	Chapter 5	Chapter 6	Chapter 4

Source: Adapted from Leslie & Caldwell, 2005.

the function words *through* and *though* could be discussed because they also include the *ou* letter sequence. This study would highlight the irregularity of the words and draw Catherine's attention to them. Looking at the last row on the orthographic error analysis chart, you are directed to Chapter 4 for instructional activities to address this need.

Progress Monitoring

An extension of your long- and short-term goals is progress monitoring. You need to have a system of monitoring your students' progress in reaching those goals. Besides

engagement LINK

Monitoring progress gives you tangible information to share with your students as you conference with them about their growth. These progress checks allow your students to see the fruits of their labor.

helping you provide evidence and guidance during your student conferences, this information is necessary for all stakeholders—the teacher, the parents, and the students. Monitoring progress over time can come in two forms: assessments at specific points during the semester (typically beginning of the year, middle of the year, and end of the year) and more frequent assessments occurring within the semester. The latter are especially critical for struggling students because no instructional time can be lost. These students are already achieving below grade level and need to make up ground. If they are not making progress, you need to be aware of this before the end of the semester so that timely instructional adjustments can be made.

Assessing Yearly Progress: Long-Term Goals

The same spelling inventory can be used several times during the year to assess progress and identify changes, if any, that need to be made for grouping or instruction. Generally, we suggest giving the same inventory three times a year. Having the same inventory allows you to truly compare apples to apples and clearly see your students' growth. Because the inventories are designed to survey across stages, you can be assured that growth can be tracked with the same inventory. You may, however, notice that students may sometimes spell a word correctly one time and later spell the same word incorrectly. This can happen when students are inventing the spelling of a word they do not have stored in memory and occasionally spell it correctly by chance.

It is important that students do not study the words on the inventories that you are using to monitor their progress. The words may naturally show up in your word study activities; however, you do not want to specifically study the words on the inventory in advance because this would inflate the results. Using the same inventory more than three or four times a year may also give your students enough exposure to the words to inflate the results.

See Figure 3.13 for Kayla's progress across the course of the year. Ms. Dishner administered the ESI three times during the school year—in September, January, and May. As you can see, Kayla ended the year with a power score of 18, which places her at the end of the syllables and affixes stage. Kayla's progress during the year therefore meets her long-term goal of achieving at the syllables and affixes stage.

Assessing Quarterly Progress: Short-Term Goals

We recommend administering spelling tests to evaluate your students' mastery of the features studied. Weekly spelling tests not only assess this mastery, but they also make it clear to your students that they are accountable for learning the features (and words) that they have worked with throughout the week. Of course, the goal is that your students will be very successful week to week on these spelling tests. If your students are missing more than a few words, you will want to spend more time on the features. Often, however, your students will do well on weekly spelling tests. The question then becomes how well they retain that knowledge. You may have already noticed that your students seem to know the words for the test but do not retain that knowledge in the following weeks. We recommend following a few steps to ensure that your weekly spelling tests give you the most reliable information about your students' mastery of the studied features.

1. Give your students a set of words to study that exemplify the targeted features each week (see Appendix D for guidelines on choosing words for study). When preparing for your spelling tests, include some of the words that have been studied but also include transfer words or words not specifically studied (making sure that they follow the target

Figure 3.13 Kayla's Progress across the Year Using the ESI

September	January	May
bed	bed	bed
ship	ship	ship
when	when	when
lump	lump	lump
float	float	float
train	train	train
place	place	place
drive	drive	drive
brite (bright)	bright	bright
shoping (shopping)	shoping (shopping)	shopping
spoyle (spoil)	spoil	spoil
serving	serving	serving
chooed (chewed)	chewed	chewed
caryes (carries)	carries	carries
martched (marched)	marched	marched
shower	shower	shower
botel (bottle)	bottel (bottle)	bottel (bottle)
faver (favor)	faver (favor)	favor
rippun (ripen)	ripen	ripen
seler (cellar)	seler (cellar)	seller (cellar)
plescher (pleasure)	plesher (pleasure)	pleasher (pleasure)
forchunate (fortunate)	forchunate (fortunate)	forchunate (fortunate)
confdant (confident)	confadant (confident)	confadant (confident)
sivulise (civilize)	civalize (civilize)	civalize (civilize)
opozishun (opposition)	oposishun (opposition)	oposition (opposition)

features). A good rule of thumb is 70 to 80 percent studied words versus 20 to 30 percent transfer words.

2. Include words on your weekly spelling tests that address previous studied features. You do not need to include many words. We recommend always having two to five additional words on your spelling tests that check for retention of previously studied features. See Figure 3.14 for a sample weekly spelling test that follows a week of hard/soft *c* study and reviews hard/soft *g*, which was an earlier unit.

3. Administer a monthly (or at least mid-semester) cumulative spelling test. This test should include words that exemplify the features you have been studying throughout the month. Cumulative tests can help you gauge your students' mastery of the features studied and can also help focus your conferences with students about their progress. The goals you and your students establish can be revisited during these conferences and the cumulative (and weekly) spelling tests can guide the conversation.

4. Provide opportunities for your students to reflect on their work. After you have given a spelling test, for example, you can have your

engagement LINK

This type of reflection provides your students with opportunities to think critically about their own learning and progress. Activities such as the reflection chart place them in the driver's seat as they analyze their own errors.

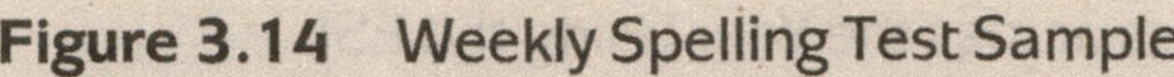

Figure 3.14 Weekly Spelling Test Sample

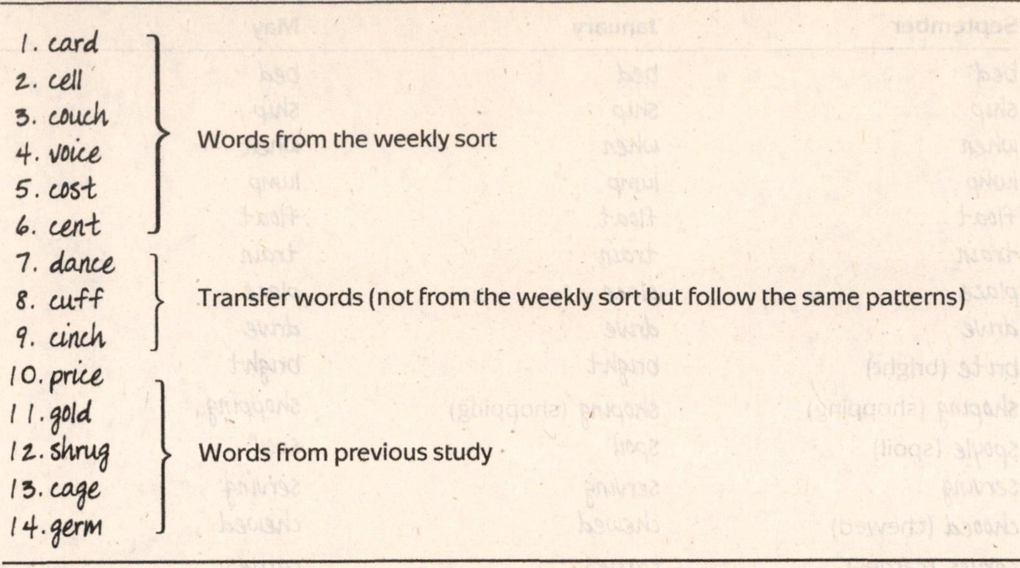

1. card
2. cell
3. couch
4. voice
5. cost
6. cent
Words from the weekly sort
7. dance
8. cuff
9. cinch
Transfer words (not from the weekly sort but follow the same patterns)
10. price
11. gold
12. shrug
13. cage
14. germ
Words from previous study

Figure 3.15 Student Reflection Chart

Word	Error	What went wrong?
forgetting	forgeting	The second syllable is accented, and the second syllable has a short vowel followed by only one final consonant. So, I need to double the final consonant.
omitted	omited	This is the same problem as forgetting. I needed to double the final consonant because the second syllable is accented and has a short vowel and only one final consonant.
benefiting	benefitting	Here I needed to not double because the final syllable is not the one that is accented. So, I didn't even need to think about if the final syllable has a short vowel and only one final consonant.

students fill out a reflection chart. See Figure 3.15 for an example. As you can see, the student records the target word, his or her misspelling, and a brief reflection about why the mistake was made. Reflection requires your students to think deeply about the spelling of the specific word and about generalizing the pattern to new words.

You can also monitor the progress your students make as they decode unknown words while reading. For those students about whom you are most concerned or who are not properly applying the information learned during word study, you can periodically complete an analysis of their oral reading errors (as shown in Figure 3.12). You could complete an error analysis not only at the beginning and end of the semester but also complete one quarterly. The frequency would be determined by the intensity of the needs of your students.

Organizing Your Classroom

Armed with your groups and instructional goals, you are ready to think about how this might be organized in your classroom. As already discussed, your students will not all be at the same stage of spelling or need the same features of study. So if you are going to deliver assessment-based, developmentally appropriate instruction, you will have to manage your groups. Teachers in the upper elementary and middle/high school grades may have a variety of classroom arrangements. We will discuss the three most common: inclusive classroom with committed language arts block, period scheduling, and block scheduling. Inclusive classrooms are generally found in the upper elementary grades, and period or block scheduling is typically found in the middle grades and high school. The upcoming examples show word study in English or language arts classes. For struggling readers, this may not be enough. If they are to ever catch up, these students must be *everyone's responsibility,* and instruction must take place all day long across all subject areas (Allington, 2005).

Routines can be engaging for students rather than laborious day-to-day practices. Purposeful routines can also contribute to your students' perceiving themselves as in control of their own learning. Everyone knows who's on first.

Within each of these arrangements, a variety of routines can be found. Some teachers deliver word study lessons during their reading groups. Others may have separate word study groups as part of group rotations. Still others conference with students in groups or individually in a mainly independent workshop routine. Regardless of the arrangement, it is important to consider the following when considering word study routines that focus on teacher-directed and student-centered learning.

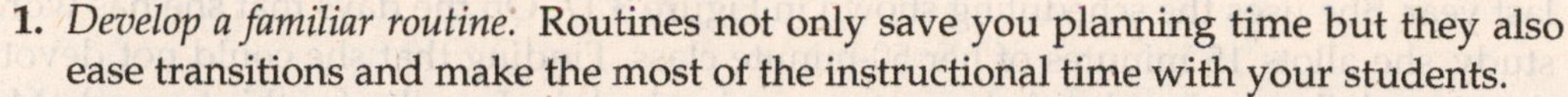

1. *Develop a familiar routine.* Routines not only save you planning time but they also ease transitions and make the most of the instructional time with your students.
2. *Schedule time for teacher-directed group work.* Students need time with you for directed word study. Not every student needs this time every day, but your struggling students most likely do.
3. *Keep it short.* Word study should be a regular part of your language arts or English time, but it should not comprise a big chunk of that time. Teacher-directed lessons introducing features may take time to implement (20 minutes on average), but follow-up lessons are often shorter.
4. *Plan for your students to work independently and with each other.* Your students need time to consider the target features on their own and should also be involved in group and partner activities.

Incorporating small-group instruction allows you to provide time for your students to work with peers in collaborative groups. Not only are these groups inherently engaging, but they also encourage a sense of community. We are a team working toward the same ultimate goal.

Inclusive Classroom

Mr. Robnolt, a fifth grade teacher, has implemented word study in his language arts block for the past three years. During the 90 minutes allotted for language arts, the teachers are expected to cover reading, writing, word study, and grammar. His schedule allows for daily word study instruction with his below-grade-level group (middle within word pattern) but not for his grade-level (late syllables and affixes) and above-grade-level groups (early derivational relations). See Figure 3.16 for his weekly word study schedule (30 minutes of his 90-minute block).

As you can see, Monday allows for extended teacher-directed time with the below-grade-level group; this group meets with him for the entire 30-minute word study section of his language arts block. On Tuesday, he meets with each group for 10 minutes. Wednesday begins with 20 minutes allotted for the below-grade-level group and 10 for the on-grade-level group; he does not meet directly with the above-grade-level group. Each group meets with Mr. Robnolt on Thursday and Friday. While the students are not with him during this half hour, they are involved in a variety of activities or projects (e.g., independent-level choice reading and a variety of independent and partner word study activities). Many word study activities appropriate for independent work can be found in Chapter 2.

Period Scheduling

Many middle and high school teachers have 50-minute periods to deliver English instruction. Students in these classes are more likely to have similar word study needs because these classes are often not as heterogeneously mixed as elementary classrooms. Still, the typical middle or high school classroom will most likely have students in at

Figure 3.16 Mr. Robnolt's Weekly Word Study Schedule

	Monday	Tuesday	Wednesday	Thursday	Friday
8:30–8:40	Below Grade Level (teacher-directed introduction)	Below Grade Level (writing sort and manipulation)	Below Grade Level (re-sort and analogy activity)	Below Grade Level (speed sort; follow-up on word hunts)	Below Grade Level (spelling test)
8:40–8:50		On Grade Level (teacher-directed introduction)		On Grade Level (speed sort with teacher)	On Grade Level (spelling test)
8:50–9:00		Above Grade Level (teacher-directed introduction)	On Grade Level (re-sort and writing sort)	Above Grade Level (speed sort with teacher)	Above Grade Level (spelling test)

least two different spelling stages. The challenge comes from the limited amount of daily time for class. Ms. Aguilar began word study groups in her eighth grade English class last year. She uses the scheduling shown in Figure 3.17. On the days that she has word study, she allots 15 minutes of her 50-minute class. Finding that she could not devote this time daily, she has decided on a two-week schedule. In order for this to work, Ms. Aguilar found that she needed to institute a two-week contract with her students to ensure that they independently completed daily word study activities. Her contract, as shown in Figure 3.18, includes re-sorting, writing sorts, speed sorts, and other activities.

On Monday, Ms. Aguilar introduces the new features or sort to her first group (below grade level) while her second group (on or above grade level) previews their words and completes an open sort. These students know the procedure of previewing prior to their open sort: After they read through the words, they guess the categories, write out their category explanations in their notebooks, and share the explanations with a partner. Tuesday is a day of review for the first group while Ms. Aguilar meets with the second group to discuss their explanations from Monday and introduce the features or sort. On Thursday and Friday Ms. Aguilar does extension work when meeting with the groups; the group not meeting with her re-sorts with a partner and then completes a writing sort. Week two begins with all students re-sorting with a partner on Monday. Ms. Aguilar moves through the room, monitoring and conferencing with partners or individual students. Tuesday and Wednesday are devoted to more extension work with Ms. Aguilar while the group not meeting with her completes a series of speed sorts.

Figure 3.17 Ms. Aguilar's Word Study Schedule

		Monday	Tuesday	Wednesday	Thursday	Friday
Week One	Group 1	Teacher-directed introduction	Contract work		Extension	Contract work
	Group 2	Contract work	Teacher-directed introduction		Contract Work	Extension
Week Two	Group 1	Re-sort	Contract work	Extension		Spelling tests
	Group 2		Extension	Contract work		

Figure 3.18 Ms. Aguilar's Independent Work Contract

<table>
<tr><td colspan="4">Week:
Don't forget to initial when you finish each job.</td></tr>
<tr><th>Monday</th><th>Tuesday</th><th>Thursday</th><th>Friday</th></tr>
<tr><td>1. Read through Words
2. Guess My Category</td><td>1. Re-Sort (check with a partner)
2. Writing Sort</td><td>1. Re-Sort (check with a partner)
2. Writing Sort</td><td>1. Word Hunt (record in categories)</td></tr>
<tr><td colspan="4">Week:
Don't forget to initial when you finish each job.</td></tr>
<tr><th>Monday</th><th>Tuesday</th><th colspan="2">Wednesday</th></tr>
<tr><td>1. Re-Sort (check with a partner)</td><td>1. Practice Sort
2. Speed Sort (at least 3 times—chart your times)</td><td colspan="2">1. Practice Sort
2. Speed Sort (at least 3 times—chart your times)</td></tr>
</table>

Block Scheduling

Mr. Wagner is a high school English teacher who has decided to incorporate word study instruction in his remedial tenth grade class. His school uses a 4 × 4 semester plan, so he has 90 minutes daily with the class for one semester (see Figure 3.19).

He typically begins his class with a whole-class meeting in which he introduces the objective for the day or reviews a continued objective, followed by a teacher-led demonstration, lecture, or discussion. The remaining 60 minutes of the class involves small-group work. Mr. Wagner meets with small groups for word study instruction during the first half of this 60 minutes and conferences with individual students during the second half. He does not meet with each of his word study groups daily. Instead, he meets with small groups for a variety of purposes and reserves at least three group meetings a week for word study. Likewise, his conferences are multipurpose. Because his classes are largely devoted to students working individually, he uses individual student contracts. These contracts map out exactly what is expected of students in terms of assignments and what is required to earn certain grades.

Figure 3.20 shows a sample student contract from Mr. Wagner's class. As you can see, the contracts cover student work for a two-week period. The English contracts are comprehensive and cover reading, word study, and writing/grammar. The word study section is highlighted. Mr. Wagner uses a word study routine in which the only portion of the contract that changes from week to week is the feature of study; the activities

Figure 3.19 Mr. Wagner's Block Schedule

Time	Activities
First 30 Minutes	Whole-Group Work: Presentation of instructional objective; teacher demonstration or lecture; teacher-led discussion
Second 30 Minutes	Small-Group Work: Students work in groups for practice, extension, investigation; teacher-led small groups
Last 30 Minutes	Small-Group Work: Students work in groups for practice, extension, investigation; teacher–student conferences

found in the "Deliverable" column remain constant. Routines such as these allow for greater independence while also providing the students with meaningful activities when not directly involved in work with the teacher. The students complete a variety of activities throughout the contractual period: re-sorts, speed sorts, word hunts, writing sorts, and spell checks. Each activity completed to satisfaction receives 5 points toward the final contract grade.

Figure 3.20 Sample Student Contract

Name: Jerry Garcia	Contract Period: 10/14–10/25	Work Due by: 10/25	
Assignment:	Deliverable:	Points Worth	Points Earned
1. Independent Reading Title: ________	5 reading log entries; ½ page each, covering pages _____ to _____	5 pts per entry	_____
2. Participation in Group Reading Lesson ______ Title/Date: ________ ________ ________	1 written summary per lesson (minimum of 1 page per summary)	5 pts per summary	
3. Leader of Group Reading Lesson Title/Date: ________	• Before reading book or background • During reading questions (stopping points marked with sticky notes) • After reading reflection and revisit	5 pts each before, during, after	
4. Complete Word Study Lesson Your feature: long-to-short vowel sound changes in related words. (ex. mine → mineral)	• Sort, check, record, and reflect (written reflection below columns) • 3 speed sorts (times recorded) • Word hunts (find at least 5 additional words) • Blind written sort • Spell check	5 pts per step	_____
5. Writing/Grammar Your focus: explications of story structure Title: ________	2-page story explication that includes —setting — tone — characters — problem — major events — resolution — theme, moral, message, or purpose	5 pts per story element	_____
Comments:			

chapter 4

The Within Word Pattern Stage

It is Thursday in Ms. Thiessen's sixth grade English/language arts class, a 90-minute uninterrupted block devoted to reading, writing, spelling, and grammar instruction. This is part of the block schedule for the middle school. For 20 minutes at the start of class each day, students are involved in contracted independent work (see Figure 4.1). One of her students, Zach, is an energetic student with many strengths and interests but has been struggling with his literacy development for many years.

Zach's group is achieving at the within word pattern stage. They are beginning the quarter working on other long vowel patterns (see Figure 4.7 later in the chapter for examples of "other" long vowels) based on their performance on the Primary Spelling Inventory (PSI). The group is comparing three options for spelling the long *a* sound: CVCe as in *cake*, CVVC as in *rain*, and CVV as in *ray*. These particular vowel patterns can be found in Zach's goals for this quarter. See Figure 4.2 to see his sort for the week. Zach has been involved in a carefully planned series of instructional activities designed to meet his needs. His week began with an explicit introduction to the features of study contrasting both by sound (comparing the sounds of short and long *a*) and pattern (comparing the *a-e*, *ai*, and *ay* spelling patterns to represent /ā/ in words). Ms. Thiessen was careful to provide opportunities for the students to have teacher-supported work,

Figure 4.1 Zach's Independent Work Contract

Independent Work Contract for ____________
Week of ____________

Monday	Tuesday	Wednesday	Thursday	Friday
Must Do: 1. Sort your words with a partner. 2. Record your feature explanations in word study notebook. Choice: 1. Read from your book set: ________ ________ 2. Writing Sort	Must Do: 1. Blind Writing Sort Choice: 1. Speed Sort 2. Writing Sort 3. Word Hunt	Must Do: 1. Sort your words with a partner. 2. Speed Sort Choice: 1. Read from your book set: ________ ________ 2. Speed Sort 3. Writing Sort 4. Word Hunt	Must Do: 1. Blind Writing Sort Choice: 1. Speed Sort 2. Writing Sort 3. Word Hunt	Must Do: 1. Blind Writing Sort Choice: 1. Read from your book set: ________ ________ 2. Review old sort.

Figure 4.2 Zach's Sort for the Week

CVCe /ā/ as in cake	CVVC /ā/ as in rain	CVV /ā/ as in tray	Oddball
blame	brain	slay	have
frame	drain	stay	said
shade	quaint	clay	they
phase	trail	way	
trade	plain	ray	

collaborative work with peers, and independent work (i.e., gradual release). These activities were designed to elicit high-level discussions and processing, as well as offer repeated practice.

Zach has chosen speed sorting for his independent work today. His competitive nature makes beating his own times a motivating activity. Ms. Thiessen's speed sorting procedure always includes working with a partner, but each partner uses words at their respective instructional levels—the same activity, but different patterns of study based on their word study areas of need. Zach and his word study partner, Kim, eagerly take out their word sort cards. Zach begins rapidly sorting the cards into their columns as Kim pushes the start button on the stopwatch. The race is on! Zach, with Kim double-checking to make sure Zach does not trade off speed for accuracy, sorts the entire deck correctly in 31 seconds. Zach pumps his fist, exclaiming "Yes!" He handily beat his Tuesday "cold" time of 1 minute, 2 seconds and records it in his word study notebook. This decrease in time is not surprising given the level of support and amount of practice Ms. Thiessen has already provided. See Zach's speed chart in Figure 4.3.

Zach and Kim will continue to take turns sorting, each time trying to lower their respective times without compromising accuracy. Ms. Thiessen checks in with the pair and notices that Zach is stumbling while reading and sorting the word *strain*. She briefly checks to make sure that Zach knows what *strain* means and then refers him back to the "keyword chart" on the wall. He points out the keyword *rain* that was introduced Monday for the *ai* pattern and immediately recognizes the word *strain*. Ms. Thiessen says, "So if you can read *rain*, you can read similar words like *strain*." She encourages Zach's higher-level processing by asking him why knowing *rain* is helpful in this situa-

Figure 4.3 Zach's Speed Sort

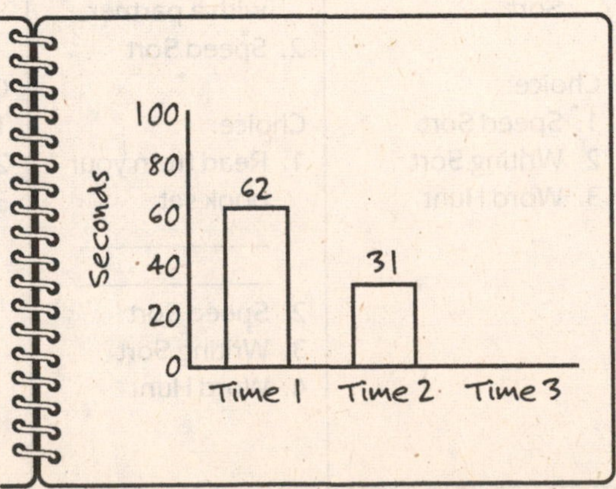

tion. Zach responds, "Well, if I remember *rain* when I see the *ai* spelling pattern, I can remember that *ai* says /ā/. Then I can use that to help me figure out the word *strain*."

"Great job, Zach," Ms. Thiessen responds. "You are right on. And you know, this lines up with one of your quarterly goals. You already have such a good understanding of long vowel patterns and wanted to work on your knowledge of these other vowel patterns. Your explanation here shows me how you are really making some progress on that goal. How are you feeling?"

"Ms. Thiessen, did you see my time for today? I cut my time in half," Zach replies.

As Zach pulls out his word study notebook, Ms. Thiessen mentally adds up the amount of practice Zach has had by the end of the 15 minutes spent sorting. He will have read his sort four times. Four speed sorts multiplied by 15 words per sort equals a total of 60 opportunities to practice reading words. Sorting definitely gives Zach a lot of bang for the buck in terms of reinforcement and repeated practice in a relatively short amount of time.

In this brief glimpse into Ms. Thiessen's class, you can already see how she is incorporating many of the principles suggested in Chapter 2 for your work with struggling adolescents:

1. She engaged her students in multiple ways, even including them in their own goal setting.
2. She planned explicit instruction to introduce features, following a gradual release model.
3. She provided opportunities for higher-level thinking and deep processing.
4. She ensured that all of her students received instruction based on their assessed needs.
5. She involved her students in multiple activities to help them connect and categorize the new features.

Reading, Writing, and Spelling Characteristics

The transitional stage of development serves as the bridge between the beginning stage in which reading and writing are labor intensive and the intermediate stage in which reading and writing become quite fluent. Chall (1983) calls this the "confirmation and fluency" stage because students are solidifying their foundational skills from the beginning stage and becoming increasingly automatic; like Zach in the vignette, they are *transitioning* into more fluent readers who automatically decode words. However, as discussed in Chapter 1, many struggling readers find themselves stuck in the stage and will not move forward without support.

To become fluent readers, students need to recognize patterns and chunks of words and reach a level of automaticity in word recognition. Instead of processing a word as series of five separate letters (*s-t-u-m-p*), they process it as a series of letter patterns (*st-ump*). This newfound ability enables the reader to decode and store words more readily (Ehri, 1997), which leads to increasing reading fluency and ultimately allows them to focus more and more on making meaning (see Figure 4.4; also see Chapter 1 for a more detailed explanation). They additionally have acquired a large bank of words that they recognize automatically, giving them the ability to read longer texts; one of Zach's current favorites is *The Chalk Box Kid* by Clyde Robert Bulla (a book written at a third grade level that appeals to older students). Attention is beginning to be freed up for higher levels of comprehension and meaning making.

Figure 4.4 From Word to Meaning

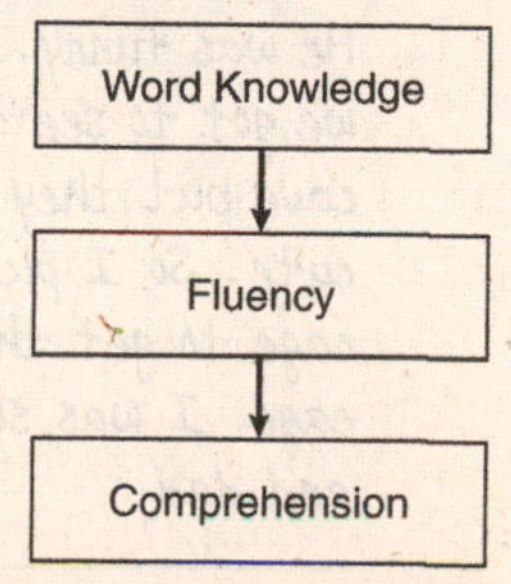

Their writing also reaches a level of fluency, with words either spelled correctly or phonetically close and readable (Bear et al., 2008).

Reading in the Transitional Stage

Transitional readers are most commonly found in grades 1 through 4 (Bear et al., 2008); however, many struggling readers in middle and even high school fall in this stage. In fact, Bear and colleagues estimate that 25 percent of the adult population functions at this stage of learning. These readers are no longer the word-by-word, monotonic readers of the beginning stage; they are more fluent and expressive. The transitional reader no longer requires the support of finger pointing and reading aloud, both markers of movement from the beginning stage. Indeed, the ability to read silently is a hallmark of transitional readers, though their silent reading rates are commensurate with their oral reading rates at the beginning of this stage of development. The movement to more phrasal reading and automatic word recognition allows the transitional reader to reach oral reading speeds of 100 words per minute (Carnine, Silbert, Kame'enui, & Tarver, 2004; Hasbrouck & Tindal, 1992). Even though they are becoming more fluent and phrasal in their reading, they are sometimes characterized as "choppy," because they are still trying out their "wings." As Bear and colleagues (2008) explain, transitional readers have limited "elevation" in their reading, meaning that they can become frustrated with their efforts at fluency, causing them to regress at times. Building fluency is a major instructional goal for readers at this stage and is often a particular need for struggling readers.

Writing in the Transitional Stage

Just as their reading becomes more fluent, so does their writing. Transitional writers have accrued a large number of words that they know how to write automatically without the pressures of working through the spelling letter by letter. Additionally, the act of writing is much more manageable, leading to the construction of relatively longer, more sophisticated pieces. Transitional writers can shift their conscious efforts from the physical act of writing to the composition of their work; they write not only with greater ease but also with more attention to their expression. See Figure 4.5 to view Zach's written sample about a birthday party at the zoo. Notice the organizational structure of this piece and the evidence of Zach's voice.

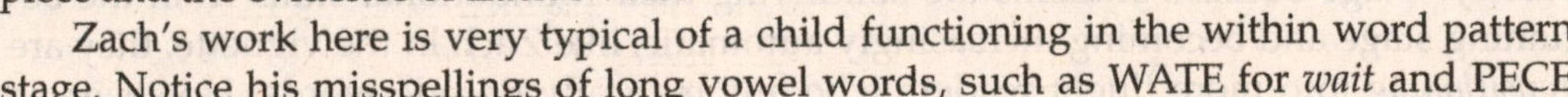

Zach's work here is very typical of a child functioning in the within word pattern stage. Notice his misspellings of long vowel words, such as WATE for *wait* and PECE

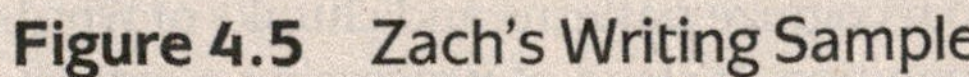

Figure 4.5 Zach's Writing Sample

At the zoo
"I can't wate to go!" I got a invatation to Coles party. He's haveing his party at the zoo. When we got thair I was so exided! We got to see the chimpanzezs first. He was funny. He cared a buked arownd and sat in it like it was a bath tub. Next we got to see a parit. We all said. "Helo!" and it coped us. We all whent to the bat cave but they were all slepping. "Yey!" Next we got to see the leamers. They are so cute. So I picked a pece of grass and tesed it. All of a sudden It got out of its cage to get the grass I was holdeing. I droped the grass and it whent back in its cage. I was so embarest evry one was looking at me but I can't wate to tell mom and dad.

for *piece.* Although Zach did not spell these words correctly, he marked the long vowel with a silent letter, evidence that he is considering long vowel patterns. Also, notice his errors related to high-frequency words (e.g., THAIR for *there* and EVRY for *every*). High-frequency word errors are commonly found in writing samples of students struggling in their literacy development. Zach also demonstrates confusion with features found in later stages, such as the consonant doubling in *dropped* (he wrote DROPED) and the *e*-drop in *having* (he wrote HAVEING).

Spelling in the Transitional Stage

Transitional readers and writers are within word pattern spellers and are typically found in the early elementary grades. However, as noted, within word spellers like Zach can be found at any age. These spellers have moved beyond the letter-by-letter spelling of the beginner where they hear a single sound and supply a single letter. Instead, these spellers begin to think of chunks of letters, or spelling patterns, found in words. When faced with writing a word like *coast,* they know to mark the long vowel in some way, even if it is not correct (e.g., *coste* using the *e*-marker or *cowst* using the *ow* vowel pattern).

Assessing your students using one of the spelling inventories from Appendix A can ensure that you are providing appropriately leveled material for your students, one of the practices that leads to engagement.

Students at the within word pattern stage of spelling development are learning to negotiate vowel patterns and three-letter blends. Please see Figure 4.6 for Zach's Primary Spelling Inventory (PSI) sample (as described in Chapter 3). He demonstrates mastery of short vowels and many consonant blends and digraphs (two letters representing a single sound). He also knows some long vowel patterns as seen in *shine* and *coach* but is confusing others (e.g., DREEM for *dream* and FRITE for *fright*). When asked to spell words with ambiguous vowels, however, Zach is unable to correctly spell any of the words. Zach sometimes marks the vowel using the wrong spelling pattern (e.g., spelling *crawl* as CRALL) but does not mark the vowel at all in other instances (e.g., spelling *chewed* as CHUED). Further evidence that Zach is in the within word pattern stage is shown by features absent in his spelling, such as the rules governing inflectional endings. He spells the doubled consonant in *clapped* as CLAPED and the *e*-drop in *riding* as RIDDING.

Once you have assessment information on your students, you should interpret the results and establish both long- and short-term goals. These goals can serve as the guiding force when you conference with students as they set their own learning goals. Ms. Thiessen, Zach's teacher, met with each of her students after she scored their spelling inventories. She also consulted writing samples from her students to confirm her findings on the spelling inventories. Looking at Zach's writing sample, she felt confident in her determination of his spelling stage and the target features for his quarterly work. At this point, she decided that other long vowel patterns should be the target for Zach this quarter.

Ms Thiessen is careful to include her students in goal setting to provide them with ownership of their own learning.

When Ms. Thiessen met with Zach to establish his goals for the quarter, she had a chart of features within his stage of development (within word pattern) to guide their discussion (see Figure 4.7). To motivate Zach, she chose a chart that listed early within word pattern features, which he could confidently mark as mastered.

She began their conversation by showing him where he was achieving on the chart. She talked to Zach about how he correctly spelled words with long vowels that had the *e*-marker as she wrote down words like *blade* and *shine,* highlighting the CVCe spelling pattern. "Zach, thanks for your hard work on the spelling assessment the other day. Your work there gave us a lot of information so that we can make some goals for our work this quarter. Let me tell you about the things we can go ahead and cross off our list. Take a look at this chart. It maps out the features of study that we will be working on this year. Let's just focus on this quarter today. I think you have a clear understanding about what a long vowel sounds like and how to use the *e*-marker like in *blade* and *shine.* These

Figure 4.6 Zach's Primary Spelling Inventory

Zach's spelling	Intended word
fan	
pet	
dig	
rob	
hope	
wait	
gum	
sled	
stick	
shine	
dreem	(dream)
blade	
coach	
frite	(fright)
chued	(chewed)
crall	(crawl)
wishes	
thorn	
shotted	(shouted)
spoel	(spoil)
grawl	(growl)
third	
capped	(camped)
tries	
claping	(clapping)
ridding	(riding)

Figure 4.7 Zach's Feature Chart for Goal Setting

Categories	**Features**	**Date Feature Mastered**
Common long vowels: *e*-marker	Long *a* with *a-e* (*cake*)	
	Long *i* with *i-e* (*bike*)	
	Long *o* with *o-e* (*bone*)	
	Long *u* with *u-e* (*cube*)	
Date Category Mastered:		
Simple *r*-controlled vowels	*ar* (*car*)	
	ir (*girl*)	
	or (*horn*)	
Date Category Mastered:		

words follow the consonant-vowel-consonant-*e* pattern (CVCe). Do you agree with this? Do you agree that you feel confident with using the *e*-marker to mark long vowels?"

Zach responded, "Yep. I feel like I know about putting *e*'s on words. But I know that I mess up. Sometimes I write a word that I know doesn't look right."

Ms. Thiessen then marked off the *e*-marker feature in that category and put the date in the chart, noting the feature as mastered. She moved the conversation to the simple *r*-controlled vowels and considered his spelling and writing samples (all simple *r*-controlled vowels were spelled correctly). "Zach, I think you also have a good understanding of the next set of features: simple *r*-controlled vowels like the *ar* in *star,* the *or* in *horn,* and the *ir* in *girl.*" She marked off the simple *r*-controlled feature as well. "Where I think we need to put our efforts is the other common long vowel pattern features. I noticed in your writing sample about the parrot that you spelled *wait* like this." Ms.Thiessen writes WATE on a dry erase board. "Is this one of those times when you look at a word and think it just doesn't look right?"

"Yes. It is. I know that isn't right."

"All right. I'd like to suggest that we begin our work this quarter with other common long vowel patterns." She pointed out the early syllables and affixes chart (Appendix B).

"Okay. So are we going to start with these, the long *a* ones?"

"Yes, like these on the chart. As we go through the quarter, we'll take a look at your weekly work, your assessments, and your writing so that we can talk about whether we are meeting our goals. And maybe even surpassing them."

As Zach works through these goals, he conferences with Ms. Thiessen to monitor his progress. The evidence used during these meetings to note mastery includes daily work in his word study notebook, weekly word study tests, writing samples, and cumulative spelling tests. One important piece of evidence is work demonstrating maintenance. Cumulative spelling tests are very helpful while looking for maintenance across time. At the end of the quarter, Ms. Thiessen gives Zach's group a cumulative spelling test of the long vowel patterns that have been covered (see Figure 4.8 for Zach's). As you can see, Zach has made significant gains. At the conference at the end of the quarter, Zach and Ms. Thiessen discuss new goals that will move him to the next main feature of study in the within word pattern sequence, long *r*-controlled vowel patterns.

Figure 4.8 Zach's Cumulative Long Vowel Pattern Test

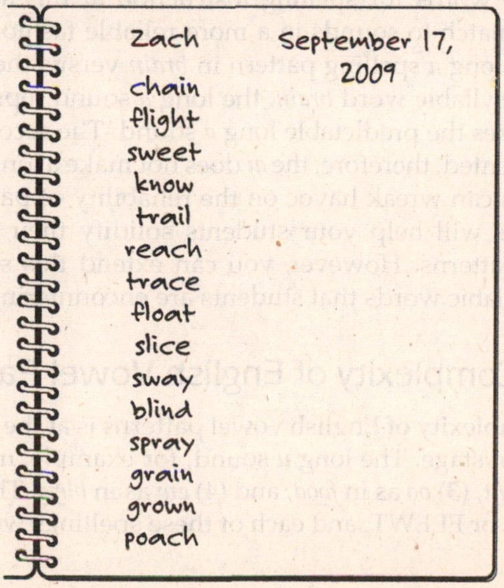

Zach September 17, 2009

chain
flight
sweet
know
trail
reach
trace
float
slice
sway
blind
spray
grain
grown
poach

The Within Word Pattern Stage: Sequence of Development

To begin instruction at the within word pattern stage, teachers reinforce the previously learned short vowels while bringing the new long vowel patterns into the instructional framework. The first long vowel pattern students typically begin to use is the silent *e*-marker. This study is followed by *r*-controlled vowel patterns (such as the *ar* in *star*) and common long vowel patterns (such as the *ee* in *sweet*). Students then move into investigating less common long vowel patterns (such as the *ew* in *chew*), complex consonant patterns (such as the *dge* in *dodge*), and ambiguous vowel patterns (such as the *ou* in *count*).

A suggested sequence can be found in Table 4.1 and words to use in this study can be found in Appendix D. This suggested pace is thorough and meant to meet the needs of struggling readers. This sequence deviates slightly from *Words Their Way* (Bear et al., 2008) because struggling students often have lingering confusions left over from the letter name–alphabetic stage, including simple *r*-controlled and schwa-*r* words. We do not have a letter name–alphabetic chapter in this book, so we included this feature in the within word pattern sequence.

Where teachers place students in this sequence depends on their performance on the spelling inventories discussed in Chapter 3. Placement should be flexible, and subsequent movement along the sequence will depend on daily student performance and indicators of transfer such as in their writing samples. Teachers must also be cognizant of student needs in order to quicken or slow down the pace when necessary. This is especially important for struggling readers, because instruction needs to honor their developmental levels while keeping an eye to acceleration. Categories can be added in order to cover more ground at once. For example, you can combine the following two categories for acceleration: (1) simple *r*-controlled vowels and schwa-*r* and (2) long vowels with the *e*-marker. However, if students are not demonstrating understanding of the orthographic features targeted, a step backward to contrasting only short vowels to the long vowel *e*-marker would be warranted, covering fewer or more obvious contrasts.

The Within Word Pattern Stage: Development and Instruction

Word study at this stage is limited to one-syllable comparisons. It is important to focus mainly on one-syllable words for spelling instruction at this stage because patterns in one-syllable words match to sounds in a more reliable fashion than in two-syllable words. Consider the *ai* long *a* spelling pattern in *brain* versus the *ai* in *fountain*. Within the one-syllable word *brain*, the long *a* sound represented by the *ai* pattern makes the predictable long *a* sound. The second syllable in *fountain* is unaccented; therefore, the *ai* does not make a long *a* sound. Unaccented syllables can wreak havoc on the reliability of patterns. Avoiding these instances will help your students solidify their understanding of the vowel patterns. However, you can extend this study to include some multisyllabic words that students are encountering in their reading.

engagement LINK

Using one-syllable words helps you support your struggling readers, resulting in fewer frustrations. This practice contributes to the developmental appropriateness of your instruction.

Negotiating the Complexity of English Vowel Patterns

Understanding the complexity of English vowel patterns is at the heart of word study in the within word pattern stage. The long *u* sound, for example, might be spelled (1) *u-e* as in *cute*, (2) *ui* as in *fruit*, (3) *oo* as in *food*, and (4) *ew* as in *blew*. Therefore, *flute* might be spelled FLUIT, FLOOT, or FLEWT, and each of these spellings would be as plausible as the correct spelling.

Table 4.1 Suggested Sequence for Within Word Pattern

Feature Sequence	Sorting Sequence	Exemplars
Common long vowels: e-marker	Short *a* vs. *a-e*	cat vs. cake
	Short *i* vs. *i-e*	pig vs. bike
	Short *o* vs. *o-e*	pot vs. bone
	Short *u* vs. *u-e*	bug vs. cube/June
	Combine all CVC vs. CVCe	cat (CVC) vs. cake (CVCe)
	Final *k, ck, ke*	bank vs. sack vs. cake
Simple *r*-controlled vowels	Short *a* vs. *a-e* vs. *ar*	cat vs. cake vs. car
	Short *i* vs. *i-e* vs. *ir*	pig vs. bike vs. girl
	Short *o* vs. *o-e* vs. *or*	pot vs. bone vs. horn
	ar vs. *or* vs. *ir*	car vs. horn vs. girl
Common and less common long vowel patterns	Short *a* vs. *a-e* vs. *ay*	cat vs. cake vs. tray
	Short *a* vs. *a-e* vs. *ai* vs. *ay*	cat vs. cake vs. rain vs. tray
	Short *i* vs. *i-e* vs. *y*	pig vs. bike vs. fly
	Short *i* vs. *i-e* vs. *igh* vs. *y*	pig vs. bike vs. light vs. fly
	Short *o* vs. *o-e* vs. *ow*	pot vs. bone vs. snow
	Short *o* vs. *o-e* vs. *oa* vs. *ow*	pot vs. bone vs. boat vs. snow
	Short *u* vs. *u-e* vs. *ew*	bug vs. cube/June vs. stew
	Short *u* vs. *u-e* vs. *ui* vs. *ew*	bug vs. cube/June vs. fruit vs. stew
	Short *u* vs. *u-e* vs. *ue* vs. *oo*	bug vs. cube/June vs. glue vs. zoo
	Short *e* vs. *ee* vs. *ea*	bed vs. sheep vs. peach
	Review all CVVC across all vowels	CVVC: long vowels
Long *r*-controlled vowels	Long *a* vs. *are* vs. *air*	cake vs. square vs. hair
	Short *e* vs. *er*	bed vs. fern
	er vs. *eer* vs. *ear*	fern vs. deer vs. ear
	Long *i* vs. *ire*	bike vs. tire
	Short *o* vs. *or* vs. *w+or*	pot vs. born vs. worm
	Long *o* vs. *oar* vs. *ore*	bone vs. oar vs. store
	Short *u* vs. *ur*	bug vs. curl
	or vs. *ur* vs. *ir*	horn vs. curl vs. girl
Complex consonant units	*kn* vs. *wr* vs. *gn*	knife vs. wren vs. gnat
	sh vs. *shr* vs. *th* vs. *thr*	shell vs. shrimp vs. thumb vs. three
	scr vs. *str* vs. *spr*	scrap vs. street vs. spray
	spl vs. *squ*	splash vs. square
	hard/soft *c* and *g*	card/cent vs. goat/gem
	dge vs. *ge*	bridge vs. stage
	ch vs. *tch*	beach vs. patch
	ce vs. *se* vs. *ve* vs. *ge*	face vs. mouse vs. glove vs. cage
Diphthongs and other ambiguous vowels	Long *o* vs. *oi* vs. *oy*	bone vs. oil vs. boy
	Short *o* vs. *ou* vs. *ow*	pot vs. cloud vs. cow
	ou vs. *ow* vs. *oo* vs. *oo*	cloud vs. cow vs. book vs. zoo
	oi vs. *oy* vs. *ou* vs. *ow*	oil vs. boy vs. cloud vs. cow
	Short *a* vs. *al* vs. *aw*	cat vs. salt vs. saw
	al vs. *au* vs. *aw*	salt vs. sauce vs. saw
	Review *ow* vs. *ew* vs. *aw*	snow vs. cow vs. stew vs. saw

Vowels pose another challenge; there are many more vowel sounds than there are letters to represent those sounds. Listen, for example, to the variety of sounds *a* can make in the following words: *track, shade, star, war, chalk, wash.* In order to spell the variety of vowel sounds, vowels are paired (e.g., the *ai* in *brain*) or a second letter is used to signal a sound variant (e.g., the silent *e* in *broke* or the *r* in *curl*). Another vowel dilemma is the difference of sound by dialect. For example, in some regions the long *i* sound as in *bike* is pronounced /bayhk/, while in other regions it is pronounced more like a vowel glide as in "bi-eke."

See Figure 4.9 for a quick reference to the various vowel sounds and their corresponding pattern options shown in Table 4.1. It is, however, important to note that not all of the patterns listed in Table 4.1 will cover every word in the English language. Sometimes words are truly exceptions, as in *was*, but often they can be explained in a category all to themselves. For example, consider the words *have* and *give*. At first sight, they appear to be exceptions because they follow the *a-e* vowel pattern, indicating that they should have a long *a* vowel sound. However, the *e* is included to accompany the *v*. Single-syllable words in English do not end with a lone *v*; the *v* is followed by an *e* as in *love*, *live*, and *curve*.

The Big Picture: A Graphic Organizer for the Features of Study

Providing your students with a visual representation of the "big picture" will help them organize and connect new features with previously learned ones. This is especially helpful at this portion of the stage where many spelling options exist for one sound: long *a* can be spelled with *a-e* (*cake*), *ai* (*rain*), *ay* (*tray*), and *ei* (*vein*). The big picture can serve as a graphic organizer for your students and a point of reference to assist during discussions. Let's revisit Zach. As his group embarks on their study of other common long vowels, Ms. Thiessen provides them with a "big picture" graphic to help them construct

Figure 4.9 Vowel Patterns

Long Vowel Patterns

Common long *a* patterns:	*a-e (cave), ai (rain), ay (play)*
Less common:	*ei (eight), ey (prey)*
Common long e patterns:	*ee (green), ea (team), e (me)*
Less common:	*ie (chief), e-e (theme)*
Common long *i* patterns:	*i-e (tribe), igh (sight), y (fly)*
Less common:	*i* followed by *nd* or *ld (mind, child)*
Common long o patterns:	*o-e (home), oa (float), ow (grow)*
Less common:	o followed by two consonants *(cold, most, jolt)*
Common long *u* patterns:	*u-e (flute), oo (moon), ew (blew)*
Less common:	*ue (blue), ui (suit)*

Consonant-Influenced Vowels

r-controlled vowels

a with *r*	*ar (car), are (care), air (fair)*
o with *r*	*or (for), ore (store), our (pour), oar (board)*
e with *r*	*er (her), eer (deer), ear (dear), ear (learn)*
i with *r*	*ir (shirt), ire (fire)*
u with *r*	*ur (burn), ure (cure)*

w influences vowels that follow: *wa (wash, warn), wo (won, word).*
l influences the *a* as heard in *al (tall, talk).*

Diphthongs and Ambiguous Vowels

o͞o (moon), o͝o (book)
oy (boy), oi (boil)
ow (brown), ou (cloud)
aw (crawl), au (caught), al (tall)

Figure 4.10 The Big Picture

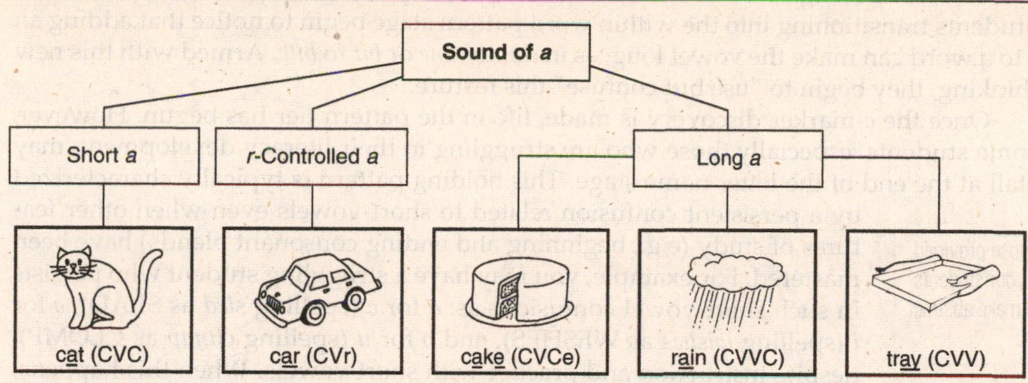

their mental organizer of the various patterns associated with long *a*. As you can see in Figure 4.10, the organizer outlines two known features (short *a* and *r*-controlled *a*) and how those features can be considered along with the new features (the *ai* and *ay* spelling patterns of long *a*). As the group works with the common spelling patterns of long *a*, Zach stumbles while spelling the word *sprain*. Ms. Thiessen is able to call their attention to the big picture to help illustrate the discussion that follows after Zach brings up to the group, "I want to write about my sprained ankle, but I'm stuck on *sprained*."

"Okay," Ms. Thiessen replies. "Let's think about our process. First, let's get to the part that is tricky for you."

"Well, that's easy. It is the long *a* sound. I know that I have to decide which pattern to use," says Zach.

Ms. Thiessen points their attention to the big picture. "I'm proud of you, Zach. You have taken the first step. Now let's think about your options here."

"Okay, so I can use *a*-consonant-*e*, *ai*, or *ay*. That's my problem."

Juan, Zach's group member, joins in the discussion, "Yeah, you are right. But I remember us sorting a lot of words that end in /ān/ that are spelled with *-ain* like *rain*. So, I'm thinking you should use that now since *sprain* ends in /ān/. Ms. Thiessen, what do you think?"

"What does the group think?" Ms. Thiessen asks as she points to the *-ain* ending highlighted on the big picture. After a few more minutes of group discussion, Zach returns to his notebook and writes a sentence about his sprained ankle.

Features for Study in Within Word Pattern

There are eight main features at this stage that we will discuss. Many of these involve negotiating vowel patterns and provide much study for students.

- Feature 1: Long vowels with the *e*-marker
- Feature 2: Simple *r*-controlled and schwa-*r* vowel patterns
- Feature 3: Other common long vowel patterns
- Feature 4: Long *r*-controlled vowel patterns
- Feature 5: Ambiguous vowels
- Feature 6: Complex consonant units
- Feature 7: Homophones/homographs
- Feature 8: Simple affixes

Feature 1: Long Vowels with the *e*-Marker

We will begin our discussion with the most common vowel pattern and the one with which students will first begin experimentation: the *e*-marker. How many times have you noticed a student overgeneralizing the *e*-marker, spelling *train* as TRANE or *coast* as COSTE or adding *e* on words that do not require any markers, spelling *hop* as HOPE? Students transitioning into the within word pattern stage begin to notice that adding an *e* to a word can make the vowel long, as in *can* to *cane* or *bit* to *bite*. Armed with this new thinking, they begin to "use but confuse" this feature.

engagement LINK

Picture and word sorts, like those provided throughout this chapter, give your students hands-on practice, as well as make abstract word concepts more concrete.

Once the *e*-marker discovery is made, life in the pattern tier has begun. However, some students, especially those who are struggling in their literacy development, may stall at the end of the letter name stage. This holding pattern is typically characterized by a persistent confusion related to short vowels even when other features of study (e.g., beginning and ending consonant blends) have been mastered. For example, you may have a struggling student who persists in such short vowel confusions as: *a* for *e* (spelling *sled* as SLAD), *e* for *i* (spelling *wishes* as WESHES), and *o* for *u* (spelling *clump* as CLOMP), despite instruction and practice with short vowels. When this happens, move on to the study of long vowel patterns and contrast each short vowel to the long vowel. Using pictures for sorting is an easy way to address sound differences with your students. Picture sorts such as the one in Figure 4.11 force your students to attend to the sound alone without the visual cue of the *e*-marker.

Figure 4.11 Short and Long *a* Picture Sort

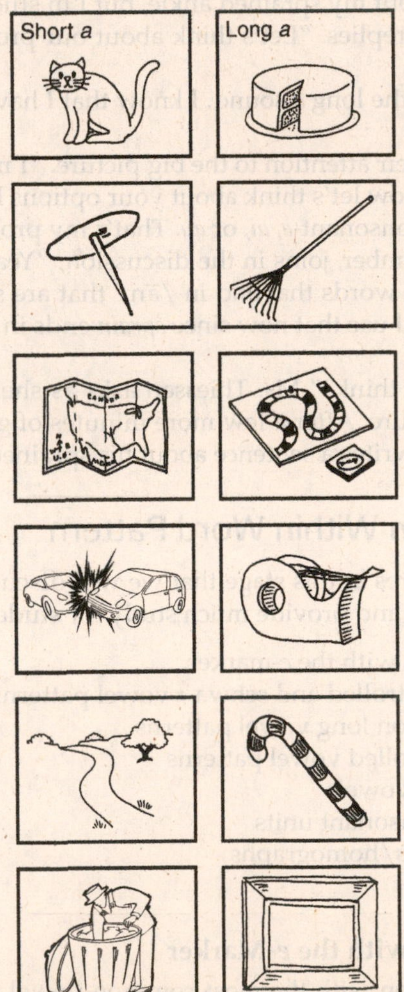

Be careful of your picture choices. Some letters influence vowels in a way that could confuse your students. These letters (*l, m, n*) actually change the sound of the preceding vowel. Say the word *cat*. Now say the word *camp*. These two *a*'s sound different because they are different. The *m* nasalizes the *a* and, subsequently, distorts its sound.

Two additional activities are critical to guiding this movement into the within word pattern stage. Sorts with very deliberate CVC patterns (such as the consonant-vowel-consonant pattern in *mad*) versus CVCe (consonant-vowel-consonant-*e* as in *made*) comparisons support the fledgling within word pattern speller. See Figure 4.12 for a sample word sort that emphasizes the *e*-marker. To make this more explicit, guide your students in changing *plan* to *plane, plane* to *mane, mane* to *man*, and so on. This type of work exaggerates the effect of the silent *e*-marker for your students in an effort to make the generalization more concrete. See the manipulation activity later in this chapter for a more complete explanation.

If your students have started to use the *e*-marker in their spelling attempts, then you can confidently begin instruction with sorts contrasting short and long vowels. You may find that moving through the entire set of CVCe comparisons found in Table 4.1 is unnecessary. Many students begin to generalize the pattern across vowels, but struggling students often require a complete study of all the vowels. Reviewing comparisons that highlight the CVC and CVCe patterns across vowels is often helpful (CVC: *brag, pick, wish;* CVCe: *shame, bite, broke*). The *e-e* pattern, as in *these*, was not included in this sequence because single-syllable words with this pattern occur infrequently. Other more common long *e* patterns (e.g., the *ee* in *need* and the *ea* in *peach*) are discussed later in the chapter.

Feature Two: Simple *r*-Controlled and Schwa-*r* Vowel Patterns

The simple *r*-controlled features (the *ar* in *cart* and the *or* in *form*) follow a study of the *e*-marker. Following up the *e*-marker with this feature can support your struggling readers for two reasons: The *r*-controlled vowel provides a distinct sound contrast to the long

Figure 4.12 Short and Long *a* Word Sort

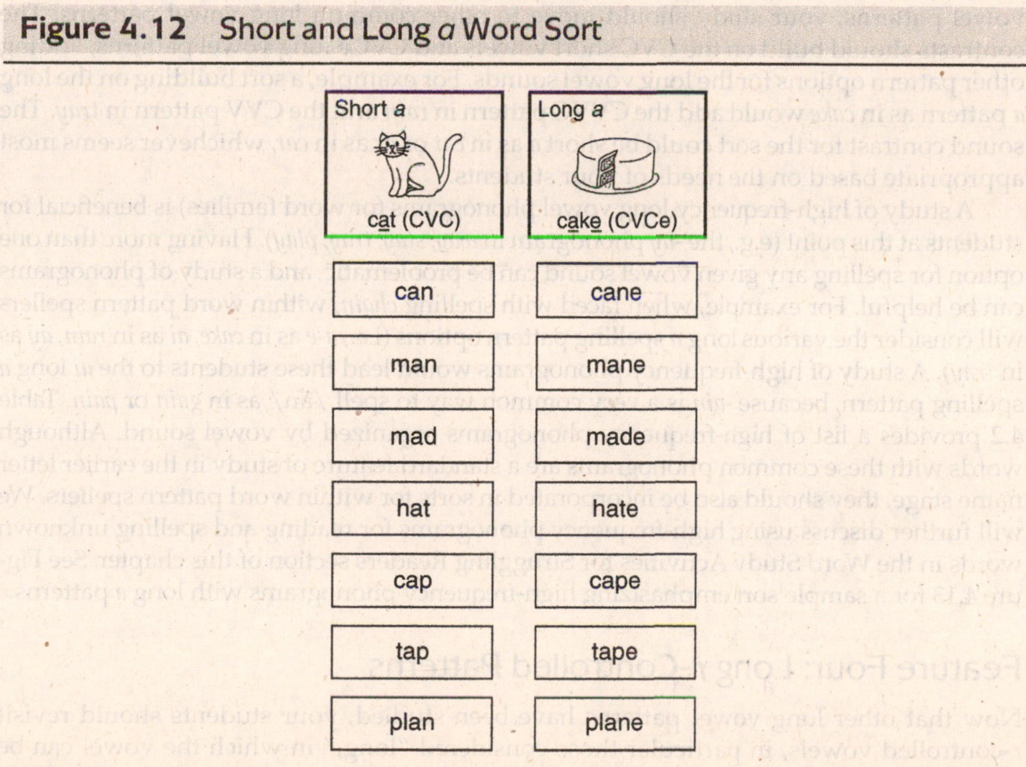

vowel for additional sound experiences, and students are provided the opportunity to continue a practice of something already taught, the *e*-marker, while learning a new vowel pattern, the *r*-controlled pattern. You may also find it necessary to include a short vowel contrast to reinforce the short and long vowel differences. For example, your contrasts might be CVC (*cat*) versus CVCe (*cake*) versus CVr/CVrC (*car/cart*).

cat	cake	car/cart
trash	trace	star
black	shake	chart
blast	shape	spark
stack	wave	yarn

Students who struggle to spell the *r*-controlled vowel patterns sometimes omit the vowel (e.g., BRD for *bird*) or reverse the letters (e.g., GRIL for *girl*) because the vowel sound cannot be separated from the *r* sound. This is commonly seen when trying to spell words with the schwa-*r* pattern: *ir* in *girl*, *ur* in *curl*, and *er* in *germ*. In addition, these patterns are often confused since they sound the same (consider *girl* spelled as GERL, *curl* spelled as CERL, and *germ* spelled as GURM).

You should start with the most common and easily differentiated *r*-controlled patterns: the *ar* in *car* and the *or* in *horn*. These patterns occur in many words and are fairly regular. To provide your students with review and extra practice, contrasts of the short vowel, the long vowel with the *e*-marker, and the *r*-controlled vowel are effective, such as *pot* versus *bone* versus *horn*. Moving to the schwa-*r* patterns may provide some confusion for your students due to the consistent sound of each. Frequency can be helpful here. One-syllable words with the *ir* and *ur* patterns are more common than *er*. A sort investigating just these three patterns can highlight this for your students and provide a backdrop to impress on them that some vowel patterns require extra attention because they are the trouble spots.

Feature Three: Other Common Long Vowel Patterns

Once your students have an understanding of the *e*-marker and simple *r*-controlled vowel patterns, your study should move to other common long vowel patterns. The contrasts should build on the CVC short vowels and CVCe long vowel patterns, adding other pattern options for the long vowel sounds. For example, a sort building on the long *a* pattern as in *cake* would add the CVVC pattern in *rain* and the CVV pattern in *tray*. The sound contrast for the sort could be short *a* as in *cat* or *ar* as in *car*, whichever seems most appropriate based on the needs of your students.

A study of high-frequency long vowel phonograms (or word families) is beneficial for students at this point (e.g., the *-ay* phonogram in *way, stay, tray, play*). Having more than one option for spelling any given vowel sound can be problematic, and a study of phonograms can be helpful. For example, when faced with spelling *chain*, within word pattern spellers will consider the various long *a* spelling pattern options (i.e., *a-e* as in *cake*, *ai* as in *rain*, *ay* as in *tray*). A study of high-frequency phonograms would lead these students to the *ai* long *a* spelling pattern, because *-ain* is a very common way to spell /ān/ as in *gain* or *pain*. Table 4.2 provides a list of high-frequency phonograms organized by vowel sound. Although words with these common phonograms are a standard feature of study in the earlier letter name stage, they should also be incorporated in sorts for within word pattern spellers. We will further discuss using high-frequency phonograms for reading and spelling unknown words in the Word Study Activities for Struggling Readers section of this chapter. See Figure 4.13 for a sample sort emphasizing high-frequency phonograms with long *a* patterns.

Feature Four: Long *r*-Controlled Patterns

Now that other long vowel patterns have been studied, your students should revisit *r*-controlled vowels, in particular those considered "long," in which the vowel can be

Table 4.2 High-Frequency Phonograms

a	e	i	o	u
ab	eak	ice	oat	ub
ace	eam	ick	ob	uck
ack	ear	id	ock	ue
ad	eat	ide	og	ug
ade	ed	ife	oil	um
ag	ee	ig	oke	ump
ail	eed	ight	old	un
ain	eel	ike	om	unk
ake	een	ile	on	up
alk	eep	ill	one	use
all	eet	im	ong	ut
am	ell	ime	ood	
ame	em	in	ook	
amp	en	ind	ool	
an	end	ine	oom	
and	ent	ing	op	
ank	er	ink	or	
ap	est	ip	ore	
ar	et	irt	orn	
ark	ew	is	ose	
art		ish	ot	
as		it	ound	
ash		ive	our	
ask			out	
at			ow	
ate			own	
ave			oy	
aw				
ay				

Source: Adapted from Adams, 1990, and Wylie & Durrell, 1970.

Figure 4.13 Long *a* Sort Sample

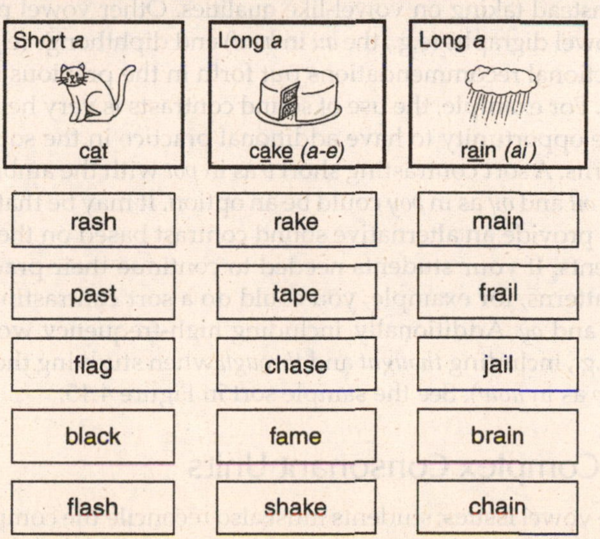

Short a
cat
Long a
cake (a-e)
Long a
rain (ai)
rash
rake
main
past
tape
frail
flag
chase
jail
black
fame
brain
flash
shake
chain

Figure 4.14 Long *r*-Controlled Sort

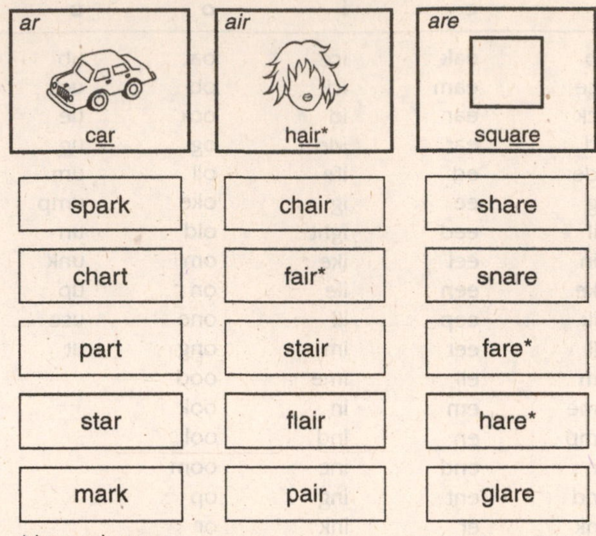

more clearly heard (e.g., *share* and *hair*). This study will provide your students with much review. Recursive instruction is especially helpful for struggling readers as they review other long vowel patterns as shown in the sort found in Figure 4.14. The more experience your students have reading and writing words with these patterns, the more confident they will be while using them. Notice that the suggested sequence of study provides you with a progression that gradually builds, adding one new long *r*-controlled pattern at a time. Special attention can also be given to words like *war* and *word*, where the *w* influences the sound of the *ar* and *or*.

ar
air
are
car
hair*
square
spark
chair
share
chart
fair*
snare
part
stair
fare*
star
flair
hare*
mark
pair
glare
* homophones

Feature Five: Ambiguous Vowels

Ambiguous vowels comprise vowels that are neither short nor long. During this feature's study, your students may become puzzled with the seemingly short vowel pattern (CVC) from their previous work. Consider *jaw, toy,* and *wall.* These words have the CVC pattern, but, in these cases, the consonants following the medial vowel are no longer acting as consonants but are instead taking on vowel-like qualities. Other vowel patterns included in this feature are vowel digraphs (e.g., the *au* in *haul*) and diphthongs (e.g., the *ou* in *sound*).

Many instructional recommendations put forth in the previous feature discussions hold here as well. For example, the use of sound contrasts is very helpful and will allow your students the opportunity to have additional practice in the sounds of certain patterns. A sort contrasting short *o* as in *pot* with the ambiguous vowels *oi* as in *oil* and *oy* as in *boy* could be an option. It may be that you would choose to provide an alternative sound contrast based on the needs of your students. If your students needed to continue their practice of long vowel patterns, for example, you could do a sort contrasting *oa* as in *boat* with *oi* and *oy.* Additionally, including high-frequency words will be helpful (e.g., including *thought* and *through* when studying the *ou* as in *mouth* and *ow* as in *now*). See the sample sort in Figure 4.15.

engagement LINK

Sorts that include oddballs, especially oddballs that are high-frequency words, are not only engaging because of their hands-on nature but also because they make these potentially troublesome words more memorable.

Feature Six: Complex Consonant Units

In addition to the vowel issues, students must also reconcile the complexity of advanced consonant units. Within word pattern spellers have solidified their knowledge of begin-

Figure 4.15 Ambiguous Vowel Sort (with Oddballs)

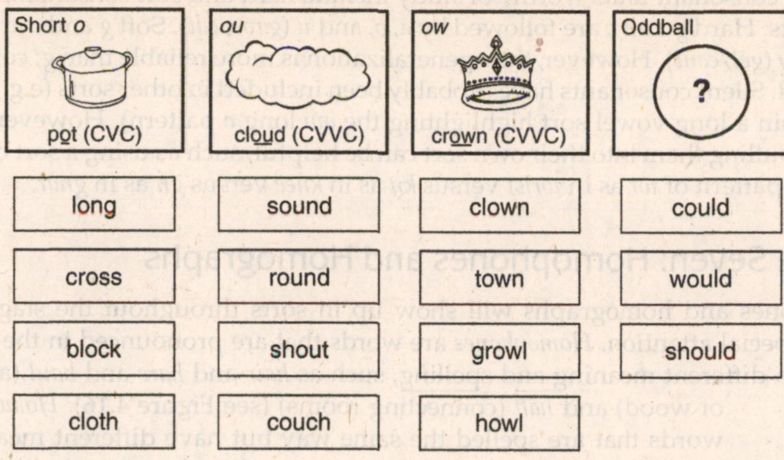

ning and ending consonant blends and digraphs such as the *sl* in *slash* and the *ch* in *chest*, but three-letter consonant blends and digraphs such as *spr* (*spray*), *scr* (*scram*), *shr* (*shrill*), *str* (*stripe*), *squ* (*squirm*), *spl* (*split*), and *thr* (*three*) are more challenging. Struggling readers may need to compare three-letter blends with related two-letter blends, such as *spr* in *sprain* versus *sp* in *spend*. *Thr* and *shr* might be contrasted with the simple digraphs *th* and *sh*, and *qu* as in *queen* can be compared to *squ* as in *squid*. Other students might simply compare *thr*, *shr*, and *squ* at one time for more accelerated study. Notice that this study affords you the opportunity for more review of previously learned patterns, such as the other long vowel pattern of *ee* in *street*.

Short o
ou
ow
Oddball
?
pot (CVC)
cloud (CVVC)
crown (CVVC)
long
sound
clown
could
cross
round
town
would
block
shout
growl
should
cloth
couch
howl

Students will benefit from the study of final complex consonant units like *dge* and *ge*. These final complex consonant units can indicate a change in vowel sound; the *dge* in *dodge* signals the reader that the *o* is short whereas the *ge* in *stage* signals the reader that the *a* is long.

***ge* ending**

- long vowels (*stage*)
- *r*-controlled vowels (*large*)
- ambiguous vowels (*lounge*)

***dge* ending**

- short vowels (*bridge, lodge, fudge*)

The only instance when the "short vowel" generalization does not apply is when the vowel is followed by a consonant (*hinge*) before ending with the *ge* pattern. Many of these words have the consonant *n* following the vowel (*cringe, lunge*, etc.).

There are other reliable consonant patterns that signal a certain vowel sound.

Patterns for the /k/ ending

- the final *ck* as in *shack* (*ck* signals short)
- the final *ke* as in *shake* (*ke* signals long)
- the final *k* as in *shook* (*k* follows vowel pairs)

Patterns for the /ch/ ending

- the final *tch* as in *notch* (*tch* signals short)
- the final *ch* as in *coach/porch/slouch* (*ch* signals other vowel patterns)

There are some exceptions, although very few, to these generalizations that can be considered as oddballs (*such, much, rich, which*).

Other consonant units worthy of study include hard and soft consonants and silent consonants. Hard *g* and *c* are followed by *a, o,* and *u* (*gave, cat*). Soft *g* and *c* are followed by *i, e,* or *y* (*gel, cent*). However, the *c* generalization is more reliable than *g*; consider *girl, give,* or *gift*. Silent consonants have probably been included in other sorts (e.g., including *know* within a long vowel sort highlighting the *ow* long *o* pattern). However, you may find that pulling them into their own sort can be helpful, such as using a sort contrasting the initial pattern of *wr* as in *wrist* versus *kn* as in *knee* versus *gn* as in *gnat*.

Feature Seven: Homophones and Homographs

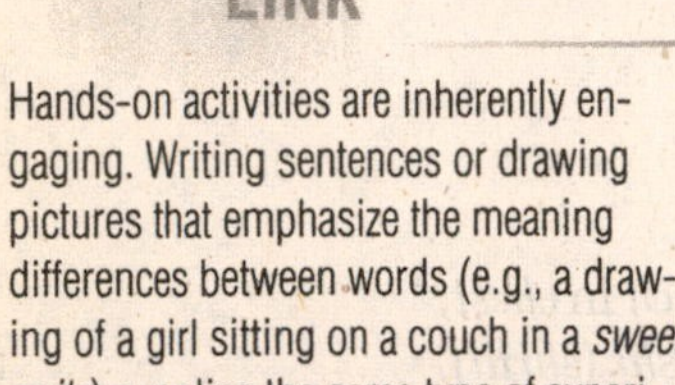

engagement LINK

Hands-on activities are inherently engaging. Writing sentences or drawing pictures that emphasize the meaning differences between words (e.g., a drawing of a girl sitting on a couch in a *sweet suite*) supplies the same type of experience with words.

Homophones and homographs will show up in sorts throughout the stage but also deserve special attention. *Homophones* are words that are pronounced in the same way but have a different meaning and spelling, such as *hair* and *hare* and *haul* (a truckload of wood) and *hall* (connecting rooms) (see Figure 4.16). *Homographs* are words that are spelled the same way but have different meanings and sometimes different pronunciations, such as *bear* (in mind)/*bear* (in the woods) and *lead* (me to the door)/*lead* (type of metal). Students can be asked to look up the meanings of homophones in a dictionary, illustrate them, or use them in sentences that demonstrate their meaning. A special challenge could involve using both in the same sentence, such as "Greg's entry in the airplane contest was very *plain* but it flew better than the other *planes*." Through an exploration of homophones, students can make generalizations about patterns, such as comparing *wait* to the uncommon *ei* pattern for long *a* in *weight*.

In addition, a study of homophones and homographs provides struggling readers with additional vocabulary study. While considering the homophones *peek* and *peak* (and even *pique*), students cannot only investigate the two patterns for representing the long *e* sound but must also consider the meaning of each word.

Feature Eight: Simple Affixes

Affixes are prefixes and suffixes that are attached to a base word or a root and affect the meaning of the word. For example, a prefix such as *re-* changes the meaning of a word, transforming *tie* into *retie*. Similarly, a suffix such as *-y* also changes meaning, turning the noun

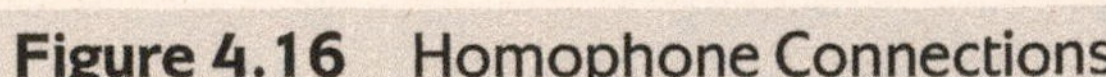

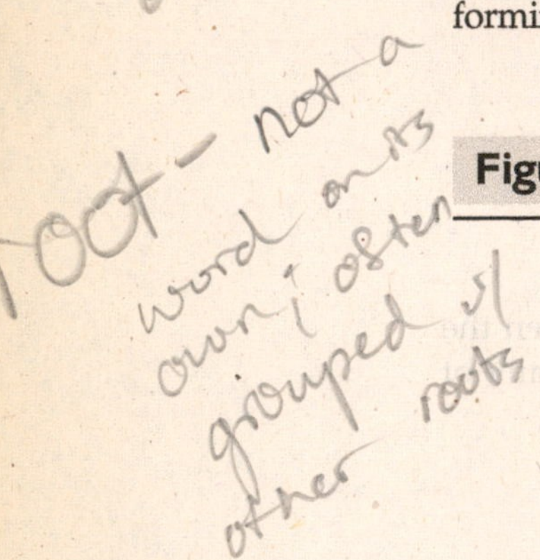

Figure 4.16 Homophone Connections

A truck *hauls* wood down a *hall*.

fun into the adjective *funny*. The next stage, syllables and affixes, is devoted to the study of prefixes and suffixes. However, many struggling adolescents in the within word pattern stage need work in this area due to content standards. In fact, standards in the elementary grades mandate the mastery of several simple affixes. Many of these affixes are extremely frequent; *un-* (meaning "not"), *re-* ("again"), *in-* ("not"), and *dis-* ("not") account for about 58 percent of all prefixes in the English language (White, Sowell, & Yanagihara, 1989).

You can use one-syllable base words that have been included in your previous study to examine affixes. For example, when investigating the prefix *un-*, you could use *unclear, unfair, unpack, untie, unreal,* and *unhook.* These base words all have patterns studied in this stage or the previous stage. Use of the *un-* prefix could be contrasted with another prefix such as *re-* (*react, reclaim, recount, research, relearn*). Additionally, you can add more than one affix, as in *unfairly* (*un* + *fair* + *ly*) or *carefully* (*care* + *ful*+ *ly*).

Considerations for English Learners

Guidelines for the Within Word Pattern Stage

During the within word pattern stage, your English learners will learn several key concepts (Bear, Helman, Templeton, Invernizzi, & Johnston, 2007). English has more vowel sounds than letters and more than one way to spell many vowel sounds. For example, students need to learn that long *i* can be spelled as *i*-consonant-*e* (*bite*), *-igh* (*fight*), *-y* (*try*), and *i*-consonant-consonant (*kind*). A student at this stage learns that although spelling *fight* as FITE would "mark" the vowel to make it long, it would not be correct. As they learn about the various vowel patterns of English, they also learn that English has oddballs, or words that do not fit the patterns being studied. English learners whose primary language is transparent may need additional support, because they do not have the "mindset" for the deep orthography of English (Bear et al., 2007). The following guidelines for word study are offered by Bear and colleagues (2007):

- Include time to discuss vocabulary and allow your students to ask questions. Check your students' understandings of the meanings as well as the features. You may need to provide support for words you might consider "common" and had not anticipated to be problematic.
- Provide opportunities for your English learners to partner with proficient English speakers, who will be good language models.
- Make sure your students are reading their words aloud and check to make sure they understand the meanings.
- Repeat sorts with your students until they are able to quickly and accurately complete them.
- Have your students record their words and meanings in word study notebooks for future reference.
- Ensure plenty of opportunities for your students to experience the patterns being studied before bringing in oddballs. They need to have positive experiences with the patterns to support their learning. When oddballs are discussed, they should be considered as to how they are different from the norm.
- Utilize the orthography of your students' primary languages if they have achieved a level of literacy in their home language. Comparisons allow them to study the similarities and differences among the languages. For example, explicit comparisons of vowel sounds might help students when learning long vowels, which often do not occur in their primary language. Therefore, your English learners will need many opportunities to compare short and long vowel sounds. It is important for them to hear the difference but not necessarily to pronounce them correctly.
- Do not forget about supporting the sounds. Although the within word pattern stage has a focus on pattern, sounds continue to play a crucial role for English learners. Many of the sounds of English do not exist in other languages. For example, many languages do not have *r*-controlled vowels, so their sounds are difficult to pronounce. Difficulty with pronunciation can cause challenges when attempting to spell the words.

A Word about Oddballs

Sometimes words do not follow the generalizations you are building with your students. You do not need to hide these exceptions, or oddballs, which is the term we prefer. Include oddballs when appropriate. During word study in the within word pattern stage, the oddball category will be used frequently. Sometimes the words you include are true exceptions such as *was* and *been*. However, sometimes these words are part of a little known category. Consider *chance, prince,* and *fence*. A student might want to consider these as long vowels because they have the *e*-marker. However, the reason for the *e* is to keep the *c* soft. Without the *e*, these words would end in a hard *c* sound like *magic*. Including these words in your sorts makes them memorable because they deviate from the pattern. This method is especially helpful with high-frequency words like *have, said,* and *their*. Calling your students' attention to the part that deviates from the pattern may help your students master the spellings of these oddballs. Appendix D provides you with lists of words to use in your work with all of the features along with oddballs for some features.

Word Study Activities for Struggling Readers at the Within Word Pattern Stage

The transitional stage of reading is a crossroads for the struggling reader. Crossing the bridge from reliance on individual sounds as the primary decoding and encoding tool to the awareness of patterns is a major feat for struggling readers in the within word pattern stage. They can sometimes find themselves spinning their wheels at this stage as they continually negotiate which pattern to use with which sound in single-syllable words, much less transfer this knowledge to two-syllable words. It is crucial to provide these students with the following:

1. Systematic and explicit instruction when moving to patterns
2. Ample opportunities to apply their phonics and spelling work to reading and writing situations
3. Scaffolded instruction that builds new information on what the student already knows

In this section, tried and true activities for struggling readers in the within word pattern stage are outlined. We will discuss teacher-directed sorts, open sorts, writing sorts, blind sorts, and word hunts. Extensions of sorting are then presented: manipulation, high-frequency words, word analysis instruction, and games. Each of the activities can be used during your weekly word study instructional routine. Some of these activities can be done in teacher-directed small groups, whereas others can be done independently or in collaborative groups. See Figure 4.17 to see Ms. Thiessen's weekly word study routine developed for the within word pattern spellers in Zach's group. Further resources can be found in Appendixes D and E. Appendix D provides you with guidelines on choosing words and has a detailed list of words that you can use for these activities. Appendix E supplies sample sorts across the features of the within word pattern stage.

engagement LINK

Ms. Thiessen's weekly routine includes time for her students to work collaboratively. She keeps that time sacred throughout the week because she knows how important collaborative work is to the model of gradual release and, ultimately, to her students' engagement.

Teacher-Directed Closed Sort

The goal of the closed sorting procedure is to explicitly set up and compare sound and pattern categories and lead students to notice similarities and differences among

Figure 4.17 Ms. Thiessen's Word Study Routine

	Monday	Tuesday	Wednesday	Thursday	Friday
Teacher-Directed Activities	Teacher-introduced closed sort		Manipulation and word analysis		Manipulation and word analysis
Collaborative or Independent Activities	Repeated Sort	Buddy Sort Word Hunt	Speed Sort	Writing Sort	Friday Test/ Writing Sort

targeted features. Let's recap the key sorting guidelines from Chapter 3: (1) Use consistent predetermined keywords that will exemplify the features of study, and (2) talk explicitly about the features of the keywords prior to sorting.

Procedure

1. *Demonstrate.* Introduce the sort by discussing keywords and the targeted features or patterns of study. Model your thinking as you sort at least two words in each column. The following is an example of language you might use when introducing the long vowel pattern *ai* (see sort in Figure 4.18):

   Teacher: When you see the letters *ai,* you know that these two letters together say /ā/ as in *rain.* So when you see the word *rain,* you can take what you know—*r, ai, n*—and put them together to make *rain.* Okay, my first word is *chain.* I know that the vowel sound in the middle of this word is long *a,* pronounced /ā/, because of the CVVC *ai* spelling pattern. So it has a long *a* sound and the CVVC *ai* pattern. I'm going to place *chain* in the category with *rain.* It looks right and it sounds right.

2. *Sort.* Have your students set up their keyword cards and sort their words. Remember to have your students name the pictures and/or read the words aloud as they sort.

Figure 4.18 Closed Sort

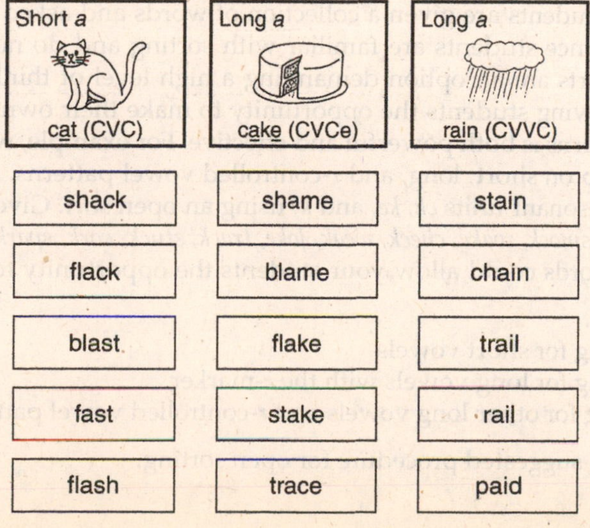

engagement LINK

Notice that even in a teacher-directed closed sort there is still teacher–student interaction and teacher questions that promote higher-level thinking.

3. *Check.* Have students read down the words under each keyword, listening for sounds while looking at the patterns. If you see any mistakes, you could say the following:

Teacher: One doesn't fit in this column [pointing to the CVCe category]. Can you find the mistake?

Student: [Student reads down column and comes to the word *plain.*] Is it this one?

Teacher: What do you think?

Student: I think it is *plain* because the pattern doesn't fit. I mean *plain* sounds the same as *cake* but it doesn't look the same.

Teacher: You are right. It doesn't look right. Where do you think it goes and tell me why?

Student: It must go in the *ai* column with *rain* because it has the *ai* spelling pattern.

Teacher: You got it. I like your thinking here.

4. *Reflect.* After students complete the sort (shown in Figure 4.18), you should initiate a reflection (either verbal or written). As each column is read, review the keywords and what each word in the category has in common, noting again the sound, pattern, and position. To reinforce student understanding of features, you can ask the following questions:

- Does it look right (or does it look the same)? This question emphasizes the pattern of the sort.
- Does it sound right (or does it sound the same)? This question emphasizes the sound feature of the sort.

You can also ask questions to generate discussion about the features:

- What did you notice about all of the words in this column?
- How are they alike in the way they sound?
- How are they alike in the patterns you can see in each word?
- What did you learn in this sort?

After these discussions, ask your students to leave up the headers and then mix the words by pushing them in from the sides (so they will be mixed up). Then ask them to sort again saying each word as they sort. This will give you a chance to assess how well they can do the sort on their own (with your support as needed). Have them check their sorts by reading down each column and then store their words for further activities, such as the writing and blind sorts described later in this section.

Open Sort

In an open sort, students are given a collection of words and asked to determine their own categories. Once students are familiar with sorting and do not need explicit instruction, open sorts are an option demanding a high level of thinking. As discussed in Chapter 2, allowing students the opportunity to make their own conclusions about orthographic patterns is both powerful and effective. For example, when your students have a good grasp on short, long, and *r*-controlled vowel patterns, you can move into a study of the consonant units *ck, ke,* and *k,* using an open sort. Give your students the following words: *smock, wake, cheek, weak, joke, track, stuck, cork, spark, shake.* An investigation of these words could allow your students the opportunity to see the following generalizations:

- *ck* as an ending for short vowels
- *ke* as an ending for long vowels with the *e*-marker
- *k* as an ending for other long vowels and *r*-controlled vowel patterns

The following is a suggested procedure for open sorting.

Procedure

1. *Introduce.* Tell your students that you are interested in their thinking about the sound and/or pattern of the sort. You can also have your students read through the words and talk about the meanings of any words they might not know (or any alternative meanings).

2. *Sort.* Have your students sort individually or collaboratively. Monitor and facilitate their thinking as they hypothesize categories. Prompt and ask questions that promote high-level thinking and deep processing:
   - What do you notice about the words?
   - What about them looks the same (or different)?
   - What about them sounds the same (or different)?
   - How are these two (or more) words related? (You might ask this question as you highlight certain words to provide more support—similar to "Guess My Category.")

3. *Reflect.* After your students have completed their sorts, have them reflect on their hypothesized categories with each other.

   Student 1: I have *smock, track,* and *stuck* in one category because they all have short vowels. Then I put *wake, joke, shake, cheek,* and *weak* in one group because they are all long vowels. And then I put *cork* and *spark* together because they are *r*-controlled.

   Student 2: I had almost the exact same categories but I ended up putting *weak* and *cheek* in another category because the spelling pattern is different. *Wake, joke,* and *shake* all have CVCe but *cheek* and *weak* have CVVC. I was thinking that the spelling pattern might make a difference.

   Teacher: Yep. I think you are on the right track here. Let's all go back to our sorts. Take a look at the patterns within your sound categories. See if you want to make any changes. [At this point, many of the students move the words to reflect the *ck, ke,* and *k* endings. See the completed sort in Figure 4.19.]

4. *Extend.* Help students place this learning in the context of previous features studied. To do this, use a big picture graphic organizer (described previously in this chapter). Reinforce these generalizations with other activities, such as writing sorts and word hunts (described later in this chapter).

Writing Sort

Writing sorts provide children with the opportunity to apply their word study work to writing. They also provide additional work categorizing sounds and patterns. Writing

Figure 4.19 Completed Open Sort

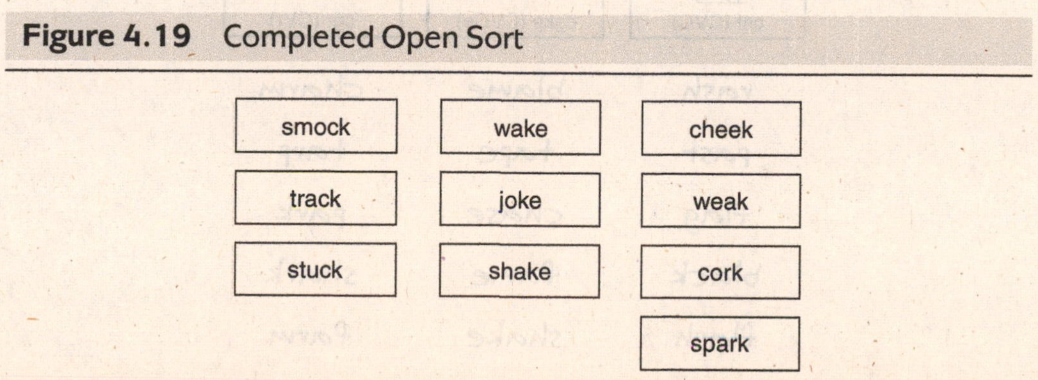

sorts can be completed by students independently or in groups with teacher support. The following provides you with a procedure for group implementation.

1. *Demonstrate.* Review the keywords and model placement of at least one word. You could use the following language when comparing short, long, and *r*-controlled *a* (e.g., *cat, cake,* and *car*).

> **Teacher:** I just picked up the word *blame* from my pack of word cards. As I look at this word, I see the CVCe spelling pattern so I know that the vowel sound in the middle is long *a*—pronounced /ā/. I'm going to write *blame* under the keyword *cake* because it has the long *a* sound and the CVCe spelling pattern. That looks right and sounds right.

2. *Sort.* This step will take your students through a three-part process: pick a word, choose the category, and spell the word. If a student has difficulty, you might take the following approach:

> **Student:** [Student can't decide where the word *charm* fits.] I'm not sure where this one goes.
> **Teacher:** What vowel sound do you hear in the middle of this word?
> **Student:** [Student slowly sounds out word.] ch-aaaar-m.
> **Teacher:** So does the middle sound in *charm* sound more like *cat, cake,* or *car*? [Teacher points to each category keyword.]
> **Student:** It sounds like *car.*
> **Teacher:** Yes, your thinking is on the right track. You can use what you know about the keyword *car* to spell and read similar words like *charm.* So, when you hear /är/, you can think of the keyword *car* and its spelling pattern *ar.*

3. *Check.* Have the students read each column after they are finished and consider each category's sound, pattern, and position. As much as possible, guide students to discover mistakes rather than telling them where they are. Your students need to then assess why a particular word is in the wrong category as well as what the appropriate category would be. You also need to find out what they are thinking.

4. *Reflect.* Regardless of whether or not a mistake was made, students need to reflect on the sort. A discussion about each category's common features is critical. For example, after reading the words *charm, tarp, park, shark,* and *farm,* you would discuss that each of

Figure 4.20 Writing Sort

Short a cat (CVC)	Long a cake (CVCe)	r-Controlled car (CVr)
rash	blame	charm
past	tape	tarp
flag	chase	park
black	fame	shark
flash	shake	farm

these words has the /ar/ sound with the spelling pattern *ar* like in *car*. They sound right and look right. Refer back to the visual of the keyword for additional support.

Blind Writing Sort

Blind sorts should be done after students have had the opportunity to sort the words for the week several times. This activity provides your students with multiple opportunities to practice and work with the features being studied as they write words without seeing them. You should model the blind sort in a group setting several times and then let students work in pairs independently.

Procedure

1. Review the categories and prepare a blank sort page for recording (i.e., a page divided into the categories with the keywords written at the top).
2. Call out the words in random order without showing the word and ask the students to write the words in the appropriate category.
3. Check the blind sort after it is completed. If this is a sort by student pairs, they can check using a sort "cheat sheet" or with a student "checker."
4. After the sort, you could have your students reflect on any errors using a student reflection chart (see Chapter 3). Or as your students do subsequent blind sorts across the week, they could chart their progress. Just as students chart decreases in time required to complete sorts during speed sorting, your students can chart increases in accuracy while doing blind sorts. See Figure 4.21 for an example of an accuracy chart.

engagement LINK

Having students hunt through their own compositions concretely illustrates one important reason for word study: to improve their writing.

Word Hunt

The goal of a word hunt is to take isolated word work and link the target features to connected text. Students are sent back to texts they have

Figure 4.21 Accuracy Chart for Blind Sorting

10			
9			
8			
7			
6			
5			
4			
3			
2			
1			
	First Time	Second Time	Third Time
	Words to work on: chain shame trait	Words to work on. blame trait	Words to work on. Got 100%!

previously read or compositions they have previously written to hunt for words that follow the same target features examined during their teacher-directed lessons. These words are then recorded in the appropriate categories.

Procedure

1. Review the keywords for the sort. For example, if your writing sort uses the features long *o* as in *bone,* /ȯi/ as in *oil,* and /ȯi/ as in *boy,* you would review the sound, pattern, and position of the target features. As you review the target sound, pattern, and position, you should always bring the discussion back to the keywords (e.g., *bone, oil,* and *boy*). See the sample word hunt in Figure 4.22.
2. Engage the students in finding words for their target categories.

Teacher: [Sitting down to conference with a student who has just completed a quarter-long study of ambiguous vowel patterns.] So today I see you did a word hunt in your draft composition to check your spelling while editing. Did you find any words that followed the spelling features we studied this quarter? Remember you get a point for finding words you spelled correctly and a point for finding words spelled incorrectly that you changed.

engagement LINK

The points collected for finding words can be applied to their final grade on the composition. This can be a powerful extrinsic motivator to use the spelling knowledge they have gained in word study and apply it to writing.

Student: I found some of each. Let me show you. [Student reads down lists showing words that were correct, like *frown,* and words that were spelled incorrectly and changed like MOWND (*mound*).]

3. After completing the hunt, review each category. Have the students read each column and verbalize what is the same about each category in terms of sound, pattern, and position.

Figure 4.22 Word Hunt

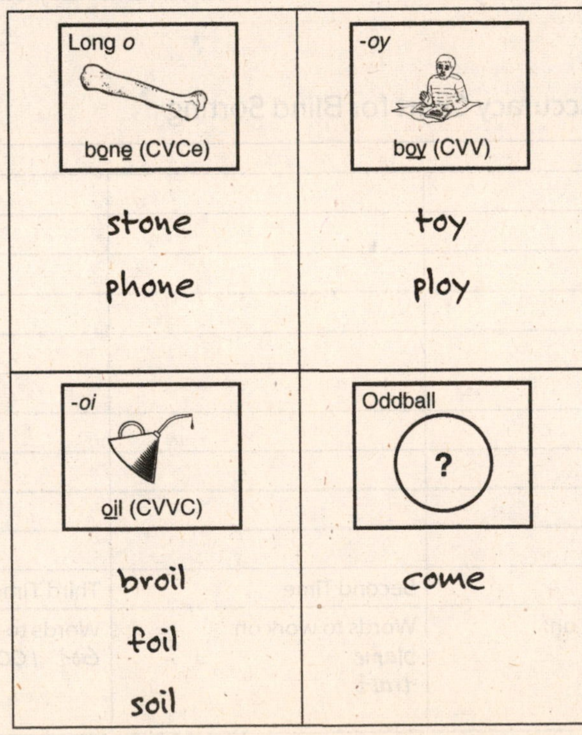

Manipulation

The goal of manipulation is to segment and blend words at the level of the phoneme (e.g., /ch/ /ā/ /n/—*chain*). Elkonin-type boxes can be used to help make the divisions of sounds more distinct. See Figure 4.23 for an example. Not only does manipulation practice help solidify phoneme-level skills but it also can help emphasize the spelling patterns that are such a presence in within word pattern features. For example, students who are beginning to work with short and long vowels can focus on the influence of the *e*-marker by changing *can* to *cane* or *hop* to *hope*. You should explicitly talk about the sounds in words, emphasizing each sound. The number of sounds in words can be discussed. For example, *chain* has three sounds —/ch/ /ā/ /n/. Words should be blended back together after segmentation.

Procedure

1. Begin the manipulation activity with a word said aloud for the students.
2. Have your students make the word using letter tiles, dry erase boards, and so on.
3. If necessary, guide your students in their thinking. You can support them by explicitly talking about sounds and connecting them to keywords.

Student: I'm not sure how to write *train*.

Teacher: What is our first step when we aren't sure how to spell a word? [Teacher refers student to a chart in her word study notebook outlining these steps.]

Student: See how many sounds are in the word. /t-r-ā-n/. That's four.

Teacher: Okay, what's your next step?

Student: Write it out and match my letter patterns to the sounds. So, the beginning is easy: *tr*. And so is the end: *n*. [Student writes the following: tr /__/ n.] It's the middle that's confusing me.

Teacher: What sound is it and what are the possible ways to spell that sound? Remember you can go back to our big picture chart.

Student: I hear a long *a*. Let's see. I know a few ways to spell long *a:* CVCe like in *cake*, CVVC like in *rain*, and CVV like in *tray*. [Student refers to the big picture chart.] It isn't CVV like in *tray* since the long *a* isn't the last sound I hear. Oh yeah, the end of the word is /ān/. It's probably *-ain* like *rain*, right?

4. Orally provide the next word. Be sure to include vowel changes in which students negotiate the vowel. Once multiple spelling patterns for the same sound are covered (e.g., the *ai* and *ay* spelling patterns for long *a*), be sure to include word sets in which these patterns "compete," forcing students to cope with multiple spelling pattern options. For

Figure 4.23 Elkonin Boxes for Manipulation

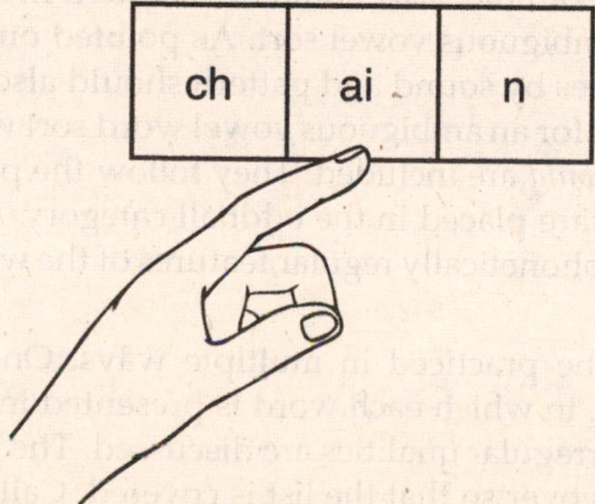

example, in the long *a* exercise, have students consider the following words: *ran, rain, pain, pay, paid, pad.*

5. If you notice your students having difficulty going from one word to the next, provide additional support. Direct them to determine whether the change is in the beginning, middle, or end of the word. Explicitly talk about the change that was made (i.e., *where* the change was made and *which letters* were switched and *why*). For example, the discussion of *pot* into *port* would point out that the change is in the middle of the word, changing short *o* into an *r*-controlled *o*. The remainder of the discussion would lead to the correct spelling pattern for the *r*-controlled *o* in *port,* bringing in the keyword, *horn.*

High-Frequency Words

It is not uncommon for older struggling readers to experience difficulty reading and spelling high-frequency words. How many times have you had a student read *through* as *though* or *thought* or *throw?* Words like these (e.g., *said, because, was*) are often referred to as "sight words"; they must be learned "by sight" because they are not entirely decodable. They are also highly frequent in the English language—it is nearly impossible to read and write with any degree of fluency without a command of these words.

Traditional approaches emphasize rote memorization of these words because they are not considered phonetically regular. This is not the whole story. For example, in the word *from,* three of the four letters *are* phonetically regular. *From* would be included as an oddball in a sort with short *o* words like *stop* and *block.* Including it in the context of this sort requires the student to focus on the only part of the word that is not regular, the *o.* Students no longer have to rely on rote memorization of the entire word but only need to attend to the fact that the *o* does not represent the regular short *o* sound. We have included many high-frequency words in Appendix D (they are noted with an asterisk) in order to assist you in planning your inclusion of these words during word study. Please notice that many of the top 200 most frequently occurring words (Dolch, 1942; Fry & Kress, 2006) should be covered by the end of the within word pattern stage.

Coverage of high-frequency words should not replace developmental word study but rather supplement such study. We offer the following guidelines about high-frequency words.

1. A cumulative list should be kept for reference either individually in personal word study notebooks or writing folders or by the classroom as a posting in the room. New words should be added to the lists as they are covered. Additionally, students may take part by selecting words they frequently use and adding them to collected lists. Students should commit to ensuring that all their written work will spell these words correctly.

2. Include high-frequency words in your weekly word study. Select words based on utility and their relationships to the features of study. Some high-frequency words are phonetically regular (e.g., *not* and *make*) and should be included in sorts when you cover a feature they follow. For example, *make* could be included in a long vowel sort or *good* could be included in an ambiguous vowel sort. As pointed out, high-frequency words that do not meet the features by sound and pattern should also be included. See Figure 4.15 for a sample word sort for an ambiguous vowel word sort where the high-frequency words *could, would,* and *should* are included. They follow the pattern of the sort but not the sound; therefore, they are placed in the oddball category. A discussion about these words should include the phonetically regular features of the words, as well as how they deviate from the feature.

3. These words should be practiced in multiple ways. One writing activity is the self-corrected test method, in which each word is presented in a written format and its phonetically regular and irregular qualities are discussed. The students write the words and then fold their papers over so that the list is covered. Call the words out while the

Figure 4.24 Sentence Bingo

B	I	N	G	O
out	away	give	now	these
some	**could**	come	again	from
place	once	around	they	because
would	under	know	should	over
work	have	other	friend	what

Could I borrow a piece of paper?

students write them again. The students can then check their spellings for accuracy by unfolding the paper. If any words are misspelled, the students write them again. The self-study method requires students to look at the word and say it, cover the word, write the word, check the word, and write the word again if it is spelled incorrectly.

4. Study high-frequency words in sets of words that are related. For example, students can also investigate *said* along with words like *laid* and *paid* where the present tense of both words is *lay* and *pay* (the present tense of *said* is *say*). This shows that the spelling pattern for the past tense of *say* is not irregular at all, but the pronunciation of it is.

5. Review of high-frequency words has historically fallen into the realm of isolated practice (e.g., flash cards, writing isolated words, etc.), but you can also work with these words in a sentence context. For example, in a modification of traditional Bingo, as seen in Figure 4.24, high-frequency words of study are written on Bingo cards, but are provided within sentences rather than as isolated words written on cards. A student might draw the sentence "Could I borrow a piece of paper?" for the word *could*. The student then finds the word *could* on his or her Bingo board. In order to make the match the student would have to correctly write the word.

Word Analysis

Struggling readers often get bogged down in the middles of words and make a guess based on the initial letters of the word and the context. Students who can break words into parts and analogize to keywords for support will have more success while decoding. Consider the following words: *rail, trail, snail, ailment,* and *detail.* A brief look is all a reader would need to realize the common letter pattern from one word to the next, the *-ail* phonogram (one of the high-frequency phonograms from Table 4.2). Once readers realize this generativity and reoccurrence of letter patterns, they can use this knowledge to help them read and spell unknown words.

When beginning a study of analogies, keywords can be helpful because they provide an anchor for the high-frequency phonogram and may help students remember the letter pattern (Gaskins et al., 1988). A study of single-syllable words to exemplify each phonogram is recommended. This encourages students to look inside the two-part structure of a syllable, the onset and the rime. The *onset* is the consonant(s) that come before the vowel in a syllable or a single-syllable word such as the *tr* in train. The *rime* is the vowel and everything that follows, such as the *ain* in train. We are only interested in rimes that share the same pronunciation and spelling patterns as in *sheep* and *beep* rather than words that share the same pronunciation but different spelling patterns as in *sheep* and *cheap*. This is why we focus on high-frequency phonograms; *eep* as in *sheep* is more frequent than *eap* as in *cheap*. Use the following guidelines to assist you in your planning of analogy instruction.

1. Use keywords to exemplify the high-frequency phonograms (or rimes) for study along with a picture cue to match the keyword. This procedure will not only help your students remember keywords for reference but will also help them remember pronunciations and letter patterns. See Table 4.1 for an optional list of keywords. For example, when covering the high-frequency phonogram *-ight*, you would use the keyword *light* with a picture cue. These keywords can be displayed in the classroom in a multitude of ways. We have organized them on posters by vowels, provided students with individualized sets on papers in their reading/writing folders, used them in sorts, and so on.

2. Explicitly demonstrate how to use the analogy strategy. Most students need help from teachers when trying to employ this strategy. For example, to help a student decode the unknown word *maintain*, think aloud by saying, "I know the word *rain*. The *-ain* in *rain* says /ā n/. So this word must be *main-tain*, because it has the same chunks *-ain* as in *rain*." Always remember to have students check their decoding by making sure that the word makes sense in the sentence.

3. Demonstrate how the onset can be changed and new words made by holding the rime (or high-frequency phonogram) constant as in the manipulations described earlier. For example, using the phonogram *-ock*, the words *block, dock, shock, clock, rock*, and many more can be made. You can even include two-syllable words like *livestock* and *stockpile* (but only if the sound and pattern match). You may want to encourage students to keep collections of words that have similar phonograms.

4. Make sure to focus on high-frequency phonograms. From a practical sense, students need to concentrate on patterns that are the most helpful, which would be the most commonly found and used phonograms. Again, please refer to Table 4.2 for the most common phonograms.

Games

Games provide the extra practice and review needed by struggling readers. Games are engaging due to the social interaction involved, and the competition aspect of games can be motivating for many adolescents. If competition is an issue for the students, you can modify the games by having students work collaboratively. For example, when playing a board game, the students could work together to move one playing piece through the game.

Many traditional and commercial games can be adapted for word study practice, especially those that involve sets of two or more. For example, the card game Slap Jack involves turning over two words simultaneously. If the words share a common sound or spelling pattern, the first player who slaps the cards gets to keep them. Similarly, the game Memory can be adapted for word pairs like homophones.

Homophone Rummy

This card game can be played with two to six players. As with the traditional card game Rummy, the object is to get the most pairs. You first need to prepare several decks of homophone pairs (52 cards, 26 pairs). Be sure to only use those words with features you have already studied. For example, if you have covered features 1, 2, and 3 (as described earlier in the chapter) only, then do not include words from features 4 and beyond. Write the words in the upper-left corners of the cards and follow the rules listed. Note that this

Figure 4.25 Homophone Rummy

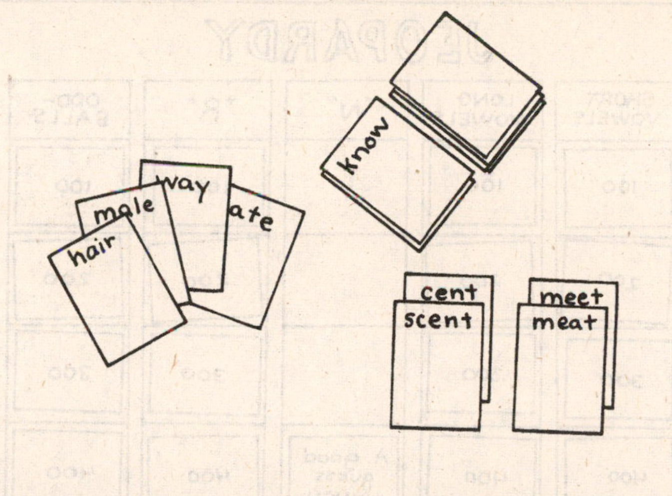

card game can be adapted in a variety of ways. For example, your students could work to create pairs of words by feature.

1. Players are dealt seven cards and begin the game by checking their hands for already existing pairs. Once a pair is discovered, it can be laid down in front of the player. The player must give the meaning for each word and use it in a sentence that makes the meaning clear.
2. The remainder of the deck is placed in a central location and the first card is turned face-up beside it to form a discard pile.
3. The person on the left of the dealer goes first. Each player draws from either the deck or the discard pile. Any new pairs are laid down and defined. The player must then discard one card to end the turn. If a card is taken from the discard pile, all the cards below are also taken and the top card must be used to make a pair.
4. A player can be challenged if another player disagrees with the definitions offered. The person who challenges looks up the words in the dictionary. Whoever is right gets to keep the pair.
5. The game is over when one player has no cards left. That player yells, "Rummy!" Then the pairs are counted up to determine the winner. An extension would be for your students to identify the sound and pattern features of their pairs. In addition, your students could keep a written record of their pairs.

Jeopardy

This take on the classic Jeopardy game, adapted by Charlotte Tucker, is designed for four or five students. During play, students must recall and spell words that follow a particular pattern. A poster board should be divided into 5-by-5-inch squares as shown in Figure 4.26. Clue cards are created and placed in each space. One side of the clue card has the clue with the answer, and the other side shows the amount. Place the cards on the board so that the amount is showing and play as follows.

1. One player is the moderator or game host. The others roll a die to determine who goes first.
2. The game begins when the first player picks a category and an amount for the moderator to read. For example, "I'll take short vowels for 100." The moderator reads the clue and the player responds by phrasing the question and spelling the word. So if the moderator reads the clue, "When struck, it produces fire," the player would

Figure 4.26 Word Jeopardy

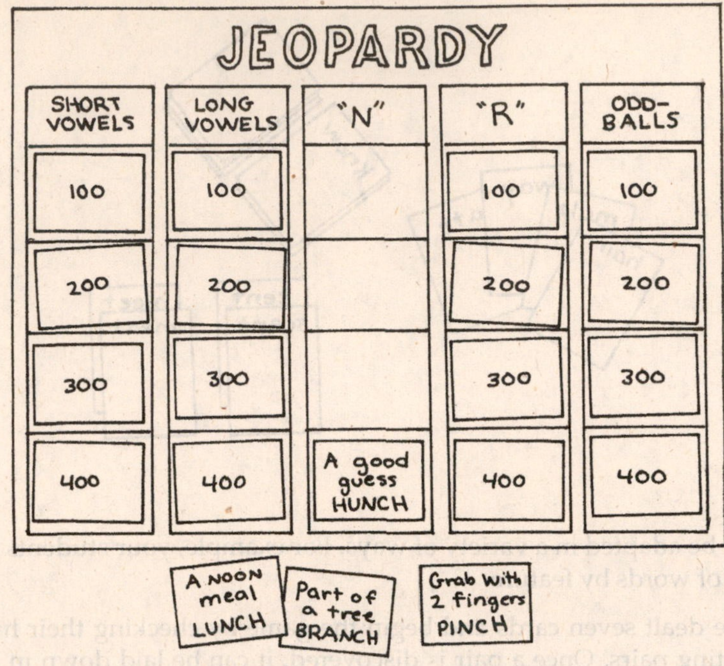

respond by saying, "What is match? *M-a-t-c-h.*" Your students could also make a written record of these words and provide an explanation of the feature

3. The player receives the card if the answer is correct. This player chooses another clue; however, players can only have two consecutive turns. If the player is incorrect, the player to the left may answer.
4. The game continues until all the clue cards are read and won or left unanswered. Players then add their points and the one accumulating the highest amount is the winner.

e Syllables
d Affixes Stage

Carson High School offers a Basic English class to students who are not yet achieving on grade level. Ms. Baker, the reading specialist, has grouped her basic reading classes by reading and word study ability levels (as assessed by performance on the Elementary Spelling Inventory—ESI); this enables her to focus instruction on the needs of the group and makes lesson planning and management much easier. To balance this homogenous grouping in the basic reading classes, these students are heterogeneously grouped in science, social studies, language arts, and specials to ensure that they interact with a diverse range of students at a variety of ability levels across the rest of the school day. Ms. Baker's first period students read at the fifth to sixth grade level instructionally and are all in the syllables and affixes stage of spelling development.

This week in word study the class is examining the doubling principle in multi-syllabic words, a primary area of need identified in her comprehensive literacy intervention plan. Specifically, they are comparing and contrasting V-CV (e.g., *pilot*), VC-CV (e.g., *basket*), and VC-V (e.g., *comet*) pattern words. Here is a sample of the word study words for this week:

V-CV (open)	**VC-CV (closed)**	**VC-V (closed)**
pilot	basket	comet
pony	cactus	robin
photo	center	never
sequel	canyon	balance
vacant	ransom	talent

Today is Monday. Ms. Baker has planned an open sort. The students will work to figure out the patterns this week on their own. At the beginning of the year, Ms. Baker was much more explicit in introducing sorts and patterns to her struggling readers. She usually began the week with a teacher-directed closed sort for each word study group. However, finding that students were starting to look for patterns in words on their own and becoming much better at applying word study to their writing and reading, she began to gradually release responsibility to the students. When she plans to bring new features to the table for study that build on previously learned features, she starts Mondays with open sorts to provide students with an opportunity to examine words independently and make their own discoveries.

For this particular week, having previously introduced the V-CV (open) and VC-CV (closed) syllable patterns, Ms. Baker was bringing in the new pattern of VC-V (closed). She chose an open sort because she felt that the students had the background knowledge necessary to support their independent sorting of the new feature. If the students needed more support, she would guide them toward an understanding of the sort when she pulled the word study group together. At this point, she would close down the sort and explicitly explain and model her thinking as she sorted the first few words. Then she would turn the sort over to the students to finish on their own.

Luisa, one of Ms. Baker's first period students, sits at her desk, cuts out the words, and begins to sort. Initially, she has a puzzled look on her face and says, "Ms. Baker, *comet* doesn't follow the V-CV pattern. Look, it's short." Ms. Baker agrees with Luisa and tells her to pull *comet* out into its own column. After a few seconds, Luisa yells, "I got it" and starts to categorize the words by the V-CV (open), VC-CV (closed), and VC-V (closed) patterns.

After students have had a chance to explore the words for about five minutes, Ms. Baker pulls the group together and begins to discuss the words and patterns with the students. When asked why he sorted the words the way he did, Will replies, "Words in these two columns, like *pilot* and *comet*, have one consonant in the middle. Words in this column, like *basket*, have two consonants in the middle." The group begins to discuss the three syllable patterns. Then Ms. Baker asks the group if these three columns *sound* different. From the lack of response, it becomes apparent that most students were sorting by sight (the visual pattern difference between V-CV and VC-CV) but weren't consciously attending to the sound difference between the columns. Ms. Baker asks students to listen to the first syllable of words like *pilot* and *comet*. She then guides the students to the understanding that the V-CV (open) column words all have long vowel sounds in the first syllable (e.g., *sequel* and *vacant*) and the VC-V (closed) column words all have short vowel sounds in the first syllable (e.g., *talent* and *robin*), like the short vowel in VC-CV (closed) column words (e.g., *canyon* and *ransom*). The consonant encloses the vowel to ensure a short vowel sound.

After asking students to gather their word cards but leave the three headers (VC-CV, VC-V, and V-CV), she tells them to re-sort the words quickly by *sight* and *sound*, asking themselves, "Does the word sound right? Does the word look right?" Ms. Baker notices Tyler struggling with the sort. She makes a mental note to give him a few extra minutes of her time and to explicitly model and think aloud while reteaching him the sort. She realizes that he may need more explicit teaching of this particular sort than the other students in the group. However, she also has many other opportunities built in during the week for struggling students to examine the words, providing Tyler and the others more chances to internalize the syllable patterns. Ms. Baker will also use Wednesday's word analysis work as another excellent opportunity to explicitly teach and model the patterns of study (see Word Analysis near the end of this chapter for a detailed explanation of this activity). During this word analysis work, students will be taught and given practice on how to apply their knowledge of syllable patterns in decoding unknown words during reading.

Ms. Baker has been very careful to include many critical elements of effective word study instruction for struggling adolescents. She engages her students in multiple ways by putting the investigation in their hands. Considering the continuum of support, she has decided that an open sort would best suit her purpose. Open sorting inherently demands higher-level thinking and deep processing. She has ensured that all of her students receive instruction based on their assessed needs, and throughout the week she involves her students in multiple activities to help them connect and categorize the features of study.

Reading, Writing, and Spelling Characteristics

The syllables and affixes stage of spelling corresponds with the intermediate stage of reading development. Students at this stage, like Ms. Baker's first period class, need to sharpen their reading strategies and broaden their reading interests. The instructional focus in the upper elementary and middle grades moves to the content area subjects and thus, a greater emphasis is placed on reading textbooks and various types of informational text. A student's background knowledge and vocabulary are crucial to their learning, much more so than at any previous stage. Previously, a student's understanding of words and how words work was the catalyst, but now a student's *world* knowledge—rather than *word* knowledge—takes center stage. Likewise, their writing is now more focused on conveying a message rather than the act of getting words on a page or constructing sentences; these skills are now effortless.

Generally, average-achieving intermediate readers are not involved in the "divide and conquer" reading of earlier stages where readers must spend cognitive energy on decoding words and constructing meaning (LaBerge & Samuels, 1974). As they gain confidence in reading and improve fluency, they expend less and less energy on decoding words so more of their cognitive energy can be devoted to understanding and learning new information. Word recognition is no longer a major challenge during reading. As Chall (1983) put it, they are clearly "reading to learn" in books like Jean Fritz's *Shh! We're Writing the Constitution* (fifth grade level), historical fiction about the Constitutional Convention of 1787. However, it is important to keep in mind that struggling readers at the intermediate stage may not fit this description. These students are able to work at a meaning level due to their age and maturity but continue to struggle at the word level, often resulting in relatively slow, disfluent reading and writing.

Reading in the Intermediate Stage

Intermediate readers are most commonly found in grades 3 through 8 (Bear et al., 2008). Rather than having the choppy quality of reading so typical of the transitional reader, the intermediate reader has a phrasal quality and smoothness to reading. They know how to interpret punctuation marks and read phrases, allowing them to pause at appropriate points in the text. These readers reach oral reading speeds of 140 words per minute or better (Carnine, Silbert, Kame'enui, & Tarver, 2004; Hasbrouck & Tindal, 1992) and have silent reading speeds approaching 200 words per minute (Morris, 2008). They read significantly faster silently compared to orally and prefer it.

Many struggling readers in the middle and high school grades, like in Ms. Baker's first period class, are also intermediate readers, who find themselves stalled in this stage. Struggling readers at this stage often still have difficulty in the area of fluency. You may see struggling students in this stage who still need work on appropriate phrasing or with their reading speed. Or you may work with a student who struggles with decoding and storing unknown multisyllabic words, requiring syllabication practice for assistance while reading (see Word Analysis on pages 155–157 for a detailed explanation of this activity).

Writing in the Intermediate Stage

Just as reading becomes more confident and fluent, so does writing. Intermediate writers are typically very fluent in their writing, only pausing when they want to consider various ways to express themselves. Their efforts are focused on conveying meaning in the most effective, creative way. They are working on their voices as writers, sometimes heavily engaged in revision, and are more aware of their audience. Additionally, these writers are more cognizant of another writer's craft. Often these students will notice another writer's style and attempt to emulate it in their own pieces. Just as fluency may continue to be an issue for struggling readers at this stage, it may continue to be an issue for them as writers. You may see this manifested in the limited lengths of their written pieces.

See Figure 5.1 to view a written piece by one of Ms. Baker's first period students, Luisa, about seeing deer in her neighborhood. Notice the evidence of voice in this piece but also notice the length of the piece. This paragraph took Luisa approximately ten minutes to write. Also notice her limited word choice, a common issue for struggling readers because of their limited spelling knowledge. They tend to stick with words they are sure they can spell. Luisa uses a variety of sentence structures, demonstrating a

Figure 5.1 Luisa's Writing Sample

Front Yard

One day I was ridding my bike up and down my driveway. When three deer ran out of the woods. There was a mom and two babies. When I slid to a stop the mom stoped and looked at me. I looked at her. As she was walking away I stomped my foot and the deer stomped her foot So I memicked her whet ever she did I did. This went on for about forty-five minets to a hour. It was vary neat to watch and do.

more sophisticated approach to writing; however, she sometimes ends up with run-on sentences in her efforts for variety and does not include internal punctuation. Her spelling errors are also reflective of a student in the syllables and affixes stage (e.g., STOPED for *stopped* and RIDDING for *riding*). High-frequency word errors are also evident (e.g., VARY for *very* and WHET for *what*). Such persistent errors are often found in the writings of struggling adolescents.

Spelling in the Intermediate Stage

Intermediate readers and writers are syllables and affixes spellers. Although they have been reading and writing multisyllable words for some time, these longer words do not become the focus of instruction until this stage. Whereas the within word pattern speller learned about the various patterns that can be used to represent the long *o* sound in single-syllable words (e.g., b<u>one</u>, b<u>oa</u>t, sn<u>ow</u>, c<u>old</u>), the syllables and affixes speller is learning how these patterns work in multisyllabic words (e.g., *expl<u>ode</u>, appr<u>oa</u>ch, bel<u>ow</u>, rev<u>olt</u>*). These readers are straddling the pattern and meaning tiers of written language. Not only must they think about patterns within multisyllabic words, but they must also connect to meaning as they consider simple affixes (prefixes and suffixes) in words like *<u>re</u>told* and *soap<u>y</u>*. They need to understand where syllable and morphemic breaks occur so they can use that information to quickly and accurately "chunk" words for reading and spelling. The word *unhappy,* for example, can be analyzed as a three-syllable word (*un-hap-py*) or as a word with two morphemic components (*un-happy*).

Luisa's spelling sample is illustrative of students at this stage (see Figure 5.2). Although she does have one long vowel pattern error (FLOTE for *float*), the majority of words with vowel patterns and letter name features are correct. The majority of her errors cluster in the early syllables and affixes stage. Notice her confusion when attempting an inflectional ending (e.g., SHOPING for *sho<u>pping</u>* and CARYIES for *carr<u>ies</u>*) or a common suffix (e.g., RIPPEN for *rip<u>en</u>*). In addition, she demonstrates difficulty when spelling unaccented syllable endings, as in her attempts to spell *cell<u>ar</u>* (CELLER) and *bott<u>le</u>* (BOTTEL).

Ms. Baker meets with Luisa after scoring and interpreting her ESI. The conference's purpose is to set long-term goals for the year and short-term goals for the quarter. Ms. Baker begins the meeting by showing Luisa a chart outlining late within word pattern and early syllables and affixes features (see Figure 5.3, p. 130). Appendix B has many goal charts that you can use for communicating with your students and their parents. Ms. Baker decides to start with vowel patterns because leading off with the student's strength is a good way to begin talking about needs. While using the chart to illustrate her points, Ms. Baker discusses Luisa's clear understanding of various vowel patterns (long, *r*-controlled, and ambiguous) found at the end of the within word pattern stage. "Luisa, when I looked at your spelling

engagement LINK

Mrs. Baker makes certain to include assessment-based instruction to ensure that Luisa receives developmentally appropriate instruction. Not only will Luisa be involved in "just right" instruction, but she will be able to make more progress than she would in grade-level material.

Figure 5.2 Luisa's Elementary Spelling Inventory

bed	
ship	
when	
lump	
flote	(float)
train	
place	
drive	
bright	
shoping	(shopping)
spoil	
serveing	(serving)
chewed	
caryies	(carries)
marched	
shower	
bottel	(bottle)
favor	
rippen	(ripen)
celler	(cellar)
plesure	(pleasure)
forchnut	(fortunate)
cofdent	(confident)
sivized	(civilized)
oposhition	(opposition)

sample from yesterday, I could see that you know a lot about vowel patterns in one-syllable words like the *ou* in *cloud*, the *oi* in *oil*, and the *au* in *sauce*." Ms. Baker points to these words on the late within word chart as she is talking. "How do you feel about using vowel patterns?"

"I don't feel like those are a problem for me at all," Luisa replies.

"I agree. So, let's move to the next chart. Good. You are on your way. Now let's talk about how things went when you spelled two-syllable words. We'll start with adding endings like *-ed* and *-ing*. I noticed that this was an area where we could do some work. In your spelling sample, you spelled *shopping* like this." She writes SHOPING on the dry erase board. "And *carries* like this." She writes CARYIES on the board. "These are both misspelled. I noticed a similar thing in your writing. Remember your story about the deer?" Ms. Baker pulls out her story. "*Stopped* and *riding* were both misspelled. Adding endings like these is an area were we can work and make some progress. What do you think?"

Figure 5.3 Goal Setting Chart for Early Syllables and Affixes

Categories	Features	Date Feature Mastered
Adding endings *-s, -es* *-ed* *-ing*	Plurals no change *(apples)*, + es *(boxes)*, *y* to *i* + es *(flies)* Adding *-ed* and *-ing* no change *(jumped, sleeping)*, e-drop *(raced, smiling)*, double *(dropped, winning)*	______ ______
Date Category Mastered:		
Syllable juncture patterns	V-CV open *(pi-lot)*	______
	VC-CV doublet *(rab-bit)*	______
	VC-CV regular *(bas-ket)*	______
	VC-V closed *(com-et)*	______
	VC-CCV *(pil-grim)*	______
	VCC-CV *(ath-lete)*	______
	V-V *(li-on)*	______
Date Category Mastered:		

"Okay. I didn't think I was wrong on those. Adding those endings seems to be so easy. I mean, I know about dropping the *e*."

"Yes, I know. It is one that you know, but there are other things to know beyond the *e* drop. I think we should focus on those as we begin the year."

"So how much do you think I can learn this year?" Luisa asks.

"What would you like for a goal?" Ms. Baker seeks Luisa's input.

"Is it possible to get through all of the things on this chart?" says Luisa.

Ms. Baker shows Luisa how they might move into the syllables and affixes stage of spelling and briefly talks about the features throughout the stage. She then makes the following recommendation. "I think we can work toward that and possibly go farther. Let's make our long-term goal to master all patterns at the syllable juncture." Ms. Baker writes the word *basket* on the dry erase board. "Like this word, *basket*. The juncture of the syllable is where the two syllables come together, *bas-ket*. We'll check for progress in our goal conferences and can change this goal if we want to . . . if you are making quicker progress and can up the ante. How does that sound?"

engagement LINK

Mrs. Baker has made Luisa a part of the process of goal setting and has created an environment of self-directed learning. Luisa has ownership of her learning; she is in the driver's seat.

Luisa agrees, and Ms. Baker writes down the long-term goal. At that point, they talk about the short-term goals for the quarter. Luisa says that she wants to learn how to add endings and asks if that would take the entire quarter. Ms. Baker tells her that she could probably move on to syllable juncture patterns. They decide to add the V-CV open and VC-CV closed syllable juncture patterns. Figure 5.4 shows the goals Luisa and Ms. Baker created for the quarter. These are taped inside her word study notebook for quick reference.

Figure 5.4 Luisa's Goals for the Quarter

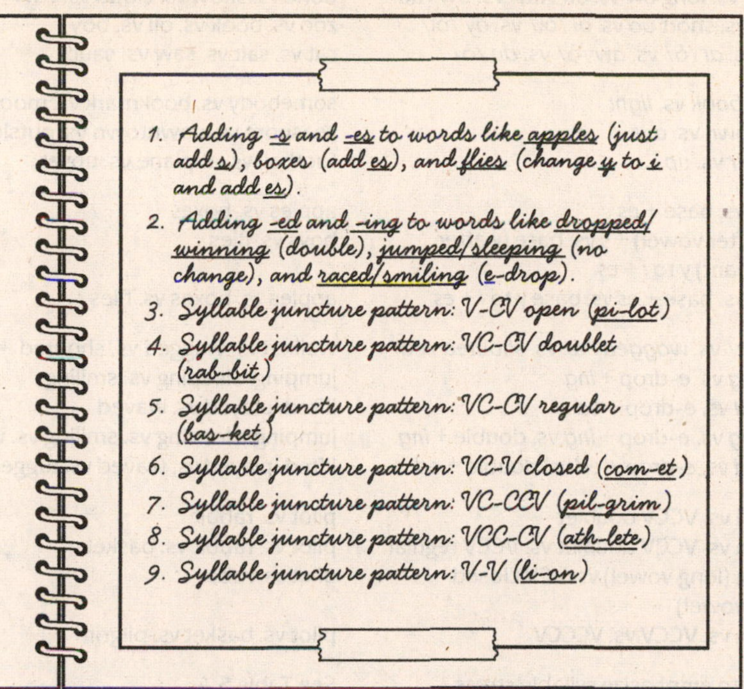

1. Adding -s and -es to words like apples (just add s), boxes (add es), and flies (change y to i and add es).
2. Adding -ed and -ing to words like dropped/winning (double), jumped/sleeping (no change), and raced/smiling (e-drop).
3. Syllable juncture pattern: V-CV open (pi-lot)
4. Syllable juncture pattern: VC-CV doublet (rab-bit)
5. Syllable juncture pattern: VC-CV regular (bas-ket)
6. Syllable juncture pattern: VC-V closed (com-et)
7. Syllable juncture pattern: VC-CCV (pil-grim)
8. Syllable juncture pattern: VCC-CV (ath-lete)
9. Syllable juncture pattern: V-V (li-on)

The Syllables and Affixes Stage: Sequence of Development

There is a lot to cover in the syllables and affixes stage, and it takes most students several years to master. You may find it necessary to quickly review ambiguous vowels, one of the last features in the within word pattern stage. Or you may find that you can move into the syllables and affixes stage with compound words. You will progress to adding plurals and other inflectional endings to one-syllable words. The sequence continues with a study of common syllable patterns, vowel patterns in accented syllables, plurals and inflectional endings in two-syllable words, final unaccented syllables, special consonants in two-syllable words, and simple affixes.

A suggested sequence can be found in Table 5.1. Note that an exemplar word is provided for each sound/pattern to be used while introducing the feature of study. Where teachers place students in this sequence depends on student performance on the spelling inventories discussed in Chapter 3. Movement after initial placement will depend on daily student performance and indicators of transfer such as in their writing samples. Teachers must also be cognizant of student needs in order to quicken or slow down the pace when necessary. This is especially important for struggling readers, because instruction needs to honor developmental needs while keeping an eye to acceleration. For example, categories can be added in order to cover more ground at one time, or sorts within categories may be skipped if the concept is grasped in fewer sorts. If students exhibit confusion, teachers can step back and cover fewer, more obvious contrasts.

The Syllables and Affixes Stage: Development and Instruction

You can provide your students with a visual representation of the features of study to help them organize and connect new features with those previously learned. This "big

Table 5.1 Suggested Sequence for Syllables and Affixes

Feature Sequence	Introductory Pace	Exemplars
Review ambiguous vowels in one-syllable words	Long *u-e* vs. *ew* vs. long *oo* /ü/ vs. short *oo* /ů/	cube/June vs. stew vs. zoo vs. book
	Long *o-e* vs. long *ow* vs. *ou* /aů/ vs. ow /aů/	bone vs. snow vs. cloud vs. cow
	Long *oo* vs. short *oo* vs. *oi* /ȯi/ vs. *oy* /ȯi/	zoo vs. book vs. oil vs. boy
	Short *a* vs. *al* /ȯ/ vs. *aw* /ȯ/ vs. *au* /ȯ/	cat vs. salt vs. saw vs. sauce
Compound words	*some* vs. *book* vs. *light*	somebody vs. bookmark vs. moonlight
	sea vs. *down* vs. *out*	seashore vs. downtown vs. outside
	foot vs. *air* vs. *up*	football vs. airplane vs. upset
Plurals in one-syllable words	Base + *s* vs. base + *es*	apples vs. boxes
	Base (*y* after vowel) + *s* vs. base (*y* after consonant) *y* to *i* + *es*	boys vs. flies
	Base + *s* vs. base + *es* vs. base *y* to *i* + *es*	apples vs. boxes vs. flies
Inflectional endings in one-syllable words	*walked* /t/ vs. *wagged* /d/ vs. *shouted* /ed/	walked vs. wagged vs. shouted
	Base + *ing* vs. e-drop + *ing*	jumping/sleeping vs. smiling
	Base + *ed* vs. e-drop + *ed*	lifted/played vs. waved
	Base + *ing* vs. e-drop + *ing* vs. double + *ing*	jumping/sleeping vs. smiling vs. winning
	Base + *ed* vs. e-drop + *ed* vs. double + *ed*	lifted/played vs. waved vs. tugged
Syllable juncture patterns	VCV open vs. VCCV doublet	pilot vs. rabbit
	VCV open vs. VCCV doublet vs. VCCV regular	pilot vs. rabbit vs. basket
	VCV open (long vowel) vs. VCV closed (short vowel)	pilot vs. robin
	VCV open vs. VCCV vs. VCCCV	pilot vs. basket vs. pilgrim
Vowel patterns in accented syllables and stress	Activities to emphasize syllable stress	See Table 5.4
	a-e vs. *ai* vs. *ay*	bracelet vs. rainbow vs. crayon
	ee vs. long *ea* vs. short *ea*	cheetah vs. easel vs. breakfast
	o-e vs. *oa* vs. *ow* vs. oCC	alone vs. toaster vs. blowhole vs. soldier
	ar vs. *are* vs. *air*	harbor vs. barefoot vs. airplane
	ir vs. *ire*	birdhouse vs. firefly
	or vs. *ore* vs. *oar* vs. *our*	corner vs. explore vs. boardwalk vs. fourteen
	o-e vs. long *oo* vs. short *oo*	alone vs. balloon vs. football
	ore vs. *ou* /aů/ vs. *ow* /aů/	explore vs. mountain vs. powder
	Long *oo* vs. short *oo* vs. *oi* /ȯi/ vs. *oy* /ȯi/	balloon vs. football vs. poison vs. royal
	a-e vs. *au* /ȯ/ vs. *aw* /ȯ/	bracelet vs. author vs. macaw
Plurals and inflectional endings in two-syllable words	Base + *s* vs. base + *es*	robots vs. eyelashes
	Base (*y* after vowel) + *s* vs. base (*y* after consonant) *y* to *i* + *es*	turkeys vs. candies
	Base + *s* vs. base + *es* vs. base *y* to *i* + *es*	robots vs. eyelashes vs. candies
	Base + *ing* vs. double + *ing*	piloting vs. forgetting
Final unaccented syllables	*er* (noun–person) vs. *er* (noun/verb)	barber vs. baker
	er (noun–person/concrete) vs. *er* (noun/verb) vs. *er* (adjective/adverb)	barber vs. baker vs. taller
	er (noun–person/concrete) vs. *or* (noun–person/concrete)	barber vs. doctor
	er (noun–person/concrete) vs. *er* (adjective/adverb) vs. or (noun) vs. ar (adjective)	barber vs. taller vs. doctor vs. circular
	ture /cher/ vs. *cher* /cher/	nature vs. teacher
	en (adjective) vs. *en* (verb) vs. *on* (noun)	golden vs. sharpen vs. apron
	en (verb) vs. *in* (noun) vs. *on* (noun)	sharpen vs. cabin vs. apron
	in (noun) vs. *on* (noun) vs. *an* (noun) vs. *ain* (noun)	cabin vs. apron vs. human vs. mountain
	le vs. *el*	angle vs. angel
	le vs. *el* vs. *al* (adjective)	angle vs. angel vs. naval
	et vs. *it*	planet vs. exit
	age vs. *idge* vs. *edge*	baggage vs. cartridge vs. knowledge
	ey vs. *ie* vs. *y*	monkey vs. birdie vs. daisy

Table 5.1 Continued

Feature Sequence	Introductory Pace	Exemplars
Special consonants in two-syllable words	Hard *g* vs. soft *g* vs. hard *c* vs. soft *c*	gorilla vs. giraffe vs. cabin vs. city
	Silent consonants	wrinkle vs. castle
	ph vs. *gh* (sounds of /f/)	dolphin vs. laughter
	ck vs. *ke* vs. *k* vs. *c* (final sounds of /k/)	hammock vs. cupcake vs. homework vs. picnic
	ck vs. *ke* vs. *que* (final sounds of /k/)	hammock vs. cupcake vs. antique
Simple prefixes	*un* vs. *re* vs. *dis*	unhappy vs. rebuild vs. disappear
	in vs. *non* vs. *mis*	infield vs. nonflammable vs. misuse
	pre vs. *ex* vs. *en*	preschool vs. explode vs. endanger
	uni vs. *bi* vs. *tri*	unicycle vs. bicycle vs. tricycle
Simple suffixes	*er* vs. *est* (no change)	taller vs. tallest
	No change + *er/est* vs. e-drop + *er/est* vs. double + *er/est*	taller/tallest vs. larger/largest vs. thinner/thinnest
	y vs. *ly*	bumpy vs. deadly
	No change + *y* vs. e-drop + *y* vs. double + *y*	bumpy vs. easy vs. starry
	ful vs. *less* vs. *ness*	colorful vs. helpless vs. kindness
	y to *i* +*er/est* vs. *y* to *i* + *ful* vs. *y* to *i* + *ness* vs. *y* to *i* + *ly*	happier vs. beautiful vs. happiness vs. easily

picture" will provide them with a sort of road map of where they are learning. You may find that you will use different variations. For example, you may have one for inflected endings but another for syllable juncture patterns. These graphic organizers can be a point of reference during your discussions and can guide conferences while monitoring goals. Ms. Baker created a big picture graphic about syllable juncture patterns with her first period class (see Figure 5.5) for this purpose.

Solidifying knowledge about consonant and vowel patterns in single-syllable words *(rain)* helps to build a foundation for navigating the patterns in multisyllabic words *(explain, complain)*. Once students have a solid foundation of pattern knowledge in single-syllable words, they are ready to begin to study multisyllabic words. They explore how consonant and vowel patterns are represented in accented syllables and how syllable stress affects the vowel sounds. As students move through this stage, they consider simple affixes and how grammar affects spelling.

engagement LINK

All of the sorts discussed in the feature sections give your students hands-on practice as they compare and contrast the features of study.

Figure 5.5 Big Picture for Syllable Juncture Patterns

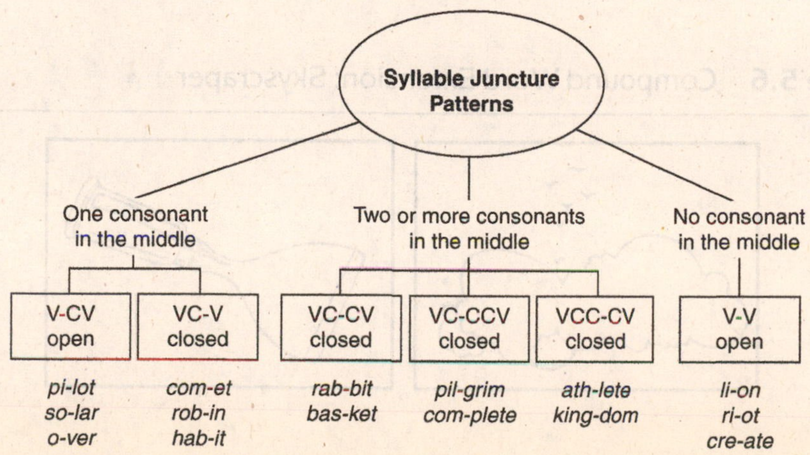

Eight main features are covered during this stage.

- Feature 1: Compound words
- Feature 2: Inflectional endings in one-syllable words
- Feature 3: Syllable juncture patterns
- Feature 4: Vowel patterns in accented syllables and stress
- Feature 5: Inflectional endings in two-syllable words
- Feature 6: Final unaccented syllables
- Feature 7: Special consonants in two-syllable words
- Feature 8: Simple affixes

Feature 1: Compound Words

A good starting place is a study of compound words made up of familiar one-syllable words. Compound words provide a stable environment for students to learn about the combinatorial features of English words. The juncture and stress issues that overshadow much of this stage are not problematic because compound words are made up of intact words. Therefore, students can get their feet wet without any concern for these potentially troublesome issues.

Students can also sort words by shared words (e.g., *bookworm, bookmark, bookshelf* versus *downhill, downstairs, downtown*) or be given a set of words (e.g., *door, head, foot, up*) with the challenge to create as many compound words as they can (e.g., *doorbell, doorknob, headlight, headdress, football, footstep, upstairs, uphill*). Another extension would be to draw a picture of the literal and actual meanings of the compound words (Ganske, 2000) as shown in Figure 5.6. This feature can be covered quickly with just a few sorts.

Because compound words are used as a way to introduce students to multisyllabic words, you should discuss what is meant by a *syllable* with your students and practice identifying syllables. Students can determine the number of syllables in their names and sort themselves into categories of one syllable (e.g., *Ben*), two syllables (e.g., *Isaac*), three syllables (e.g., *Taniqua*), and so on. Having them determine the number of syllables in interesting words like phobias is a fun challenge. For example, the fear of peanut butter sticking to the top of your mouth is called *arachibutyrophobia* (a total of nine syllables). These activities can also easily be extended into content areas using content-specific vocabulary.

Feature 2: Inflectional Endings in One-Syllable Words

Inflectional endings are suffixes added to a word as grammatical markers to indicate tense or number (e.g., *-s*, *-ed*, and *-ing*) without changing the overall meaning or part of speech (e.g., *papers, filled, walking*). Students have been using inflectional endings in their oral speech for many years but have not focused on their spellings until this stage. As an introduction, you may even find it necessary to review the meaning units and their

Figure 5.6 Compound Word Extension: Skyscraper

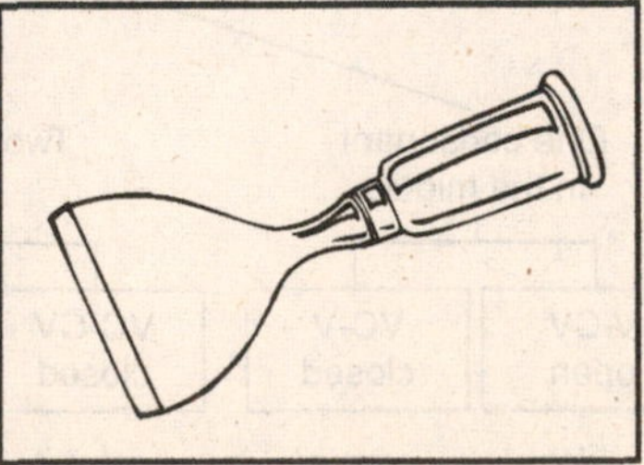

varying sounds. For example, the plural *-s* ending can have an /s/ sound as in *cats* and a /z/ sound as in *dogs*. The *-ed* past tense ending can have three different sounds: /t/ as in *walked*, /ed/ as in *strutted*, and /d/ as in *roamed*. A contrast of these varying sounds will help students realize that *-ed* is used to show past tense regardless of its pronunciation. As your students begin a study in inflectional endings, they must learn about base words (i.e., words that can stand alone after removing a prefix or suffix, like *chair* in *chairs* and *shout* in *shouted*). A study of irregular verbs, such as *went* as the past tense of *go*, should follow.

The *-s* plural ending is one of the earliest suffixes that students will learn in their written language. There are a variety of issues regarding plurals that should be addressed in a systematic fashion.

- Not only is *-s* added to words to denote plurals but *-es* is also used. You add *-es* to words that end in *ch* (*patches*), *sh* (*wishes*), *ss* (*dresses*), *s* (*buses*), and *x* (*boxes*). The *-es* is often easily heard, such as in *watches*, which can be contrasted with non-examples like *clocks*.
- The final *y* is changed to *i* before adding *-es* on words ending in a consonant plus *y*, as in *fly* to *flies*. Words that end in a vowel plus *y*, however, simply take the *-s* addition, such as in *play* to *plays*.
- Some words incur a spelling and pronunciation change as plurals. For example, words with a final *f* or *fe* require changing the *f* to *v* before adding *-es*, as in *calf* to *calves* and *wife* to *wives*. Other changes can be seen in *mouse* to *mice*.
- Some words do not require any change, such as *deer* and *sheep*.
- Two-syllable words follow these same rules. Consider *mailbox* to *mailboxes* (add *-es* because of the final *x*), *puppy* to *puppies* (change *y* to *i* and add *-es* because of the final *y*), and *monkey* to *monkeys* (add *-s* because *y* is preceded by a vowel). Two-syllable words are also addressed in the discussion of Feature 5: Inflectional Endings in Two-Syllable Words.

A summary of the various generalizations that explain adding inflectional endings can be found in Table 5.2. As you can see, the conditions can be complicated, so begin with the most common (first four items). Instruction could begin with the easiest two conditions: no change and *e*-drop. Therefore, students could first study words like *treating* (treat) and *jumping* (jump) compared to *smiling* (smile), as shown in Figure 5.7 (on p. 137). Have the students underline the base word and focus on the vowel patterns along with the vowel sounds: CVC words like *shop* need doubling as in *shopping* and *shopped* to keep the vowel short. Doubling is not needed in CVCC words (*drift/drifting* and *mark/marking*) and CVVC words (*meet/meeting* and *shout/shouting*). The *e* is dropped in CVCe words (*smile/smiling*).

Next study when words are doubled versus when they stay the same or have an *e* dropped. Doubling consonants is generally more difficult than dropping the final *e* (Henderson, 1990). An easy way to help students work through this issue is teaching them the one-one-one rule (Bear et al., 2008). When a suffix beginning with a vowel is added to a *one*-syllable base word containing *one* short vowel followed by *one* consonant, double the final consonant. Teaching your students the following three questions to ask when adding an inflectional ending will help:

1. Does the word have *one* syllable?
2. Does the word have *one* vowel?
3. Does the word end with *one* consonant?

If you answer yes to all three questions, then the final consonant should be doubled. If the answer to any of the questions is no, however, then the consonant should not be doubled.

- *Jog/jogging* is doubled because of the one syllable, one vowel, and one ending consonant.

Table 5.2 Changes to Base Words When Adding Inflectional Endings

Base Word	+ *ing*	+ *ed*	+ *s*
1. CVCe (bake, smile)	Drop final *e* (baking, smiling)	Drop final *e* (baked, smiled)	No change (bakes, smiles)
2. CVCC (hunt, rest)	No change (hunting, resting)	No change (hunted, rested)	No change (hunts, rests)
3. CVVC (wait, spoil)	No change (waiting, spoiling)	No change (waited, spoiled)	No change (waits, spoils)
4. CVC (jog, snap)	Double final letter (jogging, snapping)	Double final letter (jogged, snapped)	No change (jogs, snaps)
5. Words that end in a consonant + *y* (try, fry)	No change (trying, frying)	Change *y* to *i* (tried, fried)	Change *y* to *i* (tries, fries)
6. Words that end in a vowel + *y* (play, stray)	No change (playing, straying)	No change (played, strayed)	No change (plays, strays)
7. Two-syllable words accented on second syllable (admit, invite, apply, enjoy)	Follow rules 1–6 (admitting, inviting, applying, enjoying)	Follow rules 1–6 (admitted, invited, applied, enjoyed)	Follow rules 1–6 (admits, invites, applies, enjoys)
8. Two-syllable words accented on first syllable (pilot, purchase, copy, volley)	Follow rules 1–6 (piloting, purchasing, copying, volleying)	Follow rules 1–6 (piloted, purchased, copied, volleyed)	Follow rules 1–6 (pilots, purchases, copies, volleys)
9. Words that end in a c (mimic, picnic)	Add a *k* (mimicking, picnicking)	Add a *k* (mimicked, picnicked)	No change (mimics, picnics)

- *Jump/jumping* is not doubled because it has two ending consonants (not one).
- *Sail/sailing* is not doubled because it has two vowels (not one).
- *Skate/skating* is not doubled because it has two vowels and does not end with a consonant.

As mentioned earlier, multisyllabic words need additional consideration. This will be discussed later in the chapter.

See Figure 5.8 for an example of a sort contrasting the features that result in no change, *e*-drop, and doubling. Again, underline base words first. Next have students sort the words into the following categories:

CVC as in *hop*

CVCC as in *jump*

CVVC as in *wait*

CVCe as in *ride*

Ask your students to find the categories in which there is no change before adding *-ing*. This will lead them to combine CVCC (*jumping*) and CVVC (*sleeping*). Then ask them what happens to CVCe words, such as *smiling*. This will begin the category for *e*-drop. Last, turn your students' attention to the CVC category (*hopping*) and ask them what

Figure 5.7 No Change versus *e*-Drop Sort

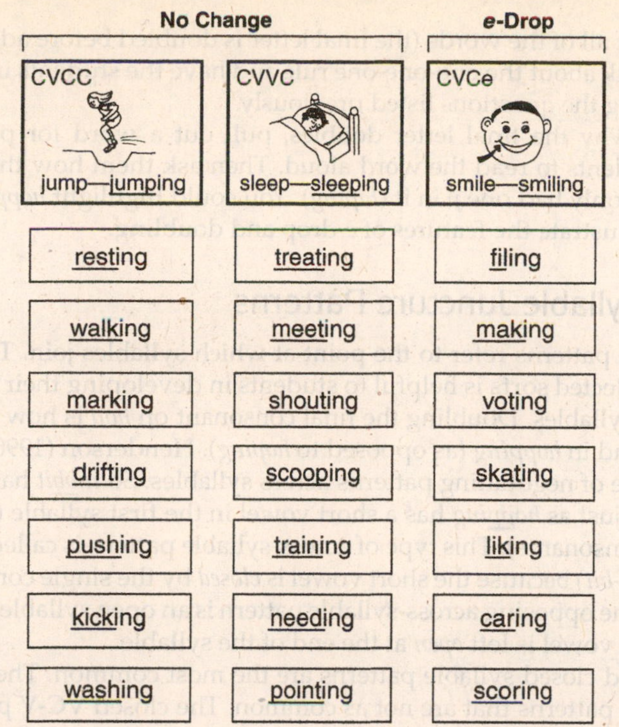

No Change
e-Drop
CVCC
jump—jumping
CVVC
sleep—sleeping
CVCe
smile—smiling
resting
treating
filing
walking
meeting
making
marking
shouting
voting
drifting
scooping
skating
pushing
training
liking
kicking
needing
caring
washing
pointing
scoring

Figure 5.8 No Change versus *e*-Drop versus Doubling Sort

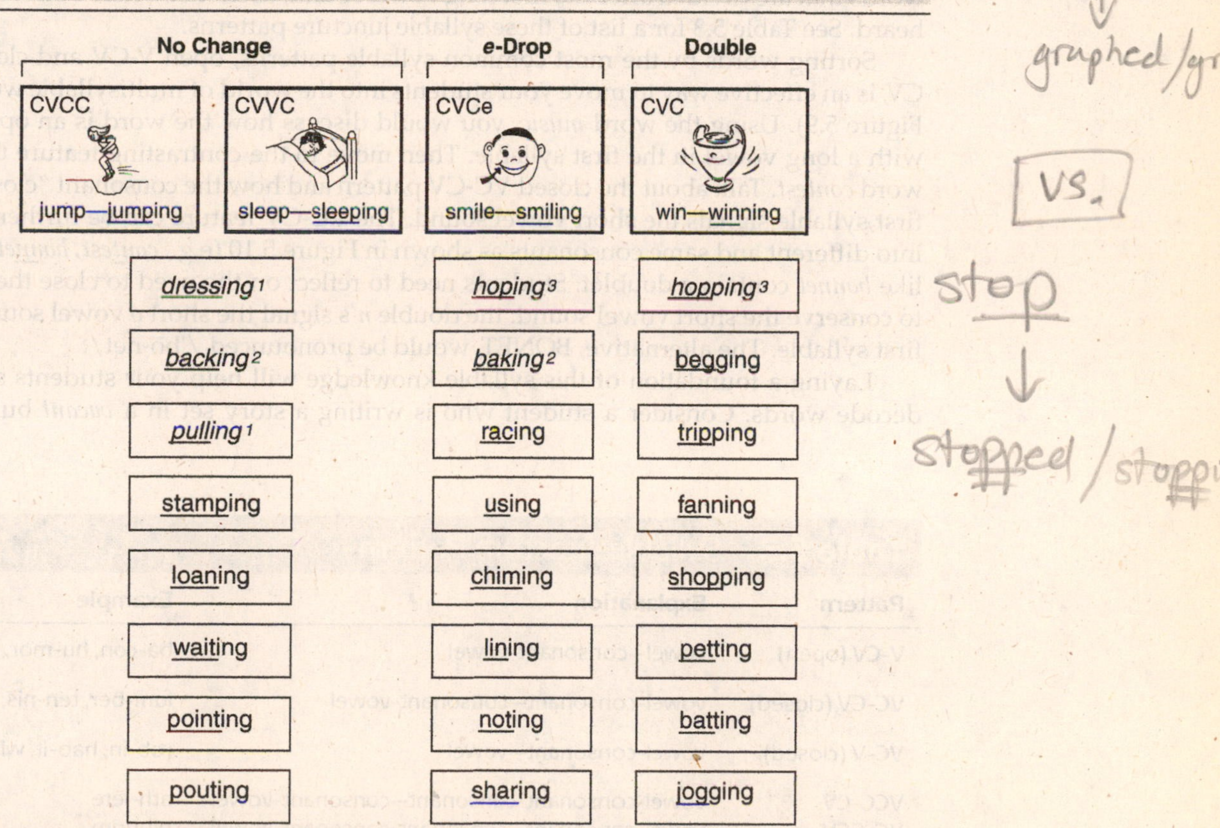

1. *dressing and pulling*—note that they follow the CVCC pattern rather than the doubling generalization.
2. *backing and baking*—note that *baking*'s base word is *bake*, which is much different from the word *back*.
3. *hoping and hopping*—note that the *p* is doubled in *hop* to make *hopping* and that *hoping* only has one *p* because its base word is *hope* (so drop the *e* and add the inflectional ending).

they notice about all of the words (the final letter is doubled before adding *-ing*). At this point, you can talk about the one-one-one rule and have the students investigate each of these words using the questions listed previously.

To explore why the final letter doubles, pull out a word for particular study—*tapping*. Ask students to read the word aloud. Then ask them how the word would be pronounced if it only had one *p* in it (*taping*). You could highlight *hopping* and *hoping* as well to further illustrate the features of *e*-drop and doubling.

Feature 3: Syllable Juncture Patterns

Syllable juncture patterns refer to the point at which syllables join. The doubling generalization in inflected sorts is helpful to students in developing their understanding of patterns across syllables. Doubling the final consonant on *hop* is how they preserve the short vowel sound in *hopping* (as opposed to *hoping*). Henderson (1990) called doubling the core principle of negotiating patterns across syllables. So *rabbit* has a short vowel in the first syllable just as *hopping* has a short vowel in the first syllable (notice the underlined doubled consonants). This type of across-syllable pattern is called a closed syllable (VC-CV as in *rab-bit*) because the short vowel is *closed* by the single consonant at the end of the syllable. The opposing across-syllable pattern is an open syllable (V-CV as in *pi-lot*) because the long vowel is left *open* at the end of the syllable.

The open and closed syllable patterns are the most common. There are three more syllable juncture patterns that are not as common. The closed VC-V pattern as in *cov-er* has only a single consonant at the juncture of the syllable after a short vowel. The closed VCCCV pattern includes words with consonant digraphs or blends at the syllable juncture, as in *ath-lete* (VCC-CV) and *mon-ster* (VC-CCV). Lastly, the V-V pattern consists of words that are divided after the first long vowel sound, as in *ri-ot* where both vowels are heard. See Table 5.3 for a list of these syllable juncture patterns.

Sorting words by the most common syllable patterns, open V-CV and closed VC-CV, is an effective way to move your students into the world of multisyllabic words (see Figure 5.9). Using the word *music*, you would discuss how the word is an open V-CV with a long vowel in the first syllable. Then move to the contrasting feature using the word *contest*. Talk about the closed VC-CV pattern and how the consonant "closing" the first syllable signals the short vowel sound. The VC-CV feature can be further divided into different and same consonants as shown in Figure 5.10 (e.g., *contest*, *bonnet*). Words like *bonnet* contain a doublet. Students need to reflect on the need to close the syllable to conserve the short vowel sound: the double *n*'s signal the short *o* vowel sound in the first syllable. The alternative, BONET, would be pronounced /'bō-net/.

Laying a foundation of this syllable knowledge will help your students spell and decode words. Consider a student who is writing a story set in a *vacant* building. A

Table 5.3 Syllable Juncture Patterns

Pattern	Explanation	Example
V-CV (open)	vowel—consonant-vowel	ba-con, hu-mor, fe-ver
VC-CV (closed)	vowel-consonant—consonant-vowel	lum-ber, ten-nis, nap-kin
VC-V (closed)	vowel-consonant—vowel	rob-in, hab-it, wiz-ard
VCC-CV	vowel-consonant-consonant—consonant-vowel	ath-lete
VC-CCV	vowel-consonant—consonant-consonant-vowel	pil-grim
VV	vowel—vowel	cre-ate, tri-al, ri-ot

Figure 5.9 V-CV versus VC-CV Sort

Figure 5.10 Subsort for the VC-CV Feature

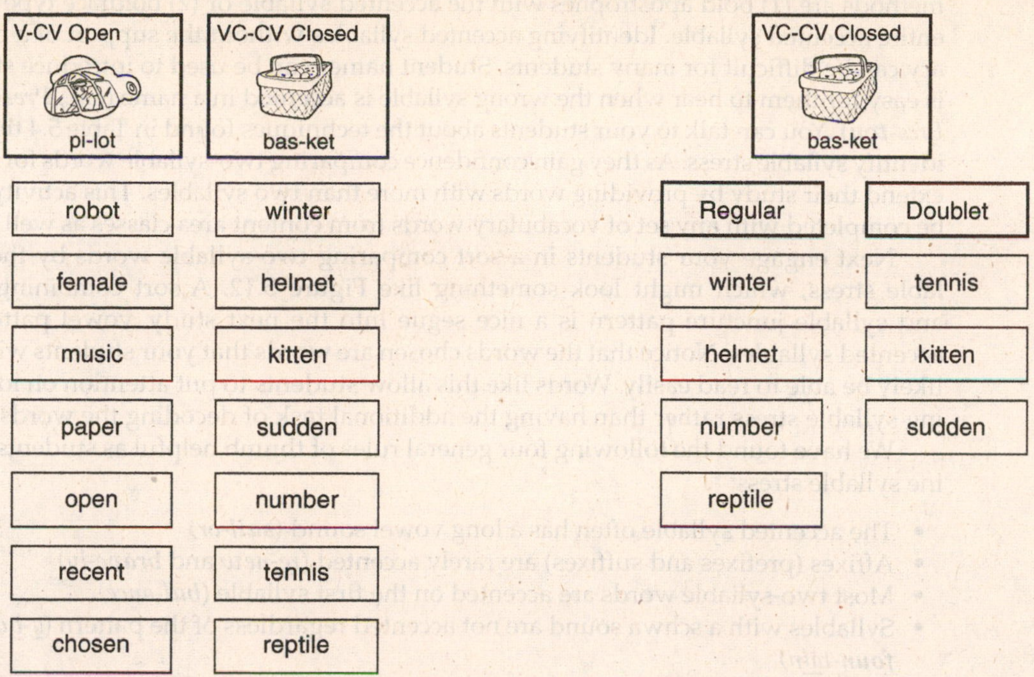

student with an awareness of the VCV versus VCCV syllable patterns will hear the open first syllable, /vā/. Thinking about the open syllable, the student will know that the consonant following the long vowel will not need to be doubled and thus will spell *vacant* with one *c*, not two. Now consider this student reading a story set on a *planet* in outer space. When attempting to decode the unknown word *planet*, the student with an awareness of syllable patterns will first try to pronounce the word using the open V-CV generalization. This would produce /ˈplā-nət/ (long *a*), which is not a real word. At this point, the student would try the less common closed VC-V pattern. The student then reads the word accurately, /ˈplan-ət/ (short *a*). This type of flexibility is just as critical as a firm awareness of how syllables are connected.

Other syllable juncture patterns should be included in your study. For example, negotiating words with two or more consonants in the middle can be especially difficult (e.g., *dol-phin* and *ham-ster*). Sorts like the one in Figure 5.11 can bring the VC-CCV and VCC-CV syllable juncture patterns to your students' attention.

Figure 5.11 VC-CCV versus VCC-CV Sort

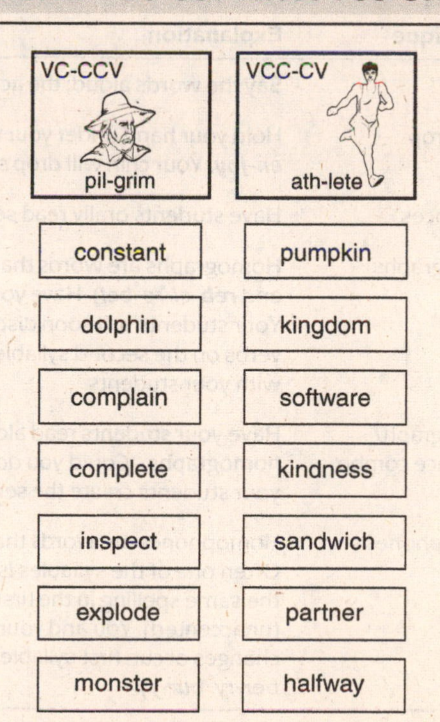

VC-CCV
pil-grim
VCC-CV
ath-lete
constant
dolphin
complain
complete
inspect
explode
monster
pumpkin
kingdom
software
kindness
sandwich
partner
halfway

Feature 4: Vowel Patterns in Accented Syllables and Stress

Now that your students are familiar with syllable juncture patterns, they should consider syllable stress. In multisyllabic words, one syllable is stressed, or accented, more than the other(s). Teach your students how dictionaries mark accented syllables. The two most common methods are (1) bold apostrophes with the accented syllable or (2) boldface type for the entire accented syllable. Identifying accented syllables without the support of a dictionary can be difficult for many students. Student names can be used to introduce stress. It is easy for them to hear when the wrong syllable is accented in a name (e.g., ***Pres**-ton* vs. *Pres-**ton***). You can talk to your students about the techniques found in Table 5.4 that help identify syllable stress. As they gain confidence comparing two-syllable words for accent, extend their study by providing words with more than two syllables. This activity could be completed with any set of vocabulary words from content area classes as well.

Next engage your students in a sort comparing two-syllable words by their syllable stress, which might look something like Figure 5.12. A sort combining stress and syllable juncture pattern is a nice segue into the next study, vowel patterns in accented syllables. Notice that the words chosen are words that your students will most likely be able to read easily. Words like this allow students to put attention on identifying syllable stress rather than having the additional task of decoding the words.

We have found the following four general rules of thumb helpful as students examine syllable stress:

- The accented syllable often has a long vowel sound (***sail**-or*)
- Affixes (prefixes and suffixes) are rarely accented (*re-**new*** and ***brave**-ly*)
- Most two-syllable words are accented on the first syllable (***bal**-ance*)
- Syllables with a schwa sound are not accented regardless of the pattern (*a-**bout*** and ***foun**-tain*)

Now that syllable stress is clear, move your students to a study of vowel patterns in the accented syllable. The vowel patterns covered in the within word pattern stage can be reexamined in this stage in two-syllable words. As previously mentioned, it is in the accented syllable that the vowel patterns are reliable (e.g., *com-**plain***). Vowels in

Table 5.4 Techniques to Illustrate Syllable Stress

Technique	Explanation
Sound	Say the words aloud; the accented syllables often sound louder.
Chin drop	Hold your hand under your chin as you say a multisyllable word such as *en-**joy***. Your chin will drop slightly more with the accented syllable.
Sentences	Have students orally read sentences using the target words. "Did you *en-**joy*** the movie?"
Homographs	Homographs are words that are spelled alike but pronounced differently (e.g., ***ad**-dress/ad-**dress*** and ***reb**-el/re-**bel***). Have your students examine how the stress changes based on meaning. Your students will soon discover that the nouns are usually accented on the first syllable and the verbs on the second syllable. Consider *address* and *rebel*. A sort is a nice way to *ad-**dress*** this with your students.
Homograph/ sentence combo	Have your students read aloud sentences that use both the noun and verb versions of homographs. "Could you *ad-**dress*** my concern about your ***ad**-dress*?" You could also have your students create the sentences. "A ***reb**-el* is a person who *re-**bels*** against something."
Homophones	Homophones are words that sound alike but are spelled differently (e.g., *coun-**sel**; coun-**cil***). Often one of the syllables is spelled alike while the other is different. *Counsel* and *council* share the same spelling in the first syllable (accented) but have different spellings in the second syllable (unaccented). You and your students can look at these words to compare where the spelling changes occur: first syllable, second syllable, or both (e.g., ***cen**-sor/**sen**-sor, na-**val**/na-**vel***, and ***ber**-ry/**bur**-y*).

unaccented syllables have the schwa sound (e.g., *foun-tain*). Many of the generalizations that your students made about vowel patterns in single-syllable words will hold true in two-syllable words. Consider the various ways to spell the long *a* sound: *cake, rain, tray, vein*). Your students will remember that position provided some assistance in making decisions previously. It can help here, too.

- The *a*-consonant-*e* long *a* spelling pattern is found at the ends of syllables (e.g., *a-maze, base-ment*).
- The *ai* long *a* spelling pattern is often found in the *-ain* ending (e.g., *main-tain, ex-plain*).
- The *ay* long *a* spelling pattern is found at the ends of syllables (e.g., *cray-on, to-day*).
- The *ei* long *a* spelling pattern is not very common (e.g., *eigh-teen, weigh-ing*).

You might sort the following words like this:

amaze	maintain	today
basement	explain	crayon
debate	rainbow	essay
bracelet	painter	maybe

Figure 5.12 Syllable Stress Combined with Pattern Sort

First Syllable Long *a*
Second Syllable Long *a*
rainbow
replace
mailbox
explain
bracelet
erase
safety
vibrate
daisy
detail
failure
delay
statement
behave
waiter
decay

Some *r*-controlled vowels from single-syllable study provided a challenge due to their similar sounds (e.g., *sir, her, fur*). This remains an issue when studying these vowel patterns in two-syllable words. (e.g., *circle, versus, sturdy*), whereas the *ar* and *or* patterns remain easier (e.g., *alarm, corner*). It is helpful for students to first sort these words by sound prior to sorting by sound and pattern. Doing the sound sort first may help your students become more mindful when faced with spelling those patterns.

Another set of vowel patterns that deserve special attention are the ambiguous vowels, due to their range of sounds and spellings. For example, the *ou* spelling pattern has four different sounds: *shout, touch, your,* and *thought*. As in the study of long vowel patterns, special attention to position can provide assistance. Your students can rely on the generalization that *oy* and *ow* are generally found at the ends of words and syllables (e.g., *con-voy, loy-al, en-dow*), whereas *oi* and *ou* are found within the syllable (e.g., *a-void, proud-ly*).

Feature 5: Inflectional Endings in Two-Syllable Words

The study of inflectional endings found earlier in this stage can be revisited at this point. Once you and your students have investigated accented syllables, review the generalizations for adding inflectional endings on single-syllable words. Words that have the stress on the second syllable—and end with a short vowel followed by a single consonant—follow the same guidelines (e.g., *admitted*). However, words that are accented on the first syllable are not doubled (e.g., *piloted*). All other generalizations hold true in two-syllable words as they did in one-syllable words. Words ending in *e* drop the *e* before adding the ending (e.g., *invited*), words ending in *-y* require students to change the *y* to *i* before adding the ending (e.g., *applied*), and words that end with consonant blends or digraphs as well as words with certain vowel patterns involve no change (e.g., *consisted, enjoyed*).

Feature 6: Final Unaccented Syllables

When the syllable is stressed, the vowel is clearly heard. However, the vowel in the unaccented syllable is reduced and becomes a schwa sound as in *vil-lage*. These unaccented syllables (e.g., *sug-ar*) can be profitably examined by students at this stage. To illustrate the reduced vowel in the unaccented syllable, Ganske (2000) suggests showing your students a few words that have the same vowel pattern, with some appearing in the accented syllable and others in the unaccented syllable. You could present your students with the following words: *contain, regain, complain, explain, refrain* and *captain, certain, bargain, villain, curtain* (p. 160). The first group of words with the *ai* spelling pattern have their second syllable accented; therefore, your students can think of the two most common ways to spell /ān/—*ain* and *ane*. The second group is accented on the first syllable, causing the *ain* to sound like /ən/ rather than /ān/ as in the first group. When this happens, your students are left with little help on how to spell the word. Conclude the discussion by calling your students' attention to how cautious they must be when spelling unaccented syllables and explaining that a study of unaccented syllables, specifically final unaccented syllables, will help. See Table 5.5 for an overview of unaccented final syllables.

Your students will have to pay close attention to unaccented syllables (and sometimes they may simply have to memorize the spelling). Meaning, however, can provide them with some assistance, and the pattern's frequency will sometimes provide a "best guess." In particular, a word's part of speech may be able to play a part in determining a certain spelling pattern in an unaccented syllable. When studying the final /ər/ in words like *actor*, emphasize the fact that agentive nouns often end with *-er* or *-or* as in *barber* and *doctor*. Adjectives are often spelled with the *-ar* pattern as in *solar*. Comparative adjectives are always spelled with *-er* as in *taller*. But overall, *-er* is simply much more common than *-or* and *-ar*. This bit of knowledge can give your students a default. When in doubt, use *-er* because that is the best bet.

Another /ər/ unaccented syllable ending worth investigating is the /cher/ ending. Begin with a discussion of base words and roots. A base word, as previously discussed, can stand on its own even when any prefix or suffix is removed. A root is also a word part left when prefixes and suffixes are removed. However, roots cannot stand alone as words (e.g., *poss* in *possible*). This distinction is important because it provides a clue into whether /chər/ is spelled with *-ture* or *-cher*. Base words are spelled with *-er*. They end in either *-ch* or *-tch* and add *-er*, ending as in *teacher* or *pitcher*. Roots, on the other hand, are generally spelled with the *-ture* ending, as in *nature* and *picture*. Also, notice the syllable break. Words with a base word ending in either *-ch* or *-tch* break after the /ch/ (*teach-er, pitch-er*); however, words ending with *-ture* break before the /ch/ (*na-ture, pic-ture*).

Final /ən/ and /əl/ sounds often prove difficult. Verbs and adjectives that end in the /ən/ sound are often spelled with the *-en* pattern, as in *golden* and *strengthen*. Nouns

Table 5.5 Common Final Unaccented Syllables

Final Unaccented Syllable	Helpful Hint	Examples
er vs. *or* vs. *ar*	Part of speech	barber, doctor, solar
ture vs. *cher*	Base word	nature, teacher
en vs. *on*	Part of speech	golden, apron
el vs. *le* vs. *al*	Part of speech Frequency Predictable patterns	naval, angel, angle
age vs. *edge* vs. *idge*	Frequency	baggage, knowledge, cartridge
ey vs. *ie* vs. *y*	Frequency Predictable patterns	monkey, birdie, daisy

with the /ən/ final sound are more commonly spelled with *-on,* like *apron.* The final /əl/ sound is also troublesome for many students. Again, parts of speech can be helpful. Adjectives are often spelled with the *-al* pattern, as in *naval.* The consonant before the ending can also be of assistance. Soft *g* and *c* provide clues. Words with a soft *c* take *-el* to keep the *e* needed for the soft pronunciation (*circle* vs. *parcel*). Frequency is another factor to consider. The *-le* pattern is much more common than the *-el* pattern. Therefore, when in doubt, go with *-le.*

Another unaccented ending worthy of particular attention is the /ij/ ending, the study of which can further emphasize to your students how meaning and frequency often provide clues about unaccented endings. This ending has three options for spelling: *-age* as in *baggage, -edge* as in *knowledge,* and *-idge* as in *cartridge.* Your students can study words ending in /ij/ by considering frequency. The *-age* ending is the most frequent by far and should be used as the default when your students are in doubt. A sort comparing these three endings can be developed to emphasize the greater frequency of *-age* (see Figure 5.13).

The unaccented long *e* final syllable is another feature to consider, as in *monkey, birdie,* and *daisy.* Your students can look at frequency as well as pattern when negotiating this ending. The final *-y* ending is the most common of the three. However, words that have a *k, l,* or *n* before the long *e* ending tend to have the final *-ey* pattern (*turkey, alley, money*).

Again, these particular endings are not the only instances where the schwa will be an issue. These highlighted features are, therefore, not exhaustive. Your students need to be aware of unaccented syllables and know of instances when meaning, frequency, or pattern can assist them. When these pieces of information will not help, your students will need to investigate the schwa sound itself. These types of investigations will help your students with the pronunciations of syllables with schwa sounds as well as impress on them the need to be cautious. Ganske (2000) suggests using sorts such as the one shown in Figure 5.14 to highlight the need for caution for your students.

Figure 5.13 Final Unaccented Syllable Sort: /ij/

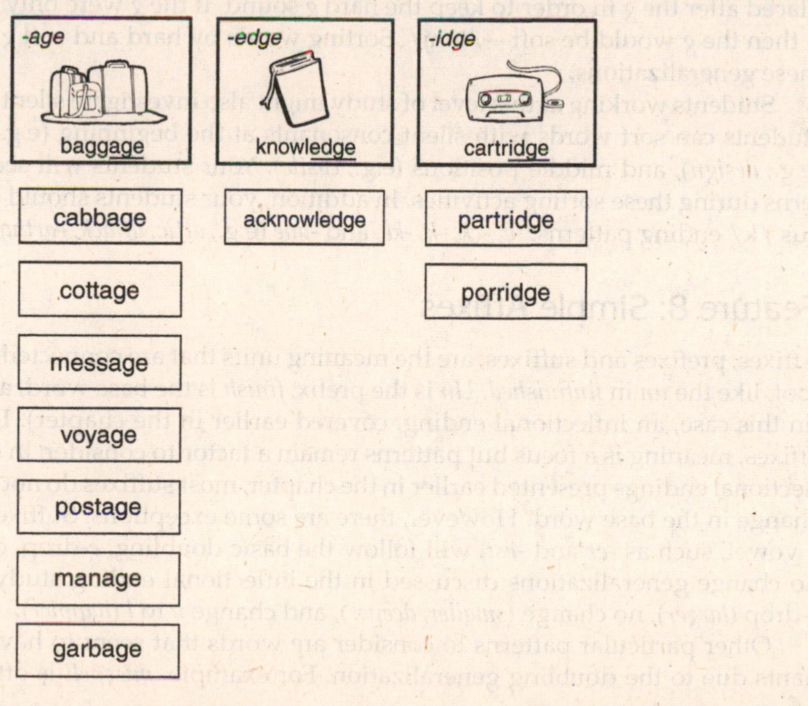

Figure 5.14 Schwa Highlight Sort

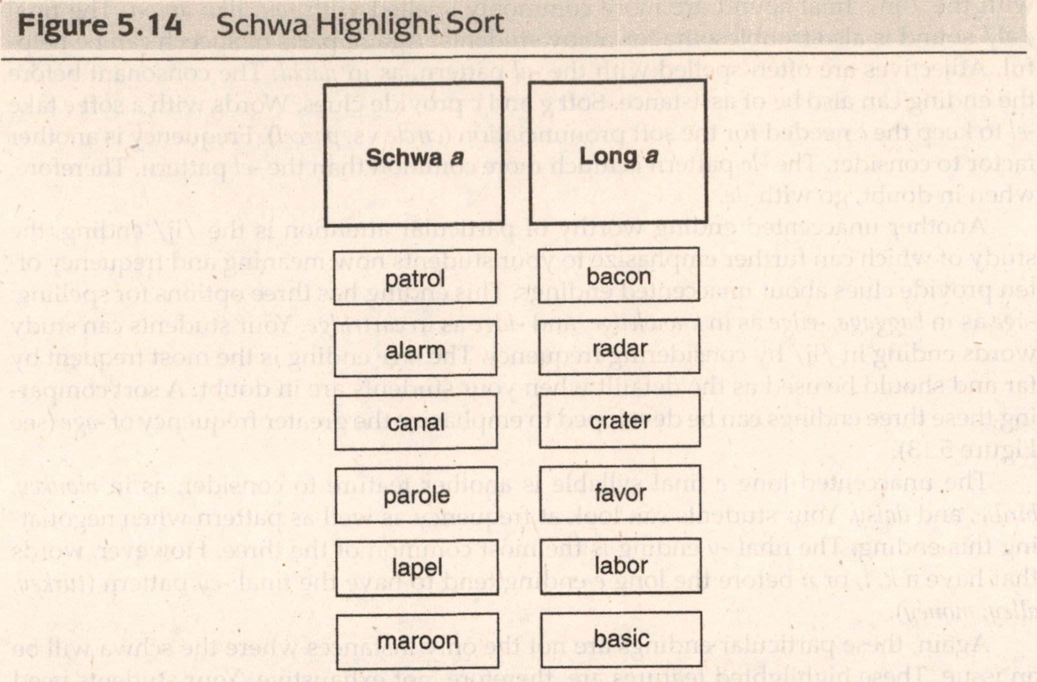

Schwa a
Long a
patrol
bacon
alarm
radar
canal
crater
parole
favor
lapel
labor
maroon
basic

Feature 7: Special Consonants in Two-Syllable Words

As your students progress in their knowledge of spelling patterns, consonants continue to be revisited. Some of the generalizations learned in the within word pattern stage can be applied to two-syllable words. Consider hard and soft *g* and *c*, which are dictated by the vowel that follows them. The vowels *a*, *o*, and *u* follow hard *g* and *c* as in *gallon* and *cozy*. The vowels *e*, *i*, and *y* follow soft *g* and *c* as in *genius* and *city*. As pointed out by Bear and colleagues (2008), interesting spellings are thus produced, but understanding the generalization reveals the logic of the spellings. Consider the word *tongue*. The *u* is placed after the *g* in order to keep the hard *g* sound. If the *g* were only followed with an *e*, then the *g* would be soft—/tonj/. Sorting words by hard and soft *g* and *c* will reveal these generalizations.

Students working at this level of study might also investigate silent consonants. Your students can sort words with silent consonants at the beginning (e.g., *wrinkle*), ending (e.g., *design*), and middle positions (e.g., *castle*). Your students will see predictable patterns during these sorting activities. In addition, your students should consider the various /k/ ending patterns: *-c*, *-ck*, *-k*, *-ke*, and *-que* (e.g., *attic, attack, earthquake, unique*).

Feature 8: Simple Affixes

Affixes, prefixes and suffixes, are the meaning units that are connected to a base word or root, like the *un* in *unfinished*. *Un* is the prefix, *finish* is the base word, and *ed* is the suffix (in this case, an inflectional ending, covered earlier in the chapter). During a study of affixes, meaning is a focus but patterns remain a factor to consider. In contrast to the inflectional endings presented earlier in the chapter, most suffixes do not require a spelling change in the base word. However, there are some exceptions. Suffixes that begin with a vowel, such as *-er* and *-est*, will follow the basic doubling, *e*-drop, change *y* to *i*, and no change generalizations discussed in the inflectional ending study: double (*bigger*), *e*-drop (*larger*), no change (*smaller, deeper*), and change *y* to *i* (*happier*).

Other particular patterns to consider are words that seem to have doubled consonants due to the doubling generalization. For example, *misspell* is often misspelled by students because only one *s* is heard in the pronunciation. The meaning connection to the prefix *mis-* will help your students in their attempts to spell this word. Include words like this in your sorts to highlight this issue for your students. For example, in a sort contrasting the prefixes *un-* and *re-*, include words like *unnoticed* and *unnamed*, or in a sort contrasting the suffixes *-ly*, *-ness*, and *-y*, include words like *finally* and *openness*. Many of the affixes in the suggested sequence discussed earlier in this chapter will be familiar to your students, but word study can highlight spelling issues that might arise when adding affixes, as well as how they affect meaning.

A Word about Oddballs

As discussed in Chapter 4 for within word pattern spellers, you should include oddballs in your sorts when appropriate. A good rule of thumb is to begin incorporating oddballs into sorts after you have introduced the feature and provided practice. Once you feel your students have a working understanding of the features, then bring oddballs to the table. Oddballs are important for two reasons: they are memorable and they force your students to really think about the sounds and patterns. Sometimes what appears to be an oddball is actually a new pattern. For example, while doing an open V-CV (*pi-lot*) and closed VC-CV (*bas-ket*) sort, you could add in words that follow the closed VC-V (*rob-in*) syllable juncture pattern. VC-V is not a true oddball because there are more words like it, but it is an oddball in that sort. Including oddballs like this will force your students to consider the feature, propelling them forward in their study as they restructure their existing schema to accommodate the new feature. Review Ms. Baker's open sort in the vignette at the beginning of the chapter.

Open sorts are engaging for many reasons. They provide hands-on practice for your students and can be done in collaborative groups. Students direct their own learning while sorting and testing their hypotheses.

Oddballs can show exceptions or introduce a little known category. For example, *senior* could be an exception oddball when studying the /er/ unaccented ending in words like *barber, doctor,* and *circular.* Adding the oddballs *fixing* and *rowing* to a sort comparing the spelling changes that occur when adding inflected endings (no change in *jumping*, *e*-drop in *baking*, and double in *hopping*) helps demonstrate a less common category. Although *fixing* and *rowing* follow the CVC pattern, the final consonant is not doubled.

fixing	waxing	chewing
boxing	rowing	snowing

Calling your students' attention to the part that deviates from the pattern may help your students master their spellings. Appendix D provides you with lists of words for all the features, along with oddballs.

Word Study Activities for Struggling Readers at the Intermediate/Syllables and Affixes Stage

In this section, more tried and true activities for struggling readers are discussed. To help students in the syllables and affixes stage, we will consider instruction using closed sorts, open sorts, writing sorts, blind writing sorts, and word hunts that will guide you along the continuum of support. Extensions of sorting are then presented: manipulation, word analysis, and games. Appendix D has a detailed list of words for these activities across the features in the syllables and affixes stage, and Appendix E provides sort samples. Ms. Baker's weekly word study routine is provided as an example of how these

Considerations for English Learners

Guidelines for the Syllables and Affixes Stage

English learners at the syllables and affixes stage may be able to quickly translate their literacy experiences in their primary language. However, they may find themselves facing unfamiliar vocabulary and content that may be overwhelming. Students at the upper levels are learning about advanced orthography that can be difficult for students whose primary language is characterized as transparent (highly regular phonetic language), such as Spanish. In contrast, students whose primary language shares similarities with the deep orthography of English may have the "mindset" for learning English spellings at this level (Bear, Helman, Templeton, Invernizzi, & Johnston, 2007). Bear and colleagues (2007) offer the following guidelines concerning word study instruction for your English learners at the syllables and affixes stage:

- Begin with teacher-directed closed sorts, making time for discussing vocabulary and asking questions. Walk through the words with your students, highlighting the morphemic units (e.g., the *re-* in *redo*, the *tele-* in *televise*, the *photo-* in *photograph*). While doing this, make the spelling–meaning connection explicit (e.g., *music* and *musician*).
- Provide your students with opportunities to work together; be sure to provide opportunities for your English learners to partner with proficient English speakers.
- Make sure your students are reading their words aloud, checking in to ensure they understand the meanings.
- Repeat sorts with your students until they are able to quickly and accurately complete them.
- Have your students record words and their meanings in word study notebooks for future reference.
- Once your students are familiar with the features, provide opportunities for them to hunt for additional examples in books and their own writing. These examples could be the exact words or shared roots. For example, your students could look for words with the root *aud* (meaning "hear"): *auditorium, audio, audience, audible, inaudible.*
- As in the within word pattern, do not forget about supporting the sounds. They continue to play a crucial role for English learners. Many of the sounds of English do not exist in other languages. For example, many languages do not have *r*-controlled vowels, making these sounds difficult to pronounce (e.g., moth<u>er</u>, doct<u>or</u>, sug<u>ar</u>). Difficulty with pronunciation can cause challenges when attempting to spell the words.

activities can be used throughout the week. Notice that teacher-directed, collaborative, and independent work are all included. Collaborative and independent work are done either in Ms. Baker's class while she works with small groups or in the mainstream English class during the contracted independent work time (see Figure 5.15).

Teacher-Directed Closed Sort

engagement LINK

All of the activities in this section are highly hands-on approaches that can be used in collaborative groups. They are also useful as activities for independent work contracts, a good way to give your students choice in their learning.

The goal of the closed sorting procedure is to emphasize similarities and differences among targeted features. Closed sorts are best used when you are introducing new concepts that might need scaffolding. Let's recap the key sorting guidelines: (1) Have consistent predetermined keywords that will exemplify the features of study and (2) talk explicitly about the keywords prior to sorting.

Procedure

1. *Demonstrate.* Introduce the sort by discussing keywords and targeted features. Model your thinking as you place at least two words in each column. For sorts at the syllables and affixes stage, you may need to call

Figure 5.15 Ms. Baker's Word Study Routine

	Monday	Tuesday	Wednesday	Thursday	Friday
Ms. Baker–Basic Reading	Teacher-directed closed sort		Manipulation Word analysis		Test
Collaborative and independent work	Repeated Sort checked with buddy	Repeated Sort checked with buddy Blind Sort	Check Word Hunt with buddy Speed Sort	Repeated Sort Speed Sort/ Beat the Teacher	Test Reflections (see Chapter 3 for detailed explanation)
Homework	Repeated Sort	Word Hunt	Blind Sort	Writing Sort	No homework

attention to grammar connections. The following example demonstrates language you might use when introducing and modeling the unaccented *-er* ending, such as with the sort in Figure 5.16.

Teacher: Okay, everyone. Today we are going to talk about the /ər/ sound at the ends of words like *teacher* and *taller*. [The teacher points to the keyword during the demonstration and highlights the features.] In our work today, the *-er* ending is used for two purposes. First, let's take the keyword *teacher*. What is the base word?

Students: *Teach.*

Teacher: What part of speech is *teach?* Is it a noun? Verb? Adjective?

Students: It is something you do . . . Verb.

engagement LINK

Teacher-directed closed sorts should have teacher–student interaction and teacher questions that promote higher-level thinking.

Figure 5.16 Final Unaccented Syllable Sort: *-er*

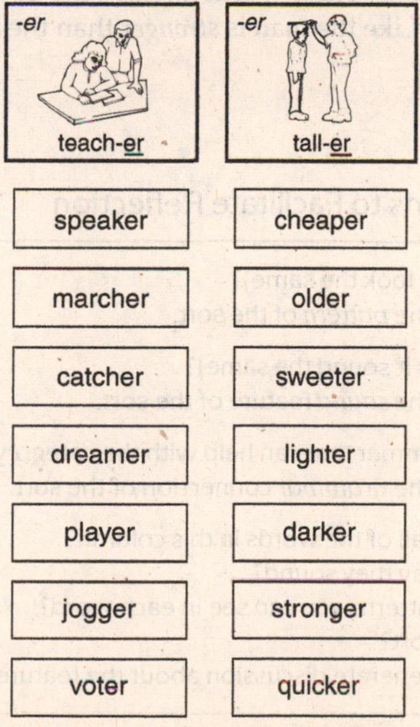

Teacher: That's right. Now let's look. When you add *-er* to *teach,* you get *teacher.* What part of speech is *teacher*?

Students: Noun.

Teacher: Yes. You can sometimes add *-er* to verbs to make a person noun. Technically, they are called agents, or people. I'm going to underline *teach,* the base word, in *teacher.* Now let's go to *taller.* Does this same thinking apply here?

Students: No. *Tall* isn't a verb. It describes.

Student 1: Yeah. And, *taller* compares one thing to another. I am *taller* than my brother.

Teacher: I like your thinking here. The *-er* on taller makes the adjective *tall* become a word that compares. I'm going to underline the base word here—*tall.* So, *-er* added to words can do two things: It can change a verb to a person noun like in *teacher* and it can change an adjective to a word that compares like in *taller.* [The teacher writes VERB → NOUN on one card that she puts under *teacher* and ADJECTIVE → COMPARE on a card that she puts under *taller.*]

2. *Sort.* Have your students set up their keyword cards and sort their words. Remember to have your students read the words aloud as they sort. In the *-er* sort, you could have them underline the base word as they sort: *cheaper, older, speaker, sweeter, marcher, lighter, catcher, darker, dreamer, stronger, player, quicker, jogger, voter.* Or you could have separate cards for base words so students can match up pairs (*quick* and *quicker*) before placing the pair in the appropriate category.

3. *Check.* Have students read down the words under each keyword, listening for sounds while looking at the patterns.

4. *Reflect.* After the sort (shown in Figure 5.16) is completed, initiate a reflection (either verbal or written). As each column is read, review the keywords and what each word in the category has in common, noting again any sound, pattern, position, or grammar connections. To reinforce student understanding of the features, you can ask questions like those presented in Figure 5.17.

Teacher: Okay, please read your first category.

Student 1: My first category is *cheaper, sweeter, lighter, darker, stronger, quicker, older.* This category is like *taller.* These words all have the *-er* to mean something is more than something else. Like the man is *stronger* than the boy.

Figure 5.17 Questions to Facilitate Reflection

- Does it look right (or does it look the same)?
  This question emphasizes the *pattern* of the sort.
- Does it sound right (or does it sound the same)?
  This question emphasizes the *sound* feature of the sort.
- Is there anything about grammar that can help with the category?
  This question emphasizes the *grammar* connection of the sort.
- What did you notice about all of the words in this column?
- How are they alike in the way they sound?
- How are they alike in the patterns you can see in each word?
- What did you learn in this sort?
  These questions can help generate discussion about the features.

Student 2: The next one is *speaker, marcher, catcher, dreamer, player, jogger, voter.* This one is for changing verbs into nouns. *Dream* becomes *dreamer*—somebody who *dreams,* like *teacher* is someone who *teaches.*

Teacher: You guys are really thinking here. Good. Now let's take a look at three words: *dreamer, jogger,* and *voter.* [The teacher pulls out the three word cards for a focused review.] Take a look at the base words: *dream, jog, vote.* [The teacher writes the base words on a dry erase board.] What patterns do you see?

Student 3: *Jog* has two *g*'s when it becomes *jogging.*

Student 2: And you drop the *e* when you add *-er* on *vote.*

Student 4: Look here. *Dream* is just the same.

Teacher: You are onto something here. Remember adding *-ed* and *-ing*?

Students: Yeah. That's just like *smiling* and *winning.* You have to drop the *e* or double.

After these discussions, keep the keywords out and mix the words. Then ask your students to sort again as they read aloud each word. This will give you a chance to assess how well they can do the sort on their own (with your support as needed). Have them discuss their categories and then store their words for further activities, such as the writing described later in this section.

Open Sort

As discussed in Chapter 2, open sorts demand a high level of thinking and can be included in your study once students are familiar with sorting and do not require explicit instruction. Therefore, open sorts may not be optimal when beginning a new (and unfamiliar) feature of study. When your students have a beginning understanding of a feature and your purpose is to extend that study, open sorting is quite effective. For example, you might include an open sort as your feature introduction of the closed VC-V syllable pattern after your students have learned the open V-CV and closed VC-CV syllable patterns, just as Ms. Baker did in the vignette at the beginning of the chapter.

Procedure

1. *Introduce.* Tell your students that you are interested in their thinking about the sound and/or pattern of the sort. For example, you may give them a set of words—*books, couches, glasses, bushes, bags, inches, lunches, wishes, dresses, bosses, cars, brushes*—and ask them to hypothesize categories. Briefly read through the words and talk about any meanings the students do not know or talk about alternate meanings (e.g., *bosses* could mean your *bosses* at work or when someone *bosses* you around).

2. *Sort.* Have your students sort individually or collaboratively as you monitor and facilitate their thinking. At this stage, pattern and sound may factor into categories but grammar may also come into play. Prompt and ask questions that promote high-level thinking and deep processing:

   - What do you notice about the words?
   - What about them looks the same (or different)?
   - What about them sounds the same (or different)?
   - Does the base word or root (or grammar) help?
   - How are these two (or more) words related? (You might ask this question as you highlight certain words to provide more support—similar to "Guess My Category.")

3. *Reflect.* After students have completed their sorts, have them reflect on their hypothesized categories with each other.

Figure 5.18 Completed Open Sort

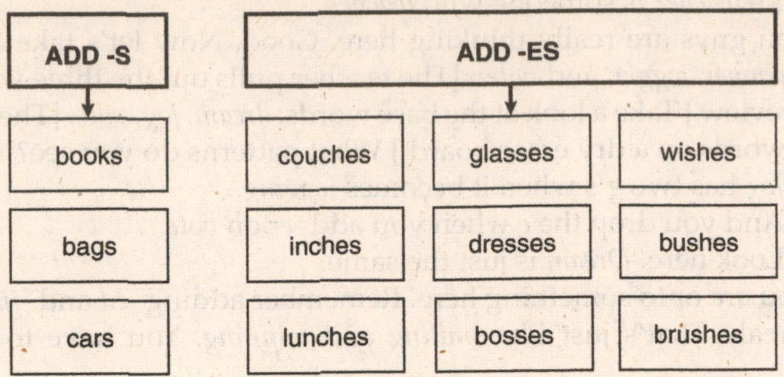

Student 1: Okay. These are all plurals. I have four categories. *Books, bags,* and *cars. Bushes, wishes,* and *brushes. Couches, inches,* and *lunches. Glasses, dresses,* and *bosses.*

Student 2: Wait a minute. I only have two categories. *Books, bags,* and *cars. Couches, glasses, bushes, inches, lunches, wishes, dresses, bosses,* and *brushes.* I have words that have just *-s* and words that have *-es.*

Student 1: That's true. I have *-s* and *-es.* But look. The *-es* category has words like *bush, inch,* and *dress.* See these words end in *-sh, -ch,* and *-ss.*

Teacher: You guys are really thinking. Keep it up. Go back to your sorts and take a closer look at your words that add *-es.* See if you want to make any changes. [At this point, many of the students move the words to create subsorts under the *-es* category. See the completed sort in Figure 5.18.]

4. *Extend.* Help students place this learning into their schema. Use a big picture graphic organizer (described previously in this chapter). Reinforce these generalizations with other activities, such as writing sorts and word hunts.

Writing Sort

Writing sorts provide children with the opportunity to apply their word study work to writing. They also provide additional work categorizing sounds and patterns. Writing sorts can be completed by students independently or in groups with teacher support.

Procedure for Group Implementation

1. *Demonstrate.* Review the keywords and model placement of at least one word. You could use the following language when comparing the various unaccented /əl/ endings (e.g., *-al* in *naval, -el* in *angel, -le* in *angle*), as shown by the sort in Figure 5.19.

Teacher: Okay. Let's review. Remember that the part of speech can help us here . . . and frequency. We have *-al* in *naval* that often notes an adjective. And then *-el* in *angel* and *-le* in *angle.* Frequency can help here: *-le* is more common. What else can help?

Students: [No response.]

Teacher: Okay. A clue . . . how about *angel* and *angle.*

Student 1: Oh. I got it. The hard and soft *g* and *c.* Like in *circle.* That's it.

Teacher: Yep. Now, I just picked up the word *parcel* from my pack of word cards. As I look at this word, I see the *-el* spelling pattern and also see (and hear) that soft

Figure 5.19 Final Unaccented Ending /el/: Writing Sort

-el angel	-le angle	-al naval
novel	able	central
label	battle	final
easel	little	bridal
	table	coastal

c. I'm going to write *parcel* under the keyword *angel* because it has the *-el* spelling pattern for the /əl/ ending. That looks right and sounds right.

2. *Sort.* This step will take your students through a three-part process: Pick a word, choose the category, and spell the word.

3. *Check.* Have the students read each column after they are finished and consider each category's sound, pattern, and part of speech characteristics, such as found in the /əl/ unaccented endings. Mistakes should be addressed and corrected. Guide students to their own discovery of mistakes. Students should address why a particular word was in the wrong category as well as what the appropriate category would be.

4. *Reflect.* Regardless of mistakes, students need to reflect on the sort. A discussion about each category's common features is a key step. For example, after reading *dental, final,* and *rural* in the category /əl/ spelled as *-al* like *naval,* discuss how each of these words is an adjective with the /əl/ sound at the end and the spelling pattern *-al.* They *sound right, look right,* and have the same *part of speech.* Refer back to the visual of the keyword for additional support. Of course, this is not always the case (e.g., *medal*), but it is a useful default.

Blind Writing Sort

As discussed in Chapter 2, blind writing sorts are done after students have had the opportunity to practice the features for the week. This activity will give your students multiple opportunities to work with the features as they write words. You may need to model a blind sort at first, but generally students can work in pairs to do this activity.

Procedure

1. Review the categories and prepare a blank sort page with the keywords at the top.
2. Call out the words without showing the word and ask students to write the words in the appropriate category.
3. Check the blind writing sort after it is completed. Give your students a sort "cheat sheet" or assign a student "checker" if they are working in pairs.
4. After the sort, you could have students reflect on any errors using a student reflection chart (see Chapter 3). Or have students chart their progress as they do subsequent blind sorts across the week, noting increases in accuracy (see Chapter 4).

5. For a spin on the blind writing sort, you could turn it into a version of the game Taboo. First, have students pair up and pick which one will be doing the guessing (the guesser) and which one will be giving the clues (the giver). The guesser should choose a card and place it on his forehead. The giver then reads the word silently and begins to give meaning clues. For example, if the word is *anchor*, the giver might say, "This thing keeps a ship in place." After successfully identifying the word, the guesser should write the word (without looking at the card) in a writing sort. The word can then be turned over to check the spelling. Another quick activity in which students write words with the target feature of study is a dictated sentence that you read aloud for students to write down on paper (e.g., The *muscular sailor* got to work *faster* on his *scooter*).

engagement LINK

Having students hunt through books they are reading concretely illustrates one important reason for word study: to improve their reading.

Word Hunt

The goal of a word hunt is to make the connection between the isolated word study work to reading and writing situations. Students "hunt" through texts they have previously read for words that follow the same target features examined during their teacher-directed lessons. These texts or text selections should be short and manageable so that the students can focus on finding appropriate words for recording.

Procedure

1. Review the keywords for the sort. For example, if your writing sort compared nouns spelled with *-or* as in *doctor*, nouns and comparatives spelled with *-er* as in *barber*, and adjectives spelled with *-ar* as in *polar*, review the sound, pattern, and part of speech of the target features. Afterward, you should always bring the discussion back to the keywords (e.g., *doctor, barber*, and *polar*). See the sample word hunt in Figure 5.20.
2. Engage the students in finding words for their target categories.

Figure 5.20 Final Unaccented Ending /er/: Word Hunt

er barber	ar polar	or doctor
taller	cellular	senator
better	familiar	humor
anger		

3. After completing the hunt, review each category. Have the students read each column and verbalize what is the same about each category in terms of sound, pattern, or part of speech.

Teacher: [Working with a group who have just completed a word hunt for the /ər/ unaccented ending in their independent work.] Let's make a list of the words you all found that fit in our categories for this week: *-er* in *barber*, *-or* in *doctor*, *-ar* in *polar*. [Students call out words for the *-ar* category as the teacher writes them down: *boxcar, lunar, cougar, muscular, particular*.]
Students: Wait. Does *boxcar* go there?
Teacher: What do you think? Why?
Student 1: No. It doesn't. You can hear the /är/. So it must be accented, right?
Teacher: Let's check. [The group looks in a dictionary.] Well, is it?
Student 2: No. It is not accented. But it is a compound word. That's why we hear it. But I have another question. What about *cougar?*
Teacher: This is a good point; *-ar* will not always signal an adjective. But it is good to think of when you are in doubt.

Manipulation

When decoding words, your students can use a strategy called "cover and connect" (O'Connor, 2007). This strategy teaches your students to delete prefixes and suffixes that may have been added to a word to help them identify the base word, which may be more familiar. Take the word *unfocused*. Your students may see the length of this word and become overwhelmed. However, "covering" or deleting the *un-* and the *-ed* leaves the student with the word *focus*, a familiar word that will at least be easily decoded (V-CV syllable pattern). Your students can then "connect" the *un-* and *-ed*, helping them produce the correct pronunciation of *unfocused*. The goal of manipulation at this stage is to highlight various parts of words that could help your students break down longer words. Your students will manipulate the parts of words that they "cover" while using the "cover and connect" strategy. Therefore, these activities should focus on a core word and then add affixes (prefixes and suffixes) to change the word's intention. Not only will these activities help your students decode unknown multisyllable words, but they will also reinforce the word study work done throughout the stage (e.g., inflectional endings, simple affixes).

Procedure

1. Begin the activity by writing a word like *handle* on a dry erase board or in a notebook, for example (see Figure 5.21). Your target words can come from anywhere; the only

Figure 5.21 Manipulation of *handle*

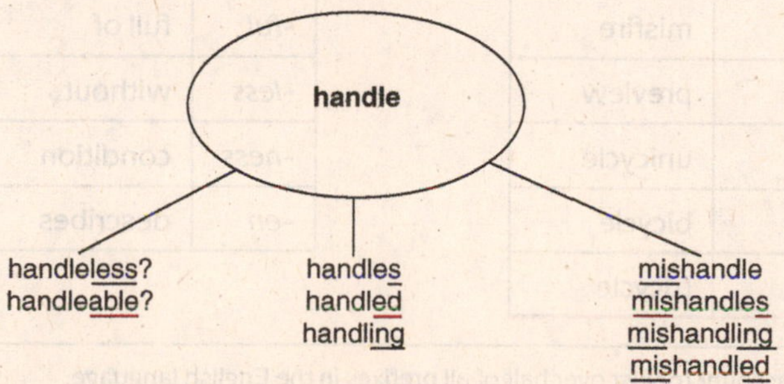

consideration is that the word is not too difficult and lends itself to the activity (a number of affixes can be connected to the word). You may bring up a word found in a book that you are reading with the class. For example, your students may have encountered the word *mishandled* while reading a shared text.

2. Direct your students to read the word and then ask about its meaning. This might bring up a discussion about how *handling* can refer to touching, feeling, carrying something in your hands, or how you deal with a situation or problem.

3. Start creating new words by adding inflectional endings. "What would I need to do to *handle* to indicate that I did it in the past? How would I indicate that I am doing it right now?" Write the words on the board in a collection: *handled, handling, handles.* Make sure that your students are recording accurately along with you. Have them underline the endings, emphasizing parts of words that can be "covered" during decoding tasks.

4. Now direct your students to add any prefixes and suffixes that may make another word. Ask them what *mishandle* means. This question should lead the group to a discussion about what *mis-* means and how it changes the meaning of *handle.* If necessary, you might say, "Remember from our vocabulary work that *mis-* means "wrong" so *mishandle* must mean that you handled something wrong. You could *mishandle* something you are carrying or touching or you could *mishandle* a situation . . . like what happened with Ruthie in our story." Have your students underline the prefix.

5. Create new words by adding inflectional endings to the new words that were created in step 4. Take the word *mishandle* and follow the same process described in step 3. These words would go into their own collection. Direct your students to underline the prefixes and endings.

6. Direct your students to think of any other endings that could be added to *handle.* You may even have a "bank" of the prefixes and suffixes that you have studied during your vocabulary work that could be of assistance to your students (see Figure 5.22). This step may leave you with some questionable words; are *handleable* and *handleless* real words? Even if your students suggest nonwords, go with it. Your students are exercising their

Figure 5.22 Bank of Prefixes and Suffixes

Prefixes (beginning)		
**un-*	not	unlock
**re-*	again	remake
**dis-*	opposite	dismiss
**in-*	in, into	indoor
mis-	not	misfire
pre-	before	preview
uni-	one	unicycle
bi-	two	bicycle
tri-	three	tricycle

Suffixes (ending)		
-y	like (adj)	jumpy
-ly	like (adv)	gladly
-er	compare (2)	taller
-est	compare (>2)	tallest
-ful	full of	graceful
-less	without	penniless
-ness	condition	happiness
-en	describes	golden

* These four prefixes account for just over half of all prefixes in the English language.

knowledge of how to add affixes and how meanings are affected all the same. Just be sure to point out that the particular words are not real words. Again, have your students underline the affixes.

7. Make the connection between this activity and decoding words very clear. To do this, you could take a word that was generated from the activity and think aloud.

Teacher: Let's take the word *mishandling*. If I were reading and came across this word without knowing it, I would look at it first to see if there were any parts of the word I could cover up. If there are, I bet I might know the base word already. I just have to get any beginnings or endings off so that I can see the base word by itself. Let's see. Well, here is one for sure. I see an *-ing* ending. I'm going to cover that up. Now I see a beginning I can cover up: *mis-*. I am going to cover that up. Now I have the word *handl*. Bet it has an *e* at the end that was taken off with the *-ing*. I know that. *Handle*. Now I'm going to connect the beginning (*mis-*) and I have *mishandle*. Now I'll put the *-ing* back on. *Mishandling*. Let me reread the sentence to make sure it makes sense.

Word Analysis

Students who do not have effective strategies for decoding unknown words will tend to get mired in their reading. These issues with decoding can negatively impact comprehension. As discussed in the previous chapter, struggling readers may use their background knowledge about a topic to compensate for deficiencies in word recognition. However, when faced with material introducing new concepts and information, students may not have background knowledge. Helping our struggling readers develop a range of strategies for word analysis is critical. In this chapter, we will focus on the strategy of syllabication. Use two-syllable words for this work. The following common syllable patterns can be used for particular study (Bear et al., 2008; Morris, 2008; O'Connor, 2007):

1. V-CV (open): *bacon, pilot, favor*
2. VC-CV (closed, regular): *number, basket, window*
3. VC-CV (closed, doublet): *bonnet, rubber, ladder*
4. VC-V (closed): *river, planet, robin*
5. Cle (unaccented ending): *angle, middle, baffle*
6. VCC-CV, VC-CCV, or VCCC-V (closed): *athlete, pilgrim, pitcher*
7. V-V (open): *create, riot, liar*

Begin this study by helping your students break words apart into syllables. Identifying the syllable break will facilitate recognition of the word. A prerequisite for this work is the mastery of one-syllable patterns (e.g., CVC, CVCe, CVVC, CVCC, etc.). The following sequence of steps, based on Morris (2008), is meant to explain how you would introduce the concept of syllabication.

1. Open and closed syllables must be explained as an initial step. Remember from our discussion earlier in the chapter that open syllables end in a vowel (the vowel is not closed by a consonant and remains open) as in *so-lar*, and the vowels are long. The pattern of one-syllable words that are open is CV (e.g., *me, go, be*). Closed syllables end with a consonant (the consonant closes the vowel) as in *bum-per*, and the vowel is short. The pattern of one-syllable words that are closed is CVC (e.g., *cat, bed, dog*). Morris (2008) suggests having your students practice reading lists of words and nonwords with open and closed syllables. Present your students with CVC and CV words on cards for them to read and place in the appropriate category (see Figure 5.23). Once your students can read and sort these words accurately and quickly, then you are ready to continue with step 2.

Figure 5.23 Closed and Open Syllable Sort

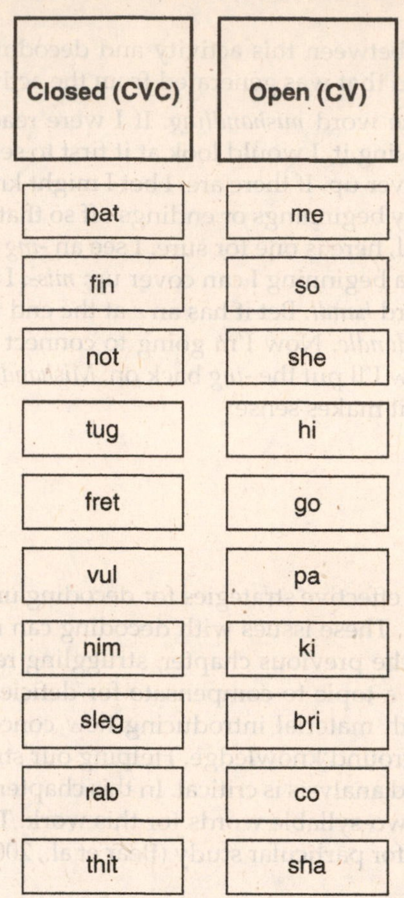

Closed (CVC)
Open (CV)
pat
me
fin
so
not
she
tug
hi
fret
go
vul
pa
nim
ki
sleg
bri
rab
co
thit
sha

2. Now you will move to a study of pattern across syllables (the seven syllable patterns outlined earlier). Begin with a study of V-CV open and VC-CV closed syllable patterns (see Figure 5.24). To begin the sort, explain the two headers: V-CV open as in *pi-lot* and VC-CV closed as in *bas-ket*.

Teacher: We are going to talk about patterns in words that have more than one syllable. The key to reading these words is deciding where the syllable breaks. The first thing you need to do is look for the consonant (there will be one or more consonants) in the word separating the vowels. Remember your vowels are *a, e, i, o, u*. Let's look at *basket*. Notice that there are two consonants in the middle of this word dividing the vowels *a* and *e*. When this happens, you divide the word between the two consonants. See our pattern: VC-CV. That is how *basket* is divided: *bas-ket* (between the two consonants). Now that we know where the syllable break occurs, we can cover up the second syllable and put our attention on the first syllable, *bas-*. [Cover up *-ket.*] What kind of syllable is this?

Students: Closed.

Teacher: Right. It is a closed CVC pattern like *cat, bed,* and *dog*. So how would you pronounce *bas-?*

Students: /bas/

Teacher: That's right. You would pronounce it with a short *a* because the syllable is closed, making the syllable /bas/. Now, let's read the whole word. [Uncover *-ket.*] That's it. The word is *basket*.

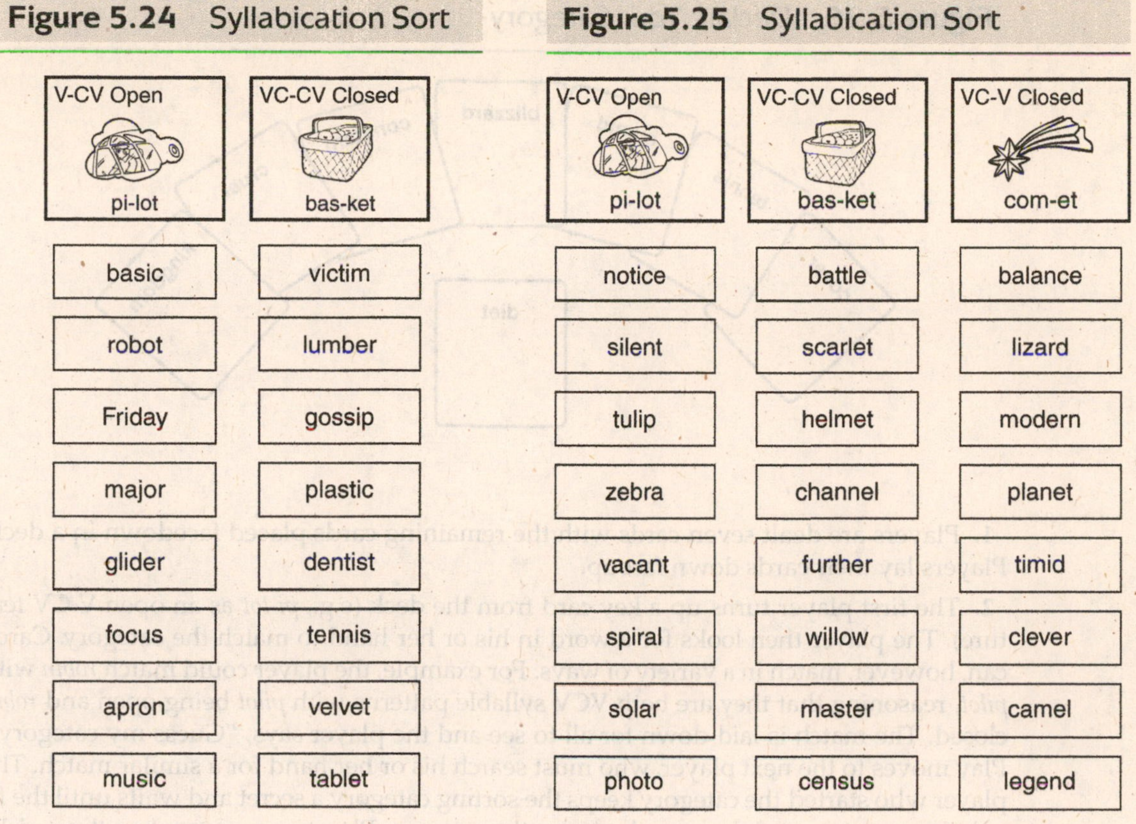

V-CV Open
pi-lot
VC-CV Closed
bas-ket
basic
robot
Friday
major
glider
focus
apron
music
victim
lumber
gossip
plastic
dentist
tennis
velvet
tablet
V-CV Open
pi-lot
VC-CV Closed
bas-ket
VC-V Closed
com-et
notice
silent
tulip
zebra
vacant
spiral
solar
photo
battle
scarlet
helmet
channel
further
willow
master
census
balance
lizard
modern
planet
timid
clever
camel
legend

Figure 5.24 Syllabication Sort

Figure 5.25 Syllabication Sort

3. Introduce the next category (V-CV open as in pilot) as in step 2.
4. Move them to the sort next, as shown in Figure 5.24. As they sort words into the two categories, make sure they are reading each word aloud.
5. After this lesson, introduce the VC-CV closed doublet syllable pattern as in *rab-bit* and include the regular and doublet in the VC-CV category. Then you can move to sorts that include other patterns like VC-V closed (*com-et*) as in Figure 5.25. You would continue following the explanation procedure introduced in step 2.

Games

Games are an engaging way to provide students with additional practice of current features as well as review of previous features. Games can also be played with or without teacher support, but keep in mind that teacher support is critical when introducing a new game. As noted in Chapter 4, you can modify games to include a more collaborative format if competition is an issue for the students. Modify games to include writing components if possible to provide students with an opportunity for application.

Declare Your Category

This game, shown in Figure 5.26, is for two to five players (three is optimal). The goal is to guess the first player's category. You will need a deck of 45 word cards with a variety of vowels and vowel patterns. Make at least four cards with any one pattern and a wild card for the pile.

Figure 5.26 Declare Your Category

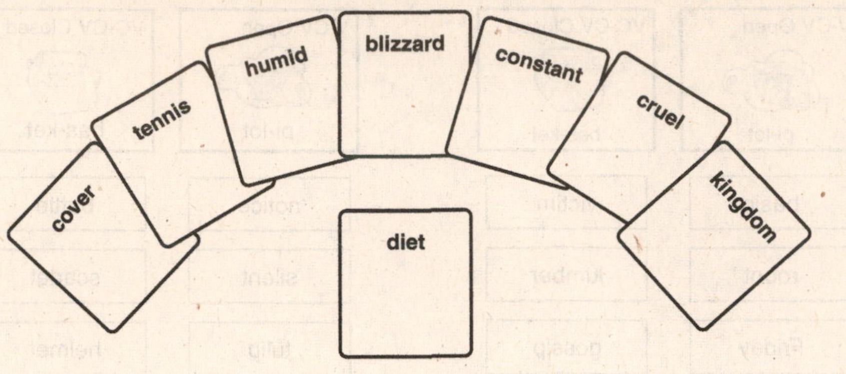

1. Players are dealt seven cards with the remaining cards placed facedown in a deck. Players lay their cards down faceup.

2. The first player turns up a key card from the deck (e.g., *pi-lot* as an open V-CV feature). The player then looks for a word in his or her hand to match the category. Cards can, however, match in a variety of ways. For example, the player could match *robin* with *pilot*, reasoning that they are both VCV syllable patterns with *pilot* being open and *robin* closed. The match is laid down for all to see and the player says, "Guess my category." Play moves to the next player, who must search his or her hand for a similar match. The player who started the category keeps the sorting category a secret and waits until the final player puts a card down and guesses the category. Players can pass when they wish.

3. If a wild card is drawn, the player has the opportunity to change the category midstream. This player must first announce the current category and then establish the new category. For example, the player might say, "Your category was the VCV syllable pattern like in *pilot* and *robin*. But *pilot* is open and *robin* is closed." The player then lays down the wild card along with his or her new card. Then the player tells the group to guess the new category.

4. If the player who set up the category does not think the next player put down an acceptable card, then she or he sends the card back and gives that player another chance. Mistakes are discussed at the end of each round.

5. The player who plays the last card has to guess the category. If correct, the player is the winner and keeps all of the cards. If the player is wrong, then the previous player gets a chance to guess the category.

6. At the end of each round, students are dealt enough cards to get them back to seven. The winner of the round turns up a card from the pile and makes up the next category.

7. The player with the most cards wins. As an enhancement, players could make a record of the cards laid in each round along with a written explanation of each category.

Scattergories

This game is a take on the popular Hasbro fast-thinking game. Two to six players participate with the objective of accruing the greatest number of points. You will need to make category cards and answer sheets with three columns of 12 blank lines for your students (or have them record answers in a notebook set up with three columns and 12 numbered lines as shown in Figure 5.27). Category cards are set up with the features (along with keywords) that you have previously covered (these cards could even cover features from a previous stage for maintenance and review). You will also need a timer.

Figure 5.27 Scattergories

Add -ing

Double	e-Drop	No Change
1. hopping	waving	jumping
2. tapping	baking	chilling
3. skipping	biking	coaching
4.	hiking	needing
5.	joking	
6.		
7.		
8.		
9.		
10.		
11.		
12.		

(12)

1. Each player is given an answer sheet. The lead player turns over the first category card and then starts the timer for one minute. In the time given, each player must think of as many words as they can that fit the category and write them on the answer sheet. For example, if the category is adding *-ing* to base words that don't change, the students could write *coaching, starting, lifting, camping, walking,* and so on.

2. When the time is up, players each read the words recorded on their answer sheets. In order for a player to get a point for a word, the word must be in the right category *and* spelled correctly. Players get a point for every word that meets those criteria.

3. Once points are tallied, the player to the left of the lead player turns over the next category card. The timer would then begin (again for one minute) once the players have read and understand the new category card. Players record answers on their answer sheet and then tally up points. Steps one and two are repeated for a third round

4. The winner is the student with the most points after three rounds of play.

For an added challenge, you could establish a rule that points are only given for words found on only one answer sheet. For example, if a player records *walking* for the "add *-ing* with no change to base word category" and one or more players have *walking* as well, then no points are given for that word.

steal

adapt

lose

chapter 6

Generative Vocabulary Instruction

Teaching Struggling Readers to Crack the Meaning Code in English

We do not have fond memories of our own high school SAT vocabulary prep instruction. Each week our well-meaning English teachers gave us a list of 30 to 40 new words to study. Organized alphabetically, in a typical week the lists might include assigned words like *boisterous, bombast,* and *brogue*—grouped not by any common meaning they shared but simply because they all happened to fall under the letter *B* in the dictionary. Figure 6.1 shows a typical list of 40 words we might have been assigned each week (Robinson & Princeton Review, 1997). Briefly read through this list and ask yourself how many words your top students might already know. Your average students? Your struggling readers?

We dutifully looked up the words in the dictionary, wrote them in sentences, and memorized their corresponding definitions for the Friday quiz. By the middle of the following week, we were so focused on learning the next slew of 40 words that we were fortunate if we remembered even half the definitions from the previous week. Now, how effective would this type of instruction be with your struggling readers? Would it engage and motivate them? Would it lead to long-term, deep understanding of vocabulary that could be readily applied in their reading and writing?

This type of word-by-word instruction, based on brute memorization and superficial word learning, is not a recipe for successfully closing the vocabulary gap for at-risk students. In fact, it is a perfect example of the "phone number syndrome" (Stahl & Nagy, 2006) described in Chapter 2, in which we memorize the telephone numbers (definitions) only long enough to dial (take the test). After that, we forget most of them. There is nothing particularly wrong with these words—in fact, many of them (such as *brusque,*

Figure 6.1 Typical Weekly List of 40 SAT Prep Vocabulary Words

bacchanal	benediction	bombast	brevity
baleful	benefactor	bon vivant	bristle
balk	benevolent	bona fide	broach
ballyhoo	benign	botch	brogue
banal	bilious	bourgeois	brouhaha
bandy	billow	bracing	brusque
baroque	blasphemy	brackish	bucolic
bastion	blatant	brandish	bulwark
bedlam	bohemian	bravado	bureaucracy
belligerent	boisterous	brazen	byzantine

bristle, and *brevity*) are exactly the types of words our students will encounter in middle grade and high school texts and are exactly the types of words we want them to use in their writing. Rather, the problems concern (a) how *many unknown* words were assigned, (b) how the words were *organized* for instruction, and (c) how the words were *taught.* Unfortunately, this word-by-word assign-and-assess type of vocabulary instruction is still the predominant method used in too many of our schools.

A Comprehensive Approach to Teaching Vocabulary

A comprehensive three-part approach to vocabulary instruction is critical in helping struggling readers close the vocabulary gap (Templeton et al., 2010):

- Overall context (reading, writing, and rich discussions)
- Direct vocabulary instruction (generative and word-specific)
- Word consciousness

If our struggling readers are to have any chance of closing the vocabulary gap, direct vocabulary instruction must occur within the *context* of wide reading, along with purposeful writing and immersion in rich oral language. This is because from approximately fourth grade on, students will acquire the majority of new vocabulary words incidentally through wide reading. Students who are *not* reading a lot or being read aloud to in more advanced texts—as is too often the case with many of our struggling readers—will *not* encounter the more sophisticated vocabulary found in these books. Therefore, a first major step in vocabulary instruction is to increase the amount of appropriate, engaged reading (and being read aloud to from more advanced texts) for our struggling readers (Cunningham & Stanovich, 1998).

In addition, struggling readers need direct vocabulary instruction. To be effective, this direct vocabulary instruction must engage students and lead to a deep understanding of specific words and how words work. It should also help develop a trait called *word consciousness* in our students—a positive disposition toward words. Finally, vocabulary instruction should be based on the student's development and prior knowledge. Chapter 8, Vocabulary Assessment and Organization, discusses how to use assessments to plan vocabulary instruction that is targeted to your students' needs, levels of development, and prior conceptual knowledge.

There are two main types of direct vocabulary instruction: generative and word-specific. *Word-specific vocabulary instruction* refers to teaching that targets specific words and the concepts they represent (e.g., teaching the concept of *photosynthesis* to a biology class). Chapter 7 will focus on this type of vocabulary teaching. *Generative vocabulary instruction,* on the other hand, refers to teaching students how words work (e.g., exploring how *photosynthesis* is related to *photocopier, telephoto,* and *photograph* and *synthesize, synthesizer,* and *synthetic*). This chapter will describe how you can help your struggling readers tap into the power of generative vocabulary instruction and "crack the meaning code" that pervades the English language.

The Power of Generative Vocabulary Instruction: Catching Up with the Classics

Wouldn't it be wonderful if there were a "secret" to teaching vocabulary? An approach that was 10 to 20 times more effective (or more) than the traditional word-by-word vocabulary instruction described earlier? A system that could help our struggling readers not only remember many more words, but also learn them more deeply and make connections among them? A method that could help them uncover the meanings of potentially tens of thousands of upper-level words independently while reading?

Incredibly, there is such a secret to vocabulary instruction. English has a built-in system of meaning—or *morphology*—that is largely based on the classic Latin and Greek origins of our language. Unfortunately, we have traditionally only let our highest performing students (the ones taking Latin and Greek or AP English classes) fully in on this secret. Students who are able to "crack the meaning code" in English and tap into this system are at a great advantage in learning new vocabulary, particularly the higher-level academic vocabulary that permeates the middle and high school curriculum. Consider the following:

- Over 60 percent of English vocabulary is created through a combination of Latin and Greek roots, prefixes, and suffixes. Some estimates go as high as 75 percent (Nagy & Anderson, 1984; Padak, Newton, Rasinski, & Newton, 2008).
- Over 90 percent of the vocabulary of the sciences and technology is created through a combination of Latin and Greek roots, prefixes, and suffixes (Green, 2008).
- "90 percent of English words with more than one syllable are Latin based. Most of the remaining 10 percent are Greek based" (Rasinski, Padak, Newton, & Newton, 2008, p. 11).
- Morphological knowledge makes a significant contribution to reading ability (Carlisle, 1995; Nagy, Berninger, & Abbott, 2006) and is correlated with reading ability through high school (Nagy, Diakidoy, & Anderson, 1993).

If 90 percent of science and technology vocabulary and 90 percent of multisyllabic words—90 percent of the very words our struggling readers need to succeed in the middle grades and high school—belong to a system, doesn't it make sense to explicitly teach our struggling readers about this system? Doesn't it make sense to provide all of our students, and particularly our struggling readers, the tools that will enable them to crack the meaning code of English? Instead of teaching our language one word at a time, we can teach our struggling readers the *meaning system that underlies our language.*

This much more mindful, productive, and engaging approach to teaching and learning vocabulary capitalizes on the generative nature of the English language—the fact that thousands of words can be constructed, or *generated,* by combining a finite number of roots, prefixes, and suffixes. For example, it makes sense to study words like *cosmic, cosmology, cosmos, cosmopolitan,* and *microcosm* together because they share the same root (*cosm* meaning "world") and thus are related in meaning. Students are much more likely to remember and use these words because knowledge of a single root provides a key to unlock the meanings of all these derivations, not to mention all the derivations they may encounter in future reading. We tell our middle and high school students that while phonics knowledge helped you decode the *sounds* of words as a beginning reader, root knowledge will help you decode the *meanings* of words as an advanced reader. Or, more simply put, phonics is to *learning to read* what generative knowledge is to *reading to learn.*

We can apply this generative principle to many of the words in the 40-word SAT vocabulary prep list from the beginning of this chapter (Figure 6.1). For example, it makes sense to examine four words from this list—*benediction* (a blessing), *benefactor* (one that gives help), *benevolent* (characterized by doing good), and *benign* (of kind and gentle disposition)—together because they all share the same Latin root and thus a common meaning derived from *bene* or *beni,* meaning "good." Words such as *beneficiary, benefit,* and *beneficial* could be added to this list. And wouldn't it make sense to study the root *bene/beni* alongside its opposite, the Latin root *mal/male* (meaning "badly")? We would include words such as *malice, malicious, malediction, malefactor, malevolent, malevolence, malign,* and *malignant*. In fact, many of the words derived from these two roots are mirror images of each other (if not all strictly antonyms):

- benediction/malediction
- benevolent/malevolent
- benevolence/malevolence

- benefactor/malefactor
- benign/malign

These examples give you a flavor for the potential power of generative vocabulary instruction. Studying high-frequency roots, prefixes, and suffixes actually gives our struggling readers a real shot at closing the daunting vocabulary gap because when they learn one word, they actually learn 10, 20, 30 words, or more (Templeton, 2007). In terms of root knowledge, a little goes a long way. For example, the following 47 words were generated from only two roots:

- *vers* ("to turn")—revert, vertex, vertigo, convert, divert, vertical, adverse, adversary, advertise, anniversary, avert, controversy, conversation, extrovert, introvert, inverse, inverted, perverted, reverse, subvert, traverse, transverse, universe, versatile, versus, vertebra.
- *miss, mitt* ("send")—transmission, remission, submission, admit, transmit, remit, submit, omit, mission, missile, demise, emission, admission, commission, emissary, intermission, intermittent, missionary, permission, promise, missive

As you read through these 47 words, notice how knowledge of only two roots can help unlock the meanings of scores of words. An *introvert* is literally someone who turns (*vert*) inward (*intro*). An *extrovert* is literally someone who turns (*vert*) outward (*extro*). An *adversary* is an enemy who opposes you by turning (*vert*) toward (*ad*) you (because they wouldn't want to turn their back to you!). What makes more sense for our struggling readers—studying 47 separate, unrelated words per week or studying two roots per week? Or over the long haul, studying 40,000 separate words (the average reading vocabulary of a high school graduate) or studying 100 high-frequency affixes and roots (see the chapter appendix for a sequence of instruction for core affixes and roots)? When we organize vocabulary instruction by meaning element and root, the vocabulary learning task for the students and the vocabulary teaching task for the teacher become much more manageable and motivating. Our struggling readers are more likely to remember these 47 words and actually use them because their meanings are part of a larger system that makes sense.

An oft-quoted aphorism states, "Give a man a fish, he can eat for a day. Teach him to fish, he can eat for a lifetime." The same holds true for vocabulary instruction. Word-specific instruction gives our students the fish; generative instruction teaches them how to fish. We understand that it is essential in the content areas to teach students individual words and the important concepts they represent, such as *biome* and *biology*—in fact, this word-specific instruction is the focus of Chapter 7. However, if this is all we do, we are simply doing the fishing for our students.

If, on the other hand, we also teach our students how *biome* and *biology* are related to *antibiotic, biography, autobiography,* and *biodegradable,* we are teaching them how to fish for words. When these students encounter unfamiliar words in their future reading that share the *bio* root (meaning "life"), like *biopsy* or *symbiotic,* they will be more likely to "hook" these words and reel them in—decoding the words' meanings, storing them solidly in memory, and using them later in speech and writing. This type of morphemic analysis provides our students the keys to unlock the meaning code that permeates the English language.

engagement LINK

Generative vocabulary instruction is inherently engaging because it puts students "in the driver's seat" by giving them the keys to independently learn new words.

Generative Instruction with Content Area Vocabulary

Teaching students about Latin and Greek prefixes, suffixes, and roots has traditionally been considered the purview of the English teacher in middle and high school. However, generative vocabulary knowledge is critical to reading comprehension and content area learning not only in English, but across the subject areas in math, social studies, and science as well.

To give you a sense of how pervasive generative vocabulary is across the subject areas, we reviewed four high school content area textbooks and found the following words that contained Latin or Greek prefixes, suffixes, or roots within the space of only two or three pages.

- *Earth Science* (Unit D—"Earth's Atmosphere") (Trefil, Calvo, & Cutler, 2005, pp. D60–62)—troposphere, altitude, crystals, cirrus, cumulus, stratus, nimbo-, nimbus, alto, medium, prefix, cirrocumulus, cirrostratus, cumulonimbus, altocumulus, altostratus, nimbostratus, precipitation, vapor, kilometers
- *Geometry: Explorations and Applications* (Aichele et al., 1998, pp. 219–220)—parallel, transversal, oxygen, combining, carbon dioxide, exhale, process, veins, intersecting, plane, points, angles, same-side interior angles, alternate-side interior angles, corresponding angles, diagrams
- *World Cultures and Geography* (Bednarz, Miyares, Schug, & White, 2005, pp. 124–126)—constitutional monarchy, monarch, legislative, legislature, laws, judicial, judiciary, justice, executive, representative, genuine, parliament, Senate, prime minister, provinces, majority, resign, dissolve, populations, geography, nations, capital, constitutional republic, president, Congress, federal, equality, democracy
- "A Wagner Matinee" by Willa Cather (in *The Language of Literature: American Literature,* Applebee et al., 2000, pp. 692–693)—tremulously, semi-somnambulant, symphony orchestra, conversed, timid, evidently, operas, respective, passive, inert, perceive, trepidation, absurdities, superficially, impersonal, solitary, conscious, veritable, matinee audience, contour, impressionist

Although you certainly do not want to point out every single Latin- or Greek-derived word that students encounter (you would never get anything else done!), it can be very helpful for students to highlight a root that is particularly prevalent in your content area or that helps your students make connections between new words they encounter and related words that they already know. Consider the following examples.

- From the earth science textbook, knowledge of a few Latin roots (*nimbus,* "rain"; *stratus,* "spread out"; and *cumulus,* "heaped or piled") can go a long way in helping students identify and remember the many different cloud types.
- From the geography textbook, knowledge of just two Latin roots (*jud,* "judge" and *leg,* "law") can help students see the meaning connections among related words on the list and additional content words like *judicial, judiciary, judge, judgement* and *legal, legislate, legislative, legislature.*
- From "A Wagner Matinee," English students can make a "new-to-known" connection with the initially daunting adjective *tremulous* (meaning "characterized by trembling, fearful"). Although your students may not know *tremulous,* you can point out a known word that shares a root and meaning—*tremble.* By connecting *tremulous* to *tremble,* students are much more likely to learn and remember the new word.

As you can see from these examples, the language of academic learning is, in a very large sense, the language of Latin and Greek. Although the bulk of generative vocabulary instruction may be directly taught by English teachers, it can and should be further exercised and guided across the content areas by math, science, and social studies teachers. One simple way to start making these connections is to hang charts of high-frequency Latin and Greek affixes and roots in all content area classrooms. During the course of lessons, teachers and students can make connections as they come up. More formally, vocabulary notebooks (see the Activities for Generative Vocabulary Instruction section at the end of this chapter) provide a motivating avenue for making these vocabulary connections across the content areas.

Figure 6.2 provides examples of some common roots found in math, social studies, and science. You can scan Appendix F in the back of this book—Word and Root Lists for

Figure 6.2 Examples of Generative Roots and Affixes across Content Areas

Mathematics	*syn-/sym-* (together, with)—symmetry, symbolic, symbol, line of symmetry
	equ- (equal)—equilaterial triangle, equation, equidistant
	gon (angle)—hexagon, pentagon, polygon, octagon, decagon, diagonal
Social studies/ history	*civ* (citizen)—civic, civil rights, civil war, city
	leg (law)—legal, legislate, legislature
	popul/pub (people)—population, populace, public, republic
Science	*therm* (heat)—thermometer, thermodynamic, geothermal, endothermic
	radi (ray)—radiate, radiation, radio wave, radioactive
	sol (sun)—solstice, solar, solar system, solar energy

Generative Activities and Word Sorts—and keep an eye out for roots that are common to your content area and curriculum. Record these roots on charts as you introduce them to students in the course of normal classroom instruction. Include the root's core meaning and examples of content vocabulary words that include this root, as in Figure 6.2. (For a more thorough discussion of generative roots found across the content areas and a more extensive version of Figure 6.2, see Templeton et al., 2010.)

Morphemic Analysis and the Spelling–Meaning Connection

Two related concepts are at the heart of generative vocabulary learning—*morphemic analysis* and the *spelling–meaning connection* (Templeton, 1983). A struggling reader in the syllables and affixes stage (see Chapter 5) attempting to read the word *biology* would most likely analyze it syllable by syllable as in *bi-ol-o-gy*. Although this syllable-by-syllable analysis might be helpful in decoding the word, it is not as helpful in uncovering the word's meaning. In contrast, a more advanced reader would most likely process this word by meaningful letter chunks *bio-logy*, which often cross syllable boundaries. We call these meaning units in language, such as the Greek root *bio* (meaning "life"), *morphemes*. Students who can analyze language by morphemes are much better equipped to learn the meanings of unfamiliar words in their reading, store these words in memory, and eventually use them in their speaking and writing. Morphemic analysis is a powerful tool for independent word learning and should be taught directly to struggling readers (Figure 6.5 on page 171 describes a step-by-step procedure for teaching students how to break down longer unknown words by morpheme).

One middle school student we worked with demonstrated the power of morphemic analysis as she attempted to break down the word *retrospect* into its morphemes. She used the following reasoning: "*Retro* . . . Hmmm . . . Isn't that like those "retro jeans" they sell today that look like the jeans they wore way back in the hippy days with the bell-bottoms? *Retro* must mean back in the old days, and we already know that *spect* means 'to look' from last week's root study. So, *retrospect* must mean looking back into the old days!" Needless to say, we were delighted with her reasoning and engagement. From examples like this, you can see the power of morphemic analysis and generative vocabulary instruction (not to mention the enthusiasm!).

Morphemes are made transparent in our language through their spellings. The spelling–meaning connection refers to the direct visual link between the spelling of a word and its meaning and is at the heart of English's meaning code (Bear et al., 2008; Templeton, 1983). Spelling is important because of the variability in how the same root can *sound* across different derivations of a word. For example, Figure 6.3 illustrates how one root—*bio*—can actually carry three different pronunciations across a number of

Figure 6.3 The Root *bio* Is Pronounced Three Different Ways

o in *bio:* short /o/ sound as in "rot"	*o* in *bio:* long /o/ sound as in "bone"	*i* in *bio:* long /e/ sound as in "keep"
antibiotic	biochemistry	amphibious
autobiography	biodegradable	symbiotic
biography	biome	
biopsy		
biology		

derived words. Read aloud the words in each column and you will hear how *bio* actually sounds different across the columns. In the left-hand column words like antibiotic, the *o* is short. In the middle-column words like biochemistry, the *o* is long. In amphibious, in the right-hand column, the *i* actually represents a long *e* sound.

Why then don't we spell these words phonetically, as they sound? Compare the following set of three words as they are actually spelled and as they might be spelled phonetically:

antibiotic	biochemistry	amphibious
antibyautic	biochemistry	amphibeeus

As you can see, if we spelled these words completely by sound, we lose the direct visual clue that our spelling system gives to readers to let them know that these words are related in meaning. If we spell completely by sound, we literally lose *sight* of the root. By keeping the spelling of the root constant across these words—despite any changes in sound—we provide a visual clue to the reader that these words are related in meaning. In other words, it is not the sound, but the spelling of the word and root that holds the meaning clue for the reader. This is why a working knowledge of high-frequency affixes and roots is so critical to vocabulary development for our struggling readers.

As students explore roots, they will come across some roots that have more than one spelling. For example, both *miss* and *mit* mean "send" in words like *transmit/transmission* and *submit/submission*. As you can see, these different spellings for the same root are usually very close, and thus easy to remember. In addition, as in the *miss/mit* example, there is often a pattern for the change in root spelling of some derived words: The change in root spelling that accompanies the /shun/affix is signaled by the change in part of speech (*mit* in *transmit* and *submit* signals a verb; *miss* in *transmission* and *submission* signals a noun).

As students explore spelling–meaning connections across words, we guide them to become explicitly aware of the spelling–meaning principle as it applies in English: Words that are related in meaning are often related in spelling as well, despite changes in sound (Chomsky, 1970; Templeton, 1983). We tell our students, "When you first learned to read you had to learn how spelling stands for sound. Now, you're going to be learning how spelling stands for meaning" (Bear et al., 2008, p. 233).

Teaching Our Students the Language of Language: Base Words, Roots, Affixes, Prefixes, and Suffixes

Educators and linguists have historically used many terms to refer to Greek and Latin word elements: *roots, root words, base words, stems, word parts,* and *combining forms,* among others. If we as teachers are not careful and consistent in our use of these terms, we run the risk of overwhelming and confusing our students. We recommend teaching and using the following terms with your struggling readers: *affixes, prefixes, suffixes, roots,* and *base words.*

An *affix* is a word part that attaches to a root or base word. There are two types of affixes—prefixes and suffixes. *Prefixes* attach at the beginning of a root or base word. *Suffixes* attach at the end of a root or base word. For example, in the word *undependable,* the prefix is *un-* ("not"), the base word is *depend,* and the suffix is *-able* ("capable of"). A morphemic analysis of this word strikes at the heart of its meaning: an *undependable* person is one who literally is not capable of being depended, or relied, on.

engagement LINK

When we give our students a common language to talk about language, we are giving them the tools to be metacognitive. They are more explicitly aware of our language system when they have been given the words and concepts to think and talk about it.

It is also important to distinquish between word parts that can stand alone and those that cannot. The consistent use of the two terms *root* and *base word* is clear and helpful to students when talking about word parts. First, we call word parts that cannot stand alone *roots.* Tell your students that just as tree roots underground cannot survive alone without attaching to the trunk, branches, and leaves above the ground, language roots like *aud* cannot stand alone as words without attaching to other word parts, as in *audible, auditorium,* and *audience.* (Notice that we use the term *root,* not *root word,* which can be confusing and something of an oxymoron to students; as one student asked, "How can *aud* be called a root *word* when you just told me a root cannot really stand alone as a word?"). Second, we tell our students that *base words* are those word parts that *can* stand alone. Word pairs like *depend/dependable* and *break/breakable* are examples of base words to which suffixes can attach to generate new, related words.

Generative Vocabulary: Sequence of Instruction for Core Affixes and Roots

Which prefixes, suffixes, and roots will give our struggling readers the most "bang for their buck" in middle and high school? Which morphological elements occur most frequently in upper-level vocabulary and across the content areas? In what order should we teach them? The appendix at the end of this chapter presents a general sequence for the most common "core" prefixes, suffixes, and Latin and Greek roots (Templeton et al., 2010).

This chart is not an ironclad sequence that you must follow in strict order but is more of a general roadmap to guide you and your students in your explorations of the affixes and roots in our language. Seize a "teachable moment" to point out morphological connections as they come up naturally in your classroom. The core elements in the chapter appendix will occur across all content areas and should be directly taught by English/language arts teachers from the intermediate grades on. We recommend that these roots be explicitly taught and directly examined by students because of their frequency and high utility. Appendix F contains additional Greek and Latin roots.

We have divided this sequence into two parts: "Strand 1: Base Words and Most Frequent Affixes," and "Strand 2: Latin and Greek Roots and Additional Affixes." The sequence within each strand and across the two strands is based on (a) the frequency of the element's occurrence and (b) the abstractness of the element's meaning. Students begin by studying higher-frequency and more concrete elements in strand 1 and move to exploring lower-frequency and more abstract elements in strand 2. In Chapter 8, Vocabulary Assessment and Organization, we discuss how you can use generative vocabulary assessments to help determine whether your students would benefit most from beginning in strand 1 or whether they have sufficient morphological knowledge to explore the more abstract affixes and roots in strand 2. In the following sections, we discuss the principles of teaching morphology in each strand and highlight certain "focus features"—prefixes, suffixes, or roots that are particularly important or might be especially difficult for struggling readers to understand.

Strand 1: Base Words and Most Frequent Affixes

In strand 1, we focus on higher-frequency affixes and concrete base words, rather than the more abstract roots. Prefixes such as *un-*, *re-*, and *non-* are taught early in strand 1 because these are the most commonly occurring prefixes in analyses of written texts from first grade through college (Zeno, Ivens, Millard, & Duvvuri, 1995). Also, when we combine these prefixes with base words, the resulting word meanings are usually clear and transparent. For example, adding *un-* ("not" or "opposite of") to the base words *even*, *broken*, and *tangle* results in *uneven*, *unbroken*, and *untangle*—words whose meanings are straightforward and easy to decode. Roots, such as the *aud* in *auditory*, are less transparent than base words and thus are not examined until strand 2.

Many of these most commonly occurring affixes in the early part of this sequence are usually part of the English/language arts curriculum as early as the third grade. However, this does not mean that struggling readers (or even most of our students) will have internalized these morphemes or be able to apply them in analyzing words while reading or writing. For this reason, it is important to target these elements again in the later grades, using words that are more appropriate for the grade level you teach.

Principles of Teaching Morphology in Strand 1: Base Words and Affixes

Use the following two principles (Templeton et al., 2010) to guide your instruction in strand 1:

- Teach prefixes and suffixes with familiar base words. Start with words in which a spelling change does not occur when the affix is added. Then examine words in which a spelling change does occur.
- Model how to flexibly apply knowledge of the new affix in context.

For example, when examining the suffix *-ion*, start with words that end in *-ct* or *-ss*, which do not change when adding *-ion* (*reject/rejection* and *transgress/transgression*). Later, move to words pairs in which the spelling of the base word does change when adding *-ion*, as in *divide/division*.

Focus Feature: Adding *-ion* to Words

Hundreds of words in the English language end with the *-ion* suffix, and because so many of these *-ion* words are familiar to students, this suffix can be examined in strand 1. Usually, the addition of /shun/ to the end of a base word changes a verb to a noun, as in *create* to *creation* or *introduce* to *introduction*. Specifically, *-ion* means "action" or "process." When the /shun/ sound has the alternate *-ian* spelling—as in the case of *music* to *musician* and *clinic* to *clinician*—common nouns become people nouns. In discussing these suffixes with your students, it is important to guide them to this understanding of what adding the *-ion* or *-ian* suffix does to the meaning of a word and its part of speech.

Figure 6.4 shows an *-ion* suffix sort. First the students pair the base word (the verb *divide*) with its derivative (the noun *division*). Next, they group the pairs by the spelling pattern to determine the generalization. The sort in Figure 6.4 also illustrates how grammar instruction can be blended into word study, as you guide your students to discovering how the addition of the *-ion* suffix changes a verb (*decide*) to a noun (*decision*).

Examining the spellings of base words is an important part of suffix study. Consider the words *election* and *decision.* Both words end with the suffix /shun/; however, /shun/ is spelled differently in each word and affects the respective base words—*elect* and *decide*—in different ways. In *elect/election*, the /t/ sound at the end of the base word *elect* changes to a /sh/ sound in *election*. In *decide/decision*, the long /i/ sound in the base word *decide* changes to a short /i/ sound in *decision*. In fact, /shun/ can be spelled many different ways (*traction*, *magician*, *decision*) in the English language. We tell our students that, when spelling the /shun/ suffix, the key is to identify the ending of the base word to help you

Figure 6.4 Word Sort to Explore the *-ion* Ending

divide	division	produce	production
delude	delusion	reduce	reduction
deride	derision	introduce	introduction
allude	allusion	reproduce	reproduction

determine the spelling. Guide your students by the following sequence in examining and exploring the generalizations that govern spelling the *-ion* suffix (Bear et al., 2008).

- Base words that end in *-ct* or *-ss* just add *-ion* (*object/objection, discuss/discussion*).
- Base words that end in *-ic* add *-ian* (*music/musican*).
- Base words that end in *-te* drop the *e* and add *-ion* (*create/creation*).
- Base words that end in *-ce* drop the *e* and add *-tion* (*produce/production*).
- Base words that end in *-de* drop those letters and add *-sion* and words that end in *-it* drop the *t* and add *-ssion* (*divide/division, submit/submission*).
- Sometimes, *-ation* is added to the base word. Because it can be heard, it causes little trouble for spellers (*transport/transportation*).

Strand 2: Latin and Greek Roots and Additional Affixes

We do not ask our students to study Greek and Latin so they can read Homer's *Odyssey* or Virgil's *Aeneid* in the original; we ask them to study Greek and Latin so that they will know the English language better. Because such a large percentage of English vocabulary (60–75%) can be traced there, it makes sense that the exploration of Greek and Latin roots is at the core of generative vocabulary instruction and remains an essential part of word study throughout the upper grades. These roots do not stand alone as base words, such as the root *dict* ("to speak") in *benediction* or the root *dorm* ("to sleep") in *dormant*. For this reason, roots might not be visually transparent to our students, particularly our struggling readers, without some direction; we need to explicitly teach and guide our students in analyzing these words and word parts. Figure 6.5 describes our "bread and butter" procedure for teaching students to decode and analyze the meanings of longer unknown words by morphemic analysis.

After students have gained a solid understanding of how prefixes and suffixes combine with base words in strand 1, they "spiral back" and examine prefixes and suffixes again in strand 2, but now in more sophisticated, more abstract forms such as absorbed prefixes. In addition, the main focus of strand 2 shifts from straightforward base words to the less transparent but incredibly powerful Latin and Greek root forms. For example, students in strand 2 examine words like *inaudible, audiologist, auditory, auditorium, audience, audition,* and *audio,* looking for the common root *aud* ("hear"). As with all Latin and Greek roots, *aud* cannot stand alone as a word like the base words examined in strand 1 but must combine with other meaning elements, making it less transparent to students. It is important to remember that the general sequence you follow is not ironclad; it represents, rather, a general blueprint for instruction. Be alert for that teachable moment in which you may wish to "jump ahead" or circle back in the sequence to make a connection for your students.

Principles of Teaching Morphology in Strand 2: Latin and Greek Roots and Affixes

Use the following three principles (Templeton et al., 2010) to guide your instruction in strand 2:

- When studying a new Latin or Greek root, begin with word meanings that students already know and affixes they have already learned.
- Next, examine unfamiliar words whose meanings are conceptually transparent from morphemic analysis—in other words, the "route" back to the "root" should be clear and straightforward for your students.
- Finally, examine words whose meanings are more challenging and abstract.

Figure 6.5 Morphemic Analysis: Decoding Longer Unknown Words

The following is our "bread and butter" process for teaching students morphemic analysis. You will likely need to model this procedure a number of times with struggling readers before it becomes internalized; however, the time and effort you invest in teaching students to analyze words by morphemes will be well worth it.

Procedure

1. When you come to a word that you don't know, first read the rest of the sentence. Read the sentences before and after. See if you can get a general gist of the word's meaning from the context. Sometimes you can, and sometimes context doesn't provide enough support. The following sentence has an unknown word: "We need to get rid of these *interlopers*—they are ruining our community." I don't know what *interloper* means, but I can tell that the character speaking in this book obviously doesn't like them. It must be some sort of a negative term for people. The context is helpful but is too vague.
2. Write the word down. Look for familiar words or word parts. "Take apart" the word by circling prefixes or suffixes and underlining any roots or base words. (If you can't write the word down, do this operation "in your head"). If you are not sure where the word parts break, or whether the word is a base or root, just make your best guess at this point. Continuing with *interloper*, I've seen the *inter* word part before, but I can't recall what it means. Maybe it's a prefix? I'll go ahead and circle it. I have no idea what *loper* means, but I'm going to guess that it is the second meaning part, so I'll underline it guessing that it is a root. So, I've got two meaning parts, *inter* and *loper*.
3. Brainstorm related words. Write these down underneath the word parts. Continuing the example, what other words have *inter* that I know? *Interrupt, international, intercollegiate, intermission.* Any common meanings that these words share? An intermission is the break between parts of an act. Intercollegiate sports are played between colleges. Maybe *inter* means "between." How would this fit into the sentence of wanting to get rid of interlopers? Maybe you wouldn't like people who somehow get between you and what you want to do?
4. Reassemble the word, thinking about the meaning contributed by the base, prefix, and suffix.
5. Try out the meaning of the word in the sentence; check to see if it makes sense in the context of the sentence and the larger context of the text that is being read.
6. If the word still does not make sense and is critical to understanding the meaning of the passage, look it up in the dictionary: *interloper*—One who interferes or intrudes in the affairs of others; a meddler. Word origin: *inter*, between; *loper*, to run. Literally, one who "runs between."
7. Think of a way to remember the word. Assign a keyword for each root. Record the word and related information in your vocabulary notebook. For the interloper example, I would write the following: "Well, if I see this word again, or any word with *inter*, I will think of my keyword for *inter*, which is *intermission*. It will be easy to remember this, because an intermission happens between acts. I know now that *lope* means to run. My teacher told me that the way wolves run is often referred to as a lope. So I can always remember wolves loping when I see *lope*."

To get a flavor for what strand 2 instruction might look like, we will follow Mrs. Manuel as she shows her students how Latin roots function within words. She begins by passing out a sheet of words and asks students to sort them. Quickly, the students discover that the words can be organized according to two word parts: *port* and *trac.* Mrs. Manuel writes the keywords *portable* and *tractor* on the board and writes the remaining words (e.g., *import, export, report, extract, contract, intractable*) in their respective columns as the students call them out.

portable	**tractor**
porter	attract
import	distract
export	extract
report	detract
deport	subtract
support	traction
transport	contract
comportment	intractable
portage	protract
rapport	
portfolio	

engagement LINK

Struggling readers are more likely to buy into classroom learning when teachers make connections to the students' background knowledge and personal experiences.

Mrs. Manuel points to *portable* and asks, "What is portable in this room?"

Students respond, "My backpack. Your laptop computer. The overhead projector."

Mrs. Manuel replies, "Good. So, any ideas on what the root *port* means yet?"

Students respond, "Able to be moved."

Mrs. Manuel responds, "Very close. I like your thinking. Jonah, you camp and canoe a lot, right? What does this word mean to you (as she points to the word *portage*)?

Jonah, eyes alight, responds, "Oh yeah. When you have to carry the canoe over land to the next lake, or past some whitewater, you have to *portage* it. So *portage* means to carry, right? We have a really heavy canoe, so I hate *portaging!*" (laughter)

Mrs. Manuel says, "Good, so Jonah thinks *port* means "to carry." Let's look at the remaining words under *port* to see if Jonah's prediction about its meaning fits in with the rest of the definitions we know."

Mrs. Manuel guides the students as they analyze the remaining words under *portable* such as *import* (to carry in), *export* (to carry out), and *porter* (one who carries), underlining the root *port* in each one to highlight the visual link among the words. During this discussion, one student comments that she remembers one of the words, *portfolio,* from a newspaper article featuring a local artist that Mrs. Manuel shared with the class last week. Mrs. Manuel encourages students to be on the lookout for words that have the *port* root in their reading and in their other content area classes. She continues to reinforce the spelling–meaning connection—how words that are spelled the same are often related in meaning. The students are engaged and amazed at the way their burgeoning knowledge of roots, prefixes, and suffixes can help them break down words and uncover meanings. The students also learn more about roots even when breaking down words they already know, like *report.* Mrs. Manuel reminds them that the prefix *re-* means "again," so to *report* means literally "to carry back and repeat something again."

Next, Mrs. Manuel points to the other keyword at the top of the second column—*tractor*—and asks the class, "What does a tractor do? What is its job?"

Students respond, "To plow. To move heavy things. To pull things." She writes these three responses on the board.

Mrs. Manuel points to the word *attracted* and continues, "When you are *attracted* to someone, what does that mean? Look at the three responses we just wrote on the board for *tractor*—to plow, to move, or to pull. Let's see if any of these three fit in with the meaning of *attracted*."

A students responds, "When you are *attracted* to someone, you like that person. So, you want to move toward that person? You are *pulled* toward them!"

Mrs. Manuel replies, "Exactly! *Tract* means 'to pull.' The *ad*- prefix, which changes to *at*- in this particular word, means 'to or toward.' So to be *attracted* means literally 'to be pulled toward someone or something.'"

Erik says, "So, Mrs. Manuel, *distract* must mean 'to be pulled away from someone or something,' like a lesson that a teacher is giving, right?" (laughter)

Mrs. Manuel continues the lesson, guiding the class in analyzing the *tract* words similarly to how they analyzed the *port* words.

This vignette highlights the five core principles of word study instruction introduced in Chapter 2: "just right" instruction, support that balances explicit instruction and student exploration, higher-level thinking activities, categorization of words and concepts, and multiple opportunities to manipulate words. By categorizing the words and attempting to deduce their meanings, the students were actively engaged in higher-level thinking. Mrs. Manuel guided the students, through example after example, to the understanding that word roots are the meaningful anchors to which prefixes and suffixes may attach. She explicitly reinforced the spelling–meaning connection throughout the lesson, making clear that words that are spelled the same often share a core meaning. She began with clear keywords that students knew (*tractor* and *portable*) and later moved to more difficult words. She gave the students multiple opportunities to analyze words they didn't know (like *intractable*) and words they already knew (like *report*), seeing the value in both types of analysis. The students left this lesson with more knowledge about specific word meanings as well as more general knowledge about how words work. (Additional lessons like this can be found in *Words Their Way: Word Sorts for Derivational Relations Spellers*.)

Focus Feature: Advanced Suffix Study

Is it spelled *dependable* or *dependible*? *Audible* or *audable*? *Breakable* or *breakible*? And does it matter? The adjective-forming *-able/-ible* suffix (along with a handful of other difficult suffixes) presents challenges for even the advanced readers and writers in our classrooms. However, as has been the case for many morphemic features discussed throughout this book, these more advanced suffixes follow patterns that can be distilled into helpful generalizations. Examine the *-ible/-able* sort that follows for a pattern. (Hint: cover up the *-ible/-able* suffix in each word, paying particular attention to the remaining root or base word.)

visible	affordable
audible	expandable
horrible	respectable
plausible	punishable

In these words, both endings sound the same—/ubel/. So how do you know when to spell the suffix *-ible* or *-able?* On examination, a fairly powerful generalization emerges: If the suffix is attached to a word root that cannot stand alone (e.g., *plaus* in *plausible*), then it is usually spelled *-ible;* if the suffix is attached to a base word that *can* stand alone (e.g., *afford* in *affordable*), then it is usually spelled *-able.* One of our students thought of the following way to easily remember this: "Remember, *able* is a stand-alone word, so spell it *-able* for stand-alone words; *-ible* is not a stand-alone word, so spell it *-ible* for roots that cannot stand alone." A few other categories emerge after further study of the *-able/-ible,* suffix. For base words that end in *e* (e.g., *debate/debatable* and *believe/believable*), we drop the *e* and add *-able.* However, we tell our students to be particularly aware of soft *c* or *g* endings, as in *changeable* and *enforceable;* in these cases, we keep the final *e* to maintain the soft sound in the derived words. Finally, some soft *c* or *g* endings may be followed by *-ible*, as in *reducible.*

The *-ant/-ance* and *-ent/-ence* suffixes can be explored next. Again, the spelling–meaning connection helps us here. A student might not be too sure how to spell *resistance* or *equivalence*. (Are they *-ance* or *-ence*?) However, advanced readers at this level are likely to know related words like *resistant* and *equivalent*. By examining the *-ant/-ance* and *-ent/-ence* suffixes across related words like *elegant/elegance* and *impatient/impatience*, students are elaborating on their understanding of the spelling–meaning connection. The connected suffixes provide an excellent opportunity to incorporate grammar instruction into word study. Guide students toward an understanding that changing *-ant* to *-ance* and *-ent* to *-ence* changes adjectives (like *elegant* and *impatient*) to nouns (*elegance* and *impatience*).

Focus Feature: Absorbed Prefixes

What's the most frequently misspelled word in the English language? It's that notorious spelling demon *accommodate*. The fact that so many people experience difficulty spelling this word points to the complex nature of *absorbed* (or *assimilated*) *prefixes* as well as the fact that *accommodate* actually has two absorbed prefixes (more on that later). Students initially explore basic prefixes in strand 1 and continue to examine them in more depth and complexity throughout strand 2. Often, prefixes are visually transparent units that are easy to see and understand, such as *un-* in *untie* and *re-* in *refill*. Notice how in both words, the prefixes do not change when attached to the base word. However, other prefixes are less visually transparent. Consider *immature* (not mature) and *immortal* (not mortal). What is the prefix here? Is it *im-*? The only clue to the original prefix *in-* is the doubled letter—*imm*. Students (and adults) may ask, "What happened to the original prefix *in-*, meaning 'not'?" Listen to Mrs. Valencia describe the process of absorbed prefixes.

> Okay, class. let's look at the word *immortal*. The word is generated from the prefix *in-*, meaning "not," and the base word *mortal*, meaning "liable or subject to death." Notice what happens when we put *in-* and *mortal* together. First, the word parts combine to form a new word, *immortal*, that means "not subject to death, everlasting." Second, the spelling of the prefix *in-* changes to *im-*. A long time ago, someone combined the prefix *in-* with the base word *mortal* to create a new word. Try saying it this way three times quickly—"*inmortal, inmortal, inmortal.*" It sounds strange, and it feels hard to say, doesn't it? Your tongue tends to trip over the beginning of the word. The more you say it, the more likely you are to start dropping the *n* when pronouncing the word—the /n/ sound literally becomes "absorbed" into the /m/ sound at the beginning of the base word, *mortal*. This is what happened in history. Eventually, the spelling of the *n* changed to an *m* to reflect this change in pronunciation. But notice that we didn't drop a letter; we still keep two letters in the prefix *im-* to indicate that there is still a prefix there. If we spelled *immortal* without the first *m*, like this—*imortal*, we would lose the visual clue that lets us know the meaning of the prefix.

Middle or high school teachers could use the next sort to examine absorbed prefixes. Students can discuss the meanings of the words first, eventually realizing that the prefixes, whether spelled *in-*, *il-*, *im-*, or *ir-*, all mean "not." Students then sort the words like this:

ineffective	illiterate	immature	irregular	impossible
inorganic	illegal	immobile	irrelevant	impatient
inactive	illogical	immortal	irrecoverable	improper
infinite	illegible	immodest	irresponsible	impartial

At this point, the teacher might ask the students, "What happens to the spelling of the prefix *in-* as it's added in each word? Do you notice a pattern?" If the students need

Considerations for English Learners

Using Cognates to Support English Learners

Cognates are words in different languages that share similar structures and meanings because they share similar origins—*cognate* literally means "to be born with or together." For example, *mother* (English), *madre* (Spanish), *mere* (French), and *mutter* (German) are all cognates. Notice how all of these words are related to the Latin *mater*. The study of cognates can be a potentially powerful way to help English learners begin to bridge the gap between their home language and English and can also be beneficial for native English speakers studying Spanish, French, or German.

Cognate knowledge can be very helpful to English learners in the content areas, particularly science and math, in which many cognates share very similar meanings and spellings. Templeton and colleagues (2010) offer the following examples of content vocabulary cognates that share the same meanings in English/Spanish: *bacteria/bacteria*, *bisect/bisectia*, and *ecosystem/ecosistema*. As with all instruction in affixes and roots, begin with more transparent cognates—in which the connection between the cognates is straightforward and the meanings and spellings are similar across languages—and move to more abstract cognates later.

An English learner's knowledge of cognates can help uncover the meanings of more difficult English vocabulary words—words that even native English speakers might not know. An example of how cognate knowledge might work occurred during a fourth grade guided reading lesson conducted by one of our undergraduate practicum students. After reading a section of the story, the practicum student asked the small group of fourth-graders what they thought the word *plumage* in the story meant. At first, none of the students responded. Then Roberto, an English learner who had moved to the United States from Mexico, said excitedly, "I think it means feather!" When asked how he knew the word *plumage*, he responded that the word looks and sounds like *pluma* in Spanish, which means feather also. Because many words in Spanish are derived from Greek and Latin, just like English, many of the same roots are used in Spanish (*spectator*–*espectador*).

more guidance, the teacher could say, "Does that pattern have anything to do with the base word that follows?"

Absorbed prefixes pose such a challenge for students because of the considerable prior knowledge required for their use: knowledge of simple Latin and Greek roots, basic spelling–meaning patterns, and the processes of adding prefixes to base words. Absorbed prefixes are generally Latin in origin and used widely across the English language. Please see Appendix F for a more extensive list of assimilated prefixes. As for *accommodate*, our original spelling demon from the beginning of this section, the *d* in the first prefix *ad-* has been assimilated into the first letter/sound of the second prefix *con-*, and the *n* in *con-* has been absorbed into the first letter/sound of the root *modate*.

Generative Vocabulary Instruction: Guidelines and Resources

In the second half of this chapter, we will describe specific activities you can do with your students to enhance their generative vocabulary knowledge. Whichever activities you use, keep the following ten general guidelines for generative vocabulary instruction in mind. These guidelines are particularly important for struggling readers and build on and extend the five core word study principles introduced in Chapter 2 (Templeton, 1989):

1. *Select words and word elements that capitalize on the generative nature of our spelling–meaning system.* Rather than teaching vocabulary as a list of discrete, unconnected terms, group words into "meaning families" for instruction. For example, when studying the different types of government in civics, it makes sense to teach *democracy, plutocracy, autocracy,* and *theocracy* together, and to point out the common root that ties them all together (*crat/cracy,* which means "rule") by spelling and meaning.

2. *Start with examples in which the "route" back to the "root" is clear and straightforward.* Select words for initial instruction based on how transparent their meaning is from the root and affixes; later on, introduce words that are more complex. For example, we will teach clearly decodable words in strand 1 such as *unworkable* before trying words in strand 2 that are more difficult to break apart, such as *audiologist.* This is particularly important for struggling readers who may need to be carefully guided from clear examples to more difficult cases.

3. *Balance teacher-directed instruction with student exploration and discussion.* Use the continuum of support (Chapter 2) as a guide in giving direction. With struggling readers, we have often found it helpful to gradually release responsibility to the student over the course of the lesson and the year. This often means beginning with more explicit instruction, but, as we fine-tune the support and guidance our students need, we cede more and more responsibility over time. Asking students to think for themselves is motivating and engaging!

4. *Use words students already know.* Students should already know the meanings (at least a basic understanding) of 50 to 75 percent of the words in a sort. These known words will serve as "anchors" to which the student can link new words. This is particularly important for struggling readers because we learn new words and concepts by linking them to known words; if all words in a sort are unknown, the student has no "anchor words" to link new words. For example, when examining the root *graph* ("to write"), we want to balance words the students probably already know (e.g., *graph, autograph, paragraph,* and *biography*) with words that may be unknown or not as familiar to the students (e.g., *seismograph, lexicographer, ethnography*). With practice, you will quickly become very good at distinguishing known "anchor words" from unknown vocabulary for your students and your grade level.

5. *Identify keywords and pictures for major roots, prefixes, and suffixes.* As with word study that targets spelling and reading, identifying keywords for high-utility affixes and roots is particularly helpful for struggling readers because it provides them a concrete reference word to examine other words that share that same feature. For example, even our best readers sometimes experience difficulty deducing that the Latin root *tract* in words like *extract, subtract,* and *contract* means "to pull." In such cases, provide a keyword. "When you think of the root *tract,* think of a tractor. What is the main job of a tractor? To *pull* things. *Tract* means "to pull." So our keyword for the root *tract* will be *tractor.*" We then ask the students to write the keyword *tractor* and draw a picture of a tractor pulling something at the top of the *tract* column in their vocabulary notebooks (or on the class word wall). The keyword *tractor* works well for the root *tract* because (a) its meaning is concrete, (b) it is known to nearly all students, and (c) the root's meaning is very close to the word's meaning.

6. *Model and think aloud.* Struggling readers do not always understand what is going on in more proficient readers' heads when they process words. And oftentimes, because processing words is so natural for them, good readers could not explain the process even if they wanted to. Our job as teachers of struggling readers is to make explicit what is implicitly going on in skilled readers' heads. One of the best ways to make this process explicit is to explain your thinking as you model the word study process—for example, "I am going to take off this *in-* at the beginning of the word *inactive.* I think I remember that the *in-* is a prefix meaning 'not.' Okay, next, I'm going to see if there is a suffix at the end I can take off."

7. *Break the process down into smaller steps.* Struggling readers may need you to break down the word analysis process into smaller steps. They may also need to be taken through a process or work with a set of words multiple times before they "get it." For example, it is fine to take two weeks to examine a set of roots if you feel this extra time provides your students the opportunity they need to really "own" the roots.

8. *Make instruction concrete and visual.* Using word study cards and pictures, asking students to circle roots and underline affixes, allowing students to physically build words from word part cards—these are all examples of making abstract words and processes concrete and visual for our students. This will help all students, but it is particularly helpful for struggling readers.

9. *Keep instruction consistent.* Use the same terminology ("What does the root mean? What does it look like?") and the same procedures consistently across the week and the year. When the teaching procedures and terminology are held constant, the struggling reader is better able to focus on the word study process.

10. *Keep instruction active.* When students are actively involved in thinking—whether sorting words, analyzing words, generating words, or playing a game—they are doing the work. Active engagement leads to deeper processing and long-term learning.

Dictionaries: A Core Resource for Generative Vocabulary Learning

With generative vocabulary instruction, your classroom dictionaries should be dog-eared from constant use by the year's end. You should explicitly teach your students about the various features of dictionaries such as parts of speech, multiple definitions, and pronunciation guides. It is particularly important to directly teach your students how to find etymological information—knowledge about a word's origins, including Latin and Greek roots and affixes that make up the word—in dictionaries and other resources, usually placed in brackets at the end of a word entry. One of the primary problems with dictionaries for struggling readers is that they define unknown words using other unknown words. For example, defining the word *radiant* with the words *incandescent, effulgent,* and *lucent* would not be much help to a student with an impoverished vocabulary. Intermediate dictionaries, with definitions that use simple, common words, are often better suited for students. The following reference resources should be readily available for your students:

- A set of dictionaries and root books that contain etymological information students can use to find the affixes and roots that make up words. *The American Heritage College Dictionary* is one example of a resource that contains this information. (See Figure 6.6 for an annotated list of resources.)
- Several copies of intermediate and collegiate dictionaries containing etymological information—enough for students to work in small groups of five or six.
- Thesaurus collection; enough for small groups of five or six students.
- Online dictionaries, such as www.yourdictionary.com, http://onelook.com, and http://dictionary.reference.com, as well as the online thesaurus, http://thesaurus.reference.com, are excellent resources.

Additional Resources for Student and Teachers

Figure 6.6 provides a list of additional resources for generative vocabulary instruction that target the Greek and Latin elements in our language. These resources will give you a sense of how the study of prefixes, suffixes, and roots is virtually endless—continuing through high school and beyond and extending across the content areas and into law, medicine, and science.

Figure 6.6 Resources for Word Study

Greek and Latin Elements

For Students and Teachers

Crutchfield, R. (1997). *English vocabulary quick reference: A comprehensive dictionary arranged by word roots.* Leesburg, VA: LexaDyne Publishing, Inc.

Danner, H., & Noel, R. (2004). *Discover it! A better vocabulary the better way* (2nd ed.). Occoquan, VA: Imprimis Books.

Fine, E. H. (2004). *Cryptomania!: Teleporting into Greek and Latin with the cryptokids.* Berkeley, CA: Tricycle Press. Illustrated by K. Donner.

Kennedy, J. (1996). *Word stems: A dictionary.* New York: Soho Press.

Moore, B., & Moore, M. (1997). *NTC's dictionary of Latin and Greek origins: A comprehensive guide to the classical origins of English words.* Chicago: NTC Publishing Group.

For Teachers

Ayers, D. M. (1986). *English words from Latin and Greek elements* (2nd ed., revised by Thomas Worthen). Tucson: The University of Arizona Press.

Fry, E. (2004). *The vocabulary teacher's book of lists.* San Francisco: Jossey-Bass.

Johnston, F., Bear, D. R., & Invernizzi, M. (2006). *Words their way: Word sorts for derivational relations spellers.* Upper Saddle River, NJ: Merrill/Prentice-Hall.

Nilsen, A. P., & Nilsen, D. L. F. (2004). *Vocabulary plus high school and up: A source-based approach.* Boston: Allyn & Bacon.

Schleifer, R. (1995). *Grow your own vocabulary.* New York: Random House.

Word Origins

For Students and Teachers

Asimov, I. (1961). *Words from the myths.* Boston: Houghton Mifflin. (The most readable and most interesting resource of this kind.)

Ayto, J. (1993). *Dictionary of word origins.* New York: Arcade.

D'Aulaire, I., & D'Aulaire, E. (1980). *D'Aulaires' book of Greek myths.* New York: Doubleday. (Of interest to third graders and up; upper intermediate reading level.)

Fisher, L. (1984). *The Olympians: Great gods and goddesses of ancient Greece.* New York: Holiday House (Of interest to third graders and up; third grade reading level.)

Gates, D. (1983). *Two queens of heaven: Aphrodite and Demeter.* New York: Puffin. (Of interest to fourth graders and up; upper intermediate reading level.)

Jones, C. F. (1999). *Eat your words: A fascinating look at the language of food.* New York: Delacorte Press. Illustrated by J. O'Brian.

Kingsley, C. (1980). *The heroes (or Greek fairy tales for my children).* Lititz, PA: BiblioBazaar. (Of interest to third graders and up; intermediate reading level.) The stories behind many present-day words that come from myths and legends help students remember the meanings of the terms and their spellings.

Merriam-Webster new book of word histories. (1995). Springfield, MA: Merriam-Webster.

For Teachers

Shipley, J. (2001). *The origins of English words.* Baltimore: Johns Hopkins University Press. (For truly dedicated wordsmiths, Shipley's book is the ultimate source. A delightful read!)

Activities for Generative Vocabulary Instruction

Across a one- or two-week unit of root study, your struggling readers should be working with words in at least three different but related ways: (a) sorting words, (b) analyzing words, and (c) generating—or building—words. We have organized the activities in this section according to these three major processes. When planning, pick at least one activity from each area to ensure that your struggling readers have practice in all three types of thinking about the affixes or roots you select for instruction. We have also added a fourth section describing motivating review games your classes can play to reinforce and extend learning. (In addition, we provide a possible two-week sequence for generative vocabulary instruction on page 259 at the end of Chapter 8, Vocabulary Assessment and Organization.)

When introducing any activity for the first time, model it and provide time in class for guided practice. Gradually release more responsibility to students as they internalize the process. Keep the continuum of support in mind. After students have demonstrated independence, you can choose whether activities are done during class, for homework, or independently during the week as part of a learning contract.

- *Word sorting* activities require students to categorize words by affixes and roots. When students sort, they compare and contrast words, analyze word parts, and look for generalizations they can apply to new words. Sometimes these sorts may focus on a spelling generalization such as adding *-ible* or *-able,* and sometimes the sorts may focus on spelling–meaning connections as in root and affix sorts.
- *Word analysis* activities teach struggling readers to decode more difficult words by morphemes (prefixes, suffixes, roots, and base words). Word analysis goes from the whole word to the parts of the word.
- *Word generation* activities focus on building words from prefixes, suffixes, and roots or base words. Word generation is the flip side of word analysis; it goes from the parts of the word to the whole word.
- *Review games* are extension activities that provide reinforcement and enrichment of root knowledge in motivating formats.

Word Sorting

As we discussed in Chapter 2, sorting words into categories is at the heart of word study because it is such a powerful way to help our students discover how words work. When our struggling readers categorize words by prefix, suffix, or root, they are comparing, contrasting, and analyzing in the search for generalizations that they can then apply to new words. The focus of generative vocabulary sorts is on word meanings. Often, teachers of middle and high school students will emphasize writing sorts and spend less time sorting with actual word sort cards. However, the act of physically moving a word sort card from one category to the next can be particularly helpful for struggling readers because it makes the abstract process of word analysis and categorization more visual and concrete.

Many of the sorts described in Chapter 2 will work when sorting words by prefix, suffix, and root, including open sorts, teacher-directed closed sorts, and word hunts (with the modifications noted). As with all sorting throughout this book, use the continuum of explicitness as your guideline for deciding how much support to provide your struggling readers in their word work. There are a number of word lists in Appendix F that are appropriate for generative vocabulary instruction and that follow the two-strand sequence described earlier in this chapter.

Teacher-Directed Closed Sorts

On the continuum of explicitness, the teacher-directed closed sort provides the most support for your students. In closed sorts, the teacher defines the categories and explicitly models the thinking process. Use teacher-directed sorts when first introducing sorting and when introducing a new feature of study that might represent a new concept or be particularly difficult (e.g., when initially moving from the more transparent base words in strand 1 to the more abstract roots in strand 2). The use of keywords and pictures can be very helpful in making this process concrete. In the following example, Mr. Rozin explicitly models the sorting process for his students.

"We are going to examine two categories of words this week. For the first part of class, I am going to show you the types of thinking I want you to do as you sort and analyze these words. Later, as you become more proficient sorting words by prefix, suffix, and root, you'll be sorting in groups or independently." Mr. Rozin points to the interactive whiteboard, where he presents the two keywords: *megaphone* and *pesticide*.

"Okay, I'll be asking myself two guiding questions as I sort and analyze words by prefix, suffix, and root." Mr. Rozin posts the following two guiding questions on the board:

- *Does the word mean the same?* (Does it share a common meaning with, or is it related in meaning to, other words in the category?)
- *Does the word look the same?* (Does it share roots with similar spellings?)

"Notice that I won't be asking you if the words sound the same—as I do when I sort words by spelling pattern or syllable—because we know that the same root can sound different in two different but related words. So when I sort by prefix, suffix, or root, these two guiding questions will help us uncover the spelling–meaning connection we've talked about."

"Let's ask ourselves the first guiding question: What do these words mean? What is a *megaphone*?" The class answers that it is a tool to help make your voice sound louder. "Good, now what is a *pesticide*?" The class answers that it is a poison used to kill bugs or other pests. "Okay, now let's look at the next word." Mr. Rozin puts the word *microphone* on the smartboard. "Now I'm going to see if *microphone* looks and/or means the same as either of our two keywords, *pesticide* or *megaphone*. Well, a *microphone* is a tool you can use to record your voice, so meaning-wise, it seems to be very closely related to *megaphone*—they both have something to do with voice or sound. Also, I see a common root—both *megaphone* and *microphone* share the same spelling at the end—*phone*." At this point in the lesson the sort on the interactive whiteboard looks like this:

megaphone	**pesticide**
microphone	

Mr. Rozin continues, "Now let's look at our next word, *insecticide*. What is our first guiding question?" The class answers, "Does the word mean the same?" "Right, what is an *insecticide*? That's right, it is a poison that kills insects. That has a very similar meaning to *pesticide*. These two words share a similar meaning, but do they look the same? Can anyone see a common root?" The class answers that both *pesticide* and *insecticide* have the same spelling at the end—*cide*. "Good, *cide* could be the root, having something to do with getting rid of or killing. Let's continue, asking ourselves the guiding questions."

Mr. Rozin continues the sort, carefully guiding his students' thinking as they categorize the words. He constantly refers back to the two guiding questions, but slowly cedes responsibility to his students over the course of the lesson as he gets the sense that they are starting to get a handle on the sorting process and the root meanings. As the students seem to be "getting it," he decides to introduce words in the sort that are not as familiar to the students. "Okay, class, has anyone seen or heard the word *genocide* before?" Class answers include hearing it connected with wars on the news but not being exactly sure what it means. "Well, let's break it down. So far, we are pretty sure that the root *cide* means to kill, right?" Mr. Rozin circles the root *cide*. So, if *genocide* has something to do with war, any idea what *geno* means? When no one answers, Mr. Rozin asks, "Do we know any other words that share *geno*, or a similar spelling? Class answers *genome, genetics, genesis,* and *genius*." Very good, these words are related, but they aren't giving us enough help with this particular word right away, so let's look this up." Mr. Rozin models looking up the word in the dictionary and finds out the root *geno* means race. "So, genocide means to kill or exterminate an entire race."

At the end of the lesson, the sort looks like this:

megaphone	**pesticide**
microphone	insecticide
headphone	fungicide
telephone	herbicide
saxophone	homicide
homophone	regicide
phonics	incise
symphony	genocide
cacophony	suicide
euphony	precise

Mr. Rozin concludes the lesson, "Okay, folks, you have done a great job sorting these words and figuring out the two roots—*phon/phone* meaning 'sound' and *cide* meaning 'to kill or to cut.' Now we are going to copy this sort on chart paper and in our vocabulary notebooks for future reference. Remember to note in your vocabulary notebook that our keyword for *phon/phone* is *megaphone*. Whenever you see the root *phon/phone* in another word while reading, I want you to think of a *megaphone*. *Megaphones* make a sound bigger, so you should always think of 'sound' when you see the root *phon/phone*." With this, Mr. Rozin quickly sketches a picture of a *megaphone* next to the word *megaphone* at the top of the sort. "We picked *megaphone* as the keyword because it will be easy to remember." Mr. Rozin then sketches a rudimentary picture of a can of *insecticide* next to the other root and briefly explains why *insecticide* will be the keyword for *cide*.

Throughout this lesson, Mr. Rozin has followed many of the principles of effective word study instruction for struggling readers:

- Explicitly modeling and thinking aloud the sorting process
- Breaking the process down into small steps
- Actively engaging the students by asking them higher-level questions that require deep processing of word parts and meanings
- Requiring the students to connect and categorize the words repeatedly throughout the lesson
- Starting with more concrete, familiar words at the beginning of the sort and moving to more abstract, less familiar words by the end of the sort
- Carefully choosing keywords whose meanings are concrete and providing a clear route back to the root (*megaphone* and *insecticide*)
- Including pictures to accompany the words
- Keeping it consistent by continually referring back to the two guiding questions for generative vocabulary sorting: *Does the word mean the same? Does the word look the same?*

Open Sorts

Because the teacher does not define the categories beforehand, open sorts are at the opposite end of the continuum of explicitness from closed sorts. Students identify their own categories and test their own hypotheses about how words work. Because of this, you will see students organize words in different ways than you may have envisioned. This open-endedness is part of the excitement of open sorts and provides valuable diagnostic information for teachers concerning what their students know about words and how they approach words. When doing open sorts with your class, remember to allow for different types of thinking as long as students can justify why they categorized words the way they did. At the same time, you can close an open sort down by simply saying something like, "I really like the different ways you analyzed and organized words. Now, I am going to show you the categories that I was looking for." Open sorts are a good match for students who are already accustomed to the sorting process.

To start an open sort, some teachers provide a mixed-up list of words on a spreadsheet that students, individually, in pairs, or in groups, cut out. Then the students physically sort the word cards into categories. Many other upper grades teachers simply list the words in random order on a handout like this:

hydrant	hydrogen	anarchy	hydrophobia
monarchy	archbishop	hydroplane	patriarch
hydrate	matriarch	hydroelectric	hydrologist
archangel	hydraulic	architect	hierarchy

Each student is given the handout. The students' job (individually, in pairs, or in small groups) is to read through the words, asking themselves the two guiding questions (see teacher-directed closed sort above) and looking for categories of roots and/or affixes. The students then rewrite the words on the bottom half of the paper in their categories. In the preceding example, students might discover the two major roots in this sort—*hydra* meaning "water" and *arch* meaning "chief."

***hydra* ("water")**	***arch* ("chief")**
hydrant	anarchy
hydrogen	monarchy
hydrophobia	archbishop
hydrate	matriarch
hydraulic	patriarch
hydroelectric	hierarchy
hydrologist	architect
hydroplane	archangel

Tips for Open Sorts

- Even if students have sorted all the words correctly by prefix, suffix, or root, it doesn't necessarily mean they have attained a deep understanding of the root or the individual word meanings. For example, in the preceding sort, students might simply sort by "sight," writing all the words with *hydra* in one column and *arch* in the other—this doesn't mean they have delved deeply into word meanings. It is critical that you engage the students in a discussion about the words to ensure that they are getting at word meanings and making the spelling–meaning connections. At this level, it is more about the *discussion* that is generated by the sort than the sort itself.
- Feel free to close an open sort down when you feel the need to direct the students toward a certain root meaning.
- You can make open sorts more supportive, such as highlighting and underlining the keywords (but not modeling your thinking as in a teacher-directed closed sort) or by simply telling the students how many categories there are.

Word Hunts

Word hunts (see Chapter 2) will look a little different when hunting for prefixes, suffixes, and roots than they did in the within word pattern and syllables and affixes chapters. This is because the words and features at this level are not as common, particularly in fiction. For example, you can read *To Kill a Mockingbird* and probably have little luck finding a word that contains the Greek root *polis* (meaning "city").

Tips for Word Hunts with Affixes and Roots

- Textbooks, particularly science texts, are more likely to contain generative words and features than works of fiction.
- Brainstorming lists of words often works better than hunting in texts. Dictionaries can be excellent places to hunt for words to supplement these brainstorming sessions.
- Online dictionaries, such as http://onelook.com, are excellent resources for word hunts. Students can use the "wild card" application by placing an asterisk before and after a word part to search for related words. For example, searching for **spect** can give you the 100 most common English words derived from this root, such as *suspect, respect, aspect,* and *specter.*
- Word hunts will extend for weeks at a time for upper-level word study. Word study notebooks or class lists of words on a class "graffiti wall" (chart paper) work well with these extended word hunts because they can be added to over time as new words turn up in students' reading and writing. These class "word walls" are particularly effective for struggling readers as they serve as a constant visual reminder of the roots and words that have been studied. We have seen (and encourage!) our struggling readers and writers to refer to these class lists both when reading and writing. When class word lists are visually available, our students' writing is more likely to contain these words.
- Some books lend themselves to upper-level word study. For example, Julia Thompson, one high school English teacher we have worked with, introduces her class to upper-level word hunts through the *Harry Potter* series. She explains that these books are full of Latin and Greek roots because J. K. Rowling uses Latin and Greek word elements to name the spells that are used repeatedly throughout these books. For example, the spell *Lumos* creates light at your wand tip (from the Latin root *lumen/lumin* meaning "light"), *Petrificus Totalus* petrifies your opponent in a body bind (from the Latin root *petra* meaning "rock"), *Incendios* starts a fire (from the Latin root *incendere* meaning "to set on fire"), and *Veritaserum* is a truth serum (from the Latin root *veritas* meaning "true"). Because most students are familiar with this series, and because of Rowling's creativity, these word hunts can be truly exciting.

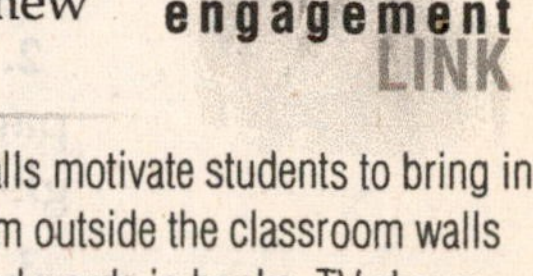

Graffiti walls motivate students to bring in words from outside the classroom walls as they find words in books, TV shows and ads, songs, and magazines.

Word Analysis Activities

Morphemic analysis activities teach students how to break words down into their meaning parts. This is a potentially very powerful process for independent word learning because when students encounter unknown words in their reading (or on the SAT or ACT), they are much better able to decode them by morpheme, unlock their meanings, and store them in long-term memory. The following activities will equip your struggling readers with an approach for analyzing more difficult multisyllabic words, or, as Edmund Henderson so elegantly put it, to "learn how to 'walk through words' with sensible expectations" (Henderson, 1985, p. 67). Remember the ultimate goal is not that students rigidly adhere to the exact sequence of steps in these activities, but that they develop a mindset for "walking through words" they can apply flexibly across the content areas whether reading a chemistry textbook, writing a persuasive essay for American history, or studying for an upcoming test in geometry. In Figure 6.5 (p. 171), we described our "bread and butter" procedure for teaching students how to analyze words by morpheme. The following additional activities help students develop their ability to break words down by their meaning parts.

Vocabulary Notebooks

We cannot imagine teaching generative vocabulary without vocabulary notebooks (Bear et al., 2008). As a place to record weekly morpheme study, note patterns and generalizations, add new words to sorts throughout the year, and investigate interesting or particularly difficult words found in reading and writing, vocabulary notebooks are an excellent tool for connecting word study to our students' reading and writing across the content areas. We have placed vocabulary notebooks in the analysis section, but we could just as easily have placed them in the generating words or sorting words sections, as they include these processes also.

Procedure

1. *Collect the word.* While reading, mark interesting, difficult, or unknown words. Sticky notes work well as placeholders for this purpose. After reading or studying, go back to the sticky notes and read the word in the context of the sentence. If possible, make a prediction about what the word might mean.

2. *Record the word and the sentence.* Write the sentence in which the word was used, the page number, and the title of the book. If the sentence is too long, write enough to get a gist of the meaning. Illustrate the word.

3. *Analyze/take apart the word into meaning chunks.* Break the word apart in the following manner. Look for prefixes and circle them. Look for suffixes and circle them. Look for roots or base words and underline them. Think about the meaning of each of these different word parts. If any of these prefixes, suffixes, or roots have already been studied, refer back to the part of your notebook that has that prefix, suffix, or root. If possible, try to put these meaning parts together to get a sense of the whole word's meaning.

4. *Generate/brainstorm related words.* Think of other words that share the same prefix. Write them down underneath the prefix. Think of other words that share the same suffix; write them under the suffix. Think of other words that share the same root or base word and write them under the root or base word. Again, try to get a sense for the word's meaning.

5. *Look up the word in the dictionary.* Find the various definitions of the word in a dictionary, identify the meaning that makes the most sense in the context of the sentence, and record the definition in a few words. Check against your prediction of the meaning in step 1. Look for similar words nearby in the dictionary and record them. If interesting and available, record the word origin.

6. *Categorize the word.* If this word shares a prefix, suffix, or root with a sort you have already studied, add this word to that weekly sort in the word study part of your vocabulary notebook.

7. *Review the words.* Periodically review your words. Ten words per week is a manageable goal. Submit these words to your teacher for any of the vocabulary games discussed later in this chapter.

An Example of the Vocabulary Notebook Process

1. Collect the word: *circumspect.*
2. Record the word and sentence: "We are always *circumspect* of 'deals' that seem too good to be true." (*Finding the Best Bargains*, p. 125)
3. Analyze the word into meaning chunks: "There don't seem to be any prefixes or suffixes that I am familiar with. However, *spect* is a root that we already studied earlier in the year—it means 'to look.' Maybe *circum* is another root? So I will break this word into two parts, underlining both <u>circum/spect.</u> This word may have something to do with looking?"
4. Generate/brainstorm related words: "Checking *spect*, I see *spectator, inspect, inspector, spectrum.* Yes, I was correct. These words all have something to do with 'looking.' *Circum—circumference.* Hmm . . . The circumference is the distance or line around a circle. Maybe *circum* means 'around'? So *circumspect* might mean 'to look around.'

Why would you want to look around when you find a deal that appears too good to be true? Maybe you don't trust it! You are looking around to be careful!"

5. Look up the word in the dictionary: circumspect—watchful, cautious, prudent. Origin: circum—around; spect—to look. "That makes sense! My prediction was close. *Circumspect* literally means to 'look around,' because when you are looking around, you are being cautious—which you would want to do with deals that appear to be too good to be true."
6. "I will add *circumspect* to the list of *spect* roots in my notebook that we studied previously. I can also create a new page with the root *circum* at the top. I will be on the lookout for more words with *circum* in the future.

"Break It Down!"

Break It Down is a highly motivating, fast-paced team game that allows students to practice the word analysis procedure just described. The format is a student favorite and can be used for any content area. The goal of the game is to "break down" unfamiliar words (e.g., *redistribution*) into prefixes, suffixes, and roots and then put these word parts back together while coming up with a definition. Teams' proposed definitions are then checked against actual dictionary definitions at the end of each round of play. Teams are awarded points not only for constructing the correct definition but also for their ability to break a word down into meaningful parts, which promotes the *process* of word analysis as well as the product. We recommend that the teacher model the word analysis procedure just described and provide some guided practice for students before playing this game.

Divide the class into teams, approximately five to six students per team. After voting for a captain and deciding on a team name, each team is given a few root books (which contain lists of common Latin and Greek prefixes, suffixes, and roots and their meanings). If you can't put your hands on root books, a list or packet of common Latin and Greek prefixes, suffixes, and roots with their meanings will suffice (copy Appendix F for students). All students should also have their word study notebooks open for quick reference. Dictionaries are *closed* at this point; all other resources are open and available, including any class lists of roots or words on the word wall—this game is an excellent forum for practicing the use of these word study resources. The game works best when teams are heterogeneously grouped in terms of language/reading/writing ability.

Procedure

1. Present a vocabulary word for teams to "break down" in a sentence. Read it twice and put the word and sentence on an overhead or screen so every student can read the word, see how it is spelled, and see how it is used in the context of the sentence. It is particularly helpful to choose words that include prefixes, suffixes, or roots that have already been studied—this ensures that your students will have enough morpheme knowledge to analyze the word. You can take these words or sentences from trade books, textbooks, newspapers, or other appropriates sources. Feel free to write the sentences yourself. You may need to rework sentences from texts to "beef up" the context for more support. For example, "The teacher was in an *irascible* mood" doesn't provide much context. However, "The teacher was in an *irascible* mood—the students weren't listening to a word she was saying" provides much richer context.

2. Call out to students, "Independent break down—Go!" For the next three to five minutes (or whatever you deem appropriate) every student on every team individually performs steps 1 through 6 from the morphemic analysis procedure just described for vocabulary notebooks. Students can work on paper or the Break It Down template presented in Appendix G. Students can refer to root books, word study notebooks, and word walls, but they cannot talk to one another during this step. Any resource *except* the dictionary is allowed at this point. This independent break down time should be silent

as students are writing down the word; circling and underlining prefixes, suffixes, and roots; writing down related words; and referring to root books and word study notebooks—all in an attempt to uncover the word's meaning. This individual time is crucial, because it ensures that every student is actively engaged in word analysis, helping mitigate one of the main problems with group activities—that certain students "coast" along, relying on teammates to do the work and carry the load. Oftentimes, these "coasters" are the struggling readers, the very students who need the most practice. Including this independent step first increases the quantity and quality of the group interaction, the next step.

3. Teacher calls out "Group break down—Go!" For the next three to five minutes, talking is allowed. The group members put their heads together and share their thinking, trying to figure out the word, using the same 6 steps, but as a group. On a whiteboard or chart paper, the team captain writes down the word, breaks the word down into word parts with their respective meanings written next to them, and then writes down the group's hypothesized definition. As you walk around, monitoring and facilitating, remind groups to use their resources to analyze the word. As in individual break down time, allowable resources include word study notebooks, root books, and class lists of word wall words, but not dictionaries. Also remind students to be relatively quiet as they discuss and try to figure out the word together; other groups can "eavesdrop" on their discussions if they get too loud. This is a nice built-in noise control. This group time can be incredibly engaging and delightful—you can "see" students' thought processes as they attempt to "walk through the words" and make sense of them! Most students are chomping at the bit to share in groups after the independent time.

engagement LINK

Games can be highly motivating for struggling readers. However, make sure the game format you choose does not involve large amounts of "down time" for any student. This is why we recommend including an individual response time for all of our team games.

4. Teacher calls out, "Answer time!" Each group holds up their chart paper or whiteboard with their word broken down by word part, with each part defined, and their predicted definition. Groups explain their thinking to each other. Prompt students to explain their thinking and praise the quality of their thinking, but don't give anything away in terms of word meanings at this point.

5. Check the definition and the meanings of the word parts. With the students, check their proposed definitions against the dictionary definition. The *American Heritage Dictionary* and http://dictionary.reference.com, which shows how words are broken down by meaningful word parts, are excellent resources for this purpose. Usually, teams are highly motivated at this point to see who has uncovered the dictionary definition.

6. Points are given in the following manner: 10 points for each word part successfully broken down by correct meaning and 30 points for constructing the correct definition of the word. For example, the word *transport* would be worth a total of 50 possible points: 10 points for identifying *trans* as a prefix that means "across," 10 more points for identifying *port* as a root that means "to carry," and 30 points for constructing the correct definition as "to literally carry something across, from one place to another." Use the Break It Down template in Appendix G to guide groups and individuals in the word analysis steps for this game.

Break It Down Classroom Example

- Step 1. The teacher calls out the word and reads the sentence twice: "*Nonconformist*. The boy was a *nonconformist* who was constantly getting in trouble for not following the school dress code."
- Steps 2 and 3. Students break down the word using the analysis procedure, first individually and then in groups. Teacher monitors and facilitates as groups fill out their answer chart.
- Step 4. Answer Time: Groups share their chart, explaining their word analysis process and how they arrived at their proposed definition of *nonconformist*. One group's

Figure 6.7 Example of Completed "Break It Down" for *Nonconformist*

Breakdown Word: *nonconformist*

How many meaning parts did you find? Four meaning parts—non–con–form–ist (write the word and circle roots, underline affixes)

How many prefixes, what were they, and what do they mean?

non (prefix, meaning "not")
con (prefix, meaning "with or jointly")

How many roots/base words, what were they, and what do they mean?

form (root meaning "the shape of a thing or person")

How many suffixes, what were they, and what do they mean?

ist (noun suffix meaning "a person who is concerned with or practices something")

Definition: Therefore, a nonconformist is someone who literally does not want to be "shaped" like others. Nonconformists do not follow the rules.

This fits the sentence because the boy did not want to follow the rules for dress in the school.

chart paper might look as shown in Figure 6.7, which can also serve as a supportive template for students to organize their thinking while analyzing unfamiliar words (see Appendix G for a blank template).

- Steps 5 and 6. The class checks the definitions and the teacher awards points to each group. The group completing the example template in Figure 6.7 would receive all 70 possible points for this word, 10 for each of the four word parts (*non, con, form, ist*) and 30 for the definition.

Break It Down Tips/Guidelines

- Allocating points in the way described rewards teams for working through the process of word analysis, as well as coming up with the product—the definition. Remind teams that even if they don't get the dictionary definition, they can still get points for analyzing the word parts. On the other hand, if a group already knows the meaning of the word, remind them that they can get additional points from their word analysis. We tell students that we can learn as much from analyzing words we know as from words we don't know.
- Because every team plays every round, each team can hypothetically attain the maximum point total for every word, provided they analyze the word accurately and come up with an appropriate definition. We have found having every team "in play" every round works well because there is no down time for any one player or team, no waiting for the other team's turn to end.
- Play continues until class time is over or a predetermined point total is reached.

Word Generation/Word Building

Word generation and *word analysis* are flip sides of the same coin. Instead of starting with a whole word and breaking it down into word elements (as in the word analysis activities), word generation activities require students to start with the word elements and put them together to construct whole words. Building whole words from roots, base words, and affixes is a student favorite because it is hands-on, active, and promotes the type of thinking about words that we want to become habitual for our students. Explain to your students that thousands of words in English were created by this process of adding word parts together.

Manipulation—Word Building

In word building (Bear et al., 2008) students create words, both "actual" words and "possible" words, in the same way. For struggling readers, it is particularly important to model this word building process first, either on an overhead or an interactive whiteboard, and explain your thinking as you build the words. This activity works well with struggling readers because it makes explicit and concrete the abstract process of word parts coming together to build words—the students can visibly see the word being constructed as the word cards are linked together (Bear et al., 2008).

Procedure

1. On a set of cards, write down prefixes (*anti-, trans-, in-, re-, pre-, ex-*), suffixes (*-ible, -able, -ion, -ant, -ent*), and roots (*rupt, spect, port, tract, chron*). As in Break It Down (see above), it works best to use word elements that students have already examined. Each group should have their own deck of cards (all decks contain the same cards).

2. Pass out the decks of cards. In groups, students see how many "real words" and how many "possible words" they can create. A recorder in each group should keep track of these words on a sheet of paper or a chart paper for later sharing—one column for actual words and another column for "possible words." Examples of words from the elements listed in item 1 could include the following:

Real Words	**"Possible" Words**
transportable	transtraction
report	antispectable
inspect	pretraction
portable	antiruptent
extract	
retract	
intractable	

3. As groups are working, encourage students to refer back to all the resources they have available—dictionaries, online dictionaries, root books, and word study notebooks. Sometimes, groups are unsure whether a word is real or "possible" and must check a dictionary to find out. Remind groups that when combining word parts to create a whole word spellings might need to change. Students must explain the meanings of the "possible words." For example, the group that created *antispectable* might define it as "unworthy of being seen or looked at" (the opposite of *respectable*).

4. Groups share with the class the words they have built. Voting for word categories such as the "most interesting actual word" or the "most creative possible word" adds a sense of excitement and competition to the activity.

engagement LINK

Because this activity is often humorous, it is particularly motivating for students. Making your own words requires deep processing of root meanings and creative thinking.

Possible Words/Dictionary of the Future

Creating "possible words"—words that are not actual words—is particularly motivating for upper grades students because it allows them to be creative and injects humor into the class discussion. The possible words could be included in a Dictionary of the Future activity (Ganske, 2000), in which you tell students to create a new word that could some day

Figure 6.8 Dictionary of the Future Example

Future word
retrochronograph

Word parts
The morpheme *retro* means "backward, behind" and *chrono* has to do with "time"; *graph* means "to write."

Definition
A *retrochronograph* is an invention that allows high school students to go back in time to retake a test that they failed the first time.

Use the word in a sentence
"The only reason Colin has straight A's this quarter is that his parents bought him a *retrochronograph* for his birthday—lucky guy."

be found in a future dictionary. They define the word, use it in a sentence, and draw a picture of it (see Figure 6.8 for a picture of an example word—*retrochronograph*). Again, asking students to vote for the most creative possible word or the word most likely to actually make it in a future dictionary adds to their motivation.

Brainburst

In Brainburst, players compete to brainstorm as many words as they can that are derived from the same root. Only unique words will earn points.

Materials

Write different roots on cards, such as *graph, phon, scope, aud, dict, port, tract, struct, spect*, and so on. Choose roots that have a wide variety of possible derivations. Each team or player needs a pencil and sheet of paper. A timer is needed, as well as a standard dictionary (condensed dictionaries may not have enough words).

Procedure

1. A card is turned over and the timer is set for two to three minutes. Each player or team tries to think of as many words as possible derived from that root.
2. When the timer goes off, players draw a line under their last word and count the number they have.
3. The player with the longest list reads the list aloud. If another player has the same word, it is crossed off of everyone's list. Any words that are not on another list are checked.
4. Each player in turn reads aloud any words that no one else has called to determine if he or she has a unique word. Disputes should be settled with the help of a dictionary.
5. The player or team with the most unique words is the winner of the round.

Variations

This game can also be played with prefixes (*ex-*, *sub-*, *pre-*, *post-*, etc.) and suffixes (*-ible*, *-able*, *-ant*, *-ent*, etc.).

Root Trees/Webs

Students make root trees or webs to see how words can grow from a common root or base word (Bear et al., 2008).

Materials

On chart paper or an interactive whiteboard, draw a picture of a tree (see Figure 6.9).

Procedure

1. Choose a base word or root to examine. Begin with roots or base words that occur frequently and that have many possible derivations. Later, you can move to less frequently occurring roots.

2. Write the base word or root at the "root" of the tree. With students, brainstorm as many derivations of the base word or root as possible. Initially, include all student-proposed words. Add additional derived words as you see fit. Write the different derivations on the branches.

3. After all words have been written, read through each word and discuss its meaning. As you read through the words and discuss their meanings, a common meaning will usually emerge. For example, a *spectator* "watches or looks," *spectacles* help you "see or look," and a *spectacle* is "something worth seeing." Eventually, with your guidance, the students will come to see how all these words share a common meaning—"to see or look." Group words that share common affixes (e.g., *inspect*, *inspection*, *inspector*).

Figure 6.9 Root Tree of *spect*

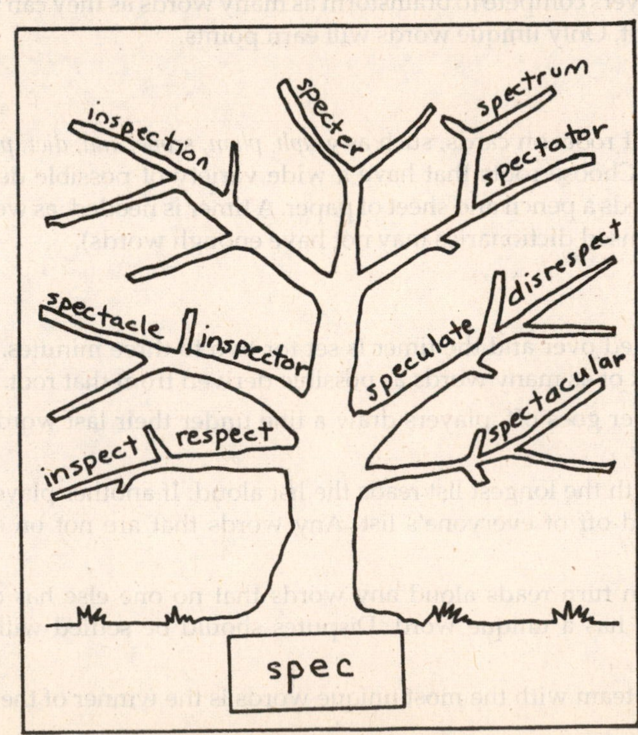

4. Some word meanings may not be directly transparent from a literal analysis of their affixes and root. Tell students that, for these more difficult words, the "route" back to the "root" might take a little more work. For example, to *respect* someone is to hold them in high esteem. How does respecting someone relate to its root *spect*, meaning "to see"? The prefix *re-* means again, so to respect someone is to hold them in such esteem that they are worth looking at again.

5. Display the root tree on the wall and have students copy it in their vocabulary notebooks for future reference. Encourage students to increase the branches on the tree by adding derivations they encounter in books they are reading, words heard on radio or television, or vocabulary from other classes (e.g., *spectrum* from a science class). Keep these word root trees up throughout the year as a visual reminder of the high-frequency roots.

Related Words Root Webs

Root webs visually represent the links between a root (or a prefix or suffix), its derivations, and related words. Related root webs take the thinking of root trees one step further by asking the students to generate synonyms, antonyms, or other types of words that are related in some way to the derived words. Because of this extra step, this activity can potentially double the number of related words students examine in a typical two-week unit.

Procedure

1. Decide on a common root or roots to examine (like *chron, graph,* or *vers*).

2. Brainstorm with the students words that are derived from this root. In Figure 6.10, you see how *adversary, introvert,* and *extrovert* are all derived from the root *vers* ("to turn").

3. Discuss the meanings of each of the derived words. Find the common meaning that the root shares. Up to this point, the process is very similar to the root tree. If you have already done a root tree with your students, you can skip steps 1 to 3 and start with step 4.

4. Brainstorm with your students synonyms or antonyms for the derived words. For example, when discussing *adversary,* your students may come up with synonyms like *foe, enemy, archenemy, nemesis,* or *opponent.* Antonyms could include *ally, compatriot, partner, colleague,* or *confederate.* To delve deeper, you can discuss the shades of meaning that differentiate these synonyms and antonyms. For example, a *colleague* usually refers to an associate in a profession or occupation, whereas *ally* refers to association in a common cause—often countries. You could also ask for words that might describe an *extrovert,* like *gregarious, outgoing,* or *sociable.* As you can see, a thesaurus is an invaluable tool for this activity.

5. Once students become proficient with this process and the use of the root dictionary and thesaurus, they can do this activity independently or in small groups for classwork or homework.

6. A vocabulary notebook is the perfect place for students to create and store root webs.

Games

As we have discussed throughout the book, there is a strong link between engagement and learning (Guthrie, 2004). The following games provide motivating contexts for your students to reinforce and extend their vocabulary knowledge.

Figure 6.10 Related Words Root Web of *vers*

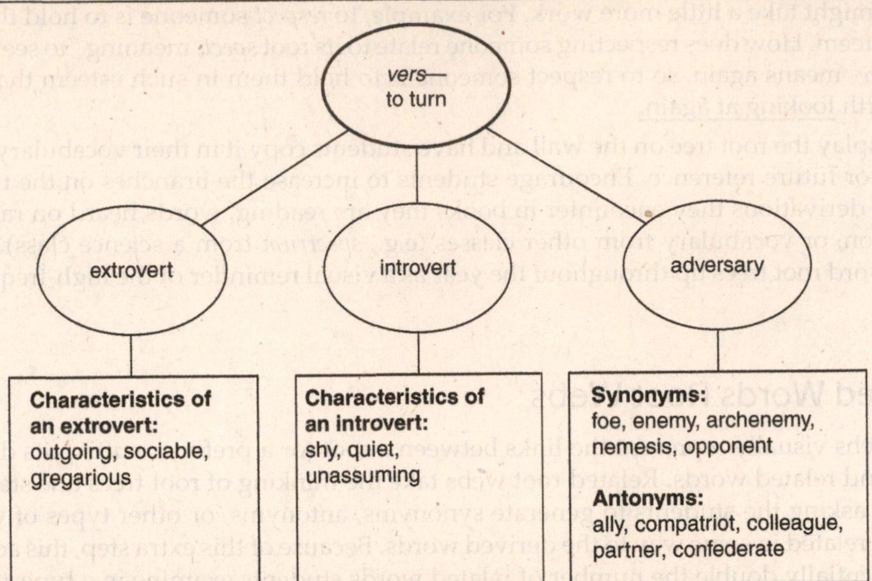

Latin and Greek Jeopardy

At least three students are needed for this game (a host and scorekeeper as well as two players), but lots more can play as well. The whole class can be divided into two teams.

Materials

Create a grid with five columns and six rows. Put headers at the top to indicate the categories. Make a clue card for each slot by writing the points on one side and the answer on the other. Turn over the square that is requested during play so the answer can be read. An alternative for a large group is to make an overhead transparency of the Latin Root Jeopardy board shown in Figure 6.11 and project it on a screen. Cover the clues with sticky notes on the transparency. On a chalkboard use tape to fix squares of paper in the correct order.

Procedure

1. The game is modeled after the "Jeopardy" television game. The clue is in the form of an answer and players must phrase their response in the form of a question:

   Answer clue: Coming from the Latin root *tract,* it means "a machine for pulling heavy loads."

   Question response: What is *tractor?*

2. Determine who will go first. The player will select the first category and point value. The host uncovers the clue and reads it aloud.

3. The first player responding correctly adds the point amount of the question to his or her total or gets to keep the card that was turned over. He or she then chooses the next category and point amount. An incorrect answer means that the points are subtracted.

4. The winner is the one with the most points.

Figure 6.11 Latin Root Jeopardy Board

LATIN ROOT JEOPARDY				
SPECT (to look)	FORM (shape)	PORT (to carry)	TRACT (to draw or pull)	DICT (to say, speak)
100 One who watches; an onlooker	100 One "form" or style of clothing such as is worn by nurses	100 Goods brought into a country from another country to be sold	100 Adjective: having power to attract; alluring; inviting	100 A book containing the words of a language explained
200 The prospect of good to come; anticipation	200 One who does not conform	200 One who carries burdens for hire	200 A powerful motor vehicle for pulling farm machinery, heavy loads, etc.	200 A speaking against, a denial
300 To regard with suspicion and mistrust	300 To form or make anew; to reclaim	300 To remove from one place to another	300 The power to grip or hold to a surface while moving, without slipping	300 A blessing often at the end of a worship service
400 Verb: to esteem Noun: regard, deference Literally: to look again	400 To change into another substance, change of form	400 To give an account of	400 An agreement: literally, to draw together	400 An order proclaimed by an authority
500 Looking around, watchful, prudent	500 Disfigurement, spoiling the shape	500 A case for carrying loose papers	500 To take apart from the rest, to deduct	500 To charge with a crime

"Questions" for Latin Root Jeopardy

	spect	*form*	*port*	*tract*	*dict*
100	spectator	uniform	import	attractive	dictionary
200	expectation	nonconformist	porter	tractor	contradiction
300	suspect	reform	transport	traction	benediction
400	respect	transform	report	contract	edict
500	circumspect	deformity	portfolio	subtract	indict

Variations

1. A round of Final Jeopardy can be added if you wish. When it is time for the Final Jeopardy question, players see the category, but not the answer. They then decide how many of their points they will risk. When they see the answer, they have 30 seconds to write the question. If they are correct, they add the number of points they risked to their total; if incorrect, that number of points is subtracted from their total.

2. Play can alternate from one player to the next or from one team to the next rather than be based on who shouts out the response first. If one player misses, the other team gets a chance to respond. If they are correct, they also get another turn.

3. Daily Doubles may be included, if desired. (The number of points for an answer is doubled and, if correct, added to the player's score; if incorrect, the doubled number of points is subtracted from the player's score.)

4. Develop a Vocabulary Jeopardy to accompany a unit of study.
   - Generate vocabulary cards from a unit of study that fit into four or five categories (for example, "Food Groups" or "Habitats").
   - Write questions that relate to facts and concepts studied on cards.
   - Teams of students play the game as a whole-class vocabulary review of unit.

It's All Greek (and Latin) to Me!

An important aspect of any vocabulary program is to extend interest in and use of vocabulary beyond the classroom and school. When our students personalize and internalize word meanings, they create deeper vocabulary knowledge. Specifically, we want students to notice roots and affixes not only in English class, but also in science, social studies, math, and while at home listening to the radio, watching TV, reading a magazine or newspaper, or talking with friends or family. It's All Greek (and Latin) to Me! provides a motivating forum that encourages this wide interest. This activity is a Latin and Greek root variation on Word Wizard, described by Beck, McKeown, and Kucan (2002) in their excellent book on effective vocabulary instruction, *Bringing Words to Life.*

Procedure

1. Tell students that approximately 70 percent of English vocabulary words and 90 percent of science and technology vocabulary words are composed of a combination of Latin or Greek prefixes, suffixes, and roots. Many of the roots and derived words they are studying will be found in their textbooks and discussions in science, social studies, and math.

2. Your class periods will compete with each other (or groups or individuals can compete within a class) to see which class can find the largest number of Latin- and Greek-derived words, or situations to which these words apply, in a single week. Alternatively, you can award extra credit points for this activity. Any of the affixes or roots studied up to that point in the year are fair game. There are three ways to earn points:
   - *Find an actual word studied in class used outside of the English classroom.* For example, if the root *dem/demos* ("people") has been studied that year, a student could use *epidemic* and *epidemiology* from the science textbook. Another student could recall discussing different world *democracies* in government class. Another student may have heard the word *demagogue* used in the news.
   - *Find a new word that was not studied, but that contains the root or affix that has been studied.* For example, if the root *phon/phone* ("sound") has been studied, a student in the school band might mention that her friend plays the *saxophone,* the conductor must use a *megaphone* to be heard during band practice, and her dad used to play violin in the *symphony.* This student would earn three points for the class!
   - *Find a situation to which the student can apply a word or root of study.* This is the most creative, and often the most fun, of the three ways to earn points. For example, a student might say, "My sister is so *malicious!* She is constantly putting me down and making fun of me. I can't understand why, because I am the kindest sister—I am always so *benevolent* toward her." Another student might say, "I always have to carry the heavy stuff for my mom and dad. I feel like their personal *porter!*" A third student could offer, "The cashier at the grocery store last night was completely *inaudible.* I couldn't understand one word she said."

3. A class receives one point for each word use or situation brought back to the classroom. The class period with the most points at the end of the week wins.

The Only Thing We Have to Fear Is . . . Phobias!

We have never met a group of students who weren't immediately engaged when talking about phobias or fears. This is a motivating and often humorous way to introduce students to how word parts connect to make meaning.

Procedure

1. Discuss with your students that the Greek root *phobia* means fear. Introduce phobias that are likely to be well-known or easy to decode, such as *arachnophobia* (fear of spiders), *technophobia* (fear of technology), *claustrophobia* (fear of enclosed places), and *octophobia* (fear of the number eight). Walk the students through the process of breaking these words down by meaning part.

2. Introduce some phobias that are less likely to be known. For example, *bibliophobia* is fear of books, *heliophobia* is fear of the sun, and *arachibutyrophobia*—one of our personal favorites—is fear of peanut butter sticking to the roof of the mouth (really!). The website http://phobialist.com lists over 500 different actual phobias found in reference books or medical papers. We recommend this website as a teacher reference, not a student website, as some of the phobias might not be appropriate for your students.

3. At this point, students usually start to share their own phobias or those of their friends and the discussion becomes lively and humorous. Encourage students to share these phobias and ask whether they can name them, or if they even have a name (one student offered that her friend was afraid of ketchup—we couldn't find a name for that one).

4. Break students into groups. Give each group a list of phobias (like the following, but without the definitions). The group's job is to look the phobia up in a dictionary or online, find out its meaning, and break it down by root. Then the group needs to generate words related to that root. For example, *aviophobia* means fear of flying, from the Latin root *avis,* meaning "bird." Related words include *aviary, aviation, aviator,* and *avian.* Groups share their findings with the whole class.

   - arithmaphobia (fear of numbers)
   - acrophobia (fear of heights)
   - aviophobia or aviatophobia (fear of flying)
   - sophophobia (fear of learning)
   - anglophobia (fear of England or English culture)
   - batrachophobia (fear of amphibians, such as frogs, newts, salamanders, etc.)
   - carnophobia (fear of meat)
   - coulrophobia (fear of clowns)
   - cyberphobia (fear of computers or working on a computer)
   - lachanophobia (fear of vegetables)
   - verbophobia (fear of words)

5. The last step, which is usually the most engaging for students, can be done the next day. Ask students to create their own phobias that have not been "discovered" yet. Groups will vote for the most creative phobia. Show the following examples of "newly discovered" phobias:

   - *spectophobia* (fear of glasses)
   - *retrotractophobia* (fear of being pulled back in time)
   - *resignaphobia* (fear of having to sign your name over and over and over again)

On chart paper, ask groups to define the new phobia, explain the meaning of the root, use it in a sentence, and draw a picture. Groups present their newfound phobias to each other. Groups vote for the most creative phobia but cannot vote for their own group's phobia. The group with the most votes wins.

APPENDIX Sequence of Instruction for Core Affixes and Roots: Intermediate, Middle, and Secondary Levels

Strand 1: Base Words and Most Frequent Affixes

The following prefixes and suffixes have usually been introduced in the primary grades, but they should be addressed in the intermediate and middle grades as they combine with the words that are appropriate at these levels:

Prefixes[1]

un-	not, opposite	*un*lock
in-	not, without	*in*correct
im-		*im*possible
il-		*il*legible
ir-		*ir*responsible
re-	again, back	*re*make
dis-	opposite, not, apart	*dis*agree *dis*like *dis*connect
non-	not	*non*fiction
mis-	badly, wrongly	*mis*fortune *mis*fire
pre-	before	*pre*view *pre*season
uni-	one	*uni*cycle
bi-	two	*bi*cycle
tri-	three	*tri*cycle

Suffixes

-y	like	lac*y*
-ly		glad*ly*
-er	comparative	cold*er*
-est	superlative	cold*est*
-less	without	penni*less*
-ness	condition	happi*ness*
-ful	full of, like	hope*ful*
-er	people who	teach*er*
-or	do things	act*or*
-ist		pian*ist*

The following prefixes and suffixes have usually been introduced in the intermediate grades, but they should be addressed in the middle grades and beyond as they combine with the words that are appropriate at these levels:

Prefixes

com-	together, with	*com*press
sub-	under	*sub*marine *sub*urban
de-	remove, opposite	*de*fuse *de*tract
post-	after	*post*game *post*season
inter-	between	*inter*continental *inter*rupt *inter*act *inter*vene
intra-	within	*intra*state *intra*mural
trans-	across	*trans*port *trans*continental
anti-	against	*anti*freeze *anti*prejudice

Suffixes

-al	like, characterized by	nation*al* natur*al*
-ous	possessing, full of	courage*ous*
-ment	result, action, or condition	develop*ment* excite*ment*
-ion[2]	action, process of, or result	inspect*ion*
-ic	of, relating to, or characterized by	angel*ic* formula*ic*
-able *-ible*	capable of, likely to	profit*able* flamm*able* cred*ible*
-ant *-ent*	performing or causing an action	observ*ant* confid*ent*
-ance *-ence*	action or process	observ*ance* confid*ence*
-ity	quality, condition	acid*ity* moral*ity*
-an *-ian*	relating to, specializing in, belonging to	Chicago*an* music*ian* Canad*ian* dietic*ian*

APPENDIX Continued

Strand 2: Latin and Greek Roots and Additional Affixes

As students read within and across different genres and content areas, they encounter an increasingly larger number of bases and roots that combine with the following prefixes and suffixes:

Prefixes

super-	over, greater	*super*vise *super*natural
counter-	opposing	*counter*act *counter*factual
contra-		*contra*dict *contra*indicate
ex-	out	*ex*it *ex*communicate *ex*cise
e-		*e*normous *e*rupt *e*mit
ex-	former	*ex*-president
fore-	before	*fore*word *fore*knowledge
pro-	in front of, forward, in favor of	*pro*active *pro*spect *pro*-American *pro*-development
in- *im-* *il-* *ir-*	in, into	*in*dent *im*plode *il*luminate *ir*radiate
en-	cause to be, in, on	*en*courage *en*able *en*circle

Suffixes

-logy *-logist*	science of, scientist	geo*logy* geo*logist*
-phobia *-phobic*	abnormal fear	claustro*phobia* aqua*phobic*
-ism	condition, belief	aut*ism* capital*ism*
-ist	one who does, believes, specializes	pian*ist* capital*ist* podiatr*ist*
-crat *-cracy*	rule	auto*crat* demo*cracy*

Absorbed Prefixes

The process of "absorbing" prefixes is examined explicitly:

in-	not, in/into	*in* + *l*iterate = *il*literate *in* + *p*ort = *im*port *in* + *r*ational = *ir*rational *in* + *m*ediate = *im*mediate

The following roots are usually introduced in the upper elementary grades, but they should be addressed in the middle grades and beyond as they combine with the words that are appropriate at these levels.

Greek Roots

tele	far, distant	*tele*vision *tele*graph *tele*gram *tele*scope *tele*photo
therm	heat	*therm*ometer *therm*ostat *therm*al exo*therm*ic

Latin Roots

aud	hear	*aud*ible *aud*ience *aud*itory	*aud*itorium *aud*io *aud*ition
spec *spic*	look	*spec*tator in*spec*t *spec*tacle	pro*spec*t su*spec*t su*spic*ious

continued

APPENDIX Continued

Strand 2 *(continued)*

Greek Roots *(continued)*

Root	Meaning	Examples
photo	light	photograph telephoto
gram	thing written	diagram monogram telegram grammar program
graph	writing	telegraph autograph biography photography telegraph graphic calligraphy polygraph digraph
micro	small	microscope micrometer microfilm microwave
scop	target, view, see	microscope microscopic telescope telescopic periscope kaleidoscope
phon	sound	telephone phonics symphonic euphony homophone
bio	life	biology biography biome biopsy
auto	self	autograph autobiography

Latin Roots *(continued)*

Root	Meaning	Examples	Examples
port	carry	import export transport	portable portfolio report
rupt	break[3]	bankrupt eruption disrupt interrupt	rupture abrupt corrupt
fract	break[3]	fracture fraction refract	
tract	drag, pull	distract tractor tractable extract detract trace	contract retract attract traction protract
mot	move	motion motivate	promotion emotion
scrib *script*	write	inscribe transcript prescribe manuscript transcribe describe	inscription transcription prescription
dict	say	dictate diction predict edict contradict	indict dictator benediction jurisdiction
vis *vid*	see	vision invisible television revise advise	vista visit supervise video provide
struct	build	construct structure	instruct destruction
gress	go	progress regress	digression aggressive

If not taught earlier, the following affixes and roots should be addressed in the middle and secondary grades:

Middle and High School Latin Affixes and Roots

Root	Meaning	Examples	Root	Meaning	Examples
pos *pon*	put, place	compose expose oppose position component exponent opponent	*cred*	believe	credo credible incredible credence incredulous creditable

APPENDIX Continued

Strand 2 *(continued)*

Middle and High School Latin Affixes and Roots *(continued)*

Root	Meaning	Examples
duc *duct*	lead	produce reduce conduct educate seduce product reduction
vers *vert*	turn	revert divert introvert adverse versatile controversy
ject	throw	project reject inject eject interject object
leg	law	legal legislate legitimate privilege
	read	legible
fer	bear, carry	transfer infer aquifer defer afferent efferent
bene	good, well	benefit beneficial benefactor benevolent
corp	body	corporation incorporate corpulent corpse corporeal
sta *stat* *stit*	stand	stable static statistics constant constitution distant
ced *ceed* *cess*	go	proceed process exceed excess intercede concede
ven *vent*	to come	intervene circumvent covenant venue
clud *clus*	close	exclude conclude include exclusion conclusion inclusion
jud	judge	prejudice judicious adjudicate
fac	make	factory facsimile factor satisfaction facilitate
fec	make	infect effect affect
fic	make	fiction efficient beneficial deficient
fy	make	beautify falsify satisfy personify objectify classify
man	hand	manual manage manufacture emancipate manacle mane
mis *mit*	send	mission missile dismiss promise transmit emit remit

continued

APPENDIX Continued

Strand 2 *(continued)*

Middle and High School Latin Affixes and Roots *(continued)*

Prefixes

mal-	bad	*mal*function *mal*adjusted *mal*content *mal*efactor *mal*aria
a- *an-*	without, not	*a*part *a*moral *an*emia *an*archy
retro-	backward, past	*retro*spect *retro*active *retro*rocket *retro*gressive
per-	through, thoroughly	*per*vasive *per*ennial

Additional Prefixes

epi-	upon, on, over, near, at, before, after	*epi*center *epi*demic *epi*dermis *epi*phenomenon
dia-	through across	*dia*gnose *dia*gram *dia*rrhea *dia*meter *dia*chronic *dia*spora
ana-	up	*ana*tomy *ana*lyze (loosen *up*)
	back/backward	*ana*chronism *ana*phora *ana*thema
	again	*Ana*baptist (baptize *again*)
ab-	off, away	*ab*sent *ab*duct *ab*stract *ab*normal *ab*hor *ab*dicate
meta-	change, beyond	*meta*morphosis *meta*phor *meta*cognitive

Absorbed Prefixes

ad-	to, toward	*ad* + *count* = *a*ccount *ad* + *firm* = *af*firm *ad* + *gress* = *ag*gress(ion) *ad* + *locate* = *al*locate *ad* + *null* = *an*nul *ad* + *point* = *ap*point *ad* + *rest* = *ar*rest *ad* + *sign* = *as*sign *ad* + *tend* = *at*tend
syn- *syl-* *sym-*	together, with	*syn* + *bol* = *sym*bol *syn* + *logistic* = *syl*logistic *syn* + *metrical* = *sym*metrical *syn* + *phonic* = *sym*phonic
com- *con-* *co-* *cor-*	together, with	*com* + *active* = *co*active *com* + *note* = *con*note *com* + *duct* = *con*duct *com* + *clude* = *con*clude *com* + *gress* = *con*gress *com* + *locate* = *col*locate *com* + *quest* = *con*quest *com* + *rupt* = *cor*rupt *com* + *spire* = *con*spire *com* + *tract* = *con*tract *com* + *vene* = *con*vene *com* + *operate* = *co*operate *com* + *educate* = *co*educate *com* + *incidence* = *co*incidence

[1]Most prefixes have more than one meaning. In this scope and sequence, notice that the meanings of prefixes are not all taught at the same time. Students need time to learn, explore, and understand how a particular meaning for the prefix consistently performs. For example, the most common meaning of *in-* is "not"; it is important that students explore, understand, and appreciate how the meaning of "not" is consistently represented across a wide range of words before later introducing the next most common meaning of *in-:* "in, into." (From a developmental perspective, it is similar to trying to teach a first- or second-grader all of the spellings of long *a* at once and expecting the student to be confident about learning all of them at the same time and being able to use the correct spelling in writing.)

[2]*-ation, -ition, -sion,* and *-tion* are all variations of *-ion.* Which spelling is used depends on the base or root to which the suffix is attached.

[3]Occasionally, more than one root from Latin with a similar meaning has come down to us, as is the case with *rupt* and *fract.* More often, however, it is the case that a root from Latin and a root from Greek have come to us with the same meaning.

chapter 7

Word-Specific Vocabulary Instruction

It is second period at Pike Run High School, planning time for two ninth grade teachers—JoAnne Pile, science, and William Chen, English. The teachers are discussing the overwhelming amount of vocabulary they are required to teach in their respective content areas (see Figure 7.1 for potential vocabulary words for instruction). Ms. Pile is planning a series of lessons on cloud formations as part of her unit Earth's Atmosphere, while Mr. Chen is wondering which vocabulary to select for the classic adventure story that his class is about to read, "The Most Dangerous Game" by Richard Connell.

During the conversation, Ms. Pile admits, "I don't know how I will be able to fit it all in. I've got 11 science terms that they absolutely need to know, and I only have three days to teach them all. I could just *cover* the vocabulary words quickly with the glossary definitions and a brief explanation, but will my students remember these words next month, or even next week? If I just cover them, will they even want to learn them in the first place? And how about my at-risk students—what are the best activities for them? I've learned interactive and motivating activities like concept mapping and semantic feature analysis in workshops, but they don't always exactly fit what I want my students to learn or the time I have to teach them."

Figure 7.1 Potential Vocabulary Words for Direct Instruction

Ms. Pile's Sequence of Lessons on Cloud Formation	Mr. Chen's Lesson on "The Most Dangerous Game"
1. cirrus	1. tangible
2. cirrocumulus	2. quarry
3. cirrostratus	3. disarming
4. cumulonimbus	4. cultivated
5. altocumulus	5. amenity
6. altostratus	6. condone
7. cumulus	7. droll
8. stratus	8. scruples
9. precipitation	9. solicitously
10. composition	10. imperative
11. troposphere	11. zealous
	12. uncanny
	13. characterization
	14. character traits
	15. character motives

Source: Adapted from Trefil, Calvo, & Cutler, 2005; and Applebee et al., 2000.

Mr. Chen chimes in, "I've got a different problem. I've had my English classes read 'The Most Dangerous Game' for a few years now and my students really get into the story. The main thing I want them to get out of this story is an appreciation for the author's skillful characterization of the two main characters: Rainsford, who is shipwrecked on an island, and General Zaroff, the evil madman who hunts Rainsford across the island. With support, most students—even my struggling readers who listen to the story on tape—can get a general grasp of the story without knowing the precise meanings of all 12 words that are recommended for instruction. In fact, those words are defined in the margins anyway! So, should I spend time preteaching them? Or will they learn them indirectly through context during reading? On the other hand, those 12 words, along with a few others from the story that I would add, *are* exactly the types of words good readers and writers need to know, at some level. Maybe we should spend time discussing them *after* the reading."

Critical Questions for Vocabulary Instruction

In the vignette, both teachers feel great pressure to quickly cover the incredible amount of vocabulary they must teach in order to stay on track with the curriculum. Too often, this rush to cover material can dampen any enthusiasm students may have toward the class or topic of study. This tension between the quality vocabulary instruction that students need and the quantity of vocabulary words to be learned in the content areas leads to critical "where the rubber meets the road" questions that the teachers in the vignette—and all content teachers—must wrestle with when planning direct vocabulary instruction.

- Which vocabulary words should I teach? Are there words I can skip directly addressing?
- How much time should I spend teaching each concept? How deep should I delve?
- When should I teach the words—before, during, or after a reading, lesson, or unit?
- What do my students already know about the concepts?
- How should I teach these words? Which activity should I use? Concept mapping? Semantic feature analysis? Glossary definitions?
- What specifically do I want students to know about each word?
- How can I get beyond merely "covering" the words and concepts in my content area and ignite an enthusiasm in my students for word learning?

The vignette illustrates a critical truth. Teaching vocabulary is not a one-size-fits-all proposition (Graves, 2008); so much depends on *your* students, *your* curriculum, and *your* goals for instruction. As well-known vocabulary researchers Blachowicz and Fisher (2000) put it, "teaching vocabulary becomes not a simple process of teaching words but one of teaching particular words to particular students for a particular purpose" (p. 517). There are no easy, cut-and-dried answers to the questions posed by Ms. Pile and Mr. Chen. However, vocabulary researchers have provided guidelines for thinking about vocabulary instruction that will help you address these important questions.

In the previous chapter, we discussed the importance of teaching students how words work—how the power of *generative vocabulary instruction* can help your struggling readers unlock the meanings of literally tens of thousands of words to potentially close the vocabulary gap. In this chapter, we focus on *word-specific instruction*—engaging and effective direct vocabulary instruction that targets specific words and the concepts they represent. We present a framework that guides you through the process of selecting vocabulary words and activities to match your students and purposes.

Matching Students, Goals, Words, and Activities

There are at least four major factors to consider when planning direct vocabulary instruction in your content area: the *students* in your classes, the nature of the *words* you plan to teach, your instructional *goals* for teaching these words, and the instructional *activities* you will use to teach the words. Teachers must balance these four factors, along with the time they have allotted for planning and teaching, when making instructional decisions. We place the students at the center of these factors in Figure 7.2 to emphasize the importance of taking into consideration our students' prior knowledge and characteristics when planning.

engagement LINK

Focusing on the few most important words or concepts will result in not only long-term, deep word knowledge, but in increased motivation to learn additional concepts later on.

For struggling readers, balancing all of these components when planning vocabulary instruction is particularly important. Often, the vocabulary load of a textbook passage, or the concepts mandated by district and state standards in a unit of study, can result in cognitive overload for struggling readers in terms of (1) the quantity of new vocabulary words to learn and (2) the depth of word knowledge required to "know" these words. Often, less is more for struggling readers. But how do you know which words/concepts are worth your valuable instructional time? The following sections will present schemes to categorize and prioritize vocabulary words for instruction.

The Nature of Words: Three Types of Vocabulary

One of the first steps in making instructional decisions regarding vocabulary is identifying the nature of the words you will teach. Words are labels for underlying ideas and concepts. For some words, students already have the basic underlying concept but lack the label; students may not have heard the word *elated* before but know the basic concept—they have probably experienced great joy as children. For other terms, both the label and the concept may be new *(nuclear fission)*—and thus take more time to teach

Figure 7.2 Matching Students, Goals, Words, and Activities

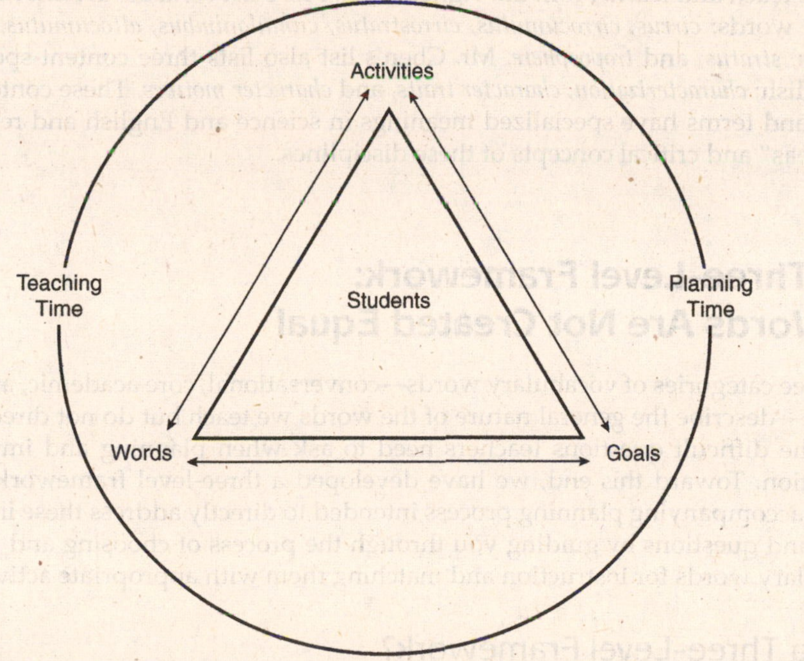

Source: Flanigan, K., & Greenwood, S. (2007). Effective content vocabulary instruction in the middle: Matching students, purposes, words, and strategies. *Journal of Adolescent and Adult Literacy, 51*(3), 226–238. Adapted with permission.

because they represent complex and unfamiliar concepts. Identifying the nature of the words you will teach can help you in planning instruction.

In Chapter 2 (Figure 2.17), we described the three major categories of words currently used by many vocabulary researchers (Beck et al., 2002; Templeton et al., 2010):

- Conversational vocabulary (tier 1)
- Core academic vocabulary (tier 2)
- Content-specific vocabulary (tier 3)

How do these three categories of words apply to Mr. Chen's and Ms. Pile's vocabulary lists? *Conversational vocabulary* includes the most frequently occurring words in our spoken language, such as *of, walk,* and *ball.* As with most middle grade and high school teachers, Mr. Chen and Ms. Pile will probably not need to directly teach the meanings of these words (however, English learners may require instruction in matching the English word to the corresponding word/concept in their native language).

Core academic vocabulary includes words that occur frequently across the content areas. Mr. Chen's list in Figure 7.1 includes 12 core academic words culled from "The Most Dangerous Game": *tangible, quarry, disarming, cultivated, amenity, condone, droll, scruples, solicitously, imperative, zealous,* and *uncanny.* Core academic words such as *cultivated* are not only found in English class, but will also be encountered across the content areas—for example, in science (to *cultivate* a strain of bacteria) or social studies (a diplomat *cultivating* a sense of trust with another county). Students usually possess the general underlying concepts that these words represent, but may lack the label (e.g., students understand the basic concept of "promoting the growth of something" but may not possess the label *cultivate* or understand its different connotations in different contexts). As the number of core academic words on Mr. Chen's list indicates, core academic vocabulary instruction is usually viewed as the primary responsibility of English or language arts teachers.

Content-specific academic vocabulary refers to specialized words and terms that are distinctive to content areas and often represent new concepts, as opposed to the more familiar concepts of core academic vocabulary, and thus will often take more time and effort to teach and learn. From the vignette, Ms. Pile's list contains at least nine content-specific words: *cirrus, cirrocumulus, cirrostratus, cumulonimbus, altocumulus, altostratus, cumulus, stratus,* and *troposphere.* Mr. Chen's list also lists three content-specific terms for English: *characterization, character traits,* and *character motives.* These content-specific words and terms have specialized meanings in science and English and represent the "big ideas" and critical concepts of these disciplines.

The Three-Level Framework: All Words Are Not Created Equal

The three categories of vocabulary words—conversational, core academic, and content-specific—describe the general nature of the words we teach but do not directly answer all of the difficult questions teachers need to ask when planning and implementing instruction. Toward this end, we have developed a three-level framework for words and an accompanying planning process intended to directly address these instructional issues and questions by guiding you through the process of choosing and prioritizing vocabulary words for instruction and matching them with appropriate activities.

Why a Three-Level Framework?

Traditional vocabulary instruction too often includes lessons in which all words are taught at the same point in the lesson (before reading), taught in the same way (copying a definition and writing a sentence), and given the same amount of time (approximately two to three minutes per word). However, this one-size-fits-all thinking does not work; different teachers with different instructional goals teaching different types of words to different students will require differing amounts of instructional time and activities. All of these factors should be taken into account.

A number of vocabulary researchers have presented guidelines to help teachers effectively organize and prioritize vocabulary words for instruction (Beck et al., 2002; Fisher and Frey, 2008b; Graves, 1984; Graves & Prenn, 1986; Stahl & Nagy, 2006). Based on their work, we have created a three-level framework for vocabulary instruction that takes into account the depth of knowledge needed to *know* a word, the instructional goals of the lesson, and when in the lesson it would be best to teach the word (see Figure 7.3). The model presented here is a modification of a method described by Flanigan and Greenwood (2007).

engagement LINK

Explicitly tell students which are the "deep knowledge" words and which are the "foot-in-the-door" words. This makes them partners in the learning process and allows them to study more effectively and efficiently.

In the three-level framework, teachers preview the passage to be read or the unit to be studied, identify the main ideas and critical concepts, and then categorize words/ concepts into one of three categories:

- Deep knowledge words
- Foot-in-the-door words
- Words not to teach

Deep Knowledge Words

Deep knowledge words are words that you deem critically important for direct instruction, for one of two reasons (Stahl & Nagy, 2006): (1) They are essential to a general understanding of the text the students are reading or the overall lesson or unit of study (often these are content-specific words), or (2) they are high-utility words that students will see in newspapers, magazines, and across the content areas (core academic words).

Criteria for Deep Knowledge Words

- These words are important enough to spend a solid chunk of classroom time directly teaching (15 minutes or more, sometimes much more) and revisiting. If you want your students to know and be able to use this word five years from now, it is probably a deep knowledge word.
- You should explicitly teach and guide students toward understanding deep knowledge words/concepts before, during, and after reading or teaching. As you will be revisiting these words again and again, choose them carefully (approximately only eight to ten per week). These words and terms might represent new concepts that need to be introduced and thoroughly taught (e.g., *scatter plot* and *outliers* in math, *magnetic repulsion* and *solubility* in science, *interior monologue* in English, or *de facto segregation* in social studies) or more precise words for basic concepts that students already know (e.g., *scuttled* for "dash off," *annihilate* for "completely destroy," or *undulate* for "rise and fall.")
- For English teachers teaching narrative stories, a large proportion of deep knowledge words are usually core academic words (Mr. Chen's *tangible, quarry, disarming, cultivated, amenity, condone, droll, scruples, solicitously, imperative, zealous,* and *uncanny*), often balanced with fewer content-specific words or terms (*characterization, character traits,* and *character motives*).
- For science, social studies, and math teachers using informational texts, the core academic versus content-specific proportion is usually reversed. The majority of words are usually content-specific words (Ms. Pile's *cirrus, cirrocumulus, cirrostratus, cumulonimbus, altocumulus, altostratus, cumulus, stratus,* and *troposphere*), balanced with possibly a few core academic words (e.g., *composition* is a word that could be introduced in science but also could be used across the content areas).

Foot-in-the-Door Words

Some words do not require deep knowledge because students only need a basic foot-in-the-door understanding of their meanings to understand the passage or lesson. For example, in a passage from a world history textbook about Muslim rule in Spain, a reader may only need to know that *mercenaries* are professional soldiers hired to fight for a foreign country.

Criteria for Foot-in-the-Door Words

- May be either content-specific or core academic words.
- Require minimal teaching time, usually a definition and brief explanation in rich context (Graves, Juel, & Graves, 2004).
- Can be developed more fully and broadly after the lesson or unit, or reading, if you decide.

Words Not to Teach

As a teacher, you know that time is one of your most precious commodities. Because you do not have the time to spend teaching every possible word, and because you want to avoid cognitive overload for your struggling readers, your rationale for selecting words not to teach is just as important as the other levels of the framework.

Criteria for Words Not to Teach

- Words your students already know (e.g., conversational vocabulary or previously examined words). This may seem obvious, but we are sometimes surprised at the words highlighted in textbooks for direct instruction that students already know.
- Words that do not serve your lesson objectives. Remember that your lesson objectives may be different from those of the textbook author.

Figure 7.3 The Three-Level Framework

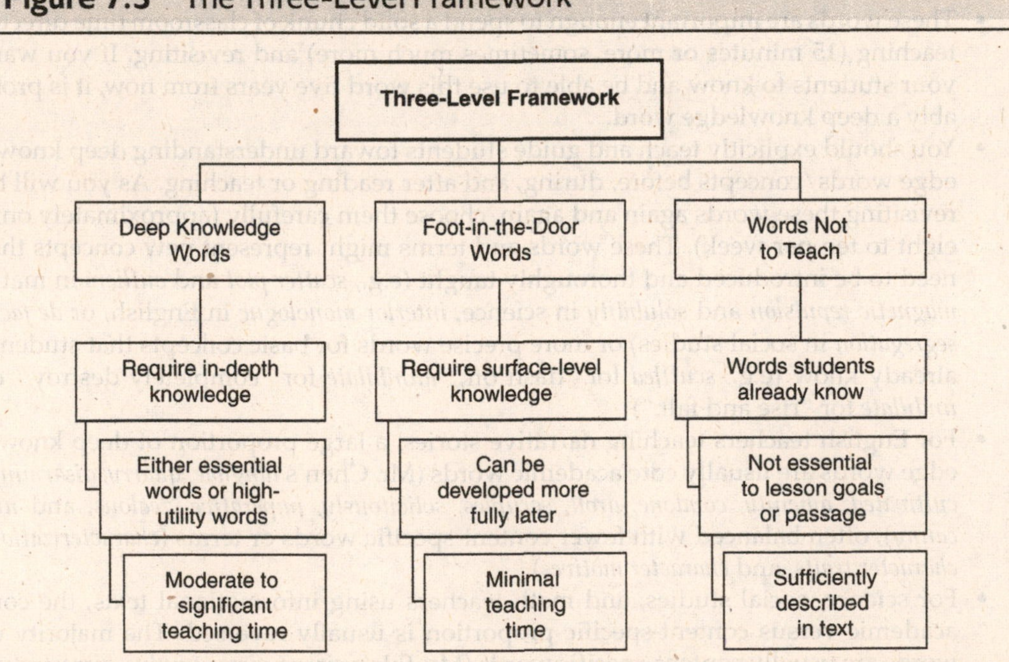

Source: Flanigan, K., & Greenwood, S. (2007). Effective content vocabulary instruction in the middle: Matching students, purposes, words, and strategies. *Journal of Adolescent and Adult Literacy, 51*(3), 226–238. Adapted with permission.

- Words that are sufficiently described in context or defined in the text. For example, in a science textbook passage on weather, *dust storms* may be described clearly enough to skip direct instruction during a lesson. If warranted, the teacher can explore this term in more depth later.
- When in doubt, remember to stick with eight to ten words per week at a maximum. Less is more, particularly for struggling readers.

A Process for Choosing, Organizing, and Prioritizing Words

So many words, so little time. This is a common refrain we hear from content area teachers. Figure 7.4 presents a process for choosing, organizing, and prioritizing words for

Figure 7.4 Process for Choosing, Organizing, and Prioritizing Vocabulary Words for Instruction

Step 1

Identify your lesson goals. What are the critical skills, strategies, and/or content that you want students to know and/or be able to do?

↓

Step 2

With the lesson goals in mind, select words or concepts that students need to know (at some level) to reach the lesson goals. These are your deep knowledge and foot-in-the-door words. The remaining words are your words not to teach.

↓

Step 3

"Chunk" instruction wherever possible. Teach related concepts as a group (e.g., compare/contrast *igneous, sedimentary,* and *metamorphic rocks*). Chunking concepts makes efficient use of your teaching time while supporting students in making connections across related concepts.

↓

Step 4

When should I teach the words? If your students absolutely need to know a word or term *before* reading a passage or participating in a lesson to successfully comprehend and learn, address these words up front. If not, address these words during or after a reading or lesson—these *during* and *after* words will now have the benefit of context.

↓

Step 5

Based on your goals, what, specifically, should students know about the words? (Do you want them to compare/contrast *mammals* and *amphibians* in depth, or do they simply need to know that a frog is a type of amphibian?) What is the learning task for the student? How are related vocabulary words conceptually connected? Answering these questions will help you decide *how* to teach the vocabulary (i.e., which activity you choose).

Source: Flanigan, K., & Greenwood, S. (2007). Effective content vocabulary instruction in the middle: Matching students, purposes, words, and strategies. *Journal of Adolescent and Adult Literacy, 51*(3), 226–238. Adapted with permission.

vocabulary instruction, using the three-level framework just described. Think of this process as a general guideline to follow rather than a strict sequence of steps you must adhere to. We describe each step of the process shown in Figure 7.4 in more depth and demonstrate the process by continuing with Mr. Chen and Ms. Pile from the vignette and the decisions they make.

When appropriate, you may want to give your students some choice in which words they study. For example, you may identify seven "teacher-chosen words" and allow students to choose from a set of remaining words to study. Or you may ask pairs or groups of students to split up the words for exploration and share with the class later. See the vocabulary self-collection strategy in Chapter 2 for an activity based on student self-selection of words.

Step 1

1. Identify the instructional goal(s) of the lesson. What do you want students to know and be able to do by the end of the lesson? Words are only important in relation to your instructional goals and the needs of your students; without these goals and knowledge of your students to guide decision making, all words tend to appear the same.

Mr. Chen wants his students to be able to analyze how the author skillfully uses character traits and character motivation to develop the two main characters, Rainsford and General Zaroff. Ms. Pile decides that the major goal is for her students to be able to identify the different cloud types and compare and contrast their defining characteristics.

Steps 2, 3, and 4

2. Based on the lesson goals, identify words/concepts that students should know (at some level) by the end of the lesson. Divide these up into deep knowledge words and foot-in-the-door words. Keep it to a maximum of eight to ten words per week. Words that don't make the cut are words not to teach.

3. Chunk instruction by teaching related concepts as a group. Think of teaching the "scheme" or structure that ties these concepts together, rather than teaching them as a series of discrete words. This will not only contextualize these concepts for your students, it will also save you valuable teaching time.

4. Which words do the students absolutely need to know in order to comprehend a reading or a lesson? Address these words up front. Remember, students may only need a foot-in-the-door knowledge of some words at the beginning of a lesson; these words can always be more fully developed afterward. Words that students don't need to know before reading can be discussed during or after reading.

Based on his lesson goal, Mr. Chen categorizes the potential words for instruction:

- *Deep knowledge words.* characterization, character traits, character motivation (content-specific words); tangible, quarry, cultivated, condone, imperative, zealous (core academic words)
- *Foot-in-the-door words.* None
- *Words not to teach.* disarming, amenity, droll, scruples, solicitously, uncanny

Mr. Chen identifies nine deep knowledge words or terms for this story: three content-specific terms that represent critical concepts in English and six core academic words that will be found across the content areas. He decides to introduce his three content-specific terms—*characterization, character traits* and *character motivation*—before his students read the story. By discussing these critical concepts up front, he knows his students will be more likely to notice the ways in which the author develops the main characters during reading. This will result in a richer discussion after reading when he can further unpack these important vocabulary concepts. Also Mr. Chen realizes that it makes sense to teach these conceptually related terms together—*character traits* and *motivations* are two specific methods authors use for *characterization.*

The remaining 12 words—all core academic words—are far too many for his students, particularly his struggling readers, to handle in a week. So, Mr. Chen narrows it down to the following six core academic words: *tangible, quarry, cultivated, condone, imperative,* and *zealous.* He chooses *tangible, cultivated,* and *zealous* because they are all words that get at the *character traits* and *motivation* of the main characters—the main goal of his lesson (e.g., General Zaroff appears *cultivated* and civilized at first). He selects *quarry* because it is used throughout the story and its meaning is central to the plot—General Zaroff hunts "human quarry" on his island. Finally, he chooses *condone* because it is a high-utility word that he feels his students will see again in academic discourse and in other content areas. Mr. Chen decides against the other potential words, like *droll,* because they are not central to the story, do not directly serve his lesson goal, and are not high-utility words compared to the other choices. As is often (but not always) the case with core academic vocabulary in narrative stories, knowledge of these words is not essential before reading to get a general grasp of the story. Therefore, Mr. Chen decides to directly teach these six words after reading. His students will be more likely to make sense of these words within the context of the just-read story.

Based on her lesson goal, Ms. Pile categorizes the potential words for instruction:

- *Deep knowledge words.* cirrus, cirrocumulus, cirrostratus, cumulonimbus, altocumulus, altostratus, cumulus, stratus, troposphere (content-specific words)
- *Foot-in-the-door words.* composition
- *Words not to teach.* precipitation

First, Ms. Pile decides that her students need only a basic foot-in-the-door understanding of the word *composition* before reading to understand the text. Therefore, she decides to address it briefly at the beginning of the lesson with a definition and a sentence with rich context. She decides not to directly teach *precipitation*—because her students already have a basic understanding of this concept and it will come up naturally in her teaching of cloud types.

Ms. Pile identifies nine deep knowledge words—including eight different types of clouds—that are specific to her content area and central to her lesson goal. She decides that her students will need relatively heavy instruction before reading in these eight concepts to understand the upcoming text. This heavy preteaching of content-specific vocabulary is not unusual for informational text. Ms. Pile also realizes that knowledge of some basic Latin roots (*cirrus, cumulus, stratus, nimbus*) can help unlock the meanings of all eight cloud words for her students, as shown in the following examples.

- *Cumulus,* from the Latin "pile" or "heap," refers to puffy-looking clouds.
- *Nimbus* or *nimbo* refers to clouds that produce precipitation.
- Therefore, *cumulonimbus* refers to the towering thunderheads that produce heavy rainfall and thunderstorms.

By capitalizing on the generative nature of English, Ms. Pile is not only saving valuable instructional time, she is also giving her students a way to hook these words into long-term memory by teaching them the morphological system that underlies how scientists classify clouds.

Step 5

5. Your final step is choosing the activity you will use. Based on your goals, what specifically should students know about the words? (Do you want them to compare/contrast *mammals* and *amphibians* in-depth, or do they simply need to know that a frog is a type of *amphibian?*) What is the learning task for the student? How are related vocabulary words conceptually connected? Answering these questions will help you decide *how* to teach the vocabulary (i.e., which activity you choose).

In Steps 1 through 4, Mr. Chen and Ms. Pile have made several important decisions.

- Which words to directly teach (and which to skip)
- The relative importance of these words

- How to chunk the words for optimal instruction
- When to most effectively teach them in the lessson

Finally, they need to decide *how* to best teach these words. Which activities will be most effective for their students? Choosing and implementing activities is the final step in the vocabulary planning process and will constitute the second half of this chapter.

Activities for Word-Specific Vocabulary Instruction

In the second part of this chapter, we (1) present a Vocabulary Activities Selection Chart to help you choose vocabulary activities to fit your instructional purposes and your students' needs (see Figure 7.5 on page 212) and (2) describe step-by-step procedures for implementing each of these vocabulary activities in your classroom. However, remember that all of the activities described in this chapter are a means to an end. This end includes igniting a love of words in your students, helping them to acquire deep word knowledge, and guiding them to use these words in written and oral language.

When employing the following approaches to word learning, your struggling readers may require additional support. Keep the following guidelines in mind when directly teaching vocabulary to struggling readers (Harmon, Hedrick, & Wood, 2005; Templeton et al., 2010). They should be particularly helpful for struggling readers, as they build on and extend the five core word study principles introduced in Chapter 2.

- Explicitly explain and model your thinking process as you guide students through vocabulary activities. Struggling readers may not be able to internalize this process without *seeing* your thinking.
- Provide at least three guided practice sessions before expecting struggling readers to internalize the process enough to apply it independently. Gradually release control to the students, using the continuum of support to guide the level of teacher support needed.
- Provide opportunities for wide reading in engaging, instructional-level material. It can be particularly helpful for struggling readers when texts or trade books connect to the content area topics being learned in the classroom—for many struggling readers, the content area textbook is too frustrating to read independently.
- Stack activities when studying a set of words. Use a variety of instructional approaches to get at a word or concept, including providing definitional and contextual information about the word, visual and graphic information, active learning, and rich discussion.
- Struggling students may need many more exposures and rich experiences with a word or concept to "own it." Choose learning activities in which students actively experience, work with, and use words over and over again in a variety of rich contexts.
- Struggling readers may not know foundational information that is assumed for learning a new concept. For example, one definition of a *prime number* is "a *positive integer* that is only *evenly divisible* by itself and one." For struggling students, we may need to back up and teach or review at least three concepts that are foundational for knowing prime numbers—*positive, integer,* and *evenly divisible.*
- Sometimes, struggling readers may have the requisite background knowledge for learning but may fail to connect this background knowledge with new information.

Considerations for English Learners
Providing a Rich Context for Vocabulary Instruction

When learning new words, we learn them best in a rich context. The more supportive this context, the more likely it is that these words will be learned deeply and flexibly. As discussed in Chapter 2, the principles and practices we describe in this book for struggling readers provide this rich context, making them also effective for English learners (with modifications needed at times). The characteristics of effective instructional practices for English learners included below (Bear, Helman, Templeton, Invernizzi, & Johnston, 2007; Echevarria et al., 2004; Freeman & Freeman 2002; Templeton et al., 2010) can be thought of as providing a richer context for learning in terms of materials, activities, oral language input, and teacher scaffolding.

- *Instructional-level teaching.* Instructional-level—"just right"—instruction is critical for struggling readers; it is equally important for English learners. Make sure that the instructional materials and activities you choose match the developmental level of the students and their level of background knowledge. Instructional-level materials and activities provide the context to support optimal learning and growth.
- *Contextualize instruction.* Use animated facial expressions and expressive body language to act out vocabulary terms (*shuffling* and *strutting* around the classroom) in skits, role plays, and games like charades. Use real-life objects and pictures as visuals. Link vocabulary terms and concepts to songs and poems. These activities can help link abstract vocabulary words and concepts to concrete experiences in the classroom.
- *Modify language.* Krashen (1985) stresses the importance of comprehensible input, which includes facing the students when talking, talking more slowly and clearly, emphasizing keywords and phrases, and avoiding idioms. You can also modify your language by providing specific examples and non-examples of vocabulary words and concepts. Create "low anxiety" situations in which students feel free to communicate.
- *Model and think aloud, using the gradual release model.* As with struggling readers, whenever you introduce a new concept, vocabulary word, or strategy, model the strategy and explicitly "think aloud" your thought processes for the students. Provide students opportunities for guided practice with feedback before expecting independence.

Therefore, it is not only critical to activate their background knowledge, but it is also important to explicitly guide them in making connections to new information.

- Older struggling readers are more likely to be apathetic about traditional approaches to learning. Therefore, it is critical that we strive to create an engaging and motivating atmosphere for vocabulary learning in our classes. One important way to do this is to provide students some choice of the words selected for instruction (see the vocabulary self-collection strategy in Chapter 2 and vocabulary notebooks in Chapter 6).

Choosing Vocabulary Activities

Instructional activities constitute the essential toolbox of any teacher. These methods of teaching are the tools of our trade, each tool designed for a very specific purpose. In the same way that we would not use a screwdriver to drive home a nail, we should not use an activity that does not fit the job we need done. Along these lines, you first need to decide *what,* specifically, you want your students to know about each word—what is your instructional goal? The same vocabulary word in two different teaching contexts might require two entirely different activities. For example, a tenth grade world history teacher may

Figure 7.5 Vocabulary Activities Selection Chart

What, specifically, do I want my students to know about the word or concept? I want my students to:	Four-Square Map or Frayer Model	Concept of Definition Map	Vocabulary Web	Vocabulary Self-Collection Strategy	Compare/Contrast Chart or Venn Diagram
Compare and contrast two or more concepts in depth					X
Know the defining features and nonfeatures of one concept in depth	X				
Develop a deep and elaborate understanding of one word or concept	X	X	X		
Differentiate shades of meaning among related words					
Organize related concepts by main ideas, subtopics, and details					
Summarize and connect related concepts					X
Self-select words and "notice" interesting words in reading				X	
Apply the word or concept beyond the classroom					
Review word definitions in a motivating format					
Gain a basic foot-in-the-door knowledge of a word in a short amount of time					

want her student to be able to compare and contrast the defining characteristics of *Athens* and *Sparta*. In this case, a compare/contrast graphic organizer or Venn diagram (described in the activities section), with a substantial chunk of time allotted for instruction, might be the best choice. However, an English teacher might decide that her students only need to know that *Athens* and *Sparta* were competing Greek city-states in order to understand a reference in a narrative story. In this case, a brief explanation might work best.

The Vocabulary Activities Selection Chart in Figure 7.5 matches instructional activities and instructional goals. We chose the particular activities because they fit the needs of older struggling readers working in the content areas. This chart is meant to guide you in choosing the many activities presented in the next section and, in a broader sense, to give you an informed way of thinking about instructional activities. Templates for a number of the activities described in this chapter, particularly the graphic organizers, can be found in Appendix G.

Using the Before, During, and After (BDA) Framework for Vocabulary Instruction

Many of the vocabulary activities we describe, particularly the graphic organizers and concept sorts, fit well into a before-during-after (BDA) instructional framework (Vacca & Vacca, 2008). The BDA framework provides a structure for planning effective, engag-

Semantic Feature Analysis	Semantic Gradient	Semantic Map	Concept Sorts	Power Map	Content Dictation/ Content Summaries	Clue Review with Vocabulary Cards	Have You Ever? (see Chapter 2, p. 56)	Definition Plus Rich Context	Word Wizard
X			X						
		X	X	X					
	X								
		X	X	X					
X					X				
							X		X
						X			
								X	

ing lessons. When applying the BDA framework to vocabulary instruction, instructional goals for each part of the lesson include the following.

Before

- *Activate related background and conceptual knowledge.* If needed, begin to build and organize the knowledge base for vocabulary terms.
- *Motivate students.* Why should I learn this concept or word?
- *Set a purpose for reading and learning.* Setting a powerful purpose motivates students, such as asking students to make a prediction or tell what they know about the vocabulary word or concept. For example, an English/language arts teacher might ask students what they think the word *stern* means from the context of a sentence. Once students predict, they will be motivated to learn more about the word *stern* to see whether their predictions are on target.

During

- *Actively engage students in learning vocabulary words and concepts.*
- *Guide students in focusing on the key aspects of vocabulary.* The particular graphic organizer that you choose will help structure student thinking on key concepts.
- *Monitor student understanding and provide feedback on their thinking during small-group work.* Graphic organizers and concept sorts provide excellent formats for focusing

small-group work and allow you to see student thinking develop as it is laid out in the graphic organizer or in the organization of the concept sort.

After

- *Extend and elaborate on student understanding.*
- *Clarify misconceptions.* Ask small groups to share their graphic organizers. While they do this, clarify misconceptions, add missing pieces of information, and help students connect vocabulary concepts. This will help deepen and broaden their understanding of the concepts.

How might the BDA framework—as applied to vocabulary instruction—look in practice? Imagine a middle school science teacher teaching a series of lessons on the humpback whale, including its physical characteristics, diet, and habitat. She might begin with a blank graphic organizer and ask students in small groups to fill in as much as they already know, or think they know, about humpback whales. (See Figure 7.6 for a student's partially completed graphic organizer about humpback whales during the before phase of instruction.)

Figure 7.6 Partially Completed "Before" Graphic Organizer on Humpback Whales

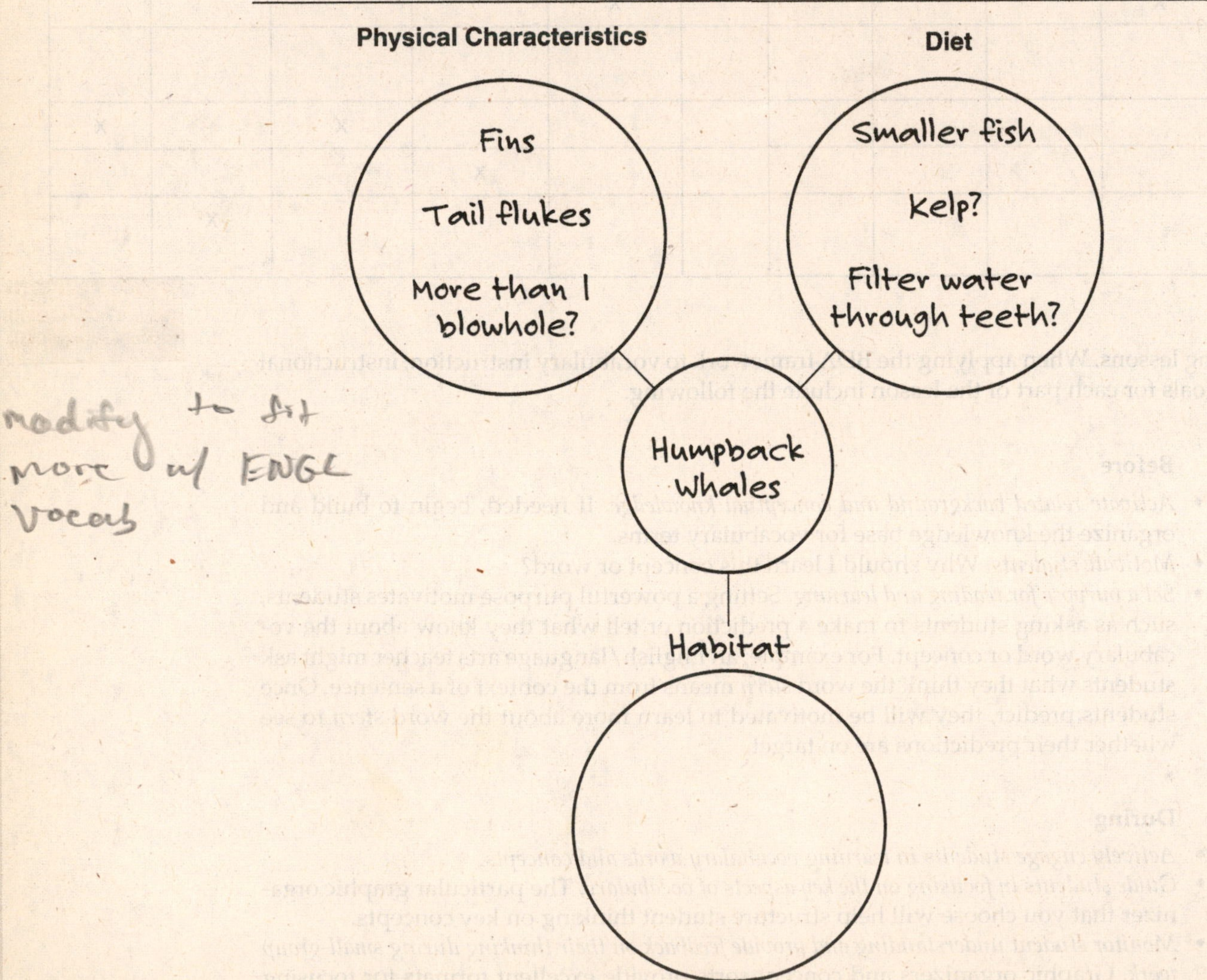

Initially, students might only tentatively pencil in information, such as "humpback whales eat smaller fish and kelp" "humpback whales have fins," and "more than 1 blowhole." This before activity (1) activates students' background knowledge (and allows the teacher to assess what students already know) and (2) sets a powerful purpose for reading and learning—students will want to see if their ideas about the whale's diet, physical characteristics, and habitat are on target. These predictions, because they *belong* to the students, also provide a powerful way to sustain motivation throughout the lesson as they learn more. In the during and after phases of the lesson, they can confirm, modify, and extend their initial predictions as they delete and add to information in the graphic organizer. For example, as students read and learn more about humpback whales, they may also add "tiny crustaceans" and "plankton" to the diet section. The graphic organizer also focuses students on the key aspects of humpback whales that the teacher is after—diet, habitat, and physical characteristics. As a final word on graphic organizers, or any of the vocabulary activities described in this book, it is the *thinking and discussion* generated by the graphic organizer that will lead to long-term deep word knowledge, not simply filling out, copying from the teacher's overhead, or completing the graphic organizer or activity.

Four-Square Concept Map

Purpose. To explore and develop a deep knowledge of one word/concept including a definition in the students' own words and examples and non-examples.

The four-square map (Eeds & Cockrum, 1985) provides teachers a format for delving deeply into concepts by asking students to contribute examples and non-examples of a concept and to produce definitions in the students' own words. Also known as the Frayer Model (Frayer, Frederick, & Klausmeier, 1969), this activity works well for many different types of words and is simple to set up—simply ask students to divide a sheet of paper into four squares. Often, the teacher will start by defining the word to get the conversation started. Then the teacher will ask students for examples, non-examples, and synonyms for the word or term, guiding the discussion and providing teacher examples as needed (see Figure 7.7 for an example). Finally, students will write definitions in their own language. We also recommend asking students, particularly struggling readers, to draw pictures of their word/concept on the backs of their papers. As with many vocabulary activities presented here, pictures help to make abstract concepts concrete.

Figure 7.7 Four-Square Concept Map

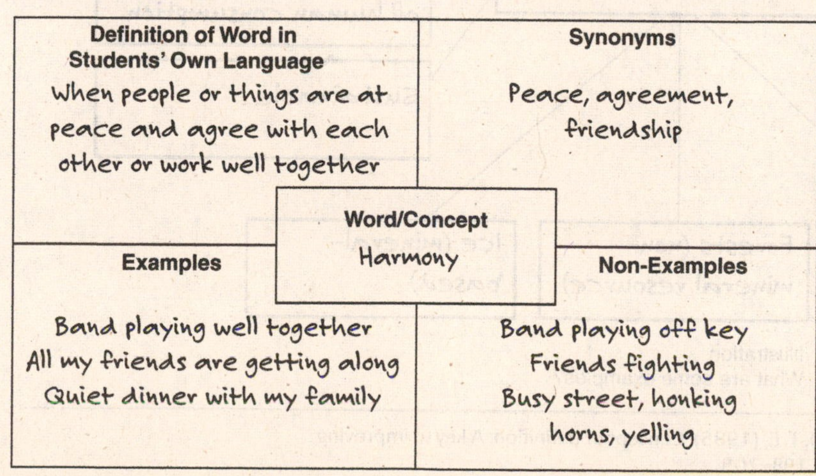

Definition of Word in Students' Own Language
When people or things are at peace and agree with each other or work well together
Synonyms
Peace, agreement, friendship
Word/Concept
Harmony
Examples
Band playing well together
All my friends are getting along
Quiet dinner with my family
Non-Examples
Band playing off key
Friends fighting
Busy street, honking horns, yelling

Concept of Definition Map

Purpose. To explore and develop a deep knowledge of one word/concept including its category and characteristics, as well as examples.

Concept of definition maps (Schwartz & Raphael, 1985) can generate rich discussion and deep thinking about a new concept that students are learning and can be adapted to explore character traits and accomplishments of people. These maps guide students to consider the following essential questions about word meaning: What is it? (category), What is it like? (characteristics), and What are some examples? Figure 7.8 presents an example of a concept of definition map from earth science. Figure 7.9 presents a modification of a concept of definition map from American history. In Figure 7.9, the modifications in the category headers and questions (Who was he? What was he like? What are some examples of his accomplishments?) show how a vocabulary activity can be part of an American history lesson about a determined leader—in this case, the African American abolitionist, author, and statesman, Frederick Douglass. Category headers and questions should always be formatted to fit the needs of your students and your lesson objectives.

Figure 7.8 Concept of Definition Map—Science Example

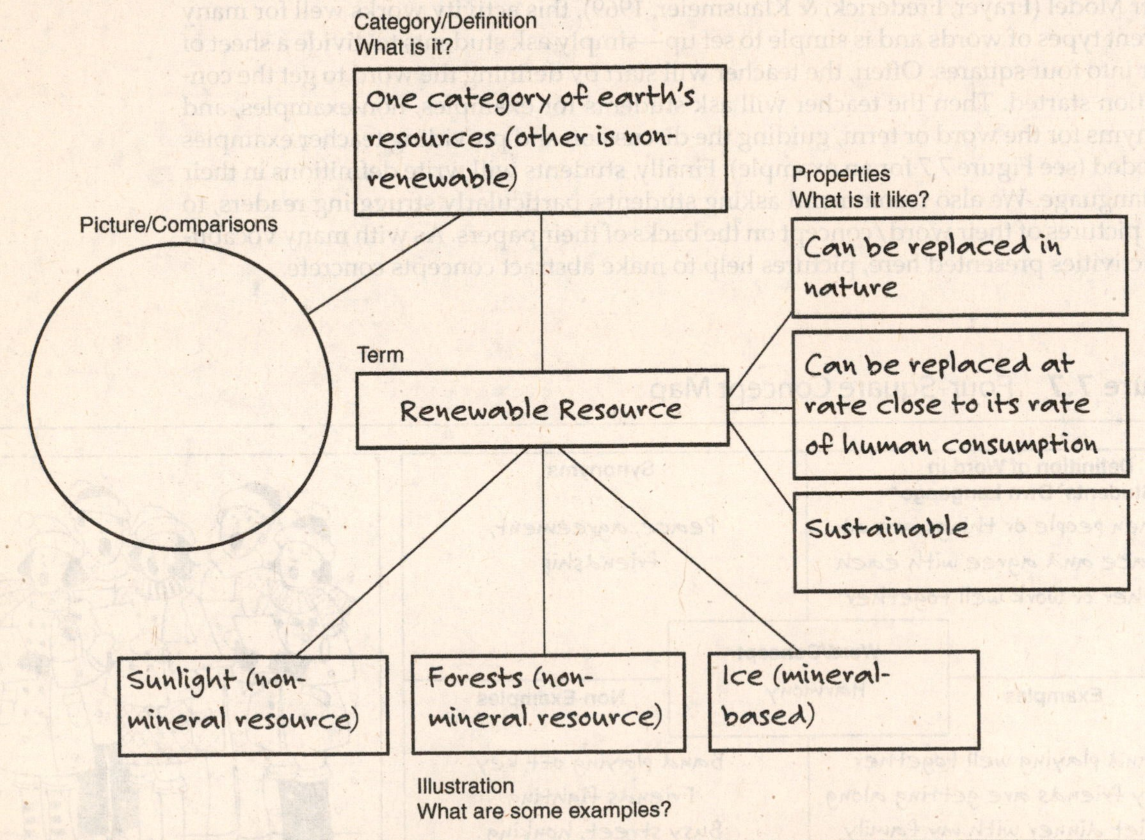

Source: Adapted from Schwartz, R. M., & Raphael, T. E. (1985). Concept of definition: A key to improving students' vocabulary. *The Reading Teacher, 39*(2), 198–205.

Figure 7.9 Modified Concept of Definition Map—Social Studies Example

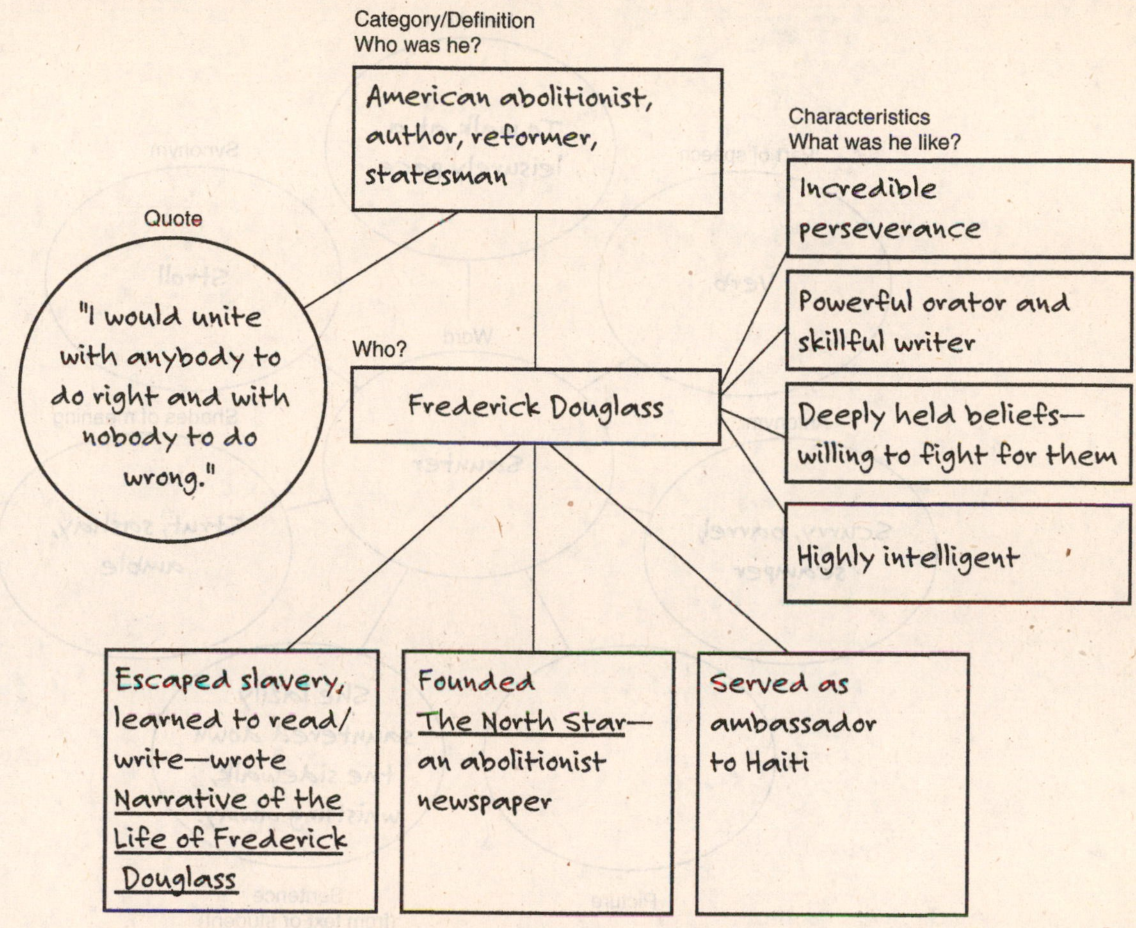
Category/Definition
Who was he?
American abolitionist, author, reformer, statesman
Characteristics
What was he like?
Incredible perseverance
Powerful orator and skillful writer
Deeply held beliefs—willing to fight for them
Highly intelligent
Quote
"I would unite with anybody to do right and with nobody to do wrong."
Who?
Frederick Douglass
Escaped slavery, learned to read/write—wrote Narrative of the Life of Frederick Douglass
Founded The North Star—an abolitionist newspaper
Served as ambassador to Haiti
What are some examples of his accomplishments?

Vocabulary Webs for Core Academic Words

Purpose. To explore and develop a deep knowledge of one word/concept, particularly core academic words, using synonyms, antonyms, and parts of speech.

A variation on concept of definition and four-square maps, vocabulary webs are graphic organizers specifically designed for core academic words (see Figure 7.10). Webs are appropriate for words introduced to the whole class by the teacher or interesting words that students find in their independent reading. As with most vocabulary activities, webs work best in groups. After students identify or are given a word to examine (e.g., *saunter*), they use their own background knowledge, the context of the sentence in which it was found, and a dictionary and thesaurus to find synonyms (*stroll*), antonyms (*barrel, scurry*), parts of speech, and related words. The original sentence (or if you prefer, a student-generated sentence) is written down.

Again, the real learning takes place not by simply filling out a graphic organizer, but in the active thinking and discussion that this activity generates. We have done this activity with middle school students, and their excitement was tangible as students *strutted, ambled, sauntered, strolled, scurried,* and *scampered* across the classroom to show their understanding of these terms and the different shades of meaning involved. You

Figure 7.10 Vocabulary Web Graphic Organizer for Core Academic Words

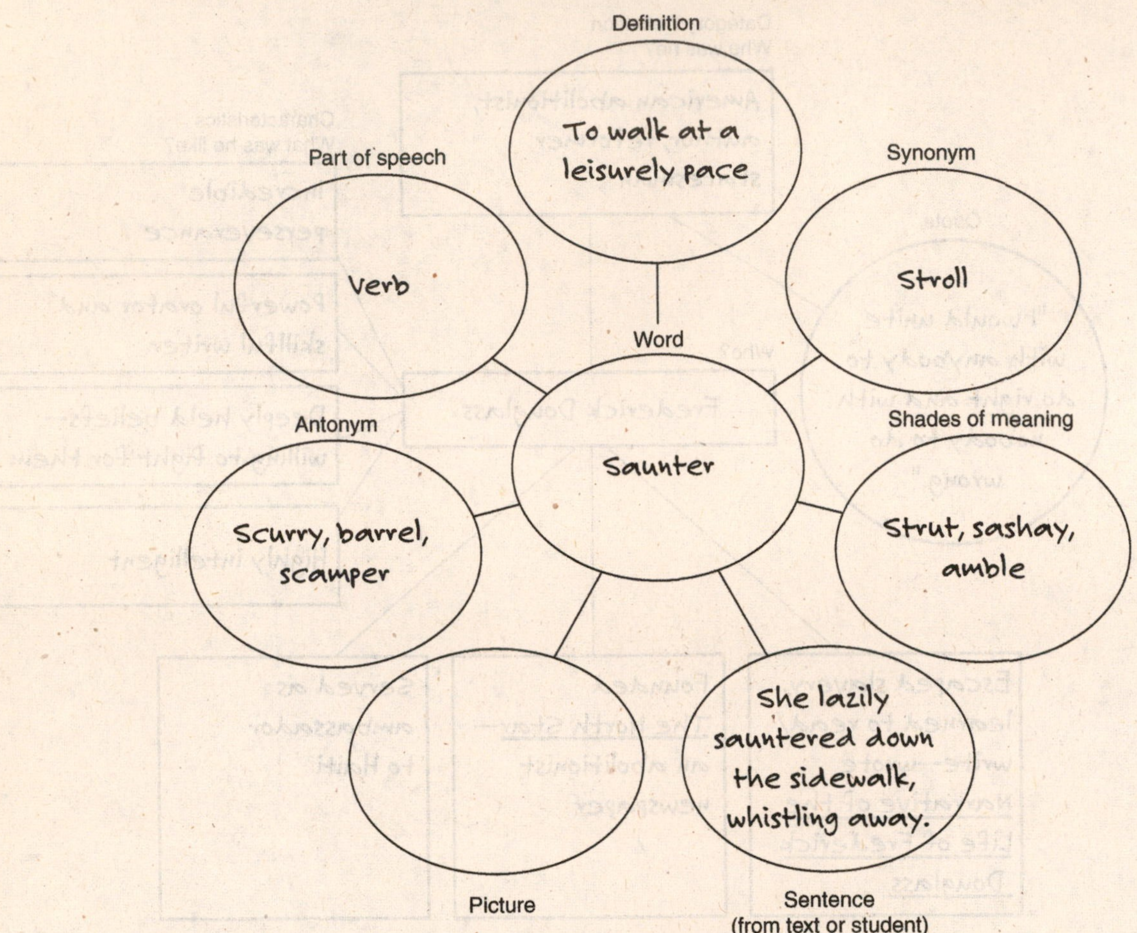

can modify the vocabulary web by adding additional categories for students to consider, such as different forms of the word (e.g., *sauntered, sauntering*), and examples and non-examples of the word.

Venn Diagrams and Compare/Contrast Graphic Organizers

Purpose. To compare and contrast two concepts in depth. Compare/contrast graphic organizers are especially helpful for struggling readers because they explicitly highlight the categories of contrast between the two concepts.

Venn diagrams have become the "go to" graphic organizer when teachers want students to compare and contrast two related concepts. Figure 7.11 shows an example of a classic Venn diagram comparing and contrasting Athens and Sparta. Compare/contrast graphic organizers are a variation on Venn diagrams that are often better suited to the needs of struggling readers and older students studying in-depth content information (Templeton et al., 2010; Vacca & Vacca, 2008). As you can see in Figure 7.12, compare/contrast charts—unlike Venn diagrams—make the features of comparison and contrast between the two concepts visually explicit for the student.

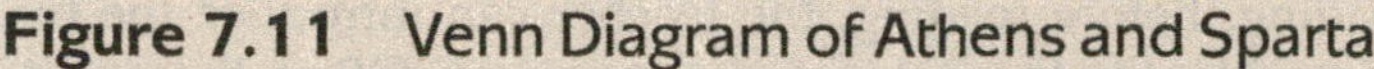

Figure 7.11 Venn Diagram of Athens and Sparta

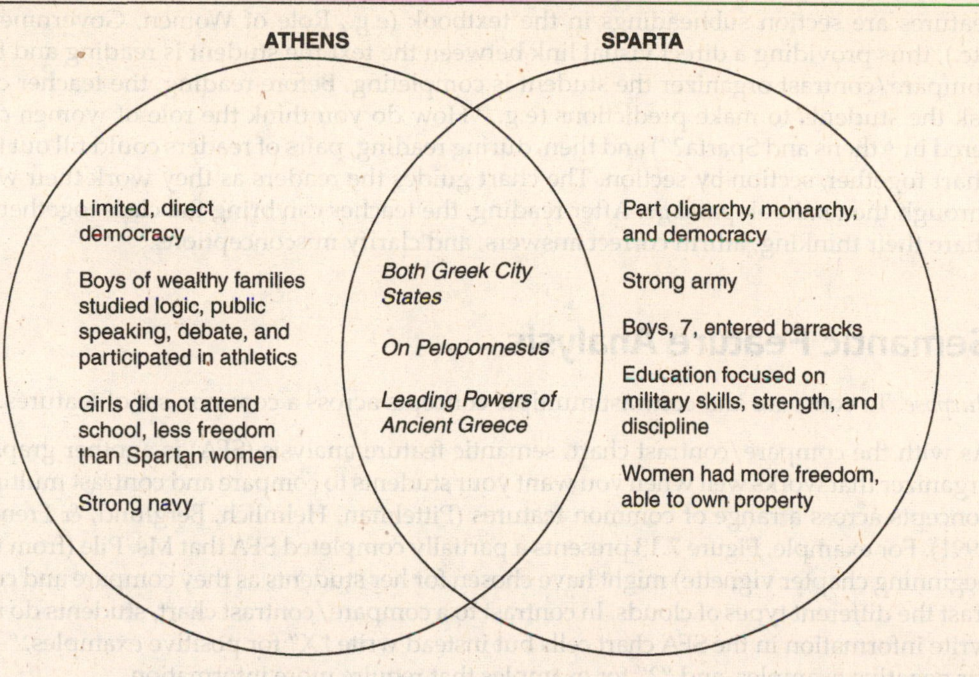

In Figure 7.12, the student not only knows that she will compare and contrast Athens and Sparta, but also knows she will compare and contrast across the following features: the role of women in society, military strength, education, and government. This level of explicitness and direction is of great help to struggling readers who may need more guidance in their thinking and reading. These compare/contrast organizers can be used

Figure 7.12 Compare/Contrast Graphic Organizer of Athens and Sparta

Athens	**FEATURES BEING CONTRASTED**	**Sparta**
Strong navy	**Military**	Strong army
Boys of wealthy families studied logic, public speaking, debate, and participated in athletics	**Education**	Boys, 7, entered barracks. Education focused on military skills, strength, and discipline
Limited, direct democracy	**Government**	Part oligarchy, monarchy, and democracy
Girls did not attend school, less freedom than Spartan women	**Role of Women**	Women had more freedom, able to own property
	FEATURES IN COMMON	
	Greek City States	
	Leading Powers of Ancient Greece	

before, during, and after reading. Before reading, the teacher can introduce the two concepts and, with the students, identify the features of comparison. Often, these same features are section subheadings in the textbook (e.g., Role of Women, Government, etc.), thus providing a direct visual link between the text the student is reading and the compare/contrast organizer the student is completing. Before reading, the teacher can ask the students to make predictions (e.g., "How do you think the role of women differed in Athens and Sparta?") and then, during reading, pairs of readers could fill out the chart together, section by section. The chart guides the readers as they work their way through the textbook passage. After reading, the teacher can bring the class together to share their thinking, affirm correct answers, and clarify misconceptions.

Semantic Feature Analysis

Purpose. To compare and contrast multiple concepts across a common set of features.

As with the compare/contrast chart, semantic feature analysis (SFA) is another graphic organizer that works well when you want your students to compare and contrast multiple concepts across a range of common features (Pittelman, Heimlich, Berglund, & French, 1991). For example, Figure 7.13 presents a partially completed SFA that Ms. Pile (from the beginning chapter vignette) might have chosen for her students as they compare and contrast the different types of clouds. In contrast to a compare/contrast chart, students do not write information in the SFA chart cells but instead write "X" for positive examples, "—" for negative examples, and "?" for examples that require more information.

This activity works best as a way to organize and clarify understandings when students have at least a partial knowledge of most of the concepts under consideration. It can also be used to guide students as they gain conceptual knowledge across a unit of study or a passage in a text. For example, before reading a passage on cloud types, Ms. Pile's students could fill out as much of the SFA as possible, after which Ms. Pile would guide a class discussion of the concepts. Ms. Pile would explain how understanding the Latin roots would help students identify cloud characteristics (e.g., *nimbo* or *nimbus* referring to clouds that produce precipitation and *cumulus* meaning clouds that "heap" or "pile up"). Students would make "predictions" about the concepts before reading by penciling in "X," "—," or "?" in the SFA cells. The SFA serves a dual purpose: (1) establishes a powerful purpose *before* reading—students want to see if their predictions about the cloud types are correct and (2) provides a clear framework to help students organize

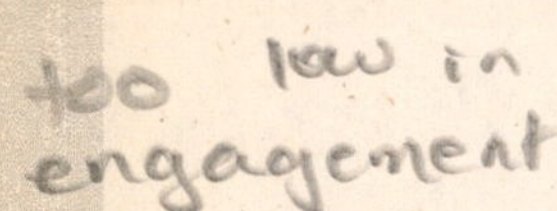

Figure 7.13 Partially Completed Semantic Feature Analysis of Cloud Types

	Cirro-cumulus	Cirro-stratus	Cumulo-nimbus	Alto-cumulus	Alto-stratus	Nimbo-stratus
Form in very cold air at high altitudes	X					
Form at medium altitudes	—					
Puffy white	X					
Usually appear in daytime in fair weather	X					
Form in layers without strong air movement	—					X
Produce precipitation	?					X

the information *during* reading—students would confirm or modify their predictions (i.e., the cells in the chart) as needed. *After* reading, Ms. Pile could bring the class back together to review the information and discuss concepts more deeply.

Word Wizard

Purpose. To apply a word/concept beyond the classroom by connecting newly learned words with students' basic underlying understandings or personal experiences.

If there is a more motivating way for taking word learning beyond the classroom walls, we have not found it. In Word Wizard (Beck et al., 2002), students earn points for finding examples of target words outside the classroom. In terms of generating sheer excitement over words, this activity is without equal. For upper elementary students, you may award points toward becoming a "word wizard." Students' names are written on a chart and tally marks are placed beside each name as students report "sightings" of words. For middle and high school students, class periods can compete against each other, or students earn points toward their grade or for extra credit.

- Tell your students that they can earn points (toward a grade, for a competition, etc.) by bringing in examples of the words they are studying.
- If students see a word, hear a word, or use a word, they earn points. For example, a student might say, "We lost the game last night. I told my mom that I was too *sullen* to play with my younger brother." One point!
- If students see an "application" of the word, they earn a point. This is often the most common, interesting, and humorous way to earn a point. This would be a perfect activity for Mr. Chen's vocabulary words from the vignette. For example, one of his students might report, "When my parents are gone, my older brother *zealously* commands us to do his chores—he is so *imperious!* Of course, my mom does not *condone* his behavior when she is around." This would earn the student three points.
- When reporting back, students must explain the context in which the word was used or applied to show their understanding of the word.

Clue Review with Vocabulary Cards

Purpose. To review and reinforce students' knowledge of vocabulary definitions in a motivating, easy-to-use game format.

As already discussed, sometimes your students only need a basic, foot-in-the-door understanding of vocabulary terms. This basic understanding often serves as a platform for deeper exploration of these terms later. Using vocabulary cards in the Clue Review game provides students with multiple experiences of a word in an active two-player format across a range of contexts. Clue Review is similar to the classic TV game show "Password," in which a celebrity gave his or her partner clues to a word—a word only known to the celebrity—in an attempt to get the partner to guess the "password." One of the great benefits of Clue Review, as opposed to many review games we have tried, is that every student is engaged 100 percent of the time—there is no down time. In some review games we have tried, such as Academic Baseball, the only students paying attention were the ones "up at bat" to answer the question and the students already getting A's in the class. Clue Review avoids this problem because of the two-player format—students are either providing clues or trying to figure them out.

engagement LINK

This is a simple, but highly motivating and effective way to review vocabulary words/concepts.

Procedure

1. Write a vocabulary word on one side of the card and the definition (and possibly the word used in rich context in a sentence) on the other side of the card.

Figure 7.14 Vocabulary Cards for Clue Review—American History Example

Front of Card	Back of Card
John Brown	Abolitionist who raided Harper's Ferry and became a martyr for the Union

Figure 7.15 Vocabulary Cards for Clue Review—Math Example

Front of Card	Back of Card
Prime Number	A positive integer that can only be divided by 1 and itself. 2, 3, 5, 7, 11, 13, 17, 19, 23

Figures 7.14 and 7.15 present examples of vocabulary cards in American history and math.

2. Students are divided into pairs: (a) clue giver and (b) "hot seat."

3. Student on the "hot seat" shuffles deck, and without looking, places the first card on her forehead, with the vocabulary term showing, and the back of the card (with definition) hidden. The clue giver can see the word but not the definition, and the "hot seat" can see neither.

4. Clue giver provides a clue. (e.g., clue giver sees *John Brown* on the vocabulary card and says, "He was an abolitionist who unsuccessfully raided Harper's Ferry. Who was he?")

5. If "hot seat" gets the word correct, she moves on to the next card. If not, clue giver provides additional clues. If partners give up on a card, students flip the card over and review the definition.

6. Pairs see how many cards they can correctly identify without needing to check the definitions on the backs of the cards.

7. After the pairs go through the deck once, students switch roles. This allows both students the opportunity to articulate a definition of the word in their own language.

Tips for Using Clue Review

- Tell students that their definitions or clues must relate to essential elements of that word/concept. We have had students try clues such as "dude with the wig" for *Thomas Jefferson* and "Sounds like marallelogram" for *parallelogram.* Needless to say, while we found these amusing, we didn't count them as correct.
- Pair up more and less proficient students. Students with stronger vocabulary knowledge and language ability can be the first clue givers to provide a language model for the

Figure 7.16 Word Bank for American History Clue Review

John Brown	Union	Confederacy
Civil War	Harper's Ferry	Abolitionist
Robert E. Lee	Frederick Douglass	Freedom

less proficient students and ELL students. The less proficient students will have a chance to provide clues after the partners switch.

- Periodically switch pairs so students can hear multiple ways of defining the same word.
- Use a word bank as a scaffold for the person in the hot seat (see Figure 7.16 for an example of a word bank from Civil War history). Students who need more support will know that the word is one of the nine words they see in the word bank.
- Assign for homework with parents or siblings as partners.
- Collect words on rings, in soap dishes, in baggies, in notebooks, or in coffee cans.

Definition Plus Rich Context

Purpose. To provide students with a basic foot-in-the-door knowledge of a word in a short amount of time.

This activity is well suited for introducing students to new words for which they already have a basic underlying concept (Graves, Juel, & Graves, 2004). It should take only a few minutes of instructional time and works well if students only need a basic understanding of the word. First provide students with a definition of the word and a sentence in which the word is used in rich context—for example, "*catastrophe*—a sudden, widespread disaster. The hurricane was a complete *catastrophe* for the small town—homes were destroyed and many people lost their lives." Discuss the word and the examples of the word with your students. If warranted, you can always examine the word in more depth later.

Using Semantic Gradients to Explore Shades of Meaning

Purpose. To differentiate shades of meaning among related words.

As teachers, we often use synonyms to help explain new vocabulary words to students. For example, we may use "very happy" or "enthusiastic" to help explain to a student the meaning of *ecstatic*. However, *ecstatic* means so much more than either of these synonyms. Someone who is ecstatic is "delirious with joy," to the point of being nearly out of control. We might explain to the student that an ecstatic person is "crazy or wild with happiness." As you can see, synonyms can serve as a starting point for discussing word meanings, but we need to dig much deeper for students to grasp the subtler shades of meaning that differentiate related words. It is precisely this type of deep word knowledge that enables our best readers to grasp the difference between *ecstatic* and *happy* and our best writers to know when to use *grapple* instead of *scuffle* or *clutch*. Semantic gradients (Blachowicz & Fisher, 2010) help generate rich discussions about shades of meaning among students around a set of related words.

Procedure

1. Provide small groups of students with a set of related terms that can be arrayed across a synonym/antonym continuum. Mix the terms up, so that they are in no apparent order to your students (e.g., *ambled, jogged, darted, sprinted, walked, strolled*). You can give these words to students either on cards or on a word bank (see Figure 7.17 for word bank and completed semantic gradient).
2. Discuss a few "anchor terms" with your students so that they have a starting point. For example, you may discuss the differences among *walked, sprinted,* and *jogged.* Which is faster? Slower? How else is *jogging* different then *sprinting?* In what situations might you *jog? Sprint?* Show me how someone who is *strolling* might look different from someone who is going for an early morning *power walk.*
3. In groups, students attempt to order the remaining terms along the continuum. This is an excellent time for students to use dictionaries and thesauruses to try to parse word meanings and delve into finer gradations of nuance among words. Discussions should be rich and lively as you monitor and facilitate the group work.
4. Bring the class back together and ask groups to share their continuums with the whole class. Ask them to explain the rationale for why they ordered the words as they did and how the words differ. Again, this is an opportune time to refer back to a dictionary or thesaurus to clarify word meanings.
5. Remember that the goal is not for each group's gradient to look exactly the same. The important thing is the discussion and thinking that are generated by the gradient, not the gradient itself. For example, at the left end of the continuum in Figure 7.17, *dawdled* and *ambled* could be flipped—one is not necessarily faster than the other. The really important point is for students to discuss the differences between the two words (both mean to walk slowly, at a leisurely pace, but *dawdled* has the additional connotation of a person moving slowly and in doing so wasting time or purposely avoiding something).

Figure 7.17 Semantic Gradient and Word Bank

Word Bank

sprinted, dawdled, moseyed, ambled, strolled, jogged, walked, swaggered, bolted

Example of Completed Semantic Gradient

dawdled ambled moseyed strolled walked swaggered jogged sprinted bolted

Semantic Mapping

Purpose. To develop a deep understanding of one overarching concept by mapping out the relations among the main ideas, subtopics, and details related to that overarching concept.

In semantic mapping (Heimlich & Pittelman, 1986), students use a graphic organizer to show how the important ideas of a topic or unit of study relate to one another. Figure 7.18 shows a semantic map from a physical science lesson on the uses of electromagnetic waves.

Procedure

1. The teacher writes the central concept in a circle on a chart paper, chalkboard, or interactive whiteboard.
2. The students brainstorm ideas and words that are related to the central concept.
3. The teacher adds key ideas and concepts that the students have not generated but that are important to the unit or topic. During this discussion the teacher guides

Figure 7.18 Semantic Map of Uses of Electromagnetic Waves

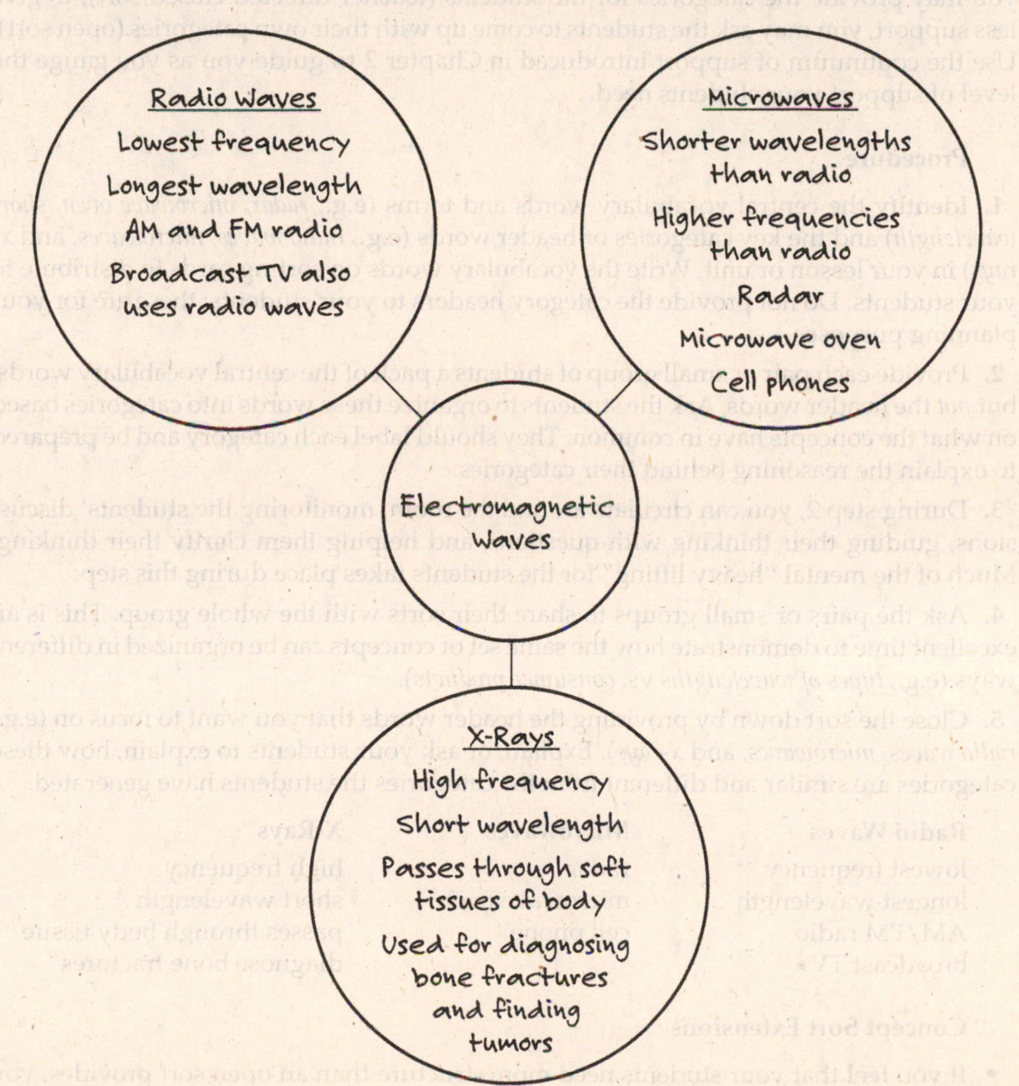

students as they discuss the relationships among the ideas and categorize the ideas according to main idea, subtopics, and details.

4. As students learn more about the topic through readings, class activities, and discussion, they can add to and modify the map.

Concept Sorts

Purpose. To develop a deep and elaborate understanding of an overarching concept by comparing, contrasting, and categorizing the subtopics and details related to that overarching concept.

We introduced concept sorting in Chapter 2 as one of our core instructional activities because it generates such high levels of student engagement and thinking and also because it can be so easily applied across grade levels, content areas, and units of study (see Chapter 2). In concept sorting, students compare, contrast, and categorize concepts by meaning. The vocabulary words may be written on index cards, sticky notes, or in a vocabulary notebook or learning log.

Concept sorts are particularly helpful for struggling readers because they make connections between abstract concepts *concrete* and *visually explicit.* To give more support, you may provide the categories for the students (teacher-directed closed sort); to give less support, you may ask the students to come up with their own categories (open sort). Use the continuum of support introduced in Chapter 2 to guide you as you gauge the level of support your students need.

Procedure

1. Identify the central vocabulary words and terms (e.g., *radar, microwave oven, short wavelength*) and the key categories or header words (e.g., *radio waves, microwaves,* and *x-rays*) in your lesson or unit. Write the vocabulary words on sorting cards to distribute to your students. Do not provide the category headers to your students; these are for your planning purposes.

2. Provide each pair or small group of students a pack of the central vocabulary words, but *not* the header words. Ask the students to organize these words into categories based on what the concepts have in common. They should label each category and be prepared to explain the reasoning behind their categories.

3. During step 2, you can circulate around the room, monitoring the students' discussions, guiding their thinking with questions, and helping them clarify their thinking. Much of the mental "heavy lifting" for the students takes place during this step.

4. Ask the pairs or small groups to share their sorts with the whole group. This is an excellent time to demonstrate how the same set of concepts can be organized in different ways (e.g., *types of wavelengths* vs. *consumer products*).

5. Close the sort down by providing the header words that you want to focus on (e.g., *radio waves, microwaves,* and *x-rays*). Explain, or ask your students to explain, how these categories are similar and different from the categories the students have generated.

Radio Waves	Microwaves	X-Rays
lowest frequency	radar	high frequency
longest wavelength	microwave oven	short wavelength
AM/FM radio	cell phone	passes through body tissue
broadcast TV		diagnose bone fractures

Concept Sort Extensions

- If you feel that your students need more structure than an open sort provides, you could simply introduce the header words before the sort and model how to sort a few vocabulary words from each category, explaining your rationale through a think-aloud. This then becomes a closed concept sort.

- Concept sorts help struggling readers because they make connections between abstract concepts concrete and visually explicit. For more support, provide the categories for the students (teacher-directed closed sort); for less, ask the students to generate their own categories (open sort). Use the continuum of support to help you decide how much scaffolding your students need.

- If you wish to activate and assess your students' background knowledge about a topic, you could use the list-group-label strategy (Taba, 1967). You would ask students to list everything they know about a topic or stimulus word (e.g., write down everything that comes to mind when you think of a "forest ecosystem"). If the students' list does not include important vocabulary terms that are critical to your lesson or unit, you can add these words to the list at this time. The remainder of the activity follows the steps of the open sort described previously.

- Notice how the concept sort about electromagnetic waves organizes *the same information* from the semantic map of electromagnetic waves in Figure 7.18. This "stacking" of activities is something we highly recommend—using a variety of activities with your struggling readers to get at the same information in different ways. For example, after small groups of students complete the sort on electromagnetic waves, they might compare/contrast it with the semantic map on electromagnetic waves they completed as a whole class earlier in the week.

- Here is another example of a concept sort from a unit on world religions in a modern world history class:

Christianity	**Hinduism**	**Islam**	**Judaism**
Bible	Vedas	Qu'ran	Torah
priest	guru	imam	rabbi
Jerusalem	Ganges River	Mecca	Western Wall
Jesus Christ	Shiva	Muhammad	Abraham
cross	sacred om	crescent moon	star of David

As students sort the words, ask them to explain the meanings of the concepts they are sorting and to explain the thinking behind their sort. We might use the following key questions to extend and elaborate our students' thinking and to enrich their discussions. Feel free to modify these questions to fit your students and your topic.

- *Why did you put this word in that category?* Why did you put the Ganges River in the Hindu category? What is important about the Ganges to Hindus?
- *How are these words connected?* (Either across categories or within a category) How are the cross, the sacred om, the crescent moon, and the star of David connected? (all are important symbols of their respective religions)
- *Could this word fit in another category? Why or why not?* Could Abraham fit into another category besides Judaism? Why or why not? Explain. (Abraham is also a key figure in the Christian and Muslim religions)
- *What is another heading or label for this category?*
- *Can you organize this same sort in a different way?* Students might come up with the following sort.

Sacred Texts	**Sacred Places**	**Leaders**	**Major Figures**	**Symbols**
Bible	Jerusalem	priests	Jesus Christ	cross
Vedas	Ganges River	gurus	Shiva	sacred om
Qu'ran	Mecca	imam	Muhammad	crescent moon
Torah	Western Wall	rabbis	Moses	star of David

- *As you organized the sort, how did you sort the information differently from the textbook? Which organizational format do you prefer? Why?* We particularly like the last two questions because they require students to conceptualize how the same information can be organized in multiple ways.

Content Dictations/Content Summaries: Using Vocabulary to Link Reading, Composing, and Content Learning

Purpose. To summarize content area information in students' own words.

Content dictations/content summaries (Bear et al., 2007) are one of our favorite teaching tools for older struggling readers who find the content textbook too difficult to read and understand. After listening to a section of the textbook read aloud by a teacher or another student, students dictate (or if they are fluent enough writers, they write) a one- to two-paragraph summary of the information, using the key vocabulary terms as a guide. This dictation is typed and becomes a student's personal textbook that can be read fluently because it is "written" in the student's own language. We have found content dictations to be a powerful and effective way to build struggling readers' comprehension, vocabulary, and language knowledge while simultaneously exercising their reading skills.

Procedure

1. Struggling readers should be provided any initial classroom activity, along with the rest of the class, to introduce the topic and build background knowledge of the central concepts and themes to be studied. Hands-on activities, instructional videos, experiments, and role-playing are just a few examples of the rich types of initiating learning experiences that can motivate students at the beginning of a unit of study in a content area. For example, a social studies teacher might begin a unit on Westward Expansion by reading aloud excerpts from vivid accounts of early American pioneers, such as *O Pioneers* by Willa Cather and *Giants in the Earth* by O. E. Rolvaag. Important vocabulary terms (e.g., *Westward Expansion, pioneers, river crossings, cholera*) should be explicitly noted and discussed.

2. After the initiating activity, read the appropriate section from the textbook aloud to the entire class or, in a pull-out setting, to the group of struggling readers. Breaking the chapter into smaller chunks will help students better "digest" the information. Reinforce the major themes, vocabulary terms, and concepts from the initiating experience by asking the students to make connections between the initiating experience and the information presented in the textbook—for example, "Did the textbook tell you anything more about the obstacles faced by the pioneers than the first-person accounts we just heard?" As an alternative, the students could listen to the textbook on tape or an aide or peer could read aloud.

3. Next, the small group of struggling readers dictates a summary of the information learned to the teacher, aide, or peer, who types the dictation directly into a computer or records it on audio for transcription later. This can be done at the end of a content class while other students are beginning independent work or in a pull-out setting with the reading specialist or special education teacher. Content dictations are often richer and more meaningful when a small group of students, instead of one student, "co-constructs" the dictation. The discussion that leads to the summary is where much of the learning takes place. Students who are independent writers can write the summary themselves, either individually, in pairs, or in small groups.

4. Struggling readers often need teacher guidance—particularly their first few tries—while constructing their dictations, sometimes skipping key concepts or experiencing

difficulty organizing their thoughts. A *vocabulary bank* can be the missing step for students who struggle with summarizing. Simply a list of the essential vocabulary terms/concepts of the lesson, a vocabulary bank is where students can find and connect the words for their summaries. Because these are the same vocabulary terms already used with the whole class in other activities, such as concept sorts, they should be familiar to the students. Order these vocabulary terms in a logical sequence, because the vocabulary bank will serve as the "backbone" for the students' summaries. It may also be helpful to add any signal words that indicate transitions (e.g., *first, next, in conclusion*) or core academic vocabulary (e.g., *population, raid*) to help the students connect the content words. You can adjust the support for the student's dictation by the amount and types of words you choose for the vocabulary bank. A fairly supportive vocabulary bank for the Westward Expansion unit might include the following terms:

> Westward Expansion (*content-specific vocabulary*), pioneers, obstacles, river crossings, cholera (*core academic vocabulary*), for example (*signal phrase*)

5. Next, ask the students to use these key vocabulary words in their dictations, connecting the keywords in a meaningful summary. As the students orally dictate their summaries, type or write down their thoughts, probing and asking questions to help students clarify their understandings. Because you have provided the students a list of the essential vocabulary terms in a logical order, they are much more likely to successfully summarize the key information. As students become more proficient with this activity, they can start writing the summaries themselves. You can highlight the key vocabulary terms in the dictation by underlining or typing in bold. A group's finished dictation might read something like this:

> During the Westward Expansion, brave pioneers traveled west to find land and better lives. They faced many obstacles along the way. For example, hundreds died during river crossings. Sometimes, there were so many people on a ferry, it sank. Another obstacle was disease. Cholera was a mysterious disease that killed a lot of people. A pioneer could go from healthy to sick to dead in just a few hours. Often there was no proper burial for these poor people.

6. More fluent writers can write the summaries themselves with the support of the vocabulary bank. This often works well in pairs. In this case, the dictation becomes a type of quick write. Next, the pairs can share their written summaries with the whole group. If warranted, you can help the whole group co-construct a group dictation based on the pairs' dictations.

7. The students' content dictation essentially becomes their own personal textbook—a textbook that they can read fluently, because they "wrote it" in their own language. As they add additional content dictations to the first one (in binders or folders selected for this purpose), their personal textbook grows. The students can now read and reread these summaries of content information several times as part of independent work or homework. Rereading not only reinforces content knowledge, but it also provides meaningful practice reading for meaning in text that they can read.

Content Dictation Extensions

- Content dictations can also be used as study guides to review for upcoming tests. Drawing a picture to accompany these definitions can be particularly helpful to help struggling readers lock abstract concepts into long-term memory (e.g., for *Emancipation Proclamation,* one student drew a simple stick figure person breaking chains. At the end of the year, the student could still remember the importance of this event). With a study partner or parent, the students can "quiz" each other on the key vocabulary terms in the content dictation summary, referring to the textbook to verify information as needed.

Power Thinking

Purpose. To organize information by main idea, subtopic, and detail. An easy-to-use and more explicit alternative to Roman numeral outlining and semantic mapping.

Power thinking (Jones, 2009; Santa, Havens, & Valdes, 2004) is one of the easiest-to-learn, clearest, and most effective ways we have found to help students organize information that is hierarchical in nature. It is particularly effective for readers who struggle with content textbooks because it helps students visually organize the types of ideas and concepts often found in expository texts in an explicit, straightforward manner. Students can usually grasp and apply this process within a few lessons. Further, it can be easily applied across the content areas in science, social studies, English/language arts, and math to organize key concepts and vocabulary terms and to actively engage students while reading informational text. Before we describe power thinking, we will place it in context by comparing it to two other popular methods for organizing information: Roman numeral outlining and semantic webbing.

Roman numeral outlining is often used in content area classrooms to help students organize information that is hierarchical in nature. However, this traditional outlining may be confusing—particularly for struggling readers—because it does not always make explicit how the different levels of ideas are related. Take the example of an eighth grade class attempting to outline information about a recent social studies field trip to historic Jamestown, Virginia. In Figure 7.19, a Roman numeral outline of this trip, students may not realize that the fort, the museum, and the ships are all on the same level of ideas—subtopics—because they are represented by three *different* Roman numerals—I, II, and III respectively. In addition, the structure of this outlining system does not always seem logical to students. For example, there is no apparent reason why Arabic numerals with parentheses—(2)—must follow lowercase letters with semiparentheses—b). In the Roman numeral outline format, students often get bogged down asking "What letter comes next?" Because of issues like these, we have seen students become confused; they are so focused on the format of the outline that they lose sight of the function—to organize information.

Semantic maps are an alternative method students can use to organize content information (see Figure 7.20 for a semantic map of Jamestown). Although semantic maps may be visually clearer than the Roman numeral outline in some respects, there is still no scheme for letting the student know specifically how ideas relate to one another. In this example, conveying all the different levels of information with the same shape—circles—does not make explicit that some ideas are "bigger" or "smaller" than other ideas. In short, semantic maps don't make the difference in idea levels (Which ideas are subtopics? Details?) easily discernable for students who may already be having a difficult time organizing the information.

Figure 7.19 Roman Numeral Outline of Jamestown

Jamestown
- I. Three Ships
  - A. *Discovery*
  - B. *Susan Constant*
  - C. *Godspeed*
- II. Fort
  - A. Musket firing
  - B. Games
  - C. Church
- III. Museum
  - A. Navigation tools
  - B. Powhatan's statue

Figure 7.20 Semantic Map of Jamestown

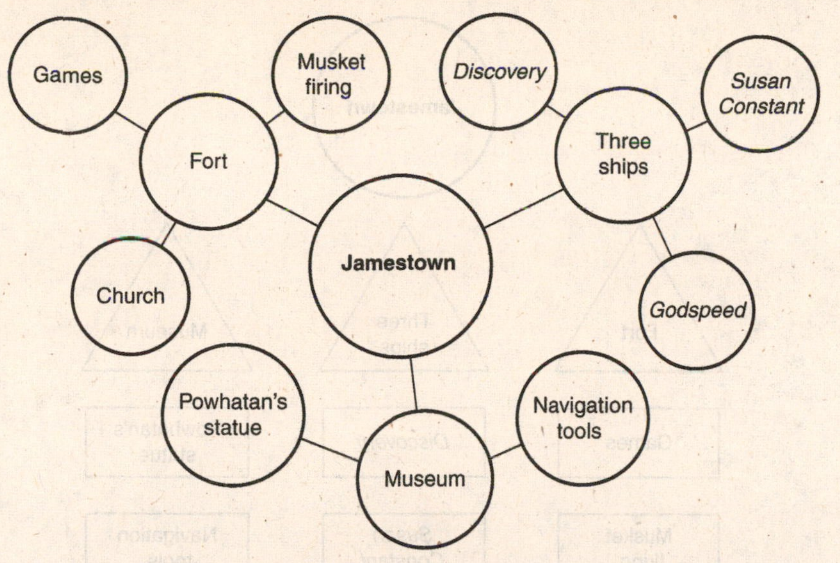

Power thinking provides a clear method to organize hierarchical information. Power 1s are main ideas, always represented by circles. Power 2s are subtopics, always represented by triangles. Power 3s are details, always represented by rectangles. See Figure 7.21 for a power map key. If students want to go to the next level of idea, they don't have to ask the English teacher what comes next. (Little Roman numerals? Lowercase letters? Semiparentheses or whole parentheses?) They go to power 4s or power 5s—assigning numbers and shapes to idea levels is simple and logical. See Figure 7.22 for a sample power map of the Jamestown outline described in Figure 7.19.

What makes power maps potentially clearer than either Roman numeral outlines or semantic webs? The shapes and the language. The shapes make visually clear to the student the level of each idea. Any consistent shape scheme can be used. In Figure 7.22, there is one circle, thus one main idea—the trip to Jamestown. Three triangles mean that there are three subtopics (the ships, the fort, and the museum). It is easy for students to see that these subtopics represent the same level of idea. Second, by using a common language (e.g., "I have a power 3, the *Susan Constant,* that goes under Ships, one of my power 2s") in conjunction with the shapes, students are reinforcing and internalizing the structure of the outline and see how "smaller" ideas fit inside "bigger" ideas. In effect,

Figure 7.21 Power Map Key

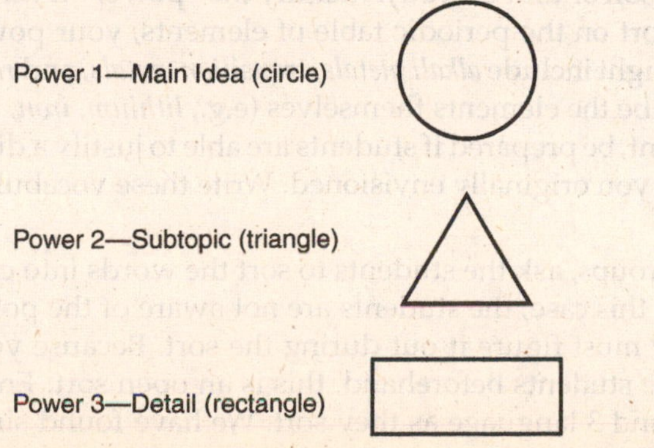

Figure 7.22 Power Map of Jamestown

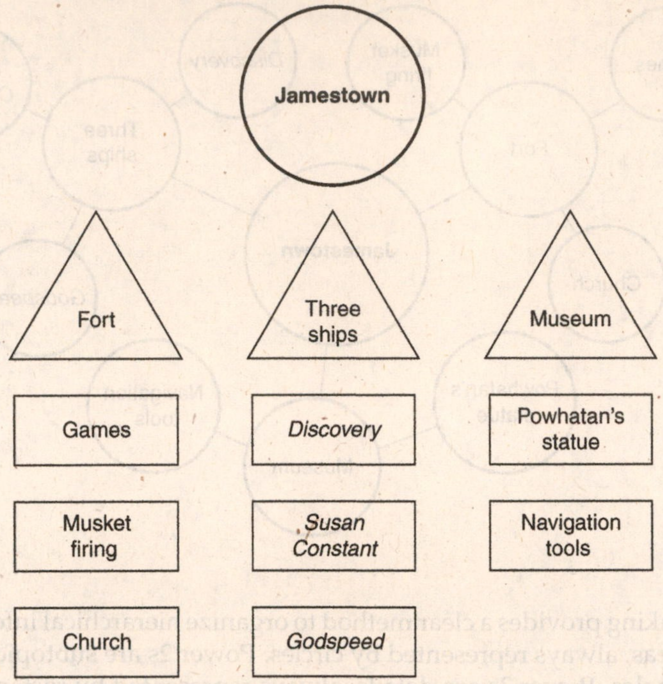

power thinking gives students a clear and easy-to-use language and format to organize their ideas; we have found it particularly effective with struggling readers who need a manageable, straightforward tool to organize their thinking and learning. With a little practice, teachers and students can use this common language for organizing in nearly any content area whether they are reading, writing, visually organizing, or discussing.

Combining Power Thinking and Concept Sorts to Organize Vocabulary

Purpose. To make concept sorting more explicit, particularly for struggling readers, by visually highlighting the differences among the differing levels of ideas (main ideas, subtopics, and details).

Procedure

1. As in the concept sort procedure we have described, identify the central vocabulary words for the lesson or unit of study. Identify the "power" level of each term or concept. In a chemistry sort on the periodic table of elements, your power 1 might be *elements,* your power 2s might include *alkali metals, transition metals,* and *rare earth metals,* and your power 3s would be the elements themselves (e.g., *lithium, iron,* and *carbon*). If appropriate to your content, be prepared if students are able to justify a different placement of key vocabulary than you originally envisioned. Write these vocabulary terms on "packs" of sorting cards.

2. In pairs or groups, ask the students to sort the words into categories based on common features. In this case, the students are not aware of the power level of the vocabulary words; they must figure it out during the sort. Because you have not defined the categories for the students beforehand, this is an open sort. Encourage students to use the power 1, 2, and 3 language as they sort. We have found simply asking students to use "power language" in their discussions goes a long way in helping make explicit the structure of the information and in clarifying their own thinking. It also gives students a common organizational framework and language to communicate with peers and the teacher.

3. For struggling readers or groups who need additional support, you might tell the students that there is one power 1 and three power 2s, but not tell them what they are. For more support, you might tell your students the power 1s and 2s (e.g., "*Periodic table* is your power 1, and *transition metals* and *earth metals* are your power 2s"), but not the power 3s. Or you might give them the power 1s and 3s, but not the power 2s. In this case, they will need to label each power 2, or each category, themselves (similar to the list-group-label approach described in this chapter). Provide as much or little structure as the students need.

4. Circulate around the room for support and guidance during student discussion; ask groups to share with the whole class at the end of the sort.

5. For an extension, ask students to take their concept sorts and create power maps in their notebooks. This can serve as an excellent graphic organizer from which to study for an upcoming test.

Combining Reading and Power Thinking

Purpose. To apply power thinking to the before, during, and after (BDA) instructional framework.

Have you ever asked your students to skim and scan the chapter before reading? Do you ever wonder what they are really doing? Are they noting the main ideas, subheadings, and key terms as an advance organizer to learning? Are they haphazardly casting their gaze here and there across the page? Are they thinking about the party they are going to this weekend? How can you ensure active engagement *before, during,* and *after* reading? Power reading is a simple variation on power thinking in which students create a power map (see previous discussion) of a text they are reading (Santa et al., 2004). It is particularly effective for struggling readers because it makes explicit what our most successful readers are already doing implicitly—it lets our struggling readers in on one of the "secrets" of engaged reading.

Procedure

1. First, ask the students to skim and scan the chapter section for power 1s (main ideas) and power 2s (subheadings) before reading. These are usually the headings and subheadings. Next, ask them to create a power map in their notebooks of just the power 1s and 2s, leaving the power 3s blank for the moment. Circulate around the room to ensure that all students have skimmed and scanned the text. Your evidence for student work will be the power maps. Ask questions: "What is the main idea in this section? How many subtopics is the author going to discuss? What are they?" Create a classroom power map on an overhead to guide the students. The prereading power map is much more concrete than assuming that students are skimming and scanning in their heads. Students transfer headings and subheadings to power 1s and 2s. Power 3s are left blank before reading.

2. Pick one power 2 (subtopic) to start with. Ask the students to predict what the author will say. "What do you think the author is going to tell us about solids? What are some characteristics or examples of solids? What is your prediction?" You can put the students' predictions about what the author will discuss on the classroom display of your power map, while they leave their own power 3s blank.

3. As the students read each section (power 2) of the text, they fill in the power 3s, or details, under that section. They can check what the author actually said against their predictions on the class power map. Initially, you can focus on one subsection at a time, until students are able to handle multiple sections at a time. Filling in the power 3s actively engages the students *during* the reading and helps them to organize their thinking section by section; we find this much more effective than waiting until the end of an entire chapter to organize information.

4. As students become more proficient at using power maps to organize information while reading, they can use power reading independently.

Review Games and Activities

Purpose. To reinforce and extend learning in motivating and engaging formats.

Periodically, you may want to review vocabulary terms and content material with your students for an upcoming end-of-chapter or unit test. Review games (Bear et al., 2008) can be highly engaging and effective ways to help your students consolidate their learning. We have two recommendations when choosing and planning review games.

1. *Know your purpose for the review game.* If you are reviewing for an upcoming test, make sure the game tests the same level of vocabulary knowledge as you will be testing. For example, if you are after definitional knowledge for certain vocabulary terms, then activities like Clue Review from this chapter might be appropriate. If you are after deeper levels of knowledge, then other review activities are probably better choices.

2. *Strive for 100 percent student engagement.* We have seen review games in which the only students who were participating at any one time were (1) the student whose turn it was in the game and (2) students who were already getting A's in the class. This led to a lot of "down time" for a majority of the class. Games in which pairs are working together (such as Clue Review) can help avoid this issue.

The following games and activities are some ways to use the activities described in the vocabulary section to review key concepts and vocabulary terms.

- *Jeopardy.* Use the same format described for Latin and Greek Root Jeopardy (Bear et al., 2008; see activities section of Chapter 6) to create your own Jeopardy review game for your content area. Divide students into groups by subtopics of your unit of study (e.g., *Legislative Branch, Executive Branch, Judicial Branch*). As part of the exam preparation, groups create 100-point to 500-point questions on their assigned topic, ranging in difficulty from easiest to most difficult. Create a board and use these exam questions in the game.
- *Clue Review.* For five to ten minutes every day or every other day, ask students to review key vocabulary words using this format. This is an excellent activity to consolidate definitional knowledge and connect related terms.
- *Break It Down.* Use the same team game format described in Chapter 6. However, instead of presenting vocabulary words for groups to break down by morphemic element, ask questions that get at the key vocabulary words your class is studying—for example, "Give me one antonym and one synonym for the word *scathing.* Independent break down, Go!"
- *Paired ten-minute review.* Ask your students to use any of the vocabulary-related graphic organizers created in class to quiz their partner, going through as many terms in five minutes as possible. Then partners switch. For example, student 1 is looking at a concept of definition map for Frederick Douglass (see example from Figure 7.9) that student 2 can't see. Student 1 asks student 2 to name three major contributions and two characteristics of Frederick Douglass. Because students are using materials that they created for review, this activity requires no additional teacher preparation.

chapter 8

Vocabulary Assessment and Organization

When we mention the term *vocabulary assessment* to middle grades and high school teachers, multiple-choice tests usually spring to mind. This is probably because the multiple-choice format was the predominant method of vocabulary assessment used for many of us in school. To get a sense of the nature of multiple-choice tests, please read the vocabulary test item in Figure 8.1. Choose the synonym that most closely matches the meaning of the underlined word in the sentence.

Figure 8.1 Vocabulary Multiple-Choice Test Item

Her resilient attitude toward life enabled her to overcome difficult situations.

A. depressing
B. dishonest
C. flexible
D. anxious

What was your answer? (We intended item C—*flexible*—as the answer). How did you arrive at your answer? As you can imagine, a student could have arrived at the correct answer in any number of ways. Consider the following three possibilities:

- *Jackie.* As an avid reader who has always had an excellent vocabulary, Jackie not surprisingly has a deep understanding of the word *resilient* and realizes that the synonym *flexible* is the closest answer. However, she also thinks to herself that there is more to *resilient* than simply being *flexible. Resilient* also carries the additional connotation of being able to "bounce back" from difficult situations. Because she doesn't see any choice that reflects this additional information, she chooses the closest answer, C. (Having taken many vocabulary tests like this, Jackie realizes that this is a common problem with the multiple-choice format—one word synonyms alone do not usually include this more precise information she often knows about words.)
- *Miller.* Although he has heard the word *resilient* before, Miller is not sure what it means beyond having a vague sense that it is a positive quality for someone to possess. In this particular case, Miller's vague sense of the word actually helps a lot; *flexible* is the only positive synonym to choose from (because *depressing, dishonest,* and *anxious* are decidedly not positive).
- *Leslie.* Although she also has never heard the word *resilient* before, Leslie realizes from the context of the sentence that *resilient* is the only choice that makes sense (because being *flexible* is the only quality that would help a person overcome difficult situations—being *depressed, anxious,* or *dishonest* wouldn't help).

As you can see, multiple-choice vocabulary tests may not assess the depth or breadth of vocabulary knowledge with the precision that you want. It is entirely possible that students could choose the correct choice for *resilient*—either through context clues or partial word knowledge—and still not be able to adequately understand the word *resilient* while reading or use it appropriately while writing. We are not against the use of multiple-choice tests; in fact, well-constructed multiple-choice tests can be useful for certain purposes, such as quickly measuring students' basic knowledge of word meanings in a whole-class format. However, if we want to move our struggling readers' vocabulary knowledge beyond a superficial level, we need a variety of assessments that are up to the task.

In this chapter, we discuss the different *purposes* you may have for assessing your students' vocabulary knowledge and different *methods* of assessment that match your purposes. The crux of this chapter centers on three principles of vocabulary assessment:

- *Identify your purpose for assessing.* Do you want to know if your students can supply basic information about a word, like the definition of a *homesteader* in an American history unit on the Westward Expansion? Or are you after more in-depth knowledge, like asking your physics students to describe Newton's first law of motion using the following key vocabulary terms—*inertia, state of motion,* and *unbalanced force?* Or are you an English teacher who is more interested in students being able to use vivid vocabulary and the "just right" word in their compositions? Identify *what* and *why* you are assessing before deciding *how* to assess.
- *Match your method of assessment to your purpose.* If your purpose is to assess students' basic definitional knowledge, then a multiple-choice test like the one described might be appropriate. If your purpose is to assess more in-depth conceptual knowledge, then assessments that tap this type of knowledge would be a better match. Match the *what* and *why* of vocabulary assessment (your purposes) to the *how* (your assessment method). Using a variety of assessment methods will give you a more complete picture of your students' vocabulary knowledge and growth.

engagement LINK

Self-assessments can be powerful motivators for struggling readers, many of whom have never been asked to share their thoughts with teachers regarding what they know and how they learn best.

- *Include students in the assessment process.* Honestly and respectfully sharing assessment results with your students, teaching your students how to self-assess and set word learning goals, and providing feedback on their growth will improve student buy-in, motivation, and learning.

Assessing Vocabulary: What Does It Mean to Know a Word?

Consider the following three words:

- ambitious
- clemency
- procrustean

Please rate your knowledge of each of these three words on the scale found in Figure 8.2. (This scale is a modified version of a vocabulary rating scale that we will describe later in this chapter as part of the Vocabulary Fist-to-Five activity [Patterson, Patterson, & Collins, 2002; Templeton et al., 2010]).

Figure 8.2 Vocabulary Knowledge Rating Scale

1 *I don't know the word.*	2 *I know a little.*	3 *I know a fair amount.*	4 *I know a lot.*
I have never heard the word before and I have no idea what you're talking about.	I have heard the word before, but I am not certain of its meaning.	When I read, I know what the word means, but I might *not* be able to use it in a conversation with precision.	I could explain the word to others and use it in writing and discussion.

Many people rate *ambitious* ("eager to achieve success, power, or wealth") as a 4—they can and do use this word in their writing and discussion. *Clemency* ("forgiveness, mercy") is often rated as a 2 or 3; the majority have either (2) heard the word before, but aren't sure of its meaning or (3) can understand it when they read it, but aren't completely comfortable using it in conversations or writing. *Procrustean* is nearly always rated a 1—most people have never heard the word before. (*Procrustean* means "inflexible; producing conformity by arbitrary means" and comes from the Greek myth of Procrustes, a horrible giant who waylaid hapless travelers and forced them to fit the exact length of his iron bed by either stretching their limbs—if they were too short—or chopping their limbs off—if they were too long.)

Assessing Developmental Word Knowledge

As you can see from the *ambitious/clemency/procrustean* example, learning a word is not like turning on a light, where one moment we do not know a word (the light is *off*), and the next moment we suddenly learn the word completely (the light is *on*). Learning word meanings is more like a dimmer switch on a light; we learn words gradually as the light slowly becomes brighter and brighter over time (Blachowicz & Fisher, 2010). Put another way, we learn and acquire words by degrees. For some words, the first step might be to learn the definition of the word. However, learning a definition is only the first step—definitional knowledge does not equal deep word knowledge. The more we see the word used in context and try to use the word ourselves, the deeper and more flexible our knowledge of that word will become. We learn words developmentally, moving on a continuum from never having heard a word before to being able to use it effectively in writing and discussion. Of course, as we mentioned before, we will probably learn new words more quickly if they represent familiar concepts.

One of the purposes of vocabulary assessments is to find out where your students are on the word learning continuum of development with respect to (1) their knowledge of specific content area words—word-specific vocabulary assessment—and (2) their knowledge of the meaning system—generative vocabulary assessment.

- For *word-specific vocabulary knowledge*, developmental assessments will help you determine how familiar your students are with respect to the keywords, terms, and concepts in your content area (e.g., using the vocabulary knowledge rating scale to find out how familiar your students are with the *Westward Expansion* in social studies, *personification* in English, or *radioactive decay* in science).
- For *generative vocabulary knowledge*, developmental assessments will help you determine approximately where your students' morphological knowledge lies on the strand 1–strand 2 continuum (i.e., determining whether they would benefit best from strand 1 instruction in basic prefixes, suffixes, and base words or strand 2 instruction in more sophisticated Latin and Greek roots).

Developmental assessments, by their very nature, are constructed to show growth. Instead of telling your struggling readers that they are still behind most of their peers—as some assessments do—developmental assessments can be motivating by showing struggling readers how far they have come in their vocabulary knowledge.

Developmental assessments that pinpoint where students are on a continuum of word knowledge are particularly important for struggling readers because they allow you to differentiate instruction based on what your students already know about words and what they are best ready to learn next. Developmental assessments, which we describe in this chapter, can also help you track your struggling readers' growth as they proceed forward along the continuum.

Specific Aspects of Vocabulary: Matching Assessments and Purposes

In addition to finding out where your students are in their word knowledge development, vocabulary assessments should also directly target the aspect of word knowledge you want to assess. What exactly do you want students to know about a word/concept? Take the example of an American history class studying *Eleanor Roosevelt.* If your purpose is to examine her many contributions to twentieth-century America, a semantic web might be the best form of assessment. If, however, you want students to compare and contrast Eleanor Roosevelt's accomplishments with other great twentieth-century humanitarians, like Martin Luther King and Gandhi, then a compare/contrast chart would better assess this type of knowledge. These two activities assess two different aspects of understanding Eleanor Roosevelt and point to the fact that there are many aspects of knowing a word or concept. Identifying the particular aspect of word knowledge you want your students to know—your purpose—enables you to match it with the appropriate activity and assessment.

Many of the vocabulary activities described in this book can also be used as vocabulary assessments. For example, we introduced concept sorting in Chapter 2 as an effective activity for vocabulary instruction. In this chapter, we describe how concept sorting can also be an extremely informative assessment of student vocabulary knowledge. Using activities as assessments is a practice that can (1) save you time in the classroom and (2) help your students see the connection between *what* you are teaching and *how* they are being assessed (because they are being tested in the same format that they are being taught).

Tables 8.1 and 8.2 are two charts that provide a framework for matching assessment purposes with assessment methods (with the page numbers where the assessments can be found noted following the assessments). Table 8.1 presents assessments that target word-specific vocabulary knowledge. Table 8.2 presents assessments that target

Table 8.1 Matching Purposes and Assessments for Word-Specific Vocabulary Learning

Assessment Purpose	Assessments
Depth of knowledge of key vocabulary terms/concepts on a continuum. Students' vocabulary growth as they proceed along a continuum of knowledge. Self-assessment.	Vocabulary self-assessment (pp. 239–240) Fist-to-Five (pp. 244–245)
Depth of knowledge of one major concept and knowledge of how supporting concepts are related.	Brainstorming (pp. 240–242) Concept sort (pp. 242–244) Power map (pp. 230–232) Four-square/Frayer model (p. 215)
Knowledge of the defining features and nonfeatures of a concept.	Four-square/Frayer model (p. 215)
Ability to compare/contrast two or more concepts across a set of features.	Venn diagram (pp. 218–220) Compare/contrast chart (pp. 218–220) Concept sort (pp. 242–244)
Depth of knowledge of academic vocabulary and, through spelling, orthographic development.	Intermediate-level academic vocabulary spelling inventory (pp. 247–249)
Ability to organize and categorize related concepts by main ideas, subtopics, and details and justify the organizational scheme.	Concept sort (pp. 242–244) Power map (pp. 230–232) Semantic map/web (pp. 225–226)
Ability to use vivid, powerful, and precise vocabulary in their writing.	Vocabulary word hunts in writing (pp. 245–246)
General growth of vocabulary over time in a portfolio format.	Vocabulary notebook (pp. 246–247)

Table 8.2 Matching Purposes and Assessments for Generative Vocabulary Learning

Assessment Purpose	Assessments
Morphological knowledge on a continuum of development.	Generating/producing words with the same prefixes and suffixes (pp. 250–251) Generating words from bases and roots (p. 251)
Knowledge of specific roots and meanings of words that contain those roots after a unit of study.	Matching Greek and Latin roots (p. 251) Word sorting (pp. 179–182)
Ability to extend word learning beyond the classroom.	Word hunt (pp. 182–183) It's All Greek (and Latin) to Me! (p. 194)
General growth of vocabulary over time in a portfolio format.	Vocabulary notebook (pp. 246–247)
Ability to generate words from a root.	Root tree (pp. 190–191) Generating/producing words with the same prefixes and suffixes (pp. 250–251) Generating words from bases and roots (p. 251)
Ability to break down/analyze a word by morpheme.	Morphemic analysis (p. 171) Break It Down (pp. 185–187)
Use of strategies to independently learn words.	Students' strategies for learning vocabulary (p. 252)

generative vocabulary knowledge. Many of the assessments are also activities that have been described in earlier chapters. In addition to the instructional activities that can be used as assessments, we introduce new assessment activities in this chapter that match a variety of assessment purposes.

Word-Specific Vocabulary Assessment and Learning

As described in Chapter 7, word-specific vocabulary knowledge refers to students' knowledge of particular words and the concepts they represent. The following assessment activities target students' knowledge of word-specific vocabulary.

Vocabulary Self-Assessment

Purpose. (1) Through self-assessment, to make students more aware of the relative depth of their knowledge of specific concepts by rating their vocabulary knowledge on a scale. (2) When used before and after a lesson or unit, to demonstrate growth in depth of knowledge of key vocabulary terms.

engagement LINK

Visibly tracking the growth of word knowledge provides struggling readers important feedback as they see the tangible results of their efforts.

As we have mentioned, knowing a word is not an either/or proposition. Rather, we learn words and concepts by degrees, from never having heard the word before to knowing it well. Based on the scales used in vocabulary assessment research (Pearson et al., 2007), the vocabulary self-assessment (Templeton et al., 2010) provides a format to rate their knowledge of key vocabulary terms on a continuum. As students progress through a unit of study, they can return to the scale to measure how their knowledge of the key concepts has grown. Figure 8.3 presents a vocabulary self-assessment used in an earth science unit, Ocean Systems. (A blank template can be found in Appendix H.)

Procedure

1. Ask students to write the key vocabulary terms/concepts from the upcoming unit or lesson in the left-hand column of the vocabulary self-assessment.

2. If this is the first time students have used the assessment, model how to complete one of the key terms. Describe your thought process. ("I've heard of *El Niño* when newscasters report bad weather in California. I think it may have something to do with the ocean's temperature, but I'm not sure, so I'll put an X in the "Have Some Ideas" column.")

3. Ask students to complete the activity with the remaining vocabulary terms. They can share their findings with others in pairs, small groups, or the whole group. Monitor and facilitate group work.

4. Periodically during the unit, students should return to the self-assessment, adding new vocabulary words and using different symbols (X, O, and +) or colors to represent growth in understanding of the key vocabulary.

5. Students can add a column to include source and page numbers to indicate where they found the information. These self-assessments can be added to a student's vocabulary notebook or quarterly folders and can be used as part of their content area grade.

Vocabulary Brainstorming

Purpose. To assess the depth of students' prior knowledge about a topic and their knowledge of how key supporting concepts are related.

We often think of brainstorming as an effective instructional activity that helps students activate their prior knowledge about a topic. In addition, brainstorming provides an excellent vehicle for assessing your students' knowledge of a topic, unit of study, or key vocabulary terms and concepts. Not only can brainstorming tell you what your students already know about a topic, it also allows you to probe their understanding of how these concepts are related to each other. Please see Figure 8.4 (p. 242) for a science example using a semantic web format to brainstorm words related to the unit Earthquakes.

Procedure

1. *Choose a topic.* Choose a keyword related to your content area or unit of study. Make sure the keyword is one that students probably have at least a moderate amount of knowledge about (or more) and will be motivated to discuss (e.g., *earthquakes*). Sometimes reading a brief vignette or part of an article from a newspaper, magazine, or powerful text can spark students' initial thinking, particularly struggling students who may not have the background knowledge of their classmates.

2. *Model.* If your students have not done this activity before, model the first few steps, explaining your thought process as you go.

Figure 8.3 Vocabulary Self-Assessment for Ocean Systems

Ocean Systems

Vocabulary Self-Assessment

Student Anwar

Dates Sept. 16 (X)

(O)

(✓)

Vocabulary	Knowledge Rating			
	Never Heard of It	Heard It	Have Some Ideas	Know It Well
ocean current				I know that there are currents in the ocean, like river currents.
surface currents			Currents on "top"?	
deep currents			Currents deep down below are different than surface currents? How are they different?	
El Niño			Something to do with bad weather in California? And ocean temp?	
desalination	X			
Gulf Stream		X		
continental shelf		X		

3. *Individual brainstorm.* Ask students to write the keyword on a piece of paper and then to each write down as many words as they can think of related to the topic. The individual step ensures that no student "cruises" through the activity, allowing other group members to shoulder the load while doing no real individual thinking.

Figure 8.4 Group Brainstorm of Earthquakes Using a Semantic Web Format

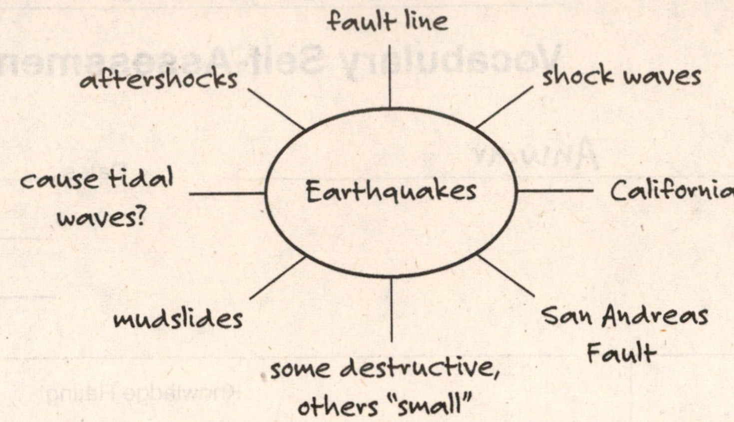

4. *Group brainstorm.* Students move into small groups and combine their ideas on chart paper. Student roles could include scribe, timekeeper, reporter, and discussion facilitator. Monitor and facilitate small-group discussions, asking students to elaborate on their thinking. Ask them how supporting ideas are connected to each other and to the main idea.

5. *Group share.* Small groups share their chart paper brainstorms with the class. Encourage groups to include new information they learn from other groups. As in the small-group step, ask students to explain how the concepts are connected. ("How could an earthquake cause a mudslide or a tidal wave?")

6. *Collect individual and group brainstorm webs.* Looking at both sets of webs allows you to assess the depth of your struggling readers' knowledge about the topic on their own as well as the collective knowledge of the group. Comparing the individual and group brainstorm webs can give you a sense of your struggling readers' background knowledge in relation to other students in the class. This will help you decide whether certain students need additional instruction in foundational concepts to better grasp an upcoming topic or concept.

Concept Sorts to Assess Content-Specific Vocabulary

Purpose. To assess students' overall knowledge of a topic that is hierarchically organized. To assess students' knowledge of how subtopics and concepts fit into the overall organization.

As with brainstorming, concept sorting is an excellent instructional activity that can also be used to effectively assess students' vocabulary knowledge (see Chapter 2 for a description of concept sorting as an instructional activity). Concept sorting is a dynamic way to assess students' conceptual knowledge as they organize, categorize, and arrange related concepts before, during, or after a lesson or unit of study. Asking students to explain their thinking, either in discussion or writing, provides valuable assessment information regarding the depth of their vocabulary knowledge and their ability to make connections across words in the sort.

As with all sorts, students should read the words, categorize the words into groups, and then share the thinking, explaining the rationale behind their sort. Ask students to set aside words that they cannot read or words whose meanings they do not know. If your assessment purpose is to see how students organize the information with no guidance, an open sort is probably your best choice. If your assessment purpose is to see how students organize key concepts according to categories you have already selected, choose a closed sort. Afterward, students can record sorts in their vocabulary notebooks with an accompanying rationale for why they sorted the way they did.

Variations

Concept sorts can be used before, during, and after a unit of study to assess students' growth in vocabulary knowledge. As students proceed through the unit of study, add word cards, key phrases, symbols, and diagrams to the sort. Include more support by providing key categories beforehand (closed sort); increase the difficulty of the sort by asking students to come up with their own categories (open sort). Timing the students can add an element of competition and challenge, requiring students to sort for accuracy and speed. Sorting accurately and quickly indicates a strong grasp of the subject matter. The following example shows a concept sort for a high school world history unit titled Indian Civilization. If this had been a closed sort, the category headers (*physical geography, religion, contributions,* and *significant figures*) would have been provided and identified by the teacher beforehand. Or for a middle ground of support between a closed and open sort, you could include these header cards in the sort, but not tell the students which cards are the header words and which are the underlying concept words. ("Here are the sort words, class. There are four header words included in the sort, but I am not going to tell you what they are. Try and figure them out as you work through the sort.")

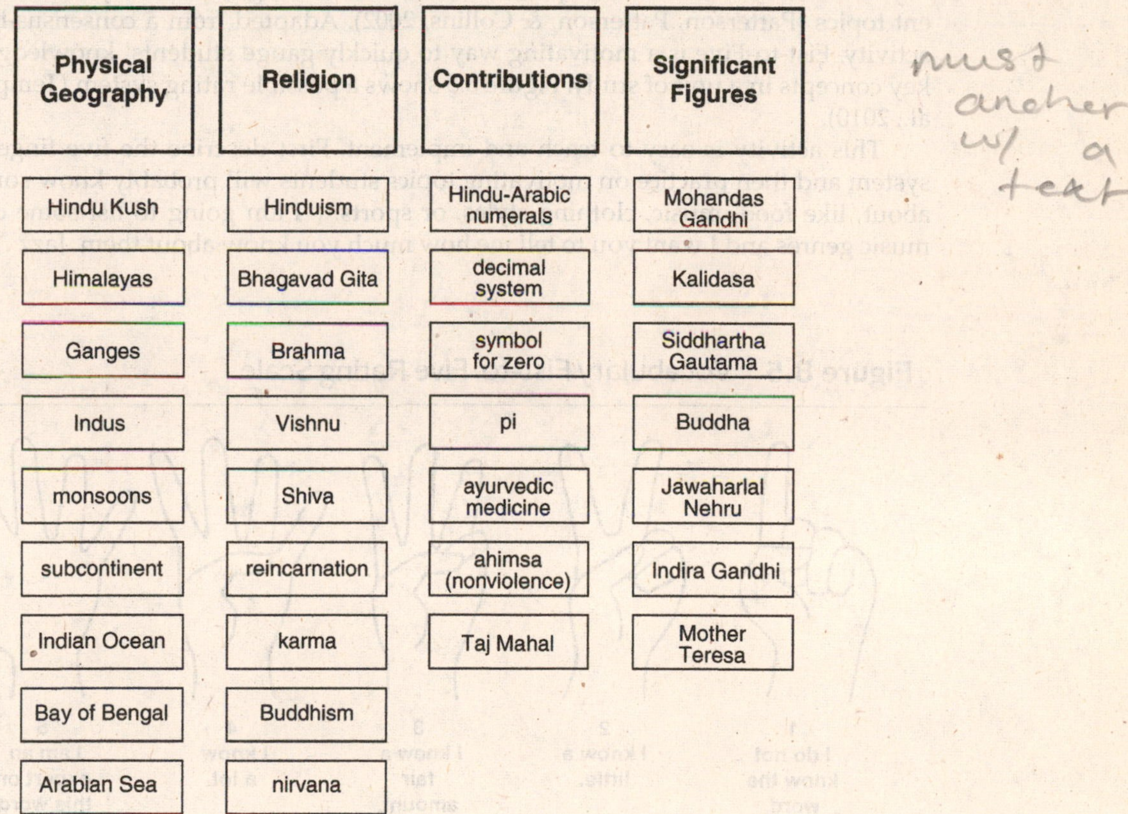

Assessing Concept Sorts

When assessing students' concept sorts, the following questions can help you gauge the depth and connectedness of your students' vocabulary knowledge:

- *Why did you organize the sort in this way?*
- *Why did you put this word in this category?* (Why did you put the Ganges in "Physical Geography"? How is this river important to India?)
- *Could you have put this word in a different category?* (Could you have put Siddartha Gautama in a different category? Why?)
- *How are these words related?* (How are *Gandhi, Mother Teresa,* and the concept of *ahimsa* related?)
- *What other connections among key vocabulary do you see?* (either within a category or across categories)

You can ask students to write their completed sorts in vocabulary notebooks for later study and for a grade. Students can write down their justifications for the sort and answer specific questions you pose, like the questions just listed. This additional step is an excellent assessment of student knowledge because it allows you to get at the specific aspects of vocabulary knowledge that you want.

Vocabulary Fist-to-Five

Purpose. To quickly and informally assess your students' depth of vocabulary knowledge in an engaging whole-class format. To give students the opportunity to self-assess.

In Fist-to-Five, students vote with their fingers to indicate how much they know about key vocabulary words or concepts or to indicate the strength of their opinions on different topics (Patterson, Patterson, & Collins, 2002). Adapted from a consensus-building activity, Fist-to-Five is a motivating way to quickly gauge students' knowledge of the key concepts in a unit of study. Figure 8.5 shows a possible rating system (Templeton et al., 2010).

This activity is easy to teach and implement. First describe the five finger rating system and then practice on motivating topics students will probably know something about, like food, music, clothing styles, or sports. ("I am going to list some different music genres and I want you to tell me how much you know about them. Jazz . . . Okay,

Figure 8.5 Vocabulary Fist-to-Five Rating Scale

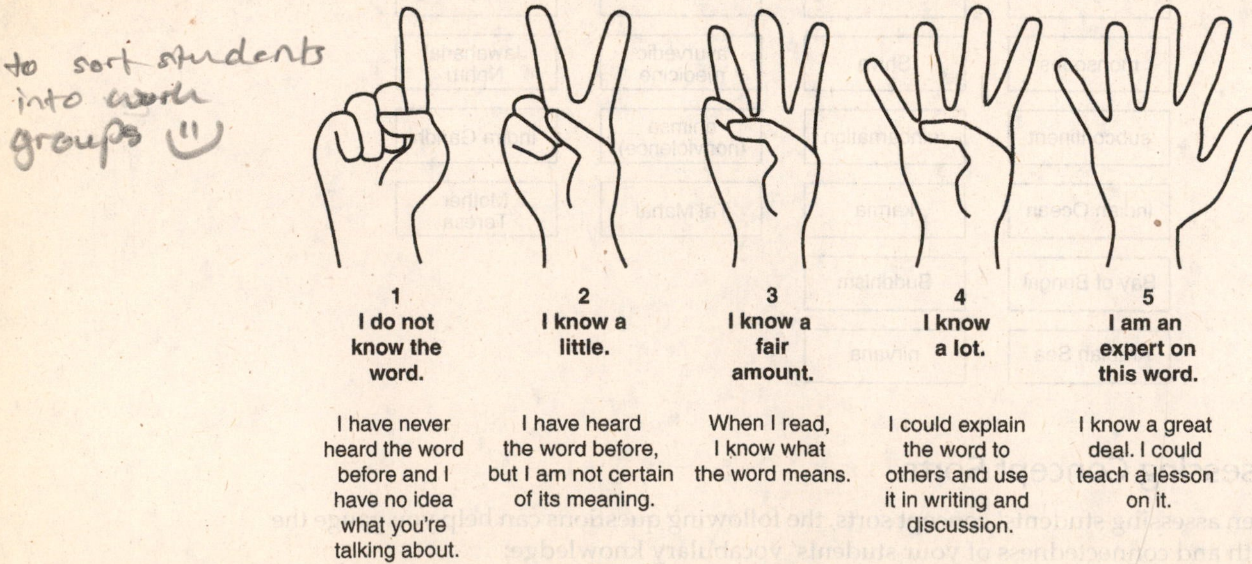
1
I do not know the word.
I have never heard the word before and I have no idea what you're talking about.
2
I know a little.
I have heard the word before, but I am not certain of its meaning.
3
I know a fair amount.
When I read, I know what the word means.
4
I know a lot.
I could explain the word to others and use it in writing and discussion.
5
I am an expert on this word.
I know a great deal. I could teach a lesson on it.

it looks like we have a few jazz aficionados in here. Rap . . . Wow, you folks know a lot about rap. Classical . . .")

Next, instruct students to vote on the five to ten vocabulary words you have chosen to examine for your unit of study. Ask students to hold up their hands long enough for you to get a sense of their knowledge and for them to see how their peers vote. During the voting, feel free to do a "play-by-play" announcement, noting concepts students appear to know a lot about as well as concepts that may be more unfamiliar. The power of this activity comes from the thinking and self-reflection generated by the voting (which immediately gets students invested in the words) and the built-in self-assessment. As students look around the room during the voting, they realize that they are not the only ones who do not know a lot about certain key concepts. This is particularly comforting to struggling readers and can reassure them that they are not alone. If you think your struggling readers may not feel comfortable in this format, you can simply change the format to an individual paper-and-pencil voting procedure.

Vocabulary Word Hunts in Writing: Assessing Students' Use of Vocabulary in Their Compositions

Purpose. To assess students' ability to incorporate rich language in their compositions.

Perhaps the most rigorous assessment of knowledge about a particular word meaning is a person's ability to use the word appropriately in context. The following example shows a student's attempt to use a vocabulary word for which he has only a superficial knowledge (Flanigan & Greenwood, 2007, p. 226).

- *Definition provided to student. expel:* to throw out
- *Student's sentence.* "The president *expelled* the first pitch at the season opener of the Washington Nationals baseball team."

As the example demonstrates, definitional knowledge does not ensure the deep, flexible word knowledge writers need when choosing the "just right" words in their compositions. Students' writing provides us with a treasure trove of information that we can use to assess their vocabulary knowledge and general literacy development. Assessing 10 to 15 minute free writes provides teachers with valuable information on students' ability to explain, relate, and apply key concepts and important vocabulary terms. The Checklist of Vocabulary in Writing found in Appendix H is an effective tool that can help struggling readers become more aware of including high-powered vocabulary in their writing. The checklist asks students and teachers to rate student compositions on a scale (*always, often, occasionally, never*) in relation to specific questions. For example, the following two questions are from the "Richness" section of the checklist. Teachers would rate the student writing in the first question; students would rate their own writing in the second question.

Richness: Colorful and descriptive vocabulary (*always, often, occasionally, never)*

Teacher question: Was the vocabulary useful and descriptive?

Student question: Did the vocabulary paint a picture and show what I was trying to say?

Procedure

1. Distribute the Checklist of Vocabulary in Writing and discuss with students how authors choose word meanings for very specific purposes. Share with students the following famous quote from Mark Twain: "The difference between the almost right word and the right word is really a large matter—it's the difference between the lightning bug and the lightning" (Mark Twain, in a letter to George Bainton,

October 15, 1888). Tell students that this checklist can help them become more aware of their use of vocabulary in writing.

2. Select a piece of text (e.g., a section of text with rich vocabulary from a story the class is reading). Read through the text once with the students. Next, model and think aloud your thought process with the students as you use the checklist to assess vocabulary usage. ("Yes, the author used the word *scuttled* to describe the beetle's movement rather than just saying *crawled*. This is a more vivid and precise word that lets us know that the beetle is moving quickly, or *scurrying*. This fits under the 'Richness' section on the vocabulary checklist, so I'll mark it there.")
3. Ask students to finish analyzing the remainder of the text with the checklist in groups, underlining descriptive vocabulary words, figurative language, and "golden words" that grab them (or words that were *not* descriptive enough and could be improved).
4. As students become more proficient, this checklist can help them assess their own use of vocabulary in writing. In fact, self-assessment of their own writing is the ultimate goal. Students can employ this checklist for the rest of the year to self-assess vocabulary usage in their own compositions and to do "vocabulary hunts" in their writing. In addition, this checklist is a way you can assess their use of vocabulary.

Vocabulary Notebooks

Purpose. To assess students' general growth in vocabulary over time in a portfolio format.

Vocabulary notebooks are a critical tool in student word learning, providing a single place for students to record word sorts, concept sorts, and graphic organizers and document other vocabulary activities described in this and other chapters in this book. Because students are collecting all of their vocabulary work in one place, vocabulary notebooks can serve as a portfolio of work—similar to an artist's portfolio—that can be used to document and assess their vocabulary growth over time. Teachers can design rubrics to grade these vocabulary notebooks, which can be in three-ring binders, spiral-bound notebooks, or composition books. Vocabulary notebooks could include any of the following:

- Weekly word sorts, with an accompanying student explanation of the pattern or meaning of the root describing how all words in a certain category are related.
- Extensions of word sorts, such as word hunts and word generation activities.
- Concept sorts, word analysis activities, and any of the graphic organizers or other vocabulary activities described in this book.
- New and interesting words that students encounter in their own reading (see steps for recording new vocabulary words in vocabulary notebooks in Chapter 6). Just as English teachers encourage students to record "golden lines" from their reading—turns of phrase that appealed to them while reading—we encourage them to be on the lookout for "golden words" that really strike them.
- Content-specific vocabulary words from science, social studies, math, and English/language arts that can be recorded in sections of the notebook divided by subject (in which students could be awarded extra credit points for finding vocabulary connections across the content areas—e.g., "We learned about *sanctuaries* as places of refuge for endangered species in science, but the word *sanctuary* was also used in a story we read in English, meaning a sacred or holy place of peace and refuge for anyone").

To give you an example of how vocabulary notebooks might look, one group of middle school English teachers we worked with planned on organizing their vocabulary notebook into the following three sections:

1. *"Back to our roots."* This section of the vocabulary notebook focuses on generative vocabulary learning, and thus is organized by meaning parts—prefixes, suffixes, and roots (e.g., *spectator, retrospect,* and *spectacles* recorded under the root *spect*). Root sorts, word hunts, It's All Greek (and Latin) to Me, and other activities described in Chapter 6 are all collected and recorded here. As students encounter new words based on a root that has already been studied (*introspection*), they record the words under that particular root.
2. *Teacher-chosen words.* In this section, students record and examine words/concepts that their teachers have chosen as important. Often these words or terms include both content-specific vocabulary required by district or state standards, like *quatrain* and *deus ex machina,* as well as core academic vocabulary gleaned from class stories, like *mesmerize, abundant,* and *hard-nosed.*
3. *MY Words.* Students love this section, because it truly is their section. They can record words they find interesting, amusing, or confusing here. Many teachers ask literature circle groups (groups reading a common story or novel) to decide on one to three words per week to nominate for weekly class examination (with four literature circles in a class, that makes roughly five to ten words per week that students can choose). This activity is engaging, as students have the power to choose words for the entire class to study—a truly motivating experience! Many teachers follow the vocabulary self-collection strategy (Haggard, 1986; Ruddell and Shearer, 2002) described in Chapter 2.

Tips for Vocabulary Notebooks

- It may be too much to expect students to work on all three sections of the notebook simultaneously.
- Encourage students to look for connections among the different sections of the vocabulary notebook, and thus among the different types of vocabulary. For example, students might notice an interesting word in a mystery novel, like *cryptograph* (a cipher; a system of secret writing) and include it in the "MY Words" section of the notebook. With teacher prompting, the student may then realize that *cryptograph* also fits in the "Back to our Roots" section under the Greek root *graph* (meaning "to write"), with related words like *telegraph* ("to write from far away") and *phonograph* ("to write with sound"). Later, in the science unit Natural Disasters, the word *seismograph* ("an instrument that measures earthquakes") may come up. From this example, you can see how vocabulary notebooks can be a powerful vehicle for not only collecting interesting and important vocabulary words, but for students to connect vocabulary learning across the school day, across content areas, and beyond the classroom walls.

Intermediate-Level Academic Vocabulary Spelling Inventory

This academic vocabulary inventory assesses the depth of students' knowledge of academic vocabulary and, through spelling, assesses their orthographic development (Townsend, Bear, & Templeton, 2009). There are two parts to the assessment found in Appendix H. First, students spell the words "the best they can" as they have done in other developmental spelling inventories. Second, they go to the top of the spelling form and, for each word, rate their knowledge of the meaning of each word and write down as many related words that they can think of (see pages 331–333 in Appendix H). For example, for the first word, *source,* students could enter *sources, resources, resourceful, sourced,* and *sourceless.* Beforehand, students are given examples different from test items as models.

What Is Academic Vocabulary?

Consider briefly what academic vocabulary tells us about students' learning. As you peruse the vocabulary of students' textbooks, notice that there is a vocabulary that is common in all of the texts no matter the content area. Students need to be able to read and understand this vocabulary to be successful in any of their classes. As examples, notice how the following academic words may appear in each subject's textbooks: *source, definition, majorities, significance,* and *occurrence.* Contrast these words with the *specialized* vocabulary peculiar to particular content areas: *mitochondria* in biology, *egalitarian* in social studies, and *sine* and *cosine* in geometry and trigonometry.

The words in this inventory were found in Coxhead's list of academic words (Coxhead, 2000) and were selected for the spelling features they contain. For example, the word *participants* was chosen for its plural *s*, the suffix *-ant,* the reduced vowel spelled with an *i,* and the stem *partic* with its soft *c* sound. Students who say they know the words and can generate two or more related words for most words (e.g., *participant, participatory, nonparticipants, participant*) are likely to have a deeper knowledge of the words, a larger vocabulary, and better reading skills than students who generate only one or no related words in the 15 seconds allotted for this task.

Scoring and Interpretation of the Inventory

Together, the spelling, students' rating of their knowledge, and their brainstorming of related words tap the depth of students' orthographic and academic vocabulary knowledge. In a study of a sample of seventh- and eighth-graders, we have found that the number of words spelled correctly and the number of related words that they generate are significantly related to standardized measures of vocabulary, reading, and spelling. This indicates that this inventory is a good resource to examine students' orthographic development and academic vocabulary.

Counting the number of words that the students spell correctly yields a power score. With this score, refer to Table 8.3 to determine a stage of spelling for each student. You can see that this table presents gradations within each stage. Once you know what stage of spelling a student is in, refer to Chapters 4 and 5 as guides to instruction in reading and word analysis instruction and Chapters 6 and 7 as guides to vocabulary instruction. It is often useful to choose the stage and gradation that is the most conservative; one of the golden rules for where to begin word study is this: When in doubt, address the stage that is one step back so that the students are secure in their learning. This gives the students a chance to become familiar with the word study schedule, and promotes students' confidence and motivation. It is also useful to examine informally the actual features that students misspell. Students who misspell the vowel pattern in s<u>ou</u>rce or the consonant blend in dist<u>inct</u> need a very different form of word study than students who spell nearly all of the words correctly but omit assimilated prefixes in o<u>cc</u>urrence or i<u>rr</u>elevance.

The second part of the assessment is scored according to the number of words students say they know, do not know, and may know, along with how many related words they are able to produce for each spelling word. Students who do not know the meanings of many of the words are often English learners who are acquiring this vocabulary in English. As you score the production of related words generated in 15 seconds, you will find that students who produce *two* or *three* related words for the items have a thorough knowledge of the vocabulary and are likely to have a well-developed vocabulary overall. Students who produce *no* or *one* related word for most words will have a less developed vocabulary and may have difficulty comprehending their texts when there is an abundance of these words in their reading. It will be important for these students to be engaged in contextualized word study with academic vocabulary words.

Table 8.3 Power Scores and Estimated Stages for the Intermediate-Level Academic Vocabulary Spelling Inventory

	Number of Words Spelled Correctly		
Gradations within Stages →	*Early Gradation*	*Middle Gradation*	*Late Gradation*
Reading and Spelling Stages ↓			
Within Word Pattern Spelling/Transitional Reading	1	2	4
Syllables and Affixes Spelling/Intermediate Reading	6	8	12
Derivational Relations Spelling/Advanced Reading	14	16	19

Given the synchrony between reading and spelling, and between reading and vocabulary, this inventory is useful in forming differentiated reading groups. The power score indicates what stage of spelling students are in, and the spelling stages are usually related to students' reading stages. As outlined in Chapters 4 and 5, students at different spelling and reading stages exhibit different reading behaviors. Students in the transitional stage account for many struggling readers; in our research and teaching, transitional readers comprise up to a third of the struggling sixth- through eighth-graders. They do not generate many related words even if they do know the meaning of the words. Students in this stage who are asked to read in middle or secondary grade-level materials will have difficulty with these materials and require the support of the activities discussed in Chapter 4. They will read their texts slowly, often reading aloud or reading silently with lip movement. Students in the syllables and affixes stage are likely to be intermediate readers; they read silently and study the spelling of how multisyllabic words combine. In the related word portion of the inventory, students in the syllables and affixes stage will likely indicate that they know the meanings of the words, but they may generate only one related word. In vocabulary study, these students need to study the meanings of harder prefixes and suffixes and study the relationships between grammar and spelling. As noted in Chapter 5, they are learning the meanings of various roots, they are predominantly reading silently, and they are learning basic outlining and other study skills, mostly with grade-level materials. Keep in mind that this inventory was created with middle school students, whom we would expect to be in the syllables and affixes stage of spelling and the intermediate stage of reading. High school students who score in the within word pattern and the early part of the syllables and affixes stage of spelling are likely to find their reading materials are at a frustration level.

Generative Vocabulary Assessment and Learning

Just as important as assessing students' knowledge of specific words is assessing their understanding of how words work. Generative vocabulary assessments measure students' *morphological knowledge*—understanding of our meaning system. This section presents a set of morphological assessments that are ordered by level of morphological difficulty:

starting with tasks measuring knowledge of easier prefixes and base words, moving to Greek and Latin roots, and finally to more difficult prefixes and suffixes. The items within many of the assessments themselves are also arranged in a developmental sequence.

Using Assessments to Inform Generative Vocabulary Instruction

The assessments we describe in this section, particularly Generating/Producing Words with the Same Prefixes and Suffixes and Generating Words from Bases and Roots, provide important information about your students' morphological knowledge. This information can help you decide whether your struggling readers would benefit most from generative vocabulary instruction with the more straightforward and concrete affixes and base words in strand 1 or the more abstract and less transparent—but incredibly powerful—roots and affixes in strand 2. In Appendix H, we provide criteria for helping you decide, based on student scores on these assessments, where to optimally begin instruction.

However, as with all assessments, it is important to keep in mind a number of factors when making the link from assessment to instruction.

- Students whose scores indicate that they should begin instruction in strand 1 can and should still be exposed to and asked to think about and discuss less transparent morphological elements—like Latin and Greek roots. This is particularly true in the content areas. For example, a student in strand 1 can (and should) still benefit greatly from a social studies discussion about how the words *democrat/democracy, autocrat/autocracy,* and *theocrat/theocracy* are all derived from the Greek root *crat/crac,* meaning "rule." However, this student will also need primary instruction in the more straightforward morphological relationships found in strand 1, giving a secure foundation from which to explore the more complex and opaque morphemes.
- As with all assessments, take into account whether your students are applying and demonstrating morphological knowledge in context—in their reading, writing, and content area learning. For example, a student who is "on the bubble" in terms of the assessment criteria, but who is struggling to make morphological connections in content learning and who experiences difficulty breaking apart simple prefixed words—like *unable*—in their reading may benefit from a "step backward" into strand 1 instruction. This student can always be moved quickly into more advanced morpheme study if warranted.

Generating/Producing Words with the Same Prefixes and Suffixes

Purpose. To assess students' morphological knowledge, particularly their ability to generate words from prefixes and suffixes.

One way to assess students' morphological knowledge is to examine their ability to produce, or *generate,* words from a given prefix or suffix. For example, students may be given the prefix *re-* and asked to produce as many words that contain the prefix as possible. The following example item, with a possible student response filled in, is taken from the Student Form for Producing Words with the Same Prefix (Templeton et al., 2010; see also Appendix H).

1. Re- (return) reuse, retire, restart, return

   Re- means: again

Developmentally, this assessment may work best with your struggling readers in the syllables and affixes stage of development. Struggling readers in the within word pattern stage of development may experience more difficulty with this assessment. Please use the Student Form for Producing Words with the Same Suffix and the accompanying form for prefixes in Appendix H for directions and student response forms. Students are given a set amount of time to produce as many words as possible with the given affix (see appendix directions for instructions about time). Students who can generate more words from the given prefixes and suffixes are more likely to have deeper morphological knowledge and larger, more flexible vocabularies.

Matching Greek and Latin Roots with Their Meanings

Purpose: To assess (1) students' knowledge of specific roots and (2) the meanings of words that contain those roots.

Matching is a commonly used format for vocabulary assessments. A matching assessment on root meanings might look like this:

_____ **1.** spect A. trust
_____ **2.** port B. carry
_____ **3.** tract C. see, look at
_____ **4.** dict D. pull
_____ **5.** fid E. speak, tell

A matching test like this can provide a quick, surface-level assessment of students' knowledge of root meanings. We recommend that you dig deeper by adding an additional step to the assessment: Call out specific words that contain these roots (e.g., *spectacular, speculate, extract, fidelity*) and ask student to define them in their own words. The test and additional step allow you to assess both general knowledge of roots and knowledge of specific word meanings that contain those roots. Appendix H, Matching Greek and Latin Roots, provides an example of this type of matching roots assessment that you can use in your classroom. Students who score 90 percent or higher are considered at mastery level; students who score below 90 percent may need more work with these roots.

Generating Words from Bases and Roots

Purpose. To assess students' morphological knowledge, particularly their ability to generate words from a given base word or root, on a continuum of development.

This activity is similar to Generating/Producing Words with the Same Prefixes and Suffixes described previously; however, instead of prefixes and suffixes, students are asked to generate words from the more complex *base words* and *roots*. Appendix H, Generating Words from Bases and Roots, presents a wide range of base words (such as *turn*), and Greek and Latin roots (such as *bio* and *tract*) that are found across the content areas. For example, students who are asked to generate words from the Latin root *tract* might answer as follows:

tract: distraction, extract, retract, traction, attract

Students who can quickly generate many words from these base words and roots probably have a relatively deep and flexible morphological knowledge. Content area teachers can easily modify this assessment to assess their students' knowledge of roots that occur frequently in their specific content areas. For example, a social studies teacher might assess students' knowledge of the following roots: civ (Latin, "citizen"): *civic, civil rights, civil war, city, civilization* and popul/pub (Latin, "people"): *population, populace, public, republic.*

Include Students in Assessment-Based Planning and Goal Setting

Your struggling readers will be more likely to buy into vocabulary instruction if they (1) understand their own strengths and areas of need and (2) have a hand in setting instructional goals based on their strengths and areas of need. Talk directly with your students, honestly and respectfully, about the results from their vocabulary assessments. The following activities can help you include students in their own assessment and goal setting.

Students' Strategies for Learning Vocabulary

Purpose. To assess students' ability to use strategies to independently learn words

One way to involve your students in the vocabulary assessment and learning process is to ask them reflect on how *they* best learn vocabulary. What strategies do they already use? For example, you can ask your students to answer the following statements on a scale, ranging from strongly agree to strongly disagree:

- I learn vocabulary best through reading.
- I prefer classroom activities that promote vocabulary growth.
- I prefer working in small groups or in pairs when studying vocabulary.
- I can think of related words to make meaning connections.

engagement LINK

Students gain more ownership over their learning when they are given the tools to self-assess and are made aware of where they are and where they need to go in terms of their vocabulary knowledge.

My Strategies for Learning Vocabulary in Appendix H presents a set of statements like the example that guide students as they self-evaluate their vocabulary learning strategies. Students can individually complete this form before a small- or whole-group class discussion. Or the form can serve as a guide to an upcoming one-on-one meeting with a student. Either way, this assessment provides the following valuable information:

- A format to begin discussing with your students how to learn vocabulary
- A way for students to develop a metacognitive stance toward learning and, by allowing students to take a step back like this, a means of letting them feel in control of their own achievement
- A vehicle by which students can share how they best learn, which immediately gives you important information about ways of learning in a lesson or unit that the students find helpful (e.g., cooperative group learning) and which also sends the powerful message to a struggling reader that learning is a partnership and that you take his or her ideas seriously

Assessing Students' Overall Content Vocabulary Knowledge from a Lesson, Unit, or Textbook

Purpose. To assess with students their overall familiarity with the key vocabulary terms and concepts in a lesson, unit of study, or textbook chapter.

In addition to knowing how students best learn vocabulary—their vocabulary learning strategies—it is very helpful to get an overall sense of the depth of your students' understanding of the key concepts and vocabulary terms in your content area. How familiar are your struggling readers with the vocabulary words in the content area textbook? How well do they understand the meanings of the vocabulary words in an upcoming lesson, story, or unit of study? The Rubric for Vocabulary Learning in Appendix H (Templeton et al., 2010) can be used before, during, or after a period of study to gauge students' initial understandings and to document conceptual growth over time. Students can skim a chapter and look over the bolded vocabulary terms, or you can present your students with a list of the key concepts in a unit. Students can then rate their overall understanding of these words using the following scale:

5—I have a complete understanding
4—I have a good understanding
3—I have some knowledge
2—I am learning the vocabulary
1—The vocabulary is new to me

As you can see, this assessment is similar to the Fist-to-Five self-assessment described earlier in the chapter, which assesses students' depth of knowledge for each vocabulary word separately. ("Class, rate your familiarity with *iambic pentameter*.") This assessment, however, asks students to rate their overall understanding of all concepts in a unit or lesson considered together. ("Class, skim through this textbook chapter, look at the bolded vocabulary words, and give me one rating that best represents your overall understanding of the vocabulary in this chapter.") There is also a section on this rubric for teacher input. If struggling readers and their teachers determine that the texts used in class are too difficult, than teachers should identify and incorporate texts and other materials at their struggling readers' instructional levels.

Including Students in Goal Setting and Self-Directed Learning

When setting vocabulary learning goals with your students, keep the following guidelines in mind:

- Differentiate between long-term goals and short-terms goals.
- Write short-term goals as clearly and specifically as possible and include a timeline. This lets your struggling readers know exactly what they need to learn, when they need to learn it by, and allows you to give feedback that is clear and specific.
- Use vocabulary assessment information to differentiate instruction, set goals, and modify goals.

As with setting goals for spelling and reading, discussed in Chapter 3, you can think of goals for vocabulary instruction as long-term goals for the year and short-term goals that will serve as stepping stones toward achieving your long-term goal. For vocabulary instruction, these short- and long-term goals will often be driven by the key vocabulary terms and concepts in your content area and as outlined by the district or state curriculum standards. In addition, you should also take into account your struggling readers' strengths and areas of need and their level of development. The following guidelines can assist in the process of setting short- and long-term goals for word-specific and generative vocabulary instruction.

Setting Goals for Word-Specific Vocabulary Instruction

The long-term goals in a content area usually include the big ideas and critical skills that are important to that discipline. For example, a world history teacher might have the following long-term goal for the year:

- *World history long-term goal.* Students will be able to use maps and globes to identify human-made and natural features, identify patterns, and make inferences based on the information in these maps and globes.

An ambitious and general long-term goal like this will take at the very least a quarter and often up to a year (or more) to accomplish. To reach these long-term goals, students must master a set of foundational, related concepts that are represented by the key vocabulary terms in the discipline. From the world history example, students will need to learn at least the following key geographical concepts, among others: *longitude, latitude, legend, hemisphere, maps, map projections,* and *globes.* However, merely listing these words on a blackboard does not make them a goal. As we discussed in Chapter 7, it is critical for you to set clear, specific vocabulary learning goals for your students. What, exactly, do you want your students to know and be able to do with the concepts of *longitude, latitude,* and *map projections?* A clear short-term goal from the key vocabulary might take the following form:

- *Short-term goal.* Students will be able to compare and contrast the defining characteristics of *maps* and *globes* and be able to decide when to use each based on their purpose (e.g., globes accurately represent relative sizes of places; it is easier to measure distance on maps).

With this more specific word learning goal in mind, it becomes much clearer which type of vocabulary activity and assessment you should use. For the short-term goal shown, a Venn diagram or compare/contrast chart (described in Chapter 7) might be an appropriate vocabulary assessment activity.

Using Assessment Information to Modify Word-Specific Goals for Struggling Readers

How can assessment information help you differentiate instruction for your struggling readers? Struggling readers may not have the foundational knowledge necessary to learn certain word-specific concepts that your curriculum requires you to teach. If this is the case, you may need to back up and solidify these foundational concepts before moving on. For example, students might not get much out of a geography lesson comparing and contrasting the different types of map projections—such as the Mercator Projection and the Robinson Projection—without having at least a basic understanding of foundational concepts about maps such as *latitude, longitude, hemisphere, prime meridian,* and *scale.* Using a vocabulary self-assessment or fist-to-five activity (described earlier in this chapter) *before* your lesson or unit can help you determine whether your students have a sufficient knowledge of foundational concepts. Although teaching these foundational concepts will require more time, simply pushing ahead with frustration-level concepts will not result in optimal learning or increased motivation to learn more later on. If you do push ahead, you will have to go back and reteach those concepts again later. Taking the time to teach what your students need *now* will save you time *later.*

Setting Goals for Generative Vocabulary Instruction

You can use a similar type of goal-setting process with generative vocabulary instruction. Long-term generative goals are often provided to English/language arts teachers as part of the curriculum. The following example shows a long-term goal for generative vocabulary instruction.

- *English/language arts long-term goal.* Students will be able to analyze words by morphemic units.

As with most long-term goals, this very general goal may take students years to accomplish. The Sequence of Instruction for Core Roots and Affixes (see the appendix to Chapter 6) shows how the study of morphemes takes place over the course of years, starting in the elementary grades and continuing through middle and high school (and beyond). Thus, it is necessary to break this important long-term goal down into manageable, reasonable short-term goals for your students. The generative vocabulary assessments described earlier in this chapter can help us do this.

Using Assessment Information to Modify Generative Goals for Struggling Readers

Use the generative assessments described earlier in this chapter to give you a sense of your struggling readers' level of morphological knowledge. This information can help you target your instruction in morphological knowledge based on your students' current level of understanding. For example, can your students quickly and easily generate words like *spectator, retrospect,* and *introspection* when give the root *spect* (from the Generating Words from Bases and Roots assessment on page 340 in Appendix H)? If so, they are probably ready for strand 2 vocabulary instruction in Latin and Greek roots. If not, they probably need to start with more basic prefixes, suffixes, and base words in strand 1. Struggling readers often benefit from instruction that begins in strand 1. Use the criteria outlined in the generative vocabulary assessments in Appendix H. When making decisions, student scores on these assessments should be balanced with your observations of their ability to apply this knowledge in context.

If your long-term goal is for students to be able to analyze words by morphemic units, how can you modify it for your struggling readers in strand 1 while still meeting this standard? The following two short-term goals (appropriate for an approximately two-week unit of study) show how you can meet this same goal for two groups of students who are developmentally in two different places (strand 1 and strand 2).

- *Short-term goal for students in strand 1.* Students will be able to accurately sort words, generate words, and analyze words that contain the following prefixes: *pre-, mis-, re-,* and *un-* (*premature, misjudge, research, unarmed*).
- *Short-term goal for students in strand 2.* Students will be able to accurately sort words, generate words, and analyze words that contain the following roots: *hydra, geo,* and *aer* (*hydroplane, geode, aerodynamic*).

You can see how assessments help target instruction based on students' needs and developmental level, while at the same time meeting the general curriculum standards. In the example, both groups are working on morpheme knowledge. However, the struggling readers (who are most likely in strand 1) are working primarily with the more basic morphemes—prefixes, suffixes, and base words—that they are optimally ready to learn.

Involving Your Students in Goal Setting

Some content teachers may question how they can involve their students in vocabulary goal setting when the content goals have already been identified in the textbook or in the local or state curriculum standards. There are a number of ways that you can involve your students in the goal-setting process and still hew to your curriculum guidelines.

- Share assessment information with your students in a goal-setting conference. Allow students the opportunity to share their own feelings about their content and vocabulary knowledge. The self-assessments described in this chapter can help students formalize their thinking in preparation for these conferences. Talking openly, honestly, and respectfully with your students about the assessment information accomplishes a number of important purposes.
  - Shows students that you respect them enough to talk with them about their strengths and needs
  - Makes them aware of their strengths and areas of need
  - Helps students see the why of the next step, setting goals

- Share with your students long-term goals for the year in your content area and short-term goals for the upcoming unit of study. Discuss with students how these short-term goals will help achieve the long-term goals.
- Ask students to add their own content subgoals and try to work at least one of their goals in per quarter. Ask questions such as "What are you interested in that relates to this unit? How can I help you apply what we are learning to your interests and life?" For example, in a physics unit on sound, a student might be interested in exploring how sound *vibrations* and *frequencies*—two key concepts—work on a guitar. Allowing the student extra credit and time to explore this area can make a *significant* difference in student motivation and learning.
- Ask students how they best learn vocabulary words and concepts. The My Strategies for Learning Vocabulary form (Templeton et al., 2010) can help students think through this general question in preparation for your goal-setting conference. Include at least one activity every unit that supports the way students learn and let students know that you are doing it. For example, if a struggling reader learns best by acting out word meanings, try to include a charades game or variation at some point in your unit.
- When possible, give students a choice of words to study. This often works best with core academic words that students choose and "nominate" for instruction in activities similar to the vocabulary self-collection strategy (Chapter 2).
- As we discussed in Chapter 3 for spelling and reading assessments, use a visual to show your students the big picture. This is relatively easy to do. For generative vocabulary instruction, copy (or create a subsection) of the appendix to Chapter 6. Students check off the prefixes, suffixes, and roots as they demonstrate mastery of them in your assessments. For word-specific instruction, copy the table of contents or use a list of the key content vocabulary terms as your checklist. Checking off these concepts gives students a sense of pride and satisfaction and shows them how these small steps are helping move them toward their long-term goals.
- Require students to periodically self-assess their growth. Meet with them on a quarterly basis to provide feedback and set, change, or modify goals.

These simple steps, while taking time, can pay dividends many times over in terms of student motivation and buy-in. When students are involved in goal setting, they are more likely to hold themselves accountable for their own learning—resulting in increased independence. They feel a sense of satisfaction as you both track their growth over time and they see the tangible results of their efforts. They also feel more in control of their own learning, resulting in increased motivation and engagement. Praise your students for persistence and hard work, acknowledging the reality of setbacks along the way.

Classroom Organization and Scheduling for Vocabulary Instruction

After assessing students' vocabulary knowledge, you will want to plan and organize instruction that meets your students' needs. When planning vocabulary activities, take into account (1) the general goals of your unit or lesson, (2) the specific word-learning goals of key vocabulary terms (what exactly you want your students to know about each word), (3) the developmental levels of your students as well as their strengths and needs, (4) the nature of the words you are teaching, and (5) the time you have allotted for instruction. Because no two teaching situations are exactly the same, there is no single generic weekly schedule of activities for vocabulary instruction that will fit every teacher's needs. The following guidelines can help as you plan vocabulary activities for your students:

- Incorporate small-group work throughout the unit. Small groups can be based on developmental level (e.g., a small group consisting of students all working on strand 1 morphemes) or a common interest or focus (a small group of students who chose the same subset of content area vocabulary terms to examine together using a four-square concept map).
- Follow the five core guidelines of word study instruction introduced in Chapter 2.
- Ensure that your struggling readers have multiple opportunities to work with and manipulate the vocabulary words in different contexts across the unit.
- "Stack" activities in a logical sequence across a unit of study, so that earlier activities provide a foundation for later activities. For example, you may start the examination of the two roots *port* and *tract* with an open sort. As the unit continues, extend student learning beyond the words found in the original sort with word hunts.
- Remember that completing a vocabulary activity is not the objective; rather, it is the thinking and discussion generated by the activity in a motivating context that will lead to deep and long-term vocabulary knowledge. High-level questions and rich discussions in engaging small- and whole-group settings are critical.

Sample Schedules for Word-Specific Vocabulary Instruction: Social Studies and English

As mentioned, there is no single perfect schedule for vocabulary instruction; so much depends on your students, your teaching goals, and the nature of the vocabulary words and concepts you and your students are examining. Other books on word study instruction discuss various classroom organization and grouping options in the middle grades and high school (Bear et al., 2008; Templeton et al., 2010). To give you a sense of what a weekly schedule might look like in particular teaching contexts, Figures 8.6 (p. 258) and 8.7 (p. 259) present two possible weekly sequences for word-specific vocabulary instruction in a social studies class and an English class, respectively. The key vocabulary terms and the planned vocabulary activities are highlighted in italics.

Social Studies Sample Schedule

An American history class is beginning a unit on the Great Depression. As a major conceptual goal for the unit, the teacher wants the students to understand the causes, consequences, and attempted solutions to the Great Depression. The bulk of the vocabulary consists of content-specific words like *Black Tuesday* and *Hoovervilles*. The teacher gradually adds vocabulary over the course of the unit as students encounter the words in the textbook reading and other related text sources. The teacher decides, based on the vocabulary selection process described in Chapter 7, whether to teach words before, during, or after the readings and lessons.

English Sample Schedule

An English class has been organized into four novel study groups (groups of five to six students reading and discussing the same text) based on two factors: (1) reading level and (2) common interest in a book. In terms of the vocabulary instruction, the teacher wants the students to notice and examine vivid, powerful core academic words used by the authors (words like *curmudgeon* and *meander*) and eventually use more vivid vocabulary in their own writing.

Sample Schedule for Generative Vocabulary Instruction

Figure 8.8 (p. 259) presents a possible two-week sequence of vocabulary activities for a group of students examining the two roots *port* ("to carry") and *tract* ("to pull"). We have found that providing two weeks to work on a set of two to four roots offers sufficient

Figure 8.6 American History Unit on the Great Depression—First Week of a Three-Week Unit

Days	Teaching Focus	Activity
1	Introduce overarching themes, concepts, and vocabulary terms of Great Depression unit. Plan experiences to assess and build background knowledge and increase student engagement and motivation.	Teacher introduces and discusses with class key vocabulary terms like *migrant workers, dust storms, Hoovervilles,* and *Black Tuesday* by • Showing students powerful pictures of Great Depression by Depression-era photographers like Dorothea Lange • Reading aloud first-person accounts from migrant workers • Showing students 15 minutes of a documentary film on Great Depression
2	Deep study of keywords and concepts introduced on day 1.	Small heterogeneous groups of five to six students choose one to two vocabulary terms each from day 1 to examine in depth using the four-square concept map format. Whole class reconvenes at end of period. Small groups share concept maps with class as teacher facilitates, clarifies misconceptions, emphasizes key points, and adds missing information. Students copy all concept maps into vocabulary notebooks.
3	Deep study of additional keywords and concepts (as class continues reading through the textbook chapter and other sources).	Small-group work continues as above with additional key terms that have been added. A modified concept of definition map for historical figures is used by small groups for an examination of important figures such as *Franklin Delano Roosevelt* and *Herbert Hoover.*
4	Organize keywords into overall conceptual framework.	Small groups complete a closed concept sort. Teacher asks students to categorize the vocabulary words studied so far this week into three categories: (1) Causes of Great Depression (e.g., *Black Tuesday*), (2) Consequences of the Great Depression (e.g., displaced *Hokies* traveling to California), and (3) Attempted Solutions (e.g., *Works Progress Administration*). Students copy completed sort into vocabulary notebooks using the power map format, in which students justify in writing why they have categorized words under certain columns.
5	Reinforce and review vocabulary words and concepts in motivating format.	Class plays Jeopardy game using vocabulary words as a whole-class review. Game uses same three categories from the concept sort on day 4 (Causes, Consequences, and Attempted Solutions of Great Depression). These same three categories will be used and added to as the class continues the unit during the next two weeks.

time for middle grade and high school students to dig deeply enough to ensure long-term learning. Notice how the students are (a) *analyzing* words (Break It Down), (b) *generating* words (Root Tree and Related Roots Web), and (c) *sorting* words (Open Sort) over the two weeks. Whichever activities you choose when planning generative vocabulary instruction, make sure students are using these three processes across the unit of study.

Figure 8.7 English Class Weekly Schedule: Novel Groups Selecting and Examining Vivid Vocabulary Words

Days	Teaching Focus	Activity
1	Select and introduce ten vivid vocabulary words for instruction from novels (students select eight words, teacher selects two words).	Each novel group selects two rich vocabulary words from previously read chapters in their novel for instruction, introduces them to the class, and explains why they were selected (with four groups, this equals eight total student-selected words) as per the vocabulary self-collection strategy. Teacher selects two rich vocabulary words for instruction, introduces them to the class, and explains why she selected them.
2	Deep study of words.	Small groups complete vocabulary webs with words using their novels, dictionaries, thesauruses, and online dictionaries. Small groups share their completed vocabulary webs with whole class at end of period. Students record the webs in their vocabulary notebooks.
3	Extend vocabulary learning beyond the classroom. Connect vocabulary terms to personal lives.	Using the word wizard format, students receive extra credit points for connecting vocabulary words to their own lives ("I was rude toward my sister last night. I have to admit, my lack of sleep turned me into a *curmudgeon.*") Word wizard continues for the next two weeks as classes and students compete against each other.
4	Continued deep study and reinforcement of words in a motivating activity.	Small groups act out words for entire class, playing charades.
5	Applying vocabulary to writing.	Small groups respond to their novels in writing based on teacher-created writing prompts, using vivid vocabulary that is important to their story in their written response. For example, if the main character in the story is a *curmudgeon,* then this vocabulary word can be used in the response.

Figure 8.8 Possible Two-Week Schedule for Class Examining Two Roots *port* and *tract*

	Monday	Tuesday	Wednesday	Thursday	Friday
Week 1	Open sort of two roots *port* and *tract* Copy completed sort in vocabulary notebook	Small-group study of word etymologies using online dictionaries and other sources. Information is shared and recorded in vocabulary notebooks.	Class creates two root trees with *port* and *tract*—adding additional words to Monday's sort		Break It Down review game
Week 2	Dictionary of the Future	Word hunt using http://onelook.com and brainstorming additional words		Related roots web—add synonyms and antonyms to root trees created the first week	Assessment—writing sort

Over the course of the two weeks, the homework includes It's All Greek (and Latin) to Me (see activities section of Chapter 6), in which students find applications of words outside class and share them in class. For example, one student might share, "My mother was intractable last night! She wouldn't budge when we repeatedly asked her if we could go out."

Sample Daily Schedule for Small-Group Instruction

At times, you will want to group students based on their developmental level. Other times you may want to group them based on your instructional focus or topic of study. Either way, a critical question teachers ask is "What are the other students doing while I'm meeting with a small group?" Figure 8.9 presents a simple, straightforward daily schedule that we have used with success for small-group work in the upper grades. This particular schedule is based on the teacher dividing the class into two groups in a 55-

Figure 8.9 Sample Daily Small-Group Schedule for Two Small Groups

Time	Group 1	Group 2
9:00–9:10	**Whole Class** (1) Set agenda for class period, (2) Assign independent work	
9:10–9:30	**Small-Group Work with Teacher** Teacher-guided vocabulary instruction (*possible activities:* closed sorts, open sorts, word hunts, etymology study, word analysis, word generation)	**Independent Work** Grouping Options • Individual • Pair • Small group Activity Options • Independent reading of novels, textbooks, or other content sources • Individual vocabulary activities • Writing responses to reading • Novel study group discussions • Composition/essay writing
9:30–9:50	**Independent Work** Grouping Options • Individual • Pair • Small group Activity Options • Independent reading of novels, textbooks, or other content sources • Individual vocabulary activities • Writing responses to reading • Novel study group discussions • Composition/essay writing	**Small Group Work with Teacher** Teacher-guided vocabulary instruction (*possible activities:* closed sorts, open sorts, word hunts, etymology study, word analysis, word generation)
9:50–9:55	**Whole Class** Assessment, set goals for next day	

minute period (e.g., group 1 working with strand 1 morphemes, group 2 working with strand 2 morphemes), but can be easily modified for work with three small groups as we discuss later. The schedule is based on a "whole group–small group–whole group" format.

- *Whole-class introduction.* The teacher begins the period with the whole class, setting the day's agenda and assigning the independent work so students know exactly what is expected of them when they are not meeting with the teacher in the small group.
- *Small-group/independent work.* The teacher meets with small group 1 while the rest of the class is working independently. After 20 minutes (or whatever the teacher deems necessary) the teacher meets with small group 2 while the group 1 students move to independent work. Teachers can decide whether this independent work is individual, in pairs, or in small groups. In terms of assigning activities, some teachers prefer to list an agenda on the board that everyone who is not with the teacher follows (e.g., everyone does independent novel reading for the first 15 minutes of independent work and then everyone begins novel response or answers textbook questions for the remaining time and finishes the activity for homework). Other teachers like to give students a list of options to choose from in the form of individual learning contracts. Students are expected to finish these contracts by the end of the week.
- *Whole-class closure.* The teacher wraps up the class in a whole group, assessing learning for the day, assigning homework, and setting the next day's agenda.

Additional Points

- Model and provide guided practice with any activity before expecting your students to perform it independently as part of their independent work.
- You don't have to use this schedule every day of the week. Some teachers choose to use it five days per week for a particular unit. Other teachers decide that they only need to meet with small groups three days per week. In the upper grades, students can perform more work independently over extended periods of time.
- If you have three groups, you can modify this schedule fairly easily. On day one, you meet with groups 1 and 2. On day two, you meet with groups 2 and 3. On day three, you meet with groups 3 and 1. Thus, each group works with you twice during a three-day rotation.

To make scheduling easier, remember that the different small groups can (and often do) perform the same activities but with different words or morphemes. Take the example of small group 1 studying prefixes and small group 2 studying roots. Both groups could follow the same schedule of activities in Figure 8.8 (open sort on Monday, root/prefix tree on Wednesday). The only difference would be that group 1 would be doing the activities with the assigned prefixes and group 2 would be doing them with the assigned roots for that week.

APPENDIXES

This section of the text contains eight segments, or Appendixes. Appendix A provides the materials you will need for assessments (described in Chapter 3). Other Appendixes contain sample sorts, word lists, and templates that you can use to create your own word study activities.

APPENDIX A

Assessment Materials

Before choosing an inventory, you may want to use the Qualitative Spelling Checklist to help you make a more informed choice (see Chapter 3 for more details). You may also use the guidelines on page 64 to choose the inventory. Students should not study the words in advance of testing. Assure students that they will not be graded on this activity and that they will be helping you plan for their needs. Ask students to number their papers. Call each word aloud and repeat it. Say each word naturally, without emphasizing phonemes or syllables. Use it in a sentence, if necessary, to be sure students know the exact word. Sample sentences are provided along with the words. After administering the inventory, use a feature guide, classroom composite, and, if desired, a spelling-by-stage classroom organization chart to complete your assessment.

Scoring the Inventory Using the Features Guides

1. Make a copy of the appropriate feature guide (PSI, p. 269; ESI, p. 272; USI, p. 275) for each student. Draw a line under the last word called if you did not use all words and adjust the possible total points at the bottom of each feature column.
2. Score the words by checking off the features spelled correctly that are listed in the cells to the right of each word. For example, if a student spells *train* as TRANE, she gets a check in the initial *tr* and the final *n* cells, but not for the long vowel pattern. Write in the vowel pattern used (*a–e* in this case), but do not give any points for it. Put a check in the "Correct" column if the word is spelled correctly. Do not count reversed letters as errors but note them in the cells. If unnecessary letters are added, give the speller credit for what is correct (e.g., if *train* is spelled TRAINE, the student still gets credit for representing the long vowel), but do not check "Correct" for spelling.
3. Add the number of checks under each feature and across for each word, double-checking the total score recorded in the last cell. Modify the ratios in the last row depending on the number of words called aloud.

Interpreting the Results of the Spelling Inventory

1. Look down each feature column to determine instructional needs. Students who miss only one can go on to other features. Students who miss two or three need some review work; students who miss more than three need careful instruction on this feature. If a student did not get any points for a feature, earlier features need to be studied first.
2. To determine a stage of development, note where students first make two or more errors under the stages listed at the top of the feature guide. Circle this stage.

Using the Class Composite and Spelling-by-Stage Form

1. Staple each feature guide to the student's spelling paper and arrange the papers in rank order from highest total points to lowest total points.
2. List students' names in this rank order in the left column of the appropriate classroom composite (PSI, p. 268; ESI, p. 271; USI, p. 274) and transfer each student's feature scores from the bottom row of the individual feature guides to the classroom composite.
3. Highlight cells where students make two or more errors on a particular feature to get a sense of your students' needs and to form groups for instruction.
4. Many teachers find it easier to form groups using the spelling-by-stage classroom organization chart. List each student under the appropriate spelling stage (the stage circled on the feature guide) and determine instructional groups.

Note. See Chapter 3 for more detailed directions for choosing, administering, scoring, interpreting, and using the inventories to form instructional groups.

Copyright © 2011 Pearson Education Inc. Reproduction is permitted for classroom use only.

Qualitative Spelling Checklist

Use this checklist to analyze students' uncorrected writing and to locate their appropriate stages of spelling development. Examples are in parentheses. The spaces for dates at the top of the checklist are used to follow students' progress. Check when certain features are observed in students' spelling. When a feature is always present, check "Yes." The last place where you check "Often" corresponds to the student's stage of spelling development.

Student ______________________ Observer ______________________

Dates ____________ ____________ ____________

	Yes	Often	No
Letter Name–Alphabetic			
Late			
• Are short vowels spelled correctly? (*bed, ship, when, lump*)	___	___	___
• Is the *m* or *n* included in front of other consonants (*lump, stand*) ?	___	___	___
Within Word Pattern			
Early			
• Are long vowels in single-syllable words used but confused? (FLOTE for *float*, TRANE for *train*)	___	___	___
Middle			
• Are most long vowel words spelled correctly, while some long vowel spelling and other vowel patterns are used but confused? (DRIEV for *drive*)	___	___	___
• Are the most common consonant digraphs and blends spelled correctly? (*sled, dream, fright*)	___	___	___
Late			
• Are the harder consonant digraphs and blends spelled correctly? (*speck, switch, smudge*)	___	___	___
• Are most other vowel patterns spelled correctly? (*spoil, chewed, serving*)	___	___	___
Syllables and Affixes			
Early			
• Are inflectional endings added correctly to base vowel patterns with short vowel patterns? (*shopping, listed*)	___	___	___
• Are junctures between syllables spelled correctly? (*cattle, cellar, carries, bottle*)	___	___	___
Middle			
• Are inflectional endings added correctly to base words? (*chewed, marched*)	___	___	___
Late			
• Are unaccented final syllables spelled correctly? (*bottle, fortunate, civilize*)	___	___	___
• Are less frequent prefixes and suffixes spelled correctly? (*confident, favor, ripen, cellar, pleasure*)	___	___	___
Derivational Relations			
Early			
• Are most polysyllabic words spelled correctly? (*fortunate, confident*)	___	___	___
Middle			
• Are unaccented vowels in derived words spelled correctly? (*confident, civilize, category*)	___	___	___
Late			
• Are words from derived forms spelled correctly? (*pleasure, opposition, criticize*)	___	___	___

Copyright © 2011 Pearson Education Inc. Reproduction is permitted for classroom use only.

Spelling-by-Stage Classroom Organization Chart

SPELLING STAGES →	EMERGENT			LETTER NAME–ALPHABETIC			WITHIN WORD PATTERN			SYLLABLES AND AFFIXES			DERIVATIONAL RELATIONS		
	EARLY	MIDDLE	LATE	EARLY	MIDDLE	LATE	EARLY	MIDDLE	LATE	EARLY	MIDDLE	LATE	EARLY	MIDDLE	LATE

Copyright © 2011 Pearson Education Inc. Reproduction is permitted for classroom use only.

Primary Spelling Inventory (PSI)

Word List

The Primary Spelling Inventory (PSI) is often used with primary or elementary-age children. The 26 words are ordered by difficulty to sample features of the letter name–alphabetic to within word pattern stages. Call out enough words so that you have at least five or six misspelled words to analyze. If any students spell more than 20 words correctly, you may want to use the Elementary Spelling Inventory.

1. fan	I could use a fan on a hot day. *fan*
2. pet	I have a pet cat who likes to play. *pet*
3. dig	He will dig a hole in the sand. *dig*
4. rob	A raccoon will rob a bird's nest for eggs. *rob*
5. hope	I hope you will do well on this test. *hope*
6. wait	You will need to wait for the letter. *wait*
7. gum	I stepped on some bubble gum. *gum*
8. sled	The dog sled was pulled by huskies. *sled*
9. stick	I used a stick to poke in the hole. *stick*
10. shine	He rubbed the coin to make it shine. *shine*
11. dream	I had a funny dream last night. *dream*
12. blade	The blade of the knife was very sharp. *blade*
13. coach	The coach called the team off the field. *coach*
14. fright	She was a fright in her Halloween costume. *fright*
15. chewed	The dog chewed on the bone until it was gone. *chewed*
16. crawl	You will get dirty if you crawl under the bed. *crawl*
17. wishes	In fairy tales wishes often come true. *wishes*
18. thorn	The thorn from the rosebush stuck me. *thorn*
19. shouted	They shouted at the barking dog. *shouted*
20. spoil	The food will spoil if it sits out too long. *spoil*
21. growl	The dog will growl if you bother him. *growl*
22. third	I was the third person in line. *third*
23. camped	We camped down by the river last weekend. *camped*
24. tries	He tries hard every day to finish his work. *tries*
25. clapping	The audience was clapping after the program. *clapping*
26. riding	They are riding their bikes to the park today. *riding*

Copyright © 2011 Pearson Education Inc. Reproduction is permitted for classroom use only.

Primary Spelling Inventory Classroom Composite

Teacher ________________ School ________________ Grade ________ Date ________

SPELLING STAGES →	EMERGENT LATE		LETTER NAME–ALPHABETIC EARLY	MIDDLE	LATE	WITHIN WORD PATTERN EARLY	MIDDLE	LATE	SYLLABLES AND AFFIXES EARLY	
Students' ↓ Names	Consonants Initial	Consonants Final	Short Vowels	Digraphs	Blends	Long Vowels	Other Vowels	Inflected Endings	Correct Spelling	Total Rank Order
Possible Points	7	7	7	7	7	7	7	7	26	82
1.										
2.										
3.										
4.										
5.										
6.										
7.										
8.										
9.										
10.										
11.										
12.										
13.										
14.										
15.										
16.										
17.										
18.										
19.										
20.										
21.										
22.										
23.										
24.										
25.										
26.										
Highlight for Instruction*										

*Highlight students who miss more than 1 on a particular feature; they will benefit from more instruction in that area.

Copyright © 2011 Pearson Education Inc. Reproduction is permitted for classroom use only.

Primary Spelling Inventory Feature Guide

Student's Name ____________ Teacher ____________ Grade ______ Date ______

Words Spelled Correctly: ____ /26 *Feature Points:* ____ /56 *Total:* ____ /82 *Spelling Stage:* ____________

SPELLING STAGES →	EMERGENT		LETTER NAME–ALPHABETIC			WITHIN WORD PATTERN		SYLLABLES AND AFFIXES		
	LATE	EARLY	MIDDLE	LATE		EARLY	MIDDLE	LATE	EARLY	
	Consonants									
Features →	Initial	Final	Short Vowels	Digraphs	Blends	Long Vowels	Other Vowels	Inflected Endings	Feature Points	Words Spelled Correctly
1. fan	f	n	a							
2. pet	p	t	e							
3. dig	d	g	i							
4. rob	r	b	o							
5. hope	h	p				o-e				
6. wait	w	t				ai				
7. gum	g	m	u							
8. sled			e		sl					
9. stick			i		st					
10. shine				sh		i-e				
11. dream					dr	ea				
12. blade					bl	a-e				
13. coach				-ch		oa				
14. fright					fr	igh				
15. chewed				ch			ew	-ed		
16. crawl					cr		aw			
17. wishes				-sh				-es		
18. thorn				th			or			
19. shouted				sh			ou	-ed		
20. spoil							oi			
21. growl							ow			
22. third				th			ir			
23. camped								-ed		
24. tries					tr			-ies		
25. clapping								-pping		
26. riding								-ding		
Totals	/7	/7	/7	/7	/7	/7	/7	/7	/56	/26

Copyright © 2011 Pearson Education Inc. Reproduction is permitted for classroom use only.

Elementary Spelling Inventory (ESI)

Word List

The Elementary Spelling Inventory (ESI) covers more stages than the PSI. It is often used across the elementary grades. The 25 words are ordered by difficulty to sample features of the letter name–alphabetic to derivational relations stages. Call out enough words so that you have at least five or six misspelled words to analyze. If any students spell more than 20 words correctly, use the Upper-Level Spelling Inventory.

1. bed	I hopped out of bed this morning. *bed*
2. ship	The ship sailed around the island. *ship*
3. when	When will you come back? *when*
4. lump	He had a lump on his head after he fell. *lump*
5. float	I can float on the water with my new raft. *float*
6. train	I rode the train to the next town. *train*
7. place	I found a new place to put my books. *place*
8. drive	I learned to drive a car. *drive*
9. bright	The light is very bright. *bright*
10. shopping	She went shopping for new shoes. *shopping*
11. spoil	The food will spoil if it is not kept cool. *spoil*
12. serving	The restaurant is serving dinner tonight. *serving*
13. chewed	The dog chewed up my favorite sweater yesterday. *chewed*
14. carries	She carries apples in her basket. *carries*
15. marched	We marched in the parade. *marched*
16. shower	The shower in the bathroom was very hot. *shower*
17. bottle	The bottle broke into pieces on the tile floor. *bottle*
18. favor	He did his brother a favor by taking out the trash. *favor*
19. ripen	The fruit will ripen over the next few days. *ripen*
20. cellar	I went down to the cellar for the can of paint. *cellar*
21. pleasure	It was a pleasure to listen to the choir sing. *pleasure*
22. fortunate	It was fortunate that the driver had snow tires. *fortunate*
23. confident	I am confident that we can win the game. *confident*
24. civilize	They wanted to civilize the forest people. *civilize*
25. opposition	The coach said the opposition would be tough. *opposition*

Copyright © 2011 Pearson Education Inc. Reproduction is permitted for classroom use only.

Elementary Spelling Inventory Classroom Composite

Teacher ______________ School ______________ Grade ________ Date ________

SPELLING STAGES →	EMERGENT LATE / EARLY	LETTER NAME–ALPHABETIC MIDDLE	LATE	WITHIN WORD PATTERN EARLY	MIDDLE	LATE	SYLLABLES AND AFFIXES EARLY	MIDDLE	LATE	DERIVATIONAL RELATIONS EARLY	MIDDLE		
Students' ↓ Names	Consonants	Short Vowels	Digraphs	Blends	Long Vowels	Other Vowels	Inflected Endings	Syllable Junctures	Unaccented Final Syllables	Harder Suffixes	Bases or Roots	Correct Spelling	Total Rank Order
Possible Points	7	5	6	7	5	7	5	5	5	5	5	25	87
1.													
2.													
3.													
4.													
5.													
6.													
7.													
8.													
9.													
10.													
11.													
12.													
13.													
14.													
15.													
16.													
17.													
18.													
19.													
20.													
21.													
22.													
23.													
24.													
25.													
26.													
Highlight for Instruction*													

*Highlight students who miss more than 1 on a particular feature; they will benefit from more instruction in that area.

Copyright © 2011 Pearson Education Inc. Reproduction is permitted for classroom use only.

Elementary Spelling Inventory Feature Guide

Student's Name ______________ Teacher ______________ Grade ________ Date ________

Words Spelled Correctly: ____ /25 *Feature Points:* ____ /62 *Total:* ____ /87 *Spelling Stage:* ______________

SPELLING STAGES →	EMERGENT LATE	LETTER NAME–ALPHABETIC EARLY	MIDDLE	LATE	WITHIN WORD PATTERN EARLY	MIDDLE	LATE	SYLLABLES AND AFFIXES EARLY	MIDDLE	LATE	DERIVATIONAL RELATIONS EARLY	MIDDLE			
	Consonants													
Features →	Initial	Final	Short Vowels	Digraphs	Blends	Long Vowels	Other Vowels	Inflected Endings	Syllable Junctures	Unaccented Final Syllables	Harder Suffixes	Bases or Roots	Feature Points	Words Spelled Correctly
1. bed	b	d	e											
2. ship		p	i	sh										
3. when			e	wh										
4. lump	l		u		mp									
5. float		t			fl	oa								
6. train		n			tr	ai								
7. place					pl	a-e								
8. drive		v			dr	i-e								
9. bright					br	igh								
10. shopping			o	sh				pping						
11. spoil					sp		oi							
12. serving							er	ving						
13. chewed				ch			ew	ed						
14. carries							ar	ies	rr					
15. marched				ch			ar	ed						
16. shower				sh			ow			er				
17. bottle									tt	le				
18. favor									v	or				
19. ripen									p	en				
20. cellar									ll	ar				
21. pleasure											ure	pleas		
22. fortunate							or				ate	fortun		
23. confident											ent	confid		
24. civilize											ize	civil		
25. opposition											tion	pos		
Totals	/7		/5	/6	/7	/5	/7	/5	/5	/5	/5	/5	/62	/25

Copyright © 2011 Pearson Education Inc. Reproduction is permitted for classroom use only.

Upper-Level Spelling Inventory (USI)

Word List

The Upper-Level Spelling Inventory (USI) can be used in upper elementary, middle, high school, and postsecondary classrooms. The 31 words are ordered by difficulty to sample features of the within word pattern to derivational relations spelling stages. With normally achieving students, you can administer the entire list, but you may stop when students misspell more than eight words and are experiencing noticeable frustration. If any students misspell five of the first eight words, use the ESI to more accurately identify within word pattern features that need instruction.

1.	switch	We can switch television channels with a remote control. *switch*
2.	smudge	There was a smudge on the mirror from her fingertips. *smudge*
3.	trapped	He was trapped in the elevator when the electricity went off. *trapped*
4.	scrape	The fall caused her to scrape her knee. *scrape*
5.	knotted	The knotted rope would not come undone. *knotted*
6.	shaving	He didn't start shaving with a razor until 11th grade. *shaving*
7.	squirt	Don't let the ketchup squirt out of the bottle too fast. *squirt*
8.	pounce	My cat likes to pounce on her toy mouse. *pounce*
9.	scratches	We had to paint over the scratches on the car. *scratches*
10.	crater	The crater of the volcano was filled with bubbling lava. *crater*
11.	sailor	When he was young, he wanted to go to sea as a sailor. *sailor*
12.	village	My Granddad lived in a small seaside village. *village*
13.	disloyal	Traitors are disloyal to their country. *disloyal*
14.	tunnel	The rockslide closed the tunnel through the mountain. *tunnel*
15.	humor	You need a sense of humor to understand his jokes. *humor*
16.	confidence	With each winning game, the team's confidence grew. *confidence*
17.	fortunate	The driver was fortunate to have snow tires on that winter day. *fortunate*
18.	visible	The singer on the stage was visible to everyone. *visible*
19.	circumference	The length of the equator is equal to the circumference of the earth. *circumference*
20.	civilization	We studied the ancient Mayan civilization last year. *civilization*
21.	monarchy	A monarchy is headed by a king or a queen. *monarchy*
22.	dominance	The dominance of the Yankees baseball team lasted for several years. *dominance*
23.	correspond	Many students correspond through e-mail. *correspond*
24.	illiterate	It is hard to get a job if you are illiterate. *illiterate*
25.	emphasize	I want to emphasize the importance of trying your best. *emphasize*
26.	opposition	The coach said the opposition would give us a tough game. *opposition*
27.	chlorine	My eyes were burning from the chlorine in the swimming pool. *chlorine*
28.	commotion	The audience heard the commotion backstage. *commotion*
29.	medicinal	Cough drops are to be taken for medicinal purposes only. *medicinal*
30.	irresponsible	It is irresponsible not to wear a seat belt. *irresponsible*
31.	succession	The firecrackers went off in rapid succession. *succession*

Copyright © 2011 Pearson Education Inc. Reproduction is permitted for classroom use only.

Upper-Level Spelling Inventory Classroom Composite

Teacher ____________ School ____________ Grade ________ Date ________

SPELLING STAGES →	WITHIN WORD PATTERN: EARLY, MIDDLE	LATE		SYLLABLES AND AFFIXES: EARLY	MIDDLE	LATE	DERIVATIONAL RELATIONS: EARLY	MIDDLE	LATE	
Students' ↓ Names	Blends and Digraphs	Vowels	Complex Consonants	Inflected Endings and Syllable Juncture	Unaccented Final Syllables	Affixes	Reduced Vowels in Unaccented Syllables	Greek and Latin Elements	Assimilated Prefixes	Total Rank Order
Possible Points	5	9	7	8	9	10	7	7	6	99
1.										
2.										
3.										
4.										
5.										
6.										
7.										
8.										
9.										
10.										
11.										
12.										
13.										
14.										
15.										
16.										
17.										
18.										
19.										
20.										
21.										
22.										
23.										
24.										
25.										
26.										
27.										
Highlight for Instruction*										

*Highlight students who miss more than 1 on a particular feature; they will benefit from more instruction in that area.

Copyright © 2011 Pearson Education Inc. Reproduction is permitted for classroom use only.

Upper-Level Spelling Inventory Feature Guide

Student's Name ______________ Teacher ______________ Grade ________ Date ________

Words Spelled Correctly: ____ */31* *Feature Points:* ____ */68* *Total:* ____ */99* *Spelling Stage:* ______________

SPELLING STAGES →	WITHIN WORD PATTERN			SYLLABLES AND AFFIXES			DERIVATIONAL RELATIONS				
	EARLY	MIDDLE	LATE	EARLY	MIDDLE	LATE	EARLY	MIDDLE	LATE		
Features →	Blends and Digraphs	Vowels	Complex Consonants	Inflected Endings and Syllable Juncture	Unaccented Final Syllables	Affixes	Reduced Vowels in Unaccented Syllables	Greek and Latin Elements	Assimilated Prefixes	Feature Points	Words Spelled Correctly
1. switch	sw	i	tch								
2. smudge	sm	u	dge								
3. trapped	tr			pped							
4. scrape		a-e	scr								
5. knotted		o	kn	tted							
6. shaving	sh			ving							
7. squirt		ir	squ								
8. pounce		ou	ce								
9. scratches		a	tch	es							
10. crater	cr			t	er						
11. sailor		ai			or						
12. village				ll	age						
13. disloyal		oy			al	dis					
14. tunnel				nn	el						
15. humor				m	or						
16. confidence						con	fid				
17. fortunate					ate			fortun			
Subtotals	/5	/9	/7	/8	/7	/2	/1	/1	/0	/40	/17

(continued)

Copyright © 2011 Pearson Education Inc. Reproduction is permitted for classroom use only.

Upper-Level Spelling Inventory Feature Guide *(continued)*

SPELLING STAGES →	WITHIN WORD PATTERN EARLY MIDDLE		LATE	SYLLABLES AND AFFIXES EARLY	MIDDLE	LATE	DERIVATIONAL RELATIONS EARLY	MIDDLE	LATE		
Features →	**Blends and Digraphs**	**Vowels**	**Complex Consonants**	**Inflected Endings and Syllable Juncture**	**Unaccented Final Syllables**	**Affixes**	**Reduced Vowels in Unaccented Syllables**	**Greek and Latin Elements**	**Assimilated Prefixes**	**Feature Points**	**Words Spelled Correctly**
18. visible						ible		vis			
19. circumference						ence		circum			
20. civilization							liz	civil			
21. monarchy								arch			
22. dominance						ance	min				
23. correspond							res		rr		
24. illiterate					ate				ll		
25. emphasize						size	pha				
26. opposition							pos		pp		
27. chlorine						ine		chlor			
28. commotion						tion			mm		
29. medicinal					al			medic			
30. irresponsible						ible	res		rr		
31. succession						sion			cc		
Subtotals	/0	/0	/0	/0	/2	/3	/6	/6	/6	/28	/14
Totals	/5	/9	/7	/8	/9	/10	/7	/7	/6	/68	/31

Copyright © 2011 Pearson Education Inc. Reproduction is permitted for classroom use only.

APPENDIX B

APPENDIX B

Goal-Setting/Monitoring Charts

The following charts are examples you can use to help (1) monitor student progress and (2) guide your conferences with students. You may also find it motivating for your students to use these for their own progress monitoring. You can find a detailed explanation in Chapter 3 and specific examples using these charts in Chapters 4 and 5. The charts are divided into:

- Early Within Word Pattern
- Middle Within Word Pattern
- Late Within Word Pattern
- Early Syllables and Affixes
- Middle Syllables and Affixes
- Late Syllables and Affixes

Early Within Word Pattern

Categories	Features	Date Feature Mastered
Common long vowels: *e*-marker	Long *a* with *a-e* (c*a*k*e*)	____________
	Long *i* with *i-e* (b*i*k*e*)	____________
	Long *o* with *o-e* (b*o*n*e*)	____________
	Long *u* with *u-e* (c*u*b*e*)	____________
Date Category Mastered:		
Simple *r*-controlled vowels	*ar* (c*ar*)	____________
	ir (g*ir*l)	____________
	or (h*or*n)	____________
Date Category Mastered:		

Copyright © 2011 Pearson Education Inc. Reproduction is permitted for classroom use only.

Middle Within Word Pattern

Categories	Features	Date Feature Mastered
Other common long vowel patterns	Long *a* patterns *ai* (*rain*), *ay* (*tray*)	________
	Long *e* patterns *ee* (*sheep*), *ea* (*peach*)	________
	Long *i* patterns *igh* (*light*), *y* (*fly*)	________
	Long *o* patterns *oa* (*boat*), *ow* (*snow*)	________
	Long *u* patterns *ue* (*glue*), *ew* (*stew*), *ui* (*fruit*)	________
Date Category Mastered:		
Long *r*-controlled vowel patterns	Long *a r*-controlled *are* (*square*), *air* (*hair*)	________
	Long *e r*-controlled *eer* (*deer*), *ear* (*ear*)	________
	Long *i r*-controlled *ire* (*tire*)	________
	Long *o r*-controlled *oar* (*oar*), *ore* (*store*)	________
	Other *r*-controlled vowels *er* (*fern*), *ur* (*curl*), *wor* (*worm*)	________
Date Category Mastered:		

Copyright © 2011 Pearson Education Inc. Reproduction is permitted for classroom use only.

Late Within Word Pattern

Categories	Features	Date Feature Mastered
Complex consonant units	Silent letters *kn* (*knife*), *wr* (*wren*), *gn* (*gnat*)	___
	Digraph units *shr* (*shrimp*), *thr* (*three*), *squ* (*square*)	___
	Three-letter blends *scr* (*scrap*), *str* (*street*), *spr* (*spray*), *spl* (*splash*)	___
	Hard/soft *c* and *g* Hard *g* (*goat*), soft *g* (*gem*), hard *c* (*card*), soft *c* (*cent*)	___
	Other consonant units *dge* (*bridge*), *tch* (*patch*)	___
	Consonant *-e* endings *ce* (*face*), *se* (*mouse*), *ve* (*glove*), *ge* (*cage*)	___
Date Category Mastered:		
Ambiguous vowels	Patterns for /oi/ *oi* (*oil*), *oy* (*boy*)	___
	Patterns for /ou/ *ou* (*cloud*), *ow* (*cow*)	___
	Patterns for /aw/ *al* (*salt*), *au* (*sauce*), *aw* (*saw*)	___
	Sounds of *oo* /oo/ in *book*, /oo/ in *zoo*	___
Date Category Mastered:		

Copyright © 2011 Pearson Education Inc. Reproduction is permitted for classroom use only.

Early Syllables and Affixes

Categories	Features	Date Feature Mastered
Adding endings	Plurals no change (*apples*), + *es* (*boxes*), *y* to *i* + *es* (*flies*) Adding -ed and -ing no change (*jumped/sleeping*), e-drop (*raced, smiling*), double (*dropped, winning*)	________ ________
Date Category Mastered:		
Syllable juncture patterns	V-CV open (*pi-lot*) VC-CV doublet (*rab-bit*) VC-CV regular (*bas-ket*) VC-V closed (*com-et*) VC-CCV (*pil-grim*) VCC-CV (*ath-lete*) V-V (*li-on*)	________ ________ ________ ________ ________ ________ ________
Date Category Mastered:		

Copyright © 2011 Pearson Education Inc. Reproduction is permitted for classroom use only.

Middle Syllables and Affixes

Categories	Features	Date Feature Mastered
Date Category Mastered:		
Vowel patterns in accented syllables	Long *a* *aCe* (*bracelet*), *ai* (*rainbow*), *ay* (*crayon*)	
	Long *e* *ee* (*cheetah*), *ea* (*easel*), *ea* (*breakfast*)	
	Long *o* *oCe* (*alone*), *oa* (*toaster*), *ow* (*blowhole*), *oCC* (*soldier*)	
	r-Controlled *ar* (*harbor*), *are* (*barefoot*), *air* (*airplane*), *ir* (*birdhouse*), *ire* (*firefly*), *or* (*corner*), *ore* (*explore*), *oar* (*boardwalk*), *our* (*fourteen*)	
	Ambiguous *oo* (*balloon*), *oo* (*football*), *ou* (*mountain*), *ow* (*powder*), *oi* (*poison*), *oy* (*royal*), *au* (*author*), *aw* (*macaw*)	
Plurals and inflectional endings in two-syllable words	Base + *s* vs. base + *es* *robots, eyelashes*	
	Base (*y* after V) + *s* vs. base (*y* after C) *y* to *i* + *es* *turkeys, candies*	
	Base + *s* vs. base + *es* vs. base *y* to *i* + *es* *robots, eyelashes, candies*	
	Base + *ing* or *ed* *forgetting, piloting*	
Date Category Mastered:		

Copyright © 2011 Pearson Education Inc. Reproduction is permitted for classroom use only.

Late Syllables and Affixes

Categories	Features	Date Feature Mastered
Final unaccented syllables	Patterns for /schwa r/ *er* (*barber, baker, taller*), *or* (*doctor*), *ar* (*circular*)	____________
	Patterns for /cher/ *nature, teacher*	____________
	Patterns for /schwa n/ *en* (*golden, sharpen*), *on* (*apron*), *in* (*cabin*), *ain* (*mountain*), *an* (*human*)	____________
	Patterns for /schwa l/ *le* (*angle*), *el* (*angel*), *al* (*naval*)	____________
	Patterns for /schwa t/ and /schwa j/ *et* (*planet*), *it* (*exit*), *age* (*baggage*)	____________
	Patterns for /E/ *ey* (*monkey*), *ie* (*birdie*), *y* (*daisy*)	____________
Special consonants in two-syllable words	Hard *g* vs. soft *g* vs. hard *c* vs. soft *c* *gorilla, giraffe, cabin, city*	____________
	Silent consonants *wrinkle, castle*	____________
	ph vs. *gh* (sounds of /f/) *dophin, laughter*	____________
	ck vs. *ke* vs. *k* vs. *c* (final sounds of /k/) *hammock, cupcake, homework, picnic, antique*	____________
Simple prefixes	un in pre uni re non ex bi dis mis en tri	____________
Simple suffixes	*er* vs. *est* *taller/tallest, larger/largest, thinner/thinnest*	____________
	y vs. *ly* *bumpy, deadly, starry, easy, easily*	____________
	ful vs. *less* vs. *ness* *colorful, beautiful, helpless, kindness, happiness*	____________
Date Category Mastered:		

Copyright © 2011 Pearson Education Inc. Reproduction is permitted for classroom use only.

APPENDIX C

Reading Error Analysis

APPENDIX C

Directions

A qualitative analysis of reading errors can be helpful in thinking about the patterns of orthographic errors your students exhibit while reading. The following error analysis was designed to target errors made while reading that can provide information about your students' orthographic knowledge. Understanding developmental word knowledge will allow you to interpret your students' reading errors and make instructional decisions. The following steps show the process of reading error analysis (see Chapter 3 for more details):

1. Take a running record of your students' oral reading, documenting their errors. These passages can come from the texts that they are reading in class, preferably instructional-level texts (texts they can read with 90 to 95 percent accuracy). Passages of 125 to 150 words have been found to be an adequate length.
2. Record all substitution errors (e.g., "she begun to run faster" instead of "she began to run faster") on the error analysis form in the "Error" column. Record the corresponding text in the "Text" column.
3. Code the errors by going across the top row of guiding questions. If you answer yes to a guiding question, then place a check in that column. If you answer no, then leave the column blank. Substitutions can be coded in a variety of ways:
   a. Consonant patterns (reading *wed* for *wedge*)
   b. Vowel patterns (reading *begun* for *began*)
   c. Syllable patterns (reading *diner* as *dinner; sumersion* for *submersion*)
   d. Morphemic units (reading *walk* for *walked; are* for *aren't*)
   e. Function words (reading *through* for *thought; what* for *went*)
4. After coding all of the errors, tally up your checks by counting the totals in each column. Write your column total in the bottom row labeled "Column Total."
5. Determine if there is a preponderance of errors of a certain type. If so, you can incorporate activities into your instruction to meet that particular need. The last row provides you with chapters in this book that will help you address those instructional needs.

Copyright © 2011 Pearson Education Inc. Reproduction is permitted for classroom use only.

Template

Text	Error	Does the error involve a consonant pattern confusion?	Does the error involve a vowel pattern confusion?	Does the error involve a syllable pattern confusion?	Does the error involve a morphemic unit confusion?	Is this a function word error?
Column Total						
Where Can I Find Out How to Teach This?		Chapter 4	Chapter 4	Chapter 5	Chapter 6	Chapter 4

Copyright © 2011 Pearson Education Inc. Reproduction is permitted for classroom use only.

APPENDIX D

Choosing Words

Guidelines

After you determine your students' stages of spelling and identify their specific goals using the qualitative spelling inventories found in Appendix A, you will need to decide on the orthographic features to target for instruction. Then you will prepare a collection of words to provide practice with the target features. Consider the feature comparison; you will want to provide your students with a sound and pattern contrast. For example, a sound and pattern contrast for the within word pattern stage might be short *a* as in *cat* versus long *a* as in *cake* (*a*-consonant-*e*), *rain* (*ai*), and *tray* (*ay*). Then you will pick words to exemplify those features. Highly frequent words should be considered first because they are words your students will read and write often; however, use your judgment. If any of these words seems too easy, do not use it. You will find an asterisk by words found on Fry's Instant Word Lists (the first 300), a list of high-frequency words. These words are important to consider because the first 100 make up approximately half of all written material, and the first 300 account for around 65 percent of all written material (Fry & Kress, 2006). You can therefore see how useful these words are.

The following lists of words are organized by features students need to study in both the within word pattern and syllables and affixes stages. Under each feature the words are generally grouped by frequency and complexity. Keywords for each are provided at the beginning of each category. For example, under short *a*, the early part of the list contains easier words (*am, ran, that*), and the latter part of the list contains words that may be obscure in meaning and/or spelled with blends or digraphs (*yam, brass, tramp*). The keyword for short *a* is found at the beginning of the feature: cat.

The lists also include oddballs that can be added to sorts. Sometimes the oddballs you include will be true exceptions (such as *said* in a sort with long *a* patterns), but other times oddballs may represent a less common spelling pattern, such as *ey* representing long *a* in *prey* and *grey*.

When you consider which of these words to include in your within word pattern sorts, you should also consider supports you are building for your students. Chapter 4 discussed the benefit of high-frequency phonograms in your vowel pattern study (e.g., *ound* in *round* and *ake* in *cake*). You may want to build sorts to highlight certain phonograms. See the sample sorts in Appendix E for examples. You may also want to include two-syllable words within sorts to advance study for your students, but keep in mind the following two important considerations:

1. Only include words where the vowel pattern is found in the accented syllable, like *arcade* and *cartoon*. If you do not consider accent, you may choose words like *cheddar* and *polar*. These are not good options because the vowel is reduced in unaccented vowels and becomes a schwa. This could confuse students.
2. These two-syllable words should be used for the reading activities of the sort, such as word sorting. Do not use them for spelling activities, such as blind writing sorts.

The first features are short vowels. Although short vowels are not included as features in the within word pattern and syllables and affixes stages, they provide a necessary sound contrast for many of your within word pattern sorts.

Copyright © 2011 Pearson Education Inc. Reproduction is permitted for classroom use only.

Word Lists

Short Vowel Words

Short *a* **cat**	Short *e* **bed**	Short *i* **pig**	Short *o* **pot**	Short *u* **bug**	*Oddball*
that*	get*	it*	not*	but*	shall*
flat	let*	quit	got*	cut*	want*
than*	yet	slit	jot	shut	what*
plan	then*	did*	plot	rub	was*
had*	when*	slid	shot	club	saw*
glad	bed*	big*	trot	shrub	laugh
drag	led	twig	job	hug	wash*
brag	bled	will*	snob	mug	child
snag	fled	chill	blob	slug	mind
clap	shed	drill	cop	plug	find*
trap	tell*	spill	mop	drug	climb
snap	help*	hip	slop	sum	of*
strap	shell	flip	flop	plum	won
crab	dwell	skip	drop	drum	son
hand*	beg	drip	shop	strum	front
stand*	leg	trip	chop	run*	for*
brand	less	chip	stop*	fun	from*
bang	guess	ship	prop	stun	cold*
hang	bless	kick	lock	duck	post
sang	dress*	sick	rock	luck	does*
rash	stress	quick	block	truck	come*
crash	deck	chick	clock	stuck	some*
smash	check	brick	smock	bump	none
flash	fleck	stick	shock	jump*	love*
back*	speck	thick	stock	stump	dove
black*	best*	click	long*	thump	glove
stack	chest	mint	song	clump	
track	guest	print	strong	sung	put*
bank	west	hint	boss	rung	push
drank	end*	thing*	toss	hung	bush
thank*	blend	bring*	cross	lung	truth
camp	trend	swing	box*	slung	
stamp	spend	sing*	odd	flung	
lamp	bent	ring	off*	cuff	
fast*	dent	if*	fond	fluff	
past	cent	is*	stomp	stuff	
last*	went	with*	lost	gruff	
plant	spent	wish*	cost	bunk	
grant	scent	him*	frost	junk	
pass	them*	his*	moth	chunk	
class	next*	this*	cloth	drunk	
glass	desk	which*	golf	stunk	
has*	left*	fish	loft	trunk	
gas	kept	swish	soft	rush	
ask*	slept	stiff		blush	
bath	shelf	lift		brush	
math	fresh	fist		crush	
fact*	flesh	limp		must*	
mask	clench	risk		just*	
raft	tenth	shift		dust	
draft	tempt	inch		trust	
shaft	melt	sixth		bunch	
		fifth		crunch	
				much*	
				such*	
				us*	
				hunt	
				thus	
				dusk	

Copyright © 2011 Pearson Education Inc. Reproduction is permitted for classroom use only.

Long *a* Words

CVCe						CVVC			CVV	CVVC
a-e **cake**						*ai* **rain**			*ay* **tray**	*ei* **vein**
made*	ate*	wake	tame	ape	pane	rain	wait	snail	day*	neigh
name*	gate	fake	fame	gape	vane	pain	bait	frail	jay	rein
same*	hate	shake	flame	grape	mane	tail	vain	praise	may*	weigh
came*	late	brake	blame	drape	slate	nail	plain	trail	play*	weight
make*	date	flake	lame	trace	scale	mail	chain	strait	say*	freight
take*	sale	base	lane	grace	stale	sail	stain	saint	stay	reign
bake	male	vase	plane	space	gaze	pail	drain	quaint	way*	veil
lake	tale	chase	cane	waste	daze	rail	grain	strain	clay	sleigh
cake	whale	race	crane	paste	blaze	fail	brain	faith	gray	beige
age	pale	lace	rate	taste	graze	jail	aim	straight	pray	
cage	fade	place	fate	haste	haze	gain	claim		tray	
page	wade	pace	crate	sake	range	main	ail	*Oddballs*	slay	
face*	shade	state	grate	quake	change	train	aide	said*		
gave*	grade	plate	bathe	drake	strange	aid	raid	again*	*ey*	*ea*
save	trade	skate	cave	phase		paid	paint	their*	they*	break
wave	shape	rage	grave	jade	*Oddballs*	maid	waist		prey	great
tape	cape	stage	slave	blade	have*	laid			grey	steak
safe	mate				dance	braid			hey	
					chance					

Long e Words

CVCe					CVVC					
e-e	*ea* **peach**				*ee* **sheep**					*ie* **chief**
eve	read*	beak	east	leave	see*	deep	tree*	sheep	spree	thief
scene	sea	leak	feast	weave	seem*	beep	flee	creep	geese	chief
scheme	eat*	weak	least	flea	bee	seep	glee	steep	cheese	grief
theme	beat	peak	clean*	peace	feed	jeep	sleep*	sweep	sneeze	brief
these*	seat	lean	steal	please*	feel	keep*	three*	creek	breeze	yield
	meat	heal	knead	cease	feet	seek	kneel	cheek	freeze	field
Open	mean	real	sneak	crease	beet	beef	steel	sleek	sleeve	shield
me*	bean	deal	creak	grease	meet	reef	wheel	speech	screen	niece
he*	seal	meal	steam	squeal	seen	eel	speed	teeth	preen	piece
we*	tea	heap	dream	league	week	heel	bleed	sleet		shriek
be*	pea	leap	cream	breathe	peek	reel	greed	greet	*Oddballs*	priest
the*	bead	seam	scream	squeak	wee	peel	breed	sheet	been*	grieve
she*	neat	each*	stream		free	deed	keen	sweet	seize	fierce
	team	teach	plead	*Oddballs*	seed	weed	green*	fleet	weird	fiend
	beam	beach	beast	head*	need	knee	queen	street	vein	siege
	lead	reach	treat	dead	peep				suite	pier
	ear*	peach		steak						
				great						*Oddballs*
				break						friend*

APPENDIX D

Copyright © 2011 Pearson Education Inc. Reproduction is permitted for classroom use only.

Long *i* Words

CVCe						CV		iCC	
			i-e bike			*ie* pie	*y/ye* fly	*igh* light	
like*	five*	while*	wide	white*	tribe	lie	my*	high*	find*
bike	mine	ice	slide	quite	scribe	pie	by*	night*	kind*
dime	fine*	mice	pride	write*	stride	tie	why*	right*	mind
time	nine	nice	tide	spite	stripe	die	fly*	light	climb
hide	vine	rice	glide	site	strike		cry	might*	child
ride*	shine	mile	wipe	lice	spine	*Oddballs*	sky	bright	wild
side	drive	file	pipe	spice	whine	buy*	try*	fight	blind
line	dive	pile	swipe	slice	prime	guy	dry	sigh	grind
live	hive	smile	spike	twice	chime	live*	shy	tight	hind
kite	life	wise	lime	price	fife	give*	sly	flight	sign
size	ripe	rise	crime	guide	knife	prince	spry	fright	bind
bite	hike	wife	pine	prize	thrive	since	dye	sight	wind
							lye	slight	rind
							rye	thigh	

Long *o* Words

CVCe					CVVC			Open	CVV	VVC	
		o-e bone				*oa* boat		*o* go	*ow* snow	*oCC* gold	
home*	wove	rove	slope	*Oddballs*	boat	foam	float	go*	bow	old*	both*
nose	drove	cove	lope	one*	coat*	roam	coach	no*	know*	gold	most*
hole	dome	stove	lone	done*	goat	goal	roach	so*	show*	hold*	folk
rope	globe	whole	stroke	none	road	coal	throat	ho	slow	cold*	roll
robe	cone	sole	throne	gone	toad	loaf	toast	yo-yo	snow	told	poll
note	zone	wrote	quote	once*	load	coax	coast		crow	fold	stroll
hose	role	choke	clothe	love	soap	loan	boast	*Oddballs*	blow	mold	scroll
hope*	stole	broke		dove	oat	moan	roast	to*	glow	sold	post
vote	doze	poke		glove	oak	groan	cloak	do*	grow*	bold	ghost
code	froze	smoke		prove	soak	moat	croak	who*	sow	scold	host
mole	pose	yoke		shove	whoa		loaves	two*	low	bolt	
pole	chose	spoke		some*					tow	colt	
joke	those*	tone		come*	*Oddballs*				flow	jolt	
stone	close*	shone		move	broad				own*	volt	
	owe	phone		lose	sew				flown		
				whose					throw		
									thrown		
									blown		
									grown		
									bowl		

Copyright © 2011 Pearson Education Inc. Reproduction is permitted for classroom use only.

Long *u* Words

CVCe			CVVC	CVVC		CVV		
u-e cube/June			*ui* fruit	*ue* glue		*ew* stew		
use*	cube	fume	fruit	blue	sue	new*	brew	*Oddballs*
cute	duke	chute	suit	due	fuel	dew	stew	do*
rude	huge	mute	bruise	clue	cruel	chew	crew	you*
rule	dude	plume	cruise	glue		drew	whew	to*
mule	nude	prune	juice	true		few	screw	two*
tune	crude	muse		flue		flew	threw	build
June	dune	spruce		hue		knew	shrewd	built
tube	flute			cue		grew	strewn	guide
								truth
								through

See also oo words

Ambiguous Vowels: ô sound

al salt	*au* sauce	*aw* saw		*o*		*ough*	*w + a*
tall	caught	saw*	gnaw	on*	loss	cough	was*
wall	taught	paw	thaw	off*	cross	ought	want*
mall	pause	law	caw	dog*	gloss	fought	wash
talk	sauce	draw	bawl	frog	cloth	bought	wand
walk	fault	claw	awe	log	moth	thought	wasp
calm	haunt	dawn	drawn	fog	broth	brought	watt
palm	launch	lawn	crawl	bog	soft	trough	swap
bald	because*	yawn	shawl	hog	loft		swat
halt		fawn	sprawl	lost	golf		watch
salt	*Oddballs*	hawk	squawk	cost	bong		
small*	aunt	raw	straw	frost	song		
fall*	laugh			boss	long		
stall				toss	strong		
stalk				moss	throng		
chalk						*Oddballs*	
						through	
						tough	
						rough	
						touch	
						young	
						could*	
						would*	
						should*	

Copyright © 2011 Pearson Education Inc. Reproduction is permitted for classroom use only.

Ambiguous Vowels/Diphthongs (*ou/ow* and *oi/oy*)

ow cow		*ou* cloud			*oo* book	*oo–u* zoo			*oi* oil	*oy* boy
how*	drown	out*	house*	*Oddballs*	book*	too*	soon*	school*	coin	boy*
now*	frown	our*	about*	could*	look*	zoo	noon	spoon	join	toy
cow	crown	loud	mouse	would*	good*	moo	moon	tooth	oil	joy
down*	crowd	pout	foul	should*	cook	boot	room	shoot	foil	enjoy
bow	fowl	ouch	mouth	touch	took*	root	zoom	smooth	soil	soy
wow	scowl	cloud	shout	young	foot	food	boom	roost	boil	ploy
town	prowl	proud	pout	cough	wood	mood	loom	proof	coil	
gown	growl	count	scout	tough	hook	tool	bloom	stool	point	
brown*	vow	round*	snout	ought	shook	cool	gloom	spook	joint	
clown		sound	stout	bought	stood	fool	loop	brood	hoist	
town*		found*	sprout	through	wool	pool	troop		moist	
owl		pound	pouch		crook	roof	whoop	*Oddballs*	toil	
howl		mound	couch		hood	goof	scoop	two*	broil	
sow		bound	crouch		hoof			blood	voice	
plow		hound	drought		soot				noise	
		wound	doubt		brook				choice	
		ground								

r-Controlled Vowels

ar car		*ar + e*	*are* square	*air* hair	*ear* ear	*eer* deer	*er* fern		
far*	dart	carve	care	fair	ear*	deer	her*	heard	*Oddballs*
car*	start*	large	bare	hair	near*	cheer	fern	earth	very*
jar	bark	starve	dare	pair	hear*	steer	herd	learn	their*
star	shark	barge	share	stair	dear*	queer	jerk	earn	there*
card	lark	charge	stare	flair	year*	jeer	term	search	were*
hard*	scar		mare	chair	fear	sneer	germ	pearl	here*
yard	mar	*Oddballs*	flare	lair	tear	steer	stern	yearn	where**
art	barb	are*	glare		clear	peer	herb		heart
part*	harp	war	rare		beard		per		bear
cart	sharp	warm*	scare		gear		perk		wear
bar	snarl		hare		spear		perch		swear
arm	scarf		snare				clerk		pear
harm	charm		blare				nerve		
dark	arch		fare				verse		
park	march		square				swerve		
spark	smart								
yarn	chart								

Copyright © 2011 Pearson Education Inc. Reproduction is permitted for classroom use only.

ur curl	*ir* girl	*ire* tire	*or* horn		*ore* store	*our* four	*oar* oar	*w + ar*	*w + or*
burn	girl*	fire	or*	storm	more*	your*	roar	warm	work*
hurt	first*	tire	for*	porch	store	four*	soar	war	word
turn*	bird	wire	born	torch	shore	pour	boar	ward	world
curl	dirt	hire	corn	force	bore	mourn	coarse	wharf	worm
curb	stir	sire	horn	north	chore	court	hoarse	quart	worth
burst	sir		worn	horse	score	fourth			worse
church	shirt		cord	forth	sore	gourd			
churn	skirt		cork	scorn	before*	source			
surf	third*		pork	chord	wore	course			
purr	birth		fort	forge	tore				
burr	firm		short	gorge	swore	*Oddballs*			
blur	swirl		nor			our*			
lurch	twirl		ford		*oor*	flour			
lurk	chirp		lord		door	hour			
spur	squirt				poor	scour			
hurl	thirst				floor	sour			
blurt	squirm								

ure
sure*
cure
pure
lure

Complex Consonants

ch beach	*tch* patch	*Cch* bench		*Hard g* goat		*Soft g* gem	*dge* bridge	*Cge* range
teach	catch	ranch	arch	frog	guide	huge	edge	range
reach	patch	branch	march	drug	guard	cage	ledge	change
beach	hatch	lunch	starch	twig	guilt	age	hedge	barge
peach	latch	bunch	search	flag	guess	page	wedge	charge
coach	match	munch	perch	shrug	guest	stage	pledge	large
speech	watch	punch	lurch	gave	ghost	rage	badge	forge
couch	ditch	bench	church	game	gone	orange	ridge	gorge
crouch	pitch	clench	birch	gain	goat	gauge	bridge	surge
pouch	witch	trench	torch	golf	gold	gem	lodge	bulge
screech	switch	wrench	porch	gulp	goose	germ	dodge	strange
	fetch	drench	scorch	gull	goof	gene	judge	
Oddballs	sketch	pinch		gust		gym	budge	
rich	clutch	finch			*Oddballs*	gyp	fudge	
such*	scratch	hunch			get*	giant	smudge	
much*	stretch	mulch			girl*	gist	trudge	
	stitch	gulch			gift		grudge	
	twitch	launch			gear			
	blotch				geese			

Copyright © 2011 Pearson Education Inc. Reproduction is permitted for classroom use only.

Complex Consonants *(continued)*

Hard *c* card	Soft *c* cent	-V*ce* face	-V*se* close	-*se* mouse	-*ze* froze	-*z* fizz	-*ve* love	Voiceless *th*	Voiced *th*
card	cell	rice	wise	cause	size	buzz	love	bath	bathe
cave	cent	face*	chase	cease	haze	fizz	dove	cloth	clothe
cast	cease	place	chose	dense	doze	jazz	shove	booth	loathe
cause	cinch	brace	close	false	prize	frizz	glove	loath	teethe
caught	cyst	slice	phase	geese	froze		have*	teeth	
couch	cite	price	muse	goose	graze	quiz	give*		
core	truce		those	loose	blaze	quartz	move		
coin	trace		these	moose	gauze	waltz	weave		
coast	since		prose	mouse	seize		leave		
cost	fence			noise	freeze		curve		
coach	peace			nurse	sneeze		nerve		
cough	juice			pause	snooze		serve		
curb	niece			purse	breeze				
curl	voice			raise	maize				
curve	sauce			sense	bronze				
cult	once			tense	wheeze				
cuff	hence			tease					
	force			rinse					
	ounce			cheese					
	dance			verse					
	chance								
	prince								

Homophones

be/bee
blue/blew
I/eye/aye
no/know
here/hear
to/too/two
hi/high
new/knew/gnu
see/sea
there/they're/their
bear/bare
by/buy*/bye
deer/dear
ate/eight*
for/four/fore
our/hour
red/read
lead/led
meat/meet
plane/plain
rode/road/rowed
sail/sale
stare/stair
we'd/weed
we'll/wheel
hole/whole
wear/ware/where
one/won
flower/flour
right/write
your/you're
lye/lie
its/it's
not/knot

hey/hay
made/maid
male/mail
nay/neigh
oh/owe
pail/pale
pair/pear/pare
peek/peak/pique
reed/read/Reid
so/sew/sow
root/route
shone/shown
aid/aide
add/ad
break/brake
cent/sent/scent
flee/flea
creak/creek
die/dye
fair/fare
hair/hare
heard/herd
night/knight
steel/steal
tail/tale
thrown/throne
fir/fur
waist/waste
week/weak
we've/weave
way/weigh
wait/weight
threw/through
vail/veil/vale

serial/cereal
cheap/cheep
days/daze
dew/do/due
doe/dough
gray/grey
heel/heal
horse/hoarse
ho/hoe
in/inn
need/kneed/knead
lone/loan
we/wee
ring/wring
peddle/petal/pedal
straight/strait
pole/poll
earn/urn
past/passed
sweet/suite
ore/or
rain/reign/rein
role/roll
sole/soul
seller/cellar
shoo/shoe
soar/sore
steak/stake
some/sum
tow/toe
vein/vane/vain
medal/metal/meddle
wrote/rote
whet/wet

Mary/marry/merry
great/grate
seem/seam
knew/new
stair/stare
hour/our
rough/ruff
poor/pour
haul/hall
piece/peace
ant/aunt
flair/flare
mist/missed
mane/main
wail/whale/wale
died/dyed
manor/manner
pier/peer
Ann/an
tacks/tax
cash/cache
rap/wrap
maze/maize
air/heir
bail/bale
ail/ale
prays/praise
base/bass
faint/feint
wade/weighed
wave/waive
knave/nave
foul/fowl
sell/cell

bred/bread
tred/tread
guessed/guest
rest/wrest
beech/beach
real/reel
peel/peal
team/teem
leak/leek
sees/seas
sheer/shear
feet/feat
hymn/him
whit/wit
scents/cents/sense
tents/tense
gilt/guilt
knit/nit
tic/tick
sight/site/cite
rye/wry
style/stile
might/mite
climb/clime
fined/find
side/sighed
tide/tied
vice/vise
awl/all
paws/pause
born/borne
chord/cord
mall/maul
mourn/morn

Copyright © 2011 Pearson Education Inc. Reproduction is permitted for classroom use only.

gate/gait
jeans/genes
time/thyme
son/sun
boy/buoy
aisle/I'll/isle
ball/bawl
beat/beet
bolder/boulder
course/coarse
forth/fourth
tea/tee
been/bin
sox/socks
board/bored
bell/belle
bowled/bold
bough/bow
browse/brows
rot/wrought
bomb/balm
bald/balled

Compound Words by Common Base Words

We have limited the list here to words that have base words across a number of compound words.

aircraft
airline
airmail
airplane
airport
airtight
anybody
anymore
anyone
anyplace
anything*
anywhere
backboard
backbone
backfire
background
backpack
backward
backyard
bareback
feedback
flashback
hatchback
paperback
piggyback
bathrobe
bathroom
bathtub
birdbath
bedrock
bedroom
bedside
bedspread
bedtime
flatbed
hotbed
sickbed
waterbed
birthday
birthmark
birthplace
birthstone
childbirth
blackberry
blackbird
blackboard
blackmail
blacksmith
blacktop
bookcase
bookkeeper
bookmark
bookworm

checkbook
cookbook
scrapbook
textbook
buttercup
butterfly
buttermilk
butterscotch
doorbell
doorknob
doorman
doormat
doorstep
doorway
backdoor
outdoor
downcast
downhill
download
downpour
downright
downsize
downstairs
downstream
downtown
breakdown
countdown
sundown
touchdown
eyeball
eyebrow
eyeglasses
eyelash
eyelid
eyesight
eyewitness
shuteye
firearm
firecracker
firefighter
firefly
firehouse
fireman
fireplace
fireproof
fireside
firewood
fireworks
backfire
bonfire
campfire
football
foothill

foothold
footlights
footnote
footprint
footstep
footstool
barefoot
tenderfoot
grandchildren
granddaughter
grandfather
grandmother
grandparent
grandson
haircut
hairdo
hairdresser
hairpin
hairstyle
handbag
handball
handbook
handcuffs
handmade
handout
handshake
handspring
handstand
handwriting
backhand
firsthand
secondhand
underhand
headache
headband
headdress
headfirst
headlight
headline
headlong
headmaster
headphones
headquarters
headstart
headstrong
headway
airhead
blockhead
figurehead
homeland
homemade
homemaker
homeroom

homesick
homespun
homestead
homework
horseback
horsefly
horseman
horseplay
horsepower
horseshoe
racehorse
sawhorse
houseboat
housefly
housewife
housework
housetop
birdhouse
clubhouse
doghouse
greenhouse
townhouse
landfill
landlady
landlord
landmark
landscape
landslide
dreamland
farmland
homeland
highland
wasteland
wonderland
lifeboat
lifeguard
lifejacket
lifelike
lifelong
lifestyle
lifetime
nightlife
wildlife
lighthouse
lightweight
daylight
flashlight
headlight
moonlight
spotlight
sunlight
mailman
doorman

snowman
fireman
gentleman
handyman
policeman
salesman
nightfall
nightgown
nightmare
nighttime
overnight
outbreak
outcast
outcome
outcry
outdated
outdo
outdoors
outfield
outfit
outgrow
outlaw
outline
outlook
outnumber
outpost
outrage
outright
outside
outsmart
outwit
blowout
carryout
cookout
handout
hideout
workout
lookout
overall
overboard
overcast
overcome
overflow
overhead
overlook
overview
playground
playhouse
playmate
playpen
playroom
playwright
rainbow

raincoat
raindrop
rainfall
rainstorm
roadblock
roadway
roadwork
railroad
sandbag
sandbar
sandbox
sandpaper
sandpiper
sandstone
seacoast
seafood
seagull
seaman
seaport
seasick
seashore
seaside
seaweed
snowball
snowflake
snowman
snowplow
snowshoe
snowstorm
somebody
someone
someday
somehow
somewhere
something
sometime
underline
undergo
underground
undermine
underwater
watercolor
waterfall
watermelon
waterproof
saltwater
windfall
windmill
windpipe
windshield
windswept
downwind
headwind

Copyright © 2011 Pearson Education Inc. Reproduction is permitted for classroom use only.

Plurals

Add *es* boxes					Change *y* to *i* + *es* flies				Change *f* to *ves* elves
ch + es	*sh + es*	*ss + es*	*x + es*	plays	flies	babies	daisies	stories	wives
arches	bushes	bosses	foxes	stays	fries	berries	guppies	buddies	knives
watches	dishes	classes	boxes	trays	cries	bodies	ladies	sixties	leaves
coaches	flashes	glasses		donkeys	tries	bunnies	parties		loaves
couches	brushes	crosses	*s + es*	monkeys	skies	cities	pennies	*Oddballs*	lives
inches	ashes	guesses	gases	jockeys	spies	copies	ponies	goalies	wolves
peaches	wishes	kisses	buses	turkeys	dries	counties	supplies	taxies	calves
notches	crashes	passes	bonuses	volleys		fairies	puppies	movies	elves
lunches	leashes	dresses		valleys		duties	bullies	cookies	scarves
	lashes								

Verbs for Inflected Ending Sorts

VCC		CVVC	CVCe		CVC				
walked		shouted	e-Drop smiling		Double wagged			Don't Double piloted	Miscellaneous Verbs
help	act	need	live	dance	stop	drip	grab	level	see/saw
jump	add	wait	time	glance	pat	fan	hug	edit	fall*/fell
want	crash	boat	name	hike	sun	flop	jam	enter	feel/felt
ask*	crack	shout	bake	hire	top	grin	kid	exit	tell/told
back	block	cook	care	serve	hop	grip	log	limit	grow/grew
talk	bowl	head*	close	score	plan	mop	map	suffer	know/knew
call	count	peek	love	solve	pot	plod	nap	appear	draw/drew
thank	brush	bloom	move	sneeze	shop	rob	nod	complain	blow/blew
laugh	bump	cool	smile	trace	trip	shrug	pin	explain	throw/threw
trick	burn	cheer	use	trade	bet	sip	dip	repeat	find/found
park	climb	clear	hate	vote	cap	skin	dim	attend	drink/drank
pick	camp	dream	hope	drape	clap	skip	rub	collect	sink/sank
plant	curl	float	ice	fade	slip	slam	beg		hear/heard
rock	dash	flood	joke	graze	snap	slap	blur	Double	break/broke
start	dust	fool	paste	praise	spot	snip	bud	forgetting	hold/held
bark	farm	oil	phone	scrape	tag	sob	chip	admit	stand/stood
work	fold	join	prove	shave	thin	strip	chop	begin	build/built
walk	growl	lean	race	shove	trap	wrap	crop	commit	ring/rang
yell	hunt	mail	scare	snare	trot	zip	strum	control	sing/sang
wish	kick	nail	share	cause	tug	brag	swap	excel	sweep/swept
guess	land	moan	skate	cease	wag	char	swat	forbid	sleep/slept
turn	learn	scream	stare	pose	drop	chug		forget	keep/kept
smell	nest	pour	taste	quote	drum	hem	*Oddballs*	omit	drive/drove
track	lick	sail	wave	rove	whiz	jog	box	permit	shine/shone
push	lock	trail	carve	blame	flap	mob	fix	rebel	feed/fed
miss	melt	zoom			flip	plot	wax	refer	bleed/bled
paint	point				scar	prop	row		lay/laid
wash	print				skim	blot	chew	e-Drop	pay/paid
wink	quack				slug	chat	sew	rattled	say/said
rest	reach				stab	scan	show	arrive	speak/spoke
					throb	slop	snow	escape	send/sent
								excuse	buy*/bought
								nibble	bring/brought
								rattle	tear/tore
								refuse	wear/wore
								amuse	
								ignore	
								retire	

Copyright © 2011 Pearson Education Inc. Reproduction is permitted for classroom use only.

Syllable Juncture

VCCV			VCV	VVCV	VCV	VV	VCCCV
Doublet rabbit	Regular basket		Open pilot	Open waiter	Closed robin	lion	pilgrim
pretty*	after*	public	over*	season	never*	create	constant
better*	under*	signal	open*	reason	present*	riot	dolphin
blizzard	number	sister*	baby	peanut	cabin	liar	bottle
blossom	chapter	subject	hoping	leader	planet	fuel	laughter
button	pencil	Sunday	writer	sneaker	finish	poem	pilgrim
cabbage	picnic	temper	basic	easy	robin	diary	instant
copper	basket	thunder	even	floated	magic	cruel	complain
cottage	cactus	trumpet	waving	waiter	limit	trial	hundred
dipper	canyon	twenty	bacon	needed	manage	diet	monster
fellow	capture	umpire	chosen	reading	prison	neon	orchard
foggy	center	walnut	moment		habit	idea	orphan
follow	window	welcome	raking	*Oddballs*	punish	video	purchase
common	compass	whimper	human	cousin	cover	meteor	complete
funny*	contest	seldom	pilot	water	promise	violin	athlete
happen	costume	winter	silent	busy	closet	annual	kitchen
mammal	doctor	wonder	vacant		camel	casual	children
message	picture	plastic	navy		cavern	radio	inspect
office	problem	fellow	music		comet		pumpkin
pattern	reptile	lumber	female		dozen		English
sudden	rescue	index	robot		habit		kingdom
tennis	sentence	insect	crater		honest		bottle
traffic	fabric	injure	climate		level		mumble
tunnel	helmet	elbow	duty		lever		
valley	husband	enter	famous		lizard		
village	master	velvet	fever		modern		
hollow	napkin	chimney	flavor		oven		
dessert	dentist		humid		palace		
butter			labor		timid		
hammer			legal		panic		
attic			local		rapid		
			pirate		visit		
			private		solid		
			program		wagon		
			recent		vanish		
			rumor		topic		
			siren		travel		
			solar				
			spiral				

Copyright © 2011 Pearson Education Inc. Reproduction is permitted for classroom use only.

a Patterns in Stressed Syllables

VCV open			VCCV	VCV				
Long *a* Accent in 1st baby	Long *a* Accent in 1st bracelet rainbow crayon	Long *a* Accent in 2nd	Short *a* Accent in 1st daddy	Short *a* Accent in 1st wagon	*ar* Accent in 1st party	*air* Accent in 1st stairway	*are* Accent in 1st barefoot	Double *r* marry
baby	rainbow	complain	attic	wagon	artist	stairway	careful	marry
nation	painter	contain	hammer	cabin	marble	fairway	careless	parrot
vapor	raisin	explain	batter	planet	garden	airport	carefree	narrow
skater	railroad	remain	happen	magic	party	dairy	barely	carrot
cradle	daisy	terrain	mammal	habit	carpet	haircut	barefoot	sparrow
lazy	dainty	exclaim	valley	camel	pardon	fairy	daredevil	narrate
bacon	sailor	refrain	cabbage	rapid	market	airplane	farewell	barrel
wafer	straighten	campaign	traffic	panic	tardy	chairman	shareable	carry*
fable	sprained	regain	pattern	panel	harvest	prairie	squarely	
raven	failure	obtain	scatter	palace	parka		warehouse	
famous	tailor	detail	ballot	cavern	charter	Accent in 2nd		
fatal	waiter	decay	daddy	manage	larva		Accent in 2nd	
ladle	traitor	dismay	gallop	vanish	garland	repair		
navy	mailbox	delay	massive	travel	parcel	despair	nightmare	
basic	maybe	portray	attach	satin	barber	unfair	prepare	
flavor	player	mistake	napkin	tragic	starchy	impair	compare	
data	crayon	parade	basket	falcon	charter	affair	beware	
crater	mayor	amaze	fabric	shadow	garlic		aware	
savor	payment	vibrate	plastic		margin		declare	
raking	prayer	replace	master		hardly		airfare	
labor	layer	dictate	cactus		partner		fanfare	
vacant	crayfish	crusade	chapter		bargain		hardware	
radar	bracelet	debate	canyon		carbon			
	pavement	behave	capture		farther		*Oddballs*	
Oddballs	basement	cascade	tadpole		jargon		toward	
any*	baseball	escape	ambush		scarlet		lizard	
many*	grateful	disgrace	lantern		parlor			
water	graceful	erase	scamper		sharpen			
	safety	essay	canvas		sparkle			
	statement	foray	package		target			
			tablet		tarnish			
		Oddballs			harbor			
		again*			partial			
		captain			marshal			
		bargain			martyr			
		postage			garbage			
					warfare			

Copyright © 2011 Pearson Education Inc. Reproduction is permitted for classroom use only.

o Patterns in Stressed Syllables

VCV open			VCCV	VCV closed			
Long *o* Accent in 1st robot	Long *o* Accent in 1st toaster blowhole	Long *o* Accent in 2nd alone	Short *o* Accent in 1st cobweb	Short *o* Accent in 1st robin	*or* Accent in 1st corner	*wor* Accent in 1st	*ore/oar/our* Accent in 1st boardwalk fourteen
robot	lonely	alone	foggy	robin	morning*	worker	boredom
pony	lonesome	explode	follow	closet	forty	worry	shoreline
chosen	hopeful	erode	copper	comet	stormy	worthy	scoreless
donate	homework	awoke	blossom	promise	story	worship	hoarsely
motor	closely	decode	cottage	honest	corner		coarsely
soda	goalie	enclose	common	modern	border	*war/quar*	hoarding
notice	loafer	dispose	office	solid	torment	warning	sources
sofa	coaster	suppose	hollow	topic	forest	warden	fourteen
frozen	toaster	compose	nozzle	volume	fortress	warrior	pouring
local	coastal	remote	bottle	body	shortage	wardrobe	mournful
moment	soapy	unload	comma	novel	torrent	quarrel	foursome
rodent	roadway	approach	cotton	profit	tortoise		courtroom
grocer	owner	afloat	hobby	chocolate	portrait		
potion	bowling	below	yonder		forfeit		Accent in 2nd
ocean	rowboat	bestow	popcorn	*Oddballs*	shorter		
rotate	snowfall	aglow	contest	wonder	order*		before*
hoping	mower	disown	costume	dolphin	normal		ignore
stolen	slowly	enroll	doctor	dozen	northern		restore
solar	towboat	behold	bonfire	oven	forward		explore
	soldier	revolt	bother	shovel	corncob		galore
Oddballs	poster	almost	cobweb	stomach	chorus		aboard
hotel	hostess		conquer	Europe	florist		ashore
only*	postage		problem	sorry	boring		adore
	smolder		posture		sporty		
	molten		monster				
	molding		congress		Accent in 2nd		
	folder						
					report		
					record		
					perform		
					inform		
					afford		
					reform		
					absorb		
					abhor		
					adorn		

Copyright © 2011 Pearson Education Inc. Reproduction is permitted for classroom use only.

i Patterns in Stressed Syllables

VCV open			VCCV	VCV				
Long *i* Accent in 1st pilot	Long *i* Accent in 1st ninety highway	Long *i* Accent in 2nd	Short *i* Accent in 1st ribbon	Short *i* Accent in 1st city	*ir* Accent in 1st birdhouse	*ire* Accent in 1st firefly	*y = i* Accent in 1st python	VV
pilot	ninety	polite	into*	finish	thirty	tiresome	typist	lion
silent	driveway	surprise	kitten	limit	firmly	firefly	dryer	dial
diner	sidewalk	decide	dipper	river	dirty	direful	flyer	diet
writer	iceberg	advice	slipper	lizard	birthday		hydrant	riot
tiger	lively	survive	mitten	timid	thirsty	Accent	bypass	pliers
siren	mighty	combine	dinner	visit	birdbath	in 2nd	nylon	diary
pirate	slightly	arrive	silly	given	circle	require	stylish	vial
private	frighten	invite	skinny	city	circus	rehire	rhyming	
spiral	lightning	describe	ribbon	sliver	stirring	attire	python	
biker	highway	divide	pillow	civil	firmly	inquire	cycle	
spider	brightly	excite	dizzy	digit	virtue	expire	tryout	
visor	higher	provide	chilly	prison	stirrup	desire	cyclone	
minus	nightmare	confide	bitter	wizard	twirler	perspire	hybrid	
rival	tighten	recline	minnow	quiver	skirmish	admire	hyphen	
bison	fighter	ignite	blizzard	figure	circuit	inspire	tyrant	
item	highlight	despite	tissue		irksome	entire	skyline	
Friday	sightsee	oblige	mixture	*Oddballs*	whirlpool	acquire	hygiene	
sinus	blindfold	divine	ignite	machine	chirping	retire		
slimy	kindness	tonight	tissue	forgive	flirting		Accent	
icy	climber	resign	mixture	liter			in 2nd	
climax	wildcat	design	fifty	mirror			defy	
	wildlife	delight	picnic	pizza			July	
		remind	picture	guitar			apply	
		rewind	chimney	spirit			rely	
		unkind	frisky				imply	
			windy				supply	
			signal				reply	
			sister					
			whimper					
			finger					
			winter					
			kidnap					
			jigsaw					
			window					

Copyright © 2011 Pearson Education Inc. Reproduction is permitted for classroom use only.

u Patterns in Stressed Syllables

VCV open			VCCV	VCV			
Long *u* Accent in 1st human	Long *u* Accent in 1st chewy	Long *u* Accent in 2nd conclude balloon	Short *u* Accent in 1st button	Short *u* Accent in 1st upon	*ur* Accent in 1st turtle	*ure* Accent in 2nd	VV
super	useful	amuse	supper	upon*	sturdy	secure	fuel
music	Tuesday	misuse	button	study	purpose	assure	cruel
ruby	juicy	confuse	funny*	punish	further	endure	annual
tuna	chewy	reduce	sudden	suburb	hurry	impure	casual
truly	dewdrop	conclude	tunnel	pumice	purple	mature	
pupil	jewel	dilute	puppet		turtle	unsure	
rumor	pewter	exclude	buddy		furnish	obscure	
human	skewer	include	butter		Thursday	manure	
humid	sewage	pollute	fuzzy		blurry	brochure	
future	poodle	excuse	guppy		turkey		
tutor	rooster	resume	puzzle		current		
tumor	moody	compute	under*		purchase		
futile	doodle	abuse	husband		burger		
student	noodle	perfume	lumber		furry		
tuba	scooter	protrude	number		murky		
tulip	toothache	salute	public		mural		
unit		dispute	Sunday		surfer		
ruler	*Oddballs*	askew	thunder		burden		
July	cougar	cartoon	trumpet		bureau		
	beauty	raccoon	umpire		burrow		
	cousin	lagoon	under		curfew		
		shampoo	hundred		hurdle		
		balloon	mumble		jury		
		baboon	lucky		murmur		
		cocoon	hungry		turnip		
		maroon	bucket		burner		
		tattoo	bundle		gurgle		

APPENDIX D

Copyright © 2011 Pearson Education Inc. Reproduction is permitted for classroom use only.

e Patterns in Stressed Syllables

VCV open

Long *e* Accent in 1st

even
female
fever
legal
meter
recent
depot
cedar
detour
veto
prefix
tepee
decent
preview
prefix
evil

Long *e* Accent in 1st — cheetah, easel

needle
freedom
freezer
breezy
cheetah
steeple
tweezers
beetle
feeble
greedy
sweeten
beaver
eager
easy
easel
season
reason
reader
feature
creature
meaning
eastern
bleachers
cleaner
eager
treaty
neatly
peanut
weasel
greasy

Long *e* Accent in 2nd

succeed
indeed
fifteen
thirteen
canteen
agree
degree
between
proceed
asleep
delete
supreme
trapeze
compete
extreme
stampede
deplete
recede
convene
mislead
disease
increase
defeat
repeat
conceal
ideal
reveal
ordeal
appeal
mislead

Long *ie* Accent in 1st — diesel

briefly
diesel

Accent in 2nd

believe
achieve
retrieve
relief
besiege
apiece
relieve
belief

Long *ei* Accent in 1st — ceiling

either
leisure
seizure
neither
ceiling

Accent in 2nd

receive
perceive
receipt
deceive
conceive
caffeine

VCCV

Short *e* Accent in 1st — tennis

better
letter*
fellow
tennis
message
penny
beggar
effect
respect
pencil
dentist
center
helmet
reptile
rescue
seldom
sentence
temper
twenty
welcome
velvet
pesky

Oddballs

people
hearty
pretty
cherry

VCV

Short *e* Accent in 1st — seven

select
medal
metal
level
lever
never
debit
denim
lemon
melon
memo
pedal
petal
seven*
clever
credit

Short *ea*

feather
heavy
steady
ready
leather
weather
pleasant
sweater
healthy
weapon
sweaty
heaven

er = *ur* Accent in 1st — mermaid

person
perfect
nervous
sermon
serpent
hermit
thermos
kernel
perky
permit
serene
sherbet
gerbil
mermaid
certain
merchant
version

ear = *ur*

early
earnings
earthworm
pearly
earnest
yearning
rehearse
research

eer/ear/ere Accent in 1st — yearbook

eerie
deerskin
cheerful
earache
fearful
earmuff
spearmint
yearbook
dreary
bleary
clearly
nearby
hearsay
teardrop
weary
merely
clearing
dearest

Accent in 2nd

career
appear
overhear
endear
adhere
austere
cashmere
revere
severe
sincere

VV

neon
create

Copyright © 2011 Pearson Education Inc. Reproduction is permitted for classroom use only.

Ambiguous Vowels in Stressed Syllables

oy/ oi
Accent in 1st
royal
poison

voyage
loyal
joyful
boycott
royal
soybean
oyster
moisture
poison
noisy
pointed
toilet

Accent in 2nd

annoy
enjoy
employ
destroy
ahoy
appoint
avoid
exploit
rejoice

ow
powder

powder
power
flower
prowler
coward
tower
drowsy
brownie
rowdy
chowder
vowel
dowdy
towel
shower
cowboy
powwow
drowning

ou
mountain

county
counter
thousand
fountain
mountain
council
lousy
scoundrel
bounty
boundary
founder
doubtful
southeast
voucher
cloudy
flounder
trousers

Accent in 2nd

about*
without
around*
announce
amount
profound

ou = short *u*
couple

trouble
double
southern
couple
cousin
touched
younger
youngster
moustache

ou = Long *u*
toucan

routine
toucan
youthful
coupon
cougar
crouton
acoustics

au
author

saucer
author
August
autumn
laundry
caution
faucet
sausage
auction
haunted
cauldron
gaudy
daughter
jaunty
naughty
slaughter
trauma
pauper

Accent in 2nd

because*

aw
macaw

awful
awkward
lawyer
awesome
awfully
gnawing
gawking
flawless
drawing
jawbone
lawless
tawny
yawning
clawed

al
hallway

also*
always*
almost
already
although
halter
salty
balky
balmy
calmly
falter
halting
hallway
waltzing

Oddballs
laughed
all right
balloon
gallon

Copyright © 2011 Pearson Education Inc. Reproduction is permitted for classroom use only.

Final Unstressed Syllables

-al naval	*-il/ile* fossil	*-el* angel	*-le* angle		*-et* planet	*-it* rabbit
central	April	angel	little*	people*	basket	audit
crystal	civil	barrel	able	hurdle	blanket	bandit
cymbal	council	bagel	ample	hustle	bucket	credit
dental	evil	bushel	angle	juggle	budget	digit
fatal	fossil	camel	ankle	jungle	carpet	edit
feudal	gerbil	cancel	apple	kettle	closet	exit
final	lentil	channel	battle	knuckle	comet	habit
focal	nostril	chapel	beagle	maple	cricket	hermit
formal	pencil	diesel	beetle	middle	faucet	limit
global	peril	flannel	bottle	needle	fidget	merit
journal	pupil	funnel	bramble	noodle	gadget	orbit
legal	stencil	gravel	bridle	noble	hatchet	profit
mammal	tonsil	hazel	bubble	paddle	helmet	rabbit
medal	docile	jewel	buckle	pebble	hornet	spirit
mental	facile	kennel	bundle	pickle	jacket	summit
metal	fertile	kernel	bugle	purple	locket	unit
nasal	fragile	label	candle	puzzle	magnet	visit
naval	futile	level	castle	riddle	midget	vomit
neutral	hostile	model	cattle	saddle	planet	
normal	missile	morsel	cable	sample	poet	
oval	mobile	nickel	chuckle	scribble	puppet	
pedal	sterile	novel	circle	settle	racket	
petal		panel	cradle	single	scarlet	
plural		parcel	cripple	steeple	secret	
rascal		quarrel	cuddle	struggle	skillet	
rival		ravel	cycle	stumble	sonnet	
royal		satchel	dimple	tackle	tablet	
rural		sequel	doodle	tickle	target	
sandal		shovel	double	title	thicket	
scandal		shrivel	eagle	triple	toilet	
signal		squirrel	fable	trouble	trumpet	
spiral		swivel	fiddle	twinkle	velvet	
tidal		tinsel	freckle	turtle	wallet	
total		towel	fumble	waffle		
vandal		travel	gamble	whistle		
vital		tunnel	gargle	wrinkle		
vocal		vessel	gentle			
		vowel	grumble			
			handle			

Copyright © 2011 Pearson Education Inc. Reproduction is permitted for classroom use only.

er number			*er* Agents barber	*er* Comparatives taller	*ar* circular	*or* doctor	
other*	poster	bother	jogger	bigger	beggar	color*	rumor
under*	printer	center	dreamer	cheaper	burglar	actor	mirror
better*	shower	copper	dancer	cleaner	scholar	author	horror
never*	timber	drawer	speaker	farther	cellar	doctor	humor
over*	toaster	finger	teacher	quicker	cedar	editor	meteor
mother*	trouser	prayer	skater	slower	cheddar	mayor	motor
another*	ladder	power	marcher	younger	collar	neighbor	razor
banner	counter	powder	shopper	older	cougar	sailor	scissors
blister	prefer	proper	racer	flatter	dollar	tailor	splendor
border	crater	quiver	grocer	plainer	grammar	traitor	sponsor
clover	cancer	roller	barber	lighter	hangar	tutor	terror
cluster	cider	rubber	peddler	darker	lunar	visitor	tractor
fiber	scorcher	sander	plumber	weaker	solar	donor	tremor
freezer	ledger	saucer	ranger	stronger	molar	armor	vapor
liter	stretcher	scooter	soldier	wilder	polar	error	cursor
litter	pitcher	shaver	usher	sweeter	sugar	favor	honor
lumber	answer		voter	cooler	nectar	anchor	
manner	blender		catcher	braver	pillar		

ture = /chər/ nature			*ch* + *er* teacher	/shoor/	/yoor/	/zhər/	/jər/
culture	nurture	mature	archer	assure	endure	leisure	conjure
capture	rapture	mixture	catcher	ensure	failure	measure	injure
creature	sculpture	moisture	butcher	insure	obscure	closure	procedure
denture	stature	picture	fetcher	pressure	secure	pleasure	
feature	stricture	pasture	pitcher	fissure	manicure	treasure	
fixture	texture	posture	launcher	brochure	insecure		
fracture	tincture	puncture	marcher	enclosure	figure	*Oddballs*	
future	torture	nature	poacher	exposure		senior	
gesture	venture	furniture	preacher	reassure		danger	
juncture	adventure	miniature	rancher	composure			
lecture	departure	premature	sketcher	disclosure			
	immature	signature	snatcher				
			researcher				

ain mountain	*an* woman	*en*–Verb sharpen	*en*–Noun chicken	*en*–Adj golden	*in* cabin	*on* apron	
again*	human	frighten	chicken	golden	basin	apron	bacon
captain	organ	listen	children	often	cabin	button	carton
certain	orphan	sharpen	garden	open*	cousin	cannon	cotton
curtain	slogan	shorten	kitten	rotten	margin	common	gallon
fountain	urban	sweeten	mitten	spoken	pumpkin	dragon	lemon
mountain	woman*	thicken	women	sunken	raisin	wagon	lesson
villain		widen	heaven	swollen	robin	pardon	prison
bargain		deafen	oxygen	wooden	dolphin	person	poison
chieftain		flatten	siren	broken	muffin	reason	ribbon
		lengthen	linen	hidden	penguin	season	weapon
		open*		chosen	satin	salmon	

(continued)

Copyright © 2011 Pearson Education Inc. Reproduction is permitted for classroom use only.

Final Unstressed Syllables *(continued)*

/ij/ baggage		/əs/ office	/əs/ necklace	*ey* monkey	*ie* birdie	*y* daisy	
voyage	sausage	justice	furnace	chimney	cookie	very*	berry
bandage	cabbage	practice	surface	donkey	movie	pretty*	body
village	rummage	service	palace	turkey	brownie	early	beauty
message	savage	office	necklace	jockey	genie	crazy	drowsy
cottage	passage	crevice	menace	valley	goalie	candy	empty
wreckage	image	notice	grimace	volley	sweetie	daisy	guilty
courage	marriage	novice	terrace	journey	zombie	forty	tidy
storage	manage	bodice		honey	birdie	envy	treaty
luggage	sewage	crisis	*Oddballs*	money*	eerie	worry	carry*
damage	language	tennis	lettuce	jersey	bootie	gravy	bossy
postage		axis	porpoise	pulley	rookie	sorry	trophy
garbage	*Oddballs*	basis	tortoise	hockey	pinkie	dizzy	stingy
hostage	knowledge	iris		galley	prairie	cherry	bury
	cartridge						

Prefixes and Suffixes

mis- misuse	*pre-* preschool	*re-* rebuild	*un-* unhappy	*dis-* disappear	*in-* "not" incorrect	*non-* nonflammable
misbehave	precook	rebound	unable	disable	incomplete	nonsense
misconduct	predate	recall	unafraid	disagreeable	incorrect	nonstop
miscount	prefix	recapture	unarmed	disappear	indecent	nonfiction
misdeed	pregame	recharge	unbeaten	disarm	indirect	nonfat
misfit	preheat	reclaim	unbroken	discharge	inexpensive	nonprofit
misgivings	prejudge	recopy	uncertain	disclose	inflexible	nondairy
misguide	premature	recount	unclean	discolor	informal	nonstick
misjudge	prepay	recycle	unclear	discomfort	inhuman	nonviolent
mislay	preschool	reelect	uncommon	discontent	injustice	nonskid
mislead	preset	refill	uncover	discover	insane	nonstandard
mismatch	preteen	refinish	undone	dishonest	invalid	
misplace	pretest	reform	unequal	disinfect	invisible	
misprint	preview	refresh	unfair	dislike		
misspell	prewash	relearn	unkind	disloyal	*in-* "in" or "into" infield	
mistake	predict	remind	unlike	disobey	indent	
mistreat	precede	remodel	unlock	disorder	indoor	
mistrust	prehistoric	renew	unpack	displace	inset	
misuse	prepare	reorder	unreal	disregard	insight	
	prevent	repay	unripe	disrespect	inside	
	precaution	reprint	unselfish	distaste	income	
	preschool	research	unstable	distrust	inmate	
		restore	unsteady	different	ingrown	
		retrace	untangle	diffuse	inboard	
		return	untie	diffident	inland	
		review	unwrap		infield	
		rewrite			inlaid	

 Copyright © 2011 Pearson Education Inc. Reproduction is permitted for classroom use only.

uni- unicycle	*bi-* bicycle	*tri-* tricycle	*fore-* forehead	*sub-* subway	*ex-* exit	*en-* enjoy
unicorn	biceps	triangle	forearm	subset	expel	enable
unicycle	bicycle	triple	forecast	subtract	express	endanger
uniform	bifocals	triceps	foretell	subdivide	explore	enact
unify	bilingual	triceratops	foresee	subgroup	exceed	enclose
union	binoculars	tricycle	foresight	submerge	excerpt	encourage
unique	bisect	trilogy	forehand	submarine	exclaim	enforce
unison	biweekly	trio	forehead	submerse	exclude	enjoy
universal		trivet	foreman	submit	excrete	enslave
universe		triplets	forethought	subway	exhale	enlarge
		tripod	foreshadow	subtotal	exile	enlist
		triad	forepaw	subtitle	expand	enrage
		trinity	foremost	sublet	explode	enrich
		trident		subsoil	exit	enroll
		triathlon		subject		entrust

-ly deadly	*-y* bumpy	*-er/-est* taller/tallest	*-less* helpless	*-ful* colorful	*-ness* kindness
badly	breezy	blacker/blackest	ageless	careful	awareness
barely	bumpy	bigger/biggest	breathless	cheerful	closeness
bravely	chilly	bolder/boldest	careless	colorful	coolness
closely	choppy	braver/bravest	ceaseless	fearful	darkness
coarsely	cloudy	calmer/calmest	endless	graceful	firmness
constantly	dirty	closer/closest	helpless	harmful	goodness
costly	dusty	cheaper/cheapest	homeless	hopeful	openness
cowardly	easy	cleaner/cleanest	lawless	lawful	ripeness
cruelly	floppy	cooler/coolest	painless	peaceful	sickness
deadly	frosty	colder/coldest	powerless	playful	sharpness
directly	gloomy	smaller/smallest	priceless	powerful	stiffness
eagerly	greasy	thinner/thinnest	reckless	tasteful	stillness
finally	grouchy	fewer/fewest	spotless	thoughtful	thinness
frequently	gritty	finer/finest	tasteless	truthful	weakness
loudly	noisy	hotter/hottest	speechless	useful	moistness
loyally	rainy	harder/hardest	thankless	wasteful	vastness
proudly	sandy	sadder/saddest	cloudless	wonderful	dullness
really	soapy	newer/newest	fruitless	youthful	
smoothly	snowy	quicker/quickest	jobless	beautiful	
kindly	stormy	lighter/lightest	scoreless	armful	
nicely	sweaty	louder/loudest	sleeveless	dreadful	
nightly	thirsty	larger/largest		respectful	
safely	windy	meaner/meanest			
	dressy	longer*/longest			
	skinny				
	speedy				

Change *y* to *i* easily	Change *y* to *i* happier/happiest	Change *y* to *i*	Change *y* to *i* happiness
lazily	noisier/noisiest	penniless	emptiness
angrily	prettier/prettiest	pitiless	laziness
busily	dirtier/dirtiest	merciless	readiness
easily	easier/easiest		fussiness
happily	juicier/juiciest		dizziness
noisily	lazier/laziest		ugliness
	funnier/funniest		happiness

Copyright © 2011 Pearson Education Inc. Reproduction is permitted for classroom use only.

APPENDIX D

Special Consonants

Hard *g* gorilla	Soft *g* giraffe	Hard *c* cabin	Soft *c* city	Final *c* picnic	*que* antique	*k / ke* homework	*ck* hammock	Silent Letters wrinkle
gadget	genie	cabin	city	attic	antique	namesake	attack	wrinkle
gallon	genius	cafe	cider	music	unique	cupcake	carsick	wreckage
gallop	genre	cactus	civil	topic	clique	earthquake	gimmick	wrestle
gamble	general	campus	cinder	zodiac	opaque	forsake	haddock	answer
garage	gentle	candle	circle	clinic	critique	keepsake	hemlock	knuckle
gully	gerbil	canyon	circus	comic	physique	mistake	potluck	knowledge
golden	gesture	cavern	citric	cynic	mystique	pancake	hammock	honest
gossip	giant	carpet	cedar	toxic	brusque	provoke	ransack	honor
guilty	ginger	cable	celery	panic		slowpoke	padlock	rhyme
gorilla	giraffe	comma	cement	picnic	***x***	turnpike		rhythm
gopher	gyro	copy	census	classic	relax	evoke		shepherd
gather	gypsy	cozy	center	critic	complex	homework		castle
gutter	gyrate	cocoa	cereal	elastic	index	embark		whistle
guitar		comet	ceiling	exotic	perplex	landmark		fasten
gobble		coffee	certain	frantic		network		listen
goggles		corner	cycle	graphic		berserk		often*
gaily		county	cynic	hectic				moisten
gallery		cubic	cymbal	garlic				daughter
		cuddle	cyclist	fabric				naughty
Oddballs		culprit	cyclone	frolic				height
giggle		curtain	cylinder	logic				weight
geyser		custom		drastic				freight
gecko				scenic				design
								resign
								gnaw
								gnarl
								gnome
								gnostic
								gnu

Copyright © 2011 Pearson Education Inc. Reproduction is permitted for classroom use only.

APPENDIX E

Creating Your Own Word Sorts

Guidelines

You can use the word lists in Appendix D to help you create sorts. Prepare word sorts by writing the selected words on a template such as the one on page 308. Many people find it easy to create computer-generated word sort sheets using the "table" function in a word processing program. The following tips may be helpful. First, set the margins all around at 0.5, and then insert a table to fit your column and row needs. Type in a word in each cell, leaving a blank line before and after each word. After typing all words, "select" the entire table and click on the "center" button. Choose a simple font (Arial and Geneva work well) and a large font size (26 works well).

Tips for Word Sorts

1. Create sorts that will help your students form generalizations about how words work. Use a collection of 15 to 25 words so that there are plenty of examples to consider.
2. Contrast at least two and up to four features in a sort. The sample sorts in this appendix will give you ideas.
3. You can also include up to three oddballs—words that have the same sound or pattern but are not consistent with the generalization that governs the other words. For example, in a long *o* sort, with words sorted by the *oa*, *o*-consonant-*e*, and *ow* patterns, the oddballs might include the words *now* and *love* because they look like they would have the long *o* sound but do not. The best oddballs are high-frequency words students might already know from reading. High-frequency words from Fry's instant word lists are marked with asterisks under "Oddballs" in the word lists in Appendix D.
4. Words in a sort can be made easier or harder in a number of ways.
   - Common words like *pain* or *store* are easier than uncommon words like *reign* or *boar.*
   - Add words with blends, digraphs, and complex consonant units (i.e., *brace, shock, scrap*) to make words harder.
   - Adding more oddballs to a sort makes the sort harder. Oddballs should not, however, constitute more than about 20 percent of the words in a sort or students might fail to see the generalizations that govern the majority of words.

The sample word sorts on the following pages are arranged sequentially by spelling stage and can be used with many of the activities described in the instructional chapters. Several points need to be made considering the use of these sorts.

- These sorts are not intended to be a sequence for all students. Chapter 3 will help you match your students to the stages of spelling. There are additional suggestions in Chapters 4 and 5 about the pacing and sequencing of word study for each stage. Choose appropriate sorts from among those presented here.
- The following is not an exhaustive list of sorts, but it does give you a starting point for creating your own. You can adapt these sorts by adding, deleting, or substituting words that are more appropriate for your students. Word lists are provided in Appendix D.

Copyright © 2011 Pearson Education Inc. Reproduction is permitted for classroom use only.

Sort Template

Copyright © 2011 Pearson Education Inc. Reproduction is permitted for classroom use only.

Within Word Pattern Sorts

Keywords are in bold and underlined. Asterisk marks the oddball category.

Short/Long *a*

cat	**cake**	*
jack	date	have
ask	race	what
slap	plane	
fast	cape	
lap	page	
flag	same	
pass	safe	
path	gave	
glad	gate	

Short/Long *a*

cat	**cake**	**rain**
last	wave	wait
plan	late	nail
sat	tape	gain
flat	bake	fail
tax	base	pail
	shade	plain
	made	sail
	maze	
	sale	

Short/Long *a* Patterns

cat	**cake**	**rain**	**tray**	*
rack	whale	pain	say	said
pack	flake	train	play	have
rash	grape	paid	may	
cash	stage	brain	pay	
fast	grade	snail	stay	
	chase	chain	clay	
	shave	tail		
	tale	waist		
	waste			

Short/Long e

bed	**sheep**	**me**
step	peel	he
west	weed	we
men	peek	she
well	speed	
help	keep	
belt	week	

Short/Long e

bed	**sheep**	**peach**	*
left	wheel	team	been
neck	sheet	deal	head
bell	need	reach	
bled	bleed	beach	
best	teeth	steam	
	creep	clean	
	speed	bean	

Short/Long e

bed	**bread**	**peach**
rest	dead	meal
bell	deaf	speak
kept	breath	meat
nest	death	treat
shell	dread	sneak
vest	head	heat

Short/Long *i*

pig	**bike**	*
chip	ride	give
king	ripe	live
whip	nice	
twin	white	
miss	dime	
dish	fine	
rich	life	

Short/Long *i*

pig	**bike**	**fly**	*
clip	price	try	eye
trick	spine	shy	buy
gift	lime	why	bye
list	wife	sky	
mitt	vine	dry	
thick	five		
swim			

Short/Long o

pot	**bone**	*
odd	slope	move
crop	note	gone
shot	hose	some
clock	vote	
shock	joke	
knob	smoke	
slot	hope	
	choke	

Short/Long o Patterns

pot	**bone**	**boat**	**snow**	*
lock	rope	road	blow	now
rock	woke	toast	grow	cow
flop	close	soap	know	
drop	stone	soak	slow	
cloth	bone	moan	throw	
	phone	loaf	low	
	broke	coach		
	hole	load		

Short/Long *u*

bug	**cube/June**	**glue**	*
bun	cute	blue	truth
fuss	rule	clue	
luck	tube	due	
lump	tune	true	
trust	huge		
plum			
crust			

Short/Long *u* Patterns

bug	**cube/June**	**fruit**	**stew**	*
dump	rude	suit	new	build
stump	crude	juice	chew	
luck	flute	bruise	drew	
just	mule	cruise	knew	
	fume		few	
	chute		dew	
	dune			
	use			

Less Common Long *a*

tray	**grey**	**vein**	*
hay	prey	eight	break
stray	they	weigh	great
pray	obey	vein	steak
sway	hey	veil	
play		freight	
		sleigh	
		neigh	

r-Controlled *a*

car	**square**	**hair**	*
star	share	pair	bear
bark	bare	air	
card	mare	chair	
far	rare		
dark	scare		
arm	hare		
start			

Less Common Long e

bed	**sheep**	**chief**	*
neck	greed	thief	friend
check	speech	field	
desk	greet	brief	
yell	creek	grief	
best	fleet	shriek	
	geese	piece	
	cheese	niece	

Copyright © 2011 Pearson Education Inc. Reproduction is permitted for classroom use only.

r-Controlled *e*

fern	ear	deer	bear	*
her	near	cheer	wear	heart
berth	clear	sneer	pear	
germ	dear	queer	swear	
jerk	year	peer		
herb	spear			
herd	beard			
perch				

Short/Long *i* Patterns

pig	bike	light	child
kick	kite	might	mind
trick	bride	night	wild
hill	write	right	kind
fill	spice	bright	blind
fist	hide	tight	find
	wipe	sight	grind
	mice		mild

r-Blends/*r*-Controlled *i*

crib	girl	tire
grin	third	hire
bring	shirt	fire
drip	dirt	wire
grill	bird	tired
trick	skirt	
drink		
brick		

Short/Long *o* Patterns

pot	cold		*
soft	roll	ghost	son
moth	cold	most	from
cost	stroll	host	
cross	mold	post	
cloth	scold		
lost	fold		
toss	told		
frost	folk		
long			

r-Controlled *o*

horn	store	door	*
for	more	floor	your
born	swore	poor	
short	chore		
porch	tore		
storm	shore		
north	score		
fort	wore		
torch			

Other Long *u*

zoo	stew	*
gloom	new	who
bloom	grew	to
roost	crew	too
smooth	flew	two
scoop	blew	
school	knew	
mood	dew	
pool		

r-Controlled *u*

curl	cure	earth
hurt	lure	heard
turn	pure	learn
church	sure	earn
burst		pearl
curl		yearn
purr		search
purse		

r-Blends/Vowels

grin	girl
grill	fork
trap	tarp
crush	curl
fry	first
price	purse
track	dark
brag	bark
drip	dirt
frog	fort

r-Controlled Vowels

car	girl/fern	horn
shark	first	short
farm	bird	corn
hard	burn	for
card	word	scorn
yard	worm	torn
scar	world	
march	dirt	
	jerk	
	her	

ck, k, ke

tack	park	cake
lick	leak	like
lack	dark	lake
tack	soak	take
snack	sleek	snake
stuck	weak	stake
stick	week	strike
whack	cork	wake

CVCe Sorts across Vowels

cake	bike	bone	cube/June
cave	drive	drove	huge
crane	while	those	fume
bake	smile	throne	prune
stage	twice	phone	chute
trade	crime	wrote	flute
brace	guide	quote	mule

CVVC across Vowels

boat	chief	rain
road	team	brain
boast	stream	strain
coach	sweet	claim
groan	queen	waist
throat	peach	faith
toast	thief	praise
roast	peace	strain
		trail

Diphthongs

boy	oil	cow	cloud
toy	coin	town	sound
joy	foil	clown	mouth
coy	boil	brown	scout
	spoil	gown	round
	noise	frown	couch
	point	howl	loud

More Diphthongs

snow	cow	cloud
row	owl	out
show	growl	found
blown	drown	shout
flown	crown	mouth
grown	plow	south
thrown	fowl	foul
	prowl	doubt

Ambiguous Vowels

salt	saw	sauce	*
bald	draw	caught	fought
chalk	lawn	cause	ought
stall	raw	taught	
false	crawl	fault	
small	claw	haul	
walk	hawk	pause	

Words Spelled with *w*

wash	war	wren
swamp	warn	wreck
swan	warm	write
wand	dwarf	wrist
swat	swarm	wrap
watch	wart	wrong

Complex Consonants

scrap	street	shrimp
scrape	strange	shrink
scratch	stretch	shred
screech	strict	shrunk
screw	string	shriek
screen	strong	shrank
scram		

ch and *tch*

patch	beach	*
witch	coach	rich
catch	peach	such
fetch	roach	
hutch	screech	
itch	pouch	
switch		
ditch		
latch		

APPENDIX E

Copyright © 2011 Pearson Education Inc. Reproduction is permitted for classroom use only.

ge and dge

bridge	**stage**
ridge	page
edge	huge
fudge	rage
badge	cage
judge	wage
hedge	seize
lodge	

Hard/Soft *c* and *g*

card/goat			**cent/gem**	
cave	coat	cute	cell	cyst
camp	coast	cup	cease	circle
cast	cost	cue	city	germ
gave	gold	gum	gym	giant
gain	golf	gush	gist	
gasp	goof			

ce, ge, ve, se

face	**cage**	**glove**	**mouse**
dance	charge	have	cheese
chance	large	give	please
prince	wedge	curve	tease
fence	dodge	shove	loose
since	ridge	live	choose
voice	edge	above	
juice	change		

Syllables and Affixes Sorts

Keywords are in bold and underlined. Asterisk marks the oddball category.

Sort for Sound of *ed*

trapped	**waited**	**played**
mixed	dotted	mailed
stopped	patted	boiled
chased	treated	raised
cracked	traded	tried
walked	ended	filled
asked	handed	seemed
jumped	needed	yelled

Plural Words (*s* and *es*)

apples	**boxes**		
cows	foxes	buses	dishes
chicks	mixes	glasses	benches
farms	axes	dresses	watches
fences	passes	lashes	gases
gates	ashes	horses	guesses
	brushes		churches

Plurals with *y*

flies	**boys**
carries	monkeys
ponies	plays
bodies	trays
pennies	donkeys
worries	enjoys
babies	turkeys
berries	valleys
parties	

Base Words + *ed* and *ing*

jump	**jumped**	**jumping**
hike	hiked	hiking
dress	dressed	dressing
wait	waited	waiting
stop	stopped	stopping
pass	passed	passing
live	lived	living
wag	wagged	wagging

Adding *ing* (double and e-drop)

wagging	**smiling**
batting	baking
shopping	skating
bragging	biting
hopping	hoping
humming	sliding
begging	waving
skipping	moving
swimming	caring

Adding *ing* (double, e-drop, nothing)

wagging	**smiling**	**jumping**	**sleeping**	*
trimming	diving	pushing	floating	mixing
running	riding	hunting	raining	taxing
popping	sliding	finding	shouting	
dragging	driving	kicking	boating	
bragging	wasting	wanting	waiting	
quitting	whining	munching	cheering	

Past-Tense Verbs

kneel	knelt	chase	chased
teach	taught	mix	mixed
bring	brought	walk	walked
deal	dealt	bake	baked
sweep	swept	shop	shopped
send	sent		
think	thought		
lend	lent		
drink	drank		

Adding *ed* (double, nothing, e-drop)

wagged	**jumped**	**smiled**
slipped	picked	traded
grabbed	called	baked
stopped	tracked	wasted
tripped	peeled	liked
knotted	watched	stared
rubbed	cheered	waved
whizzed	talked	skated
	dreamed	tasted

Adding *ing* to *k* Words (*ck*, e-drop, CVVC, VCk)

tacking	**baking**	**cooking**	**drinking**
sticking	flaking	speaking	banking
tracking	shaking	croaking	shrinking
plucking	smoking	squeaking	asking
wrecking	stroking	hooking	marking
clucking	making	looking	working
quacking	raking	leaking	frisking

Compound Words

land	**down**	**back**
landfill	downtown	backyard
homeland	downstairs	backbone
wasteland	lowdown	backpack
landlord	downcast	backward
landslide	downfall	bareback
landscape	downpour	flashback
landmark	breakdown	piggyback
mainland	countdown	paperback

Closed VCCV and Open VCV

basket	**pilot**
tablet	baby
napkin	human
happen	music
winter	fever
foggy	silent
tennis	duty
sudden	writer
fossil	rival

VCV Open and Closed

pilot	**robin**	*
meter	petal	water
human	rapid	busy
paper	punish	
lazy	magic	
even	shiver	
major	comet	
climate	river	
crater	clever	
clover	proper	
bacon	liquid	

Copyright © 2011 Pearson Education Inc. Reproduction is permitted for classroom use only.

Closed VCCV and Open VCV

rabbit	basket	pilot
funny	picture	solar
summer	expert	navy
pretty	until	nature
dollar	forget	music
butter	napkin	spoken
gossip	canyon	frozen
letter	sister	spider
pattern	army	student

le and el

angle	angel	*
fable	camel	journal
middle	model	pencil
little	gravel	
rattle	motel	
settle	bushel	
cattle	level	
nibble	pretzel	
turtle	travel	
table		

er, ar, or

barber	polar	doctor
bigger	burglar	mayor
freezer	grammar	favor
dreamer	collar	author
faster	dollar	editor
blister	lunar	tractor
jogger	solar	motor
speaker		
skater		
smaller		

er, ar, or

Comparatives	Agents	Things
sweeter	worker	cellar
thinner	teacher	meter
smarter	waiter	river
slower	voter	pillar
younger	actor	anchor
gentler	beggar	vapor
steeper	director	trailer
cheaper	barber	flower
mother		

or, ar, er and Parts of Speech

Noun	Adjective	Comparative Adjective
doctor	lunar	cooler
anchor	solar	cleaner
mirror	proper	braver
motor	similar	slower
tractor		quicker
freezer		older
lumber		lighter
ladder		stronger

Final en/on/in/ain

sharpen	apron	cabin	mountain
hidden	weapon	cousin	captain
heaven	dragon	napkin	fountain
chosen	ribbon	pumpkin	curtain
children	gallon		certain
broken	cotton		

Unaccented First Syllables

afraid	decide	beyond
away	design	begin
another	defend	between
aloud	debate	behave
agree	depend	before
again		beside
awoke		

/j/ Sound

baggage	pigeon	magic
carriage	budget	logic
voyage	agent	engine
message	angel	region
postage	gorgeous	fragile
village	danger	margin
storage	legend	
sausage	gadget	
savage	dungeon	
courage		

Changing y to i

cry	cries	cried
hurry	hurries	hurried
party	parties	partied
empty	empties	emptied
baby	babies	babied
reply	replies	replied
supply	supplies	supplied
carry	carries	carried
fry	fries	fried

Words by Part of Speech

Long i		Long e	
Verb	Noun	Adjective	Adverb
cry	celery	happy	happily
certify	candy	pretty	correctly
apply	gypsy	guilty	clearly
occupy	quarry	angry	safely
rely	country	silly	horribly
try	cemetery		hourly
	category		certainly
	copy		sensibly

Stress in Homographs

re' cord n.	re cord' v.
protest n.	protest v.
conduct n.	conduct v.
subject n.	subject v.
extract n.	extract v.
permit n.	permit v.
insert n.	insert v.
desert n.	desert v.
rebel n.	rebel v.
combat n.	combat v.
conflict n.	conflict v.

Stress in VCCV Words

per' son	hel lo'
welcome	perform
offer	support
expert	survive
harvest	escape
fellow	allow
barber	disturb
tender	suppose
common	attend
urgent	raccoon

Stress in VCV words

pi' lot	e rase'
bison	alone
major	relay
pirate	amaze
climate	remote
agent	away
fever	obey
rated	refuse
dozing	salute
raven	

Long u in Stressed Syllable

bu' gle	a muse'
future	compute
ruby	confuse
rumor	reduce
tulip	perfume
tuna	pollute
tutor	salute
super	excuse
pupil	abuse
ruler	include

Short a/Long a

cabin	bacon
canvas	agent
lantern	basic
package	cradle
tragic	fatal
attic	labor
bandage	vapor
candle	sacred
cannon	April

Copyright © 2011 Pearson Education Inc. Reproduction is permitted for classroom use only.

Patterns for Long *a*

bracelet	rainbow	crayon
debate	explain	layer
mistake	dainty	dismay
amaze	trainer	payment
parade	complain	betray
engage	acquaint	hooray
estate	raisin	decay
escape	refrain	
	painter	

Patterns for Long *u* and *o* Patterns

balloon	pollute	toaster	alone
rooster	useful	goalie	suppose
cartoon	refuse	oatmeal	decode
scooter	amuse	approach	remote
noodle	reduce	loafer	erode
	conclude	rowboat	tadpole
	perfume		lonesome
			explode

Patterns for Long *i*

ninety	highway	*
polite	lightning	believe
decide	delight	
advice	tonight	
invite	alright	
surprise	flashlight	
survive	insight	
divine		

Patterns for Long *e*

cheetah	easel	*
needle	reason	sweater
succeed	eager	
fifteen	increase	
thirteen	defeat	
canteen	season	
steeple	conceal	

Diphthongs in Two Syllables

poison	royal
moisture	joyful
appoint	boycott
pointed	employ
turquoise	soybean
moisten	oyster
pointless	voyage
broiler	annoy
embroider	enjoy
rejoice	destroy
noisy	
avoid	

More Diphthongs in Two Syllables

mountain	powder	*
county	flower	double
council	allow	
lousy	brownie	
fountain	vowel	
mouthful	shower	
scoundrel	towel	
counter	tower	
around	chowder	
bounty	coward	
foundry	drowsy	
	power	
	prowler	
	rowdy	

Words with *ure* and *er (ture, sure, cher)*

nature	treasure	teacher	*
capture	measure	archer	failure
creature	leisure	butcher	injure
fracture	pleasure	preacher	
mixture	closure	stretcher	
pasture		rancher	
texture			
future			

Spelling the /er/ Sound in Stressed and Unstressed Syllables

cer'tain	re verse'	sur prise'	lan'tern
person	observe	perhaps	concert
thirsty	alert	survive	modern
service	prefer	surround	western
hurry	emerge		govern
turkey			

Advanced Homophones

Spelling Change in Stressed Syllable		Spelling Change in Unstressed Syllable	
kernel	colonel	miner	minor
aloud	allowed	patience	patients
cinder	sender	accept	except
morning	mourning	alter	altar
berry	bury	presence	presents
roomer	rumor	council	counsel
incite	insight	hanger	hangar
vary	very	profit	prophet
censor	sensor	lesson	lessen

Prefixes

unhappy	rebuild	disappear
unfair	retell	disagree
unable	replay	distrust
uncover	retrain	disgrace
unkind	return	disarm
undress	reuse	disorder
unplug	research	disobey
unequal	regain	disable
uneven	reword	displaced
unpack	refresh	disloyal
unusual	remodel	dishonest

More Prefixes

preschool	exit	misuse
prepay	explode	misspell
preview	exceed	mistreat
prevent	expose	misplace
preheat	explore	mistrust
prefix	exile	misbehave
prepare	expand	mistake
predict	exclaim	

Number Prefixes

unicycle	bicycle	tricycle
unison	biweekly	trilogy
unicorn	bisect	triangle
unique	bilingual	tripod
uniform	biplane	triple
universe	bifocals	trio
union		triplets

Suffixes

kindness	helpless	colorful
darkness	harmless	armful
coolness	fearless	faithful
illness	homeless	dreadful
weakness	restless	thankful
freshness	ageless	thoughtful
hardness	mindless	painful
blindness	jobless	hopeful

More Suffixes

bumpy	deadly	easily
breezy	barely	lazily
frosty	fondly	angrily
dirty	finally	happily
sandy	kindly	busily
thirsty	nicely	noisily
windy	really	
speedy	proudly	
stormy		

APPENDIX E

Copyright © 2011 Pearson Education Inc. Reproduction is permitted for classroom use only.

Within Word Pattern Sample Sorts

Short *a* cat	Long *a* cake (*a-e*)	*r*-Controlled *a* car (*ar*)
CVC	*CVCe*	*CVr*
mask	make	chart
task	lane	cart
trap	tame	star
snap	cane	march
crash	game	starch
back	shake	part
Oddballs		
war	have	what

Long *o* snow (*ow*)	Other *o* cloud (*ou*)	Other *o* cow (*ow*)
CVV	*CVVC*	*CVV*
flown	sound	clown
grown	round	town
grow	found	growl
blow	pouch	prowl
mow	couch	plow
show	mouth	sow
Oddballs		
could	should	would

Copyright © 2011 Pearson Education Inc. Reproduction is permitted for classroom use only.

Syllables and Affixes Sample Sorts

V-CV Open	VC-CV Closed	VC-CV Closed
pi-lot	rab-bit	bas-ket
	doublet	*regular*
paper	tennis	after
robot	copper	under
female	valley	sister
pupil	butter	Sunday
fiber	hammer	winter
open	attic	napkin
fever	foggy	dentist
music	better	center

-ey Ending	*-y* Ending	*-ie* Ending
monkey	daisy	cookie
donkey	very	movie
turkey	early	genie
valley	crazy	brownie
honey	candy	goalie
money	forty	birdie
hockey	envy	eerie
galley	worry	prairie
jockey	carry	rookie

Copyright © 2011 Pearson Education Inc. Reproduction is permitted for classroom use only.

APPENDIX F

Word and Root Lists for Generative Activities and Word Sorts

This appendix presents lists of words that share common prefixes, suffixes, and roots (Templeton et al., 2010). These lists are particularly helpful for English/language arts teachers planning generative vocabulary instruction. They can also be very useful for content teachers as a resource in identifying roots that are common to particular content areas.

Prepare word sorts by writing the selected words on a word sort templates such as found in Appendix E on page 308. We recommend that you enlarge it 5 to 8 percent before writing in the words neatly. Many people find it easy to create computer-generated word sort sheets using the "table" function in a word processing program. The following tips may be helpful. First, set the margins all around at 0.5, and then insert at table that is three columns by six to eight rows. Type words in each cell, leaving a blank line before and after each word. After typing in all words, "select" the entire table and click on the "center" button. Choose a simple font (Arial and Geneva work well) and a large font size (26 works well). After creating the sort, save it using a name that defines the features, such as "Prefix Sort—*uni-, bi-, tri-*." You can contrast spelling patterns, prefixes, suffixes, and roots. For example, you can contrast words with the prefixes *sub-* (*subtract*), *un* (*uncertain*), and *trans-* (*transport*) or contrast words derived from the roots *aer* (*aerodynamic*) and *geo* (*geothermal*). Create a template that you can use each time.

Tips for Creating Word Sorts

1. Create sorts that will help students form their own generalizations about how words work. Use a collection of 15 to 25 words so that there are plenty of examples to consider.
2. Contrast at least two and up to four features in a sort (for example, contrasting words that share three different roots in a sort—*spect, port,* and *aud*).
3. Use a variety of activities to work with the words in the sort: (1) sorting, (2) analyzing, and (3) generating words over the course of a two-week unit of study. Refer to Chapter 6 for generative vocabulary activities that your students can use to examine the words. In grades 4 through 12, two weeks is usually a sufficient amount of time to examine words in some depth. Chapter 8, Vocabulary Assessment and Organization, presents a sample two-week schedule of generative vocabulary activities (see p. 259).

Prefixes and Suffixes

uni-	*bi-*	*tri-*	*fore-*	*sub-*	*ex-*	*en-*
unicorn	biceps	triangle	forearm	subset	expel	enable
unicycle	bicycle	triple	forecast	subtract	express	endanger
uniform	bifocals	triceps	foretell	subdivide	explore	enact
unify	bilingual	triceratops	foresee	subgroup	exceed	enclose
union	binoculars	tricycle	foresight	submerge	excerpt	encourage
unique	bisect	trilogy	forehand	submarine	exclaim	enforce
unison	biweekly	trio	forehead	submerse	exclude	enjoy
universal		trivet	foreman	subway	excrete	enslave
universe		triplets	forethought	subtotal	exhale	enlarge
		tripod	foreshadow	subtitle	exile	enlist
		triad	forepaw	sublet	expand	enrage
		trinity	foremost	subsoil	explode	enrich
		triathlon		subject	exit	entrust

Copyright © 2011 Pearson Education Inc. Reproduction is permitted for classroom use only.

mis-	*pre-*	*re-*	*un-*	*dis-*	*in-* = "not"	*non-*
misbehave	precook	rebound	unable	disable	incomplete	nonsense
misconduct	predate	recall	unafraid	disagreeable	incorrect	nonstop
miscount	prefix	recapture	unarmed	disappear	indecent	nonfiction
misdeed	pregame	recharge	unbeaten	disarm	indirect	nonfat
misfit	preheat	reclaim	unbroken	discharge	inexpensive	nonprofit
misgivings	prejudge	recopy	uncertain	disclose	inflexible	nondairy
misguide	premature	recount	unclean	discolor	informal	nonstick
misjudge	prepay	recycle	unclear	discomfort	inhuman	nonviolent
mislay	preschool	reelect	uncommon	discontent	injustice	nonskid
mislead	preset	refill	uncover	discover	insane	nonstandard
mismatch	preteen	refinish	undone	dishonest	invalid	
misplace	pretest	reform	unequal	disinfect	invisible	
misprint	preview	refresh	unfair	dislike		
misspell	prewash	relearn	unkind	disloyal	***in-* = "in" or "into"**	
mistake	predict	remind	unlike	disobey	income	
mistreat	precede	remodel	unlock	disorder	indent	
mistrust	prehistoric	renew	unpack	displace	indoor	
misuse	prepare	reorder	unreal	disregard	inset	
	prevent	repay	unripe	disrespect	insight	
	precaution	reprint	unselfish	distaste	inside	
	preschool	research	unstable	distrust	inlaid	
		restore	unsteady	different	inmate	
		retrace	untangle	diffuse	ingrown	
		return	untie	diffident	inboard	
		review	unwrap		inland	
		rewrite			infield	

Adding the suffix *-able/-ible*

Root word + *-ible*	Base word + *-able*	e-drop + *-able*	*-y* to *-i* + *-able*	Drop *-ate* in base	Oddballs (*ce/ge*)
audible	affordable	achievable	variable	tolerable	manageable
credible	agreeable	admirable	reliable	vegetable	enforceable
edible	allowable	adorable	pliable	operable	noticeable
eligible	avoidable	advisable	pitiable	navigable	changeable
feasible	breakable	believable	justifiable	abominable	
gullible	comfortable	comparable	identifiable	negotiable	
horrible	dependable	conceivable	deniable	educable	
invincible	expandable	consumable	enviable	estimable	
legible	favorable	debatable	remediable	irritable	
plausible	laughable	deplorable		appreciable	
possible	payable	desirable			
terrible	preferable	disposable			
visible	predictable	excitable			
indelible	profitable	lovable			
intangible	punishable	notable			
compatible	reasonable	pleasurable			
combustible	refillable	recyclable			
	remarkable	valuable			
	respectable				
	transferable				

Copyright © 2011 Pearson Education Inc. Reproduction is permitted for classroom use only.

Adding *-ant/-ance/-ancy* and *-ent/-ence/-ency*

-ant	*-ance*	*-ancy*
abundant	abundance	abundancy
relevant	relevance	relevancy
hesitant	hesitance	hesitancy
extravagant	extravagance	extravagancy
malignant	malignance	malignancy
petulant	petulance	petulancy
radiant	radiance	radiancy
brilliant	brilliance	brilliancy
relevant	relevance	relevancy
defiant	defiance	
reluctant	reluctance	
exuberant	exuberance	
fragrant	fragrance	
instant	instance	
elegant	elegance	
vigilant	vigilance	
resistant	resistance	
significant	significance	
tolerant	tolerance	
observant	observance	

-ent	*-ence*	*-ency*
competent	competence	competency
dependent	dependence	dependency
emergent	emergence	emergency
equivalent	equivalence	equivalency
excellent	excellence	excellency
expedient	expedience	expediency
lenient	lenience	leniency
resident	residence	residency
resilient	resilience	resiliency
violent	violence	
convenient	convenience	
different	difference	
diligent	diligence	
evident	evidence	
impatient	impatience	
independent	independence	
patient	patience	
innocent	innocence	
intelligent	intelligence	
obedient	obedience	
indulgent	indulgence	

Prefixes

***anti-* (against)**
antifreeze
antidote
antitoxin
antibiotic
anticlimactic
antisocial
antigen
antipathy
antiseptic

***auto-* (self)**
autograph
automation
autobiography
automobile
autocrat
autonomy
autopsy

***circum-* (around)**
circumference
circumvent
circumstance
circumspect
circumscribe
circumlocution
circumnavigate

***inter-* (between)**
interact
international
interfere
interloper
interchange
interject
interrupt
intercede
intermission

***intra-* (within)**
intramural
intravenous
intrastate
intracellular
intranational

***mal-* (bad)**
malice
malignant
maltreated
malpractice
maladjusted
malnutrition
malcontent
malfunction
malady

***peri-* (around)**
perimeter
period
periphery
periscope
peripatetic
periodontal

***post-* (after)**
posterior
posterity
posthumous
postpone
postscript
postmortem
postgraduate

***pro-* (in front of, forward)**
proceed
propel
produce
progress
provide
program
projector
protective
proclaim
profess
profile
promotion
prohibit
procreate
propitious
pronounce
promulgate
propensity
proficient
protracted

***super-* (over, greater)**
superpower
supervision
supermarket
supernatural
superman
supersede
supersonic
superstition
superficial
supercilious

***trans-* (across)**
transfer
transport
transmit
transplant
translate
translucent
transparent
transform
transient
transcend

Copyright © 2011 Pearson Education Inc. Reproduction is permitted for classroom use only.

Number-Related Prefixes (see *uni-*, *bi-*, and *tri-* under Prefixes and Suffixes)

mon-, mono-	***cent-***	***mil-***	***oct-***	***poly-***	***semi-***	***multi-***
monarchy	centigrade	million	octagon	polygon	semiannual	multitude
monastery	centimeter	millimeter	octopus	polygamy	semicolon	multiply
monogram	centipede	milligram	October	polychrome	semicircle	multicolored
monologue	centennial	millennium	octave	polyhedron	semisolid	multipurpose
monorail	century	millionaire	octahedron	polyglot	semiconscious	multicultural
monotone			octogenarian	polyester	semifinal	multimedia
monotonous		***deca-***		polygraph	semiweekly	multiplex
monolith		decade	***pent-***	polymath	semiprecious	multifaceted
monopoly		December	pentagon	polymers		multivitamin
monochrome		decahedron	pentameter	polyp		multifarious
monogamy		decagon	pentacle	polytechnic		multiplication

Assimilated or Absorbed Prefixes

in- meaning "not"

in-	***il-***	***im-***	***ir-***	***im-***
inaccurate	illogical	immature	irrational	impure
inefficient	illegal	immaterial	irreconcilable	impaired
inoperable	illiterate	immobile	irreparable	impartial
insecure	illegible	immodest	irregular	impossible
innumerable	illicit	immoderate	irrelevant	impediment
inactive	illustrious	immoral	irreplaceable	imperfect
inappropriate	illegitimate	immortal	irresistible	impersonal
incompetent		immovable	irresponsible	improper
indecent			irreversible	impractical

sub- meaning "under" or "lower"

sub-		***suf-***	***sup-***	***sur-***	***suc-***
subversion	subatomic	suffix	supplant	surreal	succumb
subterranean	subcommittee	suffuse	suppliant	surrender	succeed
suburban	subdivision	suffer	support	surrogate	success
substitute	submarine	suffice	supposition	surreptitious	succinct
substandard	subconscious	sufficient	suppress		
subsidize	subcontractor	suffocate	supplicant		
subclass	subjugate		supplement		
sublease	subscribe				
subscript	subscription				

com- meaning "with" or "together"

com-	***col-***	***con-***	***cor-***	***co-***
common	collection	conspire	correlate	coagulate
community	collide	concert	corroborate	coexist
combination	collision	connect	correct	coalition
committee	collage	congress	correspond	coauthor
company	collaborate	congestion	corrupted	coeducational
comply	colleague	congregation		cohabit
compress	collapse	conclude		cohesion
compound	collusion	condense		cohort
companion	collate	construct		coincide
compact	collateral	constellation		cooperate
complete	colloquial	connote		coordinate

Copyright © 2011 Pearson Education Inc. Reproduction is permitted for classroom use only.

ad- meaning "to" or "toward"

ad-	***at-***	***ac-***	***af-***	***al-***	***ap-***	***as-***
adjacent	attend	accompany	affinity	alliance	approach	assemble
adjoining	attune	acceptable	affable	alliteration	approximate	associate
addicted	attract	access	affection	allowance	appropriate	assimilate
adhesive	attach	accident	affluence	allusion	apprentice	assent
adaptation	attack	accommodate	affricative	alleviate	apprehend	assault
additional	attain	accomplish	affirmation	allotment	appreciate	assertion
adjective	attention	accumulate	***ag-***	***an-***	application	assessment
adjust	attempt	accomplish	aggregate	annex	applause	asset
admire	attitude	accrue	aggravate	annihilate	appetite	assiduous
admission	attribute	acquisition	aggression	announce	appendix	assistance
advocate	attrition	acquire	aggrieved	annul	appear	assuage
		acquisitive		annotate	appeal	assumption

dis- meaning "not," "opposite of," or "apart"

dis-		***dif-***
disadvantage	disarray	difficult
dissatisfied	disconcerted	diffusion
disillusioned	discharged	different
disaster	disclaimer	diffidence
disability	disconsolate	
disagreeable	discouraged	
disseminate	disregard	
disappoint	disenchanted	
discern	disoriented	
disdain		

ex- meaning "out" or "from"

ex-	***ef-***	***ec-***
extract	efface	ecstasy
excavate	effect	eccentric
exceed	efferent	ecclesiastical
exception	efficiency	
excerpt	effrontery	
excursion	effusive	
exhale		
exile		
expansion		
expenditure		

ob- meaning "to," "toward," or "against"

ob-			***op-***	***of-***	***oc-***
oblong	obscure	obscure	opponent	offend	occurrence
objection	observant	oblique	opposite	offensive	occasion
obligation	obstruction	obstacle	opportunity	offering	occupation
obliterate	obstreperous	obsolete	opposition	offense	occupy
oblivious	obstinate		oppress	officious	occlude

Greek Roots

aer ("air")	aerate, aerial, aerobics, aerodynamic, aeronautics, aerosol, aerospace
arch ("rule, chief")	monarchy, anarchy, archangel, archbishop, archetype, architect, hierarchy, matriarch, patriarch
aster, astr ("star")	aster, asterisk, asteroid, astrology, astronomy, astronaut, astronomical, astrophysics, disaster
bi, bio ("life")	biology, biography, autobiography, biopsy, symbiotic, biodegradable, antibiotic, amphibious, biochemistry
centr ("center")	center, central, egocentric, ethnocentric, centrifugal, concentric, concentrate, eccentric
chron ("time")	chronic, chronicle, chronological, synchronize, anachronism
cosm ("world")	cosmic, cosmology, cosmonaut, cosmopolitan, cosmos, microcosm
crat ("rule")	democrat, plutocrat, bureaucrat, idiosyncratic, technocrat
crit ("judge")	critic, criticize, critique, criterion, diacritical, hypocrite
cycl ("circle")	cycle, bicycle, cyclone, tricycle, unicycle, recycle, motorcycle, cyclical, encyclopedia
dem ("people")	demagogue, democracy, demographics, endemic, epidemic, epidemiology
derm ("skin")	dermatologist, epidermis, hypodermic, pachyderm, taxidermist, dermatitis

Copyright © 2011 Pearson Education Inc. Reproduction is permitted for classroom use only.

dont ("tooth")	orthodontist
geo ("earth")	geology, geophysics, geography, geothermal, geocentric, geode
gn(o) ("know")	cognition, recognize, incognito, cognizant, recognizance
gram ("thing written")	diagram, program, telegram, anagram, cryptogram, epigram, grammar, monogram
graph ("to write")	graph, paragraph, autograph, digraph, graphics, topography, biography, bibliography, calligraphy, choreographer, videographer, ethnography, phonograph, seismograph, lexicographer
homo ("same")	homophone, homograph, homosexual, homogeneous
hydr ("water, fluid")	hydra, hydrant, hydrate, hydrogen, hydraulic, hydroelectric, hydrology, hydroplane, hydroponics, anhydrous, hydrangea, hydrophobia
logo ("word, reason")	logic, catalogue, dialogue, prologue, epilogue, monologue
logy ("study")	biology, geology, ecology, mythology, pathology, psychology, sociology, theology, genealogy, etymology, technology, zoology
meter ("measure")	centimeter, millimeter, diameter, speedometer, thermometer, tachometer, altimeter, barometer, kilometer
micro ("small")	microscope, microphone, microwave, micrometer, microbiology, microcomputer, microcosm
ortho ("correct, straight")	orthodox, orthodontics, orthography, orthodontists, orthopedic
pan ("all")	pandemic, panorama, pandemonium, pantheon, Pan-American
path ("feeling, emotion, suffer/disease")	sympathy, antipathy, apathetic, empathize, pathogen, pathologist, pathetic, pathos, osteopath
ped ("child"; see Latin *ped* for foot)	pedagogy, pediatrician, pedophile, encyclopedia
phil ("love")	philosophy, philharmonic, bibliophile, Philadelphia, philanderer, philanthropy, philatetic, philter
phobia ("fear")	phobia, acrophobia, claustrophobia, xenophobia, arachnophobia
phon ("sound")	phonics, phonograph, cacophony, earphone, euphony, homophone, microphone, telephone, xylophone, saxophone, phoneme, symphony
photo ("light")	photograph, telephoto, photocopier, photographer, photosynthesis, photocell
phys ("nature, natural")	physics, physical, physician, physiology, physique, astrophysics, physiognomy, physiotherapy
poli ("city")	politics, police, policy, metropolis, acropolis, cosmopolitan, megalopolis, Minneapolis
psych ("spirit, soul")	psyche, psychology, psychoanalyst, psychiatry, psychedelic, psychosis, psychosomatic, psychic
scope ("see")	microscope, periscope, scope, telescope, stethoscope, gyroscope, horoscope, kaleidoscope, stereoscope
sphere ("ball")	sphere, atmosphere, biosphere, hemisphere, ionosphere, stratosphere, troposphere
tech ("art, skill, build")	technical, technician, technology, polytechnic, architect
tele ("far")	telecast, telegraph, telegram, telescope, television, telethon, teleconference, telepathy
therm ("heat")	thermal, geothermal, thermometer, thermonuclear, thermos, thermostat, thermodynamic, exothermic
typ ("to beat, to strike; impression")	typewriter, typist, typographical, archetype, daguerreotype, prototype, stereotype, typecast
zo ("animal")	zoo, zoology, protozoan, zodiac, zoologist

Latin Roots

aud ("hear")	audio, auditorium, audience, audible, audition, inaudible, audiovisual
bene ("good, well")	benefactor, benevolent, beneficial, benefit, benign, benefactress, benediction
cand, chand ("shine")	candle, chandelier, incandescent, candelabra, candid, candidate
cap ("head")	captain, capital, capitol, capitalize, capitulate, decapitate, per capita

Copyright © 2011 Pearson Education Inc. Reproduction is permitted for classroom use only.

cide ("kill, cut")	fungicide, herbicide, pesticide, insecticide, suicide, homicide, genocide, incise, incision, concise, circumcise, excise
clud/clus, clos ("close, shut")	conclude, exclude, exclusive, preclude, occlude, seclude, seclusion, recluse, closet, disclose, enclose, foreclose
corp ("body")	corpse, corporal, corporation, corpus, corpulent, incorporate, corpuscle
cred ("believe")	credible, incredible, credit, credentials, accredited, credulous
dent ("tooth")	dentist, dentures, indent
dic, dict ("speak")	dictate, diction, dictionary, predict, verdict, benediction, contradict, dedicate, edict, indict, jurisdiction, valedictorian, dictation
doc ("teach")	documentary, indoctrinate, doctorate, doctor, docent, docile, doctrine
duc, duct ("lead")	conduct, conductor, deduct, aqueduct, duct, educate, educe, induct, introduction, reduce, reproduce, viaduct, abduct
equ ("equal")	equal, equality, equation, equator, equity, equivalent, equilibrium, equivocate, equidistant, equinox
fac, fec ("do")	factory, manufacture, faculty, artifact, benefactor, confection, defect, effect, facile, facilitate, facsimile, affect, affection
fer ("carry")	ferry, transfer, prefer, reference, suffer, vociferous, inference, fertile, differ, conifer, conference, circumference
fid ("trust")	fidelity, confident, confidence, diffident, infidelity, perfidy, affidavit, bona fide, confidential
fin ("end")	final, finale, finish, infinite, definitive, finite
flex, flect ("bend, curve")	flex, flexible, inflexible, deflect, reflection, inflection, circumflex, genuflect
flu ("flow")	fluid, fluent, influx, superfluous, affluence, confluence, fluctuate, influence
form ("shape")	conform, deform, formal, formality, format, formation, formula, informal, information, malformed, platform, reform, transform, uniform
grac, grat ("pleasing, thankful")	grace, gratuity, gracious, ingrate, congratulate, grateful, gratitude, ingratiate, persona non grata, gratify
grad ("step")	graduate, gradual, gradient, grade, retrograde, centigrade, degraded, downgrade
gress ("go")	digress, aggressive, congress, egress, ingress, progress, regress, transgression
ject ("throw")	eject, injection, interject, object, objection, conjecture, abject, dejected, projection, projectile, projector, reject, subjective, trajectory
jud ("judge")	judge, judgment, prejudice, judiciary, judicial, adjudge, adjudicate, injudicious
junct ("join")	junction, juncture, injunction, conjunction, adjunct, disjunction
langu, lingu ("tongue")	language, bilingual, linguistics, linguist, linguine, lingo
lit ("letter")	literature, illiterate, literal, literacy, obliterate, alliteration, literary
loc, loq ("speak")	elocution, eloquent, loquacious, obloquy, soliloquy, ventriloquist, colloquial, interlocutor
man ("hand")	manual, manufacture, manicure, manuscript, emancipate, manacle, mandate, manipulate, manage, maneuver
mem ("memory, mindful")	remember, memory, memorize, memorial, memorandum, memento, memorabilia, commemorate
min ("small")	diminish, mince, minimize, minute, minuscule, minus, minor, minnow, minimum
miss, mit ("send")	transmission, remission, submission, admit, transmit, remit, submit, omit, mission, missile, demise, emission, admission, commission, emissary, intermission, intermittent, missionary, permission, promise
mob, mot ("move")	mobile, motion, motor, remote, automobile, promote, motivate, motel, locomotion, immobile, emotion, demote, commotion
pat ("father")	paternal, patrimony, expatriate, patron, patronize
ped ("foot")	pedal, pedestal, pedicure, pedigree, biped, centipede, millipede, moped, impede, expedite, orthopedic, pedestrian, quadruped
pens, pend ("hang")	appendage, appendix, pending, pendulum, pension, suspended, suspense, compensate, depend, dispense, expend, expensive, pensive, stipend, impending, pendant

Copyright © 2011 Pearson Education Inc. Reproduction is permitted for classroom use only.

port ("carry")	porter, portfolio, portage, portable, export, import, rapport, report, support, transport, comportment, deport, important, portmanteau
pos, pon ("put, place")	pose, position, positive, a propos, compose, composite, compost, composure, disposable, expose, impose, imposter, opposite, postpone, preposition, proponent, proposition, superimpose, suppose
prim, princ ("first")	prime, primate, primer, primeval, primitive, prima donna, primal, primary, primogeniture, primordial, primrose, prince, principal, principality, principle
quir, ques ("ask")	inquire, require, acquire, conquer, inquisition, quest, question, questionnaire, request, requisite, requisition
rupt ("break")	rupture, abrupt, bankrupt, corrupt, erupt, disrupt, interrupt, irruption
sal ("salt")	salt, saline, salary, salami, salsa, salad, desalinate
sci ("know")	science, conscience, conscious, omniscience, subconscious, conscientious
scrib, script ("write")	scribble, script, scripture, subscribe, transcription, ascribe, describe, inscribe, proscribe, postscript, prescription, circumscribe, nondescript, conscription
sect, seg ("cut")	bisect, dissect, insect, intersect, section, sector, segment
sent, sens ("feel")	sense, sensitive, sensory, sensuous, sentiment, sentimental, assent, consent, consensus, dissent, resent, sensation
sequ, sec ("follow")	sequence, sequel, sequential, consequence, consecutive, non sequitur, persecute, second, sect, subsequent
sta, sist ("stand")	stable, state, station, stationary, statistic, statue, stature, status, subsist, assist, consistent, desist, insistent, persistent, resist
son ("sound")	sonic, sonnet, sonorous, unison, ultrasonic, assonance, consonant, dissonant, resonate
spec, spic ("look")	spectacle, spectacular, specimen, prospect, respect, retrospective, speculate, suspect, suspicion, aspect, auspicious, circumspect, inspector, introspection
spir ("breathe")	spirit, respiration, perspire, transpire, inspire, conspire, aspirate, dispirited, antiperspirant
struct ("build")	construct, instruct, destruction, reconstruction, obstruct
tain, ten ("hold")	detain, obtain, pertain, retain, sustain, abstain, appertain, contain, entertain, maintain, tenacious
tang, tact ("touch")	tangible, intangible, tangent, contact, tactile
ten ("stretch")	distend, tendon, tendril, extend, intend, intensify, attend, contend, portend, superintendent
term ("end")	term, terminal, terminate, determine, exterminate, predetermine
terra ("earth")	terrain, terrarium, terrace, subterranean, terrestrial, extraterrestrial, Mediterranean, terra cotta, terra firma
tort, torq ("twist")	contort, distort, extort, torture, tortuous, torque
tract ("pull")	tractor, traction, contract, distract, subtract, retract, attract, protracted, intractable, abstract, detract
vac ("empty")	vacant, vacuum, evacuate, vacation, vacuous, vacate
val ("strong, worth")	valid, valiant, validate, evaluate, devalue, convalescent, valedictorian, invalid
ven, vent ("come")	vent, venture, venue, adventure, avenue, circumvent, convention, event, intervene, invent, prevent, revenue, souvenir, convenient
vers, vert ("turn")	revert, vertex, vertigo, convert, divert, vertical, adverse, advertise, anniversary, avert, controversy, conversation, extrovert, introvert, inverse, inverted, perverted, reverse, subvert, traverse, transverse, universe, versatile, versus, vertebra
vid, vis ("see")	video, vista, visage, visit, visual, visa, advise, audiovisual, envision, invisible, television, supervise, provision, revision, improvise
voc ("call")	vocal, vociferous, evoke, invoke, advocate, avocation, convocation, equivocal, invocation, provoke, revoke, vocabulary, vocation
vol, volv ("roll, turn")	revolve, evolve, involve, volume, convoluted, devolve

Copyright © 2011 Pearson Education Inc. Reproduction is permitted for classroom use only.

APPENDIX G

Vocabulary Templates

"Break It Down" Template

Breakdown Word: ______________________________

How many meaning parts did you find in the word?
(write the word and circle roots, underline affixes)

How many prefixes, what were they, and what do they mean?

How many suffixes, what were they, and what do they mean?

How many roots/base words, what were they, and what do they mean?

Definition: Therefore, (explain what you think the words means and how the meaning elements combine to help you construct your predicted definition)

This fits the sentence because (explain how your predicted definition fits the sentence)

Copyright © 2011 Pearson Education Inc. Reproduction is permitted for classroom use only.

Concept of Definition Map

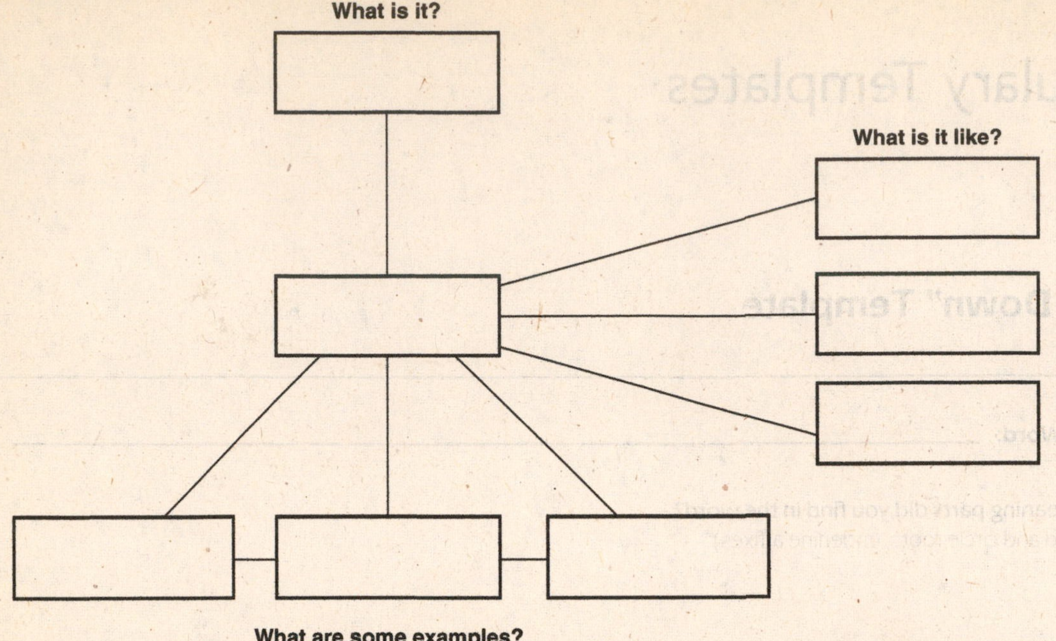

Copyright © 2010 Pearson Education Inc. Reproduction is permitted for classroom use only.

Four-Square Concept Map

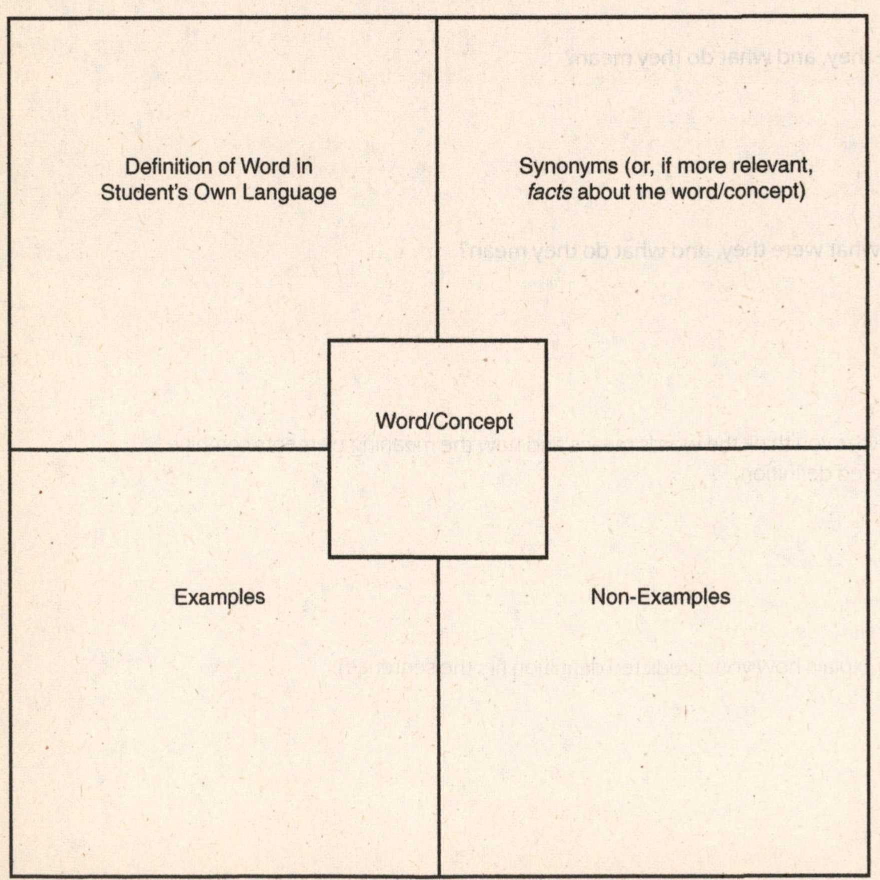

Copyright © 2011 Pearson Education Inc. Reproduction is permitted for classroom use only.

Modified Concept of Definition Map for Social Studies

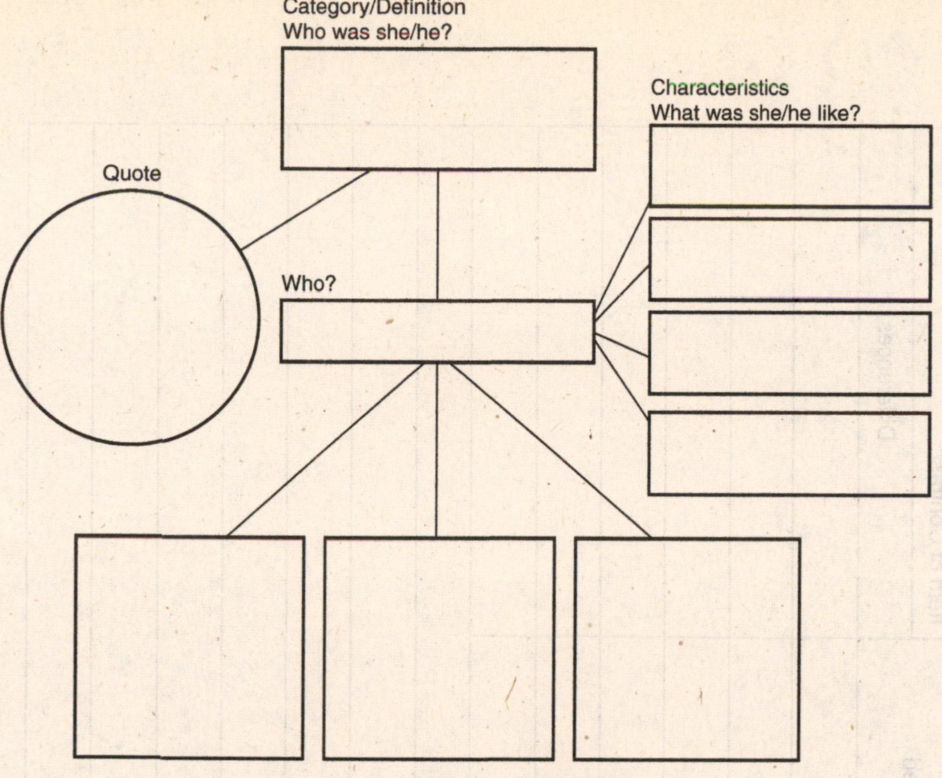

Copyright © 2010 Pearson Education Inc. Reproduction is permitted for classroom use only.

Vocabulary Web for Core Academic Words

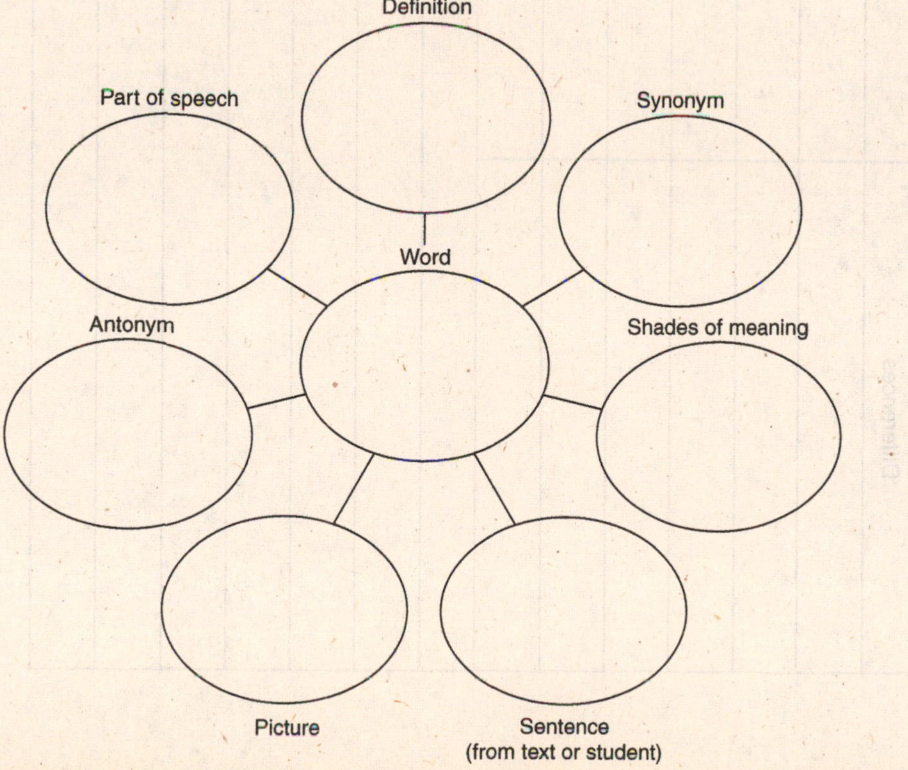

Copyright © 2011 Pearson Education Inc. Reproduction is permitted for classroom use only.

Comparison and Contrast

TOPIC ______________________________

Item of Contrast:	Feature Being Contrasted	Item of Contrast:
Differences		Differences
	Features in Common	

Copyright © 2011 Pearson Education Inc. Reproduction is permitted for classroom use only.

APPENDIX H

Vocabulary Assessment Activities

Vocabulary Self-Assessment Template

Student ______________________ Dates ______________ (X)

______________ (O)

______________ (✓)

Vocabulary	Knowledge Rating			
	Never Heard of It	Heard It	Have Some Ideas	Know It Well

Copyright © 2011 Pearson Education Inc. Reproduction is permitted for classroom use only.

Checklist of Vocabulary in Writing

Student's Name ______________________ Teacher ______________________

Period __________ Grade ______________ Date ______________________

Check the items based on writing samples.

Teacher's question: When you look at students' writing what do you usually see?

Student's question: What do I see when I look at my vocabulary? How often?

	Always	Often	Occasionally	Never
Accuracy: Vocabulary is used correctly in writing				
T: Is the vocabulary's meaning accurate in writing?	____	____	____	____
S: Did the vocabulary make sense? Did I choose the right words?	____	____	____	____
Word frequency and variety: Variety of single-syllable and polysyllabic words				
T: Were there words of 4 or more syllables in the writing?	____	____	____	____
S: How complex was the vocabulary that I used? Did I use polysyllabic words?	____	____	____	____
Word choice: Combination of common and less frequent words				
T: Were there interesting words used in the writing?	____	____	____	____
S: Did I use unusual and interesting vocabulary in my writing?	____	____	____	____
Richness: Colorful and descriptive vocabulary				
T: Was the vocabulary colorful and descriptive?	____	____	____	____
S: Did the vocabulary paint a picture and show what I was trying to say?	____	____	____	____
New vocabulary: Recently acquired vocabulary				
T: Did the writing include recently acquired vocabulary?	____	____	____	____
S: Did I use new vocabulary?	____	____	____	____
Metaphor, simile, analogy, and idioms: Figurative language				
T: Did the student use figurative language?	____	____	____	____
S: Did I use figurative language? Did I compare my ideas to others' ideas?	____	____	____	____

Other observations and examples of note:

____

____

____

____

Copyright © 2011 Pearson Education Inc. Reproduction is permitted for classroom use only.

Intermediate-Level Academic Vocabulary Spelling Inventory (Townsend, Bear, & Templeton, 2009)

Student Directions

Display or provide a copy of these directions for students to follow.

"Today we are going to take a spelling test. I am going to say a word, use it in a sentence, and then say it again. Please do your best to spell the word. Don't do anything in the columns next to where you wrote the word—we'll come back to those after we go through all 20 words."

Spelling Inventory—Spell these words the best you can.

"Write down all the sounds you hear and feel when you say the word to yourself." *Give spelling test.*

Knowledge Rating—Do I know what this word means?

"Now, let's go back to the top. I'm going to read each word again and I want you to think about a couple of things. First, think about what the word means. If you're sure you know what it means, check yes. If you have an idea what it means, but you're not quite sure, check maybe. And if you've never heard of the word or you're really not sure what it means, check no. Any questions?"

Think of Related Words—Can I think of related words?

"After you have checked the yes, no, or maybe box, look to the last column. Use this last column to write down as many real words that you think of by adding or by taking away syllables and other word parts or forms. These boxes are for you to write down other forms of the word that you can think of. Try to write other forms of the word that are actual words and not made-up words. For example, if the word *forget* were on our list, you could write *forgetful,* but not *unforgetful,* because *unforgetful* isn't a real word. Here's another example: If the word *reply* were on our list, you could write *replying,* but not *replyment.* It's OK if you can't think of other forms of each word—just do the best you can. Any questions?"

"We will now go through each word one more time. Rate how well you know the word by checking yes, no, or maybe, and write as many other forms of the word that you can think of." *The teacher will say each word. Students will have 15 seconds to rate their knowledge and think of and record related words.*

APPENDIX H

Copyright © 2011 Pearson Education Inc. Reproduction is permitted for classroom use only.

Teacher Form: Words and Sentences

Read each word and sentence, and repeat the word. After spelling all 20 words, return to the beginning to allow students to rate their knowledge and to generate related words. Say each word and give students 15 seconds to rate their knowledge and record related words.

See pages 247–249 for directions for scoring and interpretation.

1. source	The source of Earth's heat is the sun. *source*
2. traditional	The actress preferred to wear traditional clothes. *traditional*
3. distinct	There was a distinct difference between the two artists' work. *distinct*
4. restructure	The partners decided to restructure their company. *restructure*
5. requiring	The school started requiring that students wear uniforms. *requiring*
6. economical	It is more economical to shop at some stores than others. *economical*
7. residence	My grandmother's residence is on a quiet road. *residence*
8. definition	The girl gave the definition of the new vocabulary word. *definition*
9. conception	Her conception of the new gallery was different from his. *conception*
10. majorities	Presidential candidates try to win the majorities of different groups of people. *majorities*
11. participants	The participants in the game had a great time. *participants*
12. significance	The war in Iraq is of great significance to our military. *significance*
13. unapproachable	The girl did not smile and was very unapproachable. *unapproachable*
14. benefited	The whole community benefited from the new park. *benefited*
15. financially	People with large savings accounts are financially sound. *financially*
16. consequently	The team trained hard, and consequently, they won the big game. *consequently*
17. assessment	The assessment was challenging to the students, but they tried their hardest. *assessment*
18. occurrence	In Reno, snow in July would be a very strange occurrence. *occurrence*
19. perceive	The new teacher did not perceive the change in the students after vacation. *perceive*
20. irrelevance	Her argument was full of irrelevance and she lost the debate. *irrelevance*

Copyright © 2011 Pearson Education Inc. Reproduction is permitted for classroom use only.

Student Form

Spelling	Yes	Maybe	No	Write down as many related words as you can (You can use the back of the page if you need more room.)
1.				
2.				
3.				
4.				
5.				
6.				
7.				
8.				
9.				
10.				
11.				
12.				
13.				
14.				
15.				
16.				
17.				
18.				
19.				
20.				

Copyright © 2011 Pearson Education Inc. Reproduction is permitted for classroom use only.

Generating/Producing Words with the Same Suffix and Prefix

This assessment examines students' productive knowledge of prefixes and suffixes. The ability to think of related words indicates the depth of students' vocabulary knowledge and the level of their knowledge of affixes. Students are instructed to write as many words as they can with words that begin or end with these prefixes and suffixes, respectively. Two lists of ten suffixes and prefixes with examples are presented. Most of the prefixes and suffixes in Part I are more frequent and/or transparent than those in Part II. Students are asked to write the meanings of the prefixes.

Directions

The directions are printed at the top of the student copy. The time to take the assessment can vary for purpose. In whole-group settings, students can be given eight minutes to complete each part. Go on to Part II to complete the assessment if students generate at least two words for eight of the ten affixes.

Scoring and Interpretation

Score 2 points for each correct word that is also spelled correctly. Score 1 point for each word that could be correct but is misspelled. In the prefixes test, award 1 point for each prefix defined correctly.

Examine the types of suffixes and prefixes that were more difficult for students to understand to determine the types of prefixes the students would benefit from examining in vocabulary study. There should be a developmental pattern in the students' errors. Students usually produce more words for the words with common prefixes and suffixes. Instruction can begin by making the meaning connections among known affixes and explaining the explicit grammatical functions of suffixes.

In Part I of the prefix test, students who score between 30 and 40 points are likely to be in the middle of the intermediate stage of reading and in the syllables and affixes stage of spelling. Students who score between 30 and 40 points in Part II of the prefix test are likely to be in the middle of the advanced stage of reading and in the derivational relations stage of spelling. For the suffix test, students are not asked for the meanings of the suffixes. Students who score between 25 and 35 on Part I of the suffix test are likely to be in the middle of the intermediate stage of reading and in the syllables and affixes stage of spelling. Students who score between 25 and 35 on Part II of the suffix test are likely to be in the middle of the advanced stage of reading and in the derivational relations stage of spelling.

Students who score below 30 on Part I of the prefix test and below 25 on Part I of the suffix test are ready to focus on some of the easier and more common prefixes and suffixes found in strand 1. They need to look more deeply at the familiar affixes and focus on several of the affixes they do not know well.

Copyright © 2011 Pearson Education Inc. Reproduction is permitted for classroom use only.

Student Form for Producing Words with the Same Suffix

Part I. Here are ten suffixes with examples. Think of words that have the same suffix. Write up to four related words on the line. Do not include words with plurals or words that end with *s* (*basketfuls* would not count). Do not spend too much time on any one suffix. Spell the words the best you can. Your teacher will tell you how much time you have.

Student's Name ______ Teacher ______ Period/Grade ___ Date ______

	suffix	(example)	
1.	*-ful*	(basketful)	______
2.	*-ing*	(contracting)	______
3.	*-y*	(lucky)	______
4.	*-ish*	(childish)	______
5.	*-ly*	(seriously)	______
6.	*-er*	(reporter)	______
7.	*-al*	(magical)	______
8.	*-ness*	(goodness)	______
9.	*-less*	(painless)	______
10.	*-ion*	(eruption)	______

Part II. Here are ten suffixes with examples. Think of words that have the same suffix. Write up to four related words on the line. Do not include words with plurals or words that end with *s* (*punishments* would not count). Do not spend too much time on any one suffix. Spell the words the best you can. Your teacher will tell you how much time you have.

Student's Name ______ Teacher ______ Period/Grade ___ Date ______

	suffix	(example)	
1.	*-ment*	(punishment)	______
2.	*-ist*	(specialist)	______
3.	*-ial*	(presidential)	______
4.	*-ism*	(symbolism)	______
5.	*-ous*	(dangerous)	______
6.	*-ence*	(competence)	______
7.	*-ure*	(indenture)	______
8.	*-ive*	(retrospective)	______
9.	*-ous*	(poisonous)	______
10.	*-able*	(affordable)	______
	or		
	-ible	(contemptible)	______

APPENDIX H

Copyright © 2011 Pearson Education Inc. Reproduction is permitted for classroom use only.

Student Form for Producing Words with the Same Prefix

Part I. Here are ten prefixes with examples. Think of words that have the same prefix. Write up to four related words on the line. Do not include words with plurals or words that end with *s* (*returns* would not count). Write down the meaning of each prefix. Do not spend too much time on any one prefix. Spell the words the best you can. Your teacher will tell you how much time you have.

Student's Name ____________ Teacher ___________ Period/Grade ___ Date ________

prefix (example)

1. re- (return) ______________________________

re- means: ______________________________

2. *un-* (unreliable) ______________________________

un- means: ______________________________

3. *mis-* (misleading) ______________________________

mis- means: ______________________________

4. *non-* (nonfiction) ______________________________

non- means: ______________________________

5. *mono-* (monochrome) ______________________________

mono- means: ______________________________

6. *auto-* (autograph) ______________________________

auto- means: ______________________________

7. *pre-* (prejudge) ______________________________

pre- means: ______________________________

8. *semi-* (hemisphere) ______________________________

semi- means: ______________________________

9. *dis-* (discontinue) ______________________________

dis- means: ______________________________

10. *in-* (incorrect) ______________________________

in- means: ______________________________

 Copyright © 2011 Pearson Education Inc. Reproduction is permitted for classroom use only.

Part II. Here are ten prefixes with examples. Think of words that have the same prefix. Write up to four related words on the line. Do not include words with plurals or words that end with *s* (*supersonics* would not count). Write down the meaning of each prefix. Do not spend too much time on any one prefix. Spell the words the best you can. Your teacher will tell you how much time you have.

Student's Name ________ Teacher ________ Period/Grade ________ Date ________

prefix (example)

1. *super-* (supersonic) ________

   super- means: ________

2. *anti-* (antibiotic) ________

   anti- means: ________

3. *micro-* (microbiologist) ________

   micro- means: ________

4. *tri-* (triangle) ________

   tri- means: ________

5. *mal-* (malformation) ________

   mal- means: ________

6. *sub-* (subsection) ________

   sub- means: ________

7. *inter-* (interact) ________

   inter- means: ________

8. *con-/com-* (connect, company) ________

   con-/com- means: ________

9. *de-* (debug, dejected) ________

   de- means: ________

10. *trans-* (transport) ________

    trans- means: ________

APPENDIX H

Copyright © 2011 Pearson Education Inc. Reproduction is permitted for classroom use only.

Part I Answers

1. *re-*	back, again	report, realign, retract, revise, regain, reflect, rename, restate, recombine, recalculate, redo
2. *un-*	not	uncooked, unharmed, unintended, unhappy
3. *mis-*	bad, badly	misinform, misinterpret, mispronounce, misnomer, mistake, misogynist
4. *non-*	not	nonferrous, nonabrasive, nondescript, nonfat, nonfiction, nonprofit, nonsense, nonentity
5. *mono-*	single, one	monopoly, monotype, monologue, mononucleosis, monorail, monotheist
6. *auto-*	self	automobile, automatic, autograph, autonomous, autoimmune, autopilot, autobiography
7. *pre-*	before	predetermine, premeditated
8. *semi-*	half	semifinal, semiconscious, semiannual, semimonthly, semicircle
9. *dis-/dys-*	away, not, negative	dismiss, differ, disallow, disperse, dissuade, disconnect, dysfunction, disproportion, disrespect, distemper, distaste, disarray, dyslexia
10. *in-*	not	incomplete, indirect, indecent, inaccurate, inactive, independent

Part II Answers

1. *super-/ supra-*	above	superior, suprarenal, superscript, supernatural, supercede, superficial, superhero, superimpose
2. *anti-*	against	antisocial, antiseptic, antithesis, antibody, antichrist, antinomies, antifreeze, antipathy, antigen, antibiotic, antidote, antifungal, antidepressant
3. *micro-*	small	microscope, microprocessor, microfiche, micrometer, micrograph
4. *tri-*	three	triangle, trinity, trilateral, triumvirate, tribune, trilogy, tricycle, trillion
5. *mal-*	bad, badly	maladjusted, malady, malcontent, malfeasance, maleficent, malevolent, malice, malaria, malfunction, malignant
6. *sub-*	under, below	submerge, submarine, substandard, subnormal, subvert, subdivision, submersible, submit
7. *inter-*	between	international, intercept, intermission, interoffice, internal, intermittent
8. *con-/ com-*	with, together	convene, compress, contemporary, converge, compact, confluence, concatenate, conjoin, combine, convert, compatible, consequence
9. *de-*	remove, opposite	decode, deceive, definite, deduct, defend, detach
10. *trans-*	across	transaction, transform, transmit, transcribe, translate, transplant, transcontinental

APPENDIX H

Copyright © 2011 Pearson Education Inc. Reproduction is permitted for classroom use only.

Matching Greek and Latin Roots

Matching Assessment of Some Greek and Latin Roots

Matching Assessment 1

______	1. *ver*	a.	bad
______	2. *mal*	b.	breathe
______	3. *ante*	c.	all
______	4. *spir*	d.	turn
______	5. *omni*	e.	foot
______	6. *poly*	f.	before
______	7. *cap*	g.	good
______	8. *ped*	h.	life
______	9. *bene*	i.	head
______	10. *corp*	j.	many
______	11. *astr*	k.	body
______	12. *bio*	l.	star

Matching Assessment 2

______	1. *duc*	a.	flow
______	2. *sect*	b.	small
______	3. *flu*	c.	death
______	4. *gen*	d.	judge
______	5. *sequ*	e.	lead
______	6. *hydr*	f.	land
______	7. *min*	g.	water
______	8. *dent*	h.	cut
______	9. *mort*	i.	follow
______	10. *terra*	j.	tooth
______	11. *jud*	k.	hand
______	12. *man*	l.	birth

Answer Key for Matching

Matching Assessment 1

1. d 2. a 3. f 4. b 5. c 6. j 7. i 8. e 9. g 10. k 11. l 12. h

Matching Assessment 2

1. e 2. h 3. a 4. l 5. i 6. g 7. b 8. j 9. c 10. f 11. d 12. k

Words for Students to Spell and Define

Ask students to spell and define the following words.

1. consecutive
2. affluence
3. beneficial
4. malevolent
5. omnivore
6. corporal
7. aerosol
8. hydraulic
9. conspiracy
10. sectarian
11. judiciary
12. privilege
13. vertigo
14. anterior
15. equation
16. terrarium
17. asteroid
18. antibiotic
19. progeny
20. allegiance

Copyright © 2011 Pearson Education Inc. Reproduction is permitted for classroom use only.

Generating Words from Bases and Roots

Directions

Decide on a time limit; eight minutes is adequate for most students. Let students know when half the time is over, and when 30 seconds is left. If you see that students have stopped writing, you can stop the test. Read the directions aloud to students.

Scoring

Score 1 point for each correct response that is spelled correctly. Score ½ point when the word is misspelled, but is recognizable, with each syllable represented.

Here is a list of words for scoring. Consult a dictionary when in doubt.

1. *turn:* downturn, lecturn, overturn, nocturnal, return, returnable, returning, taciturn, turning, turnkeys, turnouts, turnover, turnpikes, turnstile, turntable, upturn, woodturning
2. *fuse:* confuse, confused, effuse, defuse, diffuse, diffuser, infuse, perfuse, profuse, refuse, reinfuse, suffuse, transfuse, unconfuse
3. *bio:* autobiography, biocontrol, biodiversity, biodynamic, bioelectronics, biofeedback, biographical, biography, biohazard, biological, biologist, biology, biomass, biomechanical, biometrics, bionic, biotechnology, biochemistry, biologic, biomedical, microbiology
4. *graph:* autograph, autobiography, biograph, biography, cardiograph, grapheme, graphics, graphically, lithograph, monograph, orthography, photograph, photography, pornographic, radiograph, spectrograph, telegraph, tomography, topographic
5. *spec, spect:* aspect, inspect, introspect, irrespective, prospect, respect, spectacles, spectrograph, specs, speculate, speculative, species
6. *tract:* attract, attraction, attracting, attractive, abstract, contract, contraction, contractual, detract, distraction, extract, extraction, retract, tractor
7. *tain:* retain, retaining, unattainable, contain, container, pertain, sustain, certain, certainly, certainty, distain, uncertain, tainting, tainted, taint, curtain, obtain, maintain, mountain

Interpretation

Score one point for each entry that is a real word and that is spelled correctly. These base words and roots are for advanced readers to consider. Students who score between 12 and 20 should study common prefixes and suffixes in strand 1. Students who produce three words for most items and have a score between 16 and 21 are ready to study roots and less frequent affixes in strand 2 more systematically. Students who score 22 and above are probably advanced readers who can study principles of sound change, including assimilated prefixes and vowel reduction.

Generating words related to these roots requires a flexible, quick, and deep vocabulary knowledge. Because students are thinking of the words and not hunting for them on a page, these are probably words students know.

Copyright © 2011 Pearson Education Inc. Reproduction is permitted for classroom use only.

Student Form for Generating Words

Student's Name ______________________ Teacher ______________________

Period __________ Grade ______________ Date ______________

Directions. Make as many words as you can by adding prefixes and suffixes, and by making compound words with these base words and roots. Do not include any words with plurals, words that end with *s* (*turn*s would not count). The blank spaces are for you to write your words. Spell the words the best you can. Your teacher will tell you how much time you have.

Here is an example: In item 1 below, four new words were made. Can you think of other words to make? There are four more blank spaces, and this is where you begin. Skip around as you brainstorm, and take the full time. Turn your paper over when time is called.

1. *turn* return ______ returnable ______
turned ______ downturn ______
______ ______
______ ______

2. *fuse* confuse ______ confusing ______
______ ______
______ ______
______ ______

3. *bio* ______ ______
______ ______
______ ______
______ ______

4. *graph* ______ ______
______ ______
______ ______
______ ______

5. *spec, spect* ______ ______
______ ______
______ ______
______ ______

6. *tract* ______ ______
______ ______
______ ______
______ ______

7. *tain* ______ ______
______ ______
______ ______
______ ______

APPENDIX H

Copyright © 2011 Pearson Education Inc. Reproduction is permitted for classroom use only.

My Strategies for Learning Vocabulary

Strongly agree ←——→ Strongly disagree

Do I know the meaning of the vocabulary?

I learn the vocabulary by reading the textbook. ___ ___ ___ ___ ___ ___

I learn the vocabulary in the class lectures.

I learn the vocabulary through classroom activities. ___ ___ ___ ___ ___ ___

I learn the vocabulary from reading.

Do I know how to learn new vocabulary?

I see inside words to find meaningful parts. ___ ___ ___ ___ ___ ___

I can think of related words to make meaning connections. ___ ___ ___ ___ ___ ___

I can find references and other resources to study vocabulary. ___ ___ ___ ___ ___ ___

When I read a chapter in the textbook, how many words are new to me? How many vocabulary words do I need to study?

___ 0–1 ___ 2–4 ___ 5–9 ___ 10–19 ___ ≥20

Can I read the vocabulary?

When I read, I know the meanings of most of the words. ___ ___ ___ ___ ___ ___

I can pronounce the words. ___ ___ ___ ___ ___ ___

I can read the words easily, without having to pronounce the words. ___ ___ ___ ___ ___ ___

There are a few words I do not know when I read. (≤ 5 per 100) ___ ___ ___ ___ ___ ___

There are many words I cannot read. (≥ 10 per 100) ___ ___ ___ ___ ___ ___

When I read a chapter in my textbook(s), there are words I cannot pronounce. Check how many words on a page were difficult to read:

___ 0–1 ___ 2–4 ___ 5–9 ___ ≥10

What are my next steps learning the vocabulary?

How many vocabulary words will I study each week?

___ 0–1 ___ 2–4 ___ 5–9 ___ ≥10

How many days a week will I review the vocabulary to learn the vocabulary words?

___ 0–1 ___ 2–4 ___ 5–7

I would benefit from working with others to study the vocabulary. ___ ___ ___ ___ ___ ___

I can learn the assigned vocabulary with ease. ___ ___ ___ ___ ___ ___

I benefit from having note cards. ___ ___ ___ ___ ___ ___

I need more resources to learn about the words. ___ ___ ___ ___ ___ ___

I can assist others. ___ ___ ___ ___ ___ ___

APPENDIX H

Copyright © 2011 Pearson Education Inc. Reproduction is permitted for classroom use only.

Rubric for Vocabulary Learning

Name ______________________________ Period/Grade __________

Teacher ______________________________

Dates __________ __________ __________

***Student:* How would you rate your understanding of the vocabulary?**

5 I have a complete understanding.

4 I have a good understanding.

3 I have some knowledge.

2 I am learning the vocabulary.

1 The vocabulary is very new to me.

***Teacher:* How would you rate the student's understanding of the vocabulary?**

5 Uses the vocabulary accurately in writing and speech; understands the words in various reading contexts; can explain to others; completes assignments using vocabulary; can brainstorm several closely related words; spells vocabulary accurately and easily

4 Uses the vocabulary accurately in writing and speech; understands the words in various reading contexts; learning to explain the words to others; completes assignments using the vocabulary in writing; can brainstorm two closely related words; spells most vocabulary accurately and easily

3 Learning how the vocabulary is used in speech and writing; broadening knowledge of the context in which the vocabulary is learned; takes notes on the key vocabulary; may not spell the word correctly; can recognize which words may not be spelled accurately

2 Knows the word fits in broad categories; can associate a few related words; does not spell the words accurately

1 Is hearing and seeing the vocabulary for the first time; learning to associate meanings with the words; learning to pronounce and spell all of the syllables in the words and meaning units; has an adjusted vocabulary list; receives extra instruction

Copyright © 2011 Pearson Education Inc. Reproduction is permitted for classroom use only.

References

Achieve, Inc. (2005). *Rising to the challenge: Are high school graduates prepared for college and work?* Washington, DC: Author.

ACT. (2005). *Crisis at the core: Preparing all students for college and work.* Iowa City, IA: Author.

Adams, M. J. (1990). *Beginning to read: Thinking and learning about print.* Cambridge, MA: MIT Press.

Adelman, C. (2004). *Principal indicators of student academic histories in postsecondary education, 1972–2000.* Washington, DC: U.S. Department of Education, Institute of Education Sciences.

Aichele, D. B., Hopfensperger, W. P., Leiva, A. M., Mason, M. M., Murphy, J. S., Schell, J. V., & Vheru, C. M. (1998). *Geometry: Explorations and applications.* Evanston, IL: McDougal Littell.

Alliance for Excellent Education. (2006). *Who's counted? Who's counting? Understanding high school graduation rates.* Washington, DC: Author.

Allington, R. L. (1983). The reading instruction provided readers of differing abilities. *Elementary School Journal, 83,* 548–559.

Allington, R. L. (2005). *What really matters for struggling readers: Designing research-based programs.* Boston: Allyn & Bacon.

Anderson, R. C. (1977). The notion of schemata and the educational enterprise: General discussion of the conference. In R. C. Anderson, R. J. Spiro, & W. E. Montague (Eds.), *Schooling and the acquisition of knowledge* (pp. 415–431). Mahwah, NJ: Erlbaum.

Anderson, R. C., & Freebody, P. (1981). Vocabulary knowledge. In J. Guthrie (Ed.), *Comprehension and teaching: Research reviews* (pp. 77–117). Newark, DE: International Reading Association.

Applebee, A., Bermudez, A., Blau, S., Caplan, R., Elbow, P., Hynds, S., et al. (2000). *The language of literature: American literature.* Evanston, IL: McDougal Littell.

Aronson, E. (1978). *The jigsaw classroom.* Beverly Hills, CA: Sage.

Barton, P. E. (2000). *What jobs require: Literacy, education, and training, 1940–2006.* Washington, DC: Educational Testing Service.

Bear, D. (1982). *Patterns of oral reading across stages of word knowledge.* Unpublished manuscript, University of Virginia, Charlottesville.

Bear, D. R., Helman, L., Templeton, S., Invernizzi, M., & Johnston, F. (2007). *Words their way with English learners: Word study for phonics, vocabulary, and spelling instruction.* Upper Saddle River, NJ: Pearson.

Bear, D. R., Invernizzi, M., Templeton, S., & Johnston, F. (2004). *Words their way: Word study for phonics, vocabulary, and spelling instruction.* (3rd ed.). Upper Saddle River, NJ: Pearson.

Bear, D. R., Invernizzi, M., Templeton, S., & Johnston, F. (2008). *Words their way: Word study for phonics, vocabulary, and spelling instruction* (4th ed.). Upper Saddle River, NJ: Pearson.

Bear, D., Templeton, S., & Warner, M. (1991). The development of a qualitative inventory of higher levels of orthographic knowledge. In J. Zutell & S. McCormick (Eds.), *Learner factors/teacher factors: Issues in literacy research and instruction: Fortieth yearbook of the National Reading Conference* (pp. 105–110). Chicago: National Reading Conference.

Bear, D., Truex, P., & Barone, D. (1989). In search of meaningful diagnoses: Spelling-by-stage assessment of literacy proficiency. *Adult Literacy and Basic Education, 13,* 165–185.

Beck, I. L., McKeown, M. G., & Kucan, L. (2002). *Bringing words to life: Robust vocabulary instruction.* New York: Guilford Press.

Beck, I. L., Perfetti, C. A., & McKeown, M. G. (1982). Effects of long-term vocabulary instruction on lexical access and reading comprehension. *Journal of Educational Psychology, 74,* 506–521.

Bednarz, S. W., Miyares, I. M., Schug, M. C., & White, C. S. (2005). *World cultures and geography.* Evanston, IL: McDougal Littell.

Betts, E. A. (1954). *Foundations of reading instruction with emphasis on differentiated guidance.* New York: American Book Company.

Biancarosa, C., & Snow, C. E. (2006). *Reading next—A vision for action and research in middle and high school literacy: A report to Carnegie Corporation of New York* (2nd ed.).Washington, DC: Alliance for Excellent Education.

Biemiller, A. (2003). Oral comprehension sets the ceiling on reading comprehension. *American Educator, 27,* 1–23.

Blachowicz, C. L. Z., & Fisher, P. J. (2000). Vocabulary instruction. In M. L. Kamil, P. B. Mosenthal, P. D. Pearson, & R. Barr (Eds.), *Handbook of reading research* (Vol. 3, pp. 503–523). Mahwah, NJ: Erlbaum.

Blachowicz, C., & Fisher, P. J. (2010). *Teaching vocabulary in all classrooms* (4th ed.). Boston: Allyn & Bacon.

Bruner, J. S., Goodnow, J. J., & Austin, G. A. (1966). *A study of thinking.* New York: John Wiley.

Bulla, C. R. (1987). *The chalk box kid.* New York: Random House.

Cantrell, R. J. (2001). Exploring the relationship between dialect and spelling for specific vocalic features in Appalachian first-grade children. *Linguistics and Education, 12,* 1–23.

Carlisle, J. F. (1995). Morphological awareness and early reading achievement. In L. Feldman (Ed.), *Morphological aspects of language processing* (pp. 189–209). Mahwah, NJ: Erlbaum.

Carlisle, J. F. (2000). Awareness of the structure and meaning of morphologically complex words: Impact on reading. *Reading and Writing, 12,* 169–190.

Carnegie Council on Advancing Adolescent Literacy. (2010). *Time to act: An agenda for advancing adolescent literacy for college and career success.* New York: Carnegie Corporation of New York.

Carnine, D., Silbert, J., Kame'enui, E. J., & Tarver, S. G. (2004). *Direct reading instruction.* Upper Saddle River, NJ: Merrill Prentice Hall.

Carver, R. P. (1994). Percentage of unknown vocabulary words in text as a function of the relative difficulty of the text: Implications for instruction. *Journal of Reading Behavior, 26,* 413–437.

Cataldo, S., & Ellis, N. (1988). Interactions in the development of spelling, reading, and phonological skills. *Journal of Research in Reading, 11,* 86–109.

Catts, H. W., Hogan, T. P., & Adolf, S. M. (2005). Developmental changes in reading and reading disabilities. In H. W. Catts & A. G. Kahmi (Eds.), *The connections between language and reading disabilities* (pp. 25–40). Mahwah, NJ: Erlbaum.

Center for Research on Education, Diversity and Excellence (CREDE). (2004). *Research evidence: Five standards for effective pedagogy and student outcomes* (Technical Report No. G1). Santa Cruz: University of California.

Chall, J. S. (1983). *Stages of reading development.* New York: McGraw-Hill.

Chall, J. S. (1996). *Learning to read: The great debate* (3rd ed.). New York: McGraw-Hill.

Chall, J. S., & Jacobs, V. A. (2003). Poor children's fourth-grade slump. *American Educator, 27,* 14–15.

Chapman, J. W., Tunmer, W. E., & Prochnow, J. E. (2000). Early reading-related skills and performance, reading self-concept, and the development of academic self-concept: A longitudinal study. *Journal of Educational Psychology, 92,* 703–708.

Chomsky, C. (1970). Reading, writing, and phonology. *Harvard Education Review, 40*(2), 287–309.

Chomsky, N., & Halle, M. (1968). *The sound patterns of English.* New York: Harper & Row.

Coxhead, A. (2000). A new academic word list. *TESOL Quarterly, 34,* 213–238.

Cunningham, A. E., & Stanovich, K. E. (1998). What reading does for the mind. *American Educator, 22*(1–2), 8–15.

Dale, E., O'Rourke, J., & Bamman, H. (1971). *Techniques of teaching vocabulary.* Palo Alto, CA: Field Educational Enterprises.

Davis, F. B. (1944). Fundamental factors of comprehension in reading. *Psychometrika, 9,* 185–197.

Deshler, D. D., Palincsar, A. S., Biancarosa, G., & Nair, M. (2007). *Informed choices for struggling adolescent readers: A research-based guide to instructional programs and practices.* Newark, DE: International Reading Association.

Dolch, E. W. (1942). *Better spelling.* Champaign, IL: The Garrard Press.

Duffy, G. G. (2003). *Explaining reading: A resource for teaching concepts, skills, and strategies.* New York: Guilford Press.

Duffy, G. G., Roehler, L. R., Sivan, E., Rackliffe, G., Book, C., Meloth, M. S., Vavrus, L. G., Wesselman, R., Putnam, J., & Bassiri, D. (1987). Effects of explaining the reasoning associated with using reading strategies. *Reading Research Quarterly, 22,* 347–368.

Dweck, C. S. (1987). *Children's theories of intelligence: Implications for motivation and learning.* Paper presented at the annual meeting of American Educational Research Association, Washington, DC.

Echevarria, J., Vogt, M., & Short, D. (2004). *Making content comprehensible for English learners: The SIOP model.* Boston: Allyn & Bacon.

Edwards, W. (2003). *Charting the orthographic knowledge of intermediate and advanced readers and the relationship between recognition and production of orthographic patterns.* Unpublished doctoral dissertation, University of Nevada, Reno.

Eeds, M., & Cockrum, W. (1985). Teaching word meanings by expanding schemata vs. dictionary work vs. reading in context. *Journal of Reading, 28*(6), 492–497.

Ehri, L. C. (1991). Learning to read and spell words. In L. Rieben & C. Perfetti (Eds.), *Learning to read: Basic research and its implications* (pp. 57–73). Mahwah, NJ: Erlbaum.

Ehri, L. C. (1994). Development of the ability to read words: Update. In R. Ruddell, M. Ruddell, & H. Singer (Eds.), *Theoretical models and processes of reading* (4th ed., pp. 323–358). Newark, DE: International Reading Association.

Ehri, L. C. (1997). Learning to read and learning to spell are one and the same, almost. In C. A. Perfetti, L. Rieben, & M. Fayol (Eds.), *Learning to spell: Research, theory, and practice across languages* (pp. 237–269). Mahwah, NJ: Erlbaum.

Ehri, L. C. (1998). Grapheme-phoneme knowledge is essential for learning to read words in English. In J. L. Metsala & L. C. Ehri (Eds.), *Word recognition in beginning literacy* (pp. 3–40). Mahwah, NJ: Erlbaum.

Ehri, L. C. (2000). Learning to read and learning to spell: Two sides of a coin. *Topics in Language Disorders, 20,* 19–36.

Ehri, L. C., & Wilce, L. S. (1987). Does learning to spell help beginners learn to read real words? *Reading Research Quarterly, 18,* 47–65.

Ellis, N., & Cataldo, S. (1992). Spelling is integral to learning to read. In C. M. Sterling & C. Robson (Eds.), *Psy-*

chology, spelling, and education (pp. 112–142), Clevedon, UK: Multilingual Matters.

English Standards of Learning for Virginia Public Schools. (2002). Retrieved June 10, 2009, from ww.doe.virginia.gov/VDOE/Superintendent/Sols/2002/EnglishK-12.pdf

Fisher, D., & Frey, N. (2008a). *Better learning through structured teaching: A framework for the gradual release of responsibility.* Alexandria, VA: Association for Supervision and Curriculum Development.

Fisher, D., & Frey, N. (2008b). *Word-wise and content rich: Five essential steps to teaching academic vocabulary.* Portsmouth, NH: Heinemann.

Flanigan, K., & Greenwood, S. (2007). Effective content vocabulary instruction in the middle: Matching students, purposes, words, and strategies. *Journal of Adolescent and Adult Literacy, 51*(3), 226–238.

Frayer, D. A., Frederick, W. C., & Klausmeier, H. J. (1969). *A schema for testing the level of concept mastery* (Working paper No. 16). Madison: Wisconsin Research and Development Center for Cognitive Learning.

Freeman, D., & Freeman, Y. (2002). *Between worlds: Access to second language acquisition.* Portsmouth, NH: Heinemann.

Fresch, M. J., & Wheaton, A. (2002). *Teaching and assessing spelling: A practical approach that strikes the balance between whole-group and individualized instruction.* New York: Scholastic.

Frith, U. (1985). Beneath the surface of developmental dyslexia. In K. Patterson, J. Marshall, & M. Coltheart (Eds.), *Surface dyslexia: Neuropsychological and cognitive studies of phonological reading* (pp. 301–330). London: Erlbaum.

Fritz, J. (1997). *Shh! We're writing the constitution.* New York: Putnam.

Fry, E. B., & Kress, J. E. (2006). *The reading teacher's book of lists* (5th ed.). San Francisco: Jossey-Bass.

Fullan, M., Hill, P., & Crevola, C. (2006). *Breakthrough.* Thousand Oaks, CA: Corwin Press.

Ganske, K. (1999). The developmental spelling analysis: A measure of orthographic knowledge. *Educational Assessment, 6,* 41–70.

Ganske, K. (2000). *Word journeys: Assessment-guided phonics, spelling, and vocabulary instruction.* New York: Guilford Press.

Gardiner, J. R. (1992). *Stone Fox.* New York: HarperCollins.

Gaskins, I., Downer, M., Anderson, R., Cunningham, P., Gaskins, R., Schommer, M., et al. (1988). A metacognitive approach to phonics: Using what you know to decode what you don't know. *Remedial and Special Education, 9,* 36–41.

Gill, C. (1980). *An analysis of spelling errors in French.* Unpublished doctoral dissertation, University of Virginia, Charlottesville.

Gill, C. H., & Scharer, P. L. (1996). Why do they get it on Friday and misspell it on Monday? Teachers inquiring about their students as spellers. *Language Arts, 73,* 89–96.

Gillet, J. W., & Kita, M. J. (1980). Words, kids, and categories. *The Reading Teacher, 32,* 538–542.

Graves, M. F. (1984). Selecting vocabulary to teach in the intermediate and secondary grades. In J. Flood (Ed.), *Promoting reading comprehension* (pp. 245–260). Newark, DE: International Reading Association.

Graves, M. F. (2008). Instruction on individual words: One size does not fit all. In A. E. Farstrup & S. J. Samuels (Eds.), *What research has to say about vocabulary instruction* (pp. 56–79). Newark, DE: International Reading Association.

Graves, M. F., Juel, C., & Graves, B. B. (2004). *Teaching reading in the 21st century* (3rd ed.). Boston: Allyn & Bacon.

Graves, M. F., & Prenn, M. C. (1986). Costs and benefits of various methods of teaching vocabulary. *Journal of Reading, 29,* 596–602.

Green, T. M. (2008). *The Greek and Latin roots of English* (4th ed.). Lanham, MD: Rowman & Littlefield Publishers, Inc.

Grimsley, K. D. (1995, September 29). Workplace illiteracy and the bottom line: Deteriorating skill levels are at a cost of $225 billion a year. *The Washington Post.*

Guthrie, J. T. (2004). Teaching for literacy engagement. *Journal of Literacy Research, 36,* 1–30.

Guthrie, J. T., & Wigfield, A. (2000). Engagement and motivation in reading. In M. L. Kamil, P. B. Mosenthal, P. D. Pearson, & R. Barr (Eds.), *Handbook of reading research* (Vol. 3, pp. 403–422). Mahwah, NJ: Erlbaum.

Haggard, M. R. (1985). An interactive strategies approach to content reading. *Journal of Reading, 29*(3), 204–210.

Haggard, M. R. (1986). The vocabulary self-collection strategy: Using student interest and world knowledge to enhance vocabulary growth. *Journal of Reading, 29,* 634–642.

Hanna, P. R., Hanna, J. S., Hodges, R. E., & Rudorf, H. (1966). *Phoneme-grapheme correspondences as cues to spelling improvement.* Washington, DC: United States Office of the Education Cooperative Research.

Harmon, J. M., Hedrick, W. B., & Wood, K. D. (2005). Research on vocabulary instruction in the content areas: Implications for struggling readers. *Reading and Writing Quarterly, 21,* 261–280.

Hasbrouck, J. E., & Tindal, G. (1992). Curriculum-based oral reading fluency norms for students in grades 2 through 5. *Teaching Exceptional Children, 24,* 41–44.

Heimlich, J. E., & Pittelman, S. D. (1986). *Semantic mapping: Classroom applications.* Newark, DE: International Reading Association.

Henderson, E. H. (1981). *Learning to read and spell: The child's knowledge of words.* DeKalb: Northern Illinois Press.

Henderson, E. H. (1985). *Teaching spelling.* Boston: Houghton Mifflin.

Henderson, E. H. (1990). *Teaching spelling* (2nd ed.). Boston: Houghton Mifflin.

Henderson, E. H., & Beers, J. (Eds.). (1980). *Developmental and cognitive aspects of learning to spell: A reflection of word knowledge.* Newark, DE: International Reading Association.

Henderson, V., & Dweck, C. S. (1990). Achievement and motivation in adolescence: A new model and data. In S. Feldman & G. Elliott (Eds.), *At the threshold: The developing adolescent* (pp. 308–329). Cambridge, MA: Harvard University Press.

Hock, M. F., Brasseur, I. F., Deshler, D. D., Catts, H. W., Marquis, J. G., Mark, C. A., & Stribling, J. W. (2009). What is the reading component profile of adolescent struggling readers in urban schools? *Learning Disability Quarterly, 32,* 21–38.

Holliday, W. G. (1991). Helping students learn effectively from text. In C. Santa and D. Alverman (Eds.), *Science learning: Processes and applications.* Newark, DE: International Reading Association.

Invernizzi, M. (1992). The vowel and what follows: A phonological frame of orthographic analysis. In S. Templeton & D. Bear (Eds.), *Development of orthographic knowledge and the foundations of literacy: A memorial Festschrift for Edmund H. Henderson* (pp. 106–136). Mahwah, NJ: Erlbaum.

Invernizzi, M., Meier, J., & Juel, C. (2003). *PALS 1–3: Phonological awareness literacy screening* (4th ed.). Charlottesville, VA: University Printing Services.

Invernizzi, M., & Worthy, J. W. (1989). An orthographic-specific comparison of the spelling errors of LD and normal children across four levels of spelling achievement. *Reading Psychology, 10,* 173–188.

James, W. (1958). *Talks to teachers on psychology and to students on some of life's ideals.* New York: Norton. (Original work published 1899.)

Jones, R. C. (2009). *Making sense in social studies.* Retrieved October 6, 2010, from http://readingquest.org/strat/pto.html

Kamil, M. L. (2003). *Adolescents and literacy: Reading for the 21st century.* Washington, DC: Alliance for Excellent Education.

Kistner, J. A., Osborne, M., & LeVerrier, L. (1988). Causal attributions of learning-disabled children: Developmental patterns and relation to academic progress. *Journal of Psychology, 80,* 82–89.

Klesius, J. P., & Homan, S. P. (1985). A validity and reliability upgrade on the informal reading inventory with suggestions for improvement. *Journal of Learning Disabilities, 18,* 71–75.

Krashen, S. (1985). *The input hypothesis: Issues and implications.* New York: Longman.

LaBerge, D., & Samuels, S. J. (1974). Toward a theory of automatic information processing in reading. *Cognitive Psychology, 6,* 293–323.

Leach, J. M., Scarborough, H. S., & Rescorla, L. (2003). Late-emerging reading disabilities. *Journal of Educational Psychology, 95,* 211–224.

Leslie, L., & Caldwell, J. (2005). *Qualitative reading inventory* (4th ed.). Boston: Allyn & Bacon.

Levy, F., & Murnane, R. J. (2004). *The new division of labor: How computers are creating the next job market.* New York: Russell Sage Foundation.

McKeown, M. G., Beck, I. L., Omanson, R. C., & Pople, M. T. (1985). Some effects of the nature and frequency of vocabulary instruction on the knowledge and use of words. *Reading Research Quarterly, 20,* 522–535.

Mesmer, H. A. E. (2008). *Tools for matching readers to text: Research-based practices.* New York: Guilford Press.

Miller, G. A., & Gildea, P. M. (1987). How children learn words. *Scientific American, 257,* 94–99.

Moats, L. (2000). *Speech to print: Language essentials for teachers.* Baltimore: Paul H. Brookes.

Morris, D. (2005). *The Howard Street tutoring manual* (2nd ed.). New York: Guilford Press.

Morris, D. (2008). *Diagnosis and correction of reading disabilities.* New York: Guilford Press.

Morris, D., Blanton, L., Blanton, W. E., Nowacek, J., & Perney, J. (1995). Teaching low-achieving spellers at their "instructional" level. *Elementary School Journal, 92,* 163–177.

Morris, D., Nelson, L., & Perney, J. (1986). Exploring the concept of "spelling instructional level" through the analysis of error-types. *Elementary School Journal, 87,* 181–200.

Morris, D., & Perney, J. (1984). Developmental spelling as a predictor of first-grade reading achievement. *Elementary School Journal, 84,* 441–457.

Morris, D., & Slavin, R. E. (2002). *Every child reading.* Boston: Allyn & Bacon.

Nagy, W. E., & Anderson, R. C. (1984). How many words are there in printed school English? *Reading Research Quarterly, 19,* 304–330.

Nagy, W., Berninger, V. W., & Abbott, R. D. (2006). Contributions of morphology beyond phonology to literacy outcomes of upper elementary and middle-school students. *Journal of Educational Psychology, 98*(1), 134–147.

Nagy, W. E., Diakidoy, I. N., & Anderson, R. C. (1993). The acquisition of morphology: Learning the contribution of suffixes to the meanings of derivatives. *Journal of Reading Behavior, 25*(2), 155–170.

Nagy, W. E., & Herman, P. A. (1987). Breadth and depth of vocabulary knowledge: Implications for acquisition and instruction. In M. McKeown & M. Curtis (Eds.), *The nature of vocabulary acquisition* (pp. 19–35). Mahwah, NJ: Erlbaum.

Nagy, W. E., & Scott, J. A. (2000). Vocabulary processes. In M. L. Kamil, P. B. Mosenthal, P. D. Pearson, & R. Barr (Eds.), *Handbook of reading research* (Vol. 3, pp. 269–284). Mahwah, NJ: Erlbaum.

National Center for Education Statistics (NCES). (2003). *Nation's report card: Reading 2002.* Washington, DC: U.S. Government Printing Office.

National Center for Education Statistics (NCES). (2007). *Nation's report card: Reading 2007.* Washington, DC: U.S. Government Printing Office.

National Reading Panel (2000). *Teaching children to read: An evidence-based assessment of the scientific research literature on reading and its implications for reading instruction.* Washington, DC: National Institute of Child Health and Human Development.

O'Connor, R. E. (2007). *Teaching word recognition: Effective strategies for students with learning difficulties.* New York: Guilford Press.

Ogle, D. (1986). K-W-L: A teaching model that develops active reading of expository text. *The Reading Teacher, 39,* 564–570.

Padak, N., Newton, E., Rasinski, T., & Newton, R. (2008). Getting to the root of word study: Teaching Latin and Greek word roots in elementary and middle grades. In A. E. Farstrup & S. J. Samuels (Eds.), *What research has to say about vocabulary instruction* (pp. 6–31). Newark, DE: International Reading Association.

Patterson, J., Patterson, J., & Collins, L. (2002). *Bouncing back: How your school can succeed in the face of adversity.* Larchmont, NY: Eye on Education.

Pearson, P. D., Hiebert, E. H., & Kamil, M. L. (2007). Vocabulary assessment: What we know and what we need to know. *Reading Research Quarterly, 42,* 282–296.

Perfetti, C. A. (1985). *Reading ability.* New York: Oxford University Press.

Perfetti, C. A. (1992). The representation problem in reading acquisition. In R. Treiman, L. C. Ehri, & P. B. Gough (Eds.), *Reading acquisition* (pp. 145–174). Mahwah, NJ: Erlbaum.

Piaget, J. (1926). *The language and thought of the child.* New York: Harcourt, Brace & Company.

Pittelman, S. D., Heimlich, J. E., Berglund, R. L., & French, M. P. (1991). *Semantic feature analysis: Classroom applications.* Newark, DE: International Reading Association.

Rasinksi, T., Padak, N., Newton, R., & Newton, E. (2008). *Greek and Latin roots: Keys to building vocabulary.* Huntington Beach, CA: Shell Education.

Read, C. (1971). Preschool children's knowledge of English phonology. *Harvard Educational Review, 41,* 1–34.

Robinson, A., & Princeton Review. (1997). *Word smart: Building an educated vocabulary.* New York: Random House.

Roehler, L. R., & Duffy, G. G. (1984). Direct explanation of comprehension processes. In G. G. Duffy, L. R. Roehler, & J. Mason (Eds.), *Comprehension instruction: Perspectives and suggestions* (pp. 265–280). New York: Longman.

Rosenshine, B. V. (1986). Synthesis of research on explicit teaching. *Educational Leadership, 43,* 60–69.

Ruddell, M. R., & Shearer, B. A. (2002). "Extraordinary," "tremendous," "exhilarating," "magnificent": Middle school at-risk students become avid word learners with the Vocabulary Self-Collection Strategy. *Journal of Adolescent and Adult Literacy, 45,* 352–363.

Rumelhart, D. E., Smolensky, P., McClelland, J. L., & Hinton, G. E. (1985). Models of schemata and sequential thought processes. In J. L. McClelland & D. E. Rumelhart (Eds.), *Parallel distributed processing: Explorations in the microstructure of cognition: Vol. II* (pp. 7–57). Cambridge, MA: Branford Books.

Santa, C. M., Havens, L. T., & Valdes, B. J. (2004). *Project CRISS: Creating independence through student-owned strategies* (3rd ed.). Dubuque, IA: Kendall/Hunt.

Sawyer, D. J., Wade, S., & Kim, J. K. (1999). Spelling errors as a window on variations in phonological deficits among students with dyslexia. *Annals of Dyslexia, 49,* 137–159.

Schlagal, R. (1992). Patterns of orthographic development into the intermediate grades. In S. Templeton & D. Bear (Eds.), *Development of orthographic knowledge and the foundations of literacy: A memorial Festschrift for Edmund H. Henderson* (pp. 31–52). Mahwah, NJ: Erlbaum.

Schwartz, R. M., & Raphael, T. E. (1985). Concept of definition: A key to improving students' vocabulary. *The Reading Teacher, 39*(2), 198–205.

Shaywitz, S. (2003). *Overcoming dyslexia: A new and complete science-based program for reading problems at any level.* New York: Vintage.

Smith, D., Ives, B., & Templeton, S. (2007, December). *The construction and analysis of the Degrees of Relatedness Interview: A measure of students' explicit morphological knowledge.* Paper presented at the 57th annual meeting of the National Reading Conference, Austin, TX.

Smith, M. K. (1941). Measurement of the size of general English vocabulary through the elementary grades and high school. *Genetic Psychological Monographs, 24,* 311–345.

Snow, C. E., & Biancarosa, G. (2003). *Adolescent literacy and the achievement gap: What do we know and where do we go from here?* New York: Carnegie Corporation.

Spear-Swerling, L., & Sternberg, R. J. (1996). *Off track: When poor readers become "learning disabled."* Boulder, CO: Westview Press.

Stahl, S. A., & Nagy, W. E. (2006). *Teaching word meanings.* Mahwah, NJ: Erlbaum.

Stanovich, K. (1986). Matthew effects in reading: Some consequences of individual differences in the acquisition of literacy. *Reading Research Quarterly, 21,* 360–406.

Stauffer, R. G. (1969). *Directing reading maturity as a cognitive process.* New York: Harper and Row.

Stauffer, R. G., Abrams, J. C., & Pikulski, J. J. (1978). *Diagnosis, correction, and prevention of reading disabilities.* New York: Harper & Row.

Stever, E. (1980). Dialect and spelling. In E. H. Henderson & J. W. Beers (Eds.), *Developmental and cognitive aspects in learning to spell* (pp. 46–51). Newark, DE: International Reading Association.

Taba, H. (1967). *Teacher's handbook for elementary social studies.* Reading, MA: Addison-Wesley.

Temple, C. S. (1978). *An analysis of spelling errors in Spanish.* Unpublished doctoral dissertation, University of Virginia.

Templeton, S. (1983). Using the spelling/meaning connection to develop word knowledge in older students. *Journal of Reading, 27*(1), 8–14.

Templeton, S. (1989). Tacit and explicit knowledge of derivational morphology: Foundations for a unified approach to spelling and vocabulary development in the intermediate grades and beyond. *Reading Psychology, 10,* 233–253.

Templeton, S. (2007). *Revolutionizing vocabulary instruction K–12: What does the developmental model tell us?* 22nd Annual Graham Lecture, Charlottesville, VA.

Templeton, S., & Bear, D. (Eds.). (1992). *Development of orthographic knowledge and the foundations of literacy: A memorial Festschrift for Edmund H. Henderson.* Mahwah, NJ: Erlbaum.

Templeton, S., Bear, D., Invernizzi, M., & Johnston, F. (2010). *Vocabulary their way: Word study with middle and secondary students.* Boston: Allyn & Bacon.

Templeton, S., & Spivey, E. M. (1980). The concept of "word" in young children as a function of level of cognitive development. *Research in the Teaching of English, 14,* 265–278.

Townsend, D., Bear, D. R., & Templeton, S. (2009, December). *The role of orthography in academic word knowledge and measures of academic achievement for middle school students.* Paper presented at 59th Annual Meeting of the National Reading Conference, Albuquerque, New Mexico.

Trefil, J., Calvo, R., & Cutler, K. (2005). *Earth science.* Evanston, IL: McDougal Littell.

Vacca, R. T., & Vacca, J. A. (2008). *Content area reading: Literacy and learning across the curriculum.* Boston: Allyn & Bacon.

Venezky, R. L. (1967). English orthography: Its graphical structure and its relation to sound. *Reading Research Quarterly, 2,* 75–105.

Venezky, R. L. (1970). *The structure of English orthography.* The Hague, Netherlands: Mouton.

Viise, N. (1994). *Feature word spelling lists: A diagnosis of progressing word knowledge through an assessment of spelling errors.* Unpublished doctoral dissertation, University of Virginia.

West, M. (1953). *A general service list of English words.* London: Longman.

Wexler, J., Edmonds, M., & Vaughn, S. (2008). *Effective reading strategies for adolescent struggling readers.* Portsmouth, NH: RMC Research Corporation, Center on Instruction.

White, T. G., Sowell, J., & Yanagihara, A. (1989). Teaching elementary students to use word practices. *The Reading Teacher, 42,* 302–308.

Wiggins, G. P., & McTighe, J. (2005). *Understanding by design* (2nd ed.). Alexandria, VA: Association for Supervision and Curriculum Development.

Wilbraham, A. C., Staley, D. D., & Matta, M. S. (1995). *Chemistry.* Menlo Park, CA: Addison-Wesley.

Willingham, D. T. (2009). *Why don't students like school? A cognitive scientist answers questions about how the mind works and what it means for the classroom.* San Francisco: John Wiley & Sons.

Worthy, M. J., & Invernizzi, M. (1989). Spelling errors of normal and disabled students on achievement levels one through four: Instructional implications. *Bulletin of the Orton Society, 40,* 138–149.

Worthy, M., & Viise, N. M. (1996). Morphological, phonological and orthographic differences between the spelling of normally achieving children and basic literacy adults. *Reading and Writing: An Interdisciplinary Journal, 8,* 138–159.

Wylie, R. E., & Durrell, D. D. (1970). Teaching vowels through phonograms. *Elementary English, 47,* 787–791.

Zeno, S. M., Ivens, S. H., Millard, R. T., & Duvvuri, R. (1995). *The educator's word frequency guide.* Brewster, NY: Touchstone Applied Science Associates.